Everything's An Argument

Seventh Edition

Custom Edition for The University of Oklahoma

English 1113/1213

With content from:

Habits of the Creative Mind

A Pocket Guide to Public Speaking, Fifth Edition

Andrea A. Lunsford

John J. Ruszkiewicz

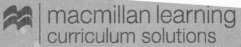

macmillan learning
curriculum solutions

bedford/st.martin's ▪ hayden-mcneil ▪ w.h. freeman ▪ worth publishers

Content taken from:
   Habits of the Creative Mind
   By Richard E. Miller and Ann Jurecic
   Copyright © 2016 by Bedford/St. Martin's

   Pocket Guide to Public Speaking, Fifth Edition
   By Dan O'Hair, Hannah Rubenstein, Rob Stewart
   Copyright © 2016 by Bedford/St. Martin's

Copyright © 2017 The University of Oklahoma for cover photography

Copyright © 2017 by Bedford/St. Martin's

Manufactured in the United States of America.

1 0 9 8 7
f

ISBN 978-1-319-08604-6

Macmillan Learning Curriculum Solutions
14903 Pilot Drive
Plymouth, MI 48170
www.macmillanlearning.com

Mountford 8604-6 F16

Acknowledgments

Text acknowledgments and works cited appear at the back of the book on pages 789–805, which constitute an extension of the copyright page. Art acknowledgments and copy-rights appear on the same page as the art selections they cover. It is a violation of the law to reproduce these selections by any means whatsoever without the written permission of the copyright holder.

CONTENTS

INTRODUCTION

Welcome to First-Year Composition at the University of Oklahoma

Welcome to First-Year Composition at OU! All of us in the First-Year Composition (FYC) Program look forward to working with you. Our goal, simply put, is to provide you with the best opportunity possible to develop as a writer and speaker. No matter your writing expertise or experience, we are dedicated to helping you get the most out of your time in our program. This means we do not view writing as a skill dependent upon natural, unlearned talent. Instead, we view writing as a tool that anyone can learn to use well. We also believe that all writers have more to learn, and we are confident that our courses will offer you innovative ways to approach rhetorical situations and deepen your critical thinking skills. Your instructors will guide you in the development of strategic writing habits that can be adapted to your educational, professional, or social interests. Our program emphasizes critical inquiry, scholarly research, rhetorical analysis, audience awareness, and good-faith deliberation in order to prepare you to write (and speak) in the public sphere, whether as a college student or as a citizen, about issues that matter to you.

Before we offer a preview of our curriculum, we want you to understand your role, the role of your instructor, and the role of the Office of First-Year Composition in your education this semester.

Your Role

- Come to class each day, fully prepared (bring assigned readings, home-work, note-taking utensils, etc.)
- Complete all homework and make a good-faith effort to learn from assignments
- Check your OU e-mail and Canvas course page regularly
- Ask questions early and often
- Dedicate yourself to challenging your assumptions, recognizing that this will be a rigorous course
- Be willing to practice new writing and speaking habits and techniques
- Take class discussions and group work seriously—our program values collaboration, and the more you put in, the more you will get out
- Communicate with your instructor about any difficulties affecting your ability to be successful

FYC Instructors' Role

- Come to class with carefully prepared lesson plans that fulfill unit and course learning objectives
- Assign homework and classwork designed to prepare you to succeed on unit projects
- Encourage questions and provide answers, guidance, or next steps
- Be available during office hours to meet with you as well as respond to your e-mails according to the policy listed in the syllabus
- Give feedback on drafts at least 48 hours before final drafts are due (incomplete drafts may not receive feedback)
- Return graded unit projects within two weeks of receiving them (grades for late or incomplete student submissions may be delayed)
- Have an optimistic view of students and be invested in your success
- Check their OU e-mail regularly, post their office hours/location on their syllabus and on Canvas, and update grades regularly on Canvas

Office of FYC's Role

- Prepare instructors to successfully teach course and unit objectives
- Design policies to support instructors and students
- Provide a safe environment for you to share concerns about your FYC classes or instructors, taking next steps when necessary
- Answer questions about FYC policies or procedures
- Have an optimistic view of students and instructors
- Check e-mail (fyc@ou.edu) regularly and keep office hours from 8:00 a.m. to 5:00 p.m. at Cate 2, Room 427

We look forward to working with you and wish you every success!

Roxanne Mountford, Director
Amanda Klinger, Associate Director
Cassandra Woody, Senior Assistant Director
Matthew Jacobson, Assistant Director
Jason Opheim, Assistant Director

Introduction to the Curriculum

At the University of Oklahoma, the First-Year Composition Program is dedicated to providing you with a rhetorical education that prepares you to write inside and outside of the university and to use writing and speaking as opportunities to contribute to the public good. We consider every writing and speaking assignment to connect an important purpose and occasion with a specific audience. That is, we won't ask you to write or speak just for us, and we won't ask you to write or speak without asking for your full engagement in the project. We treat your experiences and opinions as the catalyst for effective research, writing, and speaking, and we want you to engage the community around you by analyzing topics or issues that are of interest to you. While we consider writing to be an analytical tool of introspection and personal agency, we also want your writing to exhibit an awareness of rhetorical situations (purpose, audience, and cultural constraints). In essence, we want you to leave our classes having learned and practiced effective research, writing, and speaking habits that will help you contribute to the world around you.

In English 1113, students practice using inquiry as a tool to research and analyze the rhetorical situation of a political or social issue of importance to them, as well as the value systems that inform and are enacted by the individuals and groups participating in the issue. Building on the foundation of inquiry established in English 1113, students in English 1213 research an issue of local and national importance, crafting persuasive arguments designed to appeal to the expectations of multiple audiences.

When students complete English 1113, they will be able to:

- Use writing for discovery, comprehension, problem solving, and the construction of nuanced arguments
- Contribute, via writing or speech, to conversations mediating important social issues in a manner appropriate for the content and context specific to those issues
- Compose and deliver essays and oral presentations that demonstrate rhetorical awareness
- Develop flexible and effective strategies for organizing, revising, practicing/rehearsing, editing, and proofreading (for grammar and mechanics) to improve development and clarity of ideas
- Find, analyze, and correctly cite primary and secondary sources relevant to assignments to support and develop personal points of view and/or explore new lines of inquiry
- Develop considerate and constructive strategies for responding to peer work
- Define and practice revision strategies for essays and speeches that locate areas for improvement and effectively target them

When students complete English 1213, they will be able to:

- Compose in writing and deliver orally one major project grounded in scholarly research that responds to audience needs and expectations
- Pursue a line of inquiry to explore and intervene in an issue of public interest
- Conduct relevant secondary and primary research on a subject, effectively presenting and synthesizing research findings
- Use advanced rhetorical strategies for analyzing arguments and developing ideas
- Engage in effective peer critique
- Identify and apply revision strategies to their own writing, working with classmates, instructors, and others
- Refine speaking, writing, and visual communication skills, focusing on matters of construction, design, and delivery style

We expand on these course-level learning objectives in the section below.

Objectives for Writing at OU

Writing as Public Engagement

Students will approach writing as an opportunity to engage in meaningful public issues in a manner appropriate to the contexts and audiences involved. Students will produce writing that is relevant to their personal experiences, as well as their own academic and professional interests, enabling students to make connections from their disciplines to disparate communities. This writing will be effective in its ability to address complex issues with researched support, and persuasive when it comes to proposing solutions or calling for further inquiry. Most importantly, students will learn to view writing as a tool that can help them contribute to the public good. With that last point in mind, students will use their research and writing processes to engage thoughtfully with others in their communities in a manner that encourages, rather than curtails, further public discussion and participation.

Audience Awareness

Students will identify various stakeholders for public issues so that they can effectively understand, inform, and persuade audiences whose assumptions and beliefs about political issues are as complex as they are diverse. Students will practice developing audience awareness as a prerequisite to effective writing.

Rhetorical Strategies

Students will deploy rhetorical strategies including genre conventions, persuasive techniques, and contextual awareness. In doing so, students will begin to connect writing strategies with choice. Students will understand the ethical and political dimensions of writing, be able to analyze the rhetorical situations that produce writing, and respond to particular rhetorical situations. In addition, they will be able to respond to a writing task without being given an organizational form to follow; instead, they will be expected to discover appropriate strategies by studying examples and employing the approach that best matches their rhetorical purpose and professional or public context.

Inquiry

Students will choose topics and issues of interest to them and devise effective research questions and strategies. These research strategies aid students in developing intellectual curiosity for subjects and issues. Inquiry is a recursive process by which students explore their research, using that research to define and develop additional research questions. Through this process, students will develop skills to pursue and explore issues from multiple angles.

Research

Students will conduct secondary research, evaluate research sources (print and Web), and distinguish between informal and academic sources. Students will also become familiar with primary research methods of field research including interviews, observations, and surveys. They will also be introduced to the rich opportunities for archival research on campus, in the community, and on the Internet.

Process

Students will treat writing and speaking as an ongoing process that requires many habits and practices that work together to improve a piece of writing or a presentation. Students will learn to break down complex writing tasks; avail themselves of writing support options on campus and off; participate in workshops or collaborative writing efforts; and draft, redraft, and refine their writing.

Revision

Students will make revisions according to the needs and expectations of their audiences. Students will revise effectively by rearranging and clarifying parts of their compositions, by cutting or adding research, by sharpening the analytic frame, and by qualifying or making simplified claims more complex. Their revision will involve making substantive changes that go beyond sentence-level adjustments.

Analysis

Students will analyze how different texts are designed for different purposes. Students will also analyze how texts and/or language conventions play a role in shaping public conversations about current political/social events. They will develop researched and thoughtful claims about how writers and speakers use argument types, language conventions, rhetorical appeals, organizational strategies, and visual rhetoric in the service of an intended purpose or goal.

Synthesis

Students will place sources in conversation with one another in order to explore and complicate their own original ideas. Students will accurately interpret sources, summarize and/or paraphrase ideas, and meaningfully analyze relationships between ideas in order to produce generative claims or lines of inquiry.

Critical Thought

Students will read and analyze complex texts that meet requirements for university-level work. That is, they will read for the main idea; locate an analytic framework or structure for ideas; articulate how the idea is researched and developed; and frame questions that challenge, extend, or apply the ideas contained within the reading. They will construct an analytical framework for ideas; provide essential information; integrate information through summary, paraphrase, and quotation; and define terms.

Deliberation and Collaboration

Students will work together to investigate, discuss, brainstorm, develop, and refine their ideas. This collaboration will happen both informally—in class discussion and small group work—and formally—in peer review activities and perhaps even in research groups. Students are required to attend classes and participate, as it is their energy, curiosity, and research that bring OU's writing courses to life.

Editing

Students will use their editing skills to create a clear, functional style. They will learn that by using "strong" logical subjects and verbs, applying principles of conciseness, and selecting precise diction, they can remove distracting grammar errors in their prose. Over time, students will also learn to edit for more complex stylistic elements, that is, to fit expression to content in sentences that embody effective coordination, subordination, parallelism, balance, variety, and voice.

Citing Sources

Students will attribute and document sources honestly and correctly using a works cited page and in-text citations. Students will also be expected to introduce and establish the credibility of their sources in order to demonstrate the relevance of each source to the paper's topic or argument.

Sites for Secondary Research: Libraries and Archives

Libraries

Like all research universities, the University of Oklahoma contains a number of libraries, archives, and collections, both general and particular to disciplines and professions. Information about them is readily available: on the Internet, you can follow a link to Libraries from the OU home page (click on the "Current Students" tab and then select "Libraries" from the menu on that page), or go straight to the OU Library's homepage (https://libraries.ou.edu/) and surf collections here and elsewhere. We won't duplicate information that's so readily accessible. Rather, we'll take a tour of libraries most likely to be of use to you in your writing courses, offering impressions of their purpose and possibilities, since the very act of embarking on secondary research, of wading into the stacks, is a powerful form of direct experience.

The main resource, clearly, is **Bizzell Library**. At the North end of the South Oval, the beautiful red building presides over campus. If you're new to OU, we advise you to wander in there right away. The circulation desk sits across from an open computer lab. At the desk you can check out books and access reserved materials. At the computer lab, you can type up your notes, browse the electronic catalog, and print documents. In addition, there is a **Help Desk** on the first level, beside the computers, where you can get help or ask questions about library resources. You might also want to meet with an undergraduate services Librarian, who specializes in helping undergraduates with the kind of research you'll be doing in this course!

On Bizzell's lower level you will find the **Bookmark Cafe** and the **Helmerich Collaborative Learning Center**, where you can order a snack and coffee or rent spaces with whiteboards to meet with classmates, friends, and group members for class projects. The Collaborative Learning Center is a technology-enabled space where students can work together in groups. The OU IT service desk, within the Collaborative Learning Center, helps support the technology needs for students using the space. If you are not sure where to begin, be sure to check out the Libraries' Web site that lists the services and people to help you get started (https://libraries.ou.edu/undergraduateservices). If you're working on a multimodal project and need access to technology, or if you need help accessing online resources, the **Digital Scholarship Laboratory** on the lower level offers digital librarians, technology, and spaces to meet that support editing and presentations. If you're looking for a quiet place to read or study, we recommend checking out the **Helmerich Great Reading Room**, a favorite location on campus for industrious researchers and visitors. You can learn more about Bizzell's holdings online, as well as the hours and other special collections.

Though OU's more specialized collections aren't the sort most undergraduates will frequent (such as the John and Mary Nichols Rare Books or Bass Business collection), a few warrant special comment, since their holdings may pertain to the research your writing course requires or invites. Moreover, they are interesting places to visit and study in and of themselves:

- The **Western History Collection** includes archival materials on the American West as well as secondary sources and photographic archives. Students interested in local history or in particular groups/identities associated with Oklahoma and the American West may find interesting information here. The collection contains primary and secondary sources related to the American West, American Indians, Oklahoma, and OU history. Resource formats include documents, photographs, books, maps, source recordings, and university archives.
- Depending on your major or research question, the branch libraries (Architecture, Engineering, Fine Arts, and Geology) could be useful to you as well.
- Additional OU resources can be found through the Our Sooner Heritage Web site (https://digital.libraries.ou.edu/heritage/). This includes *Sooner Magazine*, Board of Regents Minutes, and photo archives. The *OU Daily* and *Norman Transcript* are available on microfilm in Bizzell, 4th floor East.

Beyond the OU's libraries and archives, you are lucky to have several local resources. The **Oklahoma History Center** is located in Oklahoma City. You can view many of their holdings online on their Web site (http://www.okhistory.org/research/newspapers) and through the OU libraries LibGuide (http://guides.ou.edu/ok). This guide mentions OU and digital resources the library subscribes to. You also may explore the center itself. For specific research projects, you may want to browse their holdings online before you visit, but even an informal or impromptu field trip could prove fruitful!

The **Oklahoma Department of Libraries**, also located in Oklahoma City, houses an archive of governmental documents that may also be useful to student research projects focused on the local community (http://www.odl.state.ok.us/oar/). Be sure to look at their online holdings, and if you decide to visit the archives in person, be sure to review the rules and regulations page beforehand.

Electronic Archives and Research

Electronic resources for research are proliferating at a rapid pace. Our list is suggestive (not exhaustive). Remember, also, that many of the physical archives listed above also have electronic sections. For example, the **Oklahoma Department of Libraries** has many newspaper articles available electronically (http://www.okhistory.org/research/newspapers). Sometimes you can see materials themselves online; other times, you can find detailed finding aids that help you decide whether or not an archive has information likely to be useful to you. When in doubt, don't hesitate to contact the archivists personally—they are experts and may be able to help you when you fear you have reached a dead end.

Here's a sampling of e-archives you may find interesting:

- For those of you with idiosyncratic or unique projects, you might want to browse this Wikipedia page, which lists various Oklahoma archives. Be sure to follow up with the listed organizations themselves, as Wikipedia pages can have old or incomplete information. Even so, this is a valuable list of potential resources (https://familysearch.org/wiki/en/Oklahoma_Archives_and_Libraries)

- The **Library of Congress** Web site (www.loc.gov) contains a remarkable digital archive, **American Memory**, with texts, audio, and video of cultural artifacts in all sorts of areas. They list topics, with numerous links for each. It's all readily searchable and browsable—a national digital treasure.

- If you're working on an assignment about place, you might want to go to **ePodunk** (www.epodunk.com), a Web site devoted, it says, to "the power of place." It has information, maps, and links to further sites on some 46,000 communities across the U.S., detailing parks, historic sites, museums, schools, cemeteries, and other features there and nearby.

- If you're interested in a particular social issue, citizenship and democracy could be useful themes for exploration. To that end, a stimulating electronic source is OpenDemocracy.net, billed as "an online global magazine of politics and culture." While this site is progressive in outlook (since democracy, after all, remains a progressive ideal), it is not partisan or doctrinaire but seeks rather to "publish clarifying debates which help people make up their own minds." And it is indeed restlessly global in scope, providing wider, more varied coverage and perspectives on world affairs than we are accustomed to find in our news media. These voices may inform your own; you might even seek to join them, publishing your views on this site or ones like it.

- A broadly useful research source is the **Brookings Institute** Web site (www.brookings.edu). The Brookings Institute is one of the best-known, most prestigious public affairs research institutes in the U.S. The plethora of subject areas listed on the Research home page indicates their great range of interests: Business, Cities and Suburbs, Defense, Economics, Education, Environment and Energy, Governance, Politics, Science and Technology, Social Policy.

- Another prestigious research institute, conservative in outlook, is the **Hoover Institution**, located at Stanford University. Their Web site (www.hoover.org) contains Library and Archives links useful for various projects. Other valuable information can be located through the site's Publications and Multimedia links.

These are just a few of the many possibilities for archival research on the Web. Your instructor may have further suggestions. Remember to evaluate carefully any sources you are considering using.

Further Opportunities to Develop Your Writing

After completing English 1213, you may find yourself interested in taking other courses that focus on writing prose or composing in multimedia. While you may find courses offered within your chosen major, there are plenty of opportunities to take courses that are open to any student. The following courses require only that you have successfully completed 1213.

English 1913: Writing for the Health Professions. Prerequisite: 1213. This course prepares students for the types of writing they will do in later coursework and in practice.

English 2113: Intermediate Writing. Prerequisite: 1213. The faculty who teach this course give it a theme. For example, during Spring 2016, Professor William Endres taught the course on the theme, "Style for Writers." The course is organized around the writing of non-fiction prose.

English 2133: Autobiographical Writing. Prerequisite: 1213 or EXPO 1213. Often taught by Professor Susan Kates, this course focuses on writing essays from personal experience and reading and analyzing journals, diaries, letters, and autobiographies as models for writing.

English 3113: Nature/Environment/Science Writing. Prerequisite: 1213 or EXPO 1213. This course offers students a chance to read and write about the natural world and the environment. It is attractive to students in the natural sciences and in environmental studies. The course fulfills a general education requirement (Humanities—Western Civilization).

English 3153: Technical Writing. Prerequisite: 1213. This course is open only to students in Engineering or one of the pure and applied sciences. The course focuses on the forms of report writing most frequently encountered in research and industry.

English 3183: Authoring in the Information Age. Prerequisite: 1213. If you are interested in writing for media other than print, this course is for you. The course focuses on composing for Web sites and social media, with emphasis on delivery and design of information and effective use of graphics.

English 3233: Oklahoma Writers/Writing Oklahoma. Prerequisite: 1213 or EXPO 1213. If you enjoyed writing about local and regional issues, you will enjoy this course. Taught most often by Professor Susan Kates, the course involves reading and writing about Oklahoma. The course fulfills a general education requirement (Humanities—Western Civilization).

English 4113: Magazine Editing and Publishing in the Humanities.
Prerequisite: 1213 or EXPO 1213. This course introduces students to magazine writing, editing, and publishing "scholarly and otherwise" in the humanities.

Have a great semester!

part 1

Habits of the Creative Mind

Beginning

The blank screen and the blinking cursor: for most of us, the hardest moment in the writing process is getting started. To get that cursor moving, you need to have something to say, something of interest to others. But how do you just start off being interesting? Where do interesting thoughts come from? It's a mystery—or so it seems.

The three essays in this section discuss how to begin using this book to unpack this mystery. The first essay introduces learning's central paradox: when we begin to learn something new, we simultaneously have to unlearn something familiar. A beginning is also an ending. In unlearning formulaic approaches to writing pseudo-arguments, you will be on your way to learning how to think seriously about open-ended questions.

The second and third essays discuss how to use your writing to confront what is unknown to you. In some cases, this process will involve choosing to read and write about topics that are unfamiliar. In other cases, it will involve finding ways to join an ongoing conversation among experts. In every case, you will have to contend with moments of confusion and uncertainty. The more you practice confronting what is unknown to you, the more comfortable you'll become with questions that confront all kinds of complexity and with answers that never settle things once and for all.

On Unlearning

When students enter our writing classes, they often bring with them a set of rules from high school that they use to define good writing. They know that every paragraph should start with a topic sentence that states the main point of the paragraph. And they know that all good essays have five sections or paragraphs: an introduction that states the essay's thesis; three descriptive body paragraphs, each of which discusses a different example that supports the essay's thesis; and a conclusion that restates what has been said in the previous sections. And finally, they are certain that no good essay ever uses the word *I*.

Chapter 1, "Beginning," is taken from Richard E. Miller and Ann Jurecic, *Habits of the Creative Mind*, pp. 15–33 (Part 1, "Beginning").

I—or rather we—suspect you know these rules well, since they've been repeated in writing classrooms for decades, with good grades going to those who follow them. But do they *really* produce good writing? Think about it: When was the last time you ran across a five-paragraph essay outside of school? Try looking for one in a news source, a magazine, a book, or even a collection of essays. You might find a modified version of one in an op-ed piece, but most of the writing you find will be organized quite differently. The five-paragraph essay, it turns out, is a very limited form, one best suited to the work of making simple claims and reporting or describing supporting evidence. (It's also easy to skim and easy to grade.)

In college classes, professors often expect students' writing to do a kind of work that is simply beyond the reach of the five-paragraph essay: contending with complexity. You may have had a professor who asked you to develop an argument by working with a handful of original sources, each with a competing point of view; or to support a new interpretation of a text not discussed in class; or to synthesize a semester's worth of lectures into a thoughtful reflection on a complex problem. When professors compose assignments like these, they assume you know how to use your writing to grapple with a genuine problem, puzzle, or question related to a course; they assume you've got something else in your quiver besides the formula for the five-paragraph theme.

So why don't we just give you a new set of rules, one that is capacious enough to provide directions for handling the range of writing tasks college students confront—the response paper in introductory history, the seminar project in advanced economics, the seven-to-eight-page argument for a 300-level psychology or politics or anthropology class? As appealing as that solution is, it's not available to us, because there's not one set of rules for generating good writing that works within any single discipline, let alone across multiple disciplines. The reason for this is not that any judgment of writing quality is inevitably arbitrary, as is often supposed, but rather that writing quality is always a function of context. Thus, what makes for a good paper in a literature class doesn't always make for a good paper in a history class or an econ class, or perhaps even in another literature class taught by a different professor.

How, then, does anyone in any discipline learn how to write about complex challenges? The first step involves unlearning the rules that are at the core of the five-paragraph essay. Taking that first step may seem impossible. We can't unlearn how to walk or how to talk. These habits are so deeply ingrained that a catastrophe of some kind (either psychological or physical) is required to unseat them. And we can't unlearn how to ride a bike or how to swim; we may forget how to over time, but when we return to these activities after a long hiatus, our challenge is not to learn how to do them as if for the first time, but to remember what's involved in keeping the bicycle upright or our body afloat and moving through the water.

Writing is unlike these other activities because each act of writing is not a straightforward repetition of what you've done before. Writing something new requires that you make choices about why you're writing, whom you're writing for, what you think, and what you want your writing to accomplish. So when we say you should unlearn what you learned about writing in school, we mean that we want you to actively resist the idea that writing is governed by a set of universal rules that, if followed, will clearly communicate the writer's ideas to the reader. We can't tell you to forget what you've learned (that would have the same paradoxical effect as telling you not to think about an elephant); and we can't say you shouldn't have been taught the rules governing the five-paragraph essay because, within an educational system dominated by the industry of standardized testing, you must be able to demonstrate that you can produce writing that follows those rules. Rather, we are asking you to question the two assumptions behind the formula for the five-para-graph essay: first, that the primary purpose of writing is to produce irrefutable arguments; and second, that the best writing is immediately understandable by all.

What do we propose in place of these assumptions? That you practice the habits of mind experienced writers exercise when they compose. Experienced writers tend to be curious and attentive. They choose to engage deeply with sources, ideas, people, and the world they live in. They are mentally flexible, self-reflective, and open to new ways of thinking, attributes that allow them to adapt to unfamiliar circumstances and problems. And they are persistent, resisting distraction and disappointment, accepting the fact that writing what hasn't been written before is hard work. When you commit yourself to practicing these habits—curiosity, attentiveness, openness, flexibility, reflectiveness, and persistence—you will also be committing yourself to making a habit of creativity, the practice of inventing novel and useful connections, compelling ideas, and thoughtful prose. As you delve into Part 1 of this book, you'll see that we've designed it to give you practice developing these habits. As you work your way through, you won't be working toward mastery of a formula for good writing; you'll be working on developing the habits of mind that increase your sensitivity to context and that allow you to use your writing to explore the unknown. You'll be practicing using your writing to show to others and yourself how your mind—not *any* mind, not *every* mind—works on a problem.

PRACTICE SESSION ONE

REFLECTING

When we tell students to unlearn the writing rules they learned in high school, they often ask for something—anything—to put in the place of those rules. We start our students on a path toward developing curious and creative habits of mind by telling them that their writing should show their minds at work on a problem. But what does that look like on the page?

Before you can answer that question for yourself, you need to know what kind of thinker you are. How does *your* mind work? What are your mental habits? How do you know? To answer these questions, pay attention over the course of a week to how you write and how you read.

Take notes every day on *everything* you read and write (not just in school or for school). Pay attention to all the times you process words: reading a page, a sign, a cereal box, the screen of a phone or a computer; writing a note, a Facebook post, a text message, a school assignment, a journal entry. For each instance, take note of where and when you read or wrote. Was it quiet? Were you moving? Were you alone?

At the end of the week, consider the following questions and spend at least 30 minutes composing a reflective response about what you've observed. Is the way you read and write better described as a set of rules or as a set of habits? Whichever option you choose, explain why. If you were to teach someone to read and write *the way you do*, how would you do it? What standards would apply?

PRACTICE SESSION TWO

READING

Select a reading and read it with an eye toward seeing the habits of the writer's mind at work on the page. Read the text through once and then review it, identifying evidence of the writer's habits of mind. Where do you see signs of curiosity, attentiveness, openness, flexibility, reflectiveness, persistence, and creativity?

Next, spend at least 30 minutes jotting down notes about the habits of mind on display in the reading you selected. What do the examples you've found tell you about how the writer thinks?

WRITING

The reading you chose to work with is obviously not a five-paragraph theme, and not just because it has far more than five paragraphs! Review the reading again and think about other ways the writer breaks what you thought were rules of writing. Then write an essay that considers why the writer made some surprising choices, writing in ways you thought were discouraged, or at least risky. What do these choices tell you about the writer's habits of mind?

EXPLORE

Can curiosity and creativity be learned? Unlearned? Relearned? Francine Prose recalls learning to write—outside school—by becoming a close and careful reader. In two TED videos, Ken Robinson laments the value placed on standardization and conformity in schools in the United States and United Kingdom and asks us to reimagine schools as environments that cultivate curiosity and creativity.

Prose, Francine. "Close Reading: Learning to Write by Learning to Read." *Atlantic*. 1 Aug. 2006. Web.

Robinson, Ken. "How Schools Kill Creativity." TED. Feb. 2006. Web.

———. "How to Escape Education's Death Valley." TED. April 2013. Web.

On Confronting the Unknown

In his book *Deep Survival: Who Lives, Who Dies, and Why*, Laurence Gonzales recounts the story of seventeen-year-old Juliane Koepcke who was seated next to her mother on a flight with ninety other passengers when the plane was struck by lightning, causing it to go into a nosedive. The next thing Koepcke recalled was being outside the plane, still strapped into her seat, hurtling earthward towards the canopy of the Peruvian jungle.

What would you think if you were in her place at that moment? What strikes Gonzales is Koepcke's recollection of her thoughts as she fell. Her mind was not filled with shrieking terror, or a hastily pulled together prayer, or feelings of regret. No, Koepcke remembered "thinking that the jungle trees below looked just like cauliflowers." She was moving into her new reality. She passed out while still falling, and when she regained consciousness sometime later, she was on the ground, still strapped into her chair. Her collarbone was broken. There was no sign of anyone else. She decided that the planes and helicopters she could hear flying above would never be able to see her because of the thickness of the tree canopy so she began to walk out of the jungle.

Central to Gonzales's thesis about resiliency is that those who survive a life-threatening crisis see the future as unmapped. Thus Koepcke, falling two miles upside down through a storm, didn't think the obvious thought—that her future was already clearly mapped out. Instead, she was struck by the appearance of the Peruvian forest from above. And when she came to later, having crashed through the canopy, she didn't think—or didn't only think—the obvious thought about what lay ahead for a seventeen-year-old girl without her glasses, walking alone in a jungle, barefoot, slapping the ground with her one remaining shoe to frighten off the snakes that she couldn't see well enough to avoid. She walked for eleven days while she was, as Gonzales described it, "being literally eaten alive by leeches and strange tropical insects." On the eleventh day, Koepcke found a hut and collapsed inside. The next day, as chance would have it, three hunters came by, discovered her, and got her to a doctor.

Gonzales is interested in this question: Why did Koepcke survive this crash, while "the other survivors took the same eleven days to sit down and die"? Gonzales identifies a number of reasons, besides blind luck, for Koepcke's survival. First, rather than follow rules, she improvised. Second, although she was afraid, as the other survivors surely were, she used that fear as a resource for action. And third, while many better-equipped travelers have succumbed to much lesser challenges, Koepcke had "an inner resource, a state of mind" that allowed her to make do with what the moment offered.

As Gonzales pursues his research further, he finds other traits that resilient people share in common: they use fear to focus their thoughts; they find humor in their predicaments; they remain positive. The list goes on, but the item that most interests us is Gonzales's admonition that to survive a crisis, one must "see the beauty" in the new situation:

> Survivors are attuned to the wonder of the world. The appreciation of beauty, the feeling of awe, opens the senses. When you see something beautiful, your pupils actually dilate. This appreciation not only relieves stress and creates strong motivation, but it allows you to take in new information more effectively.

After we read this, it was hard not to ask: If it's possible for someone to be attuned to the wonder of the world when confronted by a situation that is *life threatening*, could writers in far less dire circumstances cultivate this attunement as a habit of mind?

Here's why this connection suggested itself to us: from our years teaching writing, we know how terrifying and humbling the confrontation with the blank screen and the flashing cursor can be—for beginning writers and experienced writers alike. This confrontation is not life threatening, of course, but it can nevertheless trigger fears: Do I have anything worth saying? Can I make myself understood? Will the struggle with the blank screen be worth it in the end? These questions arise because the act of writing, when used as a technology for thinking new thoughts, takes us to the edge of our own well-marked path and points to the uncharted realms beyond.

Ultimately, each time a writer sits down to write, he or she chooses just how far to venture into that unknown territory. To our way of thinking, the writing prompt, properly conceived, is an invitation to embark into unmapped worlds, to improvise, to find unexpected beauty in the challenges that arise. We know from experience, though, that learning to approach writing this way takes practice, and that without such practice, the writing produced in response to a prompt tends to reject whatever is unfamiliar and huddle around whatever is obvious and easiest to defend.

We have designed the prompts in this book to help you use your writing to bring you to the edge of your understanding, to a place where you encounter what is unknown to you. The more you practice using your writing in this way, the further you will be able to take your explorations; you'll find yourself moving from writing about what is unknown to you to what is more generally unknown, and then to what is unknowable. Making this journey again and again is the essence of the examined life; the writing you do along the way tracks your ongoing encounter with the complexity of human experience. The more you do it, the more you know; and the more you know, the more connections you can make as you work through your next encounter with what is unknown to you. You'll never make it to absolute knowledge, but the more you practice, the more comfortable you'll be with saying, "I don't know, but I'm sure I can figure it out."

Or so we say.

We can pose our position as a challenge: Can you make your writing trigger an inner journey that is akin to falling from a plane over the Amazon, with everything that seemed solid and certain just moments ago suddenly giving way, question leading to question, until you land on the fundamental question, "What do I know with certainty?"

We all can count on being faced with challenges of comparable magnitude over the course of our lives—the death of a loved one; the experience of aging, disease, separation, and suffering; a crisis in faith; a betrayal of trust. Writing, properly practiced, is one way to cultivate the habits of mind found in those who are resilient in moments of crisis: openness, optimism, calm, humor, and delight in beauty.

PRACTICE SESSION ONE

WRITING

One could say that seeing the future as unmapped is something children do, and that part of growing up is learning to have reasonable expectations about what the future holds. What interests Gonzales is how a person responds, regardless of his or her age, when disaster strikes. When the plane you're on splits in half miles above the Earth, it's reasonable to assume that your future is mapped: you are going to die. Gonzales's contention is that those who respond to disaster by suspending that sense that the future is known have, perhaps paradoxically, a better chance of surviving.

The thing is, you don't know how you're going to respond to hugely significant and unexpected events until they happen. What is the most unexpected event that has taken place in your life so far? What made it unexpected? How did you respond to this confrontation with the unknown? In the event, did you settle into the moment, or did your sense of what the future held remain constant and unshaken?

Spend at least an hour writing a profile of how you responded to the unexpected. Feel free to discuss what you would do differently if given another chance, knowing now what you didn't know then.

PRACTICE SESSION TWO

REFLECTING

The kinds of crises that interest Gonzales have a cinematic quality to them: planes split apart in midair; a hiker is trapped, miles from anyone else, with his arm pinned by a boulder; a mountain climber dangles over the edge of a cliff, his partner unable to pull him to safety. (Indeed, the last two cases have been made into major motion pictures.) But writers rarely find themselves in predicaments of this kind; their crises tend to be internal and to center on getting to the heart of a matter, finding a way to express a fugitive truth, struggling to put a new thought into words.

What has been the most striking event in your *mental* life? A crisis of faith? An existential crisis? A realization that your way of thinking about love or friendship, truth or beauty, justice or politics, or any other of the concepts that are central to human experience was grounded in a false assumption? How did you respond to this confrontation with the unknown? What happened to your experience of time while this event unfolded? Did you find yourself living from moment to moment, or did your sense of what the future held remain clear?

Spend at least an hour writing a profile of how you responded to the most striking event in your mental life. Feel free to discuss what you would do differently if given another chance, knowing now what you didn't know then.

PRACTICE SESSION THREE

RESEARCHING

Choose a reading and write an essay that describes the writer's strategies for confronting the unknown. In tales of survival and resiliency, it is common to stress the hardships confronted and overcome, as well as acts of courage and ingenuity. If these terms strike you as out of place in a discussion of a writer grappling with a question, then provide terms of your own that you find more appropriate.

EXPLORE

What constitutes "the unknown" can take many forms. Jo Ann Beard writes about a radical change in her personal circumstances. Charles Mann imagines a world where people live to be 150 years old. Neil deGrasse Tyson discusses the edge of scientific understanding. And Amy Wallace looks at the deadly consequences of responding to life's uncertainties with inaction. Whatever form "the unknown" takes, writing about an encounter with it involves a confrontation with fear and an effort to get that fear under control.

Beard, Jo Ann. "The Fourth State of Matter." *New Yorker.* 24 June 1996. Web.

Mann, Charles C. "The Coming Death Shortage." *Atlantic.* May 2005. Web.

Tyson, Neil deGrasse. "The Perimeter of Ignorance." *Natural History.* Nov. 2005. Web.

Amy, Wallace. "An Epidemic of Fear: How Panicked Parents Skipping Shots Endangers Us All." *Wired Magazine.* 19 Oct. 2009. Web.

On Joining the Conversation

The literary critic Kenneth Burke described the exchange of academic ideas as a never-ending parlor conversation. "Imagine," he wrote,

> that you enter a parlor. You come late. When you arrive, others have long preceded you, and they are engaged in a heated discussion, a discussion too heated for them to pause and tell you exactly what it is about. In fact, the discussion had already begun long before any of them got there, so that no one present is qualified to retrace for you all the steps that had gone before. You listen for a while, until you decide that you have caught the tenor of the argument; then you put in your oar. Someone answers; you answer him; another comes to your defense; another aligns himself against you, to either the embarrassment or gratification of your opponent, depending upon the quality of your ally's assistance. However, the discussion is interminable. The hour grows late, you must depart. And you do depart, with the discussion still vigorously in progress.

With this extended metaphor, Burke offers us a way to think about how to write academic arguments. Preparing to write a paper about a topic that is new to you is like entering a parlor where a "heated discussion" is already taking place. For a while, all you can do is read what others have written and try to follow the debate.

Then, after a bit, you begin to figure out what's being discussed and what the different positions, conflicts, and alliances are. Eventually, after you catch the "tenor" or drift of the conversation, a moment arrives when you feel you have something to contribute to the conversation, and you "put in your oar." And so you begin writing, even as you know that you won't have the last word—that no one will ever have the last word.

Doubtless, there is much about Burke's vision of academic writing that won't surprise you: to write, you need to understand what others have written about the problem or question that intrigues you, and you must be able to represent, analyze, and synthesize those views. You also have to be interested enough in joining the conversation to develop a position of your own that responds to those sources in compelling ways. What *is* surprising about Burke's scenario is that the conversation never ends: it is "interminable." There are no decisive arguments in Burke's parlor, or even any strongly persuasive ones; there is only the ceaseless exchange of positions.

Why, it's reasonable to ask, would anyone choose to engage in a conversation without end? To answer this question, we'd like to walk you through an example of a writer working with multiple sources to explore an open-ended question.

Magazine journalist Michael Pollan writes about places where nature meets culture: "on our plates, in our farms and gardens, and in the built environment." In his article "An Animal's Place," Pollan grapples with the ideas of Peter Singer, a philosopher and the author of an influential book, *Animal Liberation*, which argues that eating meat is unethical and that vegetarianism is a moral imperative. Pollan makes his own view on meat eating clear from the very first sentence of "An Animal's Place": "The first time I opened Peter Singer's *Animal Liberation*, I was dining alone at the Palm, trying to enjoy a rib-eye steak cooked medium-rare." He's being purposely outrageous, dramatizing his resistance to what he knows of Singer's ideas. But he hasn't yet read *Animal Liberation* and he knows that engaging with Singer's text is going to be a challenge, because it's "one of those rare books that demands that you either defend the way you live or change it."

When Pollan opens *Animal Liberation* at his table at the Palm, he transforms the steakhouse into his own Burkean parlor. Having entered the conversation late, he tries to catch "the tenor of the argument." He discovers that Singer not only opposes eating meat but also objects to wearing fur, using animals in experiments, or killing animals for sport. While these practices may seem normal today, Singer argues that they will someday be seen as expressions of "speciesism," a belief system that values humans over all other beings, and that will be looked back upon, in Pollan's phrasing, as "a form of discrimination as indefensible as racism or anti-Semitism." At the core of Singer's book is this challenging question: "If possessing a higher degree of intelligence does not entitle one human to use another for his or her own ends, how can it entitle humans to exploit nonhumans for the same purpose?"

Pollan discovers that, although Singer's ideas were far from mainstream when *Animal Liberation* was first published in 1975, Singer's campaign for animal rights has since gained many intellectual, legal, and political allies. At the time that Pollan's article was published in November 2002, German lawmakers had recently granted animals the constitutional right to be treated with respect and dignity by the state, while laws in Switzerland were being amended to change the status of animals from "things" to "beings." England had banned the farming of animals for fur, and several European nations had banned the confinement of pigs and laying hens in small crates or cages. In the United States in 2002, such reforms had not yet been addressed by legislation, but today animal rights are no longer a fringe issue.

Pollan also discovers that a crowd of scholars and writers is clustered near Singer in Burke's parlor. Among them is Matthew Scully, a political conservative and former speechwriter for President George W. Bush who wrote *Dominion: The Power of Man, the Suffering of Animals, and the Call to Mercy*, a best seller about the routine cruelty toward animals in the United States. Also present is eighteenth-century philosopher Jeremy Bentham, who argued that even though animals cannot reason or speak, they are owed moral consideration because they can suffer. Beside Bentham are legal scholar Steven M. Wise and the contemporary philosophers Tom Regan and James Rachels, and off to the side is novelist J. M. Coetzee, who declares that eating meat and purchasing goods made of leather and other animal products is "a crime of stupefying proportions," akin to Germans continuing with their normal lives in the midst of the Holocaust.

Pollan wants to resist Singer's insistence on the moral superiority of vegetarianism, but before he can build his argument, he needs to find his own allies in the ongoing conversation. He is intrigued by John Berger's essay "Why Look at Animals?" which argues that humans have become deeply confused about our relationship to other animals because we no longer make eye contact with most species. This helps Pollan to explain the paradox that, even as more and more people in the United States are eager to extend rights to animals, in our factory farms "we are inflicting more suffering on more animals than at any time in history." From sources as varied as Matthew Scully's *Dominion* and farm trade magazines, Pollan learns that these farms, also known as Confined Animal Feeding Operations, or CAFOs, reduce animals to "production units" and subject them to a life of misery.

But these sources don't particularly help Pollan to stand up against Singer's insistence that everyone who considers eating meat must choose between "a lifetime of suffering for a nonhuman animal and the gastronomic preference of a human being." Unhappy with either option before him—to refuse to pay attention to the suffering of animals in factory farms or to stop eating animals—Pollan brings a completely new voice into the parlor: not a philosopher or a writer, but a farmer. Joel Salatin, owner of Polyface Farm in Virginia, raises cattle, pigs, chickens, rabbits, turkeys, and sheep on a small farm where each species, including the farmer himself, performs a unique role in the ecosystem. The cows graze in the pasture; afterward, the chickens come in and eat insect larvae and short grass; then the sheep take their turn and eat what the cows and chickens leave behind. Meanwhile, the pigs compost the cow manure in the barn. In this system, the mutual interest of humans and domestic animals is recognized, even when the animals are slaughtered for meat. In life, each animal lives according to its natural inclinations; and when it is slaughtered, its death takes place in the open. Nothing is hidden from sight. Pollan concludes that slaughtering animals, where the process can be watched is "a morally powerful idea." Salatin convinces him that animals can have respectful deaths when they are not, as they are in factory farms, "treated as a pile of protoplasm."

Pollan's visit to Polyface Farm is transformational. He decides that "what's wrong with animal agriculture—with eating animals—is the practice, not the principle." The ethical challenge, in other words, is not a philosophical issue but a practical one: Do the animals raised for meat live lives that allow them to express their natures? Do they live good lives? Pollan decides that, if he limits his consumption of meat to animals that are raised humanely, then he can eat them without ethical qualms. Pollan is so pleased with his creative solution to the problem Singer posed that he even writes to the philosopher to ask him what he thinks about the morality of eating meat that comes from farms where animals live according to their nature and appear not to suffer. Singer holds to his position that killing an animal that "has a sense of its own existence" and "preferences for its own future" (that is, a pig, but not a chicken) is wrong, but he also admits that he would not "condemn someone who purchased meat from one of these farms."

Does this mean that Pollan has won the argument? Not really. The discussion in Burke's parlor has not ended. New voices have entered to engage with both Pollan and Singer, and new ideas have emerged about sustainability, agriculture, economics, and ethics. Curious, reflective, and open-ended thinkers continue to enter, mingle, and depart, "the discussion still vigorously in progress."

PRACTICE SESSION

REFLECTING

For this exercise, we'd like you to read Michael Pollan's "An Animal's Place" and think more about how he uses sources and what it means to be "in conversation" with words on a page or screen. Read the piece with care, taking notes about where and how Pollan uses his sources to develop his own thoughts. After reading, take at least 30 minutes to write answers to these questions about entering into a conversation with sources: Where did Pollan engage with sources in ways that surprised you? Where did he use sources in ways that you'd like to emulate? What different kinds of conversations did Pollan engage in with his sources? Why did he choose to be in conversation with some sources more than others? What have you learned from these exercises about writing "in conversation" with sources?

READING

Next, we'd like you to read Harriet McBryde Johnson's "Unspeakable Conversations." Johnson's article is also in conversation with Peter Singer, but unlike Pollan, Johnson is primarily interested in Singer's controversial views on euthanasia. Read the article with care, observing the many different ways Johnson joins in conversation with her sources. To start, you might notice sources that serve as the focus of analysis; supply background or information; provide key ideas or concepts; provide positions or arguments to grapple with; or shift the direction of the conversation.

After you've read, spend at least 30 minutes making a list of the many ways Johnson uses her source material. Notice that she may name or quote some sources explicitly, while not identifying every source of information. This is one way in which journalistic writing differs significantly from academic writing, where, of course, all sources must be cited.

WRITING

Now that you've read both "An Animal's Place" and "Unspeakable Conversations," we'd like you to compose an essay in which you enter a conversation with Pollan and Johnson and answer the question: To what extent is it possible to define what makes a "good life" (or a "good death") for humans and other animals? Use Pollan's and Johnson's essays both as sources and as models of how to join a conversation in writing.

EXPLORE

Essays about ethical quandaries invite readers to join the fray. Michael Pollan challenges philosopher Peter Singer on the ethics of eating meat. Harriet McBryde Johnson also argues with Singer, but she objects to his stance on the ethics of killing severely disabled newborns. We invite you to join those conversations, and also to see how biologist Sandra Steingraber connects the words of early environmentalist Rachel Carson, author of *Silent Spring*, to current debates about the dangers of fracking.

Johnson, Harriet McBryde. "Unspeakable Conversations." *New York Times Magazine*. 16 Feb. 2003. Web.

Pollan, Michael. "An Animal's Place." *New York Times Magazine*. 10 Nov. 2002. Web.

Steingraber, Sandra. "The Fracking of Rachel Carson." *Orion Magazine*. Sept./Oct. 2012. Web.

Curiosity at Work: Rebecca Skloot's
Extra-Credit Assignment

Rebecca Skloot's best-selling book, *The Immortal Life of Henrietta Lacks,* tells the story of a poor African American woman in Baltimore who was hospitalized with cancer in 1951. Before Lacks died, a surgeon removed some of her cancer cells for research without her knowledge, and they were used to grow human cells in a lab for the first time. Lacks's cells, now known as HeLa cells, are still alive today and have been essential to medical research for more than sixty years. Every person who has received a polio vaccine or who lives in a country where polio has been eradicated, for example, is a direct beneficiary of research that used HeLa cells. And yet, before Skloot's book, few people knew of Henrietta Lacks and her immortal cells.

The path that led Skloot to write Lacks's story was long and circuitous. At age sixteen, Skloot registered for a community college biology course to make up the credit she lost when she failed the subject during her freshman year of high school. When the class was studying cell division, Skloot's teacher, Mr. Defler, told his students about HeLa cells and then wrote HENRIETTA LACKS in big letters on the blackboard. He told them that Lacks had died of cervical cancer, that a surgeon had taken a tissue sample from her tumor, and that "HeLa cells were one of the most important things that happened to medicine in the last hundred years." Before erasing the name from the board and dismissing the class for the day, Mr. Defler added one more fact: "She was a black woman."

Skloot followed her teacher back to his office, asking questions: "Where was she from? Did she know how important her cells were? Did she have any children?" Lacks's life is a mystery, Mr. Defler told her, and then he made the kind of comment teachers make: "If you're curious, go do some research, write up a little paper about what you find and I'll give you some extra credit."

That night, Skloot couldn't find any information on Lacks beyond a parenthetical reference in her biology textbook, but she didn't forget about this mysterious woman whose cells had helped protect millions from contracting polio. Some ten years later, when Skloot was working on her undergraduate degree in biology, she took her first writing course, and the teacher began by asking the students to "write for 15 minutes about something someone forgot." Skloot immediately scrawled "Henrietta Lacks" on her page and wrote about how Lacks had been forgotten by the world. Over time, Skloot resolved to write "a biography of both the cells and the woman they came from." As her commitment to her project deepened, her research became "a decade long adventure through scientific laboratories, hospitals, and mental institutions, with a cast of characters that would include Nobel laureates, grocery store clerks, convicted felons, and a professional con artist." She met Lacks's five adult children and their families, which raised new questions for her about race, ethics, and medical research, among them: If Henrietta Lacks's cells were so important to medical science and had given rise to a multibillion-dollar industry, why couldn't Lacks's children and grandchildren afford health insurance?

More than two decades after Rebecca Skloot first heard the name Henrietta Lacks, she finished her book. Putting her research skills to use once more, she tracked down the biology teacher who first told her about HeLa cells and sent him a note: "Dear Mr. Defler, here's my extra credit project. It's 22 years late, but I have a good excuse: No one knew anything about her."

Note: The quotations in this essay are from Rebecca Skloot's blog post, "What's the Most Important Lesson You Learned from a Teacher?" *Rebeccaskloot.com* 8 May 2012.

Paying Attention

I s it possible to write without paying attention? At first the question seems absurd: How could words move from your brain to your keyboard if you weren't paying attention? Writing doesn't just happen. And yet people text while walking and even while driving, which shows that writing happens all the time without one's full attention. And of course, students can now write papers while also surfing the Net and snapchatting their friends.

Funnily enough, a common response to the mistakes that happen as a result of being distracted is the command to "pay attention." You step off the curb into oncoming traffic and are pulled back to safety by a friend just before you would have been hit. "Pay attention!" You're sitting in class daydreaming when your teacher calls on you. "Pay attention!" You're in a crowd and walk directly into a stranger. "Pay attention!" In each case, the command arrives too late: it's less helpful guidance than it is a rebuke.

We want you to think of writing not as a way of proving you *were* paying attention but as a way *of* paying attention. To this end, we've populated this chapter with essays that explore how writing can be used to train the mind to focus and the eye to see. We also explore using your writing to reflect on how you think and on how you imagine the thoughts of others. When you use writing in these ways, you are practicing being engaged with and interested in the world.

On Learning to See

When Betty Edwards started teaching high school art classes in the late 1960s, she was baffled as she watched her students having trouble drawing simple, familiar objects. If they could see that the orange was *in front of* the green bottle, why did they draw the two objects *next to* each other? Why was it that the ability of her students to express themselves verbally and to reason mathematically had improved from kindergarten to high school, but their ability to draw hadn't changed much since the third grade? And when her students eventually figured out how to produce drawings that were more accurate, why did the improvement seem to take place all at once rather than gradually?

Chapter 2, "Paying Attention," is taken from Richard E. Miller and Ann Jurecic, *Habits of the Creative Mind*, pp. 34–53 (Part 3, "Paying Attention").

Around the time that Edwards was pondering why students who learned easily in academic classes had so much difficulty in art class, neuroscientists Roger W. Sperry and Michael Gazzaniga began publishing reports that suggested that the two sides of the brain did different kinds of mental work. The left hemisphere, where language was typically housed, was more systematic and linear. The right hemisphere was more visual, spatial, and synthetic. Once Sperry and Gazzaniga's research got picked up by the popular press, it was reduced to a simple binary opposition: the right brain is creative and the left brain is analytical.

Edwards used this research to make sense of the difficulty her students had seeing what was right in front of them as well as the breakthroughs they experienced when they suddenly began to see differently. In Edwards's view, students were rewarded in their academic classes for being verbal and analytical thinkers; they were required, one could say, to be left-brained. But to draw well, they needed access to visual, perceptual, and synthetic thought; they needed to find a way to see with the right brain. To trigger this apparent hemispheric shift for her students, Edwards developed exercises that quieted the verbal, analytical, and systematizing thinking rewarded elsewhere in the curriculum, so that visual, creative, and associative thinking could come to the fore. As she developed these exercises, Edwards was beginning to understand that, in order to learn how to draw, her students had to stop naming what they were trying to draw and start seeing what was in front of them in a new way—as related lines and connected spaces without names. If they stopped saying "hand," for example, they could learn to stop drawing the symbol for a hand (five stick fingers at the end of a stick arm) and could instead begin to see the intricate pattern that is made by a particular hand resting on the edge of a particular keyboard.

Edwards's explanation of the brain's two dominant operational modes makes a kind of immediate, intuitive sense; indeed, it makes it sound like all you really have to do to draw is to learn how to toggle the switch between your left brain and right brain. The truth, though, is that both the brain and learning how to draw are more complicated than the model of a sharp division between left-brain and right-brain function suggests. We now know from neuroscience that it is more accurate to say that activity in the right hemisphere is *correlated* with creative and divergent thinking and that activity in the left hemisphere is *correlated* with analytic and convergent thinking. While the right part of your brain contributes a good deal to creative potential, your whole brain has to work in concert for you to engage in creative work.

In *A Whole New Mind*, Daniel Pink describes attending a drawing class based on the methods developed by Edwards and learning just how difficult it is to get the whole brain to play along with this new way of seeing. His first attempt at drawing a self-portrait while looking at his face in a mirror was simply terrible. The eyes, nose, and lips were clumsy cartoon versions of these basic components of the human face. Pink's placement of these features in his drawing was equally cartoonish and bore little relation to where the eyes, nose, and mouth are found on a real human face. Pink couldn't draw what was right in front of him, the most familiar, recognizable part of himself, because his preconceptions about faces—which his teacher called "remembered symbols from childhood"—blinded him to the actual contours of the face looking back at him in the mirror. To draw better, Pink needed to stop naming, analyzing, and judging what he saw and practice seeing and sketching lines, patterns, relationships, and relationships between relationships. He had to practice finding increments of simplicity in complex patterns of lines and spaces.

We believe that the kind of seeing Edwards aims to trigger through her teaching practice is a specific instance of the kind of seeing that lies at the core of creative thinking. Indeed, Edwards herself says that "this ability to see things differently has many uses in life aside from drawing—not the least of which is creative problem solving." So, although it surely seems contradictory, we adapted a couple of Edwards's exercises meant to restrain the dominance of language to serve our own interest in having you think differently about the role of language in the creative process.

PRACTICE SESSION ONE

WRITING

Draw a self-portrait. Start by finding a spot with a mirror and plenty of light where you can work comfortably for at least 30 minutes. Using a pencil and a blank sheet of paper, draw your face. Do your best, and don't give up before you've got all your facial features looking back at you. The drawing may look awful, and that's okay.

Next, look carefully at the shape of the features and the relationships between features and think about how and why your portrait turned out as it did. What went right? Where did you successfully transform perception into image? What went wrong? What did you *not see* as you were drawing? How did you feel while you were completing this exercise? How did you feel when you were done? Why?

As a final step, take at least 15 minutes to write an assessment of the act of seeing that generated your self-portrait.

SEEING

For this exercise, you will use a trick of Betty Edwards's that helps you see without naming—drawing an upside-down image. We'd like you to give Edwards's exercise a try, following these instructions.

1. Gather your materials: you'll need the Egon Schiele drawing reproduced on p. 22, a pencil, an eraser, and a sheet of unlined paper. Then find a quiet place where you won't be interrupted for at least 30 minutes.

2. When you're ready to begin drawing, turn your cell phone off, close your laptop, and take off your headphones. You should do everything you can to give this exercise your undivided attention.

3. While you are making your copy of the upside-down Schiele line drawing, try not to figure out what you are looking at (and don't turn the drawing right-side up until after you're finished). You'll do a better job if you aren't trying to name what you are drawing. Focus instead on the lines in the drawing, the relationships between those lines, and the relationships between the lines and the paper's edge. Edwards tells her students: "When you come to parts that seem to force their names on you—the H-A-N-D-S and the F-A-C-E—try to focus on these parts just as shapes. You might even cover up with one hand or finger all but the specific line you are drawing and then uncover each adjacent line."

WRITING

When you are done making your copy, we'd like you to reflect upon the *experience* of drawing an upside-down image. Begin by considering the following questions: Was it difficult to stop naming and to start seeing relationships? Are there parts of your copy that are more successful than others? What happened to your sense of time while you were working on your copy?

Then, spend at least 30 minutes writing about what happened *in your mind* while you worked on your line drawing. There's no right answer here. Think of your writing as a sketch of your mind at work. Learning to see begins with learning how *you* see.

FIGURE 2.1 *Robert Muller* by Egon Schiele
© Imagno - Wien Museum/LA COLLECTION

PRACTICE SESSION TWO

REFLECTING

In the 1940s, a psychologist named Karl Duncker developed a test of problem solving that's popularly known as "the candle problem." The challenge posed to participants is to figure out how to attach a lit candle to a wall without it dripping on the floor below. To complete the challenge, participants can use only the objects pictured here:

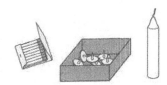

FIGURE 2.2 Karl Dunker Candle Problem.
On Problem Solving, Psychological Monographs, 58, American Psychological Association. Panel A, na

Take as much time as you need to figure out how you would solve the candle problem, and then write down your solution.

Next, watch Daniel Pink's TED talk, "The Puzzle of Motivation." Pink begins talking about the candle problem and its solution at around the two-minute mark, but we want you to listen to the talk in its entirety. Take notes while you're watching, writing down anything Pink says that surprises you.

After you've listened to Pink's TED talk, we'd like you to spend 45 minutes writing a reflective piece that considers the role seeing played in your response to the candle problem. Did solving the candle problem require a new way of seeing, a new way of thinking, or both? What do you think the implications of the candle problem are for learning?

EXPLORE

Writing about seeing is often precipitated by the experience of learning to draw. John Berger has been drawing his entire life. Adam Gopnik earned a BA and MA in art history but didn't learn to draw until middle age. A classical pianist before changing careers, Peter Mendelsund is a self-taught artist who designs book covers for a living. Each of these writers explores the relationship between how we see the world and how we put the world of our experience into words.

Berger, John. *Bento's Sketchbook: How Does the Impulse to Draw Something Begin?* New York: Pantheon, 2011. Print.

Gopnick, Adam. "Life Studies: What I Learned When I Learned to Draw." *New Yorker.* 27 June 2011. Web.

Mendelsund, Peter. *What We See When We Read.* New York: Vintage, 2014. Print.

On Looking and Looking Again

"Pay attention!"

Walk the hallways of any elementary school, and it won't be long before you hear this exasperated command. Over time, all students learn that what their teachers mean when they say "pay attention" is "sit still and be quiet." The teachers know, of course, that there's more to paying attention than being quiet, but what that "more" turns out to be is something that can't be ordered into existence by the voice of another. So students learn early on how to get their bodies to behave in class, but getting their minds to behave is another matter.

The paradox at the beginning of the process of paying attention seems irresolvable: How does mental focus emerge out of chaos, the attentive mind out of distraction? How does anyone ever learn the inner work of paying attention?

Our answer is: by practice.

But what kind of practice? How does one practice a state of mind?

The poet William Blake offers some guidance on how to think about this paradox in the opening stanza of his poem "Auguries of Innocence":

> To see a World in a Grain of Sand
> And a Heaven in a Wild Flower
> Hold Infinity in the palm of your hand
> And Eternity in an hour

On a first reading, Blake's stanza seems to offer a straightforward proposition about how to trigger a state of deep attentiveness: if you want X (to see the world in a grain of sand), then do Y (hold infinity in the palm of your hand). But if this is what it takes to pay attention, attentiveness of the kind Blake describes seems an impossibility, for how is one supposed to go about grabbing hold of infinity or experiencing "eternity in an hour"?

Perhaps we've misread the stanza. Perhaps Blake is making a statement both about what paying attention involves and what it makes possible: "To see a world in a grain of sand and heaven in a wild flower [is to] hold infinity in the palm of your hand and eternity in an hour." Read this way, Blake's verse is saying that, if you can learn to "see a world in a grain of sand" or "a heaven in a wild flower," you can gain access to realms beyond what you know and even beyond the limits of thought—you can reach the infinite and the eternal.

From Blake's poem we could conclude that the practice of writing poetry has trained Blake's mind to focus on the particular (a grain of sand, a wildflower) until it leads to something much bigger (a world, a heaven) and onward to realms beyond measure (infinity, eternity). More generally, we can say that Blake shows us that the attentive mind generates insights, connections, and beautiful objects and moves by inference, analogy, and metaphor.

Does this mean that, instead of commanding a distracted student to "pay attention" teachers should try saying, "sit still and be a poet"?

That command wouldn't work any better than the command to pay attention, of course: first, even the best poet can't be a poet on command; and second, poetry is only one possible result of paying attention.

Better by far, we think, to say, "Practice looking and looking again."

A teacher we greatly admire, Ann Berthoff, developed an exercise that we've adapted here to help you experience the kind of seeing Blake describes. To get her students to resee the natural world, Berthoff would bring to class all manner of organic objects—a starfish, the husk of a cactus, dried reeds, a pressed flower—and then have each student take one of the objects home to study for a week.

For our version of this exercise, you'll need to select your own organic object—anything from the natural world will do. You should choose something that you can hold in your hand and that you can put somewhere out of harm's way for a week.

We ask that, for seven straight days, you spend at least 10 minutes recording your *observations* of the object you've selected.

Here's an example of what a day's entry might look like, written by Erik on day five:

> Clearly the plant is dehydrated and dying, and yet, besides my dismembering it of its limbs, it still has the same form and design as it did when I first took it home. The colors of the leaves have noticeably changed, but nothing else has visibly changed as far as I can tell. Of course, the way I'm seeing this object has changed since the first day I laid my eyes upon it.

There are definitely patterns that are quite unmistakable in and on this plant. For instance, the mini-stems that connect the buds to the stem that connects back to the entire organism: there are seven of these mini-stems, and they are all about of equal length. That is interesting. If it is sunlight the buds seek, I would think that maybe one of the mini-branches would push itself considerably farther out so as to receive more energy for its own survival. But, naturally, these buds are probably not competing for energy but rather are working together for the survival and health of the entire plant.

I cannot help but draw a connection to a human body here. You can find multi facets and numerous parts and functions of parts within a single limb of a body. In fact, you can find it in one single human cell. . . . I'm reminded of a quote from Aldous Huxley [who was quoting from William Blake]: "If the doors of perception were cleansed, every thing would appear to man as it truly is, infinite." A person is not just a person with a name, a height and a weight, and a social status; each person is also composed of electricity, of a billion cells that perform who knows how many functions.

My plant here, at first glance, is just a little piece of a shrub. But if you really look at it, there is a lot going on here that makes this plant what it is. Can the physical world ever be described as infinite? Do we really actually know, in an empirical sense, of anything that is infinite? Why do we have a "word" describing something that we have never experienced? Is that evidence or a suggestion from our subconscious mind, our inner spirit, our unseen self, that there is such a thing as infinity? Is there infinity present in my little piece of shrub? I don't know, but I'm willing to bet that as more powerful microscopes are developed, there will surely be more we will be able to "see" in the physical universe around us, and this will further lend credence to the idea that, yes, with a necessary perspective, it may be possible to hold infinity in the palm of your hand. You won't know it unless you have eyes to see it, or take the time to meditate on it, and even then . . . infinity is a tough thing to swallow and ascribe to what we can perceive with our five senses. But it's not impossible.

Focusing on the plant stem, Erik makes connections to the human body, to a quote he's read in Aldous Huxley, and then back to the Blake poem we used in our writing prompt. Looking closely allows Erik to see beyond the plant back into his own mind. Thinking about how the plant is organized becomes, in this instance, a way to think about how all minds organize perceptions.

PRACTICE SESSION

WRITING

Choose an organic object from the natural world, something that you can hold in your hand and that you can keep out of harm's way for a week. Then, over seven consecutive days, write for at least 10 minutes each day about what you see.

Describe how your object is put together.

What questions does your object pose?

What does it point to?

Where did it come from?

What is it a part of?

You are free to move your object, to alter it, or to interact with it in any way that furthers your effort to understand how it is put together. You can also read and do research if questions come to mind. Your goal is to see how your object is organized within itself and how it is implicitly connected with other natural objects.

Write every day.

Ponder what your observations and explorations tell you about the object.

Write even if you're stuck.

If you try to sketch your object, does that help you see aspects you would otherwise miss? What if you photograph it?

Write even if you think you've said all there is to say about your object.

There's only one rule: don't anthropomorphize your object. Don't give it a human name. Don't invent a dialogue between yourself and your object. We've found that this approach only serves to obliterate the object—it displaces the act of looking and looking again.

REFLECTING

After you've completed your seven days of writing, reread what you've written with the following questions in mind: At the end of all your looking, how would you describe the organization of your organic object? Based on what you've written, how would you describe your own way of looking? What did you see right away? What did it take you a while to see? What kinds of questions did you ask automatically? What kinds of questions emerged late in the process?

Write an essay that reflects on what this exercise of looking and looking again has helped you to recognize about seeing in general and about paying attention in particular.

EXPLORE

Looking, learning, and rethinking can turn the ordinary into something extraordinary. Rachel Carson, Annie Dillard, and Michael Pollan each look at familiar objects or places until they become strange and surprising. Carson lingers by a sea cave that appears only at the year's lowest tide. Dillard looks for hidden treasures in the natural world: monarch pupae, flying squirrels, the streak of green light that bursts from the sun at the moment of sunset. And Pollan explores an orchard with 2,500 varieties of apple trees, including an ancient species from Kazakhstan that may be the origin of all apples.

Carson, Rachel. "The Marginal World." *The Edge of the Sea*. Boston: Houghton Mifflin, 1998. 1–7. Print. (Available on Google Books via preview.)

Dillard, Annie. "Total Eclipse." *Teaching a Stone to Talk: Expeditions and Encounters*. New York: HarperCollins, 1982. 9–28. Print. (Available on Google Books via preview.)

Pollan, Michael. "Breaking Ground: The Call of the Wild Apple." *New York Times*. 5 Nov. 1998. Web.

On Encountering Difficulty

In his essay "The Mind's Eye," the neurologist Oliver Sacks confronts the conundrum of free will: "To what extent are we—our experiences, our reactions—shaped, predetermined, by our brains, and to what extent do we shape our own brains?" He is led to this conundrum by consideration of a series of cases of individuals who were born with sight but then became blind. The point that Sacks wants to make in "The Mind's Eye" is deceptively simple: how one responds to becoming blind is idiosyncratic—that is, it is unique to the individual. Sacks did not always think this was the case. Initially, he assumed that responses to going blind were determined by the structure of the human brain and thus were essentially uniform.

Sacks begins his essay by describing an extreme example of what is thought to be the typical response to going blind, where the other senses gain heightened powers as the ability to see recedes. After John Hull, blind in one eye due to cataracts at seventeen, went completely blind at forty-eight, he steadily lost access not only to his visual memories but to what Sacks terms "the very idea of seeing." In this profound state of "deep blindness," Hull claimed that spatial references such as "here" and "there" lost meaning for him. At the same time, he became what he calls a "whole-body seer," someone whose other senses have roared to life to compensate for the loss of vision and who now experiences wholly new ways of engaging with the world.

After first writing about Hull in 1991, Sacks began to hear from others whose own experiences of becoming blind conflicted with this compensatory model of how senses covered for each other. For example, Zoltan Torey's response to going blind was the exact opposite of Hull's: instead of embracing "deep blindness" when he lost his sight in an accident at the age of twenty-one, Torey cultivated the powers of his "inner eye," self-consciously laboring to hold on to his ability to think with and manipulate visual images. What Torey has done since going blind is almost unthinkable: he learned to multiply four-figure numbers by visualizing the operations as if the calculation were written on a blackboard; he taught himself to move and manipulate three-dimensional images in his mind, breaking them apart and recombining the pieces; he even single-handedly replaced the roof on his gabled home. What motivates Torey? A deep need to retain a sense of the visual.

Then there's Sabriye Tenberken, blind since twelve, who has traveled extensively in Tibet, often alone, advocating for the blind. She has cultivated a rich synesthetic inner world, one full of color and feeling, which allows her to use words to paint elaborate and fanciful descriptions of the outside world. While Torey visualizes highly detailed maps and diagrams of the real world, Tenberken delights in holding on to an inner vision that is poetic and playful.

Sacks started out looking for a neurological explanation of these varied responses to becoming blind—i.e., that whereas Hull's visual cortex had atrophied completely, Torey was able to "stave off an otherwise inevitable loss of neuronal function in the visual cortex" as a result of his mental gymnastics. But when Sacks turns his attention to people who can see, he quickly finds a similar range in the visual imagination of sighted individuals: some seeing people can hold images in their minds and manipulate them as Torey does; some, akin to Hull, cannot generate visual images or call them to mind; others can achieve the ability to visualize in great detail only through chemical enhancement.

Where does this leave us? For Sacks, the fact that both the blind and the seeing share a spectrum of possible ways to visualize the outer world illustrates the difference between brain and mind. The power to see has a physical, neurological basis located in the brain. What happens to those impulses once the brain processes them is determined not by the brain alone but by "the higher and more personal powers of the imagination, where there is a continual struggle for concepts and form and meaning, a calling upon all the powers of the self," which we would call *the mind*. Sacks continues:

> Imagination dissolves and transforms, unifies and creates, while drawing upon the "lower" powers of memory and association. It is by such imagination, such "vision," that we create or construct our individual worlds.

Thus, at the level of the individual, there will always be a measure of mystery in the adaptations that occur in response to radical change. We see this mystery as much in Hull's embrace of deep blindness as in Torey's tending the flames of inner vision—in the interplay between the hardwiring of neurology and the software of the self. Such a mystery cannot be unraveled by science alone because the self simultaneously resides in and is created by the work of the imagination as it connects and transforms the memories and associations recorded by and stored in the brain.

To put this another way, we could say that our inner lives are both created and sustained by the imagination; and further, that in times of radical change the very survival of the self depends on imagining what was previously unimaginable—that life without sight is sensually rich, for example, or that one's blindness should be fully embraced. This observation doesn't resolve the mystery, of course, but only further sharpens it: How does one cultivate an imagination capable of such adaptation? How does one learn to live with and within new forms of embodied experience?

PRACTICE SESSION ONE

RESEARCHING

If you are blind or visually impaired, skip this exercise and go to Reflecting (for blind or visually–impaired students) on the next page. If you are sighted, visit the online *Time* magazine photo gallery *Photos by Blind Photographers*. The opening blurb says that the exhibit "raises extraordinary questions about the nature of sight." What do you see when you look at these photographs taken by photographers who are legally blind? How do the words that accompany each image influence what you see? Can you unsee the words and consider the images simply as photographs? Search the Web for other works by these photographers and for the work of other blind photographers. Follow your curiosity.

REFLECTING (FOR SIGHTED STUDENTS)

How do blind photographers teach the sighted to see? Using examples of images you have collected through your research, write a reflective essay about what you've learned about blindness and the imagination.

REFLECTING (FOR BLIND OR VISUALLY-IMPAIRED STUDENTS)

Consider what the sighted could learn about perception through a representation of your experience. John Hull offers such a representation when he describes the intensity of experiencing rain as a "whole-body seer":

> Rain has a way of bringing out the contours of everything; it throws a colored blanket over previously invisible things; instead of an intermittent and thus fragmented world, the steadily falling rain creates continuity of acoustic experience.... The sound on the path is quite different from the sound of the rain drumming into the lawn on the right, and this is different again from the blanketed, heavy, sodden feel of the large bush on the left. Further out, the sounds are less detailed. I can hear the rain falling on the road, and the swish of the cars that pass up and down.

Write a reflective essay that represents your experience of your environment. Does your experience strike you as idiosyncratic? That is, did your individual character, temperament, or will play a role in your perception of your environment?

PRACTICE SESSION TWO

WRITING

John Hull, Zoltan Torey, and Sabriye Tenberken help Sacks to see the power of the individual imagination in shaping how one responds to trauma. But what about ordinary, everyday problems? Does the imagination come into play when confronting a problem that is not life altering?

Choose a mundane problem that arises in the course of your day: a disagreement with a family member; difficulty finding parking; misplacing your keys. Does this sort of problem, in its solution, yield evidence of the uniqueness of each individual's imagination? Or do mundane problems call for mundane solutions? Write an essay that explores multiple ways of solving an everyday problem, and consider whether your example demonstrates the powers of the human imagination.

PRACTICE SESSION THREE

RESEARCHING

Choose an essay and, while reading it, mark the moments when the author encounters difficulty. When you're done, review the passages you've marked. Are all the difficulties of the same kind? Of the same importance? Of the same intensity?

How does the writer respond to these difficulties? Write an essay in which you examine the writer's approach to difficulty. Although you might be tempted to say that the writer's approach is simply "idiosyncratic," explore in greater detail how the writer responds to difficulty that's encountered in the world of ideas and words.

EXPLORE

Our essay on encountering difficulty works with four examples of how people have responded to losing the ability to see. The material we suggest here further complicates our discussion. Michael Finkel profiles a blind man who sees like a bat. Filmmakers Peter Middleton and John Spinney interpret John Hull's audio-diary of his journey into blindness. A photo gallery showcases images created by people who are legally blind.

Finkel, Michael. "The Blind Man Who Taught Himself to See." *Men's Journal*. March 2011. Web.

Hull, John. "Memory," "Panic," and "Rainfall." Supplements to Peter Middleton and John Spinney's "Notes on Blindness." Audio. *New York Times*. Web.

Middleton, Peter, and John Spinney, directors. "Notes on Blindness." *New York Times*. 16 Jan. 2014. Web.

Photos by Blind Photographers. Time n.d. Web.

Curiosity at Work: David Simon Pays Attention to the Disenfranchised

David Simon has excelled as a writer in many different roles: police reporter in Baltimore; author of two award-winning books, *Homicide: A Year on the Killing Streets* and *The Corner: A Year in the Life of an Inner-City Neighborhood;* screenwriter for *Homicide,* a television series based on his book of the same title; head writer for the HBO series *The Wire;* and cocreator and coproducer of the HBO series *Treme.* In 2010, he was awarded a no-strings-attached $625,000 MacArthur "Genius" Fellowship, which the MacArthur Foundation says "is not a reward for past accomplishment, but rather an investment in a person's originality, insight, and potential." Not bad for a guy who graduated from the University of Maryland with a C average.

What made it possible for Simon to move from cub reporter to chronicler of the collapse of American cities? The decades Simon spent on the beat in Baltimore made him comfortable with not knowing in advance what he was going to see or hear or report: "To be a decent city reporter, I had to listen to people who were different from me. I had to not be uncomfortable asking stupid questions or being on the outside. I found I had a knack for walking into situations where I didn't know anything, and just waiting." Simon learned to listen closely to the people of Baltimore and to pay attention to their multiple points of view. Because of the way he listened, he fell in love with the crime-ridden, impoverished city.

Why has Baltimore gone from being a major US port to a city with one of the highest murder rates in the country? This is a problem that can't be answered in a sound bite. It takes Simon five seasons of storytelling in *The Wire* to bring to light the multiple variables that work together in postindustrial capitalism to create the toxic conditions in which humans are worth less and less with every passing moment, while glistening new buildings rise on Baltimore's Inner Harbor. These rapacious economic and social forces can't be understood in isolation; they have to be seen in action, degrading the value of the lives of gang members as well as those who work in the police force, the failing shipping industry, the city government, the public school system, and the local newspapers. Like a contemporary Charles Dickens, Simon employs a large canvas, multiple intersecting plotlines, and memorable hard-luck characters to voice his critique of the widening gap between the haves and the have-nots.

In the four seasons of *Treme*, Simon continues exploring the fate of American cities, this time focusing on New Orleans after Hurricane Katrina. Looking beyond the image of New Orleans as the Big Easy, a place where the good times always roll, Simon tells stories about the city's recovery from the hurricane through the eyes of local musicians, a neighborhood bar owner, a "Big Chief" in the Mardi Gras parades, a civil rights attorney, and a jazz musician who has made good in New York. Why does he use storytelling and not journalism or the documentary form to do this work? Simon explains: "By referencing what is real, or historical, a fictional narrative can speak in a powerful, full-throated way to the problems and issues of our time. And a wholly imagined tale, set amid the intricate and accurate details of a real place and time, can resonate with readers in profound ways. In short, drama is its own argument."

Note: The first Simon quote is from Margaret Talbot's *New Yorker* article, "Stealing Life"; the second quote is from "HBO's 'Treme' Creator David Simon Explains It All for You," published in the *New Orleans Times-Picayune*.

Asking Questions

"There are no bad questions": this is an incantation repeated year in and year out in classrooms across the country. It represents a well-intentioned effort to establish a comfortable learning environment, but it's a hard sell, since teachers and students alike know that not only are there bad questions, but there are whole categories of questions that are unwelcome in the classroom. There are questions most teachers dread—the intrusively personal question, the cynical question, and the do-you-mind-repeating-what-you-just-said question, to name a few—and there are questions most students dread, such as the teacher's guess-what-I'm-thinking question, the teacher's fill-in-the-blank question, and the question that exposes the student who asked it to ridicule.

Rather than make the demonstrably false assertion that there are no bad questions, we prefer to ask: What is a good question? In this chapter, we introduce you to two of our favorite question posers, the hosts of *Radiolab*. We also propose an alternative to the thesis-driven writing project: writing your way to a question. And we look at how to prepare for an interview-based project. Questions you hear, questions produced by your own speculative writing, questions you put to others: we give you three different contexts for considering the roles that context, expertise, research, and curiosity play in the production of good questions.

On Asking Questions

We're devoted fans of *Radiolab*, a radio show and podcast on which the hosts, Jad Abumrad and Robert Krulwich, invite listeners to join them "on a curiosity bender." Abumrad is a composer by training and won a MacArthur Fellowship in 2011 for his work on the show, while Krulwich is a science correspondent with over three decades of broadcast experience. Working together, they make the exercise of being curious about the world *sound* like an exciting adventure.

In each show, Abumrad and Krulwich assume the air of happy amateurs who delight in having simple questions open up complex realities. They typically begin with a big question—about science, the arts, medicine, philosophy, or some other aspect

Chapter 3, "Asking Questions," is taken from Richard E. Miller and Ann Jurecic, *Habits of the Creative Mind*, pp. 54–71 (Part 4, "Asking Questions").

of human experience—and then spend an hour exploring a range of responses to the question they've posed. The questions they ask often express an open-minded wonder about the world: Why do we sleep? What is color? What is race? How do we assign blame? To help them with their explorations, they always turn to experts, but they never take what the experts have to say as the final word on the matter. They question, provoke, and at times openly disagree with their guests and with each other.

There's a common pattern in most *Radiolab* shows: Abumrad and Krulwich move back and forth between questions, big ideas, interviews, and stories, inevitably leading their listeners to new problems and new questions, and revealing in the process that the issue they started with is more complicated than it first seemed. We admire how they move from simple wonder to complex possibilities, and we like that multiple answers, insights, and solutions are entertained along the way. We also like that *Radiolab* sounds beautiful. It's important to recognize that the creative soundscapes Abumrad and Krulwich produce are more than mere entertainment. In every episode, they demonstrate how curiosity can generate beauty as well as answers and ideas.

What we admire most about *Radiolab* is that the hosts manage to express in sound and language the whole spectrum of habits of the creative mind. You can hear Abumrad's creativity as a composer in the ways he uses sound to represent ideas that might otherwise remain too abstract for listeners to grasp. You can hear how open both men are to ambiguity, the unknown, and discovery as Abumrad and Krulwich talk their way through the implications of what they're learning. You can also hear their attention to and engagement with ideas, information, and expertise in the questions they ask. And you can hear their reflectiveness as thoughts digress, reverse, and surprise. Most of all, you can hear their boundless curiosity at work in the shape and progress of each episode.

We'd like you to listen to two episodes of *Radiolab*—one scripted, one open ended—so that you can hear what curiosity as a habit of mind sounds like.

PRACTICE SESSION ONE

LISTENING

In "An Equation for Good," a chapter in *Radiolab*'s "The Good Show" podcast, Abumrad and Krulwich consider an open-ended question that has puzzled evolutionary biologists since Charles Darwin first advanced his theory that species evolve through struggle and competition. If the "fittest" survive through tooth-and-claw rivalry, how can we explain kindness, generosity, and altruism?

Find a quiet place where you can listen to "An Equation for Good" without interruption; the podcast is about 22 minutes long. Use headphones or earbuds so you don't miss a thing.

Next, listen to the podcast again, this time pausing it when necessary to write down the questions Abumrad and Krulwich ask; this is likely to take more than 30 minutes. Keep track of where each question leads. What people and sources do Abumrad and Krulwich turn to for answers? What stories do they tell? Is there a logic to the overall shape of the show? An aesthetic?

WRITING

Spend at least 30 minutes creating a visual map that illustrates the development of the hosts' thinking as "An Equation for Good" unfolds. When do their ideas move in a straight line? When do their questions cause a change in direction? Do they ever take wrong turns? If so, are any of the resulting digressions useful? By the end of "An Equation for Good," how far have Abumrad and Krulwich traveled? What do they conclude about the status of the definition of *evolution* as "the survival of the fittest"? (Note: You might want to experiment with making your map "move"; feel free to use presentation and/or animation software to bring your map to life.)

After you've created your map, pause to reflect on what you've learned. What does your map reveal about Abumrad and Krulwich's methods? Could someone else look at your map and understand what you've learned about how the show is structured? If not, how is what you've produced a map?

PRACTICE SESSION TWO

LISTENING

Next, we'd like you to listen to the *Radiolab* podcast "Secrets of Success," a conversation between Robert Krulwich and Malcolm Gladwell, author of *The Tipping Point, Blink,* and *Outliers.* This podcast shows how questions unfold when a curious person talks at length to a single expert, trying to understand the development and reach of the expert's ideas while also puzzling through whether to accept the expert's conclusions.

Find a quiet place where you can listen without interruption; the interview is about 25 minutes long. Don't forget your earbuds.

When you're done, set aside more than 30 minutes to listen to the podcast again, this time pausing to write down the questions and other prompts Krulwich uses to get Gladwell to explain his ideas about talent, practice, passion, and success.

WRITING

Set aside at least 30 minutes to create another map that illustrates the unfolding conversation between Gladwell and Krulwich. When does Krulwich move the discussion in a straight line? When does he seem to change direction? Do any apparent digressions end up looping back to serve the main argument? Are there other digressions that take the conversation off track? Are you convinced by Gladwell's responses to Krulwich's questions?

PRACTICE SESSION THREE

REFLECTING

After you've created maps for both "An Equation for Good" and "Secrets of Success," look at them side by side. Spend at least 30 minutes considering what they show you about how curiosity works and how understanding and arguments develop. What do you see that helps you to think about how you might compose a curiosity-driven essay or podcast about a big question like "How can we explain why humans sometimes go out of their way to help strangers?" or "Is there a secret to success?" What are some open-ended questions you'd like to read, listen, or write about?

EXPLORE

We're drawn to works of nonfiction that are question-driven. The podcast *Radiolab* asks questions about anything and everything, including time, tumors, blame, mosquitos, quicksand, and the power of music. While *Radiolab* jumps from topic to topic, the captivating podcast *Serial* devotes twelve episodes to one subject—an investigation into whether a man was wrongfully imprisoned for the 1999 murder of a Maryland teen. Law professor Ruthann Robson asks questions about a different kind of case, one that emerges after she is misdiagnosed with cancer, suffers through chemotherapy and medical mistreatment, and then considers both what her life is worth, and what matters more to her than money.

Radiolab. Podcast.

Robson, Ruthann. "Notes from a Difficult Case." *In Fact: The Best of Creative Nonfiction*. Ed. Lee Gutkind. New York: Norton, 2005. 226–44. Print.

Serial. Season One. Podcast.

On Writing to a Question

What's writing for? In school, the most common answer given to that question is, "To make a point." And so in school one practices having a point that can be succinctly stated in a thesis statement. "Writing is for making points" is itself an example of a succinct thesis statement.

We think the requirement to *start* an essay by committing to a thesis is a good way to kill curiosity. It turns writing into a mindless fill-in-the-blank exercise: Thesis? Check. Three examples? Check. Conclusion that summarizes the previous three paragraphs? Check. This approach to writing is a machine for arguing the obvious; it does not use writing as a tool for thinking new thoughts or for developing ideas that are new to the writer.

For your writing to become a mode of learning for you, you must begin in a state of not-knowing rather than committing yourself to a claim you came up with before you've done any curiosity-driven research. In the "Curiosity at Work" profiles in this book, we showcase a wide range of nonfiction writers who use writing as a mode of learning. Consider the divergent cases of Donovan Hohn and Rebecca Skloot.

Donovan Hohn, a high school English teacher, was reading a student's paper when he first learned about the plastic bath toys—yellow ducks, green frogs, blue turtles, and red beavers—that began washing ashore in Alaska and Australia in the early 1990s. Curious, he began to do some research online. Caught up in the mysteries, he left his job and traveled the earth to follow the path of the toys. He recorded his journey of discovery in his book *Moby-Duck*.

Rebecca Skloot was sixteen years old and taking a biology class when she learned that the first human cells ever grown in a lab were from an African American woman named Henrietta Lacks. Skloot wanted to know more about Lacks, but her teacher had no additional information, and at the time Skloot couldn't find anything more in the library. Many years later, when Skloot decided to become a writer, she tracked down Lacks's family and pieced together Henrietta Lacks's history and the history of her cell line. Then Skloot wrote the best-selling book *The Immortal Life of Henrietta Lacks*.

Neither of these writers began with a thesis that they then set out to prove. Rather, each started with a question and pushed past simplistic discussions of pollution or racism to develop a deeper, richer understanding of the situation's complexity. But where did the questions that Donovan and Skloot began with come from? Were the questions the result of inspiration or just dumb luck?

While there's always an element of chance in any research project, we think you learn how to ask the kinds of questions that stick with you for years by cultivating the habit of generating questions. How does this process work? Once you've developed the habit of generating questions about things that are taken for granted and about things unknown, you will find that you have many questions to choose from and many possible paths to explore. Some questions will seem more important than others, some will nag at you, and some will seem urgent; the very best questions will have all of these attributes.

To help our students develop the intertwined habits of curiosity and questioning, we've adopted a drafting strategy that throws out the familiar essay form. We ask our students instead to write frequent short papers in response to readings, and we tell them that these papers should not contain thesis statements.

At first they're baffled. How can you even begin an essay without a thesis? We tell them to just go ahead and give it a try. We instruct them to look in the assigned readings for moments when an author

- says something surprising or confusing;
- makes an unexpected connection;
- presents a provocative example;
- uses a familiar term in a new or peculiar way;
- or poses an idea or argument that is difficult to accept.

Freed from having to begin with a thesis statement, our students use their responses to readings to puzzle through surprising, confusing, or provocative passages. Consequently, when they write, they aren't reporting what the author said and then agreeing or disagreeing with it; they are focusing on interesting moments in which they sense a tension between their own thoughts, knowledge, or expectations and what an author has written.

Once they've written their way through a passage or a series of passages, we ask them to conclude their response papers with a reflection on what they've figured out over the course of developing their responses. Ideally, their exploration of moments of tension leads them to a compelling question or questions, which they pose in the final sentences of their responses. These should be questions that they can't presently answer and that require more thought, reading, and research—questions they are truly curious about and *want* to answer.

Right now you might be wondering, what's the point of writing to a question you can't answer? Isn't exposing your own ignorance the exact opposite of what you should be doing in school? Good questions!

We think there are many good reasons to use informal writing and drafting to arrive at a compelling question. When you write about passages or ideas in a text or set of texts that confuse or interest you, you are learning to use writing as a tool for thinking. And you'll see that writers discover what they think not *before* they write but *in the act* of writing. You'll also learn how to take more risks with your thinking. Ending with a question you don't know the answer to may feel uncomfortable at first—as if you're revealing a weakness. But openly confronting what you don't know is an essential part of learning to write well. Paradoxically, by writing to a question in a draft, you'll learn how to generate a truly interesting thesis. Once you've drafted a question that you're genuinely curious about, you're ready for the next step: figuring out how to respond to that question. Your response will be a thesis that's worth writing and reading about. Writing to a question also gives you practice with the essential habits of the creative mind: curiosity, openness to new ways of thinking, engagement with learning, and intellectual adventurousness.

PRACTICE SESSION ONE

REFLECTING

Are you a curious person? Do you express your curiosity most often in school, among your friends, at work, or elsewhere? You may not know the answers to these questions, so we'd like you to pay attention to your own curiosity for a week. Take notes every day, keeping an account of when, where, and how you pose questions, whether out loud to others or silently to yourself.

At the end of the week, spend at least 30 minutes reviewing your notes and learning about your own curiosity. When and where were you most curious? How often did you ask questions in classes? Did you pose more questions in one class or another? Did you ask questions as you read, jotting questions in the margins or in your notes? What was your most vivid experience of curiosity-driven learning in the past week? Was it in school or elsewhere?

PRACTICE SESSION TWO

READING

In the list of suggested readings in this essay's "Explore" section, on p. 41, each writer presents his or her central question in the article's subtitle: "What Should Medicine Do When It Can't Save Your Life?"; "Did American Conservationists in Africa Go Too Far?"; "Why Are We So Fat?"; "Is It a Crime?" Read one of the suggested readings, paying attention to how the writer answers the question posed in the subtitle. Trace how the writer's answer to the main question develops as the piece progresses.

Spend 30 minutes taking notes on how the answer to the question unfolds. Does the writer reverse or qualify your expectations? Are additional questions posed, explicitly or implicitly, that shift the direction of the writer's inquiry or reshape your understanding of the issue?

REFLECTING

In our essay, we describe how we ask our students to write to a question. Now we want you to give it a try.

Return to the reading you selected and review it, looking for moments in the argument that catch your attention—passages that are surprising or confusing, make an unexpected connection, present a provocative example, use a term in a new or peculiar way, or pose an idea or argument that is difficult to accept. Then write a draft in which you explore three or more parts of the reading that you find interesting or baffling—places where you feel friction between the text and your own thoughts, knowledge, or expectations.

In the final paragraph of your draft, reflect on what you've learned about the ideas or argument in the reading you selected, and pose a question that has emerged from your work with the passages you've chosen. The standard for assessing the quality of the question you've generated is this: Do you genuinely want to answer it?

WRITING

Having arrived at an interesting question, you can now write an essay that allows you to develop your thoughts and figure out your answer. Bring a version of your question into your essay's title or subtitle, as the writers of the suggested readings do. Then go about answering it, working with the reading you selected and the passages you wrote about, as well as any other passages that now seem relevant.

EXPLORE

At the beginning of Practice Session Two, we draw your attention to the subtitles of the essays listed below: each one poses a difficult question and each question leads readers into realms of ambiguity, uncertainty, and ethical confusion. It's unlikely these writers began with their questions already formed; they began instead with challenging cases: a pregnant mother who learns she is going to die; a conservation effort that leads to killings; a graph that shows an explosion in American obesity in the 1980s; a man who forgot to drop his toddler off at daycare and the terrible consequences that followed. Only after much reading, researching, drafting, and revising did the big issues crystalize: How should medicine treat the dying? What is the human cost of protecting endangered species? What has caused an "epidemic" of obesity? And can a terrible mistake also be a crime?

Gawande, Atul. "Letting Go: What Should Medicine Do When It Can't Save Your Life?" *New Yorker.* 2 Aug. 2010. Web.

Goldberg, Jeffrey. "The Hunted: Did American Conservationists in Africa Go Too Far?" *New Yorker.* 5 April 2010. Web.

Kolbert, Elizabeth. "XXXL: Why Are We So Fat?" *New Yorker.* 20 July 2009. Web.

Weingarten, Gene. "Fatal Distraction: Forgetting a Child in the Backseat of a Car Is a Horrifying Mistake. Is It a Crime?" *Washington Post.* 8 March 2009. Web.

On Interviewing

Creative nonfiction, defined by Lee Gutkind as "true stories, well told," is often focused on a personal profile: a portrait of a hero or villain, a talented athlete, or an attractive star. Some of the work in this genre features individuals who are distinctive because of their unusual interests or their exceptional abilities, but there is also work that focuses on those who have earned attention because of circumstance or an accident of history. We are particularly drawn to profiles of individuals contending with contingency, such as Anne Fadiman's account of a Hmong family struggling to take care of a gravely ill child in *The Spirit Catches You and You Fall Down* and Jon Krakauer's portrait of a young, idealistic college grad who dies while camping in Alaska in *Into the Wild*. We also admire writing that unveils mysterious, socially marginal figures, such as Susan Orlean's description of an eccentric Florida orchid hunter in *The Orchid Thief*; and Truman Capote's voyage into the minds of two murderers in the *locus classicus* of the creative nonfiction genre, *In Cold Blood*.

Capote, who is credited with inventing creative nonfiction, once said that the genre requires a writer "to empathize with personalities outside his usual imaginative range, mentalities unlike his own, kinds of people he would never have written about had he not been forced to by encountering them inside the journalistic situation." For Capote, the writer of creative nonfiction must go beyond the journalist's commitment to neutrally reporting verifiable information and must instead, via empathy, strive to reconstruct the assumptions, beliefs, and feelings of another person. For Capote, describing the murders was a relatively simple matter: two drifters break into a farmhouse, kill the owners and their two teenage children, and escape with nothing, having been misinformed about the presence on the property of a safe stuffed with cash. But finding a way into the murderers' inner worlds was a much steeper challenge. How could Capote understand the thinking of the men behind these unthinkable acts? And why would he even want to try?

Once the murderers were captured, Capote interviewed them repeatedly over a three-year period—during and after their trial, throughout their efforts to appeal their convictions, and up to the time of their executions. He also interviewed townspeople, family members of the deceased, family members of the murderers, police officers, jailers, and other inmates. To make sense of the minds behind this senseless act of violence, Capote had to work long and hard. What they had done was clear, but why they had done it could be understood only through painstaking research and leaps of the imagination.

Getting inside the heads of cold-blooded killers—that's the outer limit of the impetus driving creative nonfiction. The more general desire motivating work in this genre is a deep curiosity about how others make sense of the world—and those others can be just about anyone: a family caring for a child in a persistent coma; a young man dissatisfied with the emptiness of contemporary life; a guy who searches swamps for orchids and sells them in an international black market. The realm of creative nonfiction enables us to grapple with the most profound difference there is: what life is like in the mind of another.

The journalist's most important tool for understanding others is the interview. How does one learn to interview? The first rule is easy: be curious.

The art and craft of interviewing, like writing, takes practice. Your first few efforts might feel clumsy, but as you gain experience, conducting interviews gets easier. As you begin, these general guidelines will make the process easier and the results more useful.

Before the Interview

- Choose a time and a place for the interview that will put the interviewee at ease. You need to be able to hear each other, so select a location that doesn't distract from the conversation or invite interruptions from others.
- Draft your questions ahead of time, but before you draft them, spend time on background research. Then generate questions that your background research *can't* answer.
- Bring everything you need for note taking to the interview. You'll need paper and pencil or a laptop, of course. If the interview subject agrees to be recorded, you can also bring equipment for making an audio or a video recording. (We find that an audio recording is preferable, because the presence of a video camera often causes the interviewee to speak as if on television.) Be sure to get your subject's permission in advance to record the interview.

During the Interview Itself

- After you ask a question, pause and wait for an answer. Give your interview subject time to think. If she or he is truly stumped, ask whether you should rephrase the question.
- If your interview subject says something you don't understand or refers to something unfamiliar to you, don't be embarrassed to ask more questions.
- Listen carefully to what your interview subject says and how he or she says it.
- Give yourself permission to improvise. Your interview should feel like a conversation, not an interrogation. For this to happen, you need to be willing to stray from what you've written down and follow the interview subject down any unexpected paths the conversation has revealed.

A Cautionary Tale

A while back, we were teaching a course in which students were researching a number of nearby development projects. In one case, the developer had taken down an entire block of local businesses and was in the process of putting up a high-rise of condos and apartments. The developer agreed to meet and discuss his vision of New Brunswick with the team of students working on the case. The students did their research, and at the appointed time, they sat down with the developer in his office, the model of his redevelopment plans laid out in front of his panoramic view of the city.

The lead interviewer asked the developer about the number of apartments he anticipated renting out to students in the new high-rise.

"None," the developer told them. The high-rise wasn't being built for students.

The interview effectively ended at that point, though other questions followed. The students had done research, but their research did not help prepare them for this particular interview with this particular person. They had their one shot with a very busy local entrepreneur, and they used it to ask a question about a matter of concern to them. Unfortunately, the way their question was phrased revealed that they had not imagined a world in which students might not be the central concern. They were, in essence, asking the entrepreneur why he didn't see the world the way they did, instead of using the interview to better understand how *the entrepreneur* viewed the development project and why he viewed it that way.

To the students' credit, they realized that the interview had failed because they had not posed questions that would solicit useful material. So they started over: they drafted a whole new set of questions and requested another chance. In this instance, they were lucky enough to be granted a second interview, but interviewers can't count on their subjects giving them multiple shots, especially if, in their first shot, they seem unprepared, have chosen a poor location, or fail to show that they value the interviewee's time.

Moral?

You may only get one shot. Make it count.

PRACTICE SESSION ONE

READING

Read Gene Weingarten's "Pearls before Breakfast," which is available online at washingtonpost.com, and watch the videos embedded in the article. As you read, keep notes on the many people Weingarten interviews for his article and on how he goes about discovering what and how they think.

After you've read and thought about Weingarten's article, spend at least 30 minutes reviewing your notes and reflecting in writing on Weingarten as an interviewer. When do you think he's most successful at gathering compelling or surprising points of view? Identify instances in which Weingarten elicits a particularly important idea or revealing insight from someone he interviews. How does Weingarten use what he learns from interviews to develop his own thoughts? What does he do as an interviewer that you would like to emulate?

PRACTICE SESSION TWO

RESEARCHING

As preparation for writing a nonfiction profile, spend a week researching a little-known subculture or group at your school or in your community. The deeper the mystery, the better. (Over the years, we've had students write about underground music scenes, fire throwing—look it up!—urban gardening, religious practices, body modification, and a dance-influenced Brazilian martial art called *capoeira*.) Your research will require both observing and interviewing.

Begin by doing background research about the activity or subculture. If it's possible to attend a group activity—a performance, a practice session, a ceremony—do so. Observe, listen, and take notes. Describing the activity or subculture will be part of the challenge when you begin to write; you will need to bring the unknown and unfamiliar to light.

The other part of the challenge is getting inside the minds of the participants. You will need to interview at least one participant in depth. Conduct an interview that's at least 30 minutes long, keeping careful notes and, if your subject agrees, recording the conversation. Do your best to ask questions that invite your subject to tell stories. Try to figure out why she or he finds participation in the activity or group *meaningful*.

After you've conducted your interview, you're ready to write a profile. Compose a curiosity-driven essay that explores the subculture or group your interviewee belongs to and its meaning or value.

REFLECTING

Take at least 30 minutes to reflect on your experience as an interviewer. Review your notes and the recording you made (if there is one). Then look over the essay you wrote. Where did your use of the interview work best? What would you do differently in your next interview? What do you need to practice to get better results?

EXPLORE

There's an art to the interview. Anne Fadiman, Jon Krakauer, Janet Malcolm, and Susan Orlean each composed book-length nonfiction narratives that grew out of months, even years, of listening, learning, and asking questions. Their prose portraits display both intimate insights and evidence of the mysteries that remain after their interviews ended. We also invite you to read the transcripts of writers interviewing other writers in *The Paris Review* and *The Believer*.

The Believer. Interviews with writers from 2003 to the present. Web.

Fadiman, Anne. *The Spirit Catches You and You Fall Down*. New York: Farrar, Straus and Giroux, 1997. Print.

Krakauer, Jon. *Into the Wild*. New York: Villard, 1996. Print.

Malcolm, Janet. *The Journalist and the Murderer*. New York: Knopf/Random House, 1990. Print.

Orlean, Susan. *The Orchid Thief*. New York: Random House, 1998. Print.

The Paris Review. Interviews with writers, from 1953 to the present. Web.

Curiosity at Work: Michael Pollan Contemplates the Ethics of Eating Meat

What would history look like if it were told from the vantage point of the plant world? This provocative question drives Michael Pollan's *The Botany of Desire*, in which he considers how plants that satisfy the human desire for sweetness (apples), beauty (tulips), pleasure (marijuana), and sustenance (potatoes) have transformed the global landscape. By shifting to "a plant's-eye view," Pollan is able to see anew how the fate of the plant kingdom is inextricably linked to human desire.

In "An Animal's Place," published shortly after *The Botany of Desire*, Pollan moves from the plant world to the animal world to consider the personal, political, and moral puzzles involved in something many people take for granted: eating meat. Pollan begins his essay as a committed meat eater, one who is frustrated by the argument Peter Singer makes in *Animal Liberation* that eating, wearing, or experimenting on animals violates animals' right to live free of suffering caused by humans.

Pollan responds to his frustration with Singer by posing questions and noticing contradictions. Why is it that 51 percent of Americans believe that primates should be extended the same rights as human children, while at the same time "in our factory farms and laboratories we are inflicting more suffering on more animals than at any time in history"? Why are we so confused about our relationship to animals?

From there, Pollan's questions emerge in a steady stream. "When's the last time you saw a pig?" he asks. Is the fact that animals lack certain human characteristics a just basis for raising them for slaughter on factory farms? Pollan is especially intrigued by a question posed by eighteenth-century philosopher Jeremy Bentham, who wrote that we ought to make moral decisions about animals not by asking whether animals can reason or talk—questions that render them less than human— but rather by asking, "Can they suffer?"

And the questions keep coming. "Why treat animals more ethically than they treat one another?" "Wouldn't life in the wild be worse for these farm animals?" "Doesn't the fact that we could choose to forgo meat for moral reasons point to a crucial moral difference between animals and humans?" "What's wrong with reserving moral consideration for those able to reciprocate it?" Do "we owe animals that can feel pain any moral consideration, ... and if we do ... how can we justify eating them?" And finally, "were the walls of our meat industry to become transparent, literally or even figuratively, ... who could stand the sight?"

Pollan's train of thought leads him to a question posed in the title of critic John Berger's essay "Why Look at Animals?" Berger was concerned, says Pollan, that "the loss of everyday contact between ourselves and animals—and specifically the loss of eye contact—has left us deeply confused about the terms of our relationship to other species." Pollan agrees and concludes that if we looked animals in the eyes, and if we created the conditions in which we were also able to look without disgust or shame at how we raise and slaughter them, then we could eat animals "with the consciousness, ceremony, and respect they deserve." In two subsequent books, *The Omnivore's Dilemma* and *In Defense of Food*, Pollan has sought to better understand how to live in accordance with this insight.

Note: For additional discussion of Michael Pollan's "An Animal's Place," see "On Joining the Conversation" on p. 12.

Exploring

Our first history lessons in school are often about "the explorers." Christopher Columbus discovered America; Vasco da Gama discovered the overseas route from Europe to India; Marco Polo opened trade routes in Asia. These captivating stories involve adventure, courage, bravery, and derring-do. There are skirmishes, riches beyond imagining, kings and queens—all sorts of things to fire the imaginations of the young.

Later on, we learn that these stories have been simplified and that exploration itself is rarely the process of moving peacefully through unoccupied, unclaimed territories. Some find the revision of these earlier stories to be upsetting and somehow wrong. But we believe that those who practice being curious with their writing are learning how to explore both the worlds beyond and the worlds within the self. This isn't exploration as represented in fairytales and childhood stories of questing heroes. It's the messier, more disorienting, more complicated work that making sense of human experience and human history demands.

The first essay in this chapter likens exploration in the Internet age to Alice's trip "down the rabbit hole" and invites you to use your search engines to practice chasing ideas, thoughts, and questions wherever they may lead. In the second essay, we suggest that there is an activity called "creative reading" that parallels creative writing, and in the third essay, we show you how the process of understanding others (as opposed to conquering them) requires acts of imagination, informed by research. Why would anyone want to engage in explorations of these kinds? We close this chapter with a meditation on the mystery of motivation.

On Going down the Rabbit Hole

"Down the rabbit hole": it's a strange phrase, isn't it? If you've heard it before, it's possible that the first thing it calls to mind is the scene in *The Matrix* where Morpheus offers Neo two pills: "You take the blue pill—the story ends, you wake up in your bed and believe whatever you want to believe. You take the red pill—you stay in Wonderland,

Chapter 4, "Exploring," is taken from Richard E. Miller and Ann Jurecic, *Habits of the Creative Mind*, pp. 72–98 (Part 5, "Exploring").

and I show you how deep the rabbit hole goes." In the inside-out world of *The Matrix*, reality is an illusion and what seems illusory—that time can be slowed down, that bullets can be dodged, that gravity only applies intermittently—is actually possible in a deeper reality.

Morpheus (the name Ovid gives the god of dreams in his long poem *Metamorphoses*) refers to "Wonderland" and "the rabbit hole" on the assumption that Neo—and those watching the film—will make the connection to Lewis Carroll's *Alice's Adventures in Wonderland*. In that story, a young girl named Alice is sitting on a riverbank, bored with how the day is going, when a rabbit carrying a pocket watch rushes past her. Alice follows the rabbit, who disappears down a rabbit hole. She sticks her head in and begins to fall down the hole, and what follows is a series of adventures that has captivated generations of readers for nearly 150 years.

Think of all that happens to Alice in the few pages that make up the first chapter of her *Adventures*: when she finally hits bottom (when she sees how deep the rabbit hole goes), the rabbit is just turning a corner in another long tunnel, so she gives chase. When she turns the same corner, Alice finds herself in a long hallway with doors on each side, all of them locked. Then she discovers a key that opens a very small door, which leads to a beautiful garden on the other side. Because she is too big to fit through the door, Alice keeps exploring the hallway. She finds a bottle with a note that says DRINK ME. Alice complies, and suddenly she's "shutting up like a telescope" until she's only ten inches tall. She wants to go into the garden but can no longer reach the key to open the small door, and so she begins to cry. She looks down, discovers another small door, opens it, and finds a small cake with the words EAT ME written on top in currants. Which Alice does, of course, leading to this statement at the beginning of the second chapter:

> "Curiouser and curiouser!" cried Alice (she was so much surprised, that for the moment she quite forgot how to speak good English); "now I'm opening out like the largest telescope that ever was! Good-bye, feet!" (for when she looked down at her feet they seemed to be almost out of sight, they were getting so far off).

Why is this idea, which is at the heart of both *The Matrix* and *Alice's Adventures in Wonderland*, so appealing? Why do we take such pleasure in imagining that there's the world we experience every day and that, just beyond this everyday world (or just beneath it, assuming rabbit holes go down), there's another world where the laws of the everyday world no longer apply? One explanation for this fantasy's appeal is that the other extraordinary world is action packed: once the rules that govern the ordinary are suspended, anything can happen—rabbits can talk; bodies can bend out of the way of approaching bullets; a boy with a scar on his forehead can fight off the forces of evil. But this isn't really an explanation so much as it is a description masquerading as an explanation. Why are we drawn to the extraordinary?

Ellen Dissanayake has spent nearly five decades exploring the allure of the extraordinary. Working in evolutionary aesthetics, a field she helped to invent, Dissanayake has concluded that humans are hardwired to seek out the extraordinary; it is, she says, in our nature to do so. In making her argument, Dissanayake sets out to establish that the desire to "make special" or to "artify" (she uses both terms interchangeably) serves a number of evolutionary purposes central to the survival of the species—the most significant being that acting on this desire provides concrete responses to anxiety and uncertainty. Over time, certain ways of making special become ritualized: the wedding ceremony or the walk across the graduation stage, for example, or the gift of flowers to someone who is sick. What we find appealing about Dissanayake's thesis is the implication that art is not the set of static images you find on a wall at a museum. Rather, it is a way of doing or making; it's the practice of making special, which can manifest at anytime—at the feast for a visiting dignitary or over coffee between friends.

Is there an art to doing research? We think so. Most handbooks will send you out to do your research with a plan, an outline, or a map of some kind. The idea behind all this preplanning is to protect you from getting lost while mucking about in the endless thicket of information that's out there. That seems sensible if you think of research only as the process of predicting and then confirming results. That is, when this approach to research is followed, it's no accident that the end results are unsurprising; the whole point of this approach to doing research is that there will be no surprises!

We invite you to envision the research process not as a voyage out onto already mapped territory but as a trip down the rabbit hole. We want you to set for yourself the goal of generating research that is extraordinary—research that proceeds by "making special," by "artifying." We want your research to lead you to write something that rewards repeated acts of attention, which, after all, is just another way of defining *extraordinary*.

What does artful, special, or extraordinary research look like? Obviously, there's no formula. But we'd like to offer an example of what it can look like with an excerpt from an e-mail we received from Chris Osifchin, a former student who wrote to us a year after graduating.

> I've been really getting into Richard Linklater lately, after watching *Dazed and Confused* (my favorite movie of all time) for about the thirtieth time. I watched his movie *Slacker* and also part of *Waking Life*, and what was interesting to me was the portrayal of nothing as everything and how it is displayed in a much more explicit manner than *Dazed*.
>
> I then saw a tweet from an awesome Website, Open Culture, directing Tweeters to the films and works of Susan Sontag. Never heard of her. Isn't it funny how connections come about? As I read more about her, and more of her pieces,

I began to make a connection between Linklater's work and Sontag. The first piece of Sontag's work that I read was "Against Interpretation." I found it fascinating, and also true to a point. The best art does not try to mean anything, it just [lies] there in the glory and awe of its creation....

Next, I read a NYT review of Sontag's first novel, *The Benefactor*, and was struck by how similar it seemed to *Waking Life*. The review even says "Hippolyte also dreams numerous repetitious dreams, ponders them endlessly, and keeps encountering Frau Anders, like a guilty conscience. The intent is to present waking life as if it were a dream. And, to present dreams as concrete as daily living." This is precisely what *Waking Life* is portraying. I think the depiction of dreams as reality and reality as dreams or any combination of those is not "without motive or feeling" as the reviewer says, but rather allows you to view things from a less interpretive point of view, as Sontag might [argue for].

Now, after reading this review, I decided to see if Linklater was influenced by Sontag. I literally searched on Google "Richard Linklater influenced by Susan Sontag." Interestingly enough, and why I decided to send this email to you, Sontag mentions Linklater's *Dazed and Confused* in an article on the Abu Ghraib torture incident, "Regarding the Torture of Others." In it, Sontag mentions the increasing brutality of American culture and the increasing acceptance of violence. Not only did this make me think of [*The Ballad of Abu Ghraib*] and reading it in your class, but it also made me think of a specific moment in *Waking Life* [here he provides the link to the YouTube clip of the moment he references]. "Man wants chaos. In fact, he's gotta have it. Depression, strife, riots murder. All this dread. We're irresistibly drawn to that almost orgiastic state created out of death and destruction. It's in all of us. We revel in it!" It seems to me that this connects very well to Abu Ghraib as a whole, not just the immediate actions of the guards. Sontag's observation that "Secrets of private life that, formerly, you would have given nearly anything to conceal, you now clamor to be invited on a television show to reveal," collides at the intersection of American fantasies played out on TV screens all the time and the real world. It's an interesting comment on American society as a whole—who would have thought that reality TV would come back to bite America in a *war*? And with the extension of reality TV that is now, what I can't think to call anything but the "reality Web" (i.e., social media/networks), it is becoming more prevalent than ever. Sontag puts it better than I have—"What is illustrated by these photographs is as much the culture of shamelessness as the reigning admiration for unapologetic brutality."

For our former student, the world of ideas, like the rabbit hole in *Alice in Wonderland*, is endlessly surprising and extraordinary. He begins by writing about rewatching Richard Linklater's movie *Dazed and Confused*, and then before he knows it, he's off on an entirely self-motivated search through film, philosophy, war, and media in search of artists and thinkers who can help him better understand our "culture of shamelessness" and "unapologetic brutality." With genuine curiosity and some practice doing research, you can transform the world of ideas, as Chris did, into an astounding place in which nearly every turn inspires a new connection and thinking itself becomes both art and play.

PRACTICE SESSION

RESEARCHING

Type the words *Ellen Dissanayake* into the Google search engine. Press return.

Everyone who does this at the same time will get the same results. We can call this "ordinary research." If you click on the Wikipedia entry for Dissanayake, you'll find yourself on a page that provides a thumbnail sketch of the author and her work. Again, in gaining this foothold on Dissanayake's work, you'll be doing what any ordinary researcher starting out would do.

It's what you do next that matters. Choose one of Dissanayake's works that you find online and read it.

Your next task is to make your research into this researcher of the extraordinary extraordinary. (We composed that last sentence with *Alice's Adventures in Wonderland* in mind.) Set aside at least an hour for exploratory research. Begin by choosing a phrase, a quotation, a reference, or a footnote from the Dissanayake work you read and doing another Google search. Read two or more of the recommended links. Then choose a phrase, a quotation, a reference, or a footnote from the second set of works and do another Google search. Repeat. Repeat. And repeat again, until you've burrowed down to an insight or a question that you yourself find extraordinary.

REFLECTING

We call the process outlined above, where you move from one linked source to the next, "drilling down." Spend at least 30 minutes reflecting on this process. As you drilled down in your research, beginning with your first search about Dissanayake and ending with an extraordinary insight or question, how did you distinguish between ordinary and extraordinary moments of discovery? What choices yielded genuine surprises? Begin a list of useful strategies to include in your repertoire as a curious researcher, a list you can add to as you continue to practice drilling down.

RESEARCHING

Write an essay about your research into the extraordinary that presents a special or artful idea, insight, or question. Don't write a schoolish "report" about your research. Instead, make something special with your words; write something that rewards repeated acts of attention.

WRITING

We challenged you to write about your research into the extraordinary in a way that rewards repeated acts of attention—just as Lewis Carroll did in *Alice's Adventures in Wonderland*, and as the writers and directors Lana and Andy Wachowski did in *The Matrix*. Now spend at least 30 minutes writing and thinking about what makes *The Matrix* or *Alice's Adventures* or another work of literature, film, or art worth returning to again and again. What did you do in your own essay to reward repeated acts of attention?

EXPLORE

A rabbit hole can open up anywhere. Tim Cahill's efforts to make sense of conflicting accounts of the Jonestown Massacre lead him into the mind of a madman. Sarah Stillman's research into the war on drugs reveals the deadly consequences of police reliance on young drug informants. David Foster Wallace, dispatched to cover a lobster festival, finds himself on an existential journey to make sense of the joys of eating creatures who have been boiled alive.

Cahill, Tim. "In the Valley of the Shadow of Death: Guyana after the Jonestown Massacre." *Rolling Stone.* 25 Jan. 1979. Web.

Stillman, Sarah. "The Throwaways." *New Yorker.* 3 Sept. 2012. Web.

Wallace, David Foster. "Consider the Lobster." *Gourmet.* August 2004. Web.

On Creative Reading

Once you've learned to read, it's easy to lose sight of just what a complicated business reading actually is. You see the letters *c-a-t*, and without effort you know that together they refer to the furry, whiskered, four-legged purring thing curled before the fire. To accomplish this seemingly simple act of translation, you have had to learn a sign system (the alphabet), a host of rules governing the combination of the signs in the given system (for example, there are vowels and consonants, and they can be put together only in certain ways), and the connection between the signifier (the word that results from the orderly combination of sounds) and the signified (the object, idea, or sensation out there in the world).

Even at this most rudimentary stage, there's an inescapable arbitrariness at the heart of the reading process: Why does *c-a-t* and not some other series of letters signify that furry thing? Why *that* sound for *that* creature? And beyond the arbitrariness of the sign system, there's an even deeper mystery: How does the child watching the parent's finger point to the letters on the page ever make the leap to that moment when the sound, the letters, and the image in the picture book suddenly connect, and meaning gets made?

Solving the mystery of how and why humans developed this ability to work with sign systems is a job for evolutionary neuroscientists, and their answer, when it comes, will apply to humans in general. We're interested in a more personal issue: Once the process of reading has been routinized and internalized, why is it that different people reading the same material reach different conclusions? Or to put this another way, why is there ambiguity? Why is there misunderstanding? What happens in the movement from decoding the characters on the page or screen to creating an interpretation of what those characters, considered in context, might mean that causes one reader's mind to go in one direction and another reader's mind to go in a different direction?

The mystery of the individual response is made clear as soon as class discussion begins. Where'd *that* idea come from? How'd the teacher get *that* out of *those* words? And because students can't see inside the teacher's mind, they often conclude that the connections the teacher is making are arbitrary and, beyond that, that anything other than the reporting of facts is "just a matter of opinion." For many students, the mystery of how teachers—and experts, in general—read is never solved. For these students, the experience of higher-order literacy, where reading and writing become ways to create new ideas, remains out of reach.

Social bookmarking, a gift from the Internet, gives us a way to make visible for others some of the previously invisible workings of the creative reader's mind. Below we walk you through an example of how using social media worked in one of our classes, and then we give you some exercises to get you on your way. Although there are any number of bookmarking tools out there for you to try, we use Diigo because it allows our students to annotate the Web pages they share with the class. They can highlight passages they want to draw attention to or pose inline questions. And just like that, two previously invisible aspects of the reading process—what people read and how they respond to what they've read—become visible and available for others to consider.

So what does *creative* reading look like in practice?

Our example comes from a creative nonfiction course we taught in which the students read *On Photography*, a collection of essays by Susan Sontag that was originally published in 1977 and that remains a touchstone in discussions of how the free circulation of images changes societal norms. We were halfway through the second essay in the collection, "America, Seen through Photographs, Darkly," and had reached the point where Sontag considers the work of Diane Arbus, who presented her subjects, whether they were at the margins of society or at its center, in ways that were strange and disturbing.

Sontag's criticism of Arbus is damning: Sontag argues that Arbus used her camera to depict all of her subjects as "inhabitants of a single village … the idiot village [of] America." Here the class encountered a problem that runs throughout Sontag's *On Photography*: there are no photographs. For readers who already know the history of American photography, this isn't a problem; they can just call to mind some of Arbus's most famous images and judge for themselves whether or not Sontag's assessment is fair. But for readers who don't know Arbus's work, the only option is to treat Sontag's assessment as a fact.

Sontag's readers in the 1970s who wanted to know more about Arbus's work would not have had an easy time of it, but today any reader with access to the Internet can check out Arbus's images and assess the validity of Sontag's judgment. Without exerting any more effort than it takes to type "Diane Arbus" into a search engine, our students found the images Sontag refers to in her piece and more: Arbus's shots of circus freaks; the off-balance, bedecked socialites; the nudists; the giant man towering over his miniature parents; and of course, the twin girls.

Once she'd seen the pictures, our student Alice asked: "Well, how did people at the time react? We know Sontag didn't like Arbus's work, but did they?"

As so often happens in our classes, we didn't know the answer to the question our student had posed. (And in this instance, even if we had known, we wouldn't have said so.) Alice asked a good question—both because finding out the answer would end up requiring some creativity on her part and because wondering about how others see what you're seeing always serves to highlight the fact that meaning is both a public and a private matter. So we said, "That's a Canvas Collaboration moment," which is shorthand in our classes for, "See what you can find out and post the results to our class's collaborative Google Doc in Canvas."

Back in her room, Alice set off to answer her own question. She entered some search terms, cast about a bit, and then settled on a path that took her to *Athanor*, a journal published by Florida State University's Department of Art History, and an article by Laureen Trainer entitled "The Missing Photographs: An Examination of Diane Arbus's Images of Transvestites and Homosexuals from 1957 to 1965." Alice posted a link to the piece on Canvas and then highlighted a passage that struck her:

> However, the reaction to her images was intense anger, an emotional response prompted by the cultural war against sexual "deviants." Yuben Yee, the photo librarian at the MoMA, recalls having to come early every morning to wipe the spit off of Arbus's portraits. He recalls that, "People were uncomfortable—threatened—looking at Diane's stuff." Even within the art world, Arbus was thought to be photographing subject matter that was ahead of her time. As Andy Warhol, who had seen some of Arbus's portraits, commented, "drag queens weren't even accepted in freak circles until 1967." Arbus's images were not only disturbing to her audience on an aesthetic level, but her unabashed and unapologetic views of transvestites touched a deeper nerve in the people who viewed them.

Beneath this quote, Alice wrote about the difference between a time when people spat on images of transvestites in the Museum of Modern Art and her own experience looking at the images a half century later.

How did people respond to Arbus's work at the time? Alice made her way of answering this question visible to the rest of the class. She also found something that was new to her teachers, new to the class, and new to her; in so doing, she gave us a glimpse of what was going on in her mind while she was reading. Yes, it is true that she had just uncovered a piece of information. Yes, it is true that she had not yet done anything with this information. But meaningful engagement with information can happen only *after* one has had the experience of posing an open, exploratory question.

Alice kept looking—it's a requirement in our courses. The next source she posted to Canvas would likely raise the hackles of many teachers: Wikipedia! It's an outrage!

Well, actually, it isn't. If we grant that students are going to use Wikipedia (and SparkNotes and YouTube and, and, and), we can focus on how to use these sources productively rather than insist on unenforceable prohibitions.

So, Wikipedia: Is there a beneficial way to use an encyclopedia? How could the answer to that question be anything other than *yes*?

Alice posted the link to Wikipedia's Arbus entry as well as excerpts from the section of that entry that specifically concern the reception of Arbus's work. She deleted material that was not of interest to her; separated past reactions from more contemporary responses; added an inline comment that directly connected the Wikipedia entry to Sontag's argument; reordered the information so as to place the introductory material in this section of the Wikipedia entry at the end of her own citation; and eliminated entirely a passage where it is observed that "Sontag's essay itself has been criticized as 'an exercise in aesthetic insensibility' and 'exemplary *for its shallowness*'" (italics added).

All of this editorial activity gives us a much richer sense of what Alice did while she was reading. Alice amassed many examples of how the subjects of Arbus's images responded to being photographed; how anonymous viewers at MoMA responded when the photographs were first displayed; and how critics—those who were Arbus's contemporaries and those who came after her—responded to the photographs. Then she concluded her entry with the news that Arbus had photographed Sontag and her son.

Who was this last bit of information news to? Alice. The other students in the course. Her teachers. And given that Sontag herself does not reveal this fact anywhere in *On Photography*, it's safe to say that it would also be news to most, if not all, of Sontag's readers, past and present.

Alice posted this fact to Canvas without comment. She thought she was done.

But the practice of creative reading is never done. In this case there was a question hanging in the air, waiting to be asked. And because the Canvas Collaboration tool made what Alice was reading and how she was reading it visible to the members of the group and to her teachers, it became possible for us to pose the question that could keep the reading process going for Alice: What does the picture Arbus took of Sontag look like?

This question was posed in public for all the other students to see on the collaborative document, just below Alice's entry. And soon enough, Alice posted a link to the image. True, it was only a small, low-resolution image, but it was a start. Or rather, it was a continuation, an extension of a process that started with Alice asking, "How did others see Arbus?" and eventually led to her discovering an image of Sontag and her son looking back at the photographer Sontag describes as "not a poet delving into her entrails to relate her own pain but a photographer venturing out into the world to *collect* images that are painful."

This is one version of what happens when the purpose of reading shifts from the acquisition of information to the exploration of an open-ended question: reading begets more reading, one passage leads to another, and the original text is read and reread in a series of changing contexts, its meaning expanding and contracting depending on the use to which the reader puts it. This is the essence of higher-order reading. Some explorations will be more fruitful than others, and some more valuable for the individual than for a larger community of readers, but the movement from answers to questions, from information to ideas, remains the same.

PRACTICE SESSION ONE

REFLECTING

The example of creative reading we've described leads from a question about an essay to an image not included in or referenced in the original essay. We first want you to find a reproduction online of Diane Arbus's photograph of Susan Sontag. What light do you think Arbus's photograph of Sontag and her son sheds on Sontag's assessment of Arbus's work in "America, Seen through Photographs, Darkly"? Spend at least 20 minutes figuring out a thoughtful, compelling answer to this question. For the purposes of this exercise, work only with what we've provided. *Don't* seek out the rest of Sontag's essay or more information about Arbus. What does the photograph alone tell you?

RESEARCHING

As we've said, the work of creative reading is never done. What information can you find online about the image of Sontag and her son? About *their* relationship? About Sontag's fuller argument in "America, Seen through Photographs, Darkly"? About her argument in *On Photography*? Spend at least an hour researching and reading, keeping careful notes on your discoveries.

WRITING

Now you're ready to work on an extended essay about how to read Arbus's images creatively. Continue the research Alice began about how viewers have responded to Arbus's photographs in the forty years since Sontag's judgment, gathering information about one or more lines of response to the photographs. Then make an argument for how you think an Arbus photograph ought to be read. (Note: This series of exercises can be profitably executed using any visual artist.)

PRACTICE SESSION TWO

RESEARCHING

Once a day for a week, we'd like you to print out and annotate a page you've visited on the Web. We want you to mark those places in your reading where a question of *any kind* is raised for you. An unfamiliar word, data that seems not to compute, an interpretation that doesn't make sense, an odd sentence structure—wherever your reading is stopped, take note of it. At the end of a week, you'll have a profile of your own reading practice.

REFLECTING

Now that you have made a version of your own reading practice visible for you to consider, what do you see? Set aside at least 30 minutes to write down answers to these questions: What does your profile reveal about what kind of a reader you are? What habits do you practice currently? Are there instances when your experience of reading was more pleasurable than it was at other times? More productive? More useful? Was your practice of reading markedly different during any of these phases, or was the outcome entirely dependent on what you were reading at the time?

WRITING

Using your research and reflections on your reading practices, compose a portrait of yourself as a reader. Where are you now as a reader? Where would you like to be? What specific steps do you need to take to become a lifelong creative reader? Write an essay that analyzes the most important events in your experience as a reader up to the present moment.

Two of our suggested readings invite you to continue the creative reading of work by Susan Sontag and Diane Arbus: journalist Franklin Foer considers Sontag's critical success alongside her changing relationship to photography, while art critic Peter Schjeldahl's brief remembrance of Arbus seeks to provide a reparative reading of her work. In our third suggested reading, Nathan Chandler uses creative reading to learn about and describe the inner workings of Anonymous—a group of highly skilled hackers who are committed to remaining unknown and unfindable.

Chandler, Nathan. "How Anonymous Works." Howstuffworks.com. Web.

Foer, Franklin. "Susan Superstar: How Susan Sontag Became Seduced by Her Own Persona." Nymag.com. 14 January 2005. Web.

Schjeldahl, Peter. "Looking Back: Diane Arbus at the Met." Newyorker.com. 21 March 2005. Web.

On Imagining Others

We've all heard the proverb "Before you judge someone, walk a mile in that person's shoes." This saying is so well known because it captures the experience we've all had of making a snap judgment that then turns out to be wrong. Understanding another person's motives requires more than just trusting your intuition, and it involves more than just reviewing the evidence about that person reported to you by your own eyes and ears. It also requires an act of imagination that gives you a glimpse of what it is like to experience life as that person does.

But is the imagination really powerful enough or trustworthy enough to approximate the experience of walking a mile in another person's shoes? In our view (that is, as seen through our eyes, when walking in our shoes), the more you practice using your imagination to gain a sense of how others see the world, the better your approximations will become. We're aware that this sense, which is by definition an *approximate* understanding, is not the same thing as *complete* knowledge. Indeed, the very act of trying to produce writing that fully renders the experience of another person can lead to a deeper appreciation for how much of anyone else's experience remains out of reach of your imagination.

One of the most ambitious efforts to imagine the lives of others is the photographer Yann Arthus-Bertrand's 7 billion Others project, which seeks to promote understanding of "what separates and what unites" the world's more than seven billion people. Prior to launching the 7 billion Others project (which began as the 6 billion Others project), Arthus-Bertrand was most famous for the aerial photographs he took for his book *Earth from Above*. From up in the sky, he says, "the Earth looks like an immense area to be shared." But back on the ground, all the local impediments to sharing the earth come back into focus—problems produced by geography, culture, language, religion, wealth, health, and opportunity. To counter this immediate sense of an unshareable world, Arthus-Betrand offers spectacular image after spectacular image in *Earth from Above* of the world's rich natural resources and of the vibrant productivity of its peoples.

Confronted with the problem of how we might better understand each other, in 2003 Arthus-Bertrand and his coworkers began filming thousands of interviews in eighty-four different countries and posting these videos on their Web site. Every interview subject responded to the same list of questions (forty-five in all) about experiences, beliefs, and hopes, a list that included these conversational prompts:

What did you learn from your parents?
What would you like to hand on to your children?
What was the most difficult ordeal you have had to face in your life?
What do you think is the meaning of life?
Have you ever wanted to leave your country? Why?
Have you seen nature change since your childhood?
What does love mean to you?
What is your greatest fear?
What do you think happens after death?
What did you dream about when you were a child?

Comparing the subjects' answers to these questions to our own answers reveals both what we have in common with others and what remains puzzling and mysterious about the thoughts and lives of others.

The 7 billion Others project provides us with raw material for imagining the lives of others around the globe and across the country. But one can also find the compelling mystery of otherness across the street or across the kitchen table. Imagine, for instance, how different it might be to see the world from the perspective of a parent, sibling, grandparent, or friend, or how you would perceive the world from a wheelchair, or if you couldn't see at all. (You can even find the mystery of otherness within yourself, but that's a paradox we'll consider at another time.)

In the preface to his book *What the Dog Saw*, Malcolm Gladwell captures the sense of otherness within one's own home in a vignette from his childhood. As a young boy, Gladwell would slip into his father's study and marvel at the graph paper covered with rows of penciled numbers strewn across his father's desk. Gladwell knew his father was a mathematician, but what did that mean, really? He writes,

I would sit on the edge of his chair and look at each page with puzzlement and wonder. It seemed miraculous, first of all, that he got paid for what seemed, at the time, like gibberish. But more important, I couldn't get over the fact that someone whom I loved so dearly did something every day, inside his own head, that I could not begin to understand.

If Gladwell could "not begin to understand" what was going on in his father's mind, why did he persist in wondering about the symbols scrawled on graph paper? He persisted, he explains, because "curiosity about the interior life of other people's day-to-day work is one of the most fundamental of human impulses." Early in life, Gladwell discovered the rewards of confronting the unknown in everyday life, and he held onto his curiosity long after childhood, convinced "that everyone and everything has a story to tell." His curiosity about others' thoughts became the foundation of his career as a writer.

PRACTICE SESSION ONE

REFLECTING

Go to the 7 billion Others Web site and explore all that it makes available. Set aside at least 30 minutes to watch a few of the testimonials. Listen to how people from all over the world respond to questions about love, fear, family, and more. Then select one film on a specific topic ("After death," "Family," "Meaning of life," and so on), and watch it in its entirety.

After viewing the film, spend at least 30 minutes reflecting on what you saw and heard. Begin by reflecting on the responses of the people interviewed in the video. Then consider your own response to the topic you chose. At which points did you feel the strongest affinity with the people being interviewed? Which responses struck you as being most surprising? Does the 7 billion Others project show that there are seven billion perspectives?

PRACTICE SESSION TWO

RESEARCHING

Imagining the lives of others begins with curiosity, openness, and a commitment to listening attentively. One way to practice those habits of mind is to conduct an interview in which you listen closely and carefully to what the person being interviewed has to say. (When you conduct an interview, you should either take notes or get the interviewee's permission to record the interview.)

Option 1: Find a friend or an acquaintance—someone around your age who has a different perspective on the world than you do—and invite that person to talk with you for 30 minutes or more about one or two of the topics that most interest you from the 7 billion Others project, such as "What did you learn from your parents?" or "What do you think is the meaning of life?" Invite stories. Listen for places where your interviewee's beliefs or thoughts are different from your own, and ask questions to expand your understanding of those differences.

Option 2: Find a friend or an acquaintance who is at least twenty years older than you are, and invite that person to talk for 30 minutes or more about childhood and growing up. What was everyday life like when he or she was your age? What are the most dramatic changes that this person has observed in his or her lifetime? What does she or he miss about the past? What changes have been most welcome? Listen for places where your subject's experiences are radically different from your own, and ask questions to expand your understanding of those differences.

WRITING

After your interview, review your notes or your recording and write an essay about what it would take for you to see the world as your interview subject does. What else would you need to know about this person that you don't know from your conversation and your previous interactions? How would you know whether you had succeeded in approximating their worldview? At what point do you have to shift from what you know to what you imagine to be the case?

EXPLORE

When we imagine the experience of another person, we might focus on what it would be like to have that person's thoughts, talents, or background. With our suggested readings, we invite you to consider what it would be like either to inhabit another person's body or to be intimate friends with someone who is both enormously talented and self-destructive. Nora Ephron describes life without a plunging cleavage. Lucy Grealy describes life after half of her lower jaw was removed, at age nine, due to cancer. And Ann Patchett describes the challenges involved in being Grealy's close friend.

Ephron, Nora. "A Few Words about Breasts." *Esquire.* May 1972. Web.

Grealy, Lucy. "Mirrorings." *Harper's Magazine.* Feb. 1993. Web.

Patchett, Ann. "The Face of Pain." *New York Magazine.* 1 July 2003. Web.

On Motivation

Why write?

When posting on social media, the writer's motivation is clear: to connect with friends, or to say something others will "like." As in other kinds of "unsponsored writing," such as keeping a diary or maintaining a personal blog, the central activity is giving voice to the self. This can be pleasurable; it can teach you about yourself; it can relieve stress. While there are plenty of people who never feel the desire to engage in unsponsored writing, there's not much mystery as to why some do.

What *is* mysterious is why anyone, outside of a school assignment, voluntarily writes about anything other than the self, its interests, its desires, its travails, and so on. Why write a searching analysis of a social problem, for instance, or a book-length study of voting behaviors, or a biography of someone long dead and wholly unrelated to the writer? Why do something that requires so much time and mental energy, and for which the odds of getting published or having your work read are so low?

When cast in these terms, the motivation to write voluntarily about something other than the self does seem mysterious. But perhaps these are not the best terms for understanding how the motivation to write emerges. So let's move from the hypothetical to the particular and consider the story of how the historian Jill Lepore set out to write a book about Benjamin Franklin and ended up writing one about Jane Franklin, his virtually unknown sister. It's obvious why a historian might want to write about Ben Franklin. He's a major figure in American history; he was an inventor, an ambassador, an educator, and a philosopher; he was one of the most famous people of his time, and he interacted with others in all walks of life. If you're a scholar of American history, writing about him sounds fun.

In "The Prodigal Daughter," Lepore describes settling into reading Franklin's papers and finding herself drawn instead to the sixty-three-year-long correspondence Ben Franklin had with his younger sister Jane. Lepore discovered that Ben Franklin wrote more letters to Jane than to anyone else. "No two people in their family were more alike," Lepore came to realize, even though "their lives could hardly have been more different." Jane Franklin was nearly illiterate, and the few writing lessons her brother gave her ended after he left home when she was only eleven. Aside from letters to family and friends, the only writing she did was to record the dates of major events in a small, handmade book she called her "Book of Ages," which Lepore describes as "four sheets of foolscap between two covers to make a little book of sixteen pages." Turn the pages of this homemade book and you'll move through a list of dates and events: Jane's birth; her marriage at age fifteen; the birth of her first child, and that child's death less than a year later; the births of eleven more children and the deaths, during her lifetime, of all but one of those children.

In contrast to her brother's life, Jane Franklin's life seemed too spare and uneventful to warrant general attention. And yet when Lepore told her mother what she had learned about Ben Franklin's forgotten sister, her mother said, "Write a book about her!" Lepore thought her mother was joking. How could she write a book about a phantom? Who would want to read about her? It seemed like an impossible task, but when her mother's health began to fail, Lepore returned her attention to Jane Franklin's letters "to write the only book [her] mother ever wanted [her] to write."

Although her personal motivation for writing a book about Jane Franklin couldn't have been stronger, Lepore floundered. She tried to write a double biography that placed Jane Franklin's life story next to her brother's, but she abandoned this approach after drafting 250 pages, having found that the juxtaposition only magnified the sadness and sameness of Jane's life. Without a more compelling reason to write than pleasing her mother, Lepore put the project aside. We would say that, at this stage, Lepore had a private motive but not a public one. Her private motive was powerful enough to get her writing, but it didn't provide her with a way to present Jane Franklin's monotonous life as a puzzle, problem, or question that others might find meaningful.

Perhaps the problem was that the questions raised by Jane Franklin's life didn't merit a book-length study. Maybe what was interesting about her life could be stated much more briefly. In "Poor Jane's Almanac," a short opinion piece Lepore published in the *New York Times*, she described Jane Franklin's "Book of Ages" and the political arguments Jane had with her brother after her child-rearing days were done. By highlighting Jane's two modes of writing—the catalog of her losses and her letters to her brother—Lepore found a way to show her readers why they should be interested in her life. Jane Franklin's biography in itself isn't compelling; what is so interesting is what her life's story reveals about the connections between gender, poverty, education, and access to contraception. "Especially for women," Lepore writes, "escaping poverty has always depended on the opportunity for an education and the ability to control the size of their families," neither of which Jane had.

Lepore was stunned by the flood of letters she received in response to the *New York Times* piece. In an interview ("Out Loud: Jane Franklin's Untold American Story"), she described letters from readers about how their mothers, like Jane Franklin, swam against the "undertow of motherhood" to steal the time required to read and learn and engage with the wider world. Taken together, the mass of personal letters helped Lepore see why trying to fit Jane Franklin's life into the form of a biography hadn't worked. Lepore's readers hadn't written to her because they were moved by Jane Franklin's singular, unique life; rather, they wrote because they saw in Jane Franklin a version of their own mothers. At last, Lepore had a public motive for writing at length about Jane Franklin's life: she would use her story to show how poverty, motherhood, and limited education diminished the lives of women in the eighteenth century and rendered achievement outside the home impossible. And that's exactly what she did in *Book of Ages: The Life and Opinions of Jane Franklin*, which was nominated for a National Book Award in 2013.

We began with the question "Why write?" and have ended with a discussion of audience. How did we get here? By following the story of Jill Lepore's struggle to find a satisfying way to write about Jane Franklin's life, we've seen that the movement from a private to a public motive to write involves a shift in the imagined audience for one's writing. For personal reasons, Lepore set out to write a book about Jane Franklin with her own mother as the imagined audience; when Lepore imagined a larger audience of sympathetic readers, she realized she had to reconceive the project. It would still be about Jane Franklin, but Franklin's life story would become a case study of the challenges women in general faced in eighteenth-century America.

Given that virtually all of the writing students do in school is in response to an assignment of one kind or another, and further, that those assignments come with an external motivator (the grading system) and an intended audience (the teacher), it's highly unlikely that you have had an experience like Lepore's while writing in school. Even so, with the assignments in this book, we want you to practice imagining that the audience for your work is composed neither exclusively of your friends nor solely of those who are paid to read your work, but rather of sympathetic readers interested in seeing how your mind works on a problem. As you practice imagining a different audience for your work, you will find yourself confronting the writer's central challenge: How do I make what interests me of interest to others?

PRACTICE SESSION ONE

READING

For this exercise read Jill Lepore's "The Last Amazon: Wonder Woman Returns," or any of her other writing that is available on the Web. After you've finished reading the piece, spend at least 30 minutes considering Lepore's public motive for writing it. What is the compelling problem, question, puzzle, contradiction, or ambiguity she is exploring? At what point in the reading does she make her central project clear? What does she do to make her project compelling to her audience?

WRITING

Public and intellectual motives are often expressed as questions, or as statements that use a complicating or qualifying word such as *but, however,* or *or*. For example, Lepore's motive in *Book of Ages* can be expressed by this statement: Jane Franklin's life appears to be unexceptional, *but* her life provides a valuable example of how poverty, lack of education, and motherhood severely limited what women in the eighteenth-century United States could achieve.

We'd like you to spend at least 20 minutes reviewing the Lepore article you selected and defining the public motive of the article as clearly as you can in just one sentence. Experiment with restating the motive in a sentence that uses *but, or, however,* or some other complicating word. How does the statement you composed help to clarify Lepore's project for you?

PRACTICE SESSION TWO

RESEARCHING

We invite you to practice the motivating move that Lepore employs regularly. Specifically, we want you to use details about particular people or historical events to open up larger questions about cultural or social issues, such as motherhood, fatherhood, national identity, education, poverty, or economic opportunity.

To begin, write up a familiar anecdote from your family history. Then follow Lepore's example and consider how you could use the story to shed light on an interesting cultural or social problem, puzzle, or mystery that is bigger than your particular family. In other words, define a public motive for writing by using your family anecdote to rethink a larger issue or idea. Before you try to make a compelling connection, spend at least one hour doing research about the cultural or social issue that interests you.

After you've done sufficient research and feel ready to connect personal experience and public ideas, compose an essay that links your family history to the larger issue you've researched.

EXPLORE

Jill Lepore, whose work is the foundation for our discussion of how the motive to write evolves over time, explains in a recorded interview why she chose to write about Jane Franklin. George Orwell's discussion of motive differs from ours because it focuses instead on how writers are driven by ego, beauty, a desire for knowledge, and political purpose. Oliver Sacks further complicates explanations for motive because of what is now known about how malleable memory is; when memories change over time, motives for past actions can't be recalled with certainty.

Lepore, Jill. Interview by Sasha Weiss and Judith Thurman. "Out Loud: Jane Franklin's Untold American Story." Podcast audio. *New Yorker*. 30 June 2013. Web.

Orwell, George. "Why I Write." *Gangrel* 4 (Summer 1946). Web.

Sacks, Oliver. "Speak, Memory." *New York Review of Books*. 21 Feb. 2013. Web.

Curiosity at Work: Donovan Hohn Follows the Toys

Donovan Hohn was teaching high school English in New York when a student's paper inspired him to pursue his own open-ended research assignment. Hohn had asked his students to practice the "archaeology of the ordinary" by picking an artifact, researching its history, and writing up what they found. One student, who chose to write about his lucky rubber duck, came across a report from 1992 about twenty-eight thousand bath toys that fell off a container ship in the Pacific Ocean. A few years later, the report continued, beachcombers in Alaska began to notice the toys floating ashore—a plastic duck here, another there, arriving year after year. Hohn couldn't get this story out of his head. He started asking questions: Why had some of the toys ended up in Alaska? Where were the rest of the toys? Why didn't they all end up in the same place? He decided to look for answers.

"At the outset," Hohn writes in his book *Moby-Duck*, "I figured I'd interview a few oceanographers, talk to a few beachcombers, read up on ocean currents and Arctic geography, and then write an account of the incredible journey of the bath toys lost at sea." He thought he'd be able to do this work without leaving his desk. But Hohn didn't manage to stay seated for long. He discovered that questions

> can be like ocean currents. Wade in a little too far and they can carry you away. Follow one line of inquiry and it will lead you to another, and another. Spot a yellow duck dropped atop the seaweed at the tide line, ask yourself where it came from, and the next thing you know you're way out at sea, no land in sight, dog-paddling around in mysteries four miles deep. You're wondering when and why yellow ducks became icons of childhood. You want to know what it's like inside the toy factories of Guangdong. You're marveling at the scale of humanity's impact on this terraqueous globe and at the oceanic magnitude of your own ignorance.

In pursuit of answers to his growing list of questions, Hohn crossed the Northwest Passage in an icebreaker. He sailed on a catamaran to the Great Pacific Garbage Patch, a huge expanse of plastic soup—broken-down bits of bottles, toys, and packaging of all kinds—drawn together by ocean currents. He rode out a terrifying winter storm on the outer decks of a cargo ship in the middle of the Pacific, with "shipping containers stacked six-high overhead, … strain[ing] against their lashings, creaking and groaning and cataracting with every roll." He sped on a ferry up China's Pearl River Delta to a factory where he saw bath toys being made. He learned how to say "thank you" in Inuktitut and Cantonese.

In the end, Hohn wrote a book about many things: consumer demand for inexpensive goods, the toxins in the Chinese factories where the ducks are made and in the ocean where the toys degrade, and prospects for change. His curiosity took him all the way from an absurd image of a flotilla of plastic ducks to questions about the most pressing environmental concerns the world faces today.

Connecting

"**C**onnect the dots": this phrase used to appear atop the pages of activity books designed to help young children practice counting while they worked on improving their fine motor skills. A child, crayon in hand, would draw a line from numbered dot to numbered dot, and at the end of the process, if the child had followed the dots in order, then voilà, there was a picture. If not, there was a mess.

No one would argue that connecting the dots is creative. The child has simply followed the directions to uncover a design. But once we move from children connecting dots to students using their own writing to connect ideas discussed in what they've been reading, we enter a realm where creativity becomes possible. Any two ideas can be connected; any claim can be made; any argument can be put forward. Under such chaotic conditions, how does one make connections that matter?

The essays in this chapter will help you to resist writing formulas that preorganize your encounters with the infinite range of connections to be made. To encourage you to practice using your writing to develop new habits for engaging with and exploring what is unknown to you, we want you to think of writing itself as the act of making connections. Writers make connections with the language they use, with the questions they choose to ask, and with the sources they choose to interview. As you experiment with making connections in each of these areas, you will be engaging directly in the creative act of making meaning: the dots you connect will be your own, and the image that results will be of your own design.

On the Three Most Important Words in the English Language

How do you know you're thinking?

This is the kind of question that stops you in your tracks. First, you think, who would ask about something so obvious? And then—well, then you're left with the challenge of putting into words a central facet of your mental life.

Chapter 5, "Connecting," is taken from Richard E. Miller and Ann Jurecic, *Habits of the Creative Mind*, pp. 99–131 (Part 6, "Connecting").

When we begin discussing this question in class, we are soon deep in the murk. There's involuntary mental activity, which takes place in any brain-equipped creature—for example, the turtle sunning on a log is passively monitoring the surroundings, scanning for threats. There's instinct, the lightning-quick response to inbound data—the cat pounces on whatever is rustling in the bush, killing, as the common phrase puts it, without thinking. There's dreaming, and there's daydreaming, too. There's all this involuntary mental activity going on up there that we don't control. And then there's thought, which is, in contrast, mental activity over which we have some control. So while we can't unsee what our eyes behold or unhear the sounds that enter our ears, and we can't unsmell, untouch, or unfeel, we can change how we think about what our senses are reporting. And though we can't exactly *unthink* a thought we've had, we can change that thought by *rethinking* it.

We're interested in that stretch of mental activity that you can influence. For the moment, we ask that you grant us the following proposition:

Thinking is the intentional act of making connections.

This act of connecting can take place in language, sound, and images; chefs would doubtless say it takes place in taste, and perfumers in smell. We're open to the medium; what we want to focus on is the array of connections available to the thinker.

We are pretty sure that you'll have reservations about this proposition, but we need you to suspend those reservations for the time being. Don't worry; we'll qualify and complicate it by and by—we promise.

Beginning writers, like beginning thinkers, tend to rely on one connector: the coordinating conjunction *and*. For the beginning writer, writing is the act of connecting like to like, with thoughts or observations linked together via the explicit or implicit use of *and*:

> The house I grew up in had a garden. It also had a garage. It had two floors. *And* an attic.

In this additive mode of composing, the beginning writer can expand the composition as much as the assignment requires. All that the writer needs to supply is more of the same:

> It had two chimneys. It had three bedrooms. *And* one bathroom.

In the hands of an experienced storyteller, this additive mode of composing can serve as the foundation for an episodic epic poem:

> After the end of the Trojan War, Odysseus heads home. On the way back, he and his men sack the city of Ismarus. And then they sail to the land of the Lotus-Eaters. After they escape, they encounter the Cyclops, Polyphemus. And then, and then, and then…

Beginning writers are more likely to make connections via addition (A and B and C) than via qualification (A and B but not C). The machinery of the five-paragraph theme makes no room for thinking of this kind; there's just the thesis, the three supporting examples (A and B and C), and the conclusion. Qualification muddies the waters.

It's not that beginning writers have no access to the word *but*. Indeed, when we confer with beginning writers, we often find that their minds are abuzz with qualifications, exceptions, contradictions, and confusions. However, little of this mental activity makes it onto the page because our students have been told repeatedly that the goal of writing in school is clarity. Equating *clarity* with *simplicity*, beginning writers avoid presenting anything that might complicate their efforts to produce an argument that is straightforward and to the point. When this strategy of avoiding complications is rewarded, writing's primary function is reduced to the activity of simplification, and the goal of writing in school becomes nothing more than producing "arguments" that are clear, direct, and easy to follow.

Obviously, writing has a communicative function (moving idea X from point A to point B), but this isn't writing's sole function. Writing can also serve as a technology for thinking new thoughts—thoughts, that is, that are new to the writer. We believe that this use of writing, as a heuristic for venturing into the unknown, is as important as its communicative use. Indeed, it is through learning how to use writing for discovery, comprehension, and problem solving that we come to have ideas that are worth communicating.

Beginning writers start with a thesis and then find evidence to support their position; for them, writing is the process of reporting what fits the thesis and ignoring the rest. The problem with such writing is not that it is unclear but rather that it is, from the outset, *too* clear: it says what it's *going* to say (thesis), then it says it (three supporting examples), and then it says what it said (conclusion). Reading writing of this kind is like being plunged into the great echo chamber of nothingness.

This problem is easily solved: we just insist that our students bring the coordinating conjunction *but* into their writing. Things get messy right away, and clarity, misunderstood as simplicity, gives way to qualification and complexity. At the start, some of the qualifications are silly, and others are improbable. But the qualifications become more meaningful over time, and the prose begins to engage more productively with the complexities of lived experience. The writing begins to capture the shape of a mind at work on a problem.

But is the passkey for entry into critical thinking.

If you want to test out this assertion, we invite you to consider how different Abraham Lincoln's Gettysburg Address would be if it ended after the second paragraph:

> Four score and seven years ago our fathers brought forth on this continent, a new nation, conceived in Liberty, and dedicated to the proposition that all men are created equal.
>
> Now we are engaged in a great civil war, testing whether that nation, or any nation so conceived and so dedicated, can long endure. We are met on a great battle-field of that war. We have come to dedicate a portion of that field, as a final resting place for those who here gave their lives that that nation might live. It is altogether fitting and proper that we should do this.

Lincoln speaks at the dedication of the cemetery at Gettysburg, Pennsylvania, for the Union casualties of the Battle of Gettysburg. He invokes the nation as if it were one thing, but the nation is at war with itself. Those who have gathered for the dedication of the cemetery do so to recognize the sacrifice of those who died so that the "nation might live."

If the speech ended here, it would end with the statement that recognizing the fallen is "altogether fitting and proper." Lincoln's intent is clear: it's appropriate to recognize those who have died defending the liberties of those who are still living. He's saying aloud what everyone present already knows; the point he is making is obvious to all.

But the speech *doesn't* end here. Lincoln continues:

> But, in a larger sense, we can not dedicate—we can not consecrate—we can not hallow—this ground. The brave men, living and dead, who struggled here, have consecrated it, far above our poor power to add or detract. The world will little note, nor long remember what we say here, but it can never forget what they did here.

Everything hinges on the qualification that Lincoln introduces in the third and final paragraph of his speech. What those who are assembled are doing is "altogether fitting and proper," *but* the living do not, in fact, have the power to do what those who have died have done.

With this qualification, Lincoln is able to shift the audience's attention from an understanding of dedication as a commemorative event bounded in time to its redefinition as an open-ended activity carried out by the living in the service of a vulnerable ideal:

> It is for us the living, rather, to be dedicated here to the unfinished work which they who fought here have thus far so nobly advanced. It is rather for us to be here dedicated to the great task remaining before us—that from these honored dead we take increased devotion to that cause for which they gave the last full measure of devotion—that we here highly resolve that these dead shall not have died in vain—that this nation, under God, shall have a new birth of freedom—and that government of the people, by the people, for the people, shall not perish from the earth.

Lincoln's use of *but* at the beginning of the third paragraph of his address allows him to connect dedication as a ceremonial event to the ongoing activity of being dedicated to some higher ideal. The connection is not like to like: coming to the dedication is not the same thing as dedicating oneself to the preservation of the nation. Without the *but*, we have a speech that thanks people for coming to a battlefield; with that qualification, we have a speech that links the deaths that took place on the battlefield to a larger set of ideas, values, hopes, and aspirations.

How do you get from critical thinking to creative thinking? Here's a rubric that oversimplifies to the point of distortion:

and	Foundation for thought	Basis for black-and-white, yes/no, binary thinking
but	Foundation for critical thought	Enables qualifications, exceptions, conditions, ambiguity, uncertainty
or	Foundation for creative thought	Enables alternatives, possibilities; is future oriented

We know this table can't withstand rigorous critical examination. Indeed, we'd say the table predicts its own dismantling, since it assumes both a critical thinker who will respond to the clear-cut grid by qualifying the table's assertions and a creative thinker who will imagine other grids or other ways of modeling the relationship between coordinating conjunctions and modes of thought.

So, just like the overly simplified left brain/right brain distinction discussed in "On Learning to See" (pp. 18–24), our table doesn't fully depict how thought happens. It's just a heuristic device, a helpful strategy for identifying different mental operations; it's a way to get you to think about thinking as the process of making connections.

With those qualifications, we stand by this assertion:

> Consciously introducing *but* and *or* to your mental activity
> is a surefire way to generate new thinking.

It really is that simple.

PRACTICE SESSION ONE

REFLECTING

Find three images that are important to you. They can be pictures of you or pictures you took yourself; pictures from the Internet; pictures of historical events or pictures of historical importance; pictures of art objects; even advertisements. They need not all be important in the same way.

Place the images before you. What are the implicit connections between them—A and B and C? A or B or C? A and B but not C? A or B and C? The possibilities are not infinite, but they are multiple. Spend at least 5 minutes jotting down notes about the implicit connections—connections that are not openly expressed but that are capable of being understood—between the images as they are laid out before you.

When you've completed your reflections, change the order of the images. What happens to the implicit connections? Repeat the exercise above with the newly ordered images.

When you've completed these two reflections about connections, take at least 20 minutes to write a reflective account of what happened to the connections when you reordered the images. Why does their order make a difference?

PRACTICE SESSION TWO

READING

We'd like you to look at Ta-Nehisi Coates's essay "Fear of a Black President," found on the *Atlantic* Web site. Read it through once; then return to it and mark where Coates makes connections.

Make a list of explicit (expressed) or implicit (unexpressed) *and* connections that set information or ideas next to each other.

Then list connections that explicitly or implicitly use the word *but* to establish qualifications, exceptions, conditions, ambiguity, or uncertainty.

Next, list connections that explicitly or implicitly use the word *or* to point out alternatives or possibilities.

Finally, spend at least 30 minutes writing a reflective piece about the connections you listed in the *but* and *or* categories. Which connection is the most important? Which is the most surprising?

PRACTICE SESSION THREE

RESEARCHING

After our students compose the first draft of an essay, we often find ourselves saying something along the lines of, "Yes, you've chosen a promising topic (or made a valid observation), but the issue is more complicated than it first appears." Then we invite them to make their thinking more complex by connecting to new ideas or information using *but* or *or* instead of *and*. These objections, qualifications, and additions can't be pulled out of thin air, however. They have to be discovered through reading, research, and thought.

Ta-Nehisi Coates's article "Fear of a Black President" offers a sharp critique of the first term of Barack Obama's presidency. While it's easy to take a polarized position on Coates's argument by simply agreeing or disagreeing with him, it's more interesting to use his work as a starting place for thinking more deeply about the points he raises.

Select three or four passages that confuse, surprise, disturb, or otherwise interest you, and then spend at least 2 hours doing research into the events or history Coates presents. As you dig down into your research, pay attention to places where you learn things that deepen or complicate your understanding of Coates's argument and your own thinking. In other words, look for places where you can make new connections.

WRITING

Write an essay that discusses how your research has informed and altered your thinking about Coates's argument. As you write, use the "three most important words" (and variations) to present research that adds to, qualifies, contradicts, or suggests alternatives both to Coates's ideas *and* to your own previously held opinions.

EXPLORE

We've suggested that critical thinking begins with the word *but*. Roxane Gay feels she meets one definition of what it means to be a feminist, but not another. In Etgar Keret's short story, the narrator tells us about a crushed car he has in his living room, but something about the story—and the narrator—seems a little off. Physician Siddhartha Mukherjee knows the arguments for and against antidepressants, but he thinks both arguments distort what is currently known about the treatment of depression. Joyce Carol Oates knows there's a long tradition of writers gaining inspiration from the natural world, but she thinks differently about the ants crawling across her table.

Gay, Roxane. "Bad Feminist." *VQR* Fall 2012. Web.

Keret, Etgar. "Car Concentrate." Trans. Nathan Englander. *Granta*. 2 Jan. 2014. Web.

Mukherjee, Siddhartha. "Post-Prozac Nation: The Science and History of Treating Depression." *New York Times*. 19 April 2012. Web.

Oates, Joyce Carol. "Against Nature." *Antaeus* 57 (Autumn 1986): 236–43. Print.

On Writing by Formula

In math and science, a formula is a hard-and-fast rule or fact. The chemical formula for water, for example, is H_2O, and the algebraic formula that defines the equivalence of energy and mass is $E = mc^2$. The beauty of such formulas is that they remain true, regardless of when or where they are used. Formulas in cooking, which we usually call recipes, are sometimes more flexible. If you're making a cake and you use a little less flour than the recipe calls for, you'll still end up with a cake at the end of the process. But if you substitute an equal amount of baking soda for the baking powder listed in the recipe, you'll push kitchen chemistry past its point of flexibility; what comes out of the oven will look more like a plate than a cake.

If we shift our attention to human communication, we can see how cultural formulas differ from scientific formulas. When applied to culture, the primary meaning for *formula* is "a set form of words for use in a ceremony or ritual." Most events involving human communication—purchasing something in a store, sending a child to school, even quitting a job—aren't ceremonies or rituals and, thus, aren't governed by strict formulas. And, even when the focus is narrowed to a specific ceremony or ritual, the cultural formula for what to say isn't universal, like a scientific formula, but, rather, is context-specific and subject to change over time. Take the marriage vow: the formula for what to say depends on the country in which the ceremony is to occur, whether the vow is to be made in a secular or a religious setting, and, if the setting is religious, the denominations of the participants. In the Episcopal Church, for example, the formula for what the bride and groom vow has changed over time: prior to 1922, the bride vowed "to love, cherish, and obey" the groom; since 1922, brides and grooms have vowed "to love and to cherish" one another. As of 2012, Episcopal churches have the option of consecrating the wedding vows of same sex couples.

As this example suggests, cultural formulas loosely define the conventions that govern a given ritual or ceremony. How loosely? Enter a church of a different denomination or a mosque or a synagogue or an ashram and the formula for creating a marriage bond changes. And if you head over to City Hall to get married by a justice of the peace, where the ceremony is pared down to its essentials, you'll find that a formula still applies: the presiding authority oversees an exchange of vows; there's still an opportunity to seal the vows with a kiss; and there are still papers to be signed afterwards. Even in those ceremonies where the participants write their own vows, there's no escaping the convention of being heartfelt, sincere, and personal. Popular entertainment, for example, is often formulaic. Many of you are likely to be familiar with the formula for the horror film ("Don't go in there!"), and you may even recognize the formula for parodying horror films. ("I know only dumb people in horror movies go into places like this alone, but here I go." Screams follow.) Formulas like these, which build on audience expectations, can be picked up either by watching a bunch of popular horror films or by having someone who knows the formula tell it to you.

If the formulas that govern everything from wedding vows to movie plots are flexible, what about the formulas that govern the thoughtful essay? Are they similarly flexible? We'd be surprised if you thought so, since the tendency of writing teachers from elementary school onward is to represent the recipes or templates or rules of thumb for generating the kind of writing valued in school as hard and fast. We, on the other hand, would say that following these formulas does not produce writing that is thoughtful or compelling or reflective; it just produces writing that can be graded according to the degree to which it has followed the assigned formula. When the work at hand is delivering expected information back to the teacher, such as in an essay exam, formulaic writing is an entirely appropriate mode of response. But when the goal is independent thinking, original insights, or the production of writing that others will read voluntarily, writing that follows a formula is incapable of delivering the goods.

A formula for originality is a contradiction in terms. If your writing is going to help you to think new thoughts, it will be because you are using your writing to practice curiosity, creativity, attentiveness, and engagement. The only way to produce thoughtful prose is to actually be thoughtful; the only way to produce writing that is compelling is to feel compelled by ideas, events, and issues; the only way to produce writing that is reflective is to regularly engage in acts of reflection. In all of these realms, writing is not filling in blank spaces on a form; it is the act of exploring the possible.

At this point in our essay, we intended to demonstrate how we distinguish between writing that's formulaic and writing that's driven by curiosity. But we've discovered that a funny thing happens when you write about writing by formula: every path we've gone down to illustrate what's wrong with formulaic writing has ended up being formulaic itself. If we were teaching a class, we'd ask our students to brain-storm with us about the paths we might take after we've discussed how the meaning of "formula" changes with the context. Since we can't do that with you, our readers, we're going to ask you to join us in a thought experiment about the options available to us. We'll go through them in turn.

Show why the writing in our classes is better than the writing produced under other approaches. "Piece of cake!" we say. This was, in fact, the first path we tried. Given that we are arguing for using writing as a technology for producing thoughts that are new to the writer, it seemed only logical that we would then go on to provide our readers with an example from one of our classes that shows what "non-formulaic" writing looks like. Going in this direction felt natural, necessary, and appropriate.

It also felt familiar. And this is why, eventually, we had to admit that it didn't work. It's not that we lack examples of writing from our classes that we feel amply demonstrate the advantages of developing the habits of the creative mind. Indeed, we have showcased our students' work in a number of other essays in this book. But when we tried to frame our argument about curiosity-driven writing, we found ourselves trapped in the solipsistic activity of arguing for the superiority of writing that we ourselves have assessed as superior.

There's another problem with moving the discussion of curiosity-driven writing to examples from our own classrooms; when it comes to making our case, we hold all the cards. We don't have to show you the writing that didn't succeed; we don't have to take you through the portfolios of students who didn't make progress over the course of the semester. We just have to find examples that prove our point. And then you, the reader, have only two options: you can either agree that we've proven what we've set out to prove or you can argue that our example isn't actually writing that explores new ideas and possibilities; it's just writing to a new formula.

So much for using examples from our classes in this context. Next!

Show why the writing produced in classes that emphasize formulaic writing is bad. "Easy as pie!" we say. To head off in this direction, all we needed was an exemplary five-paragraph essay. After much research, though, we had to conclude that there was no archive of "the universally agreed upon greatest five-paragraph essays in history" for us to draw on. A sample five-paragraph theme posted on a college Web site seemed promising at first, but the sample turned out to have been copied without attribution from an online paper mill. Even the paper mill sites themselves proved to be a poor source for exemplary five-paragraph essays: it turns out these sites don't claim that the writing they are selling is actually good; they just say it's what your professors are looking for.

Our inability to find a compelling example of the five-paragraph essay led us to see that we were arguing against a phantom. We can search for "prize-winning five-paragraph essays," but no prize winners come up. We can point to a testing industry that provides models for students to emulate with clear thesis statements, clear supporting evidence and analysis, and clear structures, but we can't find compelling examples of school systems or university administrations that insist that formulaic writing of any kind is ideal for conveying important thoughts. In fact, as we continued to drill down on this problem, we were surprised to discover that the critique of formulaic writing has a long history. Michelle Tremmel, writing in 2011, found more than 120 articles published over the past fifty years in professional journals for writing teachers that were "clearly against the five-paragraph theme."

Our failed search for the exemplary five-paragraph essay showed us that we had set ourselves the wrong task. We didn't need to develop an argument against writing by formula because that argument has already been made many times over—to, as far as we can determine, very little effect. Instead, we needed to ask a different question: why is it that students are taught to excel at a form of writing that the preponderance of writing teachers agree isn't actually "good writing"? Our answer to this question, when it finally came, surprised us: teaching students to produce formulaic essays and arguments has never actually been about teaching students to write like good writers. It has instead been about teaching them to be clear and rule-abiding language users.

So, in the end, we concluded that there's actually no point in delineating the limits of the five-paragraph essay or any other writing formula because learning to be a clear and conventional language user has little to do with learning to be a writer. If familiar formulas are really just recipes for clarity, without regard for the writer's thoughts and ideas, we don't need to include them in our discussion of writing at all.

Now what?

Make a joke? We believe in the power of humor to create opportunities that reason alone can't make available. And, the truth is, we are in a funny situation: two writing teachers have given themselves the worst writing prompt ever: "make an unconventional argument against convention." Our predicament is funny in the way only contradictions, paradoxes, and koans can be: there's a fugitive meaning captured by the situation we've put ourselves in that can only be understood through the experience of being caught in the trap.

So, let's admit it's funny that, in our meditation on writing by formula, we've written ourselves into two dead ends: we can't provide unconventional evidence that our approach is better and we can't find anyone who argues convincingly that good writing requires conforming to conventions. We're Don Quixote and Sancho Panza, tilting at windmills.

If we really want to shift the conversation about writing from following a formula to practicing habits of mind, we need to take a different approach. We can't look to a single piece of student writing to bear the burden of illustrating either the habits of a creative mind or the robotic prose of a student trained to produce writing that can be assessed by machines. Instead, we need to ask some new questions: What habits of mind are being encouraged by questions that ask for the faithful reproduction of the main points in a lecture? By questions that ask the writer to agree or disagree with a simple explanation for a complex event? By an assessment system that stresses clarity over shades of meaning?

We'd like you to take some time to think about these questions and to reflect on your own experiences producing writing in school. We think your reflections are likely to support our contention that the emphasis in your education has been on order, clarity, and concision more than exploration, questioning, and the joys of digression.

Change direction. Having produced three different discussions of formulaic writing, we finally wrote ourselves to an understanding of why this particular transition has been so difficult. To comprehend how writing is based in habits of mind, one must look at the work of writers who are in the habit of writing. We want our students to ask difficult questions and get lost in the rabbit holes of research; we want them to know what it's like to get trapped in dead ends and to learn to write themselves out of such impasses. When writing this way becomes a habit, one learns the art of writing oneself into awareness of the complexity of what previously seemed straightforward, obvious, or familiar.

We realized, at last, that the best way to show you the habits of experienced writers at work is to do exactly what we've done here: document just how much work goes into resisting the allure of the familiar and the easily proven.

· · · · ·

So, a different direction.

Certain topics seem to invite predictable writing and thinking. One of the most clichéd topics in high school and college writing curricula is gun control. Given the differences between those who favor gun control and those who favor gun rights, it seems implausible that writers on either side of this debate could introduce anything that would alter where anyone stands on this issue. Pro/con, liberal/conservative, right/wrong. There doesn't appear to be a lot of room for movement.

How do experienced writers, who have made a habit of being genuinely curious, avoid reproducing predictable arguments when writing about long debated topics? To answer this question, let's consider the first few paragraphs of the introduction to *Reducing Gun Violence in America: Informing Policy with Evidence and Analysis*, an edited collection published soon after the mass shooting at Sandy Hook Elementary School in 2012.

The role of guns in violence, and what should be done, are subjects of intense debate in the United States and elsewhere. But certain facts are not debatable. More than 31,000 people died from gunshot wounds in the United States in 2010. Because the victims are disproportionately young, gun violence is one of the leading causes of premature mortality in the United States. In addition to these deaths, in 2010, there were an estimated 337,960 nonfatal violent crimes committed with guns, and 73,505 persons were treated in hospital emergency departments for nonfatal gunshot wounds. The social and economic costs of gun violence in America are also enormous.

Despite the huge daily impact of gun violence, most public discourse on gun policy is centered on mass shootings in public places. Such incidents are typically portrayed as random acts by severely mentally ill individuals which are impossible to predict or prevent. Those who viewed, heard, or read news stories on gun policy might conclude the following: (1) mass shootings, the mentally ill, and assault weapons are the primary concerns; (2) gun control laws disarm law-abiding citizens without affecting criminals' access to guns; (3) there is no evidence that gun control laws work; and (4) the public has no appetite for strengthening current gun laws. Yet all of the evidence in this book counters each of these misperceptions with facts to the contrary.

At first glance, the moves that Daniel W. Webster and Jon S. Vernick, co-authors of the introduction to *Reducing Gun Violence*, make here are likely to seem familiar. They establish the importance of their topic by referencing what they present as undebatable facts. Next, they discuss popular thinking about gun violence and legislation. And then they announce that their book will debunk the four major misperceptions about gun violence in turn.

This description of the way Webster and Vernick build their argument misses their most important move, though: they want to shift the context of the discussion of gun violence away from headline-grabbing mass shootings in order to focus their reader's attention on the high rate of gun violence in the United States. The research they have done documents the undeniable costs of this violence, both in lives lost and in medical expenses for the roughly one hundred thousand people injured or killed by guns in the United States every year. Webster and Vernick then point to one of the problems that limits our ability to discuss workable ways to reduce gun violence: *despite* the prevalence of gun violence in the United States, the only gun violence that gets sustained attention from the media is that which takes the form of a mass shooting.

What Webster and Vernick do next is further evidence of curiosity-driven minds at work on a problem: they detail the conclusions that reasonable people might make from how mass shootings are covered in the media; they *imagine* themselves in the place of such viewers and list the reasons why reducing gun violence seems impossible as a result. They haven't, in other words, produced an unsupportable "most people think" statement; they've made a connection between popular opinions and what mass media focuses on—namely mass shootings. In making this connection, Webster and Vernick have implicitly established a relationship of causality: because most people encounter information about gun violence in the context of mass shootings, they reach certain predictable conclusions about both the means and the possibility of curbing gun violence. Webster and Vernick promise to show how these conclusions no longer hold once the context is shifted from mass shootings to gun violence in general.

Can we imagine someone being persuaded to rethink gun violence as a result of Webster and Vernick's argument? In so doing, do we imagine someone who has thought about the issue a great deal? If this person *is* persuaded, would the change in position be consequential for the person? Does this personal change also have the potential to be consequential on a larger scale? We'd answer all of these questions in the affirmative. In fact, we'd go further and say that asking questions of this sort is a good way to start a conversation about how to distinguish writing that emerges from habits of the creative mind and writing that is done to confirm beliefs the writer already holds: the first kind of writing imagines readers who can consider multiple and conflicting ideas; the second seeks out readers who already agree.

Could a less experienced student writer produce something on gun control that made moves similar to those we found in the opening paragraphs of Webster and Vernick's introduction? We think so, but that writer would have to be genuinely interested in gun control as a question to be understood, rather than as an issue upon which one first takes a stand and then sets out in search of evidence supporting that stand. That student would have to want to spend time doing research that drilled down into questions about gun control, and that student would have to believe that staking out a position on gun control has consequences that extend far beyond the fulfillment of a paper assignment.

If such a student were working in a course that encouraged exploring questions rather than following a formula for putting together an argument, that student would have the chance to experience just how much is involved in understanding a complex issue in depth and what it means to use one's writing to think new thoughts. And this, finally, is why we believe that shifting the teaching of writing from formulas to habits matters. This shift encourages the creation of classroom practices that allow inexperienced writers to cultivate curiosity, to explore in wide-ranging ways, and to engage with the most pressing questions of our time.

Note: All definitions come from merriamwebster.com.

PRACTICE SESSION ONE

RESEARCHING

Using the Web as your archive, find an example of a persuasive essay that has been truly influential and that *actually changes your mind* on an issue. See if you can find an example written by a professional journalist or an experienced writer from a newspaper, an important magazine, or an academic journal. Spend at least 30 minutes searching for an essay that meets these criteria.

After you've found a truly persuasive essay, or after you've put in 30 minutes looking for one, take at least 20 minutes to write about your search. What challenges did you encounter? If you found a persuasive essay, was it about a topic that previously mattered to you, or was it about something you hadn't thought much about? What did you learn about persuasive writing as your search progressed? What's the value of doing this exercise?

PRACTICE SESSION TWO

READING

Select one of the readings suggested in the Explore section that follows. Read the article or essay and then return to the introductory paragraphs, rereading them with care. After that, spend at least 20 minutes taking notes on how the writer composes the introduction. How does the writer choose to launch the article? How does the writer get the reader interested in the topic at hand? How does the introduction differ from a conventional five-paragraph-essay introduction? Does it share any qualities with the introductions you learned to write in school?

REFLECTING

Review the article or essay you read for the Reading Practice Session taking notes about how the writer exercises curiosity; connects ideas, sources, and information in surprising ways; and keeps the reader interested from the beginning of the piece to the end. In other words, explore how the article or essay *works*.

Based on what you've discovered about how the piece you selected is put together, what would you say governed the writer's organizational decisions? Is the writer following a set of rules or a formula that you can identify? Has the writer broken rules you were taught? Spend at least 45 minutes writing about the relationship between the writer's curiosity and the structure he or she has used to organize the article or essay you've read.

EXPLORE

Is there a formula for writing against formula? Probably not. The essays we've suggested here demonstrate, instead, just how malleable the essay's form is. Annie Dillard writes lyrically about witnessing a natural event. James Baldwin reflects fearlessly on what it means to grow up black in America. John Branch uses a host of multimedia resources to help tell the story of a deadly skiing decision. And the reporters at Planet Money use video, taped interviews, and text to show how an ordinary t-shirt is the result of a global production process.

Baldwin, James. "Notes of a Native Son," *Notes of a Native Son*. Boston: Beacon Press, 1955. Print.

Branch, John. "Snow Fall: The Avalanche at Tunnel Creek." *New York Times*. 21 Dec. 2012. Web.

Dillard, Annie. "Total Eclipse," *Teaching a Stone to Talk*. New York: Harper Collins, 1982. 9–29. Print. (Available on Google Books via Preview.)

"Planet Money Makes a T-shirt: The World Behind a Simple Shirt, in Five Chapters." Video. *Planet Money*. National Public Radio. Web.

On Working with the Words of Others

Cite your sources.

It's hard to imagine a research assignment that doesn't include some version of this admonition. If you were to ask your teachers why it's important to provide full information about the sources you've used, they'd likely tell you one of two things: citation is a service to your readers because it allows them to follow up on ideas or information they encounter in your writing, or citation is a way of marking the boundaries between your work and the work of others. These answers aren't wrong, but they both imply that citation is primarily a means for defending yourself from skeptical readers—those who would doubt the quality of your sources and those who would suspect you of plagiarizing.

We acknowledge that documenting sources and preventing plagiarism are both worthy goals, but we fear that discussing citation only in these terms actively discourages students from participating in the most powerful educational experience there is—engaging deeply with the ideas of other thinkers. "To cite" a source means more than following a set of rules about how to list it in a footnote or on a works cited page; "to cite" also refers to the act of quoting, summarizing, or generally making use of material from sources.

We invite you to think of citation as an opportunity to demonstrate what you can *do* with the words of others. To cite sources is to bring other voices, other approaches, and other ideas into your work. It provides the material for you to carry on a conversation with writers whose work you find compelling. While you may have experience using sources as the object of analysis (for instance, when you've been asked to write about a literary text or primary document) or to supply background information, citation can serve your writing in a variety of other ways. It can contribute key ideas or concepts, provide positions or arguments to grapple with, or shift the direction of the conversation. We especially value citation that brings in a new perspective that questions or rejects the most obvious way of thinking, or that turns the issue, question, or problem you are working on so that you can see it from another angle.

With this understanding of citation in mind, every time you cite another writer you should ask: *What work do I want these words or ideas to do for my readers?*

To explore the value of this question, let's take a look at three examples that involve citation and consider what asking this question allows us to see about each writer's project.

· · · · ·

1.   Fareed Zakaria hosts his own show on CNN, where he discusses foreign policy and international relations. He is the author of best-selling books that consider America's fate in the altered global landscape of the twenty-first century, and he writes for *Time* magazine. On August 10, 2012, he published an editorial in *Time* entitled "The Case for Gun Control: Why Limiting Easy Access to Guns Is Intelligent and American." He was prompted to write, he says, by a mass shooting at a Sikh temple in Oak Creek, Wisconsin, that left seven dead, including the gunman, who committed suicide at the scene.

In his editorial, Zakaria refers to an influential book on the history of gun laws in the United States:

> Adam Winkler, a professor of constitutional law at UCLA, documents the actual history in *Gunfight: The Battle over the Right to Bear Arms in America*. Guns were regulated in the U.S. from the earliest years of the Republic. Laws that banned the carrying of concealed weapons were passed in Kentucky and Louisiana in 1813. Other states soon followed: Indiana in 1820, Tennessee and Virginia in 1838, Alabama in 1839, and Ohio in 1859. Similar laws were passed in Texas, Florida and Oklahoma. As the governor of Texas (Texas!) explained in 1893, the "mission of the concealed deadly weapon is murder. To check it is the duty of every self-respecting, law-abiding man."

What work does Zakaria want this citation of Winkler's work to do for his readers? Zakaria draws his readers' attention to recent scholarship, arguing that gun control in the United States has a history dating back nearly two hundred years. Zakaria clearly identifies both the author of this research and where the research can be found, should his readers care to look more deeply into this history. In referencing and summarizing work of this caliber, Zakaria is displaying his expert credentials: he knows where the best writing on gun control is, and he can succinctly represent the other author's ideas, sparing his readers the work of reading Winkler's 384-page tome on their own. So in this example, the work of citation is analogous to a display of heavy lifting.

That's one way to use citation: to digest and distill information for the reader.

There's one problem with our presenting Zakaria's writing on Winkler as exemplary of this valuable use of citation, however: the heavy lifting on display was done not by Zakaria but by Jill Lepore, whom Zakaria has failed to cite. There's an unmistakable similarity between Zakaria's paragraph and a paragraph in Lepore's April 23, 2012, *New Yorker* article, "Battleground America: One Nation, under the Gun," which she wrote in the aftermath of the shooting death of Trayvon Martin:

> As Adam Winkler, a constitutional-law scholar at U.C.L.A., demonstrates in a remarkably nuanced new book, *Gunfight: The Battle Over the Right to Bear Arms in America*, firearms have been regulated in the United States from the start. Laws banning the carrying of concealed weapons were passed in Kentucky and Louisiana in 1813, and other states soon followed: Indiana (1820), Tennessee and Virginia (1838), Alabama (1839), and Ohio (1859). Similar laws were passed in Texas, Florida, and Oklahoma. As the governor of Texas explained in 1893, the "mission of the concealed deadly weapon is murder. To check it is the duty of every self-respecting, law-abiding man."

When accusations surfaced that Zakaria had used Lepore's work without making clear that he had paraphrased and quoted from her article, CNN and *Time* suspended Zakaria pending a full review of the incident.

This appears on its face to be a clear-cut case of plagiarism. Zakaria never mentions Lepore in his piece, and he doesn't signal in any way that he is presenting her summary of Winkler's book with minor changes. He's representing Lepore's words and work as his own, which is the very definition of plagiarism. Zakaria released a statement the same day the news broke, acknowledging his responsibility for the error: "I made a terrible mistake. It is a serious lapse and one that is entirely my fault. I apologize unreservedly to her [Lepore], to my editors at *Time* and CNN, and to my readers and viewers everywhere." A week later, CNN concluded its review of Zakaria's work and determined that the error was "unintentional" and "an isolated incident." He was immediately reinstated at CNN, and he returned to *Time* after a one-month suspension.

Note that Zakaria was suspended even though his long record of publication establishes beyond a doubt that he knows how to cite in ways that do the heavy lifting for his readers; time and again, he's demonstrated that he knows how to distill long texts into concise summaries. So while we are emphasizing here that we want you to be able to (1) select an appropriately challenging source with which to work, (2) engage with an extended piece of historical scholarship, and (3) capture the author's argument succinctly, Zakaria's example shows just how important it is that you demonstrate, in *every instance*, that you are able to (4) document your sources. No one gets a free pass on that fourth requirement, no matter how long her or his record of publication!

· · · · ·

2.   For our second example of working with the words of others, we would like to draw your attention to Jonathan Lethem's "The Ecstasy of Influence: A Plagiarism." Early in his essay, Lethem illustrates his thesis that originality and copying go hand in hand during the artistic process by discussing his initial encounter with the John Donne quote that introduces his essay, "All mankind is of one author, and is one volume; when one man dies, one chapter is not torn out of the book, but translated into a better language; and every chapter must be so translated." Lethem tells us that he first came across this quote while watching the film *84 Charing Cross Road*. He then relates a convoluted tale of trying to track down the passage in its original context, turning first to the book and then the play on which the movie was based, before discovering, after many fruitless searches on the Web, that the film had misquoted Donne.

Lethem's story is an elegant example of how the meaning of strings of words (that is, quotations) changes as those strings of words travel through time and across media. There's just one thing about the example, though, as Lethem tells us in the "key" he provides at the end of his essay: "The anecdote [about tracking down the quote] is cribbed, with an elision to avoid appropriating a dead grandmother, from Jonathan Rosen's *The Talmud and the Internet*. I've never seen *84 Charing Cross Road*, nor searched the Web for a Donne quote." As Lethem's key makes clear, he has composed his essay almost entirely of uncited quotations and unattributed ideas to show what his essay has argued—the act of creation always involves copying, building on, modifying, and combining material from other sources. This is what Lethem means by "the ecstasy of influence": all originality depends on the writer having been deeply influenced by the ideas of others.

We are particularly taken with Lethem's description of the writing practice that guided him in "The Ecstasy of Influence," which appears at the end of the essay, in his introduction to the list of his unattributed sources:

> This key to the preceding essay names the source of every line I stole, warped, and cobbled together as I "wrote" (except, alas, those sources I forgot along the way). First uses of a given author or speaker are highlighted in red. Nearly every sentence I culled I also revised, at least slightly—for necessities of space, in order to produce a more consistent tone, or simply because I felt like it.

With his key, Lethem has turned our question on its head: What work does he want his *noncitation* of the words of others to do for his readers? We would say that his noncitation is a performance: since Lethem has subtitled his piece "a plagiarism," and he has provided a closing list of the citations he left uncited in the body of his essay, it's clear he isn't trying to pass off the work of others as his own. Rather, by the time Lethem is done with his key, he has documented that the work of being influenced by the ideas of others requires reading widely and deeply.

· · · · ·

Before moving to our final example, we want to acknowledge the intentionally unconventional character of our first two examples of working with the words of others. We could have pointed to Jill Lepore's distillation of Adam Winkler's book *Gunfight* as a great example of what it means to condense a lengthy text into a concise summary. Instead, we chose to highlight Zakaria's unattributed use of Lepore's writing as an example of what it means to fail to work well with the words of others. And we could have called on any number of prominent examples to further illustrate the perils of plagiarism. But instead we chose Lethem's essay, "The Ecstasy of Influence: A Plagiarism," because it complicates the notion that the process of documenting sources of inspiration or insight could ever be complete. We have started with these examples to encourage you to be thoughtful, and even creative, about working with the words of others. The primary goal of citing others' work shouldn't be to follow the rules of documentation but to extend your own thinking and show your readers that your ideas are grounded in both verifiable facts and an ongoing conversation with sources about the issues and ideas that interest you.

· · · · ·

3. For our final example, we'll look at the kind of citation that will most occupy you as a college writer: working with the words of others to complicate and enrich your own understanding of the problem, question, or mystery you've chosen to explore. To do so, we'll turn to perhaps the most generic of research topics: gun control. This was a typical research topic when we were in high school over thirty years ago, and we imagine that it will continue to be a typical research topic thirty years from now. Gun control is seen to be an ideal prompt in traditional writing class-rooms, we would say, because it lends itself so easily to for-or-against arguments.

A central point of disagreement in the debate about gun control is what James Madison meant when he wrote the Second Amendment: "A well regulated Militia, being necessary to the security of a free State, the right of the people to keep and bear Arms, shall not be infringed." Did he mean that the people, as a collective, have the right to form militias for their common defense? Or did he mean that indi-viduals have the right to own and carry guns? In our view, it is not a stretch to claim that the argument about the meaning of the Second Amendment and gun control is in part about citation. People on both sides cite the amendment, but neither side can establish, once and for all, what the amendment means. Why? Because all argu-ments about the amendment's meaning hinge on how one works with Madison's words. And so the for-or-against argument about gun control just gets repeated over and over again, without generating new insights or understandings on either side of the "debate."

A writer who practices curiosity, however, can reject the dead end of the for-or-against assignment. Consider, for example, the article we discussed above (the one Zakaria failed to cite), "Battleground America: One Nation, under the Gun," in which Jill Lepore engages with the question of whether the Second Amendment was originally intended to preserve the right of individuals to own guns. We're particularly interested in this article because of Lepore's adept and highly varied use of citation. As we noted earlier, her summary of Winkler's work is an example of citation as heavy lifting; she does the hard work of condensing a long text into a clear and concise overview. In the exercises at the end of this essay, we ask you to examine how else she works with the words of others, including Madison's. Our goal is for you to be able to use citation as Lepore does, to be able to work with the words of others in the service of exploring and exposing the complexity of a chosen question, problem, or mystery.

Lepore's discussion of the Second Amendment points to a problem all writ-ers face when they work with the words of others. Simply quoting another writer's words isn't enough to make those words do the work you want them to do. There are moments when you have to analyze those words and make a case for what you think they mean. Lepore, a historian who specializes in early US history, mines documents from the country's past, including the Articles of Confederation and the Constitution, to place the Second Amendment in the context of an eighteenth-cen-tury debate about whether the states or the newly formed federal government should have the power to maintain militias. In 1776, the Articles of Confederation included the requirement that "every *state* shall always keep up a well regulated and disciplined militia," but in 1787, when the Constitution was signed in Philadelphia, *Congress* was granted the power "to provide for calling forth the Militia to execute the Laws of the Union." When Madison drafted the Bill of Rights in 1789, he was trying to appease those who worried that the Constitution had granted too much power to the federal government. His concern, Lepore argues, was to address anxieties about a permanent federal army. By citing these original sources, Lepore means to establish that there is a historical ground for arguing that the Second Amendment originally had nothing to do with individual ownership of guns.

But if Lepore's citation of the nation's foundational documents accurately depicts Madison's original intent, how does she then account for the transformation of Madison's original concern with militias and state power into a constitutional defense of private gun ownership? Here, too, Lepore keeps her attention focused on original source material. She points out that even the National Rifle Association— founded in 1871 and now the nation's most influential lobby against gun control— did not interpret the Second Amendment as preserving a personal right to bear arms until the 1970s. What prompted this change? Lepore, citing speeches by Malcolm X and Huey Newton from the 1960s, makes the surprising case that the idea that the Second Amendment guarantees the right of private citizens to own guns was first made by black nationalists and the Black Panther Party for Self-Defense. At that point in time, following the many assassinations of that decade—of President John F. Kennedy, Malcolm X, Robert Kennedy, and Martin Luther King Jr.—the NRA actually supported the Gun Control Act of 1968. Not until 1977, on the cusp of a new conservative movement, did the NRA adopt as its new motto a quote from the Second Amendment: "The Right of the People to Keep and Bear Arms Shall Not Be Infringed." The idea that the amendment protects the rights of individual gun own-ers only went mainstream during the presidency of Ronald Reagan, after Senator Orrin Hatch and the Subcommittee on the Constitution issued a 1982 report about the Second Amendment entitled "The Right to Keep and Bear Arms."

Can we generalize about the work Lepore wants her many citations to do for the readers of "Battleground America"? Lepore does plenty of heavy lifting, summariz-ing many important scholarly sources. But what we find to be exemplary is her com-mitment to working with the words of others who are in the position to complicate her thinking. Throughout the article, Lepore demonstrates her ability to work with primary source material to cast something familiar—in this case, the debate over the Second Amendment—in a new light. Lepore does not, in other words, use citation to simplify the historical record or to flatten an issue into those who stand on one side of the question and those who stand on the other side. Rather, she weaves her many sources together into a sinuous braid supple enough to explain why repeated and horrific acts of gun violence have not yet led to meaningful legislation curbing access to guns.

PRACTICE SESSION ONE

RESEARCHING

We emphasized the importance of working with primary sources in our essay above. We'd like you to identify the primary sources Jill Lepore cites either in her essay "Battleground America" or "the Last Amazon: Wonder Woman Returns," both of which are available through the *New Yorker* Web site. After you've identified all of Lepore's primary sources, select one of the documents she mentions and go find it. If you can't access the source online, try to find it in your library. If you're reading "Battleground America," for instance, you could look at the Constitution, examples of nineteenth-century gun laws, the speech by Malcolm X that Lepore cites, or official documents of the National Rifle Association.

Read the document you've chosen and then spend at least 30 minutes writing about how a more detailed citation from the document could have further complicated Lepore's discussion. If the first document you track down doesn't yield a compelling example, search for other primary source material; once you've found something compelling, complete the assignment.

READING

Journalists who write for popular magazines or newspapers typically don't provide in-text documentation of page numbers or a list of works cited. And it's rare to come across a footnote in the *New Yorker*, *Harper's*, or the *Atlantic*. Return to the essay you read for the previous exercise and review at least three pages, paying attention to where Lepore is clear about where she found words, ideas, and information from others and where she's not. Spend at least 20 minutes making a list of where she would need to cite her sources if she had written this article for an academic class. Also note how often you were confused or unclear about whether she had taken material from a source.

REFLECTING

After reviewing how and where Lepore documents her sources, spend at least 60 minutes writing about the different citation standards of journalism and scholarly writing. Did you find evidence that caused you to trust or to doubt Lepore as a writer? Is there any way to tell whether a citation is accurate or not *without* tracking it down and checking on it yourself?

PRACTICE SESSION TWO

READING

Now we'd like you to pay attention to the variety of ways writers work with the words of others. Select an essay from the suggested readings in the Explore section that follows. Read the essay with care.

Next, spend at least 40 minutes observing, marking, and identifying the many different ways the writer works with sources. You might notice sources used to supply background information, to provide key ideas or concepts, to provide positions or arguments to grapple with, to shift the direction of the conversation, or to serve as the focus of analysis. Where did the writer work with sources in ways that impressed, surprised, or perhaps disappointed you? Were there moments when you felt a citation didn't do the work the writer wanted it to? Did the writer cite sources in ways that you'd like to emulate?

REFLECTING

Spend at least 60 minutes writing reflectively about what you've learned from this exercise about working with the words or ideas of others.

EXPLORE

As writers, we are always working with the words of others. Our suggested readings provide examples of ways of doing this work that you might want to give a try. Christopher Chabris questions the words of Malcolm Gladwell, a writer we quote a good deal in this book. Zadie Smith argues with a contemporary cultural theorist about the nature of reality. Sarah Resnick interviews a member of WikiLeaks about the collection and distribution of classified material. And John Jeremiah Sullivan evaluates the success of a half-finished work by a writer he greatly admires.

Chabris, Christopher. "The Trouble with Malcolm Gladwell." *Slate* 8. Oct. 2013. Web.

Smith, Zadie. "The Rise of the Essay." *The Guardian* 20. Nov. 2007. Web.

Resnick, Sarah. "Leave Your Cellphone at Home: Interview with Jacob Applebaum."
    n+1 10. 10 June 2013. Web

Sullivan, John Jeremiah. "Too Much Information." *GQ*. May 2011. Web.

Argument at Work: Michelle Alexander and the Power of Analogy

A decade ago, when legal scholar Michelle Alexander first noticed a bright orange poster stapled to a telephone pole that declared, in bold letters, THE DRUG WAR IS THE NEW JIM CROW, she rejected the statement as preposterous. A Stanford Law School graduate and a former clerk for Supreme Court Justice Harry Blackmun, Alexander had good reason to trust her judgment. She didn't forget that sign, though, and after years of studying how the war on drugs had been carried out, she came to believe "that mass incarceration in the United States had, in fact, emerged as a stunningly comprehensive and well-disguised system of racialized social control that functions in a manner strikingly similar to [the pre–civil rights era, "separate but equal" laws known as] Jim Crow."

Anticipating that some readers of her book *The New Jim Crow: Mass Incarceration in the Age of Colorblindness* will share her initial skepticism about the racist character of the war on drugs, Alexander uses the government's own statistics to show that, although people of all races use and sell drugs at similar rates, "black men have been admitted to prison on drug charges at rates twenty to fifty times greater than those of white men." Over time, mass incarceration leads to mass disenfranchisement, since convicted felons, regardless of their race, lose the right to vote and the right to serve on juries and may also lose access to public housing, student loans, food stamps, and other public benefits. Excluded from the mainstream economy, prisoners who have served their time fall into a status of "permanent second-class citizenship." Given the manifest disparity in rates of incarceration, Alexander argues that "laws prohibiting the use and sale of drugs are facially race neutral, but they are enforced in a highly discriminatory fashion." And this, Alexander goes on to show, has served to create "a racial caste system."

So is the drug war a new incarnation of Jim Crow? An analogy establishes a relationship of similarity, not exact equivalence. The rhetorical strength of such comparisons is realized when they shake us out of our usual ways of thinking, shift our perspectives, make us see a connection that was previously invisible. In this instance, there is evidence that Alexander has produced an argument persuasive enough to get readers who are as skeptical as she once was to reconsider their positions. Bill Frezza, a writer for the conservative magazine *Forbes*, begins his review of Alexander's book thus: "Once in a great while a writer at the opposite end of the political spectrum gets you to look at a familiar set of facts in a new way. Disconcerting as it is, you can feel your foundation shift as your mind struggles to reconcile this new point of view with long held beliefs. Michelle Alexander has done just that in her book, *The New Jim Crow*."

The raw material for Alexander's argument—government statistics on incarceration—is readily available on the Web. Anyone can cite this data, but citation alone doesn't produce a foundation-shifting argument. Alexander drills down into the data and locates her argument in history; she is skeptical of the patterns that emerge, so she tests the connections she has made and allows the results of her research to guide her thinking. In the end, she produces an argument that invites other reasonable skeptics to see the drug war as the reimplementation of Jim Crow–style institutionalized racism.

Practicing

How do you develop a habit? Through practice. But what is practice? When you're a kid practicing handwriting, you learn through repetition. You copy the letters of the alphabet over and over, mastering the block shapes first before moving on to cursive. With both types of writing, you practice certain physical gestures so that you can faithfully reproduce the conventional shape of each letter. This practice requires hand–eye coordination, fine motor control in your dominant hand, and symbol recognition. Once you've practiced these activities enough, you can reproduce all the letters of the alphabet quickly, without conscious thought. Then, in a very limited sense, you know how to write.

What do you practice if you want to become a writer? Aspiring writers are often given two pieces of well-intentioned advice: "write what you know" and "write every day." While we can quibble with this kind of advice, we'd rather have you think about what habits you should be developing through practice (that is, through writing every day). What does it mean to look at the world the way a writer does? What does it mean to read like a writer? What does it mean to ask questions like a writer? In posing these questions, we encourage you to see writing as a way of being curious about the world and your place in it.

On Seeing as a Writer

> The very reason I write is so that I might not sleepwalk through my entire life.
>
> —*Zadie Smith, "Fail Better"*

Learning how to draw, as we discussed earlier (pp. 18–24), means learning how to see without naming; this allows the visual, spatial, and synthesizing ways of thinking to guide the hand on the page. Quieting the verbal train of thought allows you to see like an artist, but what if you want to put what you see into words? How do you learn to see as a writer does?

Chapter 6, "Practicing," is taken from Richard E. Miller and Ann Jurecic, *Habits of the Creative Mind*, pp. 178–198 (Part 9, "Practicing").

Young children can be intensely observant and curious. They learn about the world by paying attention and asking lots of questions. Once we become adults, many of us stop observing so acutely and constantly—in part because so much of the previously mysterious world is now familiar to us. We go on mental autopilot during routine experiences. We see what we expect to see. And we keep our surprise and wonder in check because both take up time we don't think we have to spare.

To see as a writer does, you need to practice asking questions about what you see. So instead of quieting the verbal activity in your mind, in this process you are training yourself to question the information your eyes are reporting to you. This questioning serves two purposes: it makes you conscious of your own perspective, and it also makes clear that other perspectives are possible. And this, ultimately, is part of what seeing as a writer involves—noticing clashes, subtle tensions, or unexpected connections between differing perspectives.

What do we mean by this? Here's an example of such a conflict, which comes from the opening of an essay by Annie Stiver, a student in one of our creative nonfiction classes:

> Recently, while standing in line for a ticket at the New Brunswick train station, I witnessed a mother nudge her young son, who, after barely noticing his mother's prod, continued to look steadily at a man sitting half-awake on a bench in the corner of the station. After her eyes dropped and brows narrowed on her son, she clasped his shoulder and bent down to tell him that he is "not supposed to stare at bums." The boy turned his head forward at his mother's instruction, yet as I watched him I noticed his eyes were straining towards the right side of the room where this man was. Eventually, when it was his mother's turn at the ticket machine, the boy immediately turned his head to stare full-on at the man in tattered clothing on the train station bench. I figured that the boy was an infrequent visitor to New Brunswick.
>
> This situation got me thinking about the rate at which children are encouraged not to stare even as they are curiously struck by novel experiences and when confronted with the unexpected. How did it come to be that we are taught not to stare?
>
> A common response is that it's simply not polite to stare. But in those moments of heightened curiosity when we are told to keep our eyes from wandering on another's "business," we are, aside from being polite, affecting our own development and behavior as we repress our individual curiosities and questions about others. What happens when we stare? I would argue

that staring goes beyond seeing the "other." Rather, when we stare, we are meant to think about ourselves. Watching the boy staring at the man in the station, I remembered the familiar feeling of when I was his age during unfamiliar and curious encounters with the unknown and unexpected. We're not staring because we want to know that our way of life is more comfortable and reassuring (we can consider this impolite), but sometimes we stare because we feel instinctively that our way of life is not quite right. When this happens, we want to ask, "Why aren't more of us staring?"

This is a great start to a thoughtful essay. Rereading this passage and thinking about the choices the student made as a writer, we see that she began with close, careful observation of the scene in the train station—a mother scolds her young son for staring at a homeless person. The writer had many choices about what perspective to take on this scene, and she chose to pay attention to the tension between what the mother says—that her son is not supposed to stare—and what he does—look again and again. In so doing, the writer stages for her readers an encounter between one perspective (staring is impolite) and another (staring is evidence of curiosity). Rather than arguing that one perspective or the other is the correct one to have on the situation, the writer responds to this common experience of a parent scolding a child with a question that the scene has raised for her:

"How did it come to be that we are taught not to stare?"

The writer pushes past the obvious answer, that it's impolite. There's something more going on here than bad behavior: the child wants to stare. The writer asks another question:

"What happens when we stare?"

Again, the writer rejects the commonplace answer. Staring that involves judgment of others is rude, she concedes, but curious children may be staring for another reason. "I would argue," she writes, "that staring goes beyond seeing the 'other.' Rather, when we stare, we are meant to think about ourselves.... Sometimes we stare because we feel instinctively that our way of life is not quite right." And this line of reasoning leads the writer to the question that drives the rest of her essay:

"Why aren't more of us staring?"

As writing teachers, we look at this student's sequence of observations, inter-pretations, and questions, and we see the habits of a creative mind at work.

She began with close observation.

She asked lots of questions—and not just questions about the facts (that is, questions starting with the words *what*, *where*, or *who*), but also questions about cause and significance (questions starting with *how* or *why*).

She recognized a key concept—in this case, staring—and shifted her frame of reference to focus on what's going on when a child stares.

She shifted her perspective away from the straightforward and obvious to think from a different point of view. In this case, she thought about why the child continued to look after having been told not to.

Remembering her own childhood, she realized that a child may stare because her or his usual way of thinking has been unsettled. Staring—or merely looking thoughtfully—can lead to reflection about oneself and one's relationship to others.

This isn't a formula for seeing like a writer; rather, it shows that seeing like a writer means developing the habit of choosing—from what to focus on, to the terms of the description, to the connections made, to the other perspectives entertained. To see as a writer, one doesn't begin by choosing a topic or a theme, both of which are inert, but rather by practicing questioning what one sees, which is a never-ending activity.

Now we'd like you to practice looking from different perspectives at places and the people who inhabit them, with the goal of opening up new and compelling questions about what you see.

PRACTICE SESSION ONE

REFLECTING (ON PUBLIC SPACE)

Begin by selecting a familiar, common space in your community or on your campus, somewhere you've been dozens if not hundreds of times. Visit at a time of day when it's likely to be busy. Observe the space for at least 20 minutes. Take notes on what you see. Notice who uses the space and how they move through it. Move around, exploring different perspectives.

After you've spent 20 or more minutes observing, spend at least 15 minutes writing down questions that your observations have raised for you. How does the space signal that it's public? Is it welcoming and beautiful, or ramshackle and dirty? Is it used by a wide variety of people or by a more homogeneous group? How does the space itself shape the experiences of the people who use it? How does it encourage or enhance some activities and limit others? These questions are just to get you started; they should trigger other questions that are directly related to your observations.

Write a reflective essay that develops out of your observations and a few of your most compelling questions about the place you observed.

REFLECTING (ON PRIVATE SPACE)

Next, we'd like you to do a similar exercise with a more private place, one that's inside, known or used by few people, and rich in visual detail. (Avoid choosing your own room or any other place that's overly familiar; it's hard to see such places in new ways.) Spend at least 20 minutes observing and taking notes and photographs. Then spend another 15 minutes pondering your experience in the space and writing down questions that your observations have raised. Start with the basics: How does the place signal that it's private? What activities does the space encourage, and what activities does it discourage? Is it possible to have a perspective on this place that is uniquely your own?

Write a reflective essay that develops out of your observations and a few of the most interesting questions you asked about the place you observed. Your goal is to compose a piece that gives your readers a new way to see and understand this private space.

REFLECTING (ON NATURAL SPACE)

Repeat this exercise in a natural, uninhabited, and unlandscaped space. Once again, observe and take notes for at least 20 minutes. Then spend 15 minutes or more developing questions that are grounded in your particular perspective. Coming up with questions about a natural space may be hard at first, but that too is worth pondering. After you've gathered your notes and questions, write another reflective essay that develops out of one or more of your most interesting questions and shows your reader how to see and think about this place in a new way.

PRACTICE SESSION TWO

READING

In "On Seeing as a Writer," we examine how one of our students started to see as a writer. And we find our evidence in the words she chose to explain her experience in the train station. Select a passage from a reading you've already written about. What does this passage you've selected reveal about the writer's way of seeing?

Spend at least 30 minutes writing a profile of the writer's way of seeing based on what you can draw from the passage you've read. How is the way of seeing you've identified distinctive?

EXPLORE

In our essay, we ask you to consider the writer's way of seeing the world as something that is learned through practice. Mason Currey's blog, a compendium of the daily routines of writers and other creative people, makes it clear that seeing as a writer isn't a talent one is either born with or not, but a skill that arises from disciplined practice. Patrick Cavanagh asks: are artists and scientists wired to see the world differently? V. S. Ramachandran, looking at three cases of brain damaged patients, concludes that the ability to make abstractions, which all healthy brains have, arises because the essence of mental activity is the ceaseless making of connections via metaphor. And, finally, Joan Didion's famous riposte to George Orwell provides an electrifying account of how her acts of attention led her to turn to writing.

Cavanagh, Patrick. "The Artist as Neuroscientist." *Nature* 434 (March 17, 2005). 301–7. Print.

Currey, Mason. *Daily Routines: How Writers, Artists, and Other Interesting People Organize Their Days.* Blog.

Didion, Joan. "Why I Write." *New York Times Book Review.* 5 December 1976. Web.

Ramachandran, V. S. "Three Clues to Understanding Your Brain." TED. March 2007. Web.

On Reading as a Writer

In our writing classes, we have a couple of mantras about reading that we repeat throughout the semester:

> In order to learn how to write, you have to learn how to read *as a writer*.

> There's only one way to learn how to read well, and that's by rereading.

These mantras are connected. To read as a writer means to pay close attention to the choices other writers make. This kind of reading requires attending to lots of things at once—what the writer says, how she organizes her ideas, what types of sources she works with, and how she addresses her readers. Such multifocal reading can only be accomplished by rereading. The first time through a challenging work, you might only be able to focus on what it says; after you know how the writer gets from point A to point Z, then you can attend more carefully to the choices the writer has made along the way. As your understanding of the entire piece comes together, you can assess what works, what doesn't, and why.

If you were in a history class and were assigned Susan Sontag's essay "Looking at War," your teacher would expect you to read the essay as a student, which would entail being able to identify Sontag's thesis and to evaluate the evidence she provides to support her thesis. But if you were in one of our classes, where the focus is on becoming a writer, we would ask you to read differently: we would ask you to attend not only to Sontag's thesis and to the evidence Sontag provides in its support but also to how she presents and develops her ideas. So instead of expecting you to mark Sontag's main points with a highlighter, we would encourage you to slow down so that you can make connections, puzzle over references, and think about how the details contribute to the overarching effect of the piece.

Sontag begins her essay by telling her readers about Virginia Woolf's *Three Guineas*, a book-length essay that Woolf wrote while the Spanish Civil War was in progress. Sontag explains that Woolf framed her essay as a long-delayed response to a letter from a London lawyer who had asked her, "How in your opinion are we to prevent war?" While Woolf has sympathy for his cause, she calls into question the idea that she and the lawyer belong to the same collective "we." Even though they are both members of the same privileged social class, as a woman Woolf was denied the kind of education and professional experience that the lawyer, a man, took for granted. Woolf suggests that the two of them will only be able to find common ground by looking at photographs of war's atrocities, which are, in her view, "simply statements of fact addressed to the eye."

However different the education, the traditions behind us, our sensations are the same; and they are violent. You, Sir, call them "horror and disgust." We also call them horror and disgust. And the same words rise to our lips. War, you say, is an abomination; a barbarity; war must be stopped at whatever cost. And we echo your words.

For Sontag, the key words in this passage from Woolf's essay are, surprisingly, "us," "our," and "we." These tiny words might seem hardly worthy of comment, but Sontag wants her readers to see what work they do in the passage she's cited. Reading as a writer, Sontag notices that, when Woolf imagines herself looking with the lawyer at photographs of the war, she uses the pronoun "our" to show that the photographs evoke the same emotional responses in both of them. They agree that the images reveal war to be an abomination and a barbarity. But this alliance between them is temporary. In the final sentences quoted above, Woolf has shifted the meaning of "we" and "our." They no longer refer to Woolf and the lawyer, but to Woolf and other women. "We" *women* "echo your words." Woolf has become the voice for what she believes is a universal female opposition to war, an opposition triggered by a shared revulsion to the realities of war as depicted in photographs.

After writing several paragraphs explicating *Three Guineas*, Sontag suddenly rejects Woolf's argument. "Who believes today," Sontag asks, "that war can be abolished? No one, not even pacifists." Why does Sontag start her own essay in this curious way? If Woolf's position is wrong, why tell her readers about it at all?

Starting her essay with Woolf allows Sontag to get three common assumptions about war and photography on the table for consideration: (1) that women are unified in opposition to war; (2) that photographs are "statements of fact"; and (3) that seeing photographs of war's brutal effects will bring about an end to war. Seventy-five years after Woolf published *Three Guineas*, Sontag sees no evidence to support the contention that women naturally oppose war, and she sees no reason to stipulate that photographs present self-evident truths. To the contrary, Sontag sets out to argue that documentary photographs of war have never given rise to a political consensus against war and will never do so. Reading Woolf's essay led Sontag to formulate her own question: If it's not the function of war photography to bring about the end of war, what *is* its function?

Our discussion of Sontag's use of Woolf's essay models the importance of both reading as a writer and rereading. These practices attune us to the choices writers make as they shape their ideas and their readers' experience.

· · · · ·

We have a third mantra we repeat to our students:

Read in slow motion.

When we teach writing, we know it's more valuable for students who are learning to read as writers to read and reread a brief selection with great care than it is for them to race through a much longer text in search of some highlighter-worthy main point. Reading in slow motion means looking up unfamiliar terms, names, historical events, and images. We encourage our students to track down some of the author's sources and to read those sources as writers, which means having them explore the connections the author has made to or between those sources. We do this because we want our students to see that whatever they're reading is connected to a much larger network of meaning.

If you read Sontag's "Looking at War" in slow motion, for example, and track down the text of *Three Guineas*, you'll discover something surprising: far from being a treatise on war photography, Woolf's 144-page book includes just two paragraphs on the subject. This fact makes Sontag's decision to begin her essay with a discussion of Woolf's work curious in a different way. Is her presentation of Woolf's position a distortion? Is Sontag setting Woolf up to make her own argument look more compelling than it actually is?

After slow reading, we've decided that Sontag learned more from Woolf than she lets on. The difference between Woolf's style and Sontag's is striking: Woolf makes her arguments through stories, while Sontag makes hers with ideas, drawing on the work of preeminent thinkers in history, art, and political theory. And yet, despite her predilection for ideas over stories, Sontag arrives, late in her argument, at the idea that photographs can only "haunt us," while "narratives can make us understand." The passage that Sontag cites from *Three Guineas* at the opening of her own essay is, we realize in retrospect, a narrative. Although Sontag rejects Woolf's idea that war photography can create solidarity for peace, she recognizes that Woolf's mode of writing may well be better suited to generating insights than a discussion of abstract ideas would be.

Seeing how Sontag has used Woolf in the opening of "Looking at War" helps us to see the significance of Sontag's decision to conclude her essay by narrating a story told by a photograph. Jeff Wall's 13-by-7.5-foot photograph *Dead Troops Talk (A vision after an ambush of a Red Army patrol, near Moqor, Afghanistan, winter 1986)* shows thirteen Russian soldiers clustered on a desolate, rocky landscape. It may look at first like a documentary photograph, but it's actually a fictional scene of postbattle carnage. The men in the photograph are actors on a studio set, playing the parts of soldiers. These soldiers, it seems, have died from gruesome injuries, but most of them appear alive to each other and are talking and laughing. Sontag describes them as indifferent to the world of the living: "one could fantasize that the soldiers might turn and talk to us. But no, no one is looking out of the picture at the viewer....

These dead are supremely uninterested in the living.... Why should they seek our gaze? What would they have to say to us?"

The collective "us" at the end of Sontag's essay is not Woolf's female collective "we." Rather, at the end of "Looking at War," Sontag arrives at a new "we": "this 'we' is everyone who has never experienced anything like what [the soldiers] went through." This "we," Sontag argues, can never fully understand what this photograph depicts: "We don't get it. We truly can't imagine what it was like. We can't imagine how dreadful, how terrifying war is—and how normal it becomes. Can't understand, can't imagine." Only by reading in slow motion can we appreciate that Sontag makes her point about how little most of us know of war by translating Wall's photograph into a story. This story does not try to teach us what it's like to be in a war; instead, it teaches us that without actual experience of war, we can never know how it feels or understand its horrors.

Reading as writers, we can appreciate the arc of Sontag's essay and the elegance of her argument without being compelled to reach the same conclusions. And in fact, this is exactly how Sontag responded to Woolf's *Three Guineas*: she admired the way Woolf shifted the meaning of "we" in a single paragraph and Woolf's ability to seamlessly embed a story in her larger argument, but Sontag didn't feel bound by this admiration to agree with Woolf. Rather, she did what writers do who wish to engage fully with the ideas of another: she wrote an essay of her own.

PRACTICE SESSION ONE

READING

You can use any serious text to practice reading and rereading as a writer. For now, we recommend that you read Sontag's "Looking at War," found on the *New Yorker* Web site. Start by reading the essay from beginning to end and marking key moments in Sontag's argument. Next, read the essay again, paying attention *as a writer* to how Sontag phrases and organizes her ideas, what types of sources she uses, how and where she presents major points, and how she addresses her readers. Take notes in the margins.

What's striking about how Sontag chose to approach her topic? What parts drew you in? Are there parts of the essay that confuse you, or parts where you don't know enough about photographs or history to follow her argument? Were there any points or turns of phrase that impressed you, or sections you found yourself rereading with appreciation?

Having read Sontag's essay as a writer, identify one of the significant choices Sontag made when she composed her essay, and then spend at least 30 minutes writing about that choice. As you write, quote specific passages from Sontag's work to help your reader see what you find meaningful about how Sontag writes as well as what she writes.

RESEARCHING

Next you'll return to Sontag's work to practice a specific kind of rereading— reading in slow motion.

Sontag wrote about photographs throughout her career. Despite her enduring fascination with images, she did not include photographs in books such as *On Photography* or *Regarding the Pain of Others.* "Looking at War" is an exception to Sontag's usual practice: when the essay was originally published in the *New Yorker*, it included photographs; now that it is on the *New Yorker* Web site, the images are no longer part of the essay.

The experience of reading "Looking at War" without reproductions of the photographs obviously differs from the experience of reading the text with the images. It's important to consider why Sontag typically chose *not* to reproduce photographs in her essays about photography. But it's also important to know that you are not bound by her decisions—or by the decisions of any writer. Indeed, when reading as a writer, you are always considering both what the writer says and what the writer *doesn't* say, what the writer directs you to look at and what the writer *doesn't* draw your attention to.

Working with "Looking at War," use the Web to track down the photographs Sontag references. Seek out the highest-resolution images you can find. Look at them with care. Learn about their context by reading what others have written about them. Then return to Sontag's essay and consider what additional sources might deepen your understanding of her argument. Search more; read more. Keep track of which sources you turn to and why.

WRITING

Now that you've reread "Looking at War" in slow motion, write an essay about how slow reading altered your understanding of Sontag's work. It's likely that your research enhanced your reading of Sontag's work significantly. It's also likely that new questions or confusions arose. Again, as you write, quote specific passages from Sontag's work and your sources to show what you find meaningful about what is said and how it is said.

PRACTICE SESSION TWO

WRITING

What happens if we shift the focus from photographs to paintings? The Colombian artist Fernando Botero has created over fifty paintings that are inspired by the globally circulated images of human rights abuses committed by members of the United States Army at Abu Ghraib, in 2003. Search the Web for the highest-resolution versions of Botero's paintings you can find. Conduct your research *as a writer*, taking notes that will allow you to write an essay that is in conversation with Sontag's "Looking at War." Write an essay about the value of painting images of war in the age of digital photography.

EXPLORE

"Annotation Tuesday!" is a regular feature on *Nieman Storyboard* in which writers are interviewed about how they composed a particular essay or article. As the interviewers move through the pieces paragraph by paragraph, the writers explain their choices, often in surprising ways. We invite you to browse the archives of "Annotation Tuesday!" on the *Nieman Storyboard* Web site. We recommend, in particular or search for the interviews with writers Buzz Bissinger, Leslie Jamison, and Rachel Kaadzi Ghansa listed below.

"Annotation Tuesday! Buzz Bissinger and 'The Killing Trail.'" Interview by Elon Green. *Nieman Storyboard.* 28 Jan. 2014. Web.

"Annotation Tuesday! Leslie Jamison and the Imprisoned Ultradistance Runner." Interview by Elon Green. *Nieman Storyboard.* 2 July 2013. Web.

"Annotation Tuesday! Rachel Kaadzi Ghansa and 'If He Hollers Let Him Go.'" Interview by Elon Green. *Nieman Storyboard.* 7 Oct. 2014. Web.

On Self-Curation

The word *curate* has an interesting etymological history. According to the *Oxford English Dictionary*, *curate* entered the English language in the mid-fourteenth century as a noun signifying someone "entrusted with the cure of souls: a spiritual pastor." This nominal form of the word is linked to earlier adjectival forms in medieval Latin (*c-ur-atus*) and Italian (*curato*) and to the French noun *curé*, all of which denoted "having a cure or charge."

Some six hundred years later, *curate* made its first appearance as a verb in an English dictionary. And notice what happens to the meaning of the word when it moves from being used as a noun or an adjective to being used as a transitive verb: "to act as curator of (a museum, exhibits, etc.); to look after and preserve." So, for a very long time, a curate was a religious occupation; in the twentieth century, it became a secular activity.

Self-curation does not yet appear in the *Oxford English Dictionary* or *Merriam-Webster* or the *Cambridge Dictionary*. Nevertheless, if you search the Web for the term (with the hyphen), you'll find that this as-yet-unofficial word is currently in circulation and that it is used most frequently to refer to the conscious management of one's online life. Fancifully, we might define *self-curation* thus: "to act as curator of one's own online life; to look after and preserve an archive of one's digital existence."

We first came across the term while reading Dana Spiotta's wonderful novel *Stone Arabia*. The principle that guides the life of Nik Worth, brother of the novel's narrator, is "Self-curate or disappear." The mystery at the heart of the novel is twofold: first, what Nik has actually done is self-curate *and* disappear; and second, the self Nik has curated is an entirely fictional one. Not wanting to be remembered as an unsuccessful crank living on the margins of society, Nik spent two decades fabricating the documents, the personal journals, and the history of a forward-looking, deeply thoughtful musician. And then he left without a word. All his sister Denise can do while she waits for word from him is to make her way through the fictional journals in hopes of piecing together some understanding of what Nik had done with his life.

Nik's relationship to self-curation is pathological: he fabricates reviews of performances that never happened; he creates but never releases CDs by his fictional persona and then records the public reception of music that only he has ever heard. But Spiotta shows over the course of her novel that self-curation, understood more generally as the conscious act of placing oneself in a larger narrative, is an activity we all participate in, to a greater or lesser degree. Ada, Denise's estranged daughter, self-curates via her blog, where she foregrounds her work in documentary film. And Denise herself tries to fit the artifacts Nik has left behind into a narrative of her own life that she can understand.

In the Age of Paper, self-curation was a largely private affair. One kept a journal, perhaps, or collected shells or stamps or firearms or first editions or autographs or whatever. Now that we live in the Age of the Screen, self-curation is a largely public affair: there is the self or the selves that an individual maintains via social media; the blogging self; the photo- or video-posting self; the reviewing self. These are selves over which a person has some measure of control. And then there is the self as represented by others—via social media, via the news, via public documents.

What do you know about yourself as currently represented on the Web? Is that the version of yourself you would voluntarily give others access to? There's a practical reason for making that distinction: once something associated with your name, your face, or your work appears on the Web, it is potentially on the Web forever. Were you identified doing a keg stand on a friend's Facebook page? Did you post a comment on a local news site railing against something you now support? Have you had a run-in with the law? Any one of these events could function as a "digital tattoo" for you, ensuring that there's a public record of some past embarrassment available to anyone who is interested in digging it up. Self-curation is a practical way to counter the negative effects of the digital tattoo.

While there are good practical reasons to self-curate, we're more interested in the creative benefits that come with self-curation. If you take control of your online presence, you have the opportunity to represent yourself as a multifaceted individual with a range of interests. By self-curating as a writer, you make it that much easier for potential readers to find your work. And by making your work public, you create the opportunity to have the kind of readers all writers want—those who read voluntarily.

PRACTICE SESSION ONE

RESEARCHING

What happens when you do a Google search on your name? Do you get different results if you use Dogpile? Twitter? Facebook? Pinterest? Photobucket? Your high school's home page? Do a thorough search and document all the information about you that is publicly available on the Web. Your final dossier should include images where appropriate. Spend at least 20 minutes writing about the results of your research: What does the uncurated version of yourself, as represented on the Web, look like?

REFLECTING

What would you like people who search for you to find? What would best represent you as a thinker? A writer? A creative person? An artist? If you were to design a self-curated site, what would it include?

Spend at least 45 minutes sketching out what such a site would look like by hand or using the graphing feature on your word processing platform. Another option is to actually create a self-curated site. Regardless of which option you choose to do, you'll need to decide what tabs you would like to appear in your home page's navigation bar. Are you a writer who works in more than one genre? Have you made videos? Taken striking photographs? Started a graphic novel? Are you involved in other projects or activities that you could represent on your site? We are particularly interested in you designing a site that represents you as someone whose creativity expresses itself in production rather than consumption, so we ask that you restrict your listing of favorite books, musicians, and artists to the "About" tab on your site.

PRACTICE SESSION TWO

RESEARCHING

What happens when you do a Google search on a contemporary visual artist or writer you admire? Do you get different results if you use Dogpile? Twitter? Facebook? Pinterest? Photobucket? Spend at least 30 minutes doing a thorough search and document all the information about the artist or writer you've chosen that is publicly available on the Web. (Don't choose a celebrity, a sports star, or a politician; these figures always bring gossip, scandals, and excitable fans in their wake.) Then spend an additional 20 minutes writing about the results of your search. What does the uncurated version of the writer's or artist's self look like?

RESEARCHING

Seek out the official site or sites for the contemporary visual artist or writer you elected to research. Then take at least 45 minutes to write an essay on the difference between the official, curated self and the version of that self that emerged during your open-ended search. Drawing on your research, discuss what the artist or writer you've chosen to study might do on his or her self-curated site to engage with whatever additional unauthorized material you've discovered circulating outside the site.

PRACTICE SESSION THREE

RESEARCHING

It is now common journalistic practice to head straight to the Web in the immediate aftermath of a tragedy to see what social media can tell us about the possible victims or the possible perpetrators in the unfolding event. This practice has tended to have catastrophic results, as the pressure to be first on the scene with news has created a fertile ground for jumping to unfounded conclusions. This happened, for instance, after the tragedy in Sandy Hook and after the Boston Marathon bombing. In both cases, an innocent person was linked to the atrocity and was then quickly "convicted" online on the basis of material that was later revealed to be erroneous.

Choose a recent event that has been in the headlines and spend at least 45 minutes investigating what role social media has played in both the coverage and the interpretation of the event. Why do some responses to the event get picked up, shared, and repeated, while others are ignored? Take extensive notes, tracking key moments in the coverage of the chosen event. When you're done with your research, create a timeline that represents what you've learned about the role social media played in shaping popular understandings of the event.

WRITING

If you were to curate a site dedicated to the event you selected, what would you include? Write an essay on self-curation, the digital tattoo, and social media as they relate to the event you've chosen to research. Your piece should include your design for a site that would provide a richer understanding both of the event and of its coverage.

EXPLORE

Our suggested readings all focus on understanding how social media has changed human behavior. Ann Friedman provides a trenchant analysis of LinkedIn, the self-proclaimed largest professional network on the Web. Ariel Levy examines the role that Twitter played in the handling of the Steubenville rape trial. And Clay Shirky looks at the ways that social media is changing how citizens and their elected officials engage with each other.

Friedman, Ann. "All LinkedIn with Nowhere to Go." *The Baffler* 23 (2013). Web.

Levy, Ariel. "Trial by Twitter." *New Yorker*. 5 Aug. 2013. Web.

Shirky, Clay. "How Social Media Can Make History." TED. June 2009. Web.

Creativity at Work: Twyla Tharp and the Paradox of Habitual Creativity

The film *Amadeus* annoys dancer Twyla Tharp because it portrays Wolfgang Amadeus Mozart as a born genius. "Of course, this is hogwash," Tharp writes in her book, *The Creative Habit*. Then in large red letters she asserts, **"There are no 'natural' geniuses."**

Tharp has done her research. She knows that Mozart's father, Leopold, who was himself a composer and a musician, recognized his son's musical interest and nurtured the boy's ability by teaching him to play at a very young age. She also knows that Mozart had a strong work ethic, even as a child. And she knows that he complained in a letter to a friend that people mistakenly thought he composed without struggle; the truth was that making beautiful music took time and effort.

Tharp uses Mozart's story to begin her book about creative habits because she wants to be clear about her project: "More than anything, this book is about preparation: **In order to be creative you have to know how to prepare to be creative.**"

She understands the allure of thinking that creativity is the birthright of a lucky few, but her experience as a dancer and choreographer, as well as with the creative people who have surrounded her all her life, has shown her that creativity can be learned and that it can be taught. "There's a paradox," she writes,

> in the notion that creativity should be a habit. We think of creativity as a way of keeping everything fresh and new, while habit implies routine and repetition. That paradox intrigues me because it occupies the place where creativity and skill rub up against each other.

> It takes skill to bring something you've imagined into the world…. No one is born with that skill. It is developed through exercise, through repetition, through a blend of learning and reflection that's both painstaking and rewarding. And it takes time.

Tharp reminds her readers that Mozart, who certainly had a gift and a passion for music, composed *twenty-four* symphonies before he wrote a work that would endure: Symphony no. 25 in G Minor, which serves as the opening score for *Amadeus.*

What can we learn from the examples of Mozart and Tharp? Tharp distills her ideas in this simple statement: "Creativity is a habit; and the best creativity is a result of good work habits." So practice every day. Make a ritual of your practice. "The routine," Tharp writes, "is as much a part of the creative process as the lightning bolt of inspiration, maybe more."

CHAPTER

7

Planning and Replanning

When you undertake a writing project, one of the early steps in the process is to make an outline. The value of doing so seems self-evident: an outline, with its schematic representation of the argument you hope to make, shows you where you plan to go and keeps you on track so you don't get lost in a thicket of irrelevant details. But, the risk in the outline-driven approach is that anything that threatens to pull the project away from its predetermined destination can be dismissed as irrelevant: potential connections won't get explored, new information won't be pursued, and unsettling insights will be ignored.

In this chapter, we recommend curiosity-driven approach to planning that assumes replanning is an inevitable and essential part of the writing process. This doesn't necessarily mean abandoning the outline, so much as it means assuming that the outline is likely to get revised as the writing project develops. It means thinking of structure as malleable rather than inevitable; it means anticipating the possibility that revision will yield unforeseen insights that require starting the planning process over again from scratch; it means acknowledging that the failure of the original outline may well be proof that learning has occurred. The creative mind always has a plan, but that plan always includes planning on replanning.

On Structure

John McPhee, the author of twenty-nine books and a staff writer for the *New Yorker* since 1965, is one of the most prolific and influential writers of contemporary nonfiction—which he prefers to call "factual writing." He's written books about subjects as diverse as the geography of the western United States (*Annals of the Former World*); efforts to contain natural destruction caused by lava, water, and mountainside debris flow (*The Control of Nature*); people who work in freight transportation (*Uncommon Carriers*); and even a rogue American professor whose covert actions played a central role in preserving dissident Soviet art (*The Ransom of Russian Art*). While we admire McPhee's work, we draw your attention to him here because McPhee may well be the

---

Chapter 7, "Planning and Replanning," is taken from Richard E. Miller and Ann Jurecic, *Habits of the Creative Mind*, pp. 199–226 (Part 10, "Planning and Replanning").

best writing teacher on the planet. His former students, who collectively have published over 430 books, include David Remnick, a Pulitzer Prize winner and editor-in-chief of the *New Yorker*; Richard Stengel and Jim Kelly, each of whom has served as managing editor of *Time*; Eric Schlosser, author of *Fast Food Nation*; and Richard Preston, author of *The Hot Zone*.

Why are McPhee's students so successful?

One reason is how McPhee trains them to think about structure. In a *New Yorker* essay simply titled "Structure," McPhee offers lessons about writing and its organization that were previously reserved for the small number of Princeton University students lucky enough to get a seat in one of his seminars. He begins the essay by describing the crisis of confidence he faced early in his career when he settled in to write a long article about the Pine Barrens of New Jersey, which he'd been researching for eight months. "I had assembled enough material to fill a silo," he recalls, "and now I had no idea what to do with it." He spent two weeks lying on his back on a picnic table, stymied by panic, unable to see a way to organize his thoughts. Finally, he realized that an elderly native of the Pine Barrens, Fred Brown, had connections to most of the topics he wanted to discuss, so McPhee decided he could begin the essay by describing his first encounter with Brown and then connect each theme to various forays he and Brown made together. Having solved his structure problem, McPhee got off the picnic table and began to write. "Structure," he says, "has preoccupied me in every project I have undertaken since."

For four decades, McPhee has taught his students that structure should be "strong, sound, and artful" and that it is possible to "build a structure in such a way that it causes people to want to keep turning pages." Nonfiction, in other words, can be as absorbing as a good novel if the structure is right. To teach his students how to find the right structure, McPhee compares preparing to write to preparing to cook.

> The approach to structure in factual writing is like returning from a grocery store with materials you intend to cook for dinner. You set them out on the kitchen counter, and what's there is what you deal with, and all you deal with. If something is red and globular, you don't call it a tomato if it's a bell pepper.

In other words, to plan the structure of a piece of writing, you have to gather all the pieces of your research and lay them out so you can see them at a glance. And as you figure out the structure, you can only work with the facts in front of you.

Before he had a computer, McPhee would type all of his notes, study them, separate them into piles so that his facts were literally in front of him. Then, he would distill them into a set of several dozen index cards. On each card he would write two or three code words that indicated to him a component of the story he wanted to tell. The codes might refer to a location (UNY for upstate New York) or to an event or anecdote ("Upset Rapid"). His office furniture at the time included "a standard sheet of plywood—thirty-two square feet—on two sawhorses." He would scatter his index cards face up on the plywood, anchoring a few pieces and moving the others around until he figured out how to organize the work in ways that were both strong and artful.

Rebecca Skloot, author of *The Immortal Life of Henrietta Lacks*, regularly uses McPhee's essay "Travels in Georgia" to teach structure to her writing students. She shows her students that, if you map the narrative of "Travels in Georgia," you can see that it spirals in time: McPhee begins in the middle of the story, goes forward briefly, and then loops backward in time. By the middle of the essay, McPhee has brought his account back to where it started, and from that point on, he moves the narrative steadily forward in time. Skloot explains that McPhee calls this "the lowercase *e* structure," and she promises that once you recognize it, you'll see it everywhere—in movies, novels, and *New Yorker* articles. (Skloot's exercise teaches her students to read as writers, a topic discussed in our essay "On Reading as a Writer.")

Like McPhee, Skloot has a story about grappling for a long time with a writing task. In her case, though, she had to figure out how to organize ten years of research that she had collected for her book. She struggled because she was writing about multiple time periods and had three different narratives: the story of Henrietta Lacks, an African American woman who developed cervical cancer and died at the age of thirty-one in 1951; the story of Lacks's cancer cells, which were cultured without Lacks's consent and continue to be used to this day in medical research; and the story of Lacks's family, especially her daughter, Deborah, who for much of her life did not know that her mother's cells were alive in medical labs all over the world.

Skloot's breakthrough in organizing her research into a readable book came when she was watching *Hurricane*, a movie about the boxer Hurricane Carter, who was falsely convicted of a triple homicide in 1966. Skloot saw that the film braided three different narratives together: the story of Carter's conviction; the story of Carter's twenty years in prison; and the story of how a Brooklyn teen and three Canadian activists successfully lobbied to have Carter's case reopened. She wrote notes about the film's scenes on colored-coded index cards—one color for each of the three storylines—and laid them out on her bed according to where the scenes occurred in the film. Then she placed the color-coded index cards for the three strands of her own book on top of the cards for *Hurricane*. She saw that the film jumped more quickly between the three strands of narrative than her book manuscript did, and that the rapidity of those jumps helped sustain the momentum of each line of the intertwined narrative. When Skloot finally realized how to weave together the pieces of her own narrative, she photographed the rows of colored index cards for posterity. (See this photograph on p. 114.)

Rebecca Skloot

FIGURE 7.1 Rebecca Skloot's note cards for *The Immortal Life of Henrietta Lacks*, arranged on her bed.

For Skloot to structure her ten years of research as a braided narrative, she had to throw a lot of material away, just as McPhee did when he was sorting the siloful of material he'd collected for his article on the Pine Barrens. Neither Skloot nor McPhee thought that time spent collecting unused research was wasted, however. McPhee's former student Eric Schlosser recalled how McPhee taught him that deciding what *not* to include is a crucial and often unrecognized step in defining structure. McPhee told him, "Your writing should be like an iceberg." What ends up on the printed page is just the tip of the iceberg, while beneath the surface is all the research, reading, and writing that was done to generate the final product. The reader may not be able to see that work, but it's there—the hidden substructure of the writer's visible work.

In school, the operating assumption is often that there is one structure with which students should work: introduction, body, conclusion. Note that this approach *begins* by prescribing an organizing structure, no matter what the subject or project is, whereas the examples from McPhee and Skloot show the structure emerging after the research process is finished or well underway. In line with these examples, we think that the best time for you to make decisions about structure is *after* you've formulated the question you want to answer, the problem or puzzle you want to solve, or the idea you want to explore, and *after* you've taken time to do substantial research. Once you've gathered your materials, then you can experiment. You can move the ideas around on paper or on digital index cards, testing out possibilities. You can consider whether there's an organic order to your project. You can think about how different parts of your essay seem connected and about how you can best make those connections meaningful to your readers. Then, when you've mapped a possible structure, step back and think carefully about what you see.

Imagine that your index cards define a path readers will follow as you guide them through the development of your thoughts, and consider these questions:

- What shape is the path? Is it straight and simple because you're writing a descriptive essay ("there's this and that and the other thing")? Given the assignment or your ambitions, is this structure sufficient?

- Does the path of your project take interesting turns? Is there a step that takes your thoughts in a new direction? Are there turns that might pivot on a qualifying word or phrase such as *but, however*, or *on the other hand*?

- Does the path turn more than once? Does it double back on itself? Does it have a "lowercase *e* structure"? Does it braid three or more strands together?

- Is there a fork in the path? Is there a moment where you entertain multiple options?

- Are there gaps? Does the path abruptly change direction or miss a step between a given section and the one that follows?

- Are there pieces or ideas that don't fit anywhere? Does it make sense to include the material as a digression that eventually leads back to the main path? Would a digression contribute to the essay's overall project?

- Is there a dead end, a place where the path hits a brick wall or goes off a cliff? If so, can you use this dead end to rethink how you've addressed your essay's question or problem?

After remapping the path of your project, step back even further and consider whether the structure you've now laid out is "strong, sound, and artful." We also recommend asking the following questions:

- Where do you see evidence of your curiosity? Your creativity? Your skill at making connections between sources and ideas? Your depth of knowledge? Your mastery of detail?

- If these aren't evident, how could you rework your project? Should you do more research? Formulate a different question or problem?

- Are there places where you ignored information that would have complicated the structure or the path? Are there places where you chose the easier route?

PRACTICE SESSION ONE

RESEARCHING

We recently discovered the *Nieman Storyboard* Web site, which we recommend for a number of reasons. It not only gathers notable examples of narrative journalism but also includes a series of "Essays on Craft" in which experienced journalists explain how they have moved a story from initial idea to final publication. In addition, there's a series called "Why's This So Good?" in which writers discuss what they value in the work of a fellow writer. You can't go wrong on *Nieman Storyboard*. Explore the site for at least 20 minutes. Then select at least three essays that intrigue you and read them.

PRACTICE SESSION TWO

READING

If you search on *Nieman Storyboard*, you'll find Adam Hochschild's piece on John McPhee's craft, " 'Why's This So Good?' No. 61: John McPhee and the Archdruid." What McPhee calls "structure," Hochschild calls "engineering." Hochschild explains: "A key secret of McPhee's ability to make us care about his vast and improbable range of subject matter lies in his engineering. From the pilings beneath the foundations to the beams that support the rooftop observation deck, he is the master builder of literary skyscrapers."

As you read the essay about McPhee, pay attention to Hochschild's descriptions of the structure of his favorite works. For example, Hochschild describes *Encounters with the Archdruid* as having been built using a structure that McPhee described as:

$$\frac{ABC}{D}$$

After you've read Hochschild's essay once through, spend at least 30 minutes reviewing his descriptions of four of McPhee's other works: a profile of Thomas Hoving; the book *Levels of the Game*; and the articles "In Search of Marvin Gardens" and "A Forager." Make simple sketches to represent the structure of each of these four works.

PRACTICE SESSION THREE

READING

Select an article from the "Notable Narratives" section of *Nieman Storyboard*. Then spend at least 30 minutes making a detailed map of the essay's structure using any medium you like—a computer graphics program, pen and pencil, crayon and cardboard, or index cards on a bedspread. The map you make should highlight what surprised or impressed you about the writer's structural choices.

PRACTICE SESSION FOUR

WRITING

Go through your personal archive of papers you've written and select at least three of them. Then make a map or sketch of the structure of each one. Once you're done, step back and think about the relationship between the maps or sketches you generated for this exercise and the ones you generated for Practice Sessions Two and Three above. Your own essays will probably be shorter than Hochschild's essay or the other essays on *Nieman Storyboard*, but what other differences are there between the structure of your writing and the structure of essays by professional writers? Write an essay that uses the maps of your own writing and those you made for the previous exercises as material for speculating about the relationship between structure and thought.

EXPLORE

David Dobbs describes the structure of Michael Lewis's essay about the Greek financial crisis as "an agile manipulation of a standard trip-to-Oz story form." It can be hard to step back and see the structure of a piece of writing as a whole, but Dobbs's comparison seems obvious after the fact. To help you develop a sense for structure, we invite you to read Lewis's essay alongside Dobbs's analysis, or to read McPhee's "Structure" as well as his interview in the *Paris Review*. While Dobbs and McPhee are concerned with the big picture, the manuscript pages on Joyce Carol Oates's blog provide a more detailed picture of how a fiction writer invents and refines the shape of a novel by making sketches of towns, charts of characters, and lists of scenes and their arrangement.

Dobbs, David. " 'Why's This So Good?' No. 15: Michael Lewis' Greek Odyssey." *Nieman Storyboard*. 11 Oct. 2011. Web.

Lewis, Michael. "Beware of Greeks Bearing Bonds." *Vanity Fair*. Oct. 2010. Web.

McPhee, John. "John McPhee, The Art of Nonfiction No. 3." Interview by Peter Hessler. *Paris Review*. 192 Spring 2010. Web.

McPhee, John. "Structure." *New Yorker*. 14 Jan. 2014. Web.

Oates, Joyce Carol. "Manuscripts," "Research and Bibliography." *Celestial Timepiece: The Joyce Carol Oates Home Page*. Web.

On Revising

Every writing lesson in Part 1 of this book is implicitly connected to revision. We've repeatedly encouraged you to look and look again. (Another name for the act of reseeing is "revision.") We showed you how being curious requires that you peer around corners, disappear down rabbit holes, and explore the unknown in order to replace old assumptions or confusions with new knowledge and understanding. We showed you that creative habits of mind include being able to reflect on (that is, to resee) how you express yourself and even how you think. In a multitude of ways, reseeing and revising are fundamental practices for writers.

So why include a separate essay on revision? Two reasons, really. First, people who take writing seriously know that writing *is* revising. Indeed, the claim that "there is no such thing as good writing, only good rewriting" is so widely acknowledged by writers that it has been attributed to Robert Graves, Louis Brandeis, Isaac Bashevis Singer, William Zinsser, and Roald Dahl. Second, we know that revision is not a single stage in the writing process but a range of practices that occur throughout the writing process. The distinction is worth driving home, we've found, because many students mistakenly believe that revising is simply correcting errors and tidying up unclear sentences that a teacher marked in an essay draft. In our view this is copyediting, not revision, and it misrepresents true revision.

As writers, we know that rethinking, reseeing, and rewriting can happen at any step in producing a work of writing. In fact, before we drafted the opening paragraphs of *this* essay, we composed two different preliminary outlines and two different introductions. When we determined that neither of those versions worked, we scrapped them and started over. This example isn't an anomaly; writers regularly spiral back to rethink what they've done, entirely abandoning earlier work and beginning all over again. Moments of revision can occur as soon as you've thought your first thought or written your first word; they can occur just when you think you're writing your final sentence; and they can occur anywhere between those two points.

If revision isn't correcting grammatical mistakes and isn't a single step in a linear process, then what is it? We'd like to help you resee revision by offering descriptions and examples of a variety of ways of returning to the writing you've already completed with the goal of improving it. You won't use all of these practices every time you rewrite, but you're quite likely to use more than one as you work over what you've written.

Rethinking

As essayists and academic writers, when we contemplate a new project, we spend a lot of time reading, exploring, researching, learning, and thinking before we begin a formal draft. And yet, after composing the first pages or even the entire first draft, we may still find our work unsatisfactory because, in the process of writing about our chosen topic, we have begun to question our original position. Rethinking motivates us to revise globally—to rework our ideas rather than tinker away at surface corrections.

What's the difference between rethinking and tinkering? It's difficult to point to a published example of the former because rethinking typically occurs before publication and thus remains hidden from readers. But writer and blogger Ta-Nehisi Coates makes a practice of rethinking his opinions in public, so we'll look at a moment when he felt obligated to acknowledge that new events had shifted his perspective.

Coates's essay "Fear of a Black President" contends with a paradox at the heart of President Obama's first term in office: "As a candidate, Barack Obama said we needed to reckon with race and with America's original sin, slavery. But as our first black president, he has avoided mention of race almost entirely." To illustrate how constraining this paradox is, Coates looks at a rare public statement on race by Obama in which the president puts that topic—and his own race—at the center of the nation's attention.

On March 23, 2012, Obama was asked to comment on the shooting death of an unarmed black teenager, Trayvon Martin, that had occurred a month earlier in Florida. George Zimmerman, a member of a neighborhood watch patrol, claimed to have shot Martin in self-defense when the young man responded violently to being detained. Obama briefly addressed the uproar that followed Martin's death, saying: "When I think about this boy, I think about my own kids, and I think every parent in America should be able to understand why it is absolutely imperative that we investigate every aspect of this, and that everybody pulls together—federal, state, and local—to figure out exactly how this tragedy happened." Obama closed with the following statement: "But my main message is to the parents of Trayvon Martin. If I had a son, he'd look like Trayvon. I think they are right to expect that all of us as Americans are going to take this with the seriousness it deserves, and that we're going to get to the bottom of exactly what happened." As mild, measured, and brief as Obama's comments were, a media frenzy ensued. Radio shock jocks and cable TV pundits accused the president of lighting the match that could start a race war. Far from finding Obama's response incendiary, Coates details in "Fear of a Black President" his own frustration with Obama for making such moderate comments and for avoiding an open discussion of race.

As strong as his criticism of Obama was in "Fear of a Black President," Coates displayed his commitment to rethinking in a blog post he wrote after Obama responded to the news that George Zimmerman had been acquitted of second-degree murder and manslaughter charges on July 19, 2013. In this instance, Coates says, Obama spoke *as* an African American and *for* African Americans to explain their suffering over the verdict. We think it's worth quoting Obama's statement in full.

> You know, when Trayvon Martin was first shot I said that this could have been my son. Another way of saying that is Trayvon Martin could have been me 35 years ago. And when you think about why, in the African American community at least, there's a lot of pain around what happened here, I think it's import-ant to recognize that the African American community is looking at this issue through a set of experiences and a history that doesn't go away.

> There are very few African American men in this country who haven't had the experience of being followed when they were shopping in a department store. That includes me. There are very few African American men who haven't had the experience of walking across the street and hearing the locks click on the doors of cars. That happens to me—at least before I was a senator. There are very few African Americans who haven't had the experience of getting on an elevator and a woman clutching her purse nervously and holding her breath until she had a chance to get off. That happens often.

And I don't want to exaggerate this, but those sets of experiences inform how the African American community interprets what happened one night in Florida. And it's inescapable for people to bring those experiences to bear. The African American community is also knowledgeable that there is a history of racial disparities in the application of our criminal laws—everything from the death penalty to enforcement of our drug laws. And that ends up having an impact in terms of how people interpret the case.

Coates's blog post, "Considering the President's Comments on Racial Profiling," praises Obama for having the courage to speak out personally about the experience of racism: "No president has ever done this before. It does not matter that the competition is limited. The impact of the highest official in the country directly feeling your pain, because it is his pain, is real. And it is happening now." Coates's willingness to change his mind and express his gratitude sets him apart from many other political-opinion journalists. He's committed to presenting himself as an avid learner, and he refuses the pundit's pretense of certainty.

When you're writing for school, it may seem that you don't have the opportunity that Coates has as a blogger to rethink and rewrite; once a paper is handed in, there's usually no going back. But the truth is that every time you sit down to write, you have the opportunity to seek out new information that will complicate or alter what you were thinking before you started writing. This is the lesson we'd like you to take from Coates's work: in order to begin the process of rethinking what you've written, you need to seek out new information and be open to questioning everything, even your own certainties.

Restructuring

Often first drafts make sense to the writer, but the logic behind what has been written isn't yet clear enough for a reader to follow. This can be caused by gaps in the research or argument; lack of attention to what readers need to know and when they need to know it; too much information or too many ideas about one topic and not enough about another; or the lack of good transitions. These problems can be addressed through revision that focuses on structure.

The history of F. Scott Fitzgerald's *The Great Gatsby* reveals what a difference structural revisions can make. Fitzgerald sent the manuscript of his novel to his editor, Maxwell Perkins, who immediately saw that it was brilliant but flawed. First of all, the character of Gatsby was too physically vague. "The reader's eyes can never quite focus upon him, his outlines are dim," he wrote to Fitzgerald. "Now everything about Gatsby is more or less a mystery …, and this may be somewhat of an artistic intention, but I think it is mistaken." Fitzgerald's reply indicates that defining Gatsby's character was something he hadn't been able to accomplish in the first draft: "*I myself didn't know what Gatsby looked like or was engaged in* & you felt it." Perkins's second complaint about Fitzgerald's presentation of Gatsby was that the character's whole history—his apprenticeship on Dan Cody's yacht, his time in the army, his romance with Daisy, and his past as an "Oxford man"—all tumbled out in one long monologue in the penultimate chapter.

What to do? Perkins suggested that Fitzgerald reorganize the *whole* novel: "you can't avoid the biography altogether. I thought you might find ways to let the truth of some of his claims like 'Oxford' and his army career come out bit by bit in the course of actual narrative." Fitzgerald followed this advice, weaving bits of Gatsby's past more gracefully into earlier chapters. The result? *The Great Gatsby*, first published in 1925, has now sold over twenty-five million copies and is widely considered an enduring example of the Great American Novel.

Notice that Perkins's advice about revising *Gatsby* focused on creating a better experience for the reader. Notice, too, that Fitzgerald couldn't see what *The Great Gatsby* needed until he got the feedback that made it possible for him to view the novel through the eyes of another. (We discuss how to provide and how to respond to such feedback on p. 125.)

The Post-Draft Outline

While outside feedback is essential to the revision process, there is a way to defamiliarize your own writing to the point that you can make its implicit structure explicit and, simultaneously, produce a map that can direct your revisions. The way to do this is to produce a "post-draft outline," so called because, instead of making it before you begin to write your draft, you make it after the draft is completed. The process for making a post-draft outline is straightforward: sequentially number every paragraph in your draft, and then write a one-sentence statement about the main idea or point in each paragraph. When you're done, you'll be able to see the structure of your draft as a whole, which you can then use in a variety of ways to help you assess the quality of the experience you've created for your reader.

1. Your outline gives you a snapshot of the path your draft has taken. To develop this snapshot, read the sentences of your post-draft outline in order, and then read the post-draft outline again, this time thinking through the following questions (which also appear in our essay "On Structure" on pp. 111–116):

    • Is the path a straight line? Does it proceed by a series of *and* connections (that is, there's this and this and this)?

    • Does the path turn? Is there a paragraph that qualifies what has gone before or takes the conversation in a new direction? Are there sentences or paragraphs that pivot—or could pivot—on a qualifying word or phrase such as *but, however,* or *although*?

- Does the path turn more than once? Does it double back on itself?

- Is there a fork in the path? Is there a moment where more than one option is entertained?

- Is there a paragraph that pivots on words or phrases such as *or, perhaps,* or *what if?* that introduce more than one possible outcome or position?

- Are there gaps? Does the path abruptly change direction or miss a step between a given paragraph and the one that follows?

- Are there digressions, places where there's a loop off the path that eventually returns to the main path? If the answer is yes, does each digression contribute to the essay's overall project? (Don't assume the answer to this last question is no. In restructuring, some digressions can become central to the newly organized draft.)

- Is there a dead end, a place where the path hits a brick wall or goes off a cliff, never to return? (Again, don't assume that this is necessarily a bad thing; in restructuring, there are times when dead ends can be repurposed to improve your handling of your essay's question or problem.)

After you have a sense of the path you took in your draft you can begin to sketch plans for structural revision.

2.   Before you begin to rewrite, return to the draft and reassess it as a snapshot of your mind at work on a problem.

- Where is your curiosity in evidence? Your creativity? Your skill at putting original sources into conversation? Your interest in language? Your mastery of detail? How can these be made more evident in revision?

- Spend some time thinking about what you've left out of your draft. Are there places in the draft where you ignored ideas or information that would have complicated the journey? Where you chose to go where you were expected to go instead of where your thinking was pointing you? What can you do now to introduce ideas and information that would make your essay more interesting?

- Could anyone else have written the draft, or is it obvious to you that it's *yours?* How can you make the essay even more your own?

By using the post-draft outline in this way, you'll be serving as your own Maxwell Perkins: you'll assess both what your draft is and what it might become through structural revision.

Letting Go

Cutting sentences and paragraphs, or cutting everything and starting over from scratch: has there ever been a writer who enjoys this part of the writing process? Has there ever been a writer of note who could skip the cross-out, the toss, the "Ctrl-A, Delete"? No. But the difference between beginning writers and experienced writers is that experienced writers have practiced encountering the newly blank screen; they know that the blinking cursor can be set in motion once again and that there are always more words out there somewhere. Beginning writers, without much practice starting over, tend to fear the blank screen and to see deleted work as wasted time rather than as an unavoidable part of letting the mind work on a problem.

To encourage our students to see letting go as a habit of creative minds, we tell a story about going to hear Nobel Prize–winning writer Toni Morrison read from a work in progress. Morrison approached the lectern, paused, and then told the audience that the year before she'd completed well over a hundred pages of the novel's manuscript, but that she stood before us that night to read from the forty or so pages she had left. What had happened? Revision happened. Morrison had set out in one direction and then had to spend a year peeling off pages and pages of what she'd written until she found work that met her standards.

The Morrison anecdote can be read as an extension of the quote we opened this essay with: "there is no such thing as good writing, only good rewriting," and all good rewriting involves letting go. We hear this idea repeated in Colette's definition of an author: "Put down everything that comes into your head and then you're a writer. But an author is one who can judge his own stuff's worth, without pity, and destroy most of it." Novelist Anne Lamott makes this point about letting go in perhaps its bluntest form in her popular book *Bird by Bird*, where she asserts that all good writers write "shitty first drafts," drafts that they know will be thrown away. "This," she says, "is how they end up with good second drafts and terrific third drafts."

While Lamott's specific recommendations may not apply to all writing or to all writers, we believe there's real value in her advice to view draft after draft as practice, as work that may never see the light of day but that is valuable nonetheless. If you give yourself sufficient time to use writing to help yourself think, knowing that you are going to get rid of most of it before anyone else sees it, then maybe, as Lamott writes, you'll find "something in the very last line of the very last paragraph on page six that you just love, that is so beautiful or wild that you now know what you're supposed to be writing about, more or less, or in what direction you might go—but there was no way to get to this without first getting through the first five and a half pages."

Getting Feedback

Most writers don't publish until after they've gotten feedback from friends, colleagues, and editors. We think that getting feedback from people whose work you admire is probably *the most important revision practice of all.*

To acheive this Kerry Walk, a teacher we admire, recommends that cover letters accompany all drafts submitted for feedback. If you were to compose such a cover letter, Walk would advise you to state:

- the main question or problem your writing seeks to address;
- the idea or point you feel you've made most successfully;
- the idea or point you feel you need help with;
- your number one concern about your paper that you'd like your reader to answer for you; and
- any questions you have about how or where to start your revision.

The advantage of a cover letter of this kind is that it gives your reader a clear sense of how you see your draft and where you think it needs work. Your reader need not agree with your assessment, but the letter gives your reader a way to gauge his or her response to what you've written and to adjust that response accordingly.

Taking a Break

The best way to see your writing with fresh eyes is to set your draft aside—for a day if that's all you have, or for longer if possible. When you pick it up again, you'll be able to see more clearly what's working and what's not. And the feedback you've received, which may have caught you off guard at first, may now seem more reasonable. The point is to give yourself time to reenergize, so that you don't resort to tinkering on the edges of your writing when you really need to be rethinking and restructuring your first draft.

Prolific writer Neil Gaiman explains taking a break also allows you to return to your work as a reader, instead of as its writer. Once a draft is done, he advises, "put it away until you can read it with new eyes.... Put it in a drawer and write other things. When you're ready, pick it up and read it as if you've never read it before. If there are things you aren't satisfied with as a reader, go in and fix them as a writer: that's revision." By "fix them as a writer," he means rethinking, restructuring, letting go of what's not working, getting feedback, writing again, polishing—doing whatever it takes to move the writing forward.

PRACTICE SESSION ONE

REFLECTING

Spend at least 20 minutes reflecting on your experiences with revision and your thoughts about trying new approaches. What is your typical approach to revision? Which of the strategies that we describe in this essay have you tried before? Which approach seems easiest for you? Which approach seems most challenging or unsettling?

Now commit to setting aside the time you need to practice revision in new ways. Make a resolution to try at least three of these strategies—rethinking, restructuring, post-draft outlining, letting go, getting feedback, taking a break—before handing in your next paper. Which three do you think you'll try?

PRACTICE SESSION TWO

RESEARCHING

Do an online image search for "manuscript revisions." You'll get many pages of results. Explore, clicking on images of manuscripts that call out to you and visiting the pages where they are embedded. Look for examples from writers you admire. Then spend at least 30 minutes examining several images carefully, taking notes on how various writers revise. What can you learn about writing and revision by looking at marked-up manuscript pages?

WRITING

Write an essay that examines three or more of the manuscript revisions you find most interesting. Explain what you've learned from these specific examples about various processes for revising.

PRACTICE SESSION THREE

WRITING

Take a final draft that you wrote recently and see if you can cut it by at least 25 percent without losing the main argument or ideas. After you've cut your original piece by a quarter, compare the original version to the shorter, revised one. What's better about the more concise version? What's better about the longer one?

Then try cutting the shortened version by 25 percent again. What happens to your argument or ideas this time?

PRACTICE SESSION FOUR

REVISING

If you have a draft you're presently working on, follow the advice in "Getting Feedback" and find a tutor, teacher, or fellow student who agrees to give you feedback. Spend at least 20 minutes writing a one-page, single-spaced cover letter that explains your concerns about the draft. Give this letter to your reader with a copy of the draft, and schedule a meeting to discuss his or her feedback.

After you've received your reader's feedback, figure out what kind of revision the feedback suggests is most necessary: Should you try rethinking, restructuring, letting go, or a combination of strategies? Then revise.

EXPLORE

The word revision refers to many practices—from rethinking and restructuring to polishing sentences. For Adrienne Rich, revision is a process of reading and writing—reseeing texts from the past to make new thoughts, stories, and poems possible. Other forms of revision, especially sentence-level editing, have become essential elements of writing due to advances in technology. Craig Fehrman describes the typewriters emergence as a writing tool at the beginning of the twentieth century. You can see examples of famous writers' manuscript revisions at the *Bad Penny Review* and the *Paris Review* Web sites. At the *Paris Review*, we recommend looking at the work of Salman Rushdie and Joan Didion.

Fehrman, Craig. "Revising Your Writing Again? Blame the Modernists." *Boston Globe*. 30 June 2013. Web.

Rich, Adrienne. "When We Dead Awaken: Writing as Re-vision." *College English* 34.1 (October 1972). 18–30. Print.

"Murdering Your Darlings: Writers' Revisions." *A Bad Penny Review*. Web.

"Interviews." *Paris Review*. Web.

(To get to the manuscript files, first select an interview; then click on the "view a manuscript page" button in the menu under the title. Zoom in on the pages to read them.)

On Learning from Failure

When we watch children building a sandcastle on a summer beach, we see creativity in action. The process seems so simple. The castle grows and becomes more elaborate—with moats, towers, turrets, and carefully laid rows of shells—until late in the day it's abandoned, to be reclaimed by the tide before morning. If we watch more closely, however, we can see that the activity of building is more than just adding more and more pieces.

When we look again we notice how often things go wrong. An unexpected wave knocks down an hour's worth of building. A toddler wanders over from a neighboring beach blanket and causes more destruction. The sand dries and walls crumble. Unless disagreements and exhaustion take over, we also see the kids recover from failures. They experiment to figure out how to build a better moat to stay the tide. The toddler is distracted by collecting shells. A bucket brigade creates a pile of wetter sand. Or the construction project is moved up or down the beach to a better location. When children are at play, often enough they react to failures as opportunities for invention. They're not afraid of failure, because the stakes are low. The point is simply to have fun.

However, once we become adults, we're likely to avoid situations where the prospect of failure is high. Whether at work or school, most of us fear tackling a complex problem in front of our peers because of the possible consequences of failing: i.e. embarrassment, shame, a lower grade, a demotion. This fear of failure stifles creativity and innovation.

Not all people respond to fear of failure in the same way, though. In fact, creative people tend to have an attitude toward failure that's more like the kids on the beach than like a typical adult trying to solve a problem at work or a student trying to figure out what the teacher wants him to say. In What the Best College Students Do, Ken Bain argues that what sets the best students apart from the rest is their willingness to acknowledge failures, to explore them, and to learn from them. Unlike less creative people, they didn't deny their mistakes or get defensive about errors.

Where does this ability to bounce back from failure come from? To answer this question, Bain points to a study that compared two groups of ten-year-olds who were each given a series of puzzles. The first eight problems required the students to make real effort, but the challenges matched the students' age and education level. The next four problems were designed to be too hard for the students to solve. Over the first eight problems, there were no differences in how the groups performed; both groups talked about the problems as they worked through them, had fun, and came up with roughly the same number of correct solutions. On the second set of problems, however, the groups' reactions differed greatly from each other. The first group got frustrated, complained, and tried to change the rules; they started to make surprisingly poor choices, shifted their focus away from the problems, and gave up. By contrast, the second group continued to encourage each other, tested different approaches, and seemed to thrive on the challenge, even though they couldn't solve the hard problems either.

What caused the divergent responses? The students were grouped by researchers based on their attitudes toward intelligence. The first group had a fixed view of intelligence and the second group believed, conversely, that with effort you could become smarter. (As shorthand, we call members of the first group the "knowers" and members of the second group the "learners.") When the knowers faced failure, they looked for an escape route, because their failures called their intelligence into question; they went into mental tailspins, reverting to strategies that might be expected from preschoolers. The learners didn't take failure personally. Because they believed they could develop intelligence, working on the problems was its own reward. Even if they never found solutions, they valued learning things along the way.

Obviously, we can't just snap our fingers and change ingrained beliefs and patterns of behavior. And we can't change the fact that in some situations, when the stakes are immediate and high, it's nearly impossible to sustain an impersonal attitude toward failure. We believe, however, that it is possible to cultivate more creative attitudes toward failure through practice, and one of the most important locations for such practice in school assignments where time is allowed for experimentation and revision—such as the writing assignments (which we call "practice sessions") provided throughout Part 1 of this book. You've probably noticed that these practice sessions ask open questions or pose messy problems that can't be responded to simply with facts or by following a formula to a right answer.

In our writing classes, we encourage students to pursue what interests them, and we're thrilled when they set aside their fears and egos and risk exploring really knotty problems. In the end, even if their efforts come to naught, these students tend to learn from their mistakes. They figure out what went wrong and decide what they'll do differently the next time.

When we learn from failure, we discover that practice never ends.

PRACTICE SESSION ONE

REFLECTING

As a thought experiment, look back at what kind of student you were in middle school and in high school. Then imagine what school would have been like for you if grades hadn't mattered to parents or college admissions committees. Would you have taken more risks as a writer and learner, or would you have worked less?

Then set aside at least 30 minutes to reflect on the kind of school that could foster an environment in which students, including you, would be willing both to work hard and to "fail big." At your college, are there classes, teachers, or majors that encourage or even require students to take creative and intellectual risks?

PRACTICE SESSION TWO

READING

In "Fail Better," an essay about writing, Zadie Smith identifies the cliché as a small-scale example of literary failure. "What is a cliché," she asks, "except language passed down by Das Mann [the Man], used and shop-soiled by so many before you, and in no way the correct jumble of language for the intimate part of your vision you meant to express? With a cliché you have pandered to a shared understanding, you have taken a short-cut, you have represented what was pleasing and familiar rather than risked what was true and strange." This isn't the usual definition of failure, but it's a useful way of thinking about how to write well. While there are occasions when settling for the pleasing, familiar, and expected is the polite thing to do, success for a writer seeking new thoughts means having written something unfamiliar, unexpected, even unsettling—productively unsettling.

We'd like you to choose a reading and look for passages in which the writer is productively disruptive, rather than pleasing and familiar.

Then spend at least 40 minutes reflecting in writing about three passages from the reading that you think are particularly risky. Was the writer's risk worthwhile? Did the writer succeed or fail in Zadie Smith's terms? How about in your terms?

PRACTICE SESSION THREE

REFLECTING

We imagine it would be pretty straightforward to ask you to write about a time when you learned from failure. So instead of asking you to write up an account of a moral or educational failure that ends in self-improvement—"and ever afterwards, I was a better person"—we'd like you to write about a time when you failed to understand a concept or idea. What were the consequences of your failure? What rewards, if any, followed from overcoming that failure?

EXPLORE

We know how failure feels: we're disappointed in ourselves and ashamed of disappointing others. Catherine Tice describes the regret and loss that has accompanied her failure to become a musician. When the British daily newspaper the *Guardian* asked seven writers to reflect on failure, however, few of them expressed regret. Most wrote about failure as an inherent part of writing, inseparable from creativity. While even these writers fall into platitudes about failure as opportunity, together their comments suggest a more nuanced view: it's possible to fail *well*—to learn from failure, to make use of it, and to continue to work. Learning from failure also concerns Paul Tough, who wonders whether schools that protect students from failure in the short term ultimately set them up for failure in the long term.

"Falling Short: Seven Writers Reflect on Failure." *Guardian*. 22 June 2013. Web.

Tice, Catherine. "A Brief History of a Musical Failure." *Granta*. 2 Oct. 2013.

Tough, Paul. "What If the Secret to Success Is Failure?" *New York Times Magazine*. 18 Sept. 2011. Web.

Curiosity at Work: Alison Bechdel and the Layered Complexity of the Graphic Narrative

When Alison Bechdel began publishing her comic strip, *Dykes to Watch Out For*, in 1983, the possibility of anyone becoming a graphic memoirist—that is, someone who tells her life story using words and images—wasn't on anyone's radar. In the 1980s, the comic form was restricted largely to "the funnies" in the newspapers and to serialized stories about superheroes sold on rotating racks in convenience stores. The readers of these stories were assumed to be mostly, if not exclusively, teenage boys. A young woman just out of college composing a comic strip that followed the lives of feminists, lesbians, and gays? Not exactly a foolproof plan for success.

And yet Bechdel, inspired by Howard Cruse's *Gay Comix*, was convinced that she could use the comic form in a new way and that she could reach a different demographic with different reading interests. While she didn't set out to produce a strip that would steadily gain popularity and influence, this is exactly what Bechdel ended up doing, by dint of her ability to unite her meticulously drawn characters (some of whom were suggested to her by her avid fans) with compelling lines of narrative that crisscrossed the genres of political commentary, melodrama, and humor. (Bechdel has described the strip as "half op-ed column and half endless, serialized Victorian novel.") And this unlikely project earned Bechdel a living and numerous awards during the twenty-five years she kept *Dykes to Watch Out For* in syndication.

Bechdel's breakout work as a graphic memoirist came in 2006 when she used her cartooning skills to tell her own coming-of-age story *Fun Home: A Family Tragicomic* (the title is a play on the fact that Bechdel grew up above a funeral home). The mystery that resides at the center of *Fun Home* is her father's apparent suicide, which occurred shortly after Bechdel left home for college. Told from the dual perspective of Bechdel as a child moving into adolescence and contending with her eccentric family in rural Pennsylvania, and Bechdel as a mature, successful cartoonist reflecting on the past, *Fun Home* provided Bechdel with a means of exploring her past that simply wasn't available to her in the comic strip form.

Bechdel's sustained attention to detail, which is evident in every cell and every word of her narrative, allows her to see all of the players in this tragicomic tale in their complex humanity: her father, who was a mortician, fastidious home restorer, strict disciplinarian, and guardian of a secret life; her mother, who was an actress, distant and miserable; her brothers; the townspeople; her first female lover in college; and herself. In an interview, Bechdel described how the graphic narrative allowed her to reproduce the multiple perspectives that are ever-present in real life: "Every moment that we're living and having experiences, we're bringing to bear all of the other experiences that we've had. This is what is exciting to me about graphic narrative, that you're able to do a layered complexity that I couldn't imagine doing with just writing."

An instant success, *Fun Home* was followed in 2012 by *Are You My Mother? A Comic Drama*, Bechdel's equally incisive exploration of her mother's life in the time before and after Bechdel's father's mysterious death. In 2014, Bechdel received a MacArthur "genius" grant in recognition of her ongoing work "changing our notions of the contemporary memoir and expanding the expressive potential of the graphic form."

CHAPTER

8

Arguing

I n college, it often seems that *writing* and *arguing* are treated as synonyms. Teachers ask their students to write arguments that present interesting claims supported by evidence. But how do good, thoughtful arguments come into being? Does the act of writing move a preformulated argument from your brain to the screen? Or is an argument created through the act of writing? The distinction matters: if argument comes first, then writing is simply transcription. If writing comes first, then the argument emerges through the process of engaging with and responding to writing—one's own and the writing of others.

While it would certainly be more convenient if writing simply recorded our already-formulated thoughts, we know as writers and as teachers of writing that the best arguments emerge over time—after one has read, thought, reflected, drafted, revised, started over, and reconsidered. Thus, in this chapter we invite you to think of an argument as a compelling idea that emerges over the course of an intellectual journey. We also invite you to imagine your mental life as a drama in which there's action, excitement, and passion that can motivate your writing. And we show how three influential scholarly arguments are driven by curiosity. The emphasis throughout is on producing writing that matters.

On Argument as Journey

When professors assign papers in college classes, they typically expect their students to hand in essays that make an argument. What they mean by "an argument," however, isn't always clear to the students. Many of our students arrive in our classes believing that writing an argument is like participating in a debate: they pick a side (their thesis); they gather evidence to support the side they've chosen; and they write as if trying to show that they are right and the other side is wrong. Winning, or getting a good grade, is the goal—not thoughtfulness, not discovery, not learning.

There are contexts within which this type of writing is entirely appropriate: a legal brief, for example, or a letter of complaint. But if you listen to pundits on cable news,

Chapter 8, "Arguing," is taken from Richard E. Miller and Ann Jurecic, *Habits of the Creative Mind*, pp. 227–252 (Part 11, "Arguing").

follow congressional debates, or read the comment sections of online news sources, you'll see that such oppositional argumentation has become the norm in contemporary culture. In these venues, pushing ideas to their extremes, stirring up the emotions of one's allies and enemies, and scoring points with a pithy phrase or sound bite are more common than the reasoned exchange of ideas.

Because we have not found that practicing argument-as-debate leads to good academic writing—or to good journalism or good literary nonfiction—we propose, in its place, practicing argument as journey. What's the difference? In practicing argument as journey, you begin with the goal of answering a question or solving a problem (that's your destination); you ponder possible trajectories; you do research and rethink your plan; you learn more and more; you write, make mistakes, and head off in new and unanticipated directions; you make discoveries; you define a clearer purpose and path; you figure out how you want to answer your central question or solve your problem. Finally, the finished essay takes your readers on a journey to new ideas.

We'd like to walk you through an extended example of the argument as journey by looking at Elizabeth Kolbert's *Field Notes from a Catastrophe*, a book about global climate change. When Kolbert chose this topic, she knew she was stepping into contentious territory. Some people see climate change as an empirically verifiable threat to the future of life on this planet and others dismiss it as a false claim based in bad or inconclusive science. In the scientific community, the consensus is clear: global warming is a fact and it is caused by human activity—especially our reliance on burning carbon-based fuels such as coal, oil, wood, and natural gas. There is no such consensus in politics. Indeed as the scientific community has made it harder to deny that global warming is a fact, nonscientists of every stripe have shifted their doubt to the role humans play in changing the earth's climate. Given this political context, the project of writing about climate change poses a real challenge for Kolbert: if the National Academy of Sciences, which has been issuing warnings about impending environmental disaster since 1979, hasn't been able to convince people of the reality and danger of climate change and that humans have caused it, what could Kolbert—or any writer, for that matter—possibly say that would change readers' minds?

We admire *Field Notes from a Catastrophe* both because Kolbert sets out to see for herself the effects of climate change on the environment and because she takes her readers with her on a journey that is both physical and metaphysical. She seeks to examine evidence of climate change and also to contemplate why we have been so reluctant to acknowledge and act on signs of impending disaster. She begins by traveling above the Arctic Circle because the signs of warming are so striking there.

Kolbert visits the Alaskan village of Shishmaref, on an island off the coast of the Seward Peninsula, where native villagers once drove snowmobiles twenty miles out on the ice to hunt seals. By the time she gets there, the ice around the island is so soft that using snowmobiles is no longer safe, so the hunters use boats. The village, only twenty-two feet above sea level, has become so vulnerable to storm surges that the residents have decided to give up their way of life and relocate. Farther inland, near Fairbanks, Kolbert sees the effects of melting permafrost. Areas of ground that have been frozen since the beginning of the last glacial cycle are now threatened by thaw. Where the permafrost has been disturbed by the construction of buildings or roads, the land is especially vulnerable to warming; in some neighborhoods, foundations are degrading and houses are collapsing.

Kolbert then visits Iceland during the summer-melt season and meets members of the Icelandic Glaciological Society, who regularly survey the size of the country's three hundred or so glaciers. Though glaciers in Iceland continued to grow in the 1970s and 1980s, even as North American glaciers were shrinking, in the 1990s they, too, began to retreat. There have been glaciers on Iceland for two million years, Kolbert writes, but climate models predict that by the end of the next century there will be no more ice left to measure in Iceland.

Kolbert also travels to a research station on the Greenland ice sheet where scientists study ice cores drilled from the glacier. "A hundred and thirty-eight feet down," Kolbert writes, "there is snow that fell during the time of the American Civil War; 2,500 feet down, snow from the time of the Peloponnesian Wars, and, 5,350 feet down, snow from the days when the cave painters of Lascaux were slaughtering bison. At the very bottom, 10,000 feet down, there is snow that fell on central Greenland before the start of the last ice age, more than a hundred thousand years ago." Today, however, scientists at the research station are observing and measuring the gradual contraction of this massive glacier, which contains eight percent of the world's fresh water supply. If the Greenland ice sheet melts—and it is shrinking by twelve cubic miles each year—the consequences will be more than the loss of the history it contains. The ice sheet, Kolbert reports, contains enough water to raise sea levels around the world by twenty-three feet.

As Kolbert describes her physical journey, she also takes her readers on a journey through the science of climate change. Chapter by chapter, she carefully and clearly tells her readers how science explains the role humans have played in bringing about current warming trends and what these changes indicate about the future of the planet. After her account of Shishmaref, for instance, Kolbert summarizes the first major study of global warming, completed in 1979 by the National Academy of Sciences. A panel evaluated early studies on the effects of adding carbon dioxide to the atmosphere and concluded that continued increases in carbon dioxide would cause climate changes. They knew then that there was "no reason to believe that these changes [would] be negligible." If we had taken their warning seriously thirty years ago, we might have lessened the impact of climate change.

Later Kolbert explains why we should be concerned about the melting of perennial sea ice, which, unlike seasonal ice that forms and melts each year, remains frozen year-round. Back in 1979, perennial sea ice covered 1.7 billion acres—about the size of the continental United States. By the time Kolbert was writing her book in 2005, that area had shrunk by 250 million acres, an area about the combined size of Texas, New York, and Georgia. Why does this matter? Ice reflects sunlight away from the earth, while the dark open water of the ocean absorbs its heat. The more the perennial ice melts, exposing open ocean water, the more heat gets retained by the ocean, which then melts even more ice: the system feeds on itself, and the pace of warming speeds up. Small changes in the average temperature of ocean water, in other words, can lead to big changes in climate.

Having explained the science of the greenhouse effect and how industrialization—with its coal-burning factories, railroads, and power stations—started the process of global warming, Kolbert moves in her third chapter to discuss a contemporary symposium on climate change she attended in Iceland. None of the scientists at the symposium doubt that humans are responsible for warming the Earth's atmosphere. So Kolbert's journey through the science leads her and her readers to a *certainty* that too many politicians willingly deny: human consumption of carbon-based fuels has dramatically raised the level of carbon dioxide in the atmosphere and the consequences are changing life on earth.

Kolbert's journey does not end when she leaves the Arctic. She goes to England to see how climate change threatens the survival of butterflies and toads—and up to a quarter of the Earth's species. She learns how droughts long-ago caused the disappearance of ancient civilizations. She visits the Netherlands, where existing dikes will not hold back rising seawaters, so companies are manufacturing floating "amphibious" homes. She also travels to Burlington, Vermont, where a grassroots campaign to reduce greenhouse gas emissions by ten percent affirms the possibilities of local action, and also its limits. After all, whatever the residents of this small city accomplish is quickly offset by the rest of the world's continued expansion of energy use. Kolbert closes her book by arguing that humans have launched the planet into a new geological era. We should recognize, she says, that the Holocene, the epoch that began at the end of the Pleistocene about 11,700 years ago, is now over. We are in the dawn of the "Anthropocene," a "new age ... defined by one creature—man—who [has] become so dominant that he [is] capable of altering the planet on a geological scale."

It's obvious throughout *Field Notes from a Catastrophe* that Kolbert thinks we must end our destructive addiction to fossil fuels, but she knows this argument has been made before to little effect. So she doesn't use her book to tell us what to do. Instead, the journey she takes us on makes the argument that the problem is so far along and so deeply entrenched in human behavior that it may not be solvable. When Kolbert arrives at the conclusion that we have entered the Anthropocene, it's clear that her readers have to choose what to do now. Denial, disbelief, or despair is always an option, but if we have been affected by reading Kolbert's book, we may at least be willing to accept responsibility for the problem we've created, and we may decide that trying to halt the pace or lessen the effect of the catastrophe is surely better than doing nothing at all. Indeed, if we're capable of causing disaster on a global scale, we may also be smart, creative, and lucky enough to come up with ways to ameliorate the consequences of this disaster. If we're truly lucky, we may even manage to delay the end of the Anthropocene era.

PRACTICE SESSION ONE

READING
We've just described how Elizabeth Kolbert takes a physical journey that she then transforms into an intellectual journey for her readers. Now we'd like you to choose a reading and follow the author's intellectual journey. After you've read through the piece once, set aside at least 40 minutes to review it and take more detailed notes about how the journey unfolds. Pay attention to the sources—the people and texts the author cites. Step back and look at the decisions the author made about how to organize the text.

Then draw a map of the journey. When did it move straight ahead? When did you encounter turns of thought? Did the author send you off on digressions? Did they still feel like digressions after you'd followed them to their conclusions?

REFLECTING
Spend at least 30 minutes writing reflectively about your own journey as a reader of the essay you selected. After reading and then reviewing the article, how far have you traveled intellectually? Were there places where your own thinking diverged from the path the author provided? Did reading the piece allow you to think about its central problem or question in a new way? Did it change your mind?

PRACTICE SESSION TWO

RESEARCH ESSAY
After reading our description of *Field Notes from a Catastrophe*, you now have a sense of Kolbert's view of the environmental challenges we face. The world we know will change radically during our lifetimes and, as a consequence of our collective choices and actions, may eventually become a planet that is uninhabitable by humans. The facts are menacing and disturbing, and they raise an important question: Can we construct rational hope in the face of climate change, and if so, how?

To compose an essay that offers a thoughtful answer to this question, you will first need to do additional reading. If you go out to the Web, you will find more on climate change than any single person could read in a lifetime. How do you separate what's worth considering from what's not? How do you determine what's compelling? We'd like you to spend at least 60 minutes searching online for a fact or a set of facts about climate change that you find both powerful and worthy of further consideration.

Write up a discussion of the facts you've uncovered. What makes the facts you're presenting more convincing than other facts regarding climate change? In completing your write-up, you are likely to need to do more reading, since facts only become convincing when placed in context.

SPECULATIVE ESSAY

Thinking seriously about climate change inevitably affects one's sense of the future. Given the evidence you've uncovered in your limited research, would you say that it is possible to construct a rational hope about the future? What compelling evidence would you point to that either supports or undermines the grounds for rational hope? In composing your response, stick to evidence that you find persuasive: this isn't an invitation to trade in generalities about "human nature"; it's an opportunity to consider the relationship between evidence, reason, and the future. Take your reader on a journey that reveals your mind at work on this problem.

EXPLORE

Writers we admire often begin their work with a question about why an event occurred, how an idea came into being, or how a problem might be resolved; then they lead their readers through facts, analysis, and ideas to arrive at their own answers. The list below offers examples of such complex journeys. Brian Cathcart guides us through a London murder case while pondering race and injustice. Ta-Nehisi Coates considers the evolution of racism in the United States, from slavery to Jim Crow and from segregation to racist housing policies, asking whether a discussion about financial reparations might bring about necessary change. Joan Didion reflects on how a set of fixed political opinions led to the US invasions of Iraq and Afghanistan. Venkatesh Rao invites readers to consider how having resources to waste serves creativity. And Rebecca Solnit walks us through the collapsed city of Detroit where she finds hope in how nature quickly reclaims the landscape.

Cathcart, Brian. "The Case of Stephen Lawrence." *Granta*. 6 Jan. 2012. Web.

Coates, Ta-Nehisi. "The Case for Reparations." *Atlantic*. 21 May 2014. Web.

Didion, Joan. "Fixed Opinions, or the Hinge of History." *New York Review of Books*. 16 Jan. 2003. Web.

Rao, Venkatesh. "Waste, Creativity, and Godwin's Corollary for Technology." *Ribbonfarm*. 23 Aug. 2012. Web.

Solnit, Rebecca. "Detroit Arcadia." *Harper's Magazine*. July 2007. Web.

On the Theater of the Mind

If you do a search on the phrase "theater of the mind," you'll find it has been used in two ways. Starting in 1956, "theater of the mind" was used by those wishing to argue that listening to radio dramas required more brainpower than watching dramas on the newer medium of television. Radio dramas, the argument went, are superior to television dramas because they take place not in the sound studio where the voice actors and sound effects people convene, but in the imaginations of the listening audience. The phrase is now used more generally to describe what happens when words, whether read or heard, and/or images, whether seen or described, create a dramatic scene in the mind of the beholder. And so one could say that advertising, which has long made the programming on radio and television possible, is convened in the theater of the mind, where it continuously prods audiences to imagine the better life that comes from consumption. Indeed, this search exercise itself demonstrates just how much advertising dominates the theater of the mind: the top search results for this phrase are not links to definitions or discussions of the debate over whether radio is superior to television or vice versa; they are for the sixth studio album by the hip-hop artist Ludacris, which happens to be named … *Theater of the Mind*.

We'd like to hijack the phrase "theater of the mind" and use it for an entirely different purpose. We grant that words and images can create a virtual theater *in* the mind. What we're interested in, though, is considering what becomes possible when you think of the flow of thoughts in your mind as participating in an open-ended drama that quietly plays out as you think through and about the ideas that are most important to you. It's a drama not just *in* your mind but *of* your mind. And you can use your writing to make the theater of your mind available for others to experience. Indeed, we'd say that this is one way to define the practice of creativity. When you write, you also shape an experience in the minds of your readers; your words stage the unfolding of an idea or an argument or a narrative.

When scientific and philosophic treatises were presented as dialogues, it was easier to see that there are dramatic, comedic, and even tragic aspects to the exchange of ideas. Galileo's use of the telescope, for example, shows how a new technology can generate new information that, under the right circumstances, triggers an internal dialogue—in the theater of the mind—that in turn leads to a whole new way of thinking and seeing.

In 1609, with the aid of one of the world's first telescopes, Galileo began to collect evidence suggesting that the earth was not at the center of what we now call the solar system. He first published his results as a scientific treatise in 1610. In 1632, in his book *The Dialogue Concerning the Two Chief World Systems*, Galileo presented his argument for a sun-centered model of the universe as a dialogue between three fictional characters: Salviati, a scholar whose research supports the idea that the sun is at the center of the universe; Simplicio, who believes that the earth is at the center of the universe, an idea initially presented by Aristotle and Ptolemy more than a thousand years earlier; and Sagredo, an intelligent bystander who asks questions as Salviati and Simplicio debate the merits of the two diametrically opposed models. Galileo used the form of the dialogue to make his own thinking process accessible to the greatest number of readers, most of whom were not involved in studying the heavens. He staged what would otherwise be an arcane discussion about measuring the movements of celestial bodies as a dialogue for a general audience, one that serves up humor and insults along with explanations of the significance of his discovery of craters on the moon. With his dialogue, Galileo made it possible for his readers to imagine that the sun was at the center of the universe regardless of what the Bible said or what the Church held. While Galileo's 1610 treatise presented the same fundamental threat to the Catholic Church's worldview, it was the publication of *The Dialogue* that led to Galileo's trial for heresy in 1633, where he was forced to recant his argument for the heliocentric universe and was then sentenced to house arrest for the remainder of his life.

Were you expecting a happier ending?

Our second example comes from ancient Greece. Plato, Socrates's prolific student, presented his teacher's philosophical reflections as a series of dialogues. Here, too, one finds the exchange of ideas depicted not as the dispassionate, orderly laying out of the steps that lead to some deep truth but as a wayward back-and-forth between Socrates, who is forever searching after the Good, and one or more interlocutors, who are inevitably shown to know much less than they claim to know. In *The Republic*, the Platonic dialogue that explores whether or not the State has the power to produce good, law-abiding citizens, Socrates tells a story about the difference between the world as it is seen by average people and the world as it is seen by those who seek the truth.

Socrates asks his listeners to imagine a cave in which prisoners are chained to the ground, their gaze fixed on the cave wall before them. Behind them there is a fire, and between the fire and the prisoners is a pathway traveled by people carrying life-size cutouts of various objects. The fire casts shadows of the objects on the wall, and the prisoners, because they can't turn their heads, take these moving shadows to be reality. This, Socrates would have his listeners believe, is how unthinking people experience life: they mistake shadows for reality; they are prisoners to illusions.

Continuing his story, Socrates imagines a prisoner who breaks free of his chains, turns and sees the fire and the cutouts, and then walks from the cave into the sunlight. The former prisoner now sees things as they are, and he returns to the cave to tell the prisoners what he has seen. For Socrates, the freed prisoner is akin to the philosopher, and the return to the cave is the beginning of the philosopher's educational mission, which Socrates defines as turning the prisoners toward the light of the fire.

Then education is the craft concerned with doing this very thing, this turning around, and with how the soul can most easily and effectively be made to do it. It isn't the craft of putting sight into the soul. Education takes for granted that sight is there but that it isn't turned the right way or looking where it ought to look, and it tries to redirect it appropriately.

With Socrates's allegory of the cave, we get a nested set of theaters of the mind: there's the theater in the prisoner's mind, which is inhabited by shadows; there's the theater in the philosopher's mind, where one encounters reality; and there's Plato's theater of the mind, which stages this moment when Socrates uses a story to illustrate his view of education as the process of turning from the illusory to the real.

What we find compelling about the Allegory of the Cave and *The Dialogue Concerning the Two Chief World Systems* is that they make visible what would otherwise go unnoticed—namely, that there is a drama to the life of the mind that gets expressed in the movement from confusion to clarity, a drama that gets felt in the weight and heft of the process of changing one's mind. While the dramas that played out in the theater of Galileo's mind and the theater of Socrates's mind proved to be of global significance, we all experience a true change of mind, like a genuine change of heart, as life changing, even though the significance of the change extends no further than our own worldview.

Writing plays a central role in the theater of the mind because it makes it possible for us to see our own thoughts and then to reflect on what happens when we move those thoughts out into the world. As it happens this is why Socrates so distrusted writing: unlike an embodied dialogue between a teacher and a student, with writing there's no one there but ourselves to test the veracity of our thoughts as we express them. Despite Socrates's argument against writing, his student Plato wrote a series of dialogues featuring Socrates that have been read, discussed, and argued over for the past two thousand years. Why? Because the questions Socrates poses in Plato's dialogues cut to the very essence of what it means to be human. Indeed, for Socrates, it is the ongoing engagement with the theater of one's mind, where questions about how to live a good life are posed and reposed, that separates us from all the other animals. This sentiment, succinctly captured in Socrates's oft-quoted declaration in *The Apology* that "the unexamined life is not worth living," is, we would argue, more accurately rendered as "a life lived without ongoing self-examination is not a human life." The drama of the theater of the mind commences as soon as the question "What do I think?" is given serious consideration.

PRACTICE SESSION ONE

REFLECTING

There's a quick way to test how the idea of the theater of the mind, as we've defined it, can be of use to you: write a description of the most dramatic moment you've experienced in the realm of thought. In the theater of the mind, one deals with ideas—friendship, citizenship, truth, faith, integrity, or success, for example—and the drama is in the development of a revised understanding of the idea at the center of one's self-examination. We are not asking you to write a story about how winning an award improved your self-confidence or how an act of shoplifting led to feelings of guilt. The assignment is to focus squarely on the redefinition of an *idea* and to lead your readers through your thought process to show them why the shift in definition *matters*.

PRACTICE SESSION TWO

READING

There's a maxim in argumentation that goes like this: tell them what you're going to say; say it; tell them that you said it. This is argumentation through repetition. In the context of the current discussion, we'd say that this kind of argumentation contains no drama; there's nothing for the reader to do in the theater of the mind other than accept or reject the point that is being argued.

This is not the case for any of the readings we've included at the end of this volume. Choose a reading and observe, as you read, how the writer tries to create a theater of the mind for the readers, encouraging them to think in new ways about the topic at hand.

Set aside at least 30 minutes to take notes about places where the writer dramatizes the evolution of ideas, perhaps by refining the argument, shifting directions, or introducing new and surprising information.

WRITING

After you've read and reviewed the article, draft an essay that describes how the writer moves your thinking along from the beginning of the article to the end. Is there a drama to this movement? What has the writer done to get you to shift your thinking? Does he or she succeed?

REVISING

And now for the real challenge: revise the essay you wrote in the previous exercise so that it compellingly demonstrates your experience reading the piece you've chosen and contending with its implications. In other words, create for your reader the drama of your engagement with the writer's ideas.

EXPLORE

One of the pleasures of reading and writing is exploring the theater of other people's minds. In the *Invisibilia* podcast "The Secret History of Thoughts," you can hear the "ghost boy," who spent thirteen years in a vegetative state, describe what it was like to live entirely inside his mind. Leslie Jamison discusses how her experiences as a medical actor—i.e., playing sick for doctors in training—transformed her understanding of empathy. Cheryl Strayed offers advice to a beginning writer, Elissa Bassist, about how to overcome the internal fears that prevent getting down to work. In an interview two years later, Strayed speaks with Bassist, who has completed the book she feared she would never write.

Bassist, Elissa, and Cheryl Strayed. "How to Write Like a Mother#^@%&." *Creative Nonfiction.* #47, Winter 2013. Web.

Jamison, Leslie. "The Empathy Exams: A Medical Actor Writes Her Own Script." *The Believer.* Feb. 2014. Web.

"The Secret History of Thoughts." NPR *Invisibilia.* 9 Jan. 2015. Podcast.

Strayed, Cheryl. "Write Like a Motherfucker." *The Rumpus.* 19 Aug. 2010. Web.

On Curiosity at Work in the Academy

Throughout Part 1 of this book, we've included short entries about "Curiosity at Work"—examples of how curiosity inspires creative thought and expression. In these brief essays, we emphasize the work of contemporary nonfiction writers because they do such a good job of posing compelling questions about the world. If you're a student learning to write for school, however, you may be wondering how to connect what this book teaches you about writers' habits of mind to the kinds of papers you are asked to write for classes in particular academic disciplines. We think the best way to address that connection is to show you examples of curiosity at work in academic writing so you can see how academic articles and books emerge from the very habits of mind we've been discussing.

Academic writing differs from journalistic writing and general nonfiction in important ways. Scholarly articles and books explicitly join conversations taking place in particular branches of knowledge, and they focus on questions that are of interest to others in the same discipline; philosophers ask different kinds of questions than psychologists or anthropologists or historians ask. The various fields of study also differ from each other in their methods of research, the kinds of evidence used, and the traditions that govern how arguments, ideas, evidence, and sources are presented.

Despite these differences, academic writing has much in common with nonfiction written by generalists. Each of the three academic works we discuss below begins with the author expressing curiosity about a difficult problem, puzzle, or paradox that can be addressed through research. While the authors present their work according to the conventions of their respective academic fields, they are all motivated by a desire to advance understanding about complex issues. Reviewing these examples will make it easier for you to see three of the main moves academics make in launching their writing projects. Each writer identifies an important problem, puzzle, or paradox; joins an ongoing discussion about the problem, puzzle, or paradox; and establishes the key words in that conversation. This description may suggest that we think academic writing follows a formula. But we'd say that these writers *begin* with curiosity. The conventions become useful later as the writers shape what they've discovered for an audience of specialized readers.

· · · · ·

One of the most influential articles in the field of political theory is Michael Walzer's "Political Action: The Problem of Dirty Hands," which appeared in *Philosophy & Public Affairs* in 1973. (The full article can easily be found online.) In the introduction to his essay, Walzer immediately signals that he's joining an ongoing conversation. His first paragraph explains that he's interested in a disagreement about moral dilemmas that has already been addressed by three fellow philosophers—Thomas Nagel, Richard B. Brandt, and R. M. Hare. They disagree about "whether or not a man can ever face, or ever has to face, a moral dilemma, a situation where he must choose between two courses of action *both of which it would be wrong for him to undertake*" (emphasis added). More specifically, they're concerned about whether it's possible for a leader to govern "innocently." In other words, can a political leader resolve moral dilemmas without ever having to choose a course of action that is immoral?

Nagel thinks that, because dilemmas arise in which each possible course of action is morally wrong, a leader cannot govern innocently. Brandt argues that logical reasoning can be used to resolve such dilemmas and thus a leader can remain innocent. Hare agrees, arguing dilemmas of this kind can and should be resolved at a higher level of moral discourse.

Walzer is not satisfied with any of these answers. In the third paragraph of his article, he writes:

> My own answer is no, I don't think I could govern innocently; nor do most of us believe that those who govern us are innocent—as I shall argue below—even the best of them. But this does not mean that it isn't possible to do the right thing while governing. It means that a particular act of government (in a political party or in the state) may be exactly the right thing to do in utilitarian terms and yet leave the man who does it guilty of a moral wrong. The innocent man, afterwards, is no longer innocent. If on the other hand he remains innocent ..., he not only fails to do the right thing (in utilitarian terms), he may also fail to measure up to the duties of his office (which imposes on him a considerable responsibility for consequences and outcomes).

If you have trouble understanding what Walzer is saying the first time through, try reading this passage again, slowly, and look up the terms that are unfamiliar to you. If you look up *utilitarianism*, for example, you'll find that it is the principle of the greatest good for the greatest number. A utilitarian evaluates choices on the basis of how useful they are; the *right* choice to a utilitarian is one that is beneficial for more people.

With this definition in mind, you might assume that calculating the greatest good for the greatest number is a straightforward business, but Walzer thinks that making a utilitarian decision could be simultaneously the right course of action and a morally wrong one. For example, suppose a political leader could serve the greater good of his or her country by sacrificing the lives of bystanders to kill the head of a terrorist organization. Even if the political leader makes the "right" utilitarian choice to kill bystanders for the greater good of the country, she or he has still committed the immoral act of killing innocent people and now has dirty hands. If the leader refuses to commit this immoral act on behalf of the greater good and lets the terrorist live, then the leader has put his or her own citizens at risk. With this choice, the leader commits a different moral wrong and also has dirty hands.

Six pages into the article, Walzer fully lays out the paradox that leaders "who act for us and in our name are often killers, or seem to become killers too quickly and too easily." Even "good and decent people" who choose politics as a vocation, he writes,

> are then required to learn the lesson Machiavelli first set out to teach: "how not to be good." Some of them are incapable of learning; many more profess to be incapable. But they will not succeed unless they learn, for they have joined the terrible competition for power and glory; they have chosen to work

and struggle as Machiavelli says, among "so many who are not good." They can do no good themselves unless they win the struggle, which they are unlikely to do unless they are willing and able to use the necessary means. So we are suspicious even of the best of winners. It is not a sign of our perversity if we think them only more clever than the rest. They have not won, after all, because they were good, or not only because of that, but also because they were not good. No one succeeds in politics without getting his hands dirty. This is conventional wisdom again, and again I don't mean to insist that it is true without qualification. I repeat it only to disclose the moral dilemma inherent in the convention. For sometimes it is right to try to succeed, and then it must also be right to get one's hands dirty. But one's hands get dirty from doing what it is wrong to do. And how can it be wrong to do what is right? Or, how can we get our hands dirty by doing what we ought to do?

As this last paragraph shows, Waltzer doesn't rush to resolve the moral puzzle that fascinates him. Rather than being satisfied with the conclusion that successful leaders must have dirty hands, he continues to generate more and more questions: If having dirty hands is inevitable, when should dirty-handed leaders be held accountable? Does holding leaders accountable then dirty the hands of citizens in turn? Does everyone end up with dirty hands? Walzer concludes his essay without having answered any of these questions definitively. And yet, forty years after it was written, "Political Action: The Problem of Dirty Hands" is still being cited by scholars and taught in politics classes. Why? For two reasons: because Walzer's article presents the complex puzzle of "doing bad to do good" with remarkable clarity; and because Walzer's way of engaging with this puzzle is so lively and original that readers from across the political spectrum feel invited to join with him as he wrestles with the unsolvable challenge of leadership.

. . . . .

Edward Said's influential book *Orientalism* begins by making the same series of moves we saw Walzer's "Political Action" make above: in the introduction to Orientalism, Said joins an ongoing conversation about culture; he works to unsettle key terms; and he argues that we should understand a complicated puzzle in a new way. The introduction opens with Said staging his response to the following: "On a visit to Beirut during the terrible civil war of 1975–1976 a French journalist wrote regretfully of the gutted downtown area that 'it had once seemed to belong to … the Orient of Chateaubriand and Nerval.'" The jounalist saw only what his own country had lost. The distortions of this view of Beirut inspired Said to write a book about how the East has been seen through Western eyes.

We'd like you to read the first two paragraphs of *Orientalism* and observe how Said's curiosity about the journalist's sentence leads him to intellectually creative thoughts. It will help you understand Said's project if you know that Chateaubriand and Nerval were nineteenth-century French writers who wrote extensively about their travels to the Middle East and, more specifically, about their time in Beirut.

On a visit to Beirut during the terrible civil war of 1975–1976 a French journalist wrote regretfully of the gutted downtown area that "it had once seemed to belong to ... the Orient of Chateaubriand and Nerval." He was right about the place, of course, especially so far as a European was concerned. The Orient was almost a European invention, and had been since antiquity a place of romance, exotic beings, haunting memories and landscapes, remarkable experiences. Now it was disappearing; in a sense it had happened, its time was over. Perhaps it seemed irrelevant that Orientals themselves had some-thing at stake in the process, that even in the time of Chateaubriand and Nerval Orientals had lived there, and that now it was they who were suffering; the main thing for the European visitor was a European representation of the Orient and its contemporary fate, both of which had a privileged communal significance for the journalist and his French readers.

Americans will not feel quite the same about the Orient, which for them is much more likely to be associated very differently with the Far East (China and Japan, mainly). Unlike the Americans, the French and the British—less so the Germans, Russians, Spanish, Portuguese, Italians, and Swiss—have had a long tradition of what I shall be calling *Orientalism*, a way of coming to terms with the Orient that is based on the Orient's special place in European Western experience. The Orient is not only adjacent to Europe; it is also the place of Europe's greatest and richest and oldest colonies, the source of its civilizations and languages, its cultural contestant, and one of its deepest and most recurring images of the Other. In addition, the Orient has helped to define Europe (or the West) as its contrasting image, idea, personality, expe-rience. Yet none of this Orient is merely imaginative. The Orient is an integral part of European *material* civilization and culture. Orientalism expresses and represents that part culturally and even ideologically as a mode of discourse with supporting institutions, vocabulary, scholarship, imagery, doctrines, even colonial bureaucracies and colonial styles....

You may need to read this passage more than once and look up terms that are unfamiliar to you to understand Said's project. You could look carefully, for instance, at what Said does with the term "the Orient." For over a century, the term seemed to be culturally neutral, but Said draws our attention to how it is deeply embedded in a Western cultural perspective that casts the East as both in service to and inferior to the West. The ways the West perceives the East, he says, have far-reaching effects. The European idea of "the Orient" is embedded in the European languages, patterns of thought, and institutional structures. If we return to the journalist's description of the "gutted downtown" of Beirut that "had once seemed to belong to . . . the Orient of Chateaubriand and Nerval," we can now see what Said wants us to see—namely, the nostalgia of a Frenchman who cannot appreciate Beirut as an Eastern city and who regrets that it no longer reflects the influence of its French colonizers. With this brief example, Said takes the first step in his journey to establish that the idea of "the Orient" is a European invention. His intellectual journey ultimately inspired a generation of scholars to document the ways that European and Americans have represented Middle Eastern, African, and Asian societies and cultures over time.

. . . . .

The two examples of academic writing we've offered so far are both focused on abstract concepts, "Orientalism" and "the problem of dirty hands," and they both address how ideas and narratives shape the way we think about politics, power, culture, and cultural difference. Our third example, from the field of sociology, is less abstract, though it too examines the power of cultural narratives. "Fetal Alcohol Syndrome: The Origins of a Moral Panic," by Elizabeth M. Armstrong and Ernest L. Abel, examines the growing concern in the 1990s about fetal alcohol syndrome (FAS) as a public health issue. The writers of this article are very direct: they begin by defining fetal alcohol syndrome and then quickly cite six articles to demonstrate that they are entering an ongoing scholarly conversation about the prevalence and danger of fetal alcohol syndrome. Although their prose is unadorned, they make clear in their introduction that they've uncovered an unexpected and serious problem.

> Fetal alcohol syndrome (FAS) is a pattern of anomalies occurring in children born to alcoholic women (Jones and Smith, 1973). The main features of this pattern are pre- and/or postnatal growth retardation, characteristic facial abnormalities, and central nervous system dysfunction, including mental retardation (Stratton et al., 1996). Despite the pervasiveness of alcohol and drunkenness in human history (Abel, 1997), FAS went largely unrecognized until 1973, when it was characterized as a "tragic disorder" by Jones and Smith, the Seattle physicians who discovered it (Jones and Smith, 1973). By the 1990s, FAS had been transformed in the United States from an unrecognized condition to a

moral panic characterized as a "major public health concern" (e.g. Stratton *et al.*, 1996) and a "national health priority" (Egeland *et al.*, 1998). In this paper, we trace this evolution, paying special attention to the ways in which this moral panic has inflated fear and anxiety about the syndrome beyond levels warranted by evidence of its prevalence or impact. To acknowledge that the current level of concern about FAS is exaggerated is not to suggest that the syndrome does not exist. One of us (E. L. A.) has spent his entire professional career researching and writing about FAS and continues to be actively engaged in its prevention.

Armstrong and Abel are curious about a paradox in the history of fetal alcohol syndrome: although the syndrome was unknown before 1973, in the space of twenty years, fetal alcohol syndrome went from being invisible to being the focus of a "moral panic." They want to understand how and why the syndrome became an urgent "public health priority."

In the pages that follow the introduction, the authors reinterpret evidence that was available to everyone at the time and yet was routinely oversimplified and misunderstood by others caught up in the moral panic. They point out, for example, that highly visible prevention efforts, such as the placement of warning labels on alcohol bottles, "are doomed to fail" because all pregnant women are not, in fact, equally at risk of giving birth to children with fetal alcohol syndrome. If, as the authors say, "a small proportion of women of child-bearing age, especially those who are most disadvantaged by poverty, bear the greatest burden of risk for FAS," then the real public health concern should be identifying and helping those women who are most at risk.

This is what it means to be creative as an academic: you show your readers how to understand a problem in a new way. Armstrong and Abel have recast a seemingly intractable public health crisis so that new ways of responding to it become imaginable.

· · · · ·

These three examples of curiosity at work in the academy offer just a glimpse of how academics share their curiosity about the ways of the world with others. Academic writing poses special challenges to readers who are new to a topic or a field of study, but if you know to look for the problem, question, puzzle, or paradox that the writer is grappling with, if you can spot where the writer is joining an ongoing conversation with other scholars, and if you figure out how to define key terms and concepts, you'll be able to get your bearings, even if the language and subject matter at first seem entirely unfamiliar.

PRACTICE SESSION ONE

READING

Above we've presented examples of two kinds of curiosity-driven scholarly projects: Armstrong and Abel seek to resolve a puzzle, and Walzer and Said explore the complexity of an abstraction. For this exercise, we want you to think about other roles that curiosity can play in scholarly writing.

Begin by selecting a scholarly essay to read. You can work with one of the five articles listed in the Explore section (p. 151), or your teacher may suggest other readings. You may even be able to read an article written by one of your teachers.

Read the essay you've chosen from beginning to end, marking key moments in the argument. Then read the essay again; most academic articles need to be read more than once to be fully understood. As you reread, pay attention to how the scholar organizes ideas, works with sources, presents major points, and addresses readers. Take notes in the margins about the key moments you marked.

After you've read and reread the article with care, take at least 30 minutes to write out answers to the following questions: How did the scholar introduce his or her topic? Where did the writing draw you in? Are there parts of the essay that confused you, or sections where you didn't know enough about the topic or the sources to follow the argument? What parts of the article were particularly clear? Were there passages that prompted you to think new thoughts?

WRITING

Write an essay that reflects on how curiosity gets announced and pursued in the article you've read. Make certain to quote specific passages where you feel the focus of the scholar's curiosity is made clear. What is the status of that curiosity at the end of the article? Have the author's questions been resolved, or have they led to other questions?

PRACTICE SESSION TWO

READING

All of your teachers will have other examples of academic writing they admire. Ask some of them to recommend a few favorite academic articles, chapters, or books. Choose one and read it with an eye toward understanding the curiosity that drives the scholar's project, following the steps in the Reading section of Practice Session One: read, reread, take notes, reflect, and write. Why do you think your teacher recommended that piece of writing? Can you offer an explanation for why it has been influential?

EXPLORE

Zora Neale Hurston once wrote, "research is formalized curiosity." Although some academic prose seems dry and airless, many scholarly writers put their passion and curiosity on display. Hurston's fellow anthropologist, Ruth Behar, challenges her field to recognize ethnography as an art that engages the imagination. Douglas Hofstadter wonders about the importance of analogy in thinking, and proposes that analogy *is* cognition. Anne Harrington also examines how scientists think about thinking; she questions the assumption that neuroscience alone can account for "moral choice, existential passion, and social contracts." David Bartholomae and Shirley Brice Heath both raise questions about how teachers evaluate learning. Bartholomae insists that we rethink our assumptions about how college students learn to write academic essays, and Heath points out how strange it is that teachers judge academic ability with formulaic essays when, by design, these essays curtail "creativity, the pursuit of alternative answers, and the power of collaborative thinking in academic life."

Bartholomae, David. "Inventing the University." *When a Writer Can't Write: Studies in Writer's Block and Other Composing-Process Problems.* Ed. Mike Rose. New York: Guilford, 1985. 134–65. Print.

Behar, Ruth. "Ethnography in a Time of Blurred Genres." *Anthropology and Humanism* 32.2 (2007). 145–55. Web.

Harrington, Anne. "How to House a Mind Inside a Brain: Lessons from History." *EMBO Reports* 8, no. S1 (2007). Web.

Heath, Shirley Brice. "Rethinking the Sense of the Past: The Essay as Legacy of the Epigram." *Theory and Practice in the Teaching of Writing: Rethinking the Discipline.* Ed. Lee Odell. Carbondale: Southern Illinois UP, 1993. 105–31. Print.

Hofstadter, Douglas R. "Analogy as the Core of Cognition." Stanford Presidential Lectures in the Humanities and Arts. Web.

Argument at Work: Sonia Sotomayor and Principled Openness

On August 8, 2009, Sonia Sotomayor, who was born and raised in a working-class Puerto Rican family in the Bronx, was sworn in as the first Latina member of the United States Supreme Court. Since then, Sotomayor has written a coming-of-age memoir, *My Beloved World* (simultaneously published in Spanish as *Mi mundo adorado*), in which she describes her early years living in public housing with an alcoholic father and a distant mother, her studies at Princeton University and Yale Law School, and the steps early in her career that put her on a path to the Supreme Court.

Sotomayor credits many mentors and friends for contributing to her success, but her memoir also makes it clear that her success is due to her intellectual habits of mind, which were evident before she graduated from Cardinal Spellman High

School. As a member of that school's forensics club, Sotomayor discovered that she loved vigorous argument. She enjoyed arguing not because she was always certain of her position but because she took pleasure in the sport of rhetorical sparring and in testing her ideas against challenges.

She recalls that her manner of using argument as a tool for learning—as opposed to sticking to her original position no matter what new information and ideas she encountered—didn't always inspire the affection or admiration of her competitors. At a forensics meet during her junior year of high school, she encountered an especially hostile opponent who accused her of never being willing to take a strong stand and of thinking too much about how her position depended on context. Sotomayor thought it was valuable to be open to persuasion, but her fellow debater found it a mark of weakness because Sotomayor's position on an issue was never predictable. She accused Sotomayor of being without principles.

Sotomayor writes in her memoir's epilogue that she grappled with that accusation for decades. She concedes that she would be at fault if she truly lacked principles and had no moral center. She counts among her core values "integrity, fairness, and the avoidance of cruelty." At the same time, she reasons, "if you held to principle so passionately, so inflexibly, indifferent to the particulars of circumstance—the full range of what human beings, with all their flaws and foibles, might endure or create—if you enthroned principle above even reason, weren't you then abdicating the responsibilities of a thinking person?" Her practice as a Supreme Court justice is built on this habitual questioning and curiosity, on an openness to individual difference and a willingness to learn. She concludes: "Concern for individuals, the imperative of treating them with dignity and respect for their ideas and needs, regardless of one's own views—these too are surely principles and as worthy as any of being deemed inviolable. To remain open to understandings—perhaps even to principles—as yet not determined is the least that learning requires, its barest threshold."

part 2

Reading and Understanding Arguments

CHAPTER

9

Everything Is an Argument

On May 7, 2014, First Lady of the United States Michelle Obama turned to new media to express her concern over the kidnapping of more than 200 young Nigerian girls by the terrorist group Boko Haram. Her tweet, along with an accompanying photo highlighting the trending hashtag #BringBackOurGirls, ramped up an argument over what the international community could do to stop an organization responsible for thousands of deaths in northeastern Nigeria. In bringing her appeal to Twitter, the First Lady acknowledged the persuasive power of social media like Facebook, YouTube, Instagram, and innumerable political and social blogs. The hashtag itself, it would appear, had become a potent tool for rallying audiences around the globe to support specific ideas or causes. But to what ends?

The First Lady ✔
@FLOTUS
       Follow

Our prayers are with the missing Nigerian girls and their families. It's time to #BringBackOurGirls. -mo

Left: Pacific Press/Getty Images; right: © Akintunde Akinleye/Corbis

Just weeks before Obama's notable appeal, a U.S. State Department spokesperson Jen Psaki drew attention with a tweet of her own aimed at countering attempts by Russian social media to co-opt the U.S. State Department's #UnitedforUkraine hashtag:

The world stands #UnitedforUkraine. Let's hope that the #Kremlin & @mfa_russia will live by the promise of hashtag

The Russian government, it seems, having just annexed the Crimea region and threatening all of Ukraine, was showing more skill than Western nations at using Twitter and other social media to win propaganda points in the diplomatic crisis. Yet Psaki's response via Twitter earned her disapproval from those who interpreted her social media riposte as further evidence of U.S. weakness. For instance, Texas senator Ted Cruz tweeted in reply to Psaki:

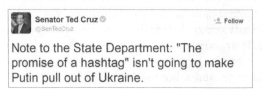

Note to the State Department: "The promise of a hashtag" isn't going to make Putin pull out of Ukraine.

Even Michelle Obama took heat for her earnest appeal on behalf of kidnapped girls the same age as her own daughters. While celebrities such as Amy Poehler and Mary J. Blige posted supportive items, Obama's tweet got quick international pushback from those who argued (in 140 characters) that the anti-terrorist use of drones by the U.S. military was no less reprehensible than the tactics of Boko Haram. And domestic critics saw Obama's message as a substitute for real action, with columnist Jeffrey Goldberg chiding well-intentioned activists with a dose of reality:

All the charity bicycle rides in the world won't get those girls back from Boko Haram. Marines, however, might work.

Clearly, social media play out on crowded, two-way channels, with claims and counterclaims whizzing by, fast and furious. Such tools reach audiences and they also create them, offering an innovative way to make and share arguments. Just as important, anyone, anywhere, with access to a phone, tablet, or other electronic device, can launch arguments that circle the globe in seconds. Social networking and digital tools are increasingly available to all.

We've opened this chapter with dramatic, perhaps troubling, examples of Twitter controversies to introduce our claim that arguments are all around us, in every medium, in every genre, in everything we do. There may be an argument on the T-shirt you put on in the morning, in the sports column you read on the bus, in the prayers you utter before an exam, in the off-the-cuff political remarks of a teacher lecturing, in the assurances of a health center nurse that "This won't hurt one bit."

The clothes you wear, the foods you eat, and the groups you join make nuanced, sometimes unspoken assertions about who you are and what you value. So an argument can be any text—written, spoken, aural, or visual—that expresses a point of view. In fact, some theorists claim that language is inherently persuasive. When you say, "Hi, how's it going?" in one sense you're arguing that your hello deserves a response. Even humor makes an argument when it causes readers to recognize—through bursts of laughter or just a faint smile—how things are and how they might be different.

More obvious as arguments are those that make direct claims based on or drawn from evidence. Such writing often moves readers to recognize problems and to consider solutions. Persuasion of this kind is usually easy to recognize:

The National Minimum Drinking Age Act, passed by Congress 30 years ago this July, is a gross violation of civil liberties and must be repealed. It is absurd and unjust that young Americans can vote, marry, enter contracts, and serve in the military at 18 but cannot buy an alcoholic drink in a bar or restaurant.

—Camille Paglia, "The Drinking Age Is Past Its Prime"

We will become a society of a million pictures without much memory, a society that looks forward every second to an immediate replication of what it has just done, but one that does not sustain the difficult labor of transmitting culture from one generation to the next.

—Christine Rosen, "The Image Culture"

RESPOND

Can an argument really be any text that expresses a point of view? What kinds of arguments—if any—might be made by the following items?

a Boston Red Sox cap

a Livestrong bracelet

the "explicit lyrics" label on a best-selling rap CD

the health warnings on a package of cigarettes

a Tesla Model S electric car

a pair of Ray-Ban sunglasses

Why We Make Arguments

In the politically divided and entertainment-driven culture of the United States today, the word *argument* may well call up negative images: the hostile scowl or shaking fist of a politician or news "opinionator" who wants to drown out other voices and prevail at all costs. This winner-take-all view turns many citizens off to the whole process of using reasoned conversation to identify, explore, and solve problems. Hoping to avoid personal conflict, many people now sidestep opportunities to speak their mind on issues shaping their lives and work. We want to counter this attitude throughout this book.

Some arguments, of course, *are* aimed at winning, especially those related to politics, business, and law. Two candidates for office, for example, vie for a majority of votes; the makers of one smartphone try to outsell their competitors by offering more features at a lower price; and two lawyers try to outwit each other in pleading to a judge and jury. In your college writing, you may also be called on to make arguments that appeal to a "judge" and "jury" (perhaps your instructor and classmates). You might, for instance, argue that students in every field should be required to engage in service learning projects. In doing so, you will need to offer better arguments or more convincing evidence than potential opponents—such as those who might regard service learning as a politicized or coercive form of education. You can do so reasonably and responsibly, no name-calling required.

There are many reasons to argue and principled ways to do so. We explore some of them in this section.

Arguments to Convince and Inform

We're stepping into an argument ourselves in drawing what we hope is a useful distinction between *convincing* and—in the next section—*persuading*. (Feel free to disagree with us.) Arguments to convince lead audiences to accept a claim as true or reasonable—based on information or evidence that seems factual and reliable; arguments to persuade then seek to move people beyond conviction to *action*. Academic arguments often combine both elements.

Many news reports and analyses, white papers, and academic articles aim to convince audiences by broadening what they know about a subject. Such fact-based arguments might have no motives beyond laying out what the facts are. Here's an opening paragraph from a 2014 news story by Anahad O'Connor in the *New York Times* that itself launched a thousand arguments (and lots of huzzahs) simply by reporting the results of a recent scientific study:

> Many of us have long been told that saturated fat, the type found in meat, butter and cheese, causes heart disease. But a large and exhaustive new analysis by a team of international scientists found no evidence that eating saturated fat increased heart attacks and other cardiac events.
>
> —*Anahad O'Connor, "Study Questions Fat and Heart Disease Link"*

Wow. You can imagine how carefully the reporter walked through the scientific data, knowing how this new information might be understood and repurposed by his readers.

Similarly, in a college paper on viability of nuclear power as an alternative source of energy, you might compare the health and safety record of a nuclear plant to that of other forms of energy. Depending upon your findings and your interpretation of the data, the result of your fact-based presentation might be to raise or alleviate concerns readers have about nuclear energy. Of course, your decision to write the argument might be driven by your conviction that nuclear power is much safer than most people believe.

Even an image can offer an argument designed both to inform and to convince. On the following page, for example, editorial cartoonist Bob Englehart finds a way to frame an issue on the minds of many students today, the burden of crushing debt. As Englehart presents it, the problem is impossible to ignore.

FIGURE 9.1 © Bob Englehart/Cagle Cartoons, Inc.

Arguments to Persuade

Today, climate change may be the public issue that best illustrates the chasm that sometimes separates conviction from persuasion. The weight of scientific research may convince people that the earth is warming, but persuading them to act on that knowledge doesn't follow easily. How then does change occur? Some theorists suggest that persuasion—understood as moving people to do more than nod in agreement—is best achieved via appeals to emotions such as fear, anger, envy, pride, sympathy, or hope. We think that's an oversimplification. The fact is that persuasive arguments, whether in advertisements, political blogs, YouTube videos, or newspaper editorials, draw upon *all* the appeals of rhetoric (see p. 172) to motivate people to act—whether it be to buy a product, pull a lever for a candidate, or volunteer for a civic organization. Here, once again, is Camille Paglia driving home her argument that the 1984 federal law raising the drinking age in the United States to 21 was a catastrophic decision in need of reversal:

> What this cruel 1984 law did is deprive young people of safe spaces where they could happily drink cheap beer, socialize, chat, and flirt in a free but controlled public environment. Hence in the 1980s we immediately got the scourge of crude binge drinking at campus fraternity keg parties, cut off from the adult world. Women in that boorish free-for-all were suddenly fighting off date rape. Club drugs—Ecstasy, methamphetamine, ketamine (a veterinary tranquilizer)—surged at raves for teenagers and on the gay male circuit scene.

Paglia chooses to dramatize her argument by sharply contrasting a safer, more supportive past with a vastly more dangerous present when drinking was forced underground and young people turned to highly risky behaviors. She doesn't hesitate to name them either: binge drinking, club drugs, raves, and, most seriously, date rape. This highly rhetorical, one might say *emotional*, argument pushes readers hard to endorse a call for serious action—the repeal of the current drinking age law.

FIGURE 9.2 Admit it, Duchess of Cornwall. You *knew* abandoned dogs need homes, but it was heartrending photos on the Battersea Dogs & Cats Home Web site that *persuaded* you to visit the shelter. WPA Pool/Getty Images

RESPOND

Apply the distinction made here between convincing and persuading to the way people respond to two or three current political or social issues. Is there a useful distinction between being convinced and being persuaded? Explain your position.

Arguments to Make Decisions

Closely allied to arguments to convince and persuade are arguments to examine the options in important matters, both civil and personal—from managing out-of-control deficits to choosing careers. Arguments to make decisions occur all the time in the public arena, where they are often slow to evolve, caught up in electoral or legal squabbles, and yet driven by a genuine desire to find consensus. In recent years, for instance, Americans have argued hard to make decisions about health care, the civil rights of same-sex couples, and the status of more than 11 million immigrants in the country. Subjects so complex aren't debated in straight lines. They get haggled over in every imaginable medium by thousands of writers, politicians, and ordinary citizens working alone or via political organizations to have their ideas considered.

For college students, choosing a major can be an especially momentous personal decision, and one way to go about making that decision is to argue your way through several alternatives. By the time you've explored the pros and cons of each alternative, you should be a little closer to a reasonable and defensible decision.

Sometimes decisions, however, are not so easy to make.

FIGURE 9.3 www.CartoonStock.com

Arguments to Understand and Explore

Arguments to make decisions often begin as choices between opposing positions already set in stone. But is it possible to examine important issues in more open-ended ways? Many situations, again in civil or personal arenas, seem to call for arguments that genuinely explore possibilities without constraints or prejudices. If there's an "opponent" in such situations at all (often there is not), it's likely to be the status quo or a current trend which, for one reason or another, puzzles just about everyone. For example, in trying to sort through the extraordinary complexities of the 2011 budget debate, philosophy professor Gary Gutting was able to show how two distinguished economists—John Taylor and Paul Krugman—draw completely different conclusions from the exact same sets of facts. Exploring how such a thing could occur led Gutting to conclude that the two economists were arguing from the same facts, all right, but that they did not have *all* the facts possible. Those missing or unknown facts allowed them to fill in the blanks as they could, thus leading them to different conclusions. By discovering the source of a paradox, Gutting potentially opened new avenues for understanding.

Exploratory arguments can also be personal, such as Zora Neale Hurston's ironic exploration of racism and of her own identity in the essay "How It Feels to Be Colored Me." If you keep a journal or blog, you have no doubt found yourself making arguments to explore issues near and dear to you. Perhaps the essential argument in any such piece is the writer's realization that a problem exists—and that the writer or reader needs to understand it and respond constructively to it if possible.

Explorations of ideas that begin by trying to understand another's perspective have been described as **invitational arguments** by researchers Sonja Foss, Cindy Griffin, and Josina Makau. Such arguments are interested in inviting others to join in mutual explorations of ideas based on discovery and respect. Another kind of argument, called **Rogerian argument** (after psychotherapist Carl Rogers), approaches audiences in similarly nonthreatening ways, finding common ground and establishing trust among those who disagree about issues. Writers who take a Rogerian approach try to see where the other person is coming from, looking for "both/and" or "win/win" solutions whenever possible. (For more on Rogerian strategies, see Chapter 15.)

"You say it's a win-win, but what if you're wrong-wrong and it all goes bad-bad?"

FIGURE 9.4 The risks of Rogerian argument
© David Sipress/The New Yorker Collection/The Cartoon Bank

RESPOND

What are your reasons for making arguments? Keep notes for two days about every single argument you make, using our broad definition to guide you. Then identify your reasons: How many times did you aim to convince? To inform? To persuade? To explore? To understand?

Occasions for Argument

In a fifth-century BCE textbook of **rhetoric** (the art of persuasion), the philosopher Aristotle provides an ingenious strategy for classifying arguments based on their perspective on time—past, future, and present. His ideas still help us to appreciate the role arguments play in society in the twenty-first century. As you consider Aristotle's occasions for argument, remember that all such classifications overlap (to a certain extent) and that we live in a world much different than his.

Arguments about the Past

Debates about what has happened in the past, what Aristotle called **forensic arguments**, are the red meat of government, courts, businesses, and academia. People want to know who did what in the past, for what reasons, and with what liability. When you argue a speeding ticket in court, you are making a forensic argument, claiming perhaps that you weren't over the limit or that the officer's radar was faulty. A judge will have to decide what exactly happened in the past in the unlikely case you push the issue that far.

More consequentially, in 2014 the federal government and General Motors found themselves deeply involved in arguments about the past as investigators sought to determine just exactly how the massive auto company had allowed a serious defect in the ignition switches of its cars to go undisclosed and uncorrected for a decade. Drivers and passengers died or were injured as engines shut down and airbags failed to go off in subsequent collisions. Who at General Motors was responsible for not diagnosing the fault? Were any engineers or executives liable for covering up the problem? And how should victims of this product defect or their families be compensated? These were all forensic questions to be thoroughly investigated, argued, and answered by regulatory panels and courts.

FIGURE 9.5 Mary Barra, the chief executive officer of General Motors, testifies before a congressional panel looking into problems with ignition switches in the company's cars. AP Photo/Ron Sachs/picture-alliance/dpa/AP Images

From an academic perspective, consider the lingering forensic arguments over Christopher Columbus's "discovery" of America. Are his expeditions cause for celebration or notably unhappy chapters in human history? Or some of both? Such arguments about past actions—heated enough to spill over into the public realm—are common in disciplines such as history, philosophy, and ethics.

Arguments about the Future

Debates about what will or should happen in the future—**deliberative arguments**—often influence policies or legislation for the future. *Should local or state governments allow or even encourage the use of self-driving cars on public roads? Should colleges and universities lend support to more dual-credit programs so that students can earn college credits while still in high school? Should coal-fired power plants be phased out of our energy grid?* These are the sorts of deliberative questions that legislatures, committees, or school boards routinely address when making laws or establishing policies.

But arguments about the future can also be speculative, advancing by means of projections and reasoned guesses, as shown in the following passage from an essay by media maven Marc Prensky. He is arguing that it is time for some college or university to be the first to ban physical, that is to say *paper*, books on its campus, a controversial proposal to say the least:

> Colleges and professors exist, in great measure, to help "liberate" and connect the knowledge and ideas in books. We should certainly pass on to our students the ability to do this. But in the future those liberated ideas—the ones in the books (the author's words), and the ones about the books (the reader's own notes, all readers' thoughts and commentaries)—should be available with a few keystrokes. So, as counterintuitive as it may sound, eliminating physical books from college campuses would be a positive step for our 21st-century students, and, I believe, for 21st-century scholarship as well. Academics, researchers, and particularly teachers need to move to the tools of the future. Artifacts belong in museums, not in our institutions of higher learning.
>
> —*Marc Prensky, "In the 21st-Century University, Let's Ban Books"*

Arguments about the Present

Arguments about the present—what Aristotle terms **epideictic** or **ceremonial arguments**—explore the current values of a society, affirming or challenging its widely shared beliefs and core assumptions. Epideictic arguments are often made at public and formal events such as inaugural addresses, sermons, eulogies, memorials, and graduation speeches. Members of the audience listen carefully as credible speakers share their wisdom. For example, as the selection of college commencement speakers has grown increasingly contentious, Ruth J. Simmons, the first African American woman to head an Ivy League college, used the opportunity of such an address (herself standing in for a rejected speaker) to offer a timely and ringing endorsement of free speech. Her words perfectly illustrate epideictic rhetoric:

> Universities have a special obligation to protect free speech, open discourse and the value of protest. The collision of views and ideologies is in the DNA of the academic enterprise. No collision avoidance technology is needed here. The noise from this discord may cause others to criticize the legitimacy of the academic enterprise, but how can knowledge advance without the questions that overturn misconceptions, push further into previously impenetrable areas of inquiry and assure us stunning breakthroughs in human knowledge? If there is anything that colleges must encourage and protect it is the persistent questioning of the status quo. Our health as a nation, our health as women, our health as an industry requires it.
>
> —Ruth J. Simmons, Smith College, 2014

Perhaps more common than Smith's impassioned address are values arguments that examine contemporary culture, praising what's admirable and blaming what's not. In the following argument, student Latisha Chisholm looks at the state of rap music after Tupac Shakur:

> With the death of Tupac, not only did one of the most intriguing rap rivalries of all time die, but the motivation for rapping seems to have changed. Where money had always been a plus, now it is obviously more important than wanting to express the hardships of Black communities. With current rappers, the positive power that came from the desire to represent Black people is lost. One of the biggest rappers now got his big break while talking about sneakers. Others announce retirement without really having done much for the soul or for Black people's morale. I equate new rappers to NFL players that don't love the game anymore. They're only in it for the money… It looks like the voice of a people has lost its heart.
>
> —Latisha Chisholm, "Has Rap Lost Its Soul?"

As in many ceremonial arguments, Chisholm here reinforces common values such as representing one's community honorably and fairly.

FIGURE 9.6 Are rappers since Tupac—like Jay Z—only in it for the money? Many epideictic arguments either praise or blame contemporary culture in this way. Michael N. Todaro/FilmMagic/Getty Images

RESPOND

In a recent magazine, newspaper, or blog, find three editorials—one that makes a forensic argument, one a deliberative argument, and one a ceremonial argument. Analyze the arguments by asking these questions: Who is arguing? What purposes are the writers trying to achieve? To whom are they directing their arguments? Then decide whether the arguments' purposes have been achieved and how you know.

Occasions for Argument

	PAST	FUTURE	PRESENT
What is it called?	Forensic	Deliberative	Epideictic
What are its concerns?	What happened in the past?	What should be done in the future?	Who or what deserves praise or blame?
What does it look like?	Court decisions, legal briefs, legislative hearings, investigative reports, academic studies	White papers, proposals, bills, regulations, mandates	Eulogies, graduation speeches, inaugural addresses, roasts

Kinds of Argument

Yet another way of categorizing arguments is to consider their status or stasis—that is, the specific *kinds of issues they address*. This approach, called **stasis theory**, was used in ancient Greek and Roman civilizations to provide questions designed to help citizens and lawyers work their way through legal cases. The status questions were posed in sequence because each depended on answers from the preceding ones. Together, the queries helped determine the point of contention in an argument—where the parties disagreed or what exactly had to be proven. A modern version of those questions might look like the following:

- Did something happen?
- What is its nature?
- What is its quality or cause?
- What actions should be taken?

Each stasis question explores a different aspect of a problem and uses different evidence or techniques to reach conclusions. You can use these questions to explore the aspects of any topic you're considering. You'll discover that we use the stasis issues to define key types of argument in Part 3.

Did Something Happen? Arguments of Fact

There's no point in arguing a case until its basic facts are established. So an **argument of fact** usually involves a statement that can be proved or disproved with specific evidence or testimony. For example, the question of pollution of the oceans — is it really occurring? — might seem relatively easy to settle. Either scientific data prove that the oceans are being dirtied as a result of human activity, or they don't. But to settle the matter, writers and readers need to ask a number of other questions about the "facts":

- Where did the facts come from?
- Are they reliable?
- Is there a problem with the facts?
- Where did the problem begin and what caused it?

For more on arguments based on facts, see Chapters 12 and 16.

What Is the Nature of the Thing? Arguments of Definition

Some of the most hotly debated issues in American life today involve questions of definition: we argue over the nature of the human fetus, the meaning of "amnesty" for immigrants, the boundaries of sexual assault. As you might guess, issues of definition have mighty consequences, and decades of debate may nonetheless leave the matter unresolved. Here, for example, is how one type of sexual assault is defined in an important 2007 report submitted to the U.S. Department of Justice by the National Institute of Justice:

> We consider as incapacitated sexual assault any unwanted sexual contact occurring when a victim is unable to provide consent or stop what is happening because she is passed out, drugged, drunk, incapacitated, or asleep, regardless of whether the perpetrator was responsible for her substance use or whether substances were administered without her knowledge. We break down incapacitated sexual assault into four subtypes....
>
> — "The Campus Sexual Assault (CSA) Study: Final Report"

The specifications of the definition go on for another two hundred words, each of consequence in determining how sexual assault on college campuses might be understood, measured, and addressed.

Of course many **arguments of definition** are less weighty than this, though still hotly contested: Is playing video games a sport? Can Batman be a tragic figure? Is Hillary Clinton a moderate or a progressive? (For more about arguments of definition, see Chapter 17.)

What Is the Quality or Cause of the Thing?
Arguments of Evaluation

Arguments of evaluation present criteria and then measure individual people, ideas, or things against those standards. For instance, a *Washington Post* story examining long-term trend lines in SAT reading scores opened with this qualitative assessment of the results:

> Reading scores on the SAT for the high school class of 2012 reached a four-decade low, putting a punctuation mark on a gradual decline in the ability of college-bound teens to read passages and answer questions about sentence structure, vocabulary and meaning on the college entrance exam...: Scores among every racial group except for those of Asian descent declined from 2006 levels. A majority of test takers—57 percent—did not score high enough to indicate likely success in college, according to the College Board, the organization that administers the test.
>
> —*Lyndsey Layton and Emma Brown,*
> *"SAT Reading Scores Hit a Four-Decade Low"*

The final sentence is particularly telling, putting the test results in context. More than half the high school test-takers may not be ready for college-level readings.

In examining a circumstance or situation like this, we are often led to wonder what accounts for it: *Why are the test scores declining? Why are some groups underperforming?* And, in fact, the authors of the brief *Post* story do follow up on some questions of cause and effect:

> The 2012 SAT scores come after a decade of efforts to raise test scores under the No Child Left Behind law, the federal education initiative crafted by President George W. Bush. Critics say the law failed to address the barriers faced by many test takers.

> "Some kids are coming to school hungry, some without the health care they need, without the vocabulary that middle-class kids come to school with, even in kindergarten," said Helen F. Ladd, a professor of public policy and economics at Duke University.

Although evaluations differ from causal analyses, in practice the boundaries between stasis questions are often porous: particular arguments have a way of defining their own issues.

For much more about arguments of evaluation, see Chapter 18; for causal arguments, see Chapter 19.

FIGURE 9.7 The No Child Left Behind Act was signed in 2002
with great hopes and bipartisan support. AFP/Getty Images

What Actions Should Be Taken? Proposal Arguments

After facts in a controversy have been confirmed, definitions agreed on, evaluations
made, and causes traced, it may be time for a **proposal argument** answering the
question *Now, what do we do about all this?* For example, in developing an argument
about out-of-control student fees at your college, you might use all the prior stasis
questions to study the issue and determine exactly how much and for what reasons
these costs are escalating. Only then will you be prepared to offer knowledgeable
suggestions for action. In examining a nationwide move to eliminate remedial
education in four-year colleges, John Cloud offers a notably moderate proposal to
address the problem:

> Students age twenty-two and over account for 43 percent of those in remedial
> classrooms, according to the National Center for Developmental Education…,
> [But] 55 percent of those needing remediation must take just one course. Is
> it too much to ask them to pay extra for that class or take it at a community
> college?
>
> —*John Cloud, "Who's Ready for College?"*

For more about proposal arguments, see Chapter 20.

STASIS QUESTIONS AT WORK

Suppose you have an opportunity to speak at a student conference on the impact of climate change. You are tentatively in favor of strengthening industrial pollution standards aimed at reducing global warming trends. But to learn more about the issue, you use the stasis questions to get started.

- **Did something happen?** Does global warming exist? *Maybe not*, say many in the oil and gas industry; at best, evidence for global warming is inconclusive. *Yes*, say most scientists and governments; climate change is real and even seems to be accelerating. To come to your conclusion, you'll weigh the facts carefully and identify problems with opposing arguments.

- **What is the nature of the thing?** Skeptics define climate change as a naturally occurring event; most scientists base their definitions on change due to human causes. You look at each definition carefully: *How do the definitions foster the goals of each group? What's at stake for each group in defining it that way?*

- **What is the quality or cause of the thing?** Exploring the differing assessments of damage done by climate change leads you to ask who will gain from such analysis: *Do oil executives want to protect their investments? Do scientists want government money for grants? Where does evidence for the dangers of global warming come from? Who benefits if the dangers are accepted as real and present, and who loses?*

- **What actions should be taken?** If climate change is occurring naturally or causing little harm, then arguably *nothing* needs to be or can be done. But if it is caused mainly by human activity and dangers, action is definitely called for (although not everyone may agree on what such action should be). As you investigate the proposals being made and the reasons behind them, you come closer to developing your own argument.

Appealing to Audiences

Exploring all the occasions and kinds of arguments available will lead you to think about the audience(s) you are addressing and the specific ways you can appeal to them. Audiences for arguments today are amazingly diverse, from the flesh-and-blood person sitting across a desk when you negotiate a student loan to your "friends" on social media, to the "ideal" reader you imagine for whatever you are writing. The figure on the following page suggests just how many dimensions an audience can have as writers and readers negotiate their relationships with a text, whether it be oral, written, or digital.

As you see there, texts usually have **intended readers**, the people writers hope and expect to address—let's say, routine browsers of a newspaper's op-ed page. But writers also shape the responses of these actual readers in ways they imagine as appropriate or desirable—for example, maneuvering readers of editorials into making focused and knowledgeable judgments about politics and culture. Such audiences, as imagined and fashioned by writers within their texts, are called **invoked readers**.

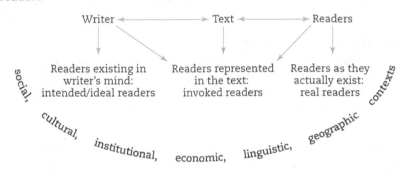

FIGURE 9.8 Readers and writers in context

Making matters even more complicated, readers can respond to writers' maneuvers by choosing to join the invoked audiences, to resist them, or maybe even to ignore them. Arguments may also attract "real" readers from groups not among those that writers originally imagined or expected to reach. You may post something on the Web, for instance, and discover that people you did not intend to address are commenting on it. (For them, the experience may be like reading private email intended for someone else: they find themselves drawn to and fascinated by your ideas!) We think about students like you whenever we write: you are our intended readers. But notice how in dozens of ways, from the images we choose to the tone of our language, we also invoke an audience of people who take writing arguments seriously. We want you to become that kind of reader.

So audiences are *very* complicated and subtle and challenging, and yet you somehow have to attract and even persuade them. As always, Aristotle offers an answer. He identified three time-tested appeals that speakers and writers can use to reach almost any audience, labeling them *pathos*, *ethos*, and *logos*—strategies as effective today as they were in ancient times, though we usually think of them in slightly different terms. Used in the right way and deployed at the right moment, emotional, ethical, and logical appeals have enormous power, as we'll see in subsequent chapters.

RESPOND

You can probably provide concise descriptions of the intended audience for most text-books you have encountered. But can you detect their invoked audiences—that is, the way their authors are imagining (and perhaps shaping) the readers they would like to have? Carefully review this entire chapter, looking for signals and strategies that might identify the audience and readers invoked by the authors of this book.

Emotional Appeals: Pathos

Emotional appeals, or **pathos**, generate emotions (fear, pity, love, anger, jealousy) that the writer hopes will lead the audience to accept a claim. Here is an alarming sentence from a book by Barry B. LePatner arguing that Americans need to make hard decisions about repairing the country's failing infrastructure:

> When the I-35W Bridge in Minneapolis shuddered, buckled, and collapsed during the evening rush hour on Wednesday, August 1, 2007, plunging 111 vehicles into the Mississippi River and sending thirteen people to their deaths, the sudden, apparently inexplicable nature of the event at first gave the appearance of an act of God.
>
> —*Too Big to Fall: America's Failing Infrastructure and the Way Forward*

If you ever drive across a bridge, LePatner has probably gotten your attention. His sober and yet descriptive language helps readers imagine the dire consequence of neglected road maintenance and bad design decisions. Making an emotional appeal like this can dramatize an issue and sometimes even create a bond between writer and readers. (For more about emotional appeals, see Chapter 10.)

Ethical Appeals: Ethos

When writers or speakers come across as trustworthy, audiences are likely to listen to and accept their arguments. That trustworthiness (along with fairness and respect) is a mark of **ethos**, or credibility. Showing that you know what you are talking about exerts an ethical appeal, as does emphasizing that you share values with and respect your audience. Once again, here's Barry LePatner from *Too Big to Fall*, shoring up his authority for writing about problems with America's roads and bridges by invoking the ethos of people even more credible:

> For those who would seek to dismiss the facts that support the thesis of this book, I ask them to consult the many professional engineers in state transportation departments who face these problems on a daily basis. These professionals understand the physics of bridge and road design, and the real problems of ignoring what happens to steel and concrete when they are exposed to the elements without a strict regimen of ongoing maintenance.

It's a sound rhetorical move to enhance credibility this way. For more about ethical appeals, see Chapter 11.

Logical Appeals: Logos

Appeals to logic, or **logos**, are often given prominence and authority in U.S. culture: "Just the facts, ma'am," a famous early TV detective on *Dragnet* used to say. Indeed, audiences respond well to the use of reasons and evidence—to the presentation of facts, statistics, credible testimony, cogent examples, or even a narrative or story that embodies a sound reason in support of an argument. Following almost two hundred pages of facts, statistics, case studies, and arguments about the sad state of American bridges, LePatner can offer this sober, logical, and inevitable conclusion:

> We can no longer afford to ignore the fact that we are in the midst of a transportation funding crisis, which has been exacerbated by an even larger and longer-term problem: how we choose to invest in our infrastructure. It is not difficult to imagine the serious consequences that will unfold if we fail to address the deplorable conditions of our bridges and roads, including the increasingly higher costs we will pay for goods and services that rely on that transportation network, and a concomitant reduction in our standard of living.

For more about logical appeals, see Chapter 12.

Bringing It Home: *Kairos* and the Rhetorical Situation

In Greek mythology, Kairos—the youngest son of Zeus—was the god of opportunity. In images, he is most often depicted as running, and his most unusual characteristic is a shock of hair on his forehead. As Kairos dashes by, you have a chance to seize that lock of hair, thereby seizing the opportune moment; once he passes you by, however, you have missed that chance.

FIGURE 9.9 Ronald Reagan at the Berlin Wall, June 12, 1987:
"Mr. Gorbachev, tear down this wall!" © Dennis Brack/PhotoShot

Kairos is also a term used to describe the most suitable time and place for making an argument and the most opportune ways of expressing it. It is easy to point to shimmering rhetorical moments, when speakers find exactly the right words to stir an audience: Franklin Roosevelt's "We have nothing to fear but fear itself," Ronald Reagan's "Mr. Gorbachev, tear down this wall," and of course Martin Luther King Jr.'s "I have a dream…" But *kairos* matters just as much in less dramatic situations, whenever speakers or writers must size up the core elements of a rhetorical situation to decide how best to make their expertise and ethos work for a particular message aimed at a specific audience. The diagram below hints at the dynamic complexity of the rhetorical situation.

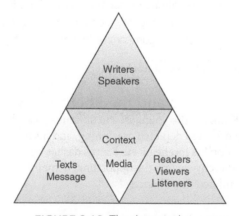

FIGURE 9.10 The rhetorical situation

But rhetorical situations are embedded in contexts of enormous social complexity. The moment you find a subject, you inherit all the knowledge, history, culture, and technological significations that surround it. To lesser and greater degrees (depending on the subject), you also bring personal circumstances into the field—perhaps your gender, your race, your religion, your economic class, your habits of language. And all those issues weigh also upon the people you write to and for.

So considering your rhetorical situation calls on you to think hard about the notion of *kairos*. Being aware of your rhetorical moment means being able to understand and take advantage of dynamic, shifting circumstances and to choose the best (most timely) proofs and evidence for a particular place, situation, and audience. It means seizing moments and enjoying opportunities, not being overwhelmed by them. Doing so might even lead you to challenge the title of this text: *is* everything an argument?

That's what makes writing arguments exciting.

RESPOND

Take a look at the bumper sticker below, and then analyze it. What is its purpose? What kind of argument is it? Which of the stasis questions does it most appropriately respond to? To what audiences does it appeal? What appeals does it make and how?

© Kevin Lamarque/Reuters/Corbis

CULTURAL CONTEXTS FOR ARGUMENT

Considering What's "Normal"

If you want to communicate effectively with people across cultures, then learn about the traditions in those cultures and examine the norms guiding your own behavior:

- Explore your assumptions! Most of us regard our ways of thinking as "normal" or "right." Such assumptions guide our judgments about what works in persuasive situations. But just because it may seem natural to speak bluntly in arguments, consider that others may find such aggression startling or even alarming.

- Remember: ways of arguing differ widely across cultures. Pay attention to how people from groups or cultures other than your own argue, and be sensitive to different paths of thinking you'll encounter as well as to differences in language.

- Don't assume that all people share your cultural values, ethical principles, or political assumptions. People across the world have different ways of defining *family, work*, or *happiness*. As you present arguments to them, consider that they may be content with their different ways of organizing their lives and societies.

- Respect the differences among individuals *within* a given group. Don't expect that every member of a community behaves—or argues—in the same way or shares the same beliefs. Avoid thinking, for instance, that there is a single Asian, African, or Hispanic culture or that Europeans are any less diverse or more predictable than Americans or Canadians in their thinking. In other words, be skeptical of stereotypes.

CHAPTER

10

Arguments Based on Emotion: Pathos

E motional appeals (*appeals to pathos*) are powerful tools for influencing what people think and believe. We all make decisions—even including the most important
ones—based on our feelings. That's what the Food and Drug Administration hoped
to capitalize on when it introduced nine tough warning labels for cigarettes, one of which
you see below. One look at the stained, rotting teeth and the lip sore may arouse emotions of fear strong enough to convince people not to smoke.

In the second panel, Bob Dorigo Jones, an opponent of lawsuit abuse, takes concerns about product liability in a different direction, publishing a book entitled *Remove
Child before Folding: The 101 Stupidest, Silliest, and Wackiest Warning Labels Ever* to
make us laugh and thereby, perhaps, to wonder why common sense seems in such short
supply. In the third panel, editorial cartoonist for the *Indianapolis Star* Gary Varvel uses
the anti-smoking meme to point out a potent irony in burgeoning campaigns to legalize
marijuana.

The arguments packed into these three images all appeal to emotion, and research has shown us that we often make decisions based on just such appeals. So when you hear that formal or academic arguments should rely solely on facts to convince us, remember that facts alone often won't carry the day, even for a worthy cause. The largely successful case made this decade for same-sex marriage provides a notable example of a movement that persuaded people equally by virtue of the reasonableness and the passion of its claims. Like many political and social debates, though, the issue provoked powerful emotions on every side—feelings that sometimes led to extreme words and tactics.

Of course, we don't have to look hard for arguments fueled with emotions such as hatred, envy, and greed, or for campaigns intended to drive wedges between economic or social groups, making them fearful or resentful. For that reason alone, writers should not use emotional appeals rashly or casually. (For more about emotional fallacies, see p. 221.)

Reading Critically for Pathos

On February 24, 2014, Senator Tom Harkin of Iowa, fresh from two "fact-finding" trips to Cuba, described his experiences on the Senate floor in a rambling, forty-minute speech, praising that island nation's accomplishments in health care and education and urging a normalization of Cuban–American relationships. Later that day, Florida senator Marco Rubio, expecting to speak about growing repression in Venezuela, found it impossible to ignore Harkin's rosy view of the "fascinating" socialist experiment ninety miles from the coast of the United States. Seizing a kairotic moment, the first-term senator delivered a passionate fifteen-minute rejoinder to Harkin without a script or teleprompter—though Rubio did use posters prepared originally for the Venezuelan talk. After a sarcastic taunt ("Sounded like he had a wonderful trip visiting what he described as a real paradise"), Rubio quickly turned serious, even angry, as he offered his take on the country Harkin had toured:

> I heard him also talk about these great doctors that they have in Cuba. I have no doubt they're very talented. I've met a bunch of them. You know where I met them? In the United States because they defected. Because in Cuba, doctors would rather drive a taxi cab or work in a hotel than be a doctor. I wonder if they spoke to him about the outbreak of cholera that they've been unable to control, or about the three-tiered system of health care that exists where foreigners and government officials get health care much better than that that's available to the general population.

The speech thereafter settles into a rhythm of patterned inquiries designed to raise doubts about what Senator Harkin had seen, Rubio's informal language rippling with contempt for his colleague's naïveté:

I heard about their [the Cubans'] wonderful literacy rate, how everyone in Cuba knows how to read. That's fantastic. Here's the problem: they can only read censored stuff. They're not allowed access to the Internet. The only newspapers they're allowed to read are *Granma* or the ones produced by the government....

He talked about these great baseball players that are coming from Cuba—and they are. But I wonder if they informed him [that] every single one of those guys playing in the Major Leagues defected. They left Cuba to play here....

So it's great to have literacy, but if you don't have access to the information, what's the point of it? So I wish somebody would have asked about that on that trip....

I wonder if anybody asked about terrorism, because Cuba is a state sponsor of terrorism....

Language this heated and pointed has risks, especially when a young legislator is taking on a genial and far more experienced colleague. But Rubio, the son of Cuban immigrants, isn't shy about allowing his feelings to show. Segueing to his original topic—growing political repression in socialist Venezuela—he uses the kind of verbal repetition common in oratory to drive home his major concern about Cuba, its influence on other nations:

Let me tell you what the Cubans are really good at, because they don't know how to run their economy, they don't know how to build, they don't know how to govern a people. What they are really good at is repression. What they are really good at is shutting off information to the Internet and to radio and television and social media. That's what they're really good at. And they're not just good at it domestically, they're good exporters of these things.

FIGURE 10.1 As originally aired on C-SPAN2 on February 24 2014

Rubio's actual audience in the U.S. Senate was very small, but today all speeches from that chamber are carried nationwide and archived by C-SPAN, and in the age of YouTube, bits and pieces of political addresses reach many listeners. Former speechwriter and *Wall Street Journal* columnist Peggy Noonan was among those who caught Rubio's remarks and blogged about them: "We have pressed in these parts for American political figures to speak clearly and with moral confidence about American sympathies in various international disputes. Rubio's speech is honest political indignation successfully deployed." You can watch the entire speech on C-SPAN's Web site (listed as "Rubio Speech on Venezuela") to see if you agree. And though Cuba and the United States did re-establish diplomatic relationships roughly ten months after the Harkin/Rubio exchange, issues raised by both senators—from health care to the immigration status of Cuban baseball players—will likely be argued for years to come.

RESPOND

Working with a classmate, make a list of reasons why speakers in highly charged situations might need to use emotional appeals cautiously, even sparingly. What consequences might heightened emotional appeals lead to? What is at stake for the speaker in such situations, in terms of credibility and ethos? What are the advantages of evoking emotions in support of your claims or ideas?

Using Emotions to Build Bridges

You may sometimes want to use emotions to connect with readers to assure them that you understand their experiences or "feel their pain," to borrow a sentiment popularized by President Bill Clinton. Such a bridge is especially important when you're writing about matters that readers regard as sensitive. Before they'll trust you, they'll want assurances that you understand the issues in depth. If you strike the right emotional note, you'll establish an important connection. That's what Apple founder Steve Jobs does in a much-admired 2005 commencement address in which he tells the audience that he doesn't have a fancy speech, just three stories from his life:

> My second story is about love and loss. I was lucky. I found what I loved to do early in life. Woz [Steve Wozniak] and I started Apple in my parents' garage when I was twenty. We worked hard and in ten years, Apple had grown from just the two of us in a garage into a $2 billion company with over four thousand employees. We'd just released our finest creation, the Macintosh, a year earlier, and I'd just turned thirty, and then I got fired. How can you get fired from a company you started? Well, as Apple grew, we hired someone who I

thought was very talented to run the company with me, and for the first year or so, things went well. But then our visions of the future began to diverge, and eventually we had a falling out. When we did, our board of directors sided with him, and so at thirty, I was out, and very publicly out....

I didn't see it then, but it turned out that getting fired from Apple was the best thing that could have ever happened to me. The heaviness of being successful was replaced by the lightness of being a beginner again, less sure about everything. It freed me to enter one of the most creative periods in my life. During the next five years I started a company named NeXT, another company named Pixar and fell in love with an amazing woman who would become my wife. Pixar went on to create the world's first computer-animated feature film, *Toy Story*, and is now the most successful animation studio in the world.

—Steve Jobs, *"You've Got to Find What You Love, Jobs Says"*

In no obvious way is Jobs's recollection a formal argument. But it prepares his audience to accept the advice he'll give later in his speech, at least partly because he's speaking from meaningful personal experiences.

A more obvious way to build an emotional tie is simply to help readers identify with your experiences. If, like Georgina Kleege, you were blind and wanted to argue for more sensible attitudes toward blind people, you might ask readers in the first paragraph of your argument to confront their prejudices. Here Kleege, a writer and college instructor, makes an emotional point by telling a story:

I tell the class, "I am legally blind." There is a pause, a collective intake of breath. I feel them look away uncertainly and then look back. After all, I just said I couldn't see. Or did I? I had managed to get there on my own—no cane, no dog, none of the usual trappings of blindness. Eyeing me askance now, they might detect that my gaze is not quite focused.... They watch me glance down, or towards the door where someone's coming in late. I'm just like anyone else.

—Georgina Kleege, *"Call It Blindness"*

Given the way she narrates the first day of class, readers are as likely to identify with the students as with Kleege, imagining themselves sitting in a classroom, facing a sightless instructor, confronting their own prejudices about the blind. Kleege wants to put her audience on the edge emotionally.

Let's consider another rhetorical situation: how do you win over an audience when the logical claims that you're making are likely to go against what many in the audience believe? Once again, a slightly risky appeal to emotions on a personal level may work. That's the tack that Michael Pollan takes in bringing readers to consider that "the great moral struggle of our time will be for the rights of animals." In introducing his lengthy exploratory argument, Pollan uses personal experience to appeal to his audience:

> The first time I opened Peter Singer's *Animal Liberation*, I was dining alone at the Palm, trying to enjoy a rib-eye steak cooked medium-rare. If this sounds like a good recipe for cognitive dissonance (if not indigestion), that was sort of the idea. Preposterous as it might seem to supporters of animal rights, what I was doing was tantamount to reading *Uncle Tom's Cabin* on a plantation in the Deep South in 1852.
>
> —*Michael Pollan, "An Animal's Place"*

In creating a vivid image of his first encounter with Singer's book, Pollan's opening builds a bridge between himself as a person trying to enter into the animal rights debate in a fair and open-minded, if still skeptical, way and readers who might be passionate about either side of this argument.

THE BIRTH OF A VEGETARIAN

FIGURE 10.2 A visual version of Michael Pollan's rhetorical situation.
© Robert Mankoff/The New Yorker Collection/The Cartoon Bank

Using Emotions to Sustain an Argument

You can also use emotional appeals to make logical claims stronger or more memorable. That is the way that photographs and other images add power to arguments. In a TV attack ad, the scowling cell phone video of a disheveled political opponent may do as much damage as the insinuation that he bought his home on the cheap from a financier convicted of fraud. In contrast, a human face smiling or showing honest emotion can sell just about any product—that's why indicted political figures now routinely smile for their mug shots. Using emotion is tricky, however. Lay on too much feeling—especially sentiments like outrage, pity, or shame, which make people uncomfortable—and you may offend the very audiences you hoped to convince.

Still, strong emotions can add energy to a passage or an entire argument, as they do when Walter Russell Mead, editor-at-large of the *American Interest*, argues about what *really* motivates Americans to donate lavishly to many colleges and universities. As you read the following excerpt, notice how the author paints vivid pictures of people at college sporting events, describes the emotions at those games, and then argues what schools really need to do to win contributions:

> But if you want to understand why so many generations of Americans have sent so much dough back to the campuses where they wasted some of the happiest years of their lives, watch the intensity of the tens of thousands of fans who attend these events. Look at the shirtless boys with faces and torsos painted in the school colors; look at the cheerleaders on the fields, the "waves" surging through the stands.
>
> American universities, those temples of reason (at their best), are tribes. The kids bond to each other and to their schools in the heat of the intense emotions that these contests generate. Those shirtless kids covered in paint, shivering in the November weather as they cheer their team on, will be prosperous, middle-aged alumni one day—and when they are, they will still be stirred by the memory of the emotions and the loyalty that brought them out to the field.
>
> If you want your alumni to give, you first have to make them fall in love with your school. This is not about having better chemistry programs or more faculty with higher name recognition than the school up the road. It is not about scoring higher on world indices of university quality. It is about competition, drama, intensity, about hope and fear, collective celebrations or collective disasters, seared into young and impressionable hearts where they will never be forgotten—and where they will be annually renewed as each sport in its season produces new highs and lows, new hopes and fears. Alumni watching

their schools' games on TV, or celebrating or mourning their schools' results each week with friends, family and colleagues, are renewing their ties with their alma maters affirming that being an "Aggie" or a "Tar Heel" is an *identity*, not a line on the resume.

This is why most of them give. It is irrational and tribal love. It is intense emotion, not a vague sense of obligation or philanthropy. They want to beat State.

—*Walter Russell Mead and The American Interest staff, "It All Begins with Football"*

Mead's claim, emotional in itself, may not be exactly what college and university administrators and faculty want to hear. But in using language this evocative, he makes his argument memorable, hoping perhaps to make general readers admit how they have felt and acted themselves.

FIGURE 10.3 Kevin C. Cox/Getty Images

It's difficult to gauge how much emotion will work in a given argument. Some issues—such as racism, immigration, abortion, and gun control—provoke strong feelings and, as a result, are often argued on emotional terms. But even issues that seem deadly dull—such as reform of federal student loan programs—can be argued passionately when proposed changes in these programs are set in human terms: reduce support for college loans and Kai, Riley, and Jayden end up in dead-end, low-paying jobs; don't reform the program and we're looking at another Wall Street–sized loan bailout and subsequent recession. Both alternatives might scare people into paying enough attention to take political action.

Using Humor

Humor has always played an important role in argument, sometimes as the sugar that makes the medicine go down. You can slip humor into an argument to put readers at ease, thereby making them more open to a proposal you have to offer. It's hard to say *no* when you're laughing. Humor also makes otherwise sober people suspend their judgment and even their prejudices, perhaps because the surprise and naughtiness of wit are combustive: they provoke laughter or smiles, not reflection. Who can resist a no-holds-barred attack on a famous personality, such as this assessment of *Twilight* star Kristen Stewart:

> The original scoffing, scowling, stammering, stuttering, gaping open mouth, temper-tantrum throwing, lip-biting, hair-flipping, plank of wood moody actress … A tape recorder in a mannequin could do her job.

Humor deployed cleverly may be why TV shows like *South Park* and *Modern Family* became popular with mainstream audiences, despite their willingness to explore controversial themes. Similarly, it's possible to make a point through humor that might not work in more sober writing. People argue endlessly about eating the right foods, typically defined by diet gurus who favor locally sourced, organically grown, and profoundly dull vegetables. *Wall Street Journal* columnist Ron Rosenbaum will have none of that. With new research suggesting that fatty diets may have unanticipated health benefits, Rosenbaum deploys some high-calorie humor to argue for the pleasures of dining lavishly:

> Preventing obesity is a laudable goal, but it has become the rationale for indiscriminate fat hunters. It can shade into a kind of bullying of the overweight, a badgering of anyone who likes butter or heavy cream. To the antifat crusaders, I say: Attack fatty junk food all you want. I'm with you. But you can deny me my roasted marrow bones when you pry them from my cold, dead hands.
>
> I'm not suggesting that we embrace these life-changing food experiences just on grounds of pure pleasure (though there's much to be said for pure pleasure). As it turns out, the science on the matter is changing as well. We are discovering that fatty delights can actually be good for you: They allow Spaniards, Italians and Greeks to live longer, and they make us satisfied with eating less. I'm speaking up not for obesity-generating fat, then, but for the kind of fatty food that leads to swooning sensual satiety.

Roast goose, for instance, is a supremely succulent, mind-alteringly flavorful fatty food. In most of America, roast goose would be viewed as the raven of cardiac mortality, hoarsely honking "never more." And listening to the doctors on cable TV, you might think that it's better to cook up a batch of meth than to cook with butter.

Eating fatty foods has become the culinary version of *Breaking Bad*: a dangerous walk on the wild side for the otherwise timid consumers of tasteless butter substitutes and Lean Cuisine.

—Ron Rosenbaum, "Let Them Eat Fat"

Our laughter testifies to what some people have thought all along: people who want us to eat tofu are the real problem. Note the pleasure Rosenbaum takes in the emotive power of words themselves: *swooning sensual satiety; the raven of cardiac mortality, hoarsely honking "never more."*

A writer or speaker can even use humor to deal with sensitive issues. For example, sports commentator Bob Costas, given the honor of eulogizing the great baseball player Mickey Mantle, couldn't ignore problems in Mantle's life. So he argues for Mantle's greatness by admitting the man's weaknesses indirectly through humor:

It brings to mind a story Mickey liked to tell on himself and maybe some of you have heard it. He pictured himself at the pearly gates, met by St. Peter, who shook his head and said, "Mick, we checked the record. We know some of what went on. Sorry, we can't let you in. But before you go, God wants to know if you'd sign these six dozen baseballs."

—Bob Costas, "Eulogy for Mickey Mantle"

Similarly, politicians may use humor to deal with issues they couldn't acknowledge in any other way. Here, for example, is former president George W. Bush at the 2004 Radio and TV Correspondents' Dinner discussing his much-mocked intellect:

Those stories about my intellectual capacity do get under my skin. You know, for a while I even thought my staff believed it. There on my schedule first thing every morning it said, "Intelligence briefing."

—George W. Bush

Not all humor is well-intentioned or barb-free. In fact, among the most powerful forms of emotional argument is ridicule—humor aimed at a particular target. Eighteenth-century poet and critic Samuel Johnson was known for his stinging and humorous put-downs, such as this comment to an aspiring writer: "Your manuscript is both good and original, but the part that is good is not original and the part that is original is not good." (Expect your own writing teachers to be kinder.) In our own time, the *Onion* has earned a reputation for its mastery of both ridicule and satire, the art of using over-the-top humor to making a serious point.

But because ridicule is a double-edged sword, it requires a deft hand to wield it. Humor that reflects bad taste discredits a writer completely, as does satire that misses its mark. Unless your target deserves riposte and you can be very funny, it's usually better to steer clear of such humor.

Using Arguments Based on Emotion

You don't want to play puppet master with people's emotions when you write arguments, but it's a good idea to spend some time early in your work thinking about how you want readers to feel as they consider your persuasive claims. For example, would readers of your editorial about campus traffic policies be more inclined to agree with you if you made them envy faculty privileges, or would arousing their sense of fairness work better? What emotional appeals might persuade meat eaters to consider a vegan diet—or vice versa? Would sketches of stage props on a Web site persuade people to buy a season ticket to the theater, or would you spark more interest by featuring pictures of costumed performers?

Consider, too, the effect that a story can have on readers. Writers and journalists routinely use what are called *human-interest stories* to give presence to issues or arguments. You can do the same, using a particular incident to evoke sympathy, understanding, outrage, or amusement. Take care, though, to tell an honest story.

RESPOND

1. To what specific emotions do the following slogans, sales pitches, and maxims appeal?

   "Just do it." (ad for Nike)

   "Think different." (ad for Apple computers)

   "Reach out and touch someone." (ad for AT&T)

   "By any means necessary." (rallying cry from Malcolm X)

   "Have it your way." (slogan for Burger King)

   "The ultimate driving machine." (slogan for BMW)

   "It's everywhere you want to be." (slogan for Visa)

   "Know what comes between me and my Calvins? Nothing!" (tag line for Calvin Klein jeans)

   "Don't mess with Texas!" (anti-litter campaign slogan)

   "American by Birth. Rebel by Choice." (slogan for Harley-Davidson)

2. Bring a magazine to class, and analyze the emotional appeals in as many full-page ads as you can. Then classify those ads by types of emotional appeal, and see whether you can connect the appeals to the subject or target audience of the magazine. Compare your results with those of your classmates, and discuss your findings. For instance, how exactly are the ads in publications such as *Cosmopolitan*, *Wired*, *Sports Illustrated*, *Motor Trend*, and *Smithsonian* adapted to their specific audiences?

3. How do arguments based on emotion work in different media? Are such arguments more or less effective in books, articles, television (both news and entertainment shows), films, brochures, magazines, email, Web sites, the theater, street protests, and so on? You might explore how a single medium handles emotional appeals or compare different media. For example, why do the comments pages of blogs seem to encourage angry outbursts? Are newspapers an emotionally colder source of information than television news programs? If so, why?

4. Spend some time looking for arguments that use ridicule or humor to make their point: check out your favorite Twitter feeds or blogs; watch for bumper stickers, posters, or advertisements; and listen to popular song lyrics. Bring one or two examples to class, and be ready to explain how the humor makes an emotional appeal and whether it's effective.

CHAPTER
11

Arguments Based on Character: Ethos

Whenever you read anything—whether it's a news article, an advertisement, a speech, or a text message—you no doubt subconsciously analyze the message for a sense of the character and credibility of the sender: *Is this someone I know and trust? Does the PBS reporter seem biased? Why should I believe an IRS official? Is this scholar really an authority on the subject?* Our culture teaches us to be skeptical of most messages, especially those that bombard us with slogans, and such reasonable doubt is a crucial skill in reading and evaluating arguments.

For that reason, people and institutions that hope to influence us do everything they can to establish their character and credibility, what ancient rhetors referred to as *ethos*. And sometimes slogans such as "All the News That's Fit to Print," "Fair & Balanced," or "Lean Forward" can be effective. At the very least, if a phrase is repeated often enough, it begins to sound plausible. Maybe CNN *is* the most trusted name in news!

But establishing character usually takes more than repetition, as marketers of all kinds know. It arises from credentials actually earned in some way. In the auto industry, for instance, companies such as Toyota, General Motors, and Nissan are hustling to present themselves as environmentally responsible producers of fuel-efficient, low-emission cars—the Prius, Volt, and Leaf. BMW, maker of "the ultimate driving machine," points to its fuel-sipping i3 and i8 cars as evidence of its commitment to "sustainable mobility." And Elon Musk (who builds rockets as well as Tesla cars) polishes his good-citizenship bona fides by sharing his electric vehicle patents with other manufacturers. All of these companies realize that their future success is linked to an ability to project a convincing ethos for themselves and their products.

Left to right: © Jon Arnold Images Ltd./Alamy; © Bernhard Classen/age fotostock; Richard Shotwell/Invision/AP

If corporations and institutions can establish an ethos, consider how much character matters when we think about people in the public arena. Perhaps no individual managed a more exceptional assertion of personal ethos than Jorge Mario Bergoglio did after he became Pope Francis on March 13, 2013, following the abdication of Benedict XVI—a man many found scholarly, cold, and out of touch with the modern world. James Carroll, writing for the *New Yorker*, identifies the precise moment when the world realized that it was dealing with a new sort of pope:

> "Who am I to judge?" With those five words, spoken in late July [2013] in reply to a reporter's question about the status of gay priests in the Church, Pope Francis stepped away from the disapproving tone, the explicit moralizing typical of popes and bishops.
>
> —James Carroll, "Who Am I to Judge?"

Carroll goes on to explain that Francis quickly established his ethos with a series of specific actions, decisions, and moments of identification with ordinary people, marking him as someone even nonbelievers might listen to and respect:

> As pope, Francis has simplified the Renaissance regalia of the papacy by abandoning fur-trimmed velvet capes, choosing to live in a two-room apartment instead of the Apostolic Palace, and replacing the papal Mercedes with a Ford Focus. Instead of the traditional red slip-ons, Francis wears ordinary black shoes.... Yet Francis didn't criticize the choices of other prelates. "He makes changes without attacking people," a Jesuit official told me. In his interview with *La Civiltà Cattolica*, Francis said, "My choices, including those related to the day-to-day aspects of life, like the use of a modest car, are related to a spiritual discernment that responds to a need that arises from looking at things, at people, and from reading the signs of the times."

In that last sentence, Francis acknowledges that ethos is gained, in part, through identification with one's audience and era. And this man, movingly photographed embracing the sick and disfigured, also posed for selfies!

You can see, then, why Aristotle treats ethos as a powerful argumentative appeal. Ethos creates quick and sometimes almost irresistible connections between readers and arguments. We observe people, groups, or institutions making and defending claims all the time and inevitably ask ourselves, *Should we pay attention to them? Can we rely on them? Do we dare to trust them?* Consider, though, that the same questions will be asked about you and your work, especially in academic settings.

FIGURE 11.1   AP Photo/L'Osservatore Romano, Riccardo Aguiari

Thinking Critically about Arguments Based on Character

Put simply, arguments based on character (ethos) depend on *trust*. We tend to accept arguments from those we trust, and we trust them (whether individuals, groups, or institutions) in good part because of their reputations. Three main elements — credibility, authority, and unselfish or clear motives — add up to *ethos*.

To answer serious and important questions, we often turn to professionals (doctors, lawyers, engineers, teachers, pastors) or to experts (those with knowledge and experience) for good advice. Based on their backgrounds, such people come with their ethos already established. Thus, appeals or arguments about character often turn on claims like these:

- A person (or group or institution) is or is not trustworthy or credible on this issue.

- A person (or group or institution) does or does not have the authority to speak to this issue.

- A person (or group or institution) does or does not have unselfish or clear motives for addressing this subject.

Establishing Trustworthiness and Credibility

Trustworthiness and credibility speak to a writer's honesty, respect for an audience and its values, and plain old likability. Sometimes a sense of humor can play an important role in getting an audience to listen to or "like" you. It's no accident that all but the most serious speeches begin with a joke or funny story: the humor puts listeners at ease and helps them identify with the speaker. Writer J. K. Rowling, for example, puts her audience (and herself) at ease early in the commencement address she delivered at Harvard in 2008 by getting real about such speeches:

> Delivering a commencement address is a great responsibility; or so I thought until I cast my mind back to my own graduation. The commencement speaker that day was the distinguished British philosopher Baroness Mary Warnock. Reflecting on her speech has helped me enormously in writing this one, because it turns out that I can't remember a single word she said. This liberating discovery enables me to proceed without any fear that I might inadvertently influence you to abandon promising careers in business, the law, or politics for the giddy delights of becoming a gay wizard.
>
> You see? If all you remember in years to come is the "gay wizard" joke, I've come out ahead of Baroness Mary Warnock. Achievable goals: the first step to self improvement.
>
> —J. K. Rowling, "The Fringe Benefits of Failure, and the Importance of Imagination"

In just a few sentences, Rowling pokes fun at herself, undercuts the expectation that graduation addresses change people's lives, slides in an allusion from her Harry Potter series, and then even offers a smidgen of advice. For an audience well disposed toward her already, Rowling has likely lived up to expectations.

But using humor to enhance your credibility may be more common in oratory than in the kind of writing you'll do in school. Fortunately, you have many options, one being simply to make plausible claims and then back them up with evidence. Academic audiences appreciate a reasonable disposition; we will discuss this approach at greater length in the next chapter.

You can also establish trustworthiness by connecting your own beliefs to core principles that are well established and widely respected. This strategy is particularly effective when your position seems to be—at first glance, at least—a threat to traditional values. For example, when former Smith College president Ruth J. Simmons describes her professional self to a commencement audience she is addressing (see Chapter 9), she presents her acquired reputation in terms that align perfectly with contemporary values:

For my part, I was cast as a troublemaker in my early career and accepted the disapproval that accompanies the expression of unpopular views: unpopular views about disparate pay for women and minorities; unpopular views about sexual harassment; unpopular views about exclusionary practices in our universities.

—Ruth J. Simmons

It's fine to be a rebel when you are on the right side of history.

Writers who establish their credibility seem trustworthy. But sometimes, to be credible, you have to admit limitations, too, as *New York Times* columnist David Brooks does as he wrestles with a problem common in our time, an inability to focus on things that matter:

Like everyone else, I am losing the attention war. I toggle over to my emails when I should be working. I text when I should be paying attention to the people in front of me. I spend hours looking at mildly diverting stuff on YouTube. ("Look, there's a bunch of guys who can play 'Billie Jean' on beer bottles!")

And, like everyone else, I've nodded along with the prohibition sermons imploring me to limit my information diet. Stop multitasking! Turn off the devices at least once a week!

And, like everyone else, these sermons have had no effect. Many of us lead lives of distraction, unable to focus on what we know we should focus on.

—David Brooks, "The Art of Focus"

Making such concessions to readers sends a strong signal that you've looked critically at your own position and can therefore be trusted when you turn to arguing its merits. Speaking to readers directly, using *I* or *you* or *us*, can also help you connect with them, as can using contractions and everyday or colloquial language—both strategies employed by Brooks. In other situations, you may find that a more formal tone gives your claims greater credibility. You'll be making such choices as you search for the ethos that represents you best.

In fact, whenever you write a paper or present an idea, you are sending signals about your credibility, whether you intend to or not. If your ideas are reasonable, your sources are reliable, and your language is appropriate to the project, you suggest to academic readers that you're someone whose ideas *might* deserve attention. Details matter: helpful graphs, tables, charts, or illustrations may carry weight with readers, as will the visual attractiveness of your text, whether in print or digital form. Obviously, correct spelling, grammar, and mechanics are important too. And though you might not worry about it now, at some point you may need letters of recommendation from instructors or supervisors. How will they remember you? Often chiefly from the ethos you have established in your work. Think about that.

Claiming Authority

When you read or listen to an argument, you have every right to ask about the writer's authority: *What does he know about the subject? What experiences does she have that make her especially knowledgeable? Why should I pay attention to this person?* When you offer an argument yourself, you have to anticipate and be prepared to answer questions like these, either directly or indirectly.

How does someone construct an authoritative ethos? In examining what he describes as "the fundamental problem with President Obama's communications ethos," Ron Fournier, editorial director of *National Journal*, explains that authority cannot be taken for granted:

> He and his advisers are so certain about their moral and political standing that they believe it's enough to make a declaration. *If we say it, the public should believe it.*
>
> That's not how it works. A president must earn the public's trust. He must teach and persuade; speak clearly, and follow word with action; show empathy toward his rivals, and acknowledge the merits of a critique. A successful president pays careful attention to how his image is projected both to U.S. voters and to the people of the world. He knows that to be strong, a leader must look strong. Image matters, especially in an era so dominated by them.
>
> —Ron Fournier, "Is the White House Lying, or Just Bad at Crisis Communications?"

Of course, writers establish their authority in various ways. Sometimes the assertion of ethos will be bold and personal, as it is when writer and activist Terry Tempest Williams attacks those who poisoned the Utah deserts with nuclear radiation. What gives her the right to speak on this subject? Not scientific expertise, but gut-wrenching personal experience:

> I belong to the Clan of One-Breasted Women. My mother, my grandmothers, and six aunts have all had mastectomies. Seven are dead. The two who survive have just completed rounds of chemotherapy and radiation.
>
> I've had my own problems: two biopsies for breast cancer and a small tumor between my ribs diagnosed as a "borderline malignancy."
>
> —Terry Tempest Williams, "The Clan of One-Breasted Women"

We are willing to listen to Williams because she has lived with the nuclear peril she will deal with in the remainder of her essay.

Other means of claiming authority are less dramatic. By simply attaching titles to their names, writers assert that they hold medical or legal or engineering degrees, or some other important credentials. Or they may mention the number of years they've worked in a given field or the distinguished positions they have held. As a reader, you'll pay more attention to an argument about global warming offered by a professor of atmospheric and oceanic science at the University of Minnesota than one by your Uncle Sid, who sells tools. But you'll prefer your uncle to the professor when you need advice about a reliable rotary saw.

When readers might be skeptical of both you and your claims, you may have to be even more specific about your credentials. That's exactly the strategy Richard Bernstein uses to establish his right to speak on the subject of "Asian culture." What gives a New York writer named Bernstein the authority to write about Asian peoples? Bernstein tells us in a sparkling example of an argument based on character:

> The Asian culture, as it happens, is something I know a bit about, having spent five years at Harvard striving for a Ph.D. in a joint program called History and East Asian Languages and, after that, living either as a student (for one year) or a journalist (six years) in China and Southeast Asia. At least I know enough to know there is no such thing as the "Asian culture."
>
> —Richard Bernstein, *Dictatorship of Virtue*

When you write for readers who trust you and your work, you may not have to make such an open claim to authority. But making this type of appeal is always an option.

Coming Clean about Motives

When people are trying to convince you of something, it's important (and natural) to ask: *Whose interests are they serving? How will they profit from their proposal?* Such suspicions go to the heart of ethical arguments.

In a hugely controversial essay published in the *Princeton Tory*, Tal Fortgang, a first-year student at the Ivy League school, argues that those on campus who used the phrase "Check your privilege" to berate white male students like him for the advantages they enjoy are, in fact, judging him according to gender and race, and not for "all the hard work I have done in my life." To challenge stereotypical assumptions about the "racist patriarchy" that supposedly paved his way to Princeton, Fortgang writes about the experiences of his ancestors, opening the paragraphs with a striking parallel structure:

Perhaps it's the privilege my grandfather and his brother had to flee their home as teenagers when the Nazis invaded Poland, leaving their mother and five younger siblings behind, running and running....

Or maybe it's the privilege my grandmother had of spending weeks upon weeks on a death march through Polish forests in subzero temperatures, one of just a handful to survive....

Perhaps my privilege is that those two resilient individuals came to America with no money and no English, obtained citizenship, learned the language and met each other....

Perhaps it was my privilege that my own father worked hard enough in City College to earn a spot at a top graduate school, got a good job, and for 25 years got up well before the crack of dawn, sacrificing precious time he wanted to spend with those he valued most—his wife and kids—to earn that living.

—Tal Fortgang, "Checking My Privilege:
Character as the Basis of Privilege"

Fortgang thus attempts to establish his own ethos and win the argument against those who make assumptions about his roots by dramatizing the ethos of his ancestors:

That's the problem with calling someone out for the "privilege" which you assume has defined their narrative. You don't know what their struggles have been, what they may have gone through to be where they are. Assuming they've benefitted from "power systems" or other conspiratorial imaginary institutions denies them credit for all they've done, things of which you may not even conceive. You don't know whose father died defending your freedom. You don't know whose mother escaped oppression. You don't know who conquered their demons, or may still [be] conquering them now.

As you might imagine, the pushback to "Checking My Privilege" was enormous, some of the hundreds of comments posted to an online version accusing Fortgang himself of assuming the very ethos of victimhood against which he inveighs. Peter Finocchiaro, a reviewer on *Slate*, is especially brutal: "Only a few short months ago he was living at home with his parents. His life experience, one presumes, is fairly limited. So in that sense, he doesn't really know any better.... He is an ignorant 19-year-old white guy from Westchester." You can see in this debate how ethos quickly raises issues of knowledge and motives. Fortgang tries to resist the stereotype others would impose on his character, but others regard the very ethos he fashions in his essay as evidence of his naïveté about race, discrimination, and, yes, privilege.

We all, of course, have connections and interests that bind us to other human beings. It makes sense that a young man would explore his social identity, that a woman might be concerned with women's issues, that members of minority groups might define social and cultural conditions on their own terms—or even that investors might look out for their investments. It's simply good strategy to let your audiences know where your loyalties lie when such information does, in fact, shape your work.

Using Ethos in Your Own Writing

- Establish your credibility by acknowledging your audience's values, showing respect for them, and establishing common ground where (and if) possible. How will you convince your audience you are trustworthy? What will you admit about your own limitations?

- Establish your authority by showing you have done your homework and know your topic well. How will you show that you know your topic well? What appropriate personal experience can you draw on?

- Examine your motives for writing. What, if anything, do you stand to gain from your argument? How can you explain those advantages to your audience?

CULTURAL CONTEXTS FOR ARGUMENT

Ethos

In the United States, students are often asked to establish authority by drawing on personal experiences, by reporting on research they or others have conducted, and by taking a position for which they can offer strong evidence. But this expectation about student authority is by no means universal.

Some cultures regard student writers as novices who can most effectively make arguments by reflecting on what they've learned from their teachers and elders—those who hold the most important knowledge and, hence, authority. When you're arguing a point with people from cultures other than your own, ask questions like:

- Whom are you addressing, and what is your relationship with that person?

- What knowledge are you expected to have? Is it appropriate or expected for you to demonstrate that knowledge—and if so, how?

- What tone is appropriate? And remember: politeness is rarely, if ever, inappropriate.

RESPOND

1. Consider the ethos of these public figures. Then describe one or two products that might benefit from their endorsements as well as several that would not.

   Edward Snowden—whistleblower

   Kaley Cuoco-Sweeting—actress

   James Earl Jones—actor

   Michael Sam—athlete

   Megyn Kelly—TV news commentator

   Miley Cyrus—singer

   Seth Meyers—late-night TV host

   Cristiano Ronaldo—soccer player

2. Opponents of Richard Nixon, the thirty-seventh president of the United States, once raised doubts about his integrity by asking a single ruinous question: *Would you buy a used car from this man?* Create your own version of the argument of character. Begin by choosing an intriguing or controversial person or group and finding an image online. Then download the image into a word-processing file. Create a caption for the photo that is modeled after the question asked about Nixon: *Would you give this woman your email password? Would you share a campsite with this couple? Would you eat lasagna that this guy fixed?* Finally, write a serious 300-word argument that explores the character flaws or strengths of your subject(s).

3. Take a close look at your Facebook page (or your page on any other social media site). What are some aspects of your character, true or not, that might be conveyed by the photos, videos, and messages you have posted online? Analyze the ethos or character you see projected there, using the advice in this chapter to guide your analysis.

CHAPTER
12
Arguments Based on Facts and Reason: Logos

These three images say a lot about the use and place of logic (*logos*) in Western and American culture. The first shows Benedict Cumberbatch from the BBC TV series *Sherlock*, just one of many actors to play Arthur Conan Doyle's much-loved fictional detective Sherlock Holmes, who solves perplexing crimes by using precise observation and impeccable logic. The second refers to an equally popular TV (and film) series character, Spock, the Vulcan officer in *Star Trek* who tries to live a life guided by reason alone—his most predicable observation being some version of "that would not be logical." The third is a cartoon spoofing a pseudo-logical argument (nine out of ten prefer X) made so often in advertising that it has become something of a joke.

These images attest to the prominent place that logic holds for most people: like Holmes, we want to know the facts on the assumption that they will help us make sound judgments. We admire those whose logic is, like Spock's, impeccable. So when arguments begin, "Nine out of ten authorities recommend," we respond favorably: those are good odds. But the three images also challenge reliance on logic alone: Sherlock Holmes and Spock are characters drawn in broad and often parodic strokes; the "nine out of ten" cartoon itself spoofs abuses of reason. Given a choice, however, most of us profess to respect and even prefer *appeals to logos*—that is, claims based on facts, evidence, and reason—but we're also inclined to read factual arguments within the context of our feelings and the ethos of people making the appeals.

"And it's recommended by nine out of ten people we believe to be doctors."

Left to right: Yui Mok/Press Association via AP Images; © NBC/Photofest, Inc.; © Frank Cotham/The New Yorker/The Cartoon Bank

Thinking Critically about Hard Evidence

Aristotle helps us out in classifying arguments by distinguishing two kinds:

Artistic Proofs	Arguments the writer/ speaker creates	Constructed arguments	Appeals to reason; common sense
Inartistic Proofs	Arguments the writer/ speaker is given	Hard evidence	Facts, statistics, testimonies, witnesses, contracts, documents

We can see these different kinds of logical appeals at work in a single paragraph from President Barack Obama's 2014 State of the Union address. Typically in such speeches — nationally televised and closely reviewed — the president assesses the current condition of the United States and then lays out an agenda for the coming years, a laundry list of commitments and goals. One of those items mentioned about halfway through the 2014 address focuses on the admirable objective of improving the conditions of working women:

> Today, women make up about half our workforce. But they still make 77 cents for every dollar a man earns. That is wrong, and in 2014, it's an embarrassment. A woman deserves equal pay for equal work. She deserves to have a baby without sacrificing her job. A mother deserves a day off to care for a sick child or sick parent without running into hardship — and you know what, a father does, too. It's time to do away with workplace policies that belong in a *Mad Men* episode. This year, let's all come together — Congress, the White House, and businesses from Wall Street to Main Street — to give every woman the opportunity she deserves. Because I firmly believe when women succeed, America succeeds.
>
> —Barack Obama, State of the Union address

As you see, Obama opens the paragraph with an important "inartistic" proof, that ratio of just 77 cents to a dollar representing what women earn in the United States compared to men. Beginning with that fact, he then offers a series of reasonable "artistic" appeals phrased as applause lines: *that is wrong; a woman deserves equal pay; a mother deserves a day off …a father does, too."* Obama then concludes the paragraph by stating the core principle behind all these claims, what we'll later describe as the *warrant* in an argument (see Chapter 15): *when women succeed, America succeeds.*

Note, then, the importance of that single number the president puts forward. It is evidence that, despite decades of political commitment to pay equity and even federal laws banning gender discrimination in employment and compensation, much work remains to be done. Who can be satisfied with the status quo in the face of that damning number? But where did that statistic come from, and *what if it is wrong?*

Now, no one expects footnotes and documentation in a presidential address. The ethos of the office itself makes the public (at least some portion of it) willing to accept a president's factual claims, if only because his remarks have surely been vetted by legions of staffers. Yet some statistics and claims assume a life of their own, repeated so often that most people—even presidents and their speechwriters—assume that they are true. Add the problem of "confirmation bias," the tendency of most people to believe evidence that confirms their views of the world, and you have numbers that will not die.

We live, however, in an age of critics and fact-checkers. Writing for the *Daily Beast*, Christina Hoff Sommers, a former professor of philosophy and no fan of contemporary feminism, complains that the president is perpetuating an error: "What is wrong and embarrassing is the President of the United States reciting a massively discredited factoid." And in case you won't believe Sommers (and most feminists and those in the president's camp wouldn't), she directs skeptics to a more objective source, the *Washington Post*, which routinely fact-checks the State of the Union and other major addresses.

Like Sommers, that paper does raise questions about the 77/100 earnings ratio, and its detailed analysis of that number suggests just how complicated evidential claims can be. Here's a shortened version of the *Post*'s statement, which you'll note cites several government sources:

> There is clearly a wage gap, but differences in the life choices of men and women—such as women tending to leave the workforce when they have children—make it difficult to make simple comparisons.
>
> Obama is using a figure (annual wages, from the Census Bureau) that makes the disparity appear the greatest. The Bureau of Labor Statistics, for instance, shows that the gap is 19 cents when looking at weekly wages. The gap is even smaller when you look at hourly wages—it is 14 cents—but then not every wage earner is paid on an hourly basis, so that statistic excludes salaried workers....
>
> Economists at the Federal Reserve Bank of St. Louis surveyed economic literature and concluded that "research suggests that the actual gender wage gap (when female workers are compared with male workers who have similar characteristics) is much lower than the raw wage gap." They cited one survey, prepared for the Labor Department, which concluded that when such differences are accounted for, much of the hourly wage gap dwindled, to about 5 cents on the dollar.

Is the entire paragraph of the president's address discredited because his hard evidence seems overstated or oversimplified? Not if we accept the *constructed* arguments he makes on the general principle of fairness for offering women—and men—more support as laborers in the job force. But he might have been more convincing at this point in a very lengthy speech if someone in the White House had taken a moment to check the government's own numbers, as the *Washington Post* did. This ongoing controversy over wage equity does, however, illustrate how closely logical arguments—whether artistic or inartistic—will be read and criticized. And so the connections between them matter.

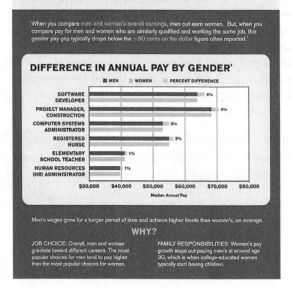

FIGURE 12.1 Factual arguments are often made or enhanced by charts, graphs, and infographics. Here PayScale, an online salary and wage information site, presents numbers to explain the pay equity issue: "Yes, men do earn more than women on average, but not that much more when they work the same job and they have similar experience and abilities." We reproduce here just a portion of the full infographic.
PayScale, Inc., by permission

RESPOND

Discuss whether the following statements are examples of hard evidence or constructed arguments. Not all cases are clear-cut.

1. Drunk drivers are involved in more than 50 percent of traffic deaths.

2. DNA tests of skin found under the victim's fingernails suggest that the defendant was responsible for the assault.

3. A psychologist testified that teenage violence could not be blamed on video games.

4. An apple a day keeps the doctor away.

5. "The only thing we have to fear is fear itself."

6. Air bags ought to be removed from vehicles because they can kill young children and small-framed adults.

Facts

Gathering factual information and transmitting it faithfully practically define what we mean by professional journalism and scholarship. We'll even listen to people we don't agree with if their evidence is really good. Below, a reviewer for the conservative *National Review* praises William Julius Wilson, a liberal sociologist, because of how well he presents his case:

> In his eagerly awaited new book, Wilson argues that ghetto blacks are worse off than ever, victimized by a near-total loss of low-skill jobs in and around inner-city neighborhoods. In support of this thesis, he *musters mountains of data, plus excerpts from some of the thousands of surveys and face-to-face interviews that he and his research team conducted among inner-city Chicagoans.* It is a book that deserves a wide audience among thinking conservatives.
>
> —John J. Dilulio Jr., "When Decency Disappears" (emphasis added)

When your facts are compelling, they may stand on their own in a low-stakes argument, supported by little more than saying where they come from. Consider the power of phrases such as "reported by the *Wall Street Journal*" or "according to FactCheck.org." Such sources gain credibility if they have reported facts accurately and reliably over time. Using such credible sources in an argument can also reflect positively on you.

In scholarly arguments, which have higher expectations for accuracy, what counts is drawing sober conclusions from the evidence turned up through detailed research or empirical studies. The language of such material may seem dryly factual to you, even when the content is inherently interesting. But presenting new knowledge dispassionately is (ideally at least) the whole point of scholarly writing, marking a contrast between it and the kind of intellectual warfare that occurs in many media forums, especially news programs and blogs. Here for example is a portion of a lengthy opening paragraph in the "Discussion and Conclusions" section of a scholarly paper arguing that people who spend a great deal of time on Facebook often frame their lives by what they observe there:

> The results of this research support the argument that using Facebook affects people's perceptions of others. For those that have used Facebook longer, it is easier to remember positive messages and happy pictures posted on Facebook; these readily available examples give users an impression that others are happier. As expected in the first hypothesis, the results show that the longer people have used Facebook, the stronger was their belief that others were happier than themselves, and the less they agreed that life is fair. Furthermore, as predicted in the second hypothesis, this research found that the more "friends" people included on their Facebook whom they did not know personally, the stronger they believed that others had better lives than themselves. In other words, looking at happy pictures of others on Facebook gives people an impression that others are "always" happy and having good lives, as evident from these pictures of happy moments. In contrast to their own experiences of life events, which are not always positive, people are very likely to conclude that others have better lives than themselves and that life is not fair.
>
> —Hui-Tzu Grace Chou, PhD, and Nicholas Edge, BS,
> "'They Are Happier and Having Better Lives Than I Am':
> The Impact of Using Facebook on Perceptions of Others' Lives"

There are no fireworks in this conclusion, no slanted or hot language, no unfair or selective reporting of data, just a faithful attention to the facts and behaviors uncovered by the study. But one can easily imagine these facts being subsequently used to support overdramatized claims about the dangers of social networks. That's often what happens to scholarly studies when they are read and interpreted in the popular media.

Of course, arguing with facts can involve challenging even the most reputable sources if they lead to unfair or selective reporting or if the stories are presented or "framed" unfairly.

In an ideal world, good information—no matter where it comes from—would always drive out bad. But you already know that we don't live in an ideal world, so sometimes bad information gets repeated in an echo chamber that amplifies the errors.

Statistics

You've probably heard the old saying "There are three kinds of lies: lies, damned lies, and statistics," and, to be sure, it is possible to lie with numbers, even those that are accurate, because numbers rarely speak for themselves. They need to be interpreted by writers—and writers almost always have agendas that shape the interpretations.

Of course, just because they are often misused doesn't mean that statistics are meaningless, but it does suggest that you need to use them carefully and to remember that your careful reading of numbers is essential. Consider the attention-grabbing map on the next page that went viral in June 2014. Created by Mark Gongloff of the *Huffington Post* in the wake of a school shooting in Oregon, it plotted the location of all seventy-four school shootings that had occurred in the United States since the Sandy Hook tragedy in December 2012, when twenty elementary school children and six adults were gunned down by a rifle-wielding killer. For the graphic, Gongloff drew on a list assembled by the group Everytown for Gun Safety, an organization formed by former New York City mayor and billionaire Michael Bloomberg to counter the influence of the National Rifle Association (NRA). Both the map and Everytown's sobering list of shootings received wide attention in the media, given the startling number of incidents it recorded.

It didn't take long before questions were raised about their accuracy. Were American elementary and secondary school children under such frequent assault as the map based on Everytown's list suggested? Well, yes and no. Guns were going off on and around school campuses, but the firearms weren't always aimed at children. The *Washington Post*, CNN, and other news outlets soon found themselves pulling back on their initial reporting, offering a more nuanced view of the controversial number. To do that, the *Washington Post* began by posing an important question:

What constitutes a school shooting?

That five-word question has no simple answer, a fact underscored by the backlash to an advocacy group's recent list of school shootings. The list, maintained by Everytown, a group that backs policies to limit gun violence, was updated last week to reflect what it identified as the 74 school shootings since the massacre in Newtown, Conn., a massacre that sparked a national debate over gun control.

Multiple news outlets, including this one, reported on Everytown's data, prompting a backlash over the broad methodology used. As we wrote in our original post, the group considered any instance of a firearm discharging on school property as a shooting—thus casting a broad net that includes homicides, suicides, accidental discharges and, in a handful of cases, shootings that had no relation to the schools themselves and occurred with no students apparently present.

—Niraj Chokshi, "Fight over School Shooting List
Underscores Difficulty in Quantifying Gun Violence"

CNN followed the same path, re-evaluating its original reporting in light of criticism from groups not on the same page as Everytown for Gun Safety:

Without a doubt, that number is startling.

So …CNN took a closer look at the list, delving into the circumstances of each incident Everytown included….

CNN determined that 15 of the incidents Everytown included were situations similar to the violence in Newtown or Oregon—a minor or adult actively shooting inside or near a school. That works out to about one such shooting every five weeks, a startling figure in its own right.

Some of the other incidents on Everytown's list included personal arguments, accidents and alleged gang activities and drug deals.

—Ashley Fantz, Lindsey Knight, and Kevin Wang, "A Closer Look:
How Many Newtown-like School Shootings since Sandy Hook?"

FIGURE 12.2 Everytown for Gun Safety Action

Other news organizations came up with their own revised numbers, but clearly the interpretation of a number can be as important as the statistic itself. And what were Mark Gongloff's Twitter reactions to these reassessments? They made an argument as well:

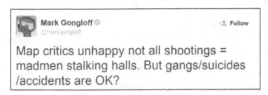

Mark Gongloff @markgongloff   Follow

Map critics unhappy not all shootings = madmen stalking halls. But gangs/suicides /accidents are OK?

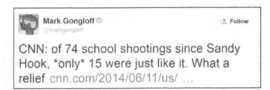

Mark Gongloff @markgongloff   Follow

CNN: of 74 school shootings since Sandy Hook, *only* 15 were just like it. What a relief cnn.com/2014/06/11/us/ …

One lesson, surely, is that when you rely on statistics in your arguments, make sure you understand where they come from, what they mean, and what their limitations might be. Check and double-check them or get help in doing so: you don't want to be accused of using fictitious data based on questionable assumptions.

RESPOND

Statistical evidence becomes useful only when interpreted fairly and reasonably. Go to the *USA Today* Web site and look for the daily graph, chart, or table called the "USA Today Snapshot." Pick a snapshot, and use the information in it to support three different claims, at least two of which make very different points. Share your claims with classmates. (The point is not to learn to use data dishonestly but to see firsthand how the same statistics can serve a variety of arguments.)

Surveys and Polls

When they verify the popularity of an idea or a proposal, surveys and polls provide strong persuasive appeals because they come as close to expressing the will of the people as anything short of an election—the most decisive poll of all. However, surveys and polls can do much more than help politicians make decisions. They can be important elements in scientific research, documenting the complexities of human behavior. They can also provide persuasive reasons for action or intervention. When surveys show, for example, that most American sixth-graders can't locate France or Wyoming on a map—not to mention Ukraine or Afghanistan—that's an appeal for better instruction in geography. It always makes sense, however, to question poll numbers, especially when they support your own point of view. Ask who commissioned the poll, who is publishing its outcome, who was surveyed (and in what proportions), and what stakes these parties might have in its outcome.

Are we being too suspicious? No. In fact, this sort of scrutiny is exactly what you might anticipate from your readers whenever you use (or create) surveys to explore an issue. You should be confident that enough subjects have been surveyed to be accurate, that the people chosen for the study were representative of the selected population as a whole, and that they were chosen randomly — not selected because of what they are likely to say. In a splendid article on how women can make research-based choices during their pregnancy, economist Emily Oster explores, for example, whether an expectant mother might in fact be able to drink responsibly. She researches not only the results of the data, but also who was surveyed, and how their participation might have influenced the results:

> It is possible to unearth research that points to light drinking as a problem, but this work is deeply flawed. One frequently cited study from the journal *Pediatrics*, published in 2001, interviewed women about their drinking while they were pregnant and then contacted them for a child behavior assessment when their children were about 6. The researchers found some evidence that lighter drinking had an impact on behavior and concluded that even one drink a day could cause behavior problems.
>
> So what's wrong with this finding?
>
> In the study, 18% of the women who didn't drink at all and 45% of the women who had one drink a day reported using cocaine during pregnancy. Presumably your first thought is, really? Cocaine? Perhaps the problem is that cocaine, not the occasional glass of Chardonnay, makes your child more likely to have behavior problems.
>
> —Emily Oster, "Take Back Your Pregnancy"

Clearly, polls, surveys, and studies need to be examined critically. You can't take even academic research at face value until you have explored its details.

The meaning of polls and surveys is also affected by the way that questions are posed. In the recent past, research revealed, for example, that polling about same-sex unions got differing responses according to how questions are worded. When people were asked whether gay and lesbian couples should be eligible for the same inheritance and partner health benefits that heterosexual couples receive, a majority of those polled said yes — unless the word *marriage* appeared in the question; then the responses are primarily negative. If anything, the differences here reveal how conflicted people may have been about the issue and how quickly opinions might shift—as they did. Remember, then, to be very careful in reviewing the wording of survey or poll questions.

Finally, always keep in mind that the date of a poll may strongly affect the results—and their usefulness in an argument. In 2010, for example, nearly 50 percent of California voters supported building more nuclear power plants. Less than a year later, that percentage had dropped to 37 percent after the meltdown of Japanese nuclear power plants in the wake of the March 2011 earthquake and tsunami. On public and political issues, you need to be sure that you are using timely information.

RESPOND

Choose an important issue and design a series of questions to evoke a range of responses in a poll. Try to design a question that would make people strongly inclined to agree, another question that would lead them to oppose the same proposition, and a third that tries to be more neutral. Then try out your questions on your classmates.

Testimonies and Narratives

Writers can support arguments by presenting human experiences in the form of narrative or testimony—particularly if those experiences are their own. In courts, judges and juries often take into consideration detailed descriptions and narratives of exactly what occurred. Look at this reporter's account of a court case in which a panel of judges decided, based on the testimony presented, that a man had been sexually harassed by another man. The narrative, in this case, supplies the evidence:

> The Seventh Circuit, in a 1997 case known as *Doe v. City of Belleville*, drew a sweeping conclusion allowing for same-sex harassment cases of many kinds…. This case, for example, centered on teenage twin brothers working a summer job cutting grass in the city cemetery of Belleville, Ill. One boy wore an earring, which caused him no end of grief that particular summer—including a lot of menacing talk among his coworkers about sexually assaulting him in the woods and sending him "back to San Francisco." One of his harassers, identified in court documents as a large former marine, culminated a verbal campaign by backing the earring-wearer against a wall and grabbing him by the testicles to see "if he was a girl or a guy." The teenager had been "singled out for this abuse," the court ruled, "because the way in which he projected the sexual aspect of his personality"—meaning his gender—"did not conform to his coworkers' view of appropriate masculine behavior."
>
> —Margaret Talbot, "Men Behaving Badly"

Personal perspectives can support a claim convincingly and logically, especially if a writer has earned the trust of readers. In arguing that Tea Party supporters of a government shutdown in 2011 had no business being offended when some opponents described them as "terrorists," Froma Harrop, one of the writers who used the term, argued logically and from experience why the characterization was appropriate:

> [T]he hurt the tea party writers most complained of was to their feelings. I had engaged in name-calling, they kept saying. One professing to want more civility in our national conversation, as I do, should not be flinging around the *terrorist* word.
>
> May I presume to disagree? Civility is a subjective concept, to be sure, but hurting people's feelings in the course of making solid arguments is fair and square. The decline in the quality of our public discourse results not so much from an excess of spleen, but a deficit of well-constructed arguments. Few things upset partisans more than when the other side makes a case that bats home.
>
> "Most of us know that effectively scoring on a point of argument opens us to the accusation of mean-spiritedness," writes Frank Partsch, who leads the National Conference of Editorial Writers' Civility Project. "It comes with the territory, and a commitment to civility should not suggest that punches will be pulled in order to avoid such accusations."
>
> —Froma Harrop, "Hurt Feelings Can Be a
> Consequence of Strong Arguments"

This narrative introduction gives a rationale for supporting the claim Harrop is making: we can expect consequences when we argue ineffectively. (For more on establishing credibility with readers, see Chapter 11.)

RESPOND

Bring to class a full review of a recent film that you either enjoyed or did not enjoy. Using testimony from that review, write a brief argument to your classmates explaining why they should see that movie (or why they should avoid it), being sure to use evidence from the review fairly and reasonably. Then exchange arguments with a classmate, and decide whether the evidence in your peer's argument helps to change your opinion about the movie. What's convincing about the evidence? If it doesn't convince you, why doesn't it?

Using Reason and Common Sense

If you don't have "hard facts," you can turn to those arguments Aristotle describes as "constructed" from reason and common sense. The formal study of such reasoning is called *logic*, and you probably recognize a famous example of deductive reasoning, called a **syllogism**:

All human beings are mortal.

Socrates is a human being.

Therefore, Socrates is mortal.

Logic: another thing that penguins aren't very good at.

FIGURE 12.3   © Randy Glasbergen/glasbergen.com

In valid syllogisms, the conclusion follows logically—and technically—from the premises that lead up to it. Many have criticized syllogistic reasoning for being limited, and others have poked fun at it, as in the cartoon above.

But we routinely see something like syllogistic reasoning operating in public arguments, particularly when writers take the time to explain key principles. Consider the step-by-step reasoning Michael Gerson uses to explain why exactly it was wrong for the Internal Revenue Service in 2010–2011 to target specific political groups, making it more difficult for them to organize politically:

> Why does this matter deserve heightened scrutiny from the rest of us? Because crimes against democracy are particularly insidious. Representative government involves a type of trade. As citizens, we cede power to public officials for important purposes that require centralized power: defending the country, imposing order, collecting taxes to promote the common good. In exchange, we expect public institutions to be evenhanded and disinterested. When the stewards of power—biased judges or corrupt policemen or politically motivated IRS officials—act unfairly, it undermines trust in the whole system.
>
> —Michael Gerson, "An Arrogant and Lawless IRS"

Gerson's criticism of the IRS actions might be mapped out by the following sequence of statements.

> Crimes against democracy undermine trust in the system.
>
> Treating taxpayers differently because of their political beliefs is a crime against democracy.
>
> Therefore, IRS actions that target political groups undermine the American system.

Few writers, of course, think about formal deductive reasoning when they support their claims. Even Aristotle recognized that most people argue perfectly well using informal logic. To do so, they rely mostly on habits of mind and assumptions that they share with their readers or listeners—as Gerson essentially does in his paragraph.

In Chapter 15, we describe a system of informal logic that you may find useful in shaping credible appeals to reason—Toulmin argument. Here, we briefly examine some ways that people use informal logic in their everyday lives. Once again, we begin with Aristotle, who used the term **enthymeme** to describe an ordinary kind of sentence that includes both a claim and a reason but depends on the audience's agreement with an assumption that is left implicit rather than spelled out. Enthymemes can be very persuasive when most people agree with the assumptions they rest on. The following sentences are all enthymemes:

> We'd better cancel the picnic because it's going to rain.
>
> Flat taxes are fair because they treat everyone the same.
>
> I'll buy a PC instead of a Mac because it's cheaper.

Sometimes enthymemes seem so obvious that readers don't realize that they're drawing inferences when they agree with them. Consider the first example:

> We'd better cancel the picnic because it's going to rain.

Let's expand the enthymeme a bit to say more of what the speaker may mean:

> We'd better cancel the picnic this afternoon because the weather bureau is predicting a 70 percent chance of rain for the remainder of the day.

Embedded in this brief argument are all sorts of assumptions and fragments of cultural information that are left implicit but that help to make it persuasive:

> Picnics are ordinarily held outdoors.
>
> When the weather is bad, it's best to cancel picnics.
>
> Rain is bad weather for picnics.
>
> A 70 percent chance of rain means that rain is more likely to occur than not.
>
> When rain is more likely to occur than not, it makes sense to cancel picnics.

For most people, the original statement carries all this information on its own; the enthymeme is a compressed argument, based on what audiences know and will accept.

CULTURAL CONTEXTS FOR ARGUMENT

Logos

In the United States, student writers are expected to draw on "hard facts" and evidence as often as possible in supporting their claims: while ethical and emotional appeals are important, logical appeals tend to hold sway in academic writing. So statistics and facts speak volumes, as does reasoning based on time-honored values such as fairness and equity. In writing to global audiences, you need to remember that not all cultures value the same kinds of appeals. If you want to write to audiences across cultures, you need to know about the norms and values in those cultures. Chinese culture, for example, values authority and often indirect allusion over "facts" alone. Some African cultures value cooperation and community over individualism, and still other cultures value religious texts as providing compelling evidence. So think carefully about what you consider strong evidence, and pay attention to what counts as evidence to others. You can begin by asking yourself questions like:

- What evidence is most valued by your audience: Facts? Concrete examples? Firsthand experience? Religious or philosophical texts? Something else?

- Will analogies count as support? How about precedents?

- Will the testimony of experts count? If so, what kinds of experts are valued most?

But sometimes enthymemes aren't self-evident:

> Be wary of environmentalism because it's religion disguised as science.

> iPhones are undermining civil society by making us even more focused on ourselves.

> It's time to make all public toilets unisex because to do otherwise is discriminatory.

In these cases, you'll have to work much harder to defend both the claim and the implicit assumptions that it's based on by drawing out the inferences that seem self-evident in other enthymemes. And you'll likely also have to supply credible evidence; a simple declaration of fact won't suffice.

Providing Logical Structures for Argument

Some arguments depend on particular logical structures to make their points. In the following pages, we identify a few of these logical structures.

Degree

Arguments based on degree are so common that people barely notice them, nor do they pay much attention to how they work because they seem self-evident. Most audiences will readily accept that *more of a good thing* or *less of a bad thing* is good. In her novel *The Fountainhead*, Ayn Rand asks: "If physical slavery is repulsive, how much more repulsive is the concept of servility of the spirit?" Most readers immediately comprehend the point Rand intends to make about slavery of the spirit because they already know that physical slavery is cruel and would reject any forms of slavery that were even crueler on the principle that *more of a bad thing is bad*. Rand still needs to offer evidence that "servility of the spirit" is, in fact, worse than bodily servitude, but she has begun with a logical structure readers can grasp. Here are other arguments that work similarly:

> If I can get a ten-year warranty on an inexpensive Kia, shouldn't I get the same or better warranty from a more expensive Lexus?

> The health benefits from using stem cells in research will surely outweigh the ethical risks.

> Better a conventional war now than a nuclear confrontation later.

FIGURE 12.4 A demonstrator at an immigrants' rights rally in New York City in 2007. Arguments based on values that are widely shared within a society—such as the idea of equal rights in American culture—have an automatic advantage with audiences. AP Photo/Seth Wenig

Analogies

Analogies, typically complex or extended comparisons, explain one idea or concept by comparing it to something else.

Here, writer and founder of literacy project 826 Valencia, Dave Eggers, uses an analogy in arguing that we do not value teachers as much as we should:

> When we don't get the results we want in our military endeavors, we don't blame the soldiers. We don't say, "It's these lazy soldiers and their bloated benefits plans! That's why we haven't done better in Afghanistan!" No, if the results aren't there, we blame the planners.... No one contemplates blaming the men and women fighting every day in the trenches for little pay and scant recognition. And yet in education we do just that. When we don't like the way our students score on international standardized tests, we blame the teachers.
>
> —Dave Eggers and Nínive Calegari, "The High Cost of Low Teacher Salaries"

Precedent

Arguments from **precedent** and arguments of analogy both involve comparisons. Consider an assertion like this one, which uses a comparison as a precedent:

> If motorists in most other states can pump their own gas safely, surely the state of Oregon can trust its own drivers to be as capable. It's time for Oregon to permit self-service gas stations.

You could tease out several inferences from this claim to explain its reasonableness: people in Oregon are as capable as people in other states; people with equivalent capabilities can do the same thing; pumping gas is not hard; and so forth. But you don't have to because most readers get the argument simply because of the way it is put together.

Here is an excerpt from an extended argument by blogger Abby Phillip, in which she argues that the Ebola outbreak that began in 2014 may not follow the same pattern as past outbreaks:

> An idea long viewed as an unlikely possibility is now becoming increasingly real: Ebola might not go away for a very long time.
>
> It has never happened before in the thirty-eight-year history of the virus. Every other time Ebola has made the unlikely jump from the animal world to the human one, it has been snuffed out within days, weeks or, at most, months.
>
> This time, though, in Guinea, Sierra Leone and Liberia, the Ebola virus is raging like a forest fire, in the words of several public health officials. And some of them are raising the possibility that the outbreak-turned-full-fledged-epidemic could become fundamentally different from any other Ebola outbreak on record, in that it might stick around.
>
> "What's always worked before — contact tracing, isolation and quarantine — is not going to work, and it's not working now," said Daniel Lucey, a professor of microbiology and immunology at Georgetown University Medical Center, who spent three weeks treating Ebola patients in Sierra Leone and will soon travel to the Liberian capital of Monrovia for another five-week stint.
>
> "In my opinion," Lucey added, "a year from now, we won't have one or two cases; we'll have many cases of Ebola."
>
> Unlike past outbreaks, in which Ebola emerged in the sparsely populated countryside of central Africa, this outbreak has become an exponentially spreading urban menace.
>
> —Abby Phillip, "This Ebola Outbreak Could Be Here to Stay"

Unfortunately, the prediction proved to be more accurate than Phillip might have preferred.

You'll encounter additional kinds of logical structures as you create your own arguments. You'll find some of them in Chapter 13, "Fallacies of Argument," and still more in Chapter 15 on Toulmin argument.

Fallacies of Argument

Do these editorial cartoons strike a chord with you? All three are complicated. The first panel pokes fun at slippery slope arguments, which aim to thwart action by predicting dire consequences: chase that Frisbee and you'll soon be pulling milk carts. The second item uses a scare tactic (a potential fallacy of argument) to raise opposition to the educational reform called "Common Core," suggesting ominously that the program's cookie-cutter approach will produce children who all think alike. And the third cartoon points to a fallacy of argument that a prominent politician has perhaps slipped into — the sentimental appeal; it alludes to Hillary Clinton's comment in a 2014 interview with Diane Sawyer that she and husband Bill "came out of the White House not only dead broke but in debt."

Fallacies are argumentative moves flawed by their very nature or structure. Because such tactics can make productive principled argument more difficult, they potentially hurt everyone involved, including the people responsible for them. The worst sorts of fallacies muck up the frank but civil conversations that people should be able to have, regardless of their differences.

Yet it's hard to deny the power in offering audiences a compelling either/or choice or a vulnerable straw man in an argument. For exactly that reason, it's important that you can recognize and point out fallacies in the work of others — and avoid them in your own writing. This chapter aims to help you meet these goals: here we'll introduce you to fallacies of argument classified according to the emotional, ethical, and logical appeals we've discussed earlier (see Chapters 10, 11, and 12).

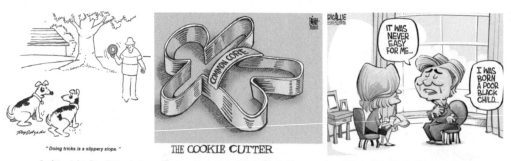

"Doing tricks is a slippery slope."   THE COOKIE CUTTER

IT WAS NEVER EASY FOR ME...   I WAS BORN A POOR BLACK CHILD...

Left to right: Roy Delgado/www.Cartoonstock.com; © Bish/Cagle Cartoons, Inc.; © Eric Allie/Cagle Cartoons, Inc.

Fallacies of Emotional Argument

Emotional arguments can be powerful and suitable in many circumstances, and most writers use them frequently. However, writers who pull on their readers' heart-strings or raise their blood pressure too often can violate the good faith on which legitimate argument depends.

Scare Tactics

Politicians, advertisers, and public figures sometimes peddle their ideas by frightening people and exaggerating possible dangers well beyond their statistical likelihood. Such ploys work because it's easier to imagine something terrible happening than to appreciate its rarity.

Scare tactics can also be used to stampede legitimate fears into panic or prejudice. Laborers who genuinely worry about losing their jobs can be persuaded to fear immigrants who might work for less money. Seniors living on fixed incomes can be convinced that minor changes to entitlement programs represent dire threats to their well-being. Such tactics have the effect of closing off thinking because people who are scared often act irrationally. Even well-intended fear campaigns—like those directed against smoking, unprotected sex, or the use of illegal drugs—can misfire if their warnings prove too shrill. People just stop listening.

Either/Or Choices

Either/or choices can be well-intentioned strategies to get something accomplished. Parents use them all the time ("Eat your broccoli, or you won't get dessert"). But they become fallacious arguments when they reduce a complicated issue to excessively simple terms or when they're designed to obscure legitimate alternatives. Here, for example, is Riyad Mansour, the Palestinian representative to the United Nations, offering the nation of Israel just such a choice in an interview with Charlie Rose in January 2014:

> It is up to them [the Israelis] to decide what kind of a state they want to be. Do they want to be a democratic state where Israel will be the state for all of its citizens? Or do they want to be a state for the Jewish people, therefore excluding 1.6 million Palestinian Arabs who are Israelis from their society? That debate is not our debate. That debate is their debate.

But Joel B. Pollak, writing for Breitbart News Network, describes Mansour's claim as a "false choice" since Israel already is a Jewish state that nonetheless allows Muslims to be full citizens. The either/or argument Mansour presents, according to Pollack, does not describe the realities of this complex political situation.

FIGURE 13.1 A false choice? © Adam Zyglis/Cagle Cartoons, Inc.

Slippery Slope

The **slippery slope** fallacy portrays today's tiny misstep as tomorrow's slide into disaster. Some arguments that aim at preventing dire consequences do not take the slippery slope approach (for example, the parent who corrects a child for misbehavior now is acting sensibly to prevent more serious problems as the child grows older). A slippery slope argument becomes wrongheaded when a writer exaggerates the likely consequences of an action, usually to frighten readers. As such, slippery slope arguments are also scare tactics. In recent years, the issue of gun ownership in America has evoked many slippery slope arguments. Here's one perspective on the tactic:

> The leadership of the NRA is exceptionally fond of the Slippery Slope argument. "Universal background checks will inevitably be followed by a national registry of gun-owners which will inevitably be followed by confiscation of all their guns." Or, "A ban on assault-style weapons and thirty+ round magazines will inevitably be followed by a ban on hand guns with ten-round magazines, that will inevitably be followed by bans on all guns, including antique dueling pistols inherited from our Founding Fathers."
>
> Problem number one with this slide down the fearsome slope is how much weaponry has changed since the days of militias with muskets. Even the NRA agrees that lines have to be drawn somewhere. They do not favor legalization of civilian use of rocket-propelled grenades, bazookas or stinger missiles. If there is a slippery slope we are starting approximately half-way down.
>
> —Michael Wolkowitz, "Slippery Slopes, Imagined and Real"

Social and political ideas and proposals do have consequences, but they aren't always as dire as writers fond of slippery slope tactics would have you believe.

Overly Sentimental Appeals

Overly **sentimental appeals** use tender emotions excessively to distract readers from facts. Often, such appeals are highly personal and individual and focus attention on heartwarming or heartrending situations that make readers feel guilty if they challenge an idea, a policy, or a proposal. Emotions become an impediment to civil discourse when they keep people from thinking clearly.

Such sentimental appeals are a major vehicle of television news, where tugging at viewers' heartstrings can mean high ratings. For example, when a camera documents the day-to-day sacrifices of a single parent trying to meet mortgage payments and keep her kids in college, the woman's on-screen struggles can seem to represent the plight of an entire class of people threatened by callous bankers and college administrators. But while such human interest stories stir genuine emotions, they seldom give a complete picture of complex social or economic issues.

FIGURE 13.2 This image, taken from a gun control protest, is designed to elicit sympathy by causing the viewer to think about the dangers guns pose to innocent children and, thus, support the cause. Tim Boyle/Getty Images

Wear pajamas.
Drink hot chocolate.
**Talk about getting
health insurance.**

#GetTalking
barackobama.com/talk

FIGURE 13.3 Some bandwagon appeals work better than others.

Bandwagon Appeals

Bandwagon appeals urge people to follow the same path everyone else is taking. Such arguments can be relatively benign and seem harmless. But they do push people to take the easier path rather than think independently about what choices to make or where to go.

Many American parents seem to have an innate ability to refute bandwagon appeals. When their kids whine, *Everyone else is going camping without chaperones*, the parents reply, *And if everyone else jumps off a cliff (or a railroad bridge or the Empire State Building), you will too?* The children groan—and then try a different line of argument.

Unfortunately, not all bandwagon approaches are so transparent. In recent decades, bandwagon issues have included a war on drugs, the nuclear freeze movement, campaigns against drunk driving, campaigns for immigration reform, bailouts for banks and businesses, and *many* fads in education from high-stakes testing to MOOCs. All these issues are too complex to permit the suspension of judgment that bandwagon tactics require.

Fallacies of Ethical Argument

Because readers give their closest attention to authors they respect or trust, writers usually want to present themselves as honest, well-informed, likable, or sympathetic. But not all the devices that writers use to gain the attention and confidence of readers are admirable. (For more on appeals based on character, see Chapter 11.)

Appeals to False Authority

Many academic research papers find and reflect on the work of reputable authorities and introduce these authorities through direct quotations or citations as credible evidence. (For more on assessing the reliability of sources, see Chapter 27.) **False authority**, however, occurs when writers offer themselves or other authorities as sufficient warrant for believing a claim:

Claim	X is true because I say so.
Warrant	What I say must be true.

Claim	X is true because Y says so.
Warrant	What Y says must be true.

Though they are seldom stated so baldly, claims of authority drive many political campaigns. American pundits and politicians are fond of citing the U.S. Constitution and its Bill of Rights (Canadians have their Charter of Rights and Freedoms) as ultimate authorities, a reasonable practice when the documents are interpreted respectfully. However, the rights claimed sometimes aren't in the texts themselves or don't mean what the speakers think they do. And most constitutional matters are debatable—as volumes of court records prove. Likewise, religious believers often base arguments on books or traditions that wield great authority in a particular religious community. But the power of such texts is usually limited to that group and less capable of persuading others solely on the grounds of authority.

In short, you should pay serious attention to claims supported by respected authorities, such as the Centers for Disease Control, the National Science Foundation, or the *Globe and Mail*. But don't accept information simply because it is put forth by such offices and agencies. To quote a Russian proverb made famous by Ronald Reagan, "Trust, but verify."

Dogmatism

A writer who asserts or assumes that a particular position is the *only one* that is conceivably acceptable is expressing **dogmatism**, a fallacy of character that undermines the trust that must exist between those who make and listen to arguments. When people or organizations write dogmatically, they imply that no arguments are necessary: the truth is self-evident and needs no support. Here is an extreme example of such an appeal, quoted in an *Atlantic* story by Tracy Brown Hamilton and describing an anti-smoking appeal made by the Third Reich:

> "Brother national socialist, do you know that your Fuhrer is against smoking and thinks that every German is responsible to the whole people for all his deeds and omissions, and does not have the right to damage his body with drugs?"
>
> —From Tracy Brown Hamilton, "The Nazis'
> Forgotten Anti-Smoking Campaign"

Subjects or ideas that can be defended with facts, testimony, and good reasons ought not to be off the table in a free society. In general, whenever someone suggests that even raising an issue for debate is totally unacceptable—whether on the grounds that it's racist, sexist, unpatriotic, blasphemous, insensitive, or offensive in some other way—you should be suspicious.

Ad Hominem Arguments

Ad hominem (Latin for "to the man") **arguments** attack the character of a person rather than the claims he or she makes: when you destroy the credibility of your opponents, you either destroy their ability to present reasonable appeals or distract from the successful arguments they may be offering. Such attacks, of course, aren't aimed at men only, as columnist Jamie Stiehm proved when she criticized Supreme Court Justice Sonia Sotomayor for delaying an Obamacare mandate objected to by the Little Sisters of the Poor, a Catholic religious order. Stiehm directly targets Sotomayor's religious beliefs:

> Et tu, Justice Sonia Sotomayor? Really, we can't trust you on women's health and human rights? The lady from the Bronx just dropped the ball on American women and girls as surely as she did the sparkling ball at midnight on New Year's Eve in Times Square. Or maybe she's just a good Catholic girl.
>
> —Jamie Stiehm, "The Catholic Supreme Court's War on Women"

Stiehm then widens her *ad hominem* assault to include Catholics in general:

> Sotomayor's blow brings us to confront an uncomfortable reality. More than WASPs, Methodists, Jews, Quakers or Baptists, Catholics often try to impose their beliefs on you, me, public discourse and institutions. Especially if "you" are female.

Arguably, *ad hominem* tactics like this turn arguments into two-sided affairs with good guys and bad guys (or gals), and that's unfortunate, since character often really *does* matter in argument. People expect the proponent of peace to be civil, a secretary of the treasury to pay his or her taxes, and the champion of family values to be a faithful spouse. But it's fallacious to attack an idea by uncovering the foibles of its advocates or by attacking their motives, backgrounds, or unchangeable traits.

Stacking the Deck

Just as gamblers try to stack the deck by arranging cards so they are sure to win, writers **stack the deck** when they show only one side of the story—the one in their favor. In a Facebook forum on the documentary film *Super Size Me* (which followed a 32-year-old man who ate three meals a day at McDonald's for thirty days with drastic health consequences), one student points out an example of stacking the deck:

One of the fallacies was stacking the deck. Spurlock stated many facts and gave plenty of evidence of what can happen if you eat fast food in abundance. Weight gain, decline in health, habit forming, and a toll on your daily life. But he failed to show what could happen if you ate the fast food and participated in daily exercise and took vitamins. The fallacy is that he does not show us both sides of what can happen. Possibly you could eat McDonald's for three meals a day for thirty days and if you engaged in daily exercise and took vitamins maybe your health would be just fine. But we were not ever shown that side of the experiment.

—Heather Tew Alleman, on a Facebook forum

In the same way, reviewers have been critical of documentaries by Michael Moore and Dinesh D'Souza that resolutely show only one side of a story or prove highly selective in their coverage. When you stack the deck, you take a big chance that your readers will react like Alleman and decide not to trust you: that's one reason it's so important to show that you have considered alternatives in making any argument.

Fallacies of Logical Argument

You'll encounter a problem in any argument when the claims, warrants, or proofs in it are invalid, insufficient, or disconnected. In theory, such problems seem easy enough to spot, but in practice, they can be camouflaged by a skillful use of words or images. Indeed, logical fallacies pose a challenge to civil argument because they often seem reasonable and natural, especially when they appeal to people's self-interests.

Hasty Generalization

A **hasty generalization** is an inference drawn from insufficient evidence: because *my* Fiat broke down, then *all* Fiats must be junk. It also forms the basis for most stereotypes about people or institutions: because *a few* people in a large group are observed to act in a certain way, *all* members of that group are inferred to behave similarly. The resulting conclusions are usually sweeping claims of little merit: *women are bad drivers*; *men are slobs*; *English teachers are nitpicky*; *computer jocks are…* , and on and on.

To draw valid inferences, you must always have sufficient evidence (see Chapter 26) and you must qualify your claims appropriately. After all, people do need generalizations to make reasonable decisions in life. Such claims can be offered legitimately if placed in context and tagged with sensible qualifiers—*some, a few, many, most, occasionally, rarely, possibly, in some cases, under certain circumstances, in my limited experience.*

Faulty Causality

In Latin, **faulty causality** is known as *post hoc, ergo propter hoc*, which translates as "after this, therefore because of this" — the faulty assumption that because one event or action follows another, the first causes the second. Consider a lawsuit commented on in the *Wall Street Journal* in which a writer sued Coors (unsuccessfully), claiming that drinking copious amounts of the company's beer had kept him from writing a novel.

Some actions do produce reactions. Step on the brake pedal in your car, and you move hydraulic fluid that pushes calipers against disks to create friction that stops the vehicle. In other cases, however, a supposed connection between cause and effect turns out to be completely wrong. For example, doctors now believe that when an elderly person falls and breaks a hip or leg, the injury usually caused the fall rather than the other way around.

That's why overly simple causal claims should always be subject to scrutiny. In summer 2008, writer Nicholas Carr posed a simple causal question in a cover story for the *Atlantic*: "Is Google Making Us Stupid?" Carr essentially answered yes, arguing that "as we come to rely on computers to mediate our understanding of the world, it is our own intelligence that flattens" and that the more one is online the less he or she is able to concentrate or read deeply.

But others, like Jamais Cascio (senior fellow at the Institute for Ethics and Emerging Technologies), soon challenged that causal connection: rather than making us stupid, Cascio argues, Internet tools like Google will lead to the development of "'fluid intelligence' — the ability to find meaning in confusion and to solve new problems, independent of acquired knowledge." The final word on this contentious causal relationship — the effects on the human brain caused by new technology — has yet to be written, and will probably be available only after decades of complicated research.

Begging the Question

Most teachers have heard some version of the following argument: *You can't give me a C in this course; I'm an A student.* A member of Congress accused of taking kickbacks can make much the same argument: *I can't be guilty of accepting such bribes; I'm an honest person.* In both cases, the claim is made on grounds that can't be accepted as true because those grounds themselves are in question. How can the accused bribe-taker defend herself on grounds of honesty when that honesty is in doubt? Looking at the arguments in Toulmin terms helps to see the fallacy:

Claim	You can't give me a C in this course . . .
Reason	. . . because I'm an A student.
Warrant	An A student is someone who can't receive Cs.

Claim	Representative X can't be guilty of accepting bribes . . .
Reason	. . . because she's an honest person.
Warrant	An honest person cannot be guilty of accepting bribes.

With the warrants stated, you can see why **begging the question**— assuming as true the very claim that's disputed — is a form of circular argument that goes nowhere. (For more on Toulmin argument, see Chapter 15.)

Equivocation

Equivocations— half truths or arguments that give lies an honest appearance— are usually based on tricks of language. Consider the plagiarist who copies a paper word for word from a source and then declares that "I wrote the entire paper myself"— meaning that she physically copied the piece on her own. But the plagiarist is using *wrote* equivocally and knows that most people understand the word to mean composing and not merely copying words.

Parsing words carefully can sometimes look like equivocation or be the thing itself. For example, early in 2014 Internal Revenue Service Commissioner John Koskinen promised to turn over to a committee of the House of Representatives all the relevant emails in a scandal involving the agency. Subsequently, the agency revealed that some of those requested emails had been destroyed by the failure of a computer's hard drive. But Koskinen defended his earlier promise by telling the chair of the committee, "I never said I would provide you emails we didn't have." A simple statement of fact or a slick equivocation?

Non Sequitur

A **non sequitur** is an argument whose claims, reasons, or warrants don't connect logically. You've probably detected a non sequitur when you react to an argument with a puzzled, "Wait, that doesn't follow." Children are adept at framing non sequiturs like this one: *You don't love me or you'd buy me a new bicycle!* It doesn't take a parental genius to realize that love has little connection with buying children toys.

Non sequiturs often occur when writers omit steps in an otherwise logical chain of reasoning. For example, it might be a non sequitur to argue that since postsecondary education now costs so much, it's time to move colleges and university instruction online. Such a suggestion *may* have merit, but a leap from brick-and-mortar schools to virtual ones is extreme. Numerous issues and questions must be addressed step-by-step before the proposal can be taken seriously.

Politicians sometimes resort to non sequiturs to evade thorny issues or questions. Here for example is presidential candidate Mitt Romney in a 2011 CNBC Republican primary debate turning moderator John Harwood's question about changing political positions into one about demonstrating personal integrity:

> *Harwood:*...Your opponents have said you switched positions on many issues.... What can you say to Republicans to persuade them that the things you say in the campaign are rooted in something deeper than the fact that you are running for office?

> *Romney:* John, I think people know me pretty well.... I think people understand that I'm a man of steadiness and constancy. I don't think you are going to find somebody who has more of those attributes than I do. I have been married to the same woman for ...42 years.... I have been in the same church my entire life.

Conservative writer Matt K. Lewis took Romney to task for this move, pointing out that a steady personal life is no guarantor of a consistent political philosophy:

> This, of course, is not to say that values and character do not matter—they *do*—but it is to say that Romney's answer was a non sequitur. Everyone knows Mitt Romney is a decent, respectable person. The question is whether or not he can be trusted to advance conservatism as president.

Straw Man

Those who resort to the **straw man** fallacy attack arguments that no one is really making or portray opponents' positions as more extreme or far less coherent than they actually are. The speaker or writer thus sets up an argument that is conveniently easy to knock down (like a man of straw), proceeds to do so, and then claims victory over an opponent who may not even exist.

Straw men are especially convenient devices for politicians who want to characterize the positions of their opponents as more extreme than they actually are: consider obvious memes such as "war on women" and "war on Christmas." But straw man arguments are often more subtle. For instance, Steven Novella of Yale

University argues that political commentator Charles Krauthammer slips into the fallacy when he misconstrues the meaning of "settled science" in a column on climate change. Novella rebuts Krauthammer's assertion that "There is nothing more anti-scientific than the very idea that science is settled, static, impervious to challenge" by explaining why such a claim is deceptive:

> Calling something an established scientific fact means that it is reasonable to proceed with that fact as a premise, for further research or for policy. It does not mean "static, impervious to challenge." That is the straw man. Both evolution deniers and climate change deniers use this tactic to misinterpret scientific confidence as an anti-scientific resistance to new evidence or arguments. It isn't. It does mean that the burden of proof has shifted to those opposing the theory that is now well-established (because it has already met a significant burden of proof).

> —Steven Novella, *NeuroLogica Blog*, February 25, 2014

In other words, Krauthammer's definition of *science* is not one that most scientists use.

Red Herring

This fallacy gets its name from the old British hunting practice of dragging a dried herring across the path of the fox in order to throw the hounds off the trail. A **red herring** fallacy does just that: it changes the subject abruptly or introduces an irrelevant claim or fact to throw readers or listeners off the trail. For example, people skeptical about climate change will routinely note that weather is always changing and point to the fact that Vikings settled in Greenland one thousand years ago before harsher conditions drove them away. True, scientists will say, but the point is irrelevant to arguments about worldwide global warming caused by human activity.

The red herring is not only a device writers and speakers use in the arguments they create, but it's also a charge used frequently to undermine someone else's arguments. Couple the term "red herring" in a Web search to just about any political or social cause and you'll come up with numerous articles complaining of someone's use of the device.

climate change + red herring

common core + red herring

immigration reform + red herring

"Red herring" has become a convenient way of saying "I disagree with your argument" or "your point is irrelevant." And perhaps making a too-easy rebuttal like that can itself be a fallacy?

Faulty Analogy

Comparisons can help to clarify one concept by measuring it against another that is more familiar. Consider the power and humor of this comparison attributed to Mark Twain, an implicit argument for term limits in politics:

> Politicians and diapers must be changed often, and for the same reason.

When comparisons such as this one are extended, they become *analogies*—ways of understanding unfamiliar ideas by comparing them with something that's better known (see p. 217). But useful as such comparisons are, they may prove false if either taken on their own and pushed too far, or taken too seriously. At this point, they turn into **faulty analogies**—inaccurate or inconsequential comparisons between objects or concepts. Economist Paul Krugman provides an eye-opening analysis of a familiar but, as he sees it, false analogy between personal and government debt:

> Deficit-worriers portray a future in which we're impoverished by the need to pay back money we've been borrowing. They see America as being like a family that took out too large a mortgage, and will have a hard time making the monthly payments.
>
> This is, however, a really bad analogy in at least two ways.
>
> First, families have to pay back their debt. Governments don't—all they need to do is ensure that debt grows more slowly than their tax base. The debt from World War II was never repaid; it just became increasingly irrelevant as the U.S. economy grew, and with it the income subject to taxation.
>
> Second—and this is the point almost nobody seems to get—an overborrowed family owes money to someone else; U.S. debt is, to a large extent, money we owe to ourselves.

Whether you agree with the Nobel laureate or not, his explanation offers insight into how analogies work (or fail) and how to think about them critically.

RESPOND

1. Examine each of the following political slogans or phrases for logical fallacies.

    "Resistance is futile." (Borg message on *Star Trek: The Next Generation*)

    "It's the economy, stupid." (sign on the wall at Bill Clinton's campaign headquarters)

    "Make love, not war." (antiwar slogan popularized during the Vietnam War)

    "A chicken in every pot." (campaign slogan)

    "Guns don't kill, people do." (NRA slogan)

    "Dog Fighters Are Cowardly Scum." (PETA T-shirt)

    "If you can't stand the heat, get out of the kitchen." (attributed to Harry S Truman)

2. Choose a paper you've written for a college class and analyze it for signs of fallacious reasoning. Then find an editorial, a syndicated column, and a news report on the same topic and look for fallacies in them. Which has the most fallacies—and what kind? What may be the role of the audience in determining when a statement is fallacious?

3. Find a Web site that is sponsored by an organization (the Future of Music Coalition, perhaps), a business (Coca-Cola, Pepsi), or another group (the Democratic or Republican National Committee), and analyze the site for fallacious reasoning. Among other considerations, look at the relationship between text and graphics and between individual pages and the pages that surround or are linked to them.

4. Political blogs such as Mother Jones and *InstaPundit* typically provide quick responses to daily events and detailed critiques of material in other media sites, including national newspapers. Study one such blog for a few days to see whether and how the site critiques the articles, political commentary, or writers it links to. Does the blog ever point out fallacies of argument? If so, does it explain the problems with such reasoning or just assume readers will understand the fallacies? Summarize your findings in a brief oral report to your class.

Rhetorical Analysis

I f you watched the 2013 Super Bowl between the Baltimore Ravens and the San Francisco 49ers, you may remember the commercial. For two solemn minutes, still photographs of rural America and the people who work there moved across the screen accompanied by the unmistakable voice of the late Paul Harvey reading words he had first delivered in 1978. Maria Godoy of NPR described it this way: "It may not have been as dramatic as the stadium blackout that halted play for more than a half-hour, or as extravagant as Beyonce's halftime show. But for many viewers of Super Bowl XLVII, one of the standout moments was a deceptively simple ad for the Dodge Ram called 'God Made a Farmer.'" It was a fourth quarter interrupted by cattle, churches, snowy farmyards, bales of hay, plowed fields, hardworking men, and a few sturdy women. Occasionally, a slide discreetly showed a Ram truck, sponsor of the video, but there were no overt sales pitches—only a product logo in the final frame. Yet visits to the Ram Web site spiked immediately, and sales of Ram pickups did too. (The official video has been viewed on YouTube more than 17 million times.)

All images © Andy Anderson, Lone River Productions

So how to account for the appeal of such an unconventional and unexpected commercial? That would be the work of a **rhetorical analysis**, the close reading of a text or, in this case, a video commercial, to figure out exactly how it functions. Certainly, the creators of "God Made a Farmer" counted on the strong emotional appeal of the photographs they'd commissioned, guessing perhaps that the expert images and Harvey's spellbinding words would contrast powerfully with the frivolity and emptiness of much Super Bowl ad fare:

> God said, "I need somebody willing to sit up all night with a newborn colt. And watch it die. Then dry his eyes and say, 'Maybe next year.'"

They pushed convention, too, by the length of the spot and the muted product connection, doubtless hoping to win the goodwill of a huge audience suddenly all teary-eyed in the midst of a football game. And they surely gained the respect of a great many truck-buying farmers.

Rhetorical analyses can also probe the contexts that surround any argument or text — its impact on a society, its deeper implications, or even what it lacks or whom it excludes. Predictably, the widely admired Ram commercial (selected #1 Super Bowl XLVII spot by *Adweek*) acquired its share of critics, some attacking it for romanticizing farm life, others for ignoring the realities of industrial agriculture. And not a few writers noted what they regarded as glaring absences in its representation of farmers. Here, for instance, is copywriter and blogger Edye Deloch-Hughes, offering a highly personal and conflicted view of the spot in what amounts to an informal rhetorical analysis:

> …I was riveted by the still photography and stirring thirty-five-year-old delivery of legendary radio broadcaster Paul Harvey. But as I sat mesmerized, I waited to see an image that spoke to my heritage. What flashed before me were close-ups of stoic white men whose faces drowned out the obligatory medium shots of a minority token or two; their images minimized against the amber waves of grain.

> God made a Black farmer too. Where was my Grandpa, Grandma and Great Granny? My Auntie and Uncle Bolden? And didn't God make Hispanic and Native American farmers? They too were under-represented.

> I am the offspring of a century and a half of African-American caretakers of the land, from Arkansas, Mississippi and Louisiana, who experienced their toils and troubles, their sun ups and sun downs. Their injustices and beatdowns. I wrestled with my mixed emotions; loving the commercial and feeling dejected at the same time.

…Minimizing positive Black imagery and accomplishments is as American as wrestling cattle. We're often footnotes or accessories in history books, TV shows, movies and magazines as well as TV commercials. When content is exceptional, the omission is harder to recognize or criticize. Some friends of mine saw—or rather *felt*—the omission as I did. Others did not. I say be aware and vocal about how you are represented—if represented at all, otherwise your importance and relevance will be lost.

—Edye Deloch-Hughes, "So God Made a Black Farmer Too"

As this example suggests, whenever you undertake a rhetorical analysis, follow your instincts and look closely. Why does an ad for a cell phone or breakfast sandwich make people want one immediately? How does an op-ed piece in the *Washington Post* suddenly change your long-held position on immigration? A rhetorical analysis might help you understand. Dig as deep as you can into the context of the item you are analyzing, especially when you encounter puzzling, troubling, or unusually successful appeals—ethical, emotional, or logical. Ask yourself what strategies a speech, editorial, opinion column, film, or ad spot employs to move your heart, win your trust, and change your mind—or why, maybe, it fails to do so.

Composing a Rhetorical Analysis

You perform a rhetorical analysis by analyzing how well the components of an argument work together to persuade or move an audience. You can study arguments of any kind—advertisements (as we've seen), editorials, political cartoons, and even songs, movies, or photographs. In every case, you'll need to focus your rhetorical analysis on elements that stand out or make the piece intriguing or problematic. You could begin by exploring *some* of the following issues:

- What is the purpose of this argument? What does it hope to achieve?

- Who is the audience for this argument? Who is ignored or excluded?

- What appeals or techniques does the argument use—emotional, logical, ethical?

- What type of argument is it, and how does the genre affect the argument? (You might challenge the lack of evidence in editorials, but you wouldn't make the same complaint about bumper stickers.)

- Who is making the argument? What ethos does it create, and how does it do so? What values does the ethos evoke? How does it make the writer or creator seem trustworthy?

- What authorities does the argument rely on or appeal to?

- What facts, reasoning, and evidence are used in the argument? How are they presented?

- What claims does the argument make? What issues are raised—or ignored or evaded?

- What are the contexts—social, political, historical, cultural—for this argument? Whose interests does it serve? Who gains or loses by it?

- How is the argument organized or arranged? What media does the argument use and how effectively?

- How does the language or style of the argument persuade an audience?

In answering questions like these, try to show *how* the key devices in an argument actually make it succeed or fail. Quote freely from a written piece, or describe the elements in a visual argument. (Annotating a visual text is one option.) Let readers know where and why an argument makes sense and where it falls apart. If you believe that an argument startles, challenges, insults, or lulls audiences, explain why that is the case and provide evidence. Don't be surprised when your rhetorical analysis itself becomes an argument. That's what it should be.

Understanding the Purpose of Arguments You Are Analyzing

To understand how well any argument works, begin with its purpose: Is it to sell running shoes? To advocate for limits to college tuition? To push a political agenda? In many cases, that purpose may be obvious. A conservative blog will likely advance right-wing causes; ads from a baby food company will likely show happy infants delighted with stewed prunes.

But some projects may hide their persuasive intentions. Perhaps you've responded to a mail survey or telephone poll only to discover that the questions are leading you to switch your cable service or buy apartment insurance. Do such stealthy arguments succeed? Do consumers resent the intrusion? Answering questions like these provides material for useful rhetorical analyses that assess the strengths, risks, and ethics of such strategies.

Understanding Who Makes an Argument

Knowing *who* is claiming *what* is key to any rhetorical analysis. That's why persuasive appeals usually have a name attached to them. Remember the statements included in TV ads during the last federal election: "Hello, I'm X—and I approve this ad"? Federal law requires such statements so we can tell the difference between ads a candidate endorses and ones sponsored by groups not even affiliated with the campaigns. Their interests and motives might be very different.

But knowing a name is just a starting place for analysis. You need to dig deeper, and you could do worse than to Google such people or groups to discover more about them. What else have they produced? Who publishes them: the *Wall Street Journal*, the blog *The Daily Kos*, or even a LiveJournal celebrity gossip site such as *Oh No They Didn't*? Check out related Web sites for information about goals, policies, contributors, and funding.

FIGURE 14.1 Funny, offensive, or both? © Chris Maddaloni/CQ Roll Call

RESPOND

Describe a persuasive moment that you can recall from a speech, an editorial, an advertisement, a YouTube clip, or a blog posting. Or research one of the following famous persuasive moments and describe the circumstances—the historical situation, the issues at stake, the purpose of the argument—that make it so memorable.

Abraham Lincoln's Gettysburg Address (1863)

Elizabeth Cady Stanton's Declaration of Sentiments at the Seneca Falls Convention (1848)

Chief Tecumseh's address to General William Henry Harrison (1810)

Winston Churchill's radio addresses to the British people during World War II (1940)

Martin Luther King Jr.'s "Letter from Birmingham Jail" (1963)

Ronald Reagan's tribute to the *Challenger* astronauts (1986)

Toni Morrison's speech accepting the Nobel Prize (1993)

Will.i.am's "Yes We Can" song/collage on YouTube (2008)

Identifying and Appealing to Audiences

Most arguments are composed with specific audiences in mind, and their success depends, in part, on how well their strategies, content, tone, and language meet the expectations of that audience. So your rhetorical analysis of an argumentative piece should identify its target readers or viewers (see "Appealing to Audiences," p. 172) if possible, or make an educated guess about the audience, since most arguments suggest whom they intend to reach and in what ways.

Both a flyer stapled to a bulletin board in a college dorm ("Why you shouldn't drink and drive") and a forty-foot billboard for Bud Light might be aimed at the same general population—college students. But each will adjust its appeals for the different moods of that group in different moments. For starters, the flyer will appeal to students in a serious vein, while the beer ad will probably be visually stunning and virtually text-free.

You might also examine how a writer or an argument establishes credibility with an audience. One effective means of building credibility is to show respect for your readers or viewers, especially if they may not agree with you. In introducing an article on problems facing African American women in the workplace, editor in chief of *Essence* Diane Weathers considers the problems that she faced with respecting all her potential readers:

> We spent more than a minute agonizing over the provocative cover line for our feature "White Women at Work." The countless stories we had heard from women across the country told us that this was a workplace issue we had to address. From my own experience at several major magazines, it was painfully obvious to me that Black and White women are not on the same track. Sure, we might all start out in the same place. But early in the game, most sisters I know become stuck—and the reasons have little to do with intelligence or drive. At some point we bump our heads against that ceiling. And while White women may complain of a glass ceiling, for us, the ceiling is concrete.
>
> So how do we tell this story without sounding whiny and paranoid, or turning off our White-female readers, staff members, advertisers and girlfriends? Our solution: Bring together real women (several of them highly successful senior corporate executives), put them in a room, promise them anonymity and let them speak their truth.
>
> —Diane Weathers, "Speaking Our Truth"

Both paragraphs affirm Weathers's determination to treat audiences fairly *and* to deal honestly with a difficult subject. The strategy would merit attention in any rhetorical analysis.

FIGURE 14.2 Retailers like Walmart build their credibility by simple "straight talk" to shoppers: our low prices make your life better. Beth Hall/Bloomberg News/Getty Images

Look, too, for signals that writers share values with readers or at least understand an audience. In the following passage, writer Jack Solomon is clear about one value that he hopes readers have in common—a preference for "straight talk":

> There are some signs in the advertising world that Americans are getting fed up with fantasy advertisements and want to hear some straight talk. Weary of extravagant product claims ..., consumers trained by years of advertising to distrust what they hear seem to be developing an immunity to commercials.
>
> —Jack Solomon, "Masters of Desire:
> The Culture of American Advertising"

But straight talk still requires common sense. If ever a major television ad seriously misread its audience, it may have been a spot that ran during the 2014 Winter Olympics for Cadillac's pricey new plug-in hybrid, the ELR. The company seemed to go out of its way to offend a great many people, foreign and domestic. As is typical strategy in rhetorical analyses, *Huffington Post*'s Carolyn Gregoire takes care to describe in detail the item she finds offensive:

> The opening shot shows a middle-aged man, played by the actor Neal McDonough, looking out over his backyard pool, asking the question: "Why do we work so hard? For this? For stuff?"

As the ad continues, it becomes clear that the answer to this rhetorical question is actually a big fat YES. And it gets worse. "Other countries, they work," he says. "They stroll home. They stop by the cafe. They take August off. Off."

Then he reveals just what it is that makes Americans better than all those lazy, espresso-sipping foreigners.

"Why aren't you like that?" he says. "Why aren't we like that? Because we're crazy, driven, hard-working believers, that's why."

> —Carolyn Gregoire, "Cadillac Made a Commercial about
> the American Dream, and It's a Nightmare"

Her conclusion then is blistering, showing how readily a rhetorical analysis becomes an argument — and subject to criticism itself:

> Cadillacs have long been a quintessentially American symbol of wealth and status. But as this commercial proves, no amount of wealth or status is a guarantee of good taste. Now, the luxury car company is selling a vision of the American Dream at its worst: Work yourself into the ground, take as little time off as possible, and buy expensive sh*t (specifically, a 2014 Cadillac ELR).

Examining Arguments Based on Emotion: Pathos

Some emotional appeals are just ploys to win over readers with a pretty face, figurative or real. You've seen ads promising an exciting life and attractive friends if only you drink the right soda or wear a particular brand of clothes. Are you fooled by such claims? Probably not, if you pause to think about them. But that's the strategy — to distract you from thought just long enough to make a bad choice. It's a move worth commenting on in a rhetorical analysis.

Yet emotions can add real muscle to arguments, too, and that's worth noting. For example, persuading people not to drink and drive by making them fear death, injury, or arrest seems like a fair use of an emotional appeal. The public service announcement on p. 242 uses an emotion-laden image to remind drivers to think of the consequences.

In a rhetorical analysis, you might note the juxtaposition of image with text, leading readers to connect casual notes left on windshields with the very serious consequences of drunk driving.

FIGURE 14.3 How well does the emotional appeal here work?

In analyzing emotional appeals, judge whether the emotions raised—anger, sympathy, fear, envy, joy, love, lust—advance the claims offered. Consider how columnist Ron Rosenbaum (whom we met in Chapter 10) makes the reasonable argument he offers for fatty foods all the more attractive by larding it with voluptuous language:

> The foods that best hit that sweet spot and "overwhelm the brain" with pleasure are high-quality fatty foods. They discourage us from overeating. A modest serving of short ribs or Peking duck will be both deeply pleasurable and self-limiting. As the brain swoons into insensate delight, you won't have to gorge a still-craving cortex with mediocre sensations. "Sensory-specific satiety" makes a slam-dunk case (it's science!) for eating reasonable servings of superbly satisfying fatty foods.
>
> —Ron Rosenbaum, "Let Them Eat Fat"

Does the use of evocative language ("swoons," "insensate delight," "superbly satisfying," "slam-dunk") convince you, or does it distract from considering the scientific case for "sensory-specific satiety"? Your task in a rhetorical analysis is to study an author's words, the emotions they evoke, and the claims they support and then to make this kind of judgment.

FIGURE 14.4 Health food? Kittipojn Pravalpatkul/Shutterstock

RESPOND

Browse YouTube or another Web site to find an example of a powerful emotional argument that's made visually, either alone or using words as well. In a paragraph, defend a claim about how the argument works. For example, does an image itself make a claim, or does it draw you in to consider a verbal claim? What emotion does the argument generate? How does that emotion work to persuade you?

Examining Arguments Based on Character: Ethos

It should come as no surprise: readers believe writers who seem honest, wise, and trustworthy. So in analyzing the effectiveness of an argument, look for evidence of these traits. Does the writer have the experience or authority to write on this subject? Are all claims qualified reasonably? Is evidence presented in full, not tailored to the writer's agenda? Are important objections to the author's position acknowledged and addressed? Are sources documented? Above all, does the writer sound trustworthy?

When a Norwegian anti-immigration extremist killed seventy-six innocent people in July 2011, Prime Minister Jens Stoltenberg addressed the citizens of Norway (and the world), and in doing so evoked the character or ethos of the entire nation:

> We will not let fear break us! The warmth of response from people in Norway and from the whole world makes me sure of this one thing: evil can kill a single person, but never defeat a whole people. The strongest weapon in the world—that is freedom of expression and democracy.

In analyzing this speech, you would do well to look at the way this passage deploys the deepest values of Norway—freedom of expression and democracy—to serve as a response to fear of terrorism. In doing so, Stoltenberg evokes ethical ideals to hold onto in a time of tragedy.

Or take a look at the following paragraph from a blog posting by Timothy Burke, a teacher at Swarthmore College and parent of a preschool child who is trying to think through the issue of homework for elementary school kids:

> So I've been reading a bit about homework and comparing notes with parents. There is a lot of variation across districts, not just in the amount of homework that kids are being asked to do, but in the kind of homework. Some districts give kids a lot of time-consuming busywork; other districts try to concentrate on having homework assignments be substantive work that is best accomplished independently. Some give a lot from a very early point in K-12 education; some give relatively little. As both a professional educator and an individual with personal convictions, I'd tend to argue against excessive amounts of homework and against assigning busywork. But what has ultimately interested me more about reading various discussions of homework is how intense the feelings are swirling around the topic and how much that intensity strikes me as a problem in and of itself. Not just as a symptom of a kind of civic illness, an inability to collectively and democratically work through complex issues, but also in some cases as evidence of an educational failure in its own right.

Burke establishes his ethos by citing his reading and his talks with other parents.

He underscores his right to address the matter.

He expresses concern about immoderate arguments and implies that he will demonstrate an opposite approach.

In considering the role of ethos in rhetorical analyses, pay attention to the details right down to the choice of words or, in an image, the shapes and colors. The modest, tentative tone that Burke uses in his blog is an example of the kind of choice that can shape an audience's perception of ethos. But these details need your interpretation. Language that's hot and extreme can mark a writer as either passionate or loony. Work that's sober and carefully organized can paint an institution as competent or overly cautious. Technical terms and abstract phrases can make a writer seem either knowledgeable or pompous.

Examining Arguments Based on
Facts and Reason: Logos

In analyzing most arguments, you'll have to decide whether an argument makes a plausible claim and offers good reasons for you to believe it. Not all arguments will package such claims in a single neat sentence, or **thesis**—nor should they. A writer may tell a story from which you have to infer the claim. Visual arguments may work the same way: viewers have to assemble the parts and draw inferences in order to get the point.

Some conventional arguments (like those on an editorial page) may be perfectly obvious: writers stake out a claim and then present reasons that you should consider, or they may first present reasons and lay out a case that leads you to accept a claim in the conclusion. Consider the following example. In a tough opinion piece in *Time*, political commentator John McWhorter argues that filmmaker Spike Lee is being racist when he rails against hipsters moving into Fort Greene, a formerly all-black neighborhood in Brooklyn, New York. Lee fears that the whites are raising housing prices, pushing out old-time residents and diminishing the African American character of Fort Greene. McWhorter, an African American like Lee, sees matters differently:

> Basically, black people are getting paid more money than they've ever seen in their lives for their houses, and a once sketchy neighborhood is now quiet and pleasant. And this is a bad thing …why?

> Lee seems to think it's somehow an injustice whenever black people pick up stakes. But I doubt many of the blacks now set to pass fat inheritances on to their kids feel that way. This is not the old story of poor blacks being pushed out of neighborhoods razed down for highway construction. Lee isn't making sense.

> —John McWhorter, "Spike Lee's Racism Isn't Cute"

When you encounter explicit charges like these, you analyze whether and how the claims are supported by good reasons and reliable evidence. A lengthy essay may, in fact, contain a series of claims, each developed to support an even larger point. Here's McWhorter, for instance, expanding his argument by suggesting that Lee's attitudes toward whites are irreconcilable.

> "Respect the culture" when you move in, Lee growls. But again, he isn't making sense. We can be quite sure that if whites "respected" the culture by trying to participate in it, Lee would be one of the first in line to call it "appropriation." So, no whites better open up barbecue joints or spoken word cafes or try to be rappers. Yet if whites walk on by the culture in "respectful" silence, then the word on the street becomes that they want to keep blacks at a distance.

FIGURE 14.5 An anti-fur protestor in London makes a rather specific claim.
© Charles Platiau/Reuters/Corbis

Indeed, every paragraph in an argument may develop a specific and related idea. In a rhetorical analysis, you need to identify all these separate propositions and examine the relationships among them: Are they solidly linked? Are there inconsistencies that the writer should acknowledge? Does the end of the piece support what the writer said (and promised) at the beginning?

You'll also need to examine the quality of the information presented in an argument, assessing how accurately such information is reported, how conveniently it's displayed (in charts or graphs, for example), and how well the sources cited represent a range of *respected* opinions on a topic. (For more information on the use of evidence, see Chapter 12.)

Knowing how to judge the quality of sources is more important now than ever before because the digital universe is full of junk. In some ways, the computer terminal has become the equivalent of a library reference room, but the sources available online vary widely in quality and have not been evaluated by a library professional. As a consequence, you must know the difference between reliable, firsthand, or fully documented sources and those that don't meet such standards. (For using and documenting sources, see Chapters 27, 28, and 30.)

Examining the Arrangement and Media of Arguments

Aristotle carved the structure of logical argument to its bare bones when he observed that it had only two parts:

- statement
- proof

You could do worse, in examining an argument, than to make sure that every claim a writer makes is backed by sufficient evidence. Some arguments are written on the fly in the heat of the moment. Most arguments that you read and write, however, will be more than mere statements followed by proofs. Some writers will lay their cards on the table immediately; others may lead you carefully through a chain of claims toward a conclusion. Writers may even interrupt their arguments to offer background information or cultural contexts for readers. Sometimes they'll tell stories or provide anecdotes that make an argumentative point. They'll qualify the arguments they make, too, and often pause to admit that other points of view are plausible.

In other words, there are no formulas or acceptable patterns that fit all successful arguments. In writing a rhetorical analysis, you'll have to assess the organization of a persuasive text on its own merits.

It's fair, however, to complain about what may be *absent* from an argument. Most arguments of proposal (see Chapter 20), for example, include a section that defends the feasibility of a new idea, explaining how it might be funded or managed. In a rhetorical analysis, you might fault an editorial that supports a new stadium for a city without addressing feasibility issues. Similarly, analyzing a movie review that reads like an off-the-top-of-the-head opinion, you might legitimately ask what criteria of evaluation are in play (see Chapter 18).

Rhetorical analysis also calls for you to look carefully at an argument's transitions, headings and subheadings, documentation of sources, and overall tone or voice. Don't take such details for granted, since all of them contribute to the strength—or weakness—of an argument.

Nor should you ignore the way a writer or an institution uses media. Would an argument originally made in a print editorial, for instance, work better as a digital presentation (or vice versa)? Would a lengthy paper have more power if it included more images? Or do these images distract from a written argument's substance?

Finally, be open to the possibility of new or nontraditional structures of arguments. The visual arguments that you analyze may defy conventional principles of logic or arrangement—for example, making juxtapositions rather than logical transitions between elements or using quick cuts, fades, or other devices to link ideas. Quite often, these nontraditional structures will also resist the neatness of a thesis, leaving readers to construct at least a part of the argument in their heads. As we saw with the "God Made a Farmer" spot at the beginning of this chapter, advertisers are growing fond of soft-sell multimedia productions that can seem like something other than what they really are—product pitches. We may be asked not just to buy a product but also to live its lifestyle or embrace its ethos. Is that a reasonable or work-able strategy for an argument? Your analysis might entertain such possibilities.

Looking at Style

Even a coherent argument full of sound evidence may not connect with readers if it's dull, off-key, or offensive. Readers naturally judge the credibility of arguments in part by how stylishly the case is made—even when they don't know exactly what style is (for more on style, see Chapter 21). Consider how these simple, blunt sentences from the opening of an argument shape your image of the author and probably determine whether you're willing to continue to read the whole piece:

> We are young, urban, and professional. We are literate, respectable, intelli-gent, and charming. But foremost and above all, we are unemployed.
>
> —Julia Carlisle, "Young, Privileged, and Unemployed"

The strong, straightforward tone and the stark juxtaposition of being "intelligent" with "unemployed" set the style for this letter to the editor.

Now consider the brutally sarcastic tone of Nathaniel Stein's hilarious parody of the Harvard grading policy, a piece he wrote following up on a professor's complaint of out-of-control grade inflation at the school. Stein borrows the formal language of a typical "grading standards" sheet to mock the decline in rigor that the professor has lamented:

> The A+ grade is used only in very rare instances for the recognition of truly exceptional achievement.
>
> For example: A term paper receiving the A+ is virtually indistinguishable from the work of a professional, both in its choice of paper stock and its font. The student's command of the topic is expert, or at the very least intermediate, or beginner. Nearly every single word in the paper is spelled correctly; those that are not can be reasoned out phonetically within minutes. Content from Wikipedia is integrated with precision. The paper contains few, if any, death threats....
>
> An overall course grade of A+ is reserved for those students who have not only demonstrated outstanding achievement in coursework but have also asked very nicely.

Finally, the A+ grade is awarded to all collages, dioramas and other art projects.

—Nathaniel Stein, "Leaked! Harvard's Grading Rubric"

Both styles probably work, but they signal that the writers are about to make very different kinds of cases. Here, style alone tells readers what to expect.

Manipulating style also enables writers to shape readers' responses to their ideas. Devices as simple as repetition, parallelism, or even paragraph length can give sentences remarkable power. Consider this passage from an essay by Sherman Alexie in which he explores the complex reaction of straight men to the announcement of NBA star Jason Collins that he is gay:

Homophobic basketball fans will disparage his skills, somehow equating his NBA benchwarmer status with his sexuality. But let's not forget that Collins is still one of the best 1,000 basketball players in the world. He has always been better than his modest statistics would indicate, and his teams have been dramatically more efficient with him on the court. He is better at hoops than 99.9 percent of you are at anything you do. He might not be a demigod, but he's certainly a semi-demigod. Moreover, his basketball colleagues universally praise him as a physically and mentally tough player. In his prime, he ably battled that behemoth known as Shaquille O'Neal. Most of all, Collins is widely regarded as one of the finest gentlemen to ever play the game. Generous, wise, and supportive, he's a natural leader. And he has a degree from Stanford University.

In other words, he's a highly attractive dude.

—Sherman Alexie,
"Jason Collins Is the Envy of Straight Men Everywhere"

In this passage, Alexie uses a sequence of short, direct, and roughly parallel sentences ("He is …He might …He ably battled …He has") to present evidence justifying the playful point he makes in a pointedly emphatic, one-sentence paragraph. The remainder of his short essay then amplifies that point.

In a rhetorical analysis, you can explore such stylistic choices. Why does a formal style work for discussing one type of subject matter but not another? How does a writer use humor or irony to underscore an important point or to manage a difficult concession? Do stylistic choices, even something as simple as the use of contractions or personal pronouns, bring readers close to a writer, or do technical words and an impersonal voice signal that an argument is for experts only?

FIGURE 14.6 Jason Collins © Gary A. Vasquez/USA Today Sports Images

To describe the stylistic effects of visual arguments, you may use a different vocabulary and talk about colors, camera angles, editing, balance, proportion, fonts, perspective, and so on. But the basic principle is this: the look of an item—whether a poster, an editorial cartoon, or a film documentary—can support the message that it carries, undermine it, or muddle it. In some cases, the look will *be* the message. In a rhetorical analysis, you can't ignore style.

FIGURE 14.7 This poster, promoting travel to the bicycle-friendly city of Münster, Germany, demonstrates visually the amount of space needed to transport the same number of people by car, bicycle, and bus. Foto Presseamt Münster, City of Münster, Press Office

RESPOND

Find a recent example of a visual argument, either in print or on the Internet. Even though you may have a copy of the image, describe it carefully in your paper on the assumption that your description is all readers may have to go on. Then make a judgment about its effectiveness, supporting your claim with clear evidence from the "text."

Examining a Rhetorical Analysis

On the following pages, well-known political commentator and columnist for the *New York Times* David Brooks argues that today's college graduates have been poorly prepared for life after school because of what he sees as a radical excess of supervision. Responding to his argument with a detailed analysis is Rachel Kolb, a student at Stanford University.

It's Not about You

DAVID BROOKS

© David Levene/eyevine/Redux Pictures

Over the past few weeks, America's colleges have sent another class of graduates off into the world. These graduates possess something of inestimable value. Nearly every sensible middle-aged person would give away all their money to be able to go back to age 22 and begin adulthood anew.

But, especially this year, one is conscious of the many ways in which this year's graduating class has been ill served by their elders. They enter a bad job market, the hangover from decades of excessive borrowing. They inherit a ruinous federal debt.

More important, their lives have been perversely structured. This year's graduates are members of the most supervised generation in American history. Through their childhoods and teenage years, they have been monitored, tutored, coached and honed to an unprecedented degree.

Yet upon graduation they will enter a world that is unprecedentedly wide open and unstructured. Most of them will not quickly get married, buy a home and have kids, as previous generations did. Instead, they will confront amazingly diverse job markets, social landscapes and lifestyle niches. Most will spend a decade wandering from job to job and clique to clique, searching for a role.

No one would design a system of extreme supervision to prepare people for a decade of extreme openness. But this is exactly what has emerged in modern America. College students are raised in an environment that demands one set of navigational skills, and they are then cast out into a different environment requiring a different set of skills, which they have to figure out on their own.

Worst of all, they are sent off into this world with the whole baby-boomer theology ringing in their ears. If you sample some of the commencement addresses being broadcast on C-Span these days, you see that many graduates are told to: Follow *your* passion, chart *your* own course, march to the beat of *your* own drummer, follow *your* dreams and find *yourself*. This is the litany of expressive individualism, which is still the dominant note in American culture.

But, of course, this mantra misleads on nearly every front.

College grads are often sent out into the world amid rapturous talk of limitless possibilities. But this talk is of no help to the central business of adulthood, finding serious things to tie yourself down to. The successful young adult is beginning to make sacred commitments—to a spouse, a community and calling—yet mostly hears about freedom and autonomy.

Today's graduates are also told to find their passion and then pursue their dreams. The implication is that they should find themselves first and then go off and live their quest. But, of course, very few people at age 22 or 24 can take an inward journey and come out having discovered a developed self.

Most successful young people don't look inside and then plan a life. They look outside and find a problem, which summons their life. A relative suffers from Alzheimer's and a young woman feels called to help cure that disease. A young man works under a miserable boss and must develop management skills so his department can function. Another young woman finds herself confronted by an opportunity she never thought of in a job category she never imagined. This wasn't in her plans, but this is where she can make her contribution.

Most people don't form a self and then lead a life. They are called by a problem, and the self is constructed gradually by their calling.

The graduates are also told to pursue happiness and joy. But, of course, when you read a biography of someone you admire, it's rarely the things that made them happy that compel your admiration. It's the things they did to court unhappiness—the things they did that were arduous and miserable, which sometimes cost them friends and aroused hatred. It's excellence, not happiness, that we admire most.

Finally, graduates are told to be independent-minded and to express their inner spirit. But, of course, doing your job well often means suppressing yourself. As Atul Gawande mentioned during his countercultural address ...at Harvard Medical School, being a good doctor often means being part of a team, following the rules of an institution, going down a regimented checklist.

Today's grads enter a cultural climate that preaches the self as the center of a life. But, of course, as they age, they'll discover that the tasks of a life are at the center. Fulfillment is a byproduct of how people engage their tasks, and can't be pursued directly. Most of us are egotistical and most are self-concerned most of the time, but it's nonetheless true that life comes to a point only in those moments when the self dissolves into some task. The purpose in life is not to find yourself. It's to lose yourself.

Understanding Brooks's Binaries

RACHEL KOLB

Courtesy of
Rachel Kolb

Connects
article to
personal
experience
to create an
ethical appeal.

Provides brief
overview
of Brooks's
argument.

States Brooks's
central claim.

As a high school and college student, I was given an incredible range of educational and extracurricular options, from interdisciplinary studies to summer institutes to student-organized clubs. Although today's students have more opportunities to adapt their educations to their specific personal goals, as I did, David Brooks argues that the structure of the modern educational system nevertheless leaves young people ill-prepared to meet the challenges of the real world. In his *New York Times* editorial "It's Not about You," Brooks illustrates excessive supervision and uncontrolled individualistic rhetoric as opposing problems that complicate young people's entry into adult life, which then becomes less of a natural progression than an outright paradigm shift. Brooks's argument itself mimics the pattern of moving from "perversely structured" youth to "unprecedentedly wide open" adulthood: it operates on the basis of binary oppositions, raising familiar notions about how to live one's life and then dismantling them. Throughout, the piece relies less on factual evidence than on Brooks's own authoritative tone and skill in using rhetorical devices.

Transition
sentence.

Comments
critically on
author's use of
evidence.

In his editorial, Brooks objects to mainstream cultural messages that sell students on individuality, but bases his conclusions more on general observations than on specific facts. His argument is, in itself, a loose form of rhetorical analysis. It opens by telling us to "sample some of the commencement addresses being broadcast on C-Span these days," where we will find messages such as: "Follow *your* passion, chart *your* own course, march to the beat of *your* own drummer, follow *your* dreams and find *yourself.*" As though moving down a checklist, it then scrutinizes the problems with this rhetoric of "expressive individualism." Finally, it turns to Atul Gawande's "countercultural address" about working collectively, en route to confronting the individualism of modern America. C-Span and Harvard Medical School aside, however, Brooks's argument is astonishingly short on external sources. He cites no basis for claims such as "this year's graduates are members of the most supervised generation in American history" or "most successful young people don't look inside and then plan a life," despite the fact that these claims are fundamental to his observations. Instead, his argument persuades through painting a picture — first of "limitless possibilities," then of young men and women called into action by problems that "summon their life" — and hoping that we will find the illustration familiar.

Instead of relying on the logos of his argument, Brooks assumes that his position as a baby boomer and *New York Times* columnist will provide a sufficient enough ethos to validate his claims. If this impression of age and social status did not enter our minds along with his bespectacled portrait, Brooks reminds us of it. Although he refers to the theology of the baby boomer generation as the "worst of all," from the beginning of his editorial he allots himself as another "sensible middle-aged person" and distances himself from college graduates by referring to them as "they" or as "today's grads," contrasting with his more inclusive reader-directed "you." Combined with his repeated use of passive sentence constructions that create a confusing sense of responsibility ("The graduates are sent off into the world"; "graduates are told"), this sense of distance could be alienating to the younger audiences for which this editorial seems intended. Granted, Brooks compensates for it by embracing themes of "excellence" and "fulfillment" and by opening up his message to "most of us" in his final paragraph, but nevertheless his self-defined persona has its limitations. Besides dividing his audience, Brooks risks reminding us that, just as his observations belong only to this persona, his arguments apply only to a subset of American society. More specifically, they apply only to the well-educated middle to upper class who might be more likely to fret after the implications of "supervision" and "possibilities," or the readers who would be most likely to flip through the *New York Times*.

Brooks overcomes his limitations in logos and ethos through his piece's greatest strength: its style. He effectively frames cultural messages in binaries in order to reinforce the disconnect that exists between what students are told and what they will face as full members of society. Throughout his piece, he states one assumption after another, then prompts us to consider its opposite. "Serious things" immediately take the place of "rapturous talk"; "look[ing] inside" replaces "look[ing] outside"; "suppressing yourself" becomes an alternative to being "independent-minded." Brooks's argument is consumed with dichotomies, culminating with his statement "It's excellence, not happiness, that we admire most." He frames his

Analyzes author's intended audience.

Closely analyzes Brooks's style.

ideas within a tight framework of repetition and parallel structure, creating muscular prose intended to engage his readers. His repeated use of the phrase "but, of course" serves as a metronomic reminder, at once echoing his earlier assertions and referring back to his air of authority.

Brooks illustrates the power of words in swaying an audience, and in his final paragraph his argument shifts beyond commentary. Having tested our way of thinking, he now challenges us to change. His editorial closes with one final binary, the claim that "The purpose in life is not to find yourself" but "to lose yourself." And, although some of Brooks's previous binaries have clanged with oversimplification, this one rings truer. In accordance with his adoption of the general "you," his concluding message need not apply only to college graduates. By unfettering its restrictions at its climax, Brooks liberates his argument. After all, only we readers bear the responsibility of reflecting, of justifying, and ultimately of determining how to live our lives.

Analyzes author's conclusion.

Work Cited

Brooks, David. "It's Not about You." *Everything's an Argument.* By Andrea A. Lunsford and John J. Ruszkiewicz. 7th ed. Boston: Bedford, 2016. 106–8. Print. Rpt. of "It's Not about You." *New York Times* 30 May 2011.

GUIDE TO WRITING A RHETORICAL ANALYSIS

Finding a Topic

A rhetorical analysis is usually assigned: you're asked to show how an argument works and to assess its effectiveness. When you can choose your own subject for analysis, look for one or more of the following qualities:

- a complex verbal or visual argument that challenges you — or disturbs or pleases you

- a text that raises current or enduring issues of substance

- a text that you believe should be taken more seriously

Look for arguments to analyze in the editorial and op-ed pages of any newspaper, political magazines such as the *Nation* or *National Review*, Web sites of organizations and interest groups, political blogs such as *Huffington Post* or *Power Line*, corporate Web sites that post their TV ad spots, videos and statements posted to YouTube, and so on.

Researching Your Topic

Once you've got a text to analyze, find out all you can about it. Use library or Web resources to explore:

- who the author is and what his or her credentials are

- if the author is an institution, what it does, what its sources of funding are, who its members are, and so on

- who is publishing or sponsoring the piece, and what the organization typically publishes

- what the leanings or biases of the author and publisher might be

- what the context of the argument is — what preceded or provoked it and how others have responded to it

Formulating a Claim

Begin with a hypothesis. A full thesis might not become evident until you're well into your analysis, but your final thesis should reflect the complexity of the piece that you're studying. In developing a thesis, consider questions such as the following:

- How can I describe what this argument achieves?

- What is the purpose, and is it accomplished?

- What audiences does the argument address and what audiences does it ignore, and why?

- Which of its rhetorical features will likely influence readers most: ethos of the author? emotional appeals? logical progression? style?

- What aspects of the argument work better than others?

- How do the rhetorical elements interact?

Here's the hardest part for most writers of rhetorical analyses: whether you agree or disagree with an argument usually doesn't matter in a rhetorical analysis. You've got to stay out of the fray and pay attention only to how — and to how well — the argument works.

Examples of Possible Claims for a Rhetorical Analysis

- Some people admire the directness and confidence of Hillary Clinton; others are put off by her bland and sometimes tone-deaf rhetoric. A close look at several of her speeches and public appearances will illuminate both sides of this debate.

- Today's editorial in the *Daily Collegian* about campus crimes may scare first-year students, but its anecdotal reporting doesn't get down to hard numbers — and for a good reason. Those statistics don't back the position taken by the editors.

- The imageboard 4chan has been called an "Internet hate machine," yet others claim it as a great boon to creativity. A close analysis of its homepage can help to settle this debate.

- The original design of New York's Freedom Tower, with its torqued surfaces and evocative spire, made a stronger argument about American values than its replacement, a fortress-like skyscraper stripped of imagination and unable to make any statement except "I'm 1,776 feet tall."

Preparing a Proposal

If your instructor asks you to prepare a proposal for your rhetorical analysis, here's a format you might use:

- Provide a copy of the work you're analyzing, whether it's a print text, a photograph, a digital image, or a URL, for instance.

- Offer a working hypothesis or tentative thesis.

- Indicate which rhetorical components seem especially compelling and worthy of detailed study and any connections between elements. For example, does the piece seem to emphasize facts and logic so much that it becomes disconnected from potential audiences? If so, hint at that possibility in your proposal.

- Indicate background information you intend to research about the author, institution, and contexts (political, economic, social, and religious) of the argument.

- Define the audience you'd like to reach. If you're responding to an assignment, you may be writing primarily for a teacher and classmates. But they make up a complex audience in themselves. If you can do so within the spirit of the assignment, imagine that your analysis will be published in a local newspaper, Web site, or blog.

- Conclude by briefly discussing the key challenges you anticipate in preparing a rhetorical analysis.

Considering Format and Media

Your instructor may specify that you use a particular format and/or medium. If not, ask yourself these questions to help you make a good choice:

- What format is most appropriate for your rhetorical analysis? Does it call for an academic essay, a report, an infographic, a brochure, or something else?

- What medium is most appropriate for your analysis? Would it be best delivered orally to a live audience? Presented as an audio essay or podcast? Presented in print only or in print with illustrations?

- Will you need visuals, such as moving or still images, maps, graphs, charts—and what function will they play in your analysis? Make sure they are not just "added on" but are necessary components of the analysis.

Thinking about Organization

Your rhetorical analysis is likely to include the following:

- Facts about the text you're analyzing: Provide the author's name; the title or name of the work; its place of publication or its location; the date it was published or viewed.

- Contexts for the argument: Readers need to know where the text is coming from, to what it may be responding, in what controversies it might be embroiled, and so on. Don't assume that they can infer the important contextual elements.

- A synopsis of the text that you're analyzing: If you can't attach the original argument, you must summarize it in enough detail so that a reader can imagine it. Even if you attach a copy of the piece, the analysis should include a summary.

- Some claim about the work's rhetorical effectiveness: It might be a simple evaluative claim or something more complex. The claim can come early in the paper, or you might build up to it, providing the evidence that leads toward the conclusion you've reached.

- A detailed analysis of how the argument works: Although you'll probably analyze rhetorical components separately, don't let your analysis become a dull roster of emotional, ethical, and logical appeals. Your rhetorical analysis should be an argument itself that supports a claim; a simple list of rhetorical appeals won't make much of a point.

- Evidence for every part of the analysis.

- An assessment of alternative views and counterarguments to your own analysis.

Getting and Giving Response: Questions for Peer Response

If you have access to a writing center, discuss the text that you intend to analyze with a writing consultant before you write the paper. Try to find people who agree with the argument and others who disagree, and take notes on their observations. Your instructor may assign you to a peer group for the purpose of reading and responding to one another's drafts; if not, share your draft with someone on your own. You can use the following questions to evaluate a draft. If you're evaluating someone else's draft, be sure to illustrate your points with examples. Specific comments are always more helpful than general observations.

The Claim

- Does the claim address the rhetorical effectiveness of the argument itself rather than the opinion or position that it takes?

- Is the claim significant enough to interest readers?

- Does the claim indicate important relationships between various rhetorical components?

- Would the claim be one that the creator of the piece would regard as serious criticism?

Evidence for the Claim

- Is enough evidence given to support all your claims? What evidence do you still need?

- Is the evidence in support of the claim simply announced, or are its significance and appropriateness analyzed? Is a more detailed discussion needed?

- Do you use appropriate evidence, drawn from the argument itself or from other materials?

- Do you address objections readers might have to the claim, criteria, or evidence?

- What kinds of sources might you use to explain the context of the argument? Do you need to use sources to check factual claims made in the argument?

- Are all quotations introduced with appropriate signal phrases (for instance, "As Áida Álvarez points out"), and do they merge smoothly into your sentences?

Organization and Style

- How are the parts of the argument organized? How effective is this organization? Would some other structure work better?

- Will readers understand the relationships among the original text, your claims, your supporting reasons, and the evidence you've gathered (from the original text and any other sources you've used)? If not, what could be done to make those connections clearer? Are more transitional words and phrases needed? Would headings or graphic devices help?

- Are the transitions or links from point to point, sentence to sentence, and paragraph to paragraph clear and effective? If not, how could they be improved?

- Is the style suited to the subject and appropriate to your audience? Is it too formal? Too casual? Too technical? Too bland or boring?

- Which sentences seem particularly effective? Which ones seem weakest, and how could they be improved? Should some short sentences be combined, or should any long ones be separated into two or more sentences?

- How effective are the paragraphs? Do any seem too skimpy or too long? Do they break the analysis at strategic points?

- Which words or phrases seem particularly effective, accurate, and powerful? Do any seem dull, vague, unclear, or inappropriate for the audience or your purpose? Are definitions provided for technical or other terms that readers might not know?

Spelling, Punctuation, Mechanics, Documentation, and Format

- Check the spelling of the author's name, and make sure that the name of any institution involved with the work is correct. Note that the names of many corporations and institutions use distinctive spelling and punctuation.

- Get the title of the text you're analyzing right.

- Are there any errors in spelling, punctuation, capitalization, and the like?

- Does the assignment require a specific format? Check the original assignment sheet to be sure.

RESPOND

Find an argument on the editorial page or op-ed page in a recent newspaper. Then analyze it rhetorically, using principles discussed in this chapter. Show how it succeeds, fails, or does something else entirely. Perhaps you can show that the author is unusually successful in connecting with readers but then has nothing to say. Or perhaps you discover that the strong logical appeal is undercut by a contradictory emotional argument. Be sure that the analysis includes a summary of the original essay and basic publication information about it (its author, place of publication, and publisher).

part 3

Writing
Arguments

Structuring Arguments

These two sets of statements illustrate the most basic ways in which Western culture structures logical arguments. The first piles up specific examples and draws a conclusion from them: that's **inductive reasoning** and structure. The second sets out a general principle (the major premise of a syllogism) and applies it to a specific case (the minor premise) in order to reach a conclusion: that's **deductive reasoning** and structure. In everyday reasoning, we often omit the middle statement, resulting in what Aristotle called an *enthymeme*: "Since dairy products make me sick, I better leave that ice cream alone." (See p. 214 for more on enthymemes.)

But the arguments you will write in college call for more than just the careful critical thinking offered within inductive and deductive reasoning. You will also need to define claims, explain the contexts in which you are offering them, consider counterarguments fairly and carefully, defend your assumptions, offer convincing evidence, appeal to particular audiences, and more. And you will have to do so using a clear structure that moves your argument forward. This chapter introduces you to three helpful ways to structure arguments. Feel free to borrow from all of them!

I get hives after eating ice cream. My mouth swells up when I eat cheese. Yogurt triggers my asthma. ↓ Dairy products make me sick.	Dairy products make me sick. Ice cream is a dairy product. ↓ Ice cream makes me sick.

The Classical Oration

The authors of this book once examined a series of engineering reports and found that—to their great surprise—these reports were generally structured in ways similar to those used by Greek and Roman rhetors two thousand years ago. Thus, this ancient structuring system is alive and well in twenty-first-century culture. The classical oration has six parts, most of which will be familiar to you, despite their Latin names:

Exordium: You try to win the attention and goodwill of an audience while introducing a topic or problem.

Narratio: You present the facts of the case, explaining what happened when, who is involved, and so on. The *narratio* puts an argument in context.

Partitio: You divide up the topic, explaining what the claim is, what the key issues are, and in what order they will be treated.

Confirmatio: You offer detailed support for the claim, using both logical reasoning and factual evidence.

Refutatio: You carefully consider and respond to opposing claims or evidence.

Peroratio: You summarize the case and move the audience to action.

That's Life used with the permission of Mike Twohy and The Cartoonist Group. All rights reserved.

This structure is powerful because it covers all the bases: readers or listeners want to know what your topic is, how you intend to cover it, and what evidence you have to offer. And you probably need a reminder to present a pleasing *ethos* when beginning a presentation and to conclude with enough *pathos* to win an audience over completely. Here, in outline form, is a five-part updated version of the classical pattern, which you may find useful on many occasions:

Introduction

- gains readers' interest and willingness to listen
- establishes your qualifications to write about your topic
- establishes some common ground with your audience
- demonstrates that you're fair and even-handed
- states your claim

Background

- presents information, including personal stories or anecdotes that are important to your argument

Lines of Argument

- presents good reasons, including logical and emotional appeals, in support of your claim

Alternative Arguments

- carefully considers alternative points of view and opposing arguments
- notes the advantages and disadvantages of these views
- explains why your view is preferable to others

Conclusion

- summarizes the argument
- elaborates on the implications of your claim
- makes clear what you want the audience to think or do
- reinforces your credibility and perhaps offers an emotional appeal

Not every piece of rhetoric, past or present, follows the structure of the oration or includes all its components. But you can identify some of its elements in successful arguments if you pay attention to their design. Here are the words of the 1776 Declaration of Independence:

> When in the Course of human events, it becomes necessary for one people to dissolve the political bands which have connected them with another, and to assume among the powers of the earth, the separate and equal station to which the Laws of Nature and of Nature's God entitle them, a decent respect to the opinions of mankind requires that they should declare the causes which impel them to the separation.

— Opens with a brief *exordium* explaining why the document is necessary, invoking a broad audience in acknowledging a need to show "a decent respect to the opinions of mankind." Important in this case, the lines that follow explain the assumptions on which the document rests.

> We hold these truths to be self-evident, that all men are created equal, that they are endowed by their Creator with certain unalienable Rights, that among these are Life, Liberty, and the pursuit of Happiness — that to secure these rights, Governments are instituted among Men, deriving their just powers from the consent of the governed — That whenever any Form of Government becomes destructive to these ends, it is the Right of the People to alter or to abolish it and to institute new Government, laying its Foundation on such principles and organizing its powers in such form, as to them shall seem most likely to effect their Safety and Happiness. Prudence, indeed, will dictate that Governments long established should not be changed for light and transient causes; and accordingly all experience hath shewn that mankind are more disposed to suffer, while evils are sufferable, than to right themselves by abolishing the forms to which they are accustomed. But when a long train of abuses and usurptions, pursuing invariably the same Object evinces a design to reduce them under absolute Despotism, it is their right, it is their duty, to throw off such Government and to provide new Guards for their future security. — Such has been the patient sufferance of these Colonies; and such is now the necessity which constrains them to alter their former Systems

— A *narratio* follows, offering background on the situation: because the government of George III has become destructive, the framers of the Declaration are obligated to abolish their allegiance to him.

of Government. The history of the present King of Great Britain is
a history of repeated injuries and usurpations, all having in direct
object the establishment of an absolute Tyranny over these States.
To prove this, let Facts be submitted to a candid world.

—Declaration of Independence, July 4, 1776

Arguably, the *partitio* begins here, followed by the longest part of the document (not reprinted here), a *confirmatio* that lists the "long train of abuses and usurpations" by George III.

The authors might have structured this argument by beginning with the last two sentences of the excerpt and then listing the facts intended to prove the king's abuse and tyranny. But by choosing first to explain the purpose and "self-evident" assumptions behind their argument and only then moving on to demonstrate how these "truths" have been denied by the British, the authors forge an immediate connection with readers and build up to the memorable conclusion. The structure is both familiar and inventive—as your own use of key elements of the oration should be in the arguments you compose.

FIGURE 15.1 The Declaration of Independence National Archives

Rogerian and Invitational Arguments

In trying to find an alternative to confrontational and angry arguments like those that so often erupt in legislative bodies around the world, scholars and teachers of rhetoric have adapted the nonconfrontational principles employed by psychologist Carl Rogers in personal therapy sessions. In simple terms, Rogers argued that people involved in disputes should not respond to each other until they could fully, fairly, and even sympathetically state the other person's position. Scholars of rhetoric Richard E. Young, Alton L. Becker, and Kenneth L. Pike developed a four-part structure that is now known as Rogerian argument:

1. **Introduction:** You describe an issue, a problem, or a conflict in terms rich enough to show that you fully understand and respect any alternative position or positions.

2. **Contexts:** You describe the contexts in which alternative positions may be valid.

3. **Writer's position:** You state your position on the issue and present the circumstances in which that opinion would be valid.

4. **Benefits to opponent:** You explain to opponents how they would benefit from adopting your position.

The key to Rogerian argumentation is a willingness to think about opposing positions and to describe them fairly. In a Rogerian structure, you have to acknowledge that alternatives to your claims exist and that they might be reasonable under certain circumstances. In tone, Rogerian arguments steer clear of heated and stereotypical language, emphasizing instead how all parties in a dispute might gain from working together.

In the same vein, feminist scholars Sonja Foss and Cindy Griffin have outlined a form of argument they label "invitational," one that begins with careful attention to and respect for the person or the audience you are in conversation with. Foss and Griffin show that such listening — in effect, walking in the other person's shoes — helps you see that person's points of view more clearly and thoroughly and thus offers a basis for moving together toward new understandings. The kind of argument they describe is what another rhetorician, Krista Ratcliffe, calls "rhetorical listening," which helps to establish productive connections between people and thus helps enable effective cross-cultural communications.

Invitational rhetoric has as its goal not winning over opponents but getting people and groups to work together and identify with each other; it strives for connection, collaboration, and the mutually informed creation of knowledge. As feminist scholar Sally Miller Gearhart puts it, invitational argument offers a way to disagree without hurting one another, to disagree with respect. This kind of argument is especially important in a society that increasingly depends on successful collaboration to get things done. In college, you may have opportunities to practice invitational rhetoric in peer-review sessions, when each member of a group listens carefully in order to work through problems and issues. You may also practice invitational rhetoric looking at any contested issue from other people's points of view, taking them into account, and engaging them fairly and respectfully in your own argument. Students we know who are working in high-tech industries also tell us how much such arguments are valued, since they fuel innovation and "out of the box" thinking.

Invitational arguments, then, call up structures that more resemble good two-way conversations or free-ranging dialogues than straight-line marches from thesis to conclusion. Even conventional arguments benefit from invitational strategies by giving space early on to a full range of perspectives, making sure to present them thoroughly and clearly. Remember that in such arguments your goal is enhanced understanding so that you can open up a space for new perceptions and fresh ideas.

Consider how Frederick Douglass tried to broaden the outlook of his audiences when he delivered a Fourth of July oration in 1852. Most nineteenth-century Fourth of July speeches followed a pattern of praising the Revolutionary War heroes and emphasizing freedom, democracy, and justice. Douglass, a former slave, had that tradition in mind as he delivered his address, acknowledging the "great principles" that the "glorious anniversary" celebrates. But he also asked his (white) listeners to see the occasion from another point of view:

> Fellow-citizens, pardon me, allow me to ask, why am I called upon to speak here today? What have I, or those I represent, to do with your national independence? Are the great principles of political freedom and natural justice, embodied in the Declaration of Independence, extended to us? And am I, therefore, called upon to bring our humble offering to the national altar, and to confess the benefits and express devout gratitude for the blessings resulting from your independence to us? ... I say it with a sad sense of the disparity between us. I am not included within the pale of this glorious anniversary! Your high independence only reveals the immeasurable distance between us. The blessings in which you, this day, rejoice, are not enjoyed in common. The rich inheritance of justice, liberty, prosperity and independence, bequeathed by your fathers, is shared by you, not by me. The sunlight that brought life and healing to you, has brought stripes and death to me. This Fourth of July is yours, not mine. You may rejoice, I must mourn.

> —Frederick Douglass, "What to the Slave Is the Fourth of July?"

FIGURE 15.2 Frederick Douglass © World History Archive/Alamy

Although his speech is in some ways confrontational, Douglass is also inviting his audience to see a version of reality that they could have discovered on their own had they dared to imagine the lives of African Americans living in the shadows of American liberty. Issuing that invitation, and highlighting its consequences, points a way forward in the conflict between slavery and freedom, black and white, oppression and justice, although response to Douglass's invitation was a long time in coming.

In May 2014, First Lady Michelle Obama used elements of invitational argument in delivering a speech to high school graduates from several high schools in Topeka, Kansas. Since the speech occurred on the sixtieth anniversary of the Supreme Court's decision to disallow "separate but equal" schools in the landmark *Brown v. Board of Education* case, which was initiated in Topeka, Mrs. Obama invited the audience to experience the ups and downs of students before and after the decision, putting themselves in the places of the young African Americans who, in 1954, desperately wanted the freedom to attend well-funded schools open to white students. So she tells the stories of some of these young people, inviting those there to walk a while in their shoes. And she concludes her speech with a call for understanding and cooperation:

> Every day, you have the same power to choose our better history—by opening your hearts and minds, by speaking up for what you know is right, by sharing the lessons of *Brown v. Board of Education*, the lessons you learned right here in Topeka, wherever you go for the rest of our lives. I know you all can do it. I am so proud of all of you, and I cannot wait to see everything you achieve in the years ahead.

FIGURE 15.3 Michelle Obama speaking in Topeka, Kansas AP Photo/Orlin Wagner

In this speech, Mrs. Obama did not castigate audience members for failing to live up to the ideals of *Brown v. Board of Education* (though she could have done so), nor does she dwell on current ills in Topeka. Rather, she invokes "our better history" and focuses on the ways those in Topeka have helped to write that history. She identifies with her audience and asks them to identify with her — and she aims to inspire the young graduates to follow her example.

The use of invitational argument and careful listening in contemporary political life are rare, but in spite of much evidence to the contrary (think of the repeatedly demonstrated effectiveness of political attack ads), the public claims to prefer nonpartisan and invitational rhetoric to one-on-one, winner-take-all battles, suggesting that such an approach strikes a chord in many people, especially in a world that is increasingly open to issues of diversity. The lesson to take from Rogerian or invitational argument is that it makes good sense in structuring your own arguments to learn opposing positions well enough to state them accurately and honestly, to strive to understand the points of view of your opponents, to acknowledge those views fairly in your own work, and to look for solutions that benefit as many people as possible.

RESPOND

Choose a controversial topic that is frequently in the news, and decide how you might structure an argument on the subject, using the general principles of the classical oration. Then look at the same subject from a Rogerian or invitational perspective. How might your argument differ? Which approach would work better for your topic? For the audiences you might want to address?

Toulmin Argument

In *The Uses of Argument* (1958), British philosopher Stephen Toulmin presented structures to describe the way that ordinary people make reasonable arguments. Because Toulmin's system acknowledges the complications of life—situations when we qualify our thoughts with words such as *sometimes*, *often*, *presumably*, *unless*, and *almost*—his method isn't as airtight as formal logic that uses syllogisms (see p. 265 in this chapter and p. 213 in Chapter 12). But for that reason, Toulmin logic has become a powerful and, for the most part, practical tool for understanding and shaping arguments in the real world.

Toulmin argument will help you come up with and test ideas and also figure out what goes where in many kinds of arguments. Let's take a look at the basic elements of Toulmin's structure:

Claim	the argument you wish to prove
Qualifiers	any limits you place on your claim
Reason(s)/ Evidence	support for your claim
Warrants	underlying assumptions that support your claim
Backing	evidence for warrant

If you wanted to state the relationship between them in a sentence, you might say:

> My claim is true, to a qualified degree, because of the following reasons, which make sense if you consider the warrant, backed by these additional reasons.

These terms—claim, evidence, warrants, backing, and qualifiers—are the building blocks of the Toulmin argument structure. Let's take them one at a time.

Making Claims

Toulmin arguments begin with claims, debatable and controversial statements or assertions you hope to prove.

A claim answers the question *So what's your point?* or *Where do you stand on that?* Some writers might like to ignore these questions and avoid stating a position. But when you make a claim worth writing about, then it's worth standing up and owning it.

Is there a danger that you might oversimplify an issue by making too bold a claim? Of course. But making that sweeping claim is a logical first step toward eventually saying something more reasonable and subtle. Here are some fairly simple, undeveloped claims:

Congress should enact legislation that establishes a path to citizenship for illegal immigrants.

It's time for the World Health Organization (WHO) to exert leadership in coordinating efforts to stem the Ebola epidemic in West Africa.

NASA should launch a human expedition to Mars.

Veganism is the most responsible choice of diet.

Military insurance should not cover the cost of sex change surgery for service men and women.

Good claims often spring from personal experiences. You may have relevant work or military or athletic experience—or you may know a lot about music, film, sustainable agriculture, social networking, inequities in government services—all fertile ground for authoritative, debatable, and personally relevant claims.

RESPOND

Claims aren't always easy to find. Sometimes they're buried deep within an argument, and sometimes they're not present at all. An important skill in reading and writing arguments is the ability to identify claims, even when they aren't obvious.

Collect a sample of six to eight letters to the editor of a daily newspaper (or a similar number of argumentative postings from a political blog). Read each item, and then identify every claim that the writer makes. When you've compiled your list of claims, look carefully at the words that the writer or writers use when stating their positions. Is there a common vocabulary? Can you find words or phrases that signal an impending claim? Which of these seem most effective? Which ones seem least effective? Why?

Offering Evidence and Good Reasons

You can begin developing a claim by drawing up a list of reasons to support it or finding evidence that backs up the point.

Evidence and Reason(s) ⎯⎯⎯⎯⎯⎯⎯⎯→ So Claim

One student writer wanted to gather good reasons in support of an assertion that his college campus needed more official spaces for parking bicycles. He did some research, gathering statistics about parking-space allocation, numbers of people using particular designated slots, and numbers of bicycles registered on campus. Before he went any further, however, he listed his primary reasons for wanting to increase bicycle parking:

- **Personal experience:** At least twice a week for two terms, he was unable to find a designated parking space for his bike.

- **Anecdotes:** Several of his friends told similar stories. One even sold her bike as a result.

- **Facts:** He found out that the ratio of car to bike parking spaces was 100 to 1, whereas the ratio of cars to bikes registered on campus was 25 to 1.

- **Authorities:** The campus police chief told the college newspaper that she believed a problem existed for students who tried to park bicycles legally.

On the basis of his preliminary listing of possible reasons in support of the claim, this student decided that his subject was worth more research. He was on the way to amassing a set of good reasons and evidence that were sufficient to support his claim.

In shaping your own arguments, try putting claims and reasons together early in the writing process to create enthymemes. Think of these enthymemes as test cases or even as topic sentences:

Bicycle parking spaces should be expanded because the number of bikes on campus far exceeds the available spots.

It's time to lower the driving age because I've been driving since I was fourteen and it hasn't hurt me.

National legalization of marijuana is long overdue since it is already legal in over twenty states, has shown to be less harmful than alcohol, and provides effective relief from pain associated with cancer.

Violent video games should be carefully evaluated and their use monitored by the industry, the government, and parents because these games cause addiction and psychological harm to players.

As you can see, attaching a reason to a claim often spells out the major terms of an argument.

**"I know your type, you're the type who'll
make me prove every claim I make."**

FIGURE 15.4 Anticipate challenges to your claims.
© 2009 Charles Barsotti/The New Yorker Collection/The Cartoon Bank

But your work is just beginning when you've put a claim together with its supporting reasons and evidence—because readers are certain to begin questioning your statement. They might ask whether the reasons and evidence that you're offering really do support the claim: should the driving age really be changed just because you've managed to drive since you were fourteen? They might ask pointed questions about your evidence: exactly how do you know that the number of bikes on campus far exceeds the number of spaces available? Eventually, you've got to address potential questions about the quality of your assumptions and the quality of your evidence. The connection between claim and reason(s) is a concern at the next level in Toulmin argument.

Determining Warrants

Crucial to Toulmin argument is appreciating that there must be a logical and persuasive connection between a claim and the reasons and data supporting it. Toulmin calls this connection the warrant. It answers the question *How exactly do I get from the data to the claim?* Like the warrant in legal situations (a search warrant, for example), a sound warrant in an argument gives you authority to proceed with your case.

The warrant tells readers what your (often unstated) assumptions are—for example, that any practice that causes serious disease should be banned by the government. If readers accept your warrant, you can then present specific evidence to develop your claim. But if readers dispute your warrant, you'll have to defend it before you can move on to the claim itself.

Stating warrants can be tricky because they can be phrased in various ways. What you're looking for is the general principle that enables you to justify the move from a reason to a specific claim—the bridge connecting them. The warrant is the assumption that makes the claim seem believable. It's often a value or principle that you share with your readers. Here's an easy example:

> Don't eat that mushroom: it's poisonous.

The warrant supporting this enthymeme can be stated in several ways, always moving from the reason (*it's poisonous*) to the claim (*Don't eat that mushroom*):

> Anything that is poisonous shouldn't be eaten.

> If something is poisonous, it's dangerous to eat.

Here's the relationship, diagrammed:

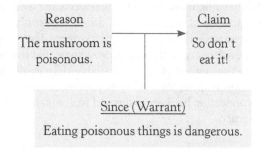

FIGURE 15.5 A simple icon—a skull and crossbones—can make a visual argument that implies a claim, a reason, and a warrant. PhotoLink/Getty Images

Perfectly obvious, you say? Exactly—and that's why the statement is so convincing. If the mushroom in question is a death cap or destroying angel (and you might still need expert testimony to prove that it is), the warrant does the rest of the work, making the claim that it supports seem logical and persuasive.

Let's look at a similar example, beginning with the argument in its basic form:

> We'd better stop for gas because the gauge has been reading empty for more than thirty miles.

In this case, you have evidence that is so clear (a gas gauge reading empty) that the reason for getting gas doesn't even have to be stated: the tank is almost empty. The warrant connecting the evidence to the claim is also pretty obvious:

> If the fuel gauge of a car has been reading empty for more than thirty miles, then that car is about to run out of gas.

Since most readers would accept this warrant as reasonable, they would also likely accept the statement the warrant supports.

Naturally, factual information might undermine the whole argument: the fuel gauge might be broken, or the driver might know that the car will go another fifty miles even though the fuel gauge reads empty. But in most cases, readers would accept the warrant.

Now let's consider how stating and then examining a warrant can help you determine the grounds on which you want to make a case. Here's a political enthymeme of a familiar sort:

> Flat taxes are fairer than progressive taxes because they treat all taxpayers in the same way.

Warrants that follow from this enthymeme have power because they appeal to a core American value—equal treatment under the law:

> Treating people equitably is the American way.
>
> All people should be treated in the same way.

You certainly could make an argument on these grounds. But stating the warrant should also raise a flag if you know anything about tax policy. If the principle is obvious and universal, then why do federal and many progressive state income taxes require people at higher levels of income to pay at higher tax rates than people at lower income levels? Could the warrant not be as universally popular as it seems at first glance? To explore the argument further, try stating the contrary claim and warrants:

> Progressive taxes are fairer than flat taxes because people with more income can afford to pay more, benefit more from government, and shelter more of their income from taxes.

> People should be taxed according to their ability to pay.

> People who benefit more from government and can shelter more of their income from taxes should be taxed at higher rates.

Now you see how different the assumptions behind opposing positions really are. If you decided to argue in favor of flat taxes, you'd be smart to recognize that some members of your audience might have fundamental reservations about your position. Or you might even decide to shift your entire argument to an alternative rationale for flat taxes:

> Flat taxes are preferable to progressive taxes because they simplify the tax code and reduce the likelihood of fraud.

Here, you have two stated reasons that are supported by two new warrants:

> Taxes that simplify the tax code are desirable.

> Taxes that reduce the likelihood of fraud are preferable.

Whenever possible, you'll choose your warrant knowing your audience, the context of your argument, and your own feelings.

Be careful, though, not to suggest that you'll appeal to any old warrant that works to your advantage. If readers suspect that your argument for progressive taxes really amounts to *I want to stick it to people who work harder than I*, your credibility may suffer a fatal blow.

Examples of Claims, Reasons, and Warrants

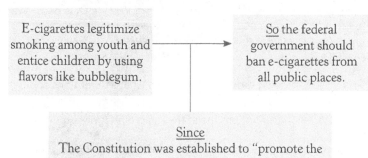

E-cigarettes legitimize smoking among youth and entice children by using flavors like bubblegum. ⟶ So the federal government should ban e-cigarettes from all public places.

Since
The Constitution was established to "promote the general welfare," and citizens are thus entitled to protection from harmful actions by others.

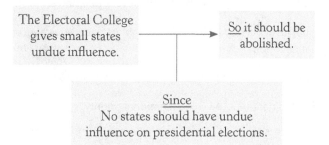

The Electoral College gives small states undue influence. ⟶ So it should be abolished.

Since
No states should have undue influence on presidential elections.

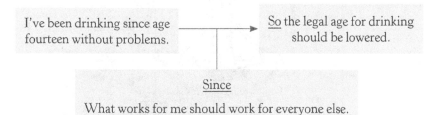

I've been drinking since age fourteen without problems. ⟶ So the legal age for drinking should be lowered.

Since
What works for me should work for everyone else.

RESPOND

At their simplest, warrants can be stated as "X is good" or "X is bad." Return to the letters to the editor or blog postings that you analyzed in the exercise on p. 275, this time looking for the warrant that is behind each claim. As a way to start, ask yourself these questions:

> If I find myself agreeing with the letter writer, what assumptions about the subject matter do I share with him/her?
>
> If I disagree, what assumptions are at the heart of that disagreement?

The list of warrants you generate will likely come from these assumptions.

Offering Evidence: Backing

The richest, most interesting part of a writer's work — backing — remains to be done after the argument has been outlined. Clearly stated claims and warrants show you how much evidence you will need. Take a look at this brief argument, which is both debatable and controversial, especially in tough economic times:

> NASA should launch a human expedition to Mars because Americans need a unifying national goal.

Here's one version of the warrant that supports the enthymeme:

> What unifies the nation ought to be a national priority.

FIGURE 15.6 Sticker honoring the retirement of the Space Shuttle program
© Steven Barrymore

To run with this claim and warrant, you'd first need to place both in context. Human space exploration has been debated with varying intensity following the 1957 launch of the Soviet Union's Sputnik satellite, after the losses of the U.S. space shuttles Challenger (1986) and Columbia (2003), and after the retirement of the Space Shuttle program in 2011. Acquiring such background knowledge through reading, conversation, and inquiry of all kinds will be necessary for making your case. (See Chapter 11 for more on gaining authority.)

There's no point in defending any claim until you've satisfied readers that questionable warrants on which the claim is based are defensible. In Toulmin argument, evidence you offer to support a warrant is called **backing**.

Warrant
What unifies the nation ought to be a national priority.

Backing
Americans want to be part of something bigger than themselves. (Emotional appeal as evidence)

In a country as diverse as the United States, common purposes and values help make the nation stronger. (Ethical appeal as evidence)

In the past, government investments such as the Hoover Dam and the *Apollo* moon program enabled many—though not all—Americans to work toward common goals. (Logical appeal as evidence)

In addition to evidence to support your warrant (backing), you'll need evidence to support your claim:

Argument in Brief (Enthymeme/Claim)
NASA should launch a human expedition to Mars because Americans now need a unifying national goal.

Evidence
The American people are politically divided along lines of race, ethnicity, religion, gender, and class. (Fact as evidence)

A common challenge or problem often unites people to accomplish great things. (Emotional appeal as evidence)

A successful Mars mission would require the cooperation of the entire nation—and generate tens of thousands of jobs. (Logical appeal as evidence)

A human expedition to Mars would be a valuable scientific project for the nation to pursue. (Appeal to values as evidence)

As these examples show, appeals to values and emotions can be just as appropriate as appeals to logic and facts, and all such claims will be stronger if a writer presents a convincing ethos. In most arguments, appeals work together rather than separately, reinforcing each other. (See Chapter 11 for more on ethos.)

Using Qualifiers

Experienced writers know that qualifying expressions make writing more precise and honest. Toulmin logic encourages you to acknowledge limitations to your argument through the effective use of qualifiers. You can save time if you qualify a claim early in the writing process. But you might not figure out how to limit a claim effectively until after you've explored your subject or discussed it with others.

Qualifiers

few	more or less	often
it is possible	in some cases	perhaps
rarely	many	under these conditions
it seems	typically	possibly
some	routinely	for the most part
it may be	most	if it were so
sometimes	one might argue	in general

Never assume that readers understand the limits you have in mind. Rather, spell them out as precisely as possible, as in the following examples:

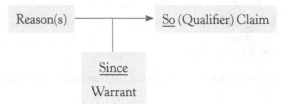

Reason(s) ──────→ So (Qualifier) Claim

Since

Warrant

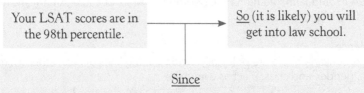

Your LSAT scores are in the 98th percentile. ──────→ So (it is likely) you will get into law school.

Since

High LSAT scores are an important factor in law school admissions.

Unqualified Claim	People who don't go to college earn less than those who do.
Qualified Claim	*In most cases*, people who don't go to college earn less than those who do.

Understanding Conditions of Rebuttal

In the Toulmin system, potential objections to an argument are called **conditions of rebuttal**. Understanding and reacting to these conditions are essential to support your own claims where they're weak and also to recognize and understand the reasonable objections of people who see the world differently. For example, you may be a big fan of the Public Broadcasting Service (PBS) and the National Endowment for the Arts (NEA) and prefer that federal tax dollars be spent on these programs. So you offer the following claim:

Claim	The federal government should support the arts.

You need reasons to support this thesis, so you decide to present the issue as a matter of values:

Argument in Brief	The federal government should support the arts because it also supports the military.

Now you've got an enthymeme and can test the warrant, or the premises of your claim:

Warrant	If the federal government can support the military, then it can also support other programs.

But the warrant seems frail: you can hear a voice over your shoulder saying, "In essence, you're saying that *Because we pay for a military, we should pay for everything!*" So you decide to revise your claim:

Revised Argument	If the federal government can spend huge amounts of money on the military, then it can afford to spend moderate amounts on arts programs.

Now you've got a new warrant, too:

Revised Warrant	A country that can fund expensive programs can also afford less expensive programs.

This is a premise that you can defend, since you believe strongly that the arts are just as essential as a strong military is to the well-being of the country. Although the warrant now seems solid, you still have to offer strong grounds to support your specific and controversial claim. So you cite statistics from reputable sources, this time comparing the federal budgets for the military and the arts. You break them down in ways that readers can visualize, demonstrating that much less than a penny of every tax dollar goes to support the arts.

FIGURE 15.7 The new NEA logo

But then you hear those voices again, saying that the "common defense" is a federal mandate; the government is constitutionally obligated to support a military, and support for the arts is hardly in the same league! Looks like you need to add a paragraph explaining all the benefits the arts provide for very few dollars spent, and maybe you should suggest that such funding falls under the constitutional mandate to "promote the general welfare." Though not all readers will accept these grounds, they'll appreciate that you haven't ignored their point of view: you've gained credibility by anticipating a reasonable objection.

Dealing with conditions of rebuttal is an essential part of argument. But it's important to understand rebuttal as more than mere opposition. Anticipating objections broadens your horizons, makes you more open to alternative viewpoints, and helps you understand what you need to do to support your claim.

Within Toulmin argument, conditions of rebuttal remind us that we're part of global conversations: Internet newsgroups and blogs provide potent responses to positions offered by participants in discussions; instant messaging and social networking let you respond to and challenge others; links on Web sites form networks that are infinitely variable and open. In cyberspace, conditions of rebuttal are as close as your screen.

RESPOND

Using an essay or a project you are composing, do a Toulmin analysis of the argument. When you're done, see which elements of the Toulmin scheme are represented. Are you short of evidence to support the warrant? Have you considered the conditions of rebuttal? Have you qualified your claim adequately? Next, write a brief revision plan: How will you buttress the argument in the places where it is weakest? What additional evidence will you offer for the warrant? How can you qualify your claim to meet the conditions of rebuttal? Then show your paper to a classmate and have him/her do a Toulmin analysis: a new reader will probably see your argument in different ways and suggest revisions that may not have occurred to you.

Outline of a Toulmin Argument

Consider the claim that was mentioned on p. 281:

Claim	The federal government should ban e-cigarettes.
Qualifier	The ban would be limited to public spaces.
Good Reasons	E-cigarettes have not been proven to be harmless.
	E-cigarettes legitimize smoking and also are aimed at recruiting teens and children with flavors like bubblegum and cotton candy.
Warrants	The Constitution promises to "promote the general welfare." Citizens are entitled to protection from harmful actions by others.
Backing	The United States is based on a political system that is supposed to serve the basic needs of its people, including their health.
Evidence	Analysis of advertising campaigns that reveal direct appeals to children
	Lawsuits recently won against e-cigarette companies, citing the link between e-cigarettes and a return to regular smoking
	Examples of bans on e-cigarettes already imposed in many public places
Authority	Cite the FDA and medical groups on effect of e-cigarette smoking.
Conditions of Rebuttal	E-cigarette smokers have rights, too.
	Smoking laws should be left to the states.
	Such a ban could not be enforced.
Responses	The ban applies to public places; smokers can smoke in private.

A Toulmin Analysis

You might wonder how Toulmin's method holds up when applied to an argument that is longer than a few sentences. Do such arguments really work the way that Toulmin predicts? In the following short argument, well-known linguist and author Deborah Tannen explores the consequences of a shift in the meaning of one crucial word: *compromise*. Tannen's essay, which originally appeared as a posting on Politico.com on June 15, 2011, offers a series of interrelated claims based on reasons, evidence, and warrants that culminate in the last sentence of the essay. She begins by showing that the word *compromise* is now rejected by both the political right and the political left and offers good reasons and evidence to support that claim. She then moves back to a time when "a compromise really was considered great," and offers three powerful pieces of evidence in support of that claim. The argument then comes back to the present, with a claim that the compromise and politeness of the nineteenth century have been replaced by "growing enmity." That claim is supported with reasoning and evidence that rest on an underlying warrant that "vituperation and seeing opponents as enemies is corrosive to the human spirit." The claims in the argument—that *compromise* has become a dirty word and that enmity and an adversarial spirit are on the rise—lead to Tannen's conclusion: rejecting compromise breaks the trust necessary for a democracy and thus undermines the very foundation of our society. While she does not use traditional qualifying words, she does say that the situation she describes is a "threat" to our nation, which qualifies the claim to some extent: the situation is not the "death" of our nation but rather a "threat." Tannen's annotated essay follows.

Why Is "Compromise" Now a Dirty Word?

DEBORAH TANNEN

Photo: Stephen
Voss, courtesy of
Deborah Tannen

Contextual
information
leading up to
initial claim

When did the word "compromise" get compromised?

When did the negative connotations of "He was caught in a compromising position" or "She compromised her ethics" replace the positive connotations of "They reached a compromise"?

House Speaker John Boehner said it outright on *60 Minutes* last year. When talking about "compromise," Boehner said, "I reject the word."

"When you say the word 'compromise,'" he explained, "…a lot of Americans look up and go, 'Uh-oh, they're gonna sell me out.'" His position is common right now.

In the same spirit, Tony Perkins wrote in a recent CNN.com op-ed piece, "When it comes to conservative principles, compromise is the companion of losers."

The political right is particularly vehement when it comes to compromise. Conservatives are now strongly swayed by the tea party movement, whose clarion call is a refusal to compromise, regardless of the practical consequences.

But the rejection of compromise is more widespread than that. The left regularly savages President Barack Obama for compromising too soon, too much or on the wrong issues. Many who fervently sought universal health coverage, for example, could not celebrate its near accomplishment because the president gave up the public option.

The death of compromise has become a threat to our nation as we confront crucial issues such as the debt ceiling and that most basic of legislative responsibilities: a federal budget. At stake is the very meaning of what had once seemed unshakable: "the full faith and credit" of the U.S. government.

Initial claim

Reason

Back when the powerful nineteenth-century senator Henry Clay was called "the great compromiser," achieving a compromise really was considered great. On three occasions, the Kentucky statesman helped the Senate preserve the Union by crafting compromises between the deadlocked slave-holding South and the Northern free states. In 1820, his Missouri Compromise stemmed the spread of slavery. In 1833, when the South was poised to defy federal tariff

Evidence

laws favored by the North and the federal government was about to authorize military action, Clay found a last-minute compromise. And his Compromise of 1850 averted civil war for at least a decade.

It was during an 1850 Senate debate that Clay stated his conviction: "I go for honorable compromise whenever it can be made." Something else he said then holds a key to how the dwindling respect for compromise is related to larger and more dangerous developments in our nation today.

Warrant

"All legislation, all government, all society," Clay said, "is formed upon the principle of mutual concession, politeness, comity, courtesy; upon these, everything is based."

Claim

Concession, politeness, comity, courtesy—none of these words could be uttered now with the assurance of listeners' approval. The word "comity" is rarely heard; "concession" sounds weak; "politeness" and "courtesy" sound quaint—much like the contemporary equivalent, "civility."

Reason

That Clay lauded both compromise and civil discourse in the same speech reveals the link between, on the one hand, the word "compromise" falling into disrepute, and, on the other, the glorification of aggression that I wrote about in my book, *The Argument Culture: Stopping America's War of Words.*

Evidence

Today we have an increasing tendency to approach every task—and each other—in an ever more adversarial spirit. Nowhere is this more evident, or more destructive, than in the Senate.

Claim

Though the two-party system is oppositional by nature, there is plenty of evidence that a certain (yes) comity has been replaced by growing enmity. We don't have to look as far back as Clay for evidence. In 1996, for example, an unprecedented fourteen incumbent senators announced that they would not seek reelection. And many, in farewell essays, described an increase in vituperation and partisanship that made it impossible to do the work of the Senate.

Rebuttal

Evidence

"The bipartisanship that is so crucial to the operation of Congress," Howell Heflin of Alabama wrote, "especially the Senate, has been abandoned." J. James Exon of Nebraska described an "ever-increasing vicious polarization of the electorate" that had "all but swept aside the former preponderance of reasonable discussion."

Evidence

But this is not happening only in the Senate. There is a rising adversarial spirit among the people and the press. It isn't only the obvious invective on TV and radio. A newspaper story that

Claim

criticizes its subject is praised as "tough"; one that refrains from criticism is scorned as a "puff piece."

The notion of "balance" today often leads to a search for the most extreme opposing views — so they can be presented as "both sides," leaving no forum for subtlety, multiple perspectives or the middle ground, where most people stand. Framing issues in this polarizing way reinforces the impression that Boehner voiced: that compromising is selling out.

Being surrounded by vituperation and seeing opponents as enemies is corrosive to the human spirit. It's also dangerous to our democracy. The great anthropologist Margaret Mead explained this in a 1962 speech.

"We are essentially a society which must be more committed to a two-party system than to either party," Mead said. "The only way you can have a two-party system is to belong to a party formally and to fight to the death . . ." not for your party to win but "for the right of the other party to be there too."

Today, this sounds almost as quaint as "comity" in political discourse.

Mead traced our two-party system to our unique revolution: "We didn't kill a king and we didn't execute a large number of our people, and we came into our own without the stained hands that have been associated with most revolutions."

With this noble heritage, Mead said, comes "the obligation to keep the kind of government we set up" — where members of each party may "disagree mightily" but still "trust in each other and trust in our political opponents."

Losing that trust, Mead concluded, undermines the foundation of our democracy. That trust is exactly what is threatened when the very notion of compromise is rejected.

What Toulmin Teaches

As Tannen's essay demonstrates, few arguments you read have perfectly sequenced claims or clear warrants, so you might not think of Toulmin's terms in building your own arguments. Once you're into your subject, it's easy to forget about qualifying a claim or finessing a warrant. But remembering what Toulmin teaches will always help you strengthen your arguments:

- Claims should be clear, reasonable, and carefully qualified.

- Claims should be supported with good reasons and evidence. Remember that a Toulmin structure provides the framework of an argument, which you fill out with all kinds of data, including facts, statistics, precedents, photographs, and even stories.

- Claims and reasons should be based on assumptions your audience will likely accept. Toulmin's focus on warrants can be confusing because it asks us to look at the assumptions that underlie our arguments—something many would rather not do. Toulmin pushes us to probe the values that support any argument and to think of how those values relate to particular audiences.

- Effective arguments respectfully anticipate objections readers might offer. Toulmin argument acknowledges that any claim can crumble under certain conditions, so it encourages a complex view that doesn't demand absolute or unqualified positions.

It takes considerable experience to write arguments that meet all these conditions. Using Toulmin's framework brings them into play automatically. If you learn it well enough, constructing good arguments can become a habit.

CULTURAL CONTEXTS FOR ARGUMENT

Organization

As you think about organizing your argument, remember that cultural factors are at work: patterns that you find persuasive are probably ones that are deeply embedded in your culture. In the United States, many people expect a writer to "get to the point" as directly as possible and to articulate that point efficiently and unambiguously. The organizational patterns favored by many in business hold similarities to the classical oration — a highly explicit pattern that leaves little or nothing unexplained — introduction and thesis, background, overview of the parts that follow, evidence, other viewpoints, and conclusion. If a piece of writing follows this pattern, American readers ordinarily find it "well organized."

So it's no surprise that student writers in the United States are expected to make their structures direct and their claims explicit, leaving little unspoken. Their claims usually appear early in an argument, often in the first paragraph.

But not all cultures take such an approach. Some expect any claim or thesis to be introduced subtly, indirectly, and perhaps at the end of a work, assuming that audiences will "read between the lines" to understand what's being said. Consequently, the preferred structure of arguments (and face-to-face negotiations, as well) may be elaborate, repetitive, and full of digressions. Those accustomed to such writing may find more direct Western styles overly simple, childish, or even rude.

When arguing across cultures, look for cues to determine how to structure your presentations effectively. Here are several points to consider:

- Do members of your audience tend to be very direct, saying explicitly what they mean? Or are they restrained, less likely to call a spade a spade? Consider adjusting your work to the expectations of the audience.

- Do members of your audience tend to respect authority and the opinions of groups? They may find blunt approaches disrespectful or contrary to their expectations.

- Consider when to state your thesis: At the beginning? At the end? Somewhere else? Not at all?

- Consider whether digressions are a good idea, a requirement, or an element to avoid.

Arguments of Fact

Many people believe that extensive use of the Internet, and especially social media, is harmful to memory and to learning, but recent research by scholars of literacy provides evidence suggesting that they are probably wrong.

In the past, female screen stars like Marilyn Monroe could be buxom and curvy, less concerned about their weight than actresses today. Or so the legend goes. But measuring the costumes worn by Monroe and other actresses reveals a different story.

When an instructor announces a tough new attendance policy for her course, a student objects that there is no evidence that students who regularly attend classes perform any better than those who do not. The instructor begs to differ.

Left to right: Zoonar/N.Sorokin/age fototstock; Alfred Eisenstaedt/Getty Images; © David R. Frazier, Photolibrary, Inc./Alamy

Understanding Arguments of Fact

Factual arguments come in many varieties, but they all try to establish whether something is or is not so, answering questions such as *Is a historical legend true? Has a crime occurred?* or *Are the claims of a scientist accurate?* At first glance, you might object that these aren't arguments at all but just a matter of looking things up and then writing reports. And you'd be correct to an extent: people don't usually argue factual matters that are settled or undisputed (*The earth revolves around the sun*), that might be decided with simple research (*The Mendenhall Glacier has receded 1.75 miles since 1958*), or that are the equivalent of a rule (*One mile measures 5,280 feet*). Reporting facts, you might think, should be free of the friction of argument.

Yet facts become arguments whenever they're controversial on their own or challenge people's beliefs and lifestyles. Disagreements about childhood obesity, endangered species, or energy production ought to have a kind of clean, scientific logic to them. But that's rarely the case because the facts surrounding them must be interpreted. Those interpretations then determine what we feed children, where we can build a dam, or how we heat our homes. In other words, serious factual arguments almost always have consequences. *Can we rely on wind and solar power to solve our energy needs? Will the Social Security trust fund really go broke? Is it healthy to eat fatty foods?* People need well-reasoned factual arguments on subjects of this kind to make informed decisions. Such arguments educate the public.

For the same reason, we need arguments to challenge beliefs that are common in a society but held on the basis of inadequate or faulty information. Corrective arguments appear daily in the media, often based on studies written by scientists or researchers that the public would not encounter on their own. Many people, for example, believe that talking on a cell phone while driving is just like listening to the radio. But their intuition is not based on hard data: scientific studies show that using a cell phone in a car is comparable to driving under the influence of alcohol. That's a fact. As a result, fourteen states (and counting) have banned the use of handheld phones in cars.

Factual arguments also routinely address broad questions about how we understand the past. For example, are the accounts that we have of the American founding—or the Civil War, Reconstruction, or the heroics of the "Greatest Generation" in World War II—accurate? Or do the "facts" that we teach today sometimes reflect the perspectives and prejudices of earlier times or ideologies? The telling of history is almost always controversial and rarely settled: the British and Americans will always tell different versions of what happened in North America in 1776.

FIGURE 16.1 © Bagley/Cagle Cartoons, Inc.

The Internet puts mountains of information at our fingertips, but we need to be sure to confirm whether or not that information is fact, using what Howard Rheingold calls "crap detection," the ability to distinguish between accurate information and inaccurate information, misinformation, or disinformation. (For more on "crap detection," see Chapter 27, "Evaluating Sources.")

As you can see, arguments of fact do much of the heavy lifting in our world. They report on what has been recently discovered or explore the implications of that new information. They also add interest and complexity to our lives, taking what might seem simple and adding new dimensions to it. In many situations, they're the precursors to other forms of analysis, especially causal and proposal arguments. Before we can explore why things happen as they do or solve problems, we need to do our best to determine the facts.

RESPOND

For each topic in the following list, decide whether the claim is worth arguing to a college audience, and explain why or why not.

Earthquakes are increasing in number and intensity.

Many people die annually of heart disease.

Fewer people would be obese if they followed the Paleo Diet.

Japan might have come to terms more readily in 1945 if the Allies in World War II hadn't demanded unconditional surrender.

Boys would do better in school if there were more men teaching in elementary and secondary classrooms.

The sharp drop in oil prices could lead drivers to go back to buying gas-guzzling trucks and SUVs.

There aren't enough high-paying jobs for college graduates these days.

Hydrogen may never be a viable alternative to fossil fuels because it takes too much energy to change hydrogen into a usable form.

Proponents of the Keystone Pipe Line have exaggerated the benefits it will bring to the American economy.

Characterizing Factual Arguments

Factual arguments are often motivated by simple human curiosity or suspicion: *Are people who earn college degrees happier than those who don't? If being fat is so unhealthy, why aren't mortality rates rising?* Researchers may notice a pattern that leads them to look more closely at some phenomenon or behavior, exploring questions such as *What if?* or *How come?* Or maybe a writer first notes something new or different or unexpected and wants to draw attention to that fact: *Contrary to expectations, suicide rates are much higher in rural areas than in urban ones.*

Such observations can lead quickly to **hypotheses**—that is, toward tentative and plausible statements of fact whose merits need to be examined more closely. *Maybe being a little overweight isn't as bad for people as we've been told? Maybe people in rural areas have less access to mental health services?* To support such hypotheses, writers then have to uncover evidence that reaches well beyond the casual observations that triggered an initial interest—like a news reporter motivated to see whether there's a verifiable story behind a source's tip.

For instance, the authors of *Freakonomics*, Stephen J. Dubner and Steven D. Levitt, were intrigued by the National Highway Traffic Safety Administration's claim that car seats for children were 54 percent effective in preventing deaths in auto crashes for children below the age of four. In a *New York Times* op-ed column entitled "The Seat-Belt Solution," they posed an important question about that factual claim:

> But 54 percent effective compared with what? The answer, it turns out, is this: Compared with a child's riding completely unrestrained.

Their initial question about that claim led them to a more focused inquiry, then to a database on auto crashes, and then to a surprising conclusion: for kids above age twenty-four months, those in car seats were statistically safer than those without any protection but weren't safer than those confined by seat belts (which are much simpler, cheaper, and more readily available devices). Looking at the statistics every which way, the authors wonder if children older than two years would be just as well off physically—and their parents less stressed and better off financially—if the government mandated seat belts rather than car seats for them.

What kinds of evidence typically appear in sound factual arguments? The simple answer might be "all sorts," but a case can be made that factual arguments try to rely more on "hard evidence" than do "constructed" arguments based on logic and reason (see Chapter 12). Even so, some pieces of evidence are harder than others!

Developing a Factual Argument

Entire Web sites are dedicated to finding and posting errors from news and political sources. Some, like Media Matters for America and Accuracy in Media, take overtly partisan stands. Here's a one-day sampling of headlines from Media Matters:

> Hillary Clinton Overcompensates on Foreign Policy Because She's a Woman
>
> Fox Host Defends Calling Michelle Obama Fat
>
> Fox News Decries Granting Undocumented Children Their Right to Public Education

And here's a listing from Accuracy in Media:

> An Inside Look at How Democrats Rig the Election Game
>
> Why Obamacare Is Unfixable
>
> The American Left: Friends to Our Country's Enemies

It would be hard to miss the blatant political agendas at work on these sites.

Other fact-checking organizations have better reputations when it comes to assessing the truths behind political claims and media presentations. Though both are also routinely charged with bias, Pulitzer Prize–winning PolitiFact.com and FactCheck.org at least make an effort to be fair-minded across a broader political spectrum. FactCheck, for example, provides a detailed analysis of the claims it investigates in relatively neutral and denotative language, and lists the sources its researchers used—just as if its writers were doing a research paper. At its best, FactCheck.org demonstrates what one valuable kind of factual argument can accomplish.

Any factual argument that you might compose—from how you state your claim to how you present evidence and the language you use—should be similarly shaped by the occasion for the argument and a desire to serve the audiences that you hope to reach. We can offer some general advice to help you get started.

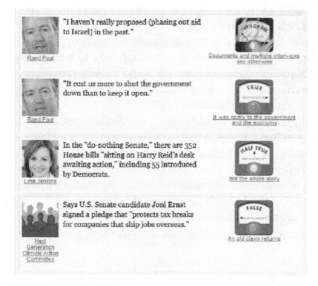

FIGURE 16.2 PolitiFact uses a meter to rate political claims from "True" to "Pants on Fire." Tampa Bay Times, all rights reserved

RESPOND

The Annenberg Public Policy Center at the University of Pennsylvania hosts FactCheck.org, a Web site dedicated to separating facts from opinion or falsehood in the area of politics. It claims to be politically neutral. Find a case that interests you, either a recent controversial item listed on its homepage or another from its archives. Carefully study the item. Pay attention to the devices that FactCheck uses to suggest or ensure objectivity and the way that it handles facts and statistics. Then offer your own brief *factual* argument about the site's objectivity.

Identifying an Issue

To offer a factual argument of your own, you need to identify an issue or problem that will interest you and potential readers. Look for situations or phenomena—local or national—that seem out of the ordinary in the expected order of things. For instance, you might notice that many people you know are deciding not to attend college. How widespread is this change, and who are the people making this choice?

Or follow up claims that strike you as at odds with the facts as you know them or believe them. Maybe you doubt explanations being offered for your favorite sport team's current slump or for the declining number of minority men in your college courses. Or you might give a local spin to factual questions that other people have already formulated on a national level. Do people in your town seem to be flocking to high-MPG vehicles or resisting bans on texting while driving or smoking in public places outdoors? You will likely write a better paper if you take on a factual question that genuinely interests you.

In fact, whole books are written when authors decide to pursue factual questions that intrigue them. But you want to be careful not to argue matters that pose no challenge for you or your audiences. You're not offering anything new if you just try to persuade readers that smoking is harmful to their well-being. So how about something fresh in the area of health?

Quick preliminary research and reading might allow you to move from an intuition to a hypothesis, that is, a tentative statement of your claim: *Having a dog is good for your health.* As noted earlier, factual arguments often provoke other types of analysis. In developing this claim, you'd need to explain what "good for your health" means, potentially an argument of definition. You'd also likely find yourself researching causes of the phenomenon if you can demonstrate that it is factual. As it turns out, your canine hypothesis would have merit if you defined "good for health" as "encouraging exercise." Here's the lead to a *New York Times* story reporting recent research:

> If you're looking for the latest in home exercise equipment, you may want to consider something with four legs and a wagging tail.
>
> Several studies now show that dogs can be powerful motivators to get people moving. Not only are dog owners more likely to take regular walks, but new research shows that dog walkers are more active overall than people who don't have dogs.
>
> One study even found that older people are more likely to take regular walks if the walking companion is canine rather than human.
>
> —Tara Parker-Pope, "Forget the Treadmill. Get a Dog," March 14, 2011

As always, there's another side to the story: what if people likely to get dogs are the very sort already inclined to be more physically active? You could explore that possibility as well (and researchers have) and then either modify your initial hypothesis or offer a new one. That's what hypotheses are for. They are works in progress.

Moving is the best medicine.
Keeping active and losing weight are just two of the ways that you can fight osteoarthritis pain. In fact, for every pound you lose, that's four pounds less pressure on each knee. For information on managing pain, go to fightarthritispain.org.

FIGURE 16.3 Here's an actual ad based on the claim that exercise (and dog ownership) is good for health.

Researching Your Hypothesis

How and where you research your subject will depend, naturally, on your subject. You'll certainly want to review Chapter 26, "Finding Evidence," Chapter 27, "Evaluating Sources," and Chapter 28, "Using Sources," before constructing an argument of fact. Libraries and the Web will provide you with deep resources on almost every subject. Your task will typically be to separate the best sources from all the rest. The word *best* here has many connotations: some reputable sources may be too technical for your audiences; some accessible sources may be pitched too low or be too far removed from the actual facts.

You'll be making judgment calls like this routinely. But do use primary sources whenever you can. For example, when gathering a comment from a source on the Web, trace it whenever possible to its original site, and read the comment in its full context. When statistics are quoted, follow them back to the source that offered them first to be sure that they're recent and reputable. Instructors and librarians can help you appreciate the differences. Understand that even sources with pronounced biases can furnish useful information, provided that you know how to use them, take their limitations into account, and then share what you know about the sources with your readers.

Sometimes, you'll be able to do primary research on your own, especially when your subject is local and you have the resources to do it. Consider conducting a competent survey of campus opinions and attitudes, for example, or study budget documents (often public) to determine trends in faculty salaries, tuition, student fees, and so on. Primary research of this sort can be challenging because even the simplest surveys or polls have to be intelligently designed and executed in a way that samples a representative population (see Chapter 12). But the work could pay off in an argument that brings new information to readers.

Refining Your Claim

As you learn more about your subject, you might revise your hypothesis to reflect what you've discovered. In most cases, these revised hypotheses will grow increasingly complex and specific. Following are three versions of essentially the same claim, with each version offering more information to help readers judge its merit:

- Americans really did land on the moon, despite what some people think!

- Since 1969, when the *Eagle* supposedly landed on the moon, some people have been unjustifiably skeptical about the success of the United States' *Apollo* program.

- Despite plentiful hard evidence to the contrary—from *Saturn V* launches witnessed by thousands to actual moon rocks tested by independent labs worldwide—some people persist in believing falsely that NASA's moon landings were actually filmed on deserts in the American Southwest as part of a massive propaganda fraud.

The additional details about the subject might also suggest new ways to develop and support it. For example, conspiracy theorists claim that the absence of visible stars in photographs of the moon landing is evidence that it was staged, but photographers know that the camera exposure needed to capture the foreground—astronauts in their bright space suits—would have made the stars in the background too dim to see. That's a key bit of evidence for this argument.

'...And, of course, there are the conspiracy theorists
who say that it was all a big hoax and I didn't jump
over it at all.'

FIGURE 16.4 © KES/CartoonStock.com

As you advance in your research, your thesis will likely pick up even more
qualifying words and expressions, which help you to make reasonable claims.
Qualifiers—words and phrases such as *some, most, few, for most people, for a few
users, under specific conditions, usually, occasionally, seldom,* and so on—will be
among your most valuable tools in a factual argument. (See p. 284 in Chapter 15
for more on qualifiers.)

Sometimes it is important to set your factual claim into a context that helps
explain it to others who may find it hard to accept. You might have to concede
some ground initially in order to see the broader picture. For instance, professor of
English Vincent Carretta anticipated strong objections after he uncovered evidence
that Olaudah Equiano—the author of *The Interesting Narrative* (1789), a much-
cited autobiographical account of his Middle Passage voyage and subsequent life as
a slave—may actually have been born in South Carolina and not in western Africa.
Speaking to the *Chronicle of Higher Education* about why Equiano may have fabricated his African origins to serve a larger cause, Carretta explains:

> "Whether [Equiano] invented his African birth or not, he knew that what that
> movement needed was a first-person account. And because they were going
> after the slave trade, it had to be an account of someone who had been born
> in Africa and was brought across the Middle Passage. An African American
> voice wouldn't have done it."

> —Jennifer Howard, "Unraveling the Narrative"

Carretta asks readers to appreciate that the new facts that he has discovered about *The Interesting Narrative* do not undermine the work's historical significance. If anything, his research has added new dimensions to its meaning and interpretation.

Deciding Which Evidence to Use

In this chapter, we've blurred the distinction between factual arguments for scientific and technical audiences and those for the general public (in magazines, blogs, social media sites, television documentaries, and so on). In the former kind of arguments, readers will expect specific types of evidence arranged in a formulaic way. Such reports may include a hypothesis, a review of existing research on the subject, a description of methods, a presentation of results, and finally a formal discussion of the findings. If you are thinking "lab report," you are already familiar with an academic form of a factual argument with precise standards for evidence.

Less scientific factual arguments — claims about our society, institutions, behaviors, habits, and so on — are seldom so systematic, and they may draw on evidence from a great many different media. For instance, you might need to review old newspapers, scan videos, study statistics on government Web sites, read transcripts of congressional hearings, record the words of eyewitnesses to an event, glean information by following experts on Twitter, and so on. Very often, you will assemble your arguments from material found in credible, though not always concurring, authorities and resources — drawing upon the factual findings of scientists and scholars, but perhaps using their original insights in novel ways.

For example, you might be intrigued by a comprehensive report from the Kaiser Family Foundation (2010) providing the results of a study of more than 2,000 eight- to eighteen-year-old American children:

> The study found that the average time spent reading books for pleasure in a typical day rose from 21 minutes in 1999 to 23 minutes in 2004, and finally to 25 minutes in 2010. The rise of screen-based media has not melted children's brains, despite ardent warnings otherwise: "It does not appear that time spent using screen media (TV, video games and computers) displaces time spent with print media," the report stated. Teens are not only reading more books, they're involved in communities of like-minded book lovers.
>
> —Hannah Withers and Lauren Ross,
> "Young People Are Reading More Than You"

Reading about these results, however, may raise some new questions for you: Is twenty-five minutes of reading a day really something to be happy about? What is the quality of what these young people are reading? Such questions might lead you to do a new study that could challenge the conclusion of the earlier research by bringing fresh facts to the table.

Often, you may have only a limited number of words or pages in which to make a factual argument. What do you do then? You present your best evidence as powerfully as possible. But that's not difficult. You can make a persuasive factual case with just a few examples: three or four often suffice to make a point. Indeed, going on too long or presenting even good data in ways that make it seem uninteresting or pointless can undermine a claim.

Presenting Your Evidence

In *Hard Times* (1854), British author Charles Dickens poked fun at a pedagogue he named Thomas Gradgrind, who preferred hard facts before all things human or humane. When poor Sissy Jupe (called "girl number twenty" in his awful classroom) is unable at his command to define *horse*, Gradgrind turns to his star pupil:

> "Bitzer," said Thomas Gradgrind. "Your definition of a horse."
>
> "Quadruped. Graminivorous. Forty teeth, namely twenty-four grinders, four eyeteeth, and twelve incisive. Sheds coat in the spring; in marshy countries, sheds hoofs, too. Hoofs hard, but requiring to be shod with iron. Age known by marks in mouth." Thus (and much more) Bitzer.
>
> "Now girl number twenty," said Mr. Gradgrind. "You know what a horse is."
>
> —Charles Dickens, *Hard Times*

But does Bitzer? Rattling off facts about a subject isn't quite the same thing as knowing it, especially when your goal is, as it is in an argument of fact, to educate and persuade audiences. So you must take care how you present your evidence.

Factual arguments, like any others, take many forms. They can be as simple and pithy as a letter to the editor (or Bitzer's definition of a horse) or as comprehensive and formal as a senior thesis or even a dissertation. Such a thesis might have just two or three readers mainly interested in the facts you are presenting and the competence of your work. So your presentation can be lean and relatively simple.

But to earn the attention of readers in some more public forum, you may need to work harder to be persuasive. For instance, Pew Research Center's May 2014 formal report, *Young Adults, Student Debt, and Economic Well-Being*, which spends time introducing its authors and establishing their expertise, is twenty-three pages long, cites a dozen sources, and contains sixteen figures and tables. Like many such studies, it also includes a foreword, an overview, and a detailed table of contents. All these elements help readers find the facts they need while also establishing the ethos of the work, making it seem serious, credible, well conceived, and worth reading.

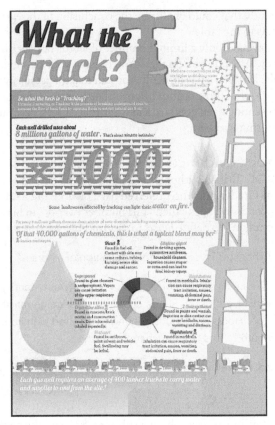

FIGURE 16.5 "What the Frack?" uses images to present
its case against fracking. © Jess Nelson Design

Considering Design and Visuals

When you prepare a factual argument, consider how you can present your evidence most effectively. Precisely because factual arguments often rely on evidence that can be measured, computed, or illustrated, they benefit from thoughtful, even artful presentation of data. If you have lots of examples, you might arrange them in a list (bulleted or otherwise) and keep the language in each item roughly parallel. If you have an argument that can be translated into a table, chart, or graph (see Chapter 22), try it. And if there's a more dramatic medium for your factual argument—a Prezi slide show, a multimedia mashup, a documentary video posted via a social network—experiment with it, checking to be sure it would satisfy the assignment.

FIGURE 16.6 Infographics like this one turn facts and data into arguments. USAID

Images and photos—from technical illustrations to imaginative re-creations—have the power to document what readers might otherwise have to imagine, whether actual conditions of drought, poverty, or a disaster like devastating typhoon Haiyan that displaced over 4 million people in the Philippines in 2013, or the dimensions of the Roman forum as it existed in the time of Julius Caesar. Readers today expect the arguments they read to include visual elements, and there's little reason not to offer this assistance if you have the technical skills to create them.

Consider the rapid development of the genre known as infographics—basically data presented in bold visual form. These items can be humorous and creative, but many, such as "Learning Out of Poverty" on the preceding page, make powerful factual arguments even when they leave it to viewers to draw their own conclusions. Just search "infographics" on the Web to find many examples.

GUIDE TO WRITING AN ARGUMENT OF FACT

Finding a Topic

You're entering an argument of fact when you:

- make a claim about fact or existence that's controversial or surprising: *Climate change is threatening species in all regions by extending the range of non-native plants and animals.*

- correct an error of fact: *The overall abortion rate is not increasing in the United States, though rates are increasing in some states.*

- challenge societal myths: *Many Mexicans fought alongside Anglos in battles that won Texas its independence from Mexico.*

- wish to discover the state of knowledge about a subject or examine a range of perspectives and points of view: *The rationales of parents who homeschool their children reveal some surprising differences.*

Researching Your Topic

Use both a library and the Web to locate the information you need. A research librarian is often a valuable resource, as are experts or eyewitnesses. Begin research by consulting the following types of sources:

- scholarly books on your subject

- newspapers, magazines, reviews, and journals (online and print)

- online databases

- government documents and reports

- Web sites, blogs, social networking sites, and listservs or newsgroups

- experts in the field, some of whom might be right on your campus

Do field research if appropriate—a survey, a poll, or systematic observation. Or invite people with a stake in the subject to present their interpretations of the facts. Evaluate all sources carefully, making sure that each is authoritative and credible.

Formulating a Hypothesis

Don't rush into a thesis. Instead, begin with a hypothesis that expresses your beliefs at the beginning of the project but that may change as you learn more. It's OK to start with a question to which you don't have an answer or with a broad, general interest in a subject:

- **Question:** Have higher admissions standards at BSU reduced the numbers of entering first-year students from small, rural high schools?
- **Hypothesis:** Higher admissions standards at BSU are reducing the number of students admitted from rural high schools, which tend to be smaller and less well-funded than those in suburban and urban areas.
- **Question:** Have music sites like Pandora and Spotify reduced the amount of illegal downloading of music?
- **Hypothesis:** Services like Pandora and Spotify may have done more than lawsuits by record companies to discourage illegal downloads of music.
- **Question:** How dangerous is nuclear energy, really?
- **Hypothesis:** The danger posed by nuclear power plants is far less than that attributable to other viable energy sources.
- **Question:** Why can't politicians and citizens agree about the threat posed by the huge federal deficit?
- **Hypothesis:** People with different points of view read different threats into the budget numbers and so react differently.

Examples of Arguable Factual Claims

- A campus survey that shows that far more students have read *Harry Potter and the Prisoner of Azkaban* than *Hamlet* indicates that our current core curriculum lacks depth.
- Evidence suggests that the European conquest of the Americas may have had more to do with infectious diseases than any superiority in technology or weaponry.
- In the long run, dieting may be more harmful than moderate overeating.

Preparing a Proposal

If your instructor asks you to prepare a proposal for your project, here's a format that may help:

State your thesis or hypothesis completely. If you are having trouble doing so, try outlining it in Toulmin terms:

Claim:

Reason(s):

Warrant(s):

Alternatively, you might describe the complications of a factual issue you hope to explore in your project, with the thesis perhaps coming later.

- Explain why the issue you're examining is important, and provide the context for raising the issue. Are you introducing new information, making available information better known, correcting what has been reported incorrectly, or complicating what has been understood more simply?

- Identify and describe those readers you most hope to reach with your argument. Why is this group of readers most appropriate for your project? What are their interests in the subject? How might you involve them in the paper?

- Discuss the kinds of evidence you expect to use in the project and the research the paper will require.

- Briefly discuss the key challenges you anticipate in preparing your argument.

Considering Format and Media

Your instructor may specify that you use a particular format and/or medium. If not, ask yourself these questions to help you make a good choice:

- What format is most appropriate for your argument of fact? Does it call for an academic essay, a report, an infographic, a brochure, or something else?

- What medium is most appropriate for your argument? Would it be best delivered orally to a live audience? Presented as an audio essay or podcast? Presented in print only or in print with illustrations?

- Will you need visuals, such as moving or still images, maps, graphs, charts—and what function will they play in your argument? Make sure they are not just "added on" but are necessary components of the argument.

Thinking about Organization

The simplest structure for a factual argument is to make a claim and then prove it. But even a basic approach needs an introductory section that provides a context for the claim and a concluding section that assesses the implications of the argument. A factual argument that corrects an error or provides an alternative view of some familiar concept or historical event will also need a section early on explaining what the error or the common belief is. Be sure your opening section answers the *who, what, where, when, how,* and (maybe) *why* questions that readers will bring to the case.

Factual arguments offered in some academic fields follow formulas and templates. A format favored in the hard sciences and also in the social and behavioral sciences is known by its acronym, IMRAD, which stands for Introduction, Methods, Research, and Discussion. Another typical format calls for an abstract, a review of literature, a discussion of method, an analysis, and a references list. When you have flexibility in the structure of your argument, it makes sense to lead with a striking example to interest readers in your subject and then to conclude with your strongest evidence. Pay particular attention to transitions between key points.

If you are defending a specific claim, anticipate the ways people with different points of view might respond to your argument. Consider how to address such differences respectfully in the body of your argument. But don't let a factual argument with a persuasive thesis end with concessions or refutations, especially in pieces for the general public. Such a strategy leaves readers thinking about problems with your claim at precisely the point when they should be impressed by its strengths. On the other hand, if your factual argument becomes exploratory, you may find yourself simply presenting a range of positions.

Getting and Giving Response: Questions for Peer Response

Your instructor may assign you to a group for the purpose of reading and responding to each other's drafts. If not, ask for responses from serious readers or consultants at a writing center. Use the following questions to evaluate a colleague's draft. Since specific comments help more than general observations, be sure to illustrate your comments with examples. Some of the questions below assume a conventional, thesis-driven project, but more exploratory or invitational arguments of fact also need to be clearly phrased, organized, and supported with evidence.

The Claim

- Does the claim clearly raise a serious and arguable factual issue?

- Is the claim as clear and specific as possible?

- Is the claim qualified? If so, how?

Evidence for the Claim

- Is the evidence provided enough to persuade readers to believe your claim? If not, what additional evidence would help? Does any of the evidence seem inappropriate or ineffective? Why?

- Is the evidence in support of the claim simply announced, or do you explain its significance and appropriateness? Is more discussion needed?

- Are readers' potential objections to the claim or evidence addressed adequately? Are alternative positions understood thoroughly and presented fairly?

- What kinds of sources are cited? How credible and persuasive will they be to readers? What other kinds of sources might work better?

- Are all quotations introduced with appropriate signal phrases (such as "As Tyson argues, …") and blended smoothly into the writer's sentences?

- Are all visuals titled and labeled appropriately? Have you introduced them and commented on their significance?

Organization and Style

- How are the parts of the argument organized? Is this organization effective?

- Will readers understand the relationships among the claims, supporting reasons, warrants, and evidence? If not, how might those connections be clearer? Is the function of every visual clear? Are more transitions needed? Would headings or graphic devices help?

- Are the transitions or links from point to point, sentence to sentence, and paragraph to paragraph clear and effective? If not, how could they be improved?

- Are all visuals carefully integrated into the text? Is each visual introduced and commented on to point out its significance? Is each visual labeled as a figure or a table and given a caption as well as a citation?

- Is the style suited to the subject? Is it too formal, casual, or technical? Can it be improved?

- Which sentences seem effective? Which ones seem weaker, and how could they be improved? Should short sentences be combined, and any longer ones be broken up?

- How effective are the paragraphs? Too short or too long? How can they be improved?

- Which words or phrases seem effective? Do any seem vague or inappropriate for the audience or the writer's purpose? Are technical or unfamiliar terms defined?

Spelling, Punctuation, Mechanics, Documentation, and Format

- Are there any errors in spelling, punctuation, capitalization, and the like?

- Is an appropriate and consistent style of documentation used for parenthetical citations and the list of works cited or references? (See Chapter 30.)

- Does the paper or project follow an appropriate format? Is it appropriately designed and attractively presented? How could it be improved?

PROJECTS

1. Turn a database of information you find in the library or online into a traditional argument or, alternatively, into an infographic that offers a variety of potential claims. FedStats, a government Web site, provides endless data, but so can the sports or financial sections of a newspaper. Once you find a rich field of study, examine the data and draw your ideas from it, perhaps amplifying these ideas with material from other related sources of information. If you decide to create an infographic, you'll find good examples at VizWorld or Cool Infographics online. Software tools you can use to create infographics include Piktochart and Google Public Data. Have fun.

2. Write an argument about one factual matter you are confident—based on personal experience or your state of knowledge—that most people get wrong, time and again. Use your expertise to correct this false impression.

3. Tough economic and political times sometimes reinforce and sometimes undermine cultural myths. With your classmates, generate a list of common beliefs about education, employment, family life, marriage, social progress, technology, and so on that seem to be under unusual scrutiny today. *Does it still pay to invest in higher education? Do two-parent households matter as much as they used to? Can children today expect to do better than their parents? Is a home still a good investment?* Pick one area to explore in depth, narrow the topic as much as you can, and then gather facts that inform it by doing research, perhaps working collaboratively to expand your findings. Turn your investigation into a factual argument.

4. Since critic and writer Nicholas Carr first asked "Is Google Making Us Stupid?" many have answered with a resounding "yes," arguing that extensive time online is reducing attention spans and leaving readers less critical than ever. Others have disagreed, saying that new technologies are doing just the opposite—expanding our brain power. Do some research on this controversy, on the Web or in the library, and consult with a wide range of people interested in the subject, perhaps gathering them together for a discussion or panel discussion. Then offer a factual argument based on what you uncover, reflecting the range of perspectives and opinions you have encountered.

Two Sample Factual Arguments

Why You Should Fear Your Toaster More Than Nuclear Power

Readers will certainly notice the title.

TAYLOR PEARSON

For the past month or so, headlines everywhere have been warning us of the horrible crises caused by the damaged Japanese nuclear reactors. Titles like "Japan Nuclear Disaster Tops Scale" have fueled a new wave of protests against anything nuclear — namely, the construction of new nuclear plants or even the continued operation of existing plants. However, all this reignited fear of nuclear energy is nothing more than media sensationalism. We need nuclear energy. It's clean, it's efficient, it's economic, and it's probably the only thing that will enable us to quickly phase out fossil fuels.

A recent nuclear disaster in Japan provides a challenging context for Pearson's claim: we need nuclear energy.

The first-person plural point of view (we) helps Pearson to connect with his audience.

Death Toll

First, let's address what is probably everyone's main concern about nuclear energy: the threat it poses to us and the likelihood of a nuclear power plant killing large numbers of people. The actual number of deaths caused by nuclear power plant accidents, even in worst-case scenarios, have been few. Take the Chernobyl accident — the worst and most lethal nuclear incident to date. As tragic as it was, the incident has killed only eighty-two people. More specifically, according to a 2005 release by the World Health Organization, thirty-two were killed in the effort to put out the fires caused by the meltdown and thirty-eight died within months of the accident as a result of acute radiation poisoning. Since the accident occurred in 1986, an additional twelve people have died from the radiation they were exposed to during the accident. Almost all deaths were highly exposed rescue workers. Other nuclear power accidents have been few and never resulted in more than ten deaths per incident. Still think that's too dangerous? To provide some perspective, let's consider an innocuous household appliance, the toaster: over three

Pearson deflates fears by putting deaths caused by nuclear plants in perspective.

Taylor Pearson wrote "Why You Should Fear Your Toaster More Than Nuclear Power" while he was a sophomore at the University of Texas at Austin. The assignment asked for a public argument — one good enough to attract readers who could put it down if they lost interest. In other words, a purely academic argument wouldn't work. So Pearson allows himself to exercise his sense of humor. Nor did the paper have to be formally documented. However, Pearson was expected to identify crucial sources the way writers do in magazines and newspapers. The paper provides an example of a factual argument with a clear thesis: "We need nuclear energy."

thousand people died from toaster accidents the first year the appliances were produced and sold in the 1920s, and they still cause around fifty accident-related deaths every year in the United States. So your toaster is far more likely to kill you than any nuclear power plant and subsequently give you a painfully embarrassing epitaph.

In fact, in comparison to the other major means of energy production in the United States, nuclear power is remarkably safe. According to the U.S. Department of Labor, coal mining currently causes about sixty-five deaths and eleven thousand injuries per year, while oil drilling is responsible for approximately 125 deaths per year in the United States. Annual death tolls fluctuate depending upon the demand for these resources and the subsequent drilling or mining required, but the human cost is still exponentially more than that of nuclear energy. However, in the decades that nuclear power has been used in the United States, there have been zero deaths caused by nuclear power accidents — none at all. That's much better than the thousands of lives coal, oil, and toasters have cost us. If you care about saving human lives, then you should like nuclear energy.

Radiation

Despite nuclear energy causing remarkably few deaths, people are also terrified of another aspect of nuclear power — radiation. Everyone's scared of developing a boulder-size tumor or our apples growing to similar size as a result of the awful radiation given off by nuclear power plants or their potential meltdowns. However, it should comfort you to know (or perhaps not) that you receive more radiation from a brick wall than from a nuclear power plant.

The argument uses technical terms but makes sure they are accessible to readers.

We live in a radioactive world — nearly everything gives off at least a trace amount of radiation; that includes brick walls. Yes, while such a wall emits about 3.5 millirems of radiation per year, a nuclear power plant gives off about .3 millirems per year. (Millirem is just a unit of radiation dosage.) Of course, this low level of emission is a result of the numerous safeguards set up around the reactors to suppress radiation. So what happens if those safeguards fail? Will everyone surrounding the plant turn into a mutant?

To answer that question, let's examine the reactor failures in the recent Japanese nuclear crisis following several devastating earthquakes. The damage from the quakes took out the power to several nuclear plants, which caused their core cooling systems to go offline.

To prevent reactor meltdowns, workers had to douse the failing reactors in thousands of gallons of seawater to cool the fuel rods, which contain all the radioactive materials. Worries about the resulting radioactive seawater contaminating the ocean and sea life flared as a result. But just how radioactive is the water? Officials from Tokyo Electric Power Company said the water "would have to be drunk for a whole year in order to accumulate one millisievert." People are generally exposed to about 1 to 10 millisieverts each year from background radiation caused by substances in the air and soil. "You would have to eat or drink an awful lot to get any level of radiation that would be harmful," said British nuclear expert Laurence Williams. You get exposed to 5 millisieverts during a coast-to-coast flight across the United States. According to the U.S. Food and Drug Administration, you receive between 5 and 60 millisieverts in a CAT scan, depending on the type. So drinking water for a year that was in direct contact with containers of radioactive material used in those Japanese nuclear plants will expose you to a fifth of the radiation you would get from the weakest CAT scan. How dangerous!

> The argument is full of data and statistics from what seem to be reputable authorities and sources.

Waste

But even if we have little to fear from nuclear power plants themselves, what about the supposedly deadly by-products of these plants? Opponents of nuclear energy cite the fact that while nuclear power plants don't emit greenhouse gases, they do leave behind waste that remains radioactive for thousands of years. However, this nuclear waste problem is exaggerated. According to Professor Emeritus of Computer Science at Stanford University, John McCarthy, a 1,000-megawatt reactor produces only 1.5 cubic meters of waste after a year of operation. The current solution is to put the waste in protective containers and store them in caverns cut in granite. At the very least, with such a small amount of waste per reactor, the caverns don't have to be dug very fast.

> As the argument explores various aspects of nuclear energy, headings keep the reader on track.

> Pearson strategically concedes a downside of nuclear energy.

Nuclear power plants do produce waste that needs to be kept away from living things, but the actual amount of waste produced is small and therefore manageable. If the United States got all its power from nuclear plants, the amount of waste produced would be equivalent to one pill of aspirin per person, per year — tiny compared to the amount of waste produced by plants that use fossil fuels; the U.S. Energy Information Administration notes that coal alone produces about 1.8 billion metric tons of CO_2 emissions per year.

Quantity is not the only factor that has been exaggerated—the amount of time the waste remains dangerously radioactive has also been inflated. After about five hundred years, the fission products' radiation levels drop to below the level at which we typically find them in nature; the thousands of years opponents of nuclear energy refer to are the years the waste will be radioactive, not excessively so. You don't want to stand right next to this material even after those first five hundred years, but if it can exist in nature without doing any noticeable damage, then it doesn't pose any serious threat. Essentially, everything is radioactive; to criticize something for being radioactive without specifying the level of radioactivity means nothing.

Meeting Our Energy Demands

Although I've done a lot here in an attempt to defend nuclear energy, I still acknowledge it's not perfect. While the nuclear waste problem isn't something to be too worried about, it would still be better if we could satisfy our demand for energy without producing waste, radioactive or otherwise. However, I believe nuclear energy is the only realistic option we have to one day achieve an entirely clean energy reality.

We live in an age dominated by energy—to power our cars, our homes, and our computers. Let's face it: we're not going to give up the lifestyle that energy gives us. But under the current means of energy production—primarily coal in the United States—we're pumping out billions of tons of greenhouse gases that will eventually destroy our planet. So we have a dilemma. While we want to do something about global warming, we don't want to change our high-energy-consumption way of life. What are our options?

The concluding paragraphs compare nuclear power to potential alternatives.

Currently, completely clean sources of energy haven't been developed enough to make them a realistic option to supply all our energy needs. For solar energy to match the energy production of nuclear power plants presently in use, we would have to cover an area the size of New Jersey with solar panels. That's not a realistic option; we're not going to build that many panels just to get ourselves off of our addiction to fossil fuels. The same is true of the other renewable energy sources: wind, geothermal, hydroelectric, etc. The technologies simply aren't mature enough.

However, nuclear power *is* realistic. We have the means and the technology to make enough nuclear power plants to satisfy our electricity demands. Nuclear plants produce a lot of power with relatively little waste. Moving from coal to nuclear plants could provide us with adequate power until we develop more efficient renewable sources of electricity.

So what's stopping us? Of course, those heavily invested in coal and other fossil fuels lobby the government to keep their industries profitable, but a large source of opposition is also the American public. Because of the atom bombs of World War II, the Cold War, and Chernobyl, we're scared of all things nuclear. Anytime we hear the word "radiation," images of mushroom clouds and fallout enter our minds. But nuclear power plants aren't bombs. No matter what happens to them, they will never explode. Strong as it might be, our fear of nuclear power is overblown and keeping us from using a source of energy that could literally save our planet. We need to stop the fearmongering before we burn our planet to a crisp.

Of course, that's if our toasters don't kill us first.

Pearson ends his argument by asking readers to acknowledge that their fears of nuclear power aren't based in fact.

What the Numbers Show about N.F.L. Player Arrests

NEIL IRWIN

Off-the-field violence by professional football players is coming under new focus this week after the release of a video involving the star Baltimore Ravens running back Ray Rice, followed by a bungled response by the National Football League.

But what do the numbers show about N.F.L. players' tangles with the law more broadly? Are some teams' players more likely to get into legal trouble? Are arrests rising or falling? What are the most common offenses?

USA Today maintains a database of arrests, charges, and citations of N.F.L. players for anything more serious than a traffic citation. Maintained by Brent Schrotenboer, it goes back to 2000 and covers, to date, 713 instances in which pro football players have had a run-in with the law that was reported by the news media.

The data set is imperfect; after all, it depends on news media outlets finding out about every time a third-string offensive lineman is pulled over for driving drunk, and so some arrests may well fall through the cracks. Moreover, arrests are included even if charges are dropped or the player is found not guilty, so it presumably includes legal run-ins in which the player did nothing wrong.

Finally, for purposes of these tabulations, a simple drug possession charge in which no one was hurt counts the same as a case like that of Mr. Rice, who is on tape punching his fiancée out cold (she is now his wife), or even that of the former New England Patriot Aaron Hernandez, who is in jail awaiting trial on murder charges.

FIGURE 16.7 Ray Rice was arraigned on domestic violence charges in May 2014. He was fired by the Baltimore Ravens in September 2014.

AP Photo/The Philadelphia Inquirer, Tom Gralish, Pool

But with those caveats aside, here's what the data show about how pro football players are interacting with the law. The numbers show a league in which drunk-driving arrests are a continuing problem and domestic violence charges are surprisingly common; in which the teams that have the most players getting in legal trouble don't always fit the impressions fans might have; and in which teams with high arrest rates tend to stay that way over time.

One N.F.L. player in 40 is arrested in a given year. There are 32 teams, each with 53 players on its roster plus another eight on its practice squad (plus more players who show up for training camp but do not make the team, but we didn't attempt to account for them). Thus over the nearly 15 years that the *USA Today* data goes back, the 713 arrests mean that 2.53 percent of players have had a serious run-in with the law in an average year. That may sound bad, but the arrest rate is lower than the national average for men in that age range.

Arrests peaked in the mid-2000s, and are way down this year. The peak year for arrests of N.F.L. players was 2006, followed closely by 2007 and 2008. (These are calendar years, not N.F.L. seasons.) One important caveat: The apparent increase could be a result of increased coverage of professional athletes' legal troubles by Internet media. In other words, we don't know for sure whether more N.F.L. players were being arrested in those years, or whether TMZ and other outlets were better positioned to find out about it.

Despite the Ray Rice episode, 2014 is on track to be the year with the fewest arrests of N.F.L. players on record. Through Sept. 10, there had only been 21. If the final four months of the year proceed at the same pace of arrests as the first eight, that will come to 28, well below the previous low of 36 in 2004.

The most common accusation is driving while drunk, but domestic violence is a big problem. Some 28 percent of the arrests in the database were for driving under the influence, with 202 incidents. Other frequent categories of charges include assault and battery (88 cases) and drug-related offenses (82). This data is also a reminder that domestic violence has been a problem among N.F.L. players since long before Ray and Janay Rice got on that Atlantic City elevator: There have been 85 charges for domestic violence and related offenses since 2000.

The Minnesota Vikings have had the most players arrested since 2000. The number of arrests by team range from a low of 11 (tie between the Arizona Cardinals and St. Louis Rams) versus a high of 44 (the Vikings), with the Cincinnati Bengals and Denver Broncos close behind. (The Houston Texans also have 11 but started playing in 2002.)

To look at it a different way, across the league from 2000 through 2013, 2.53 percent of players were arrested per year, but for the Vikings, that number is 5 percent. For the teams tied for fewest arrests, it is 1.3 percent.

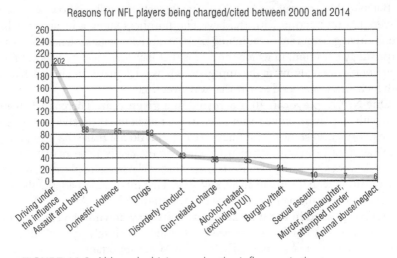

FIGURE 16.8 Although driving under the influence is the top reason NFL players ran into trouble with the law, the next three biggest reasons are very concerning. Data from *USA Today*

The Ravens have received negative publicity over Rice, whom they fired, and over other players' legal troubles this year, but their 22 player arrests since 2000 make them right at the leaguewide average. The Oakland Raiders have cultivated an image of being a franchise for tough, rowdy bad boys. The team's players, however, have had 19 scrapes with the law since 2000, below average.

The frequency of arrests in a franchise tends to be consistent over time. One might imagine that the number of players from a given franchise who are arrested is a random phenomenon. Maybe, in the rankings above, for example, the Vikings and the Bengals were just unlucky and the Cardinals and Rams were just lucky.

But there's a simple way to test that. If the results were random, you would expect there to be no correlation between the number of player arrests in one time period with a subsequent time period. You could even imagine a negative correlation, if teams that had a run of players getting in trouble took extra care not to sign players reputed to have character issues.

But that is not what happened over the last 14 years. If you chart the number of arrests of players from each franchise in the first seven years of the data, 2000 to 2006, versus the number of arrests that franchise experienced from 2007 to 2013, the correlation is a pretty solid 53 percent. [This] shows a clear pattern in which those franchises with high numbers of arrests in the early years also tended to have high numbers of arrests in later years and vice versa.

The data don't tell us anything about why these patterns are so persistent, but there are two possibilities that seem to stand out. First, there could be club culture. The top management of a franchise may send a message to personnel scouts and coaches that they are either more or less tolerant of signing players who have had legal problems in the past. (One might imagine that the personal style of the coach could play a role as well, but coaches tend not to have long tenures in the modern N.F.L.; no coach has led his team continuously for the entirety of the time covered by this arrest data, though the Patriots' Bill Belichick misses that honor by only a few weeks, having been hired in late January 2000.)

Second, there is geography. Different cities have different patterns of living and different approaches to law enforcement. Perhaps players for the Jets and the Giants (both with persistently low arrest rates) are at less risk of arrest for D.U.I. because people are less likely to need to drive themselves to nightclubs in Manhattan. Or perhaps in some cities, young African-American men driving expensive cars attract more police attention than in others.

Regardless of the reasons, a handful of franchises have persistently higher numbers of players who end up being arrested, and may want to learn from their rivals in other cities as to why.

Arguments of Definition

A student writes a cookbook for her master's thesis, hoping to make it easier for people to eat good, healthy food for less money. Her work helps redefine current definitions of *thesis*.

A panel of judges must decide whether computer-enhanced images will be eligible in a contest for landscape photography. At what point is an electronically manipulated image no longer a *photograph*?

A conservative student group accuses the student government on campus of sponsoring a lecture series featuring a disproportionate number of "left-wing" writers and celebrities. A spokesperson for the student government defends its program by questioning the definition of *left-wing* used to classify some of the speakers.

Left to right: AP Photo/Seth Wenig; Bill Wight/Getty Images; Frederick M. Brown/Getty Images

Understanding Arguments of Definition

Definitions matter. Just ask a scientist, a mathematician, an engineer, a judge—or just an everyday person who wants to marry someone of the same sex. In 1996, the Congress passed, and President Clinton signed, the Defense of Marriage Act (DOMA), which defined marriage in federal law this way:

> In determining the meaning of any Act of Congress, or of any ruling, regulation, or interpretation of the various administrative bureaus and agencies of the United States, the word "marriage" means only a legal union between one man and one woman as husband and wife, and the word "spouse" refers only to a person of the opposite sex who is a husband or a wife. 1 U.S.C. 7.

This decision and its definitions of *marriage* and *spouse* have been challenged over and over again in the ensuing decades, leading eventually to another Supreme Court decision, in the summer of 2013, that declared DOMA unconstitutional. The majority opinion, written by Justice Kennedy, found that the earlier law was discriminatory and that it labeled same-sex unions as "less worthy than the marriage of others." In so ruling, the court affirmed that the federal government cannot differentiate between a "marriage" of heterosexuals and one of homosexuals. Laws regarding marriage—and thus attempting to define or redefine the term—are still ongoing, and you might want to check the status of such controversies in your own state.

In any case, such decisions demonstrate that arguments of definition aren't abstract academic exercises: they are contentious and very often have important consequences for ordinary people. That's because they wield the power to say what someone or something is or can be. Such arguments can both include or exclude: A wolf in Montana either is an endangered species or it isn't. An unsolicited kiss is or is not sexual harassment. A person merits official political refugee status in the United States or doesn't. Another way of approaching definitional arguments, however, is to think of what falls between *is* and *is not* in a definitional claim. In fact, many definitional disputes occur in that murky realm.

Consider the controversy over how to define *human intelligence.* Some argue that human intelligence is a capacity that is measured by tests of verbal and mathematical reasoning. In other words, it's defined by IQ and SAT scores. Others define *intelligence* as the ability to perform specific practical tasks. Still others interpret *intelligence* in emotional terms as a competence in relating to other people. Any of these positions could be defended reasonably, but perhaps the wisest approach would be to construct a definition of *intelligence* that is rich enough to incorporate all these perspectives—and maybe more.

The fact is that crucial political, social, and scientific terms—such as *intelligence, social justice, war,* or *marriage*—are reargued, reshaped, and updated for the times.

The use of drones in air strikes—and the loss of civilian lives involved—has led to a heated national controversy. Commenting in *The Daily Kos*, MinistryOfTruth wrote:

> We all cringe when we hear of the innocent lives lost at war and civilians caught in the crossfire. These civilian deaths are always sad and tragic reminders of the cost of war. The Military/Industrial Complex doesn't like that. Reports of civilian deaths make the wars unpopular, and that's not the right way to continue to justify an ever growing military budget full of expensive drone missiles and the longest war in American history, is it? Nope. So what do they do? Re-define the dead civilians.
>
> —MinistryOfTruth, in *The Daily Kos*

Blogger MinistryOfTruth goes on to quote from a lengthy article in the *New York Times* concluding that the administration "embraced a disputed method for counting civilian casualties that ... in effect counts all military-age males in a strike zone as combatants, ... unless there is explicit intelligence posthumously proving them innocent." As this example illustrates, during war times it is especially important to watch how definitions get shifted and changed to shape or change reality.

FIGURE 17.1 Red DaxLuma Gallery/Shutterstock

The argument over how to define *militants* and *combatants* will not be settled simply by consulting a dictionary, no matter how up to date it is. In fact, dictionaries inevitably reflect the way that particular groups of people use words at a specified time and place. And like any form of writing, these reference books mirror the prejudices of their makers—as shown, perhaps most famously, in the entries of lexicographer Samuel Johnson (1709–1784), who gave the English language its first great dictionary. Johnson, no friend of the Scots, defined *oats* as "a grain which in England is generally given to horses, but in Scotland supports the people." (To be fair, he also defined *lexicographer* as "a writer of dictionaries, a harmless drudge.") Thus, it's possible to disagree with dictionary definitions or to regard them merely as starting points for arguments.

FIGURE 17.2 The *Dictionary for Landlubbers* defines words according to their point of view! Excerpted from *SAILING: A Dictionary for Landlubbers, Old Salts, & Armchair Drifters.* Copyright © 1981 by Henry Beard and Roy McKie. Used by permission of Workman Publishing Co., Inc., New York. All rights reserved.

RESPOND

Briefly discuss how you might define the italicized terms in the following controversial claims of definition. Compare your definitions of the terms with those of your classmates.

Graphic novels are *serious literature*.

Burning a nation's flag is a *hate crime*.

Matt Drudge and Arianna Huffington aren't *journalists*.

College sports programs have become *big businesses*.

Plagiarism can be an act of *civil disobedience*.

Satanism is a *religion* properly protected by the First Amendment.

Campaign contributions are acts of *free speech* that should never be regulated.

The District of Columbia should not have all the privileges of an American *state*.

Polygamous couples should have the legal privileges of *marriage*.

Kinds of Definition

Because there are different kinds of definitions, there are also different ways to make a definition argument. Fortunately, identifying a particular type of definition is less important than appreciating when an issue of definition is at stake. Let's explore some common definitional issues.

Formal Definitions

Formal definitions are what you find in dictionaries. Such definitions place a term in its proper **genus** and **species**—first determining its class and then identifying the features or criteria that distinguish it from other members of that class. That sounds complicated, but a definition will help you see the principle. To define *hybrid car*, you might first place it in a general class—*passenger vehicles*. Then the formal definition would distinguish hybrid cars from other passenger vehicles: *they can move using two or more sources of power, either separately or in combination*. So the full definition might look like this: *a hybrid car is a passenger vehicle* (genus) *that can operate using two or more sources of power, separately or in combination* (species).

Many arguments involve deciding whether an object meets the criteria set by a formal definition. For instance, suppose that you are considering whether a Toyota Prius and a Honda Insight are comparable hybrid vehicles. Both are clearly passenger cars, so the genus raises no questions. But not all vehicles that claim to be hybrids are powered by two sources: some of them are just electrically *assisted* versions of a regular gasoline car. That's the species question. Looking closely, you discover that a Prius can run on either gas or electric power alone. But does the Insight have that flexibility? Not quite. It has an electric motor that assists its small gas engine, but the vehicle never runs on electricity alone. So technically the Insight is labeled a *mild hybrid* whereas the Prius is called a *full hybrid*. This definitional distinction obviously has consequences for consumers concerned about CO_2 emissions.

FIGURE 17.3 2014 Honda Insight: fully hybrid or something else?
PHOTOEDIT/PhotoEdit, Inc.

Operational Definitions

Operational definitions identify an object or idea by what it does or by what conditions create it. For example, someone's offensive sexual imposition on another person may not meet the technical definition of *harassment* unless it is considered *unwanted, unsolicited,* and *repeated.* These three conditions then define what makes an act that might be acceptable in some situations turn into harassment. But they might also then become part of a highly contentious debate: were the conditions actually present in a given case? For example, could an offensive act really be harassment if the accused believed sexual interest was mutual and therefore solicited?

As you might imagine, arguments arise from operational definitions whenever people disagree about what the conditions define or whether these conditions have been fulfilled. Here are some examples of those types of questions:

Questions Related to Conditions

- Can institutional racism occur in the absence of specific and individual acts of racism?
- Can someone who is paid for their community service still be called a volunteer?
- Can an offensive act be termed harassment if the accused believed sexual interest was mutual and therefore solicited?

Questions Related to Fulfillment of Conditions

- Has an institution supported traditions or policies that have led to widespread racial inequities?
- Was the compensation given to a volunteer really "pay" or simply "reimbursement" for expenses?
- Should a person be punished for harassment if he or she believed the offensive action to be solicited?

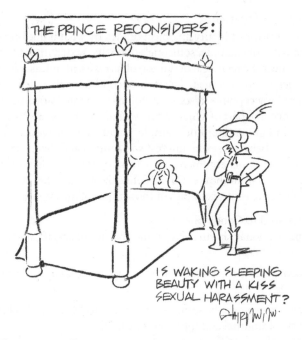

FIGURE 17.4 Prince Charming considers whether an action would fulfill the conditions for an operational definition. Cartoonstock Ltd./www.CartoonStock.com

RESPOND

This chapter opens with several rhetorical situations that center on definitional issues. Select one of these situations, and then, using the strategy of formal definition, set down some criteria of definition. For example, identify the features of a photograph that make it part of a larger class (*art, communication method, journalistic technique*). Next, identify the features that make it distinct from other members of that larger class. Then use the strategy of operational definition to establish criteria for the same object: what does it do? Remember to ask questions related to conditions (*Is a computer-scanned photograph still a photograph?*) and questions related to fulfillment of conditions (*Does a good photocopy of a photograph achieve the same effect as the photograph itself?*).

Definitions by Example

Resembling operational definitions are **definitions by example**, which define a class by listing its individual members. Such definitions can be helpful when it is easier to illustrate or show what related people or things have in common than to explain each one in precise detail. For example, one might define the broad category of *tablets* by listing the major examples of these products or define *heirloom tomatoes* by recalling all those available at the local farmers' market.

Arguments of this sort may focus on who or what may be included in a list that defines a category — *classic movies, worst natural disasters, groundbreaking painters*. Such arguments often involve comparisons and contrasts with the items that most readers would agree belong in this list. One could ask why Washington, D.C., is denied the status of a state: how does it differ from the fifty recognized American states? Or one might wonder why the status of planet is denied to asteroids, when both planets and asteroids are bodies that orbit the sun. A comparison between planets and asteroids might suggest that size is one essential feature of the eight recognized planets that asteroids don't meet. (In 2006, in a famous exercise in definitional argument, astronomers decided to deny poor Pluto its planetary classification.)

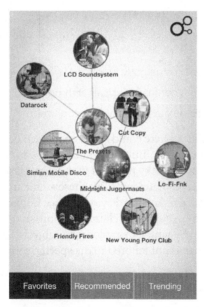

FIGURE 17.5 An app like Discovr Music defines musical styles by example when it connects specific artists or groups to others who make similar sounds. Discovr Music 2012

Developing a Definitional Argument

Definitional arguments don't just appear out of the blue; they often evolve out of daily life. You might get into an argument over the definition of *ordinary wear and tear* when you return a rental car with some soiled upholstery. Or you might be asked to write a job description for a new position to be created in your office: you have to define the job position in a way that doesn't step on anyone else's turf. Or maybe employees on your campus object to being defined as *temporary workers* when they've held their same jobs for years. Or someone derides one of your best friends as *just a nerd*. In a dozen ways every day, you encounter situations that are questions of definition. They're so frequent and indispensable that you barely notice them for what they are.

Formulating Claims

In addressing a question of definition, you'll likely formulate a *tentative claim*—a declarative statement that represents your first response to such situations. Note that such initial claims usually don't follow a single definitional formula.

Claims of Definition

A person paid to do public service is not a *volunteer*.

Institutional racism can exist—maybe even thrive—in the absence of overt civil rights violations.

Political bias has been consistently practiced by the mainstream media.

Theatergoers shouldn't confuse *musicals* with *operas*.

White lies are hard to define but easy to recognize.

None of the statements listed here could stand on its own because it likely reflects a first impression and gut reaction. But that's fine because making a claim of definition is typically a starting point, a cocky moment that doesn't last much beyond the first serious rebuttal or challenge. Statements like these aren't arguments until they're attached to reasons, data, warrants, and evidence (see Chapter 15).

Finding good reasons to support a claim of definition usually requires formulating a general definition by which to explore the subject. To be persuasive, the definition must be broad and not tailored to the specific controversy:

A volunteer is …

Institutional racism is …

Political bias is …

A musical is … but an opera is …

A white lie is …

Now consider how the following claims might be expanded with a general definition to become full-fledged definitional arguments:

Arguments of Definition

Someone paid to do public service is not a volunteer because volunteers are people who …

Institutional racism can exist even in the absence of overt violations of civil rights because, by definition, institutional racism is …

Political bias in the media is evident when …

Musicals focus on words first while operas …

The most important element of a white lie is its destructive nature; the act of telling one hurts both the receiver and the sender.

Notice, too, that some of the issues can involve comparisons between things — such as operas and musicals.

Crafting Definitions

Imagine that you decide to tackle the concept of *paid volunteer* in the following way:

Participants in the federal AmeriCorps program are not really volunteers because they receive "education awards" for their public service. Volunteers are people who work for a cause without receiving compensation.

In Toulmin terms, as explained in Chapter 15, the argument looks like this:

Claim	Participants in AmeriCorps aren't volunteers …
Reason	… because they are paid for their service.
Warrant	People who are compensated for their services are, ordinarily, employees.

As you can see, the definition of *volunteers* will be crucial to the shape of the argument. In fact, you might think you've settled the matter with this tight little formulation. But now it's time to listen to the readers over your shoulder (again, see Chapter 15), who are pushing you further. Do the terms of your definition account for all pertinent cases of volunteerism — in particular, any related to the types of public service AmeriCorps members might be involved in? What do you do with unpaid interns: how do they affect your definition of *volunteers*? Consider, too, the word *cause* in your original claim of the definition:

Volunteers are people who work for a cause without receiving compensation.

Cause has political connotations that you may or may not intend. You'd better clarify what you mean by *cause* when you discuss its definition in your paper. Might a phrase such as *the public good* be a more comprehensive or appropriate substitute for *a cause*? And then there's the matter of *compensation* in the second half of your definition:

> Volunteers are people who work for a cause without receiving compensation.

Aren't people who volunteer to serve on boards, committees, and commissions sometimes paid, especially for their expenses? What about members of the so-called all-volunteer military? They're financially compensated during their years of service, and they enjoy benefits after they complete their tours of duty.

As you can see, you can't just offer up a definition as part of an argument and expect that readers will accept it. Every part of a definition has to be interrogated, critiqued, and defended. So investigate your subject in the library, on the Internet, and in conversation with others, including experts if you can. You might then be able to present your definition in a single paragraph, or you may have to spend several pages coming to terms with the complexity of the core issue.

After conducting research of this kind, you'll be in a better position to write an extended definition that explains to your readers what you believe makes a volunteer a volunteer, how to identify institutional racism, or how to distinguish between a musical and an opera.

Matching Claims to Definitions

Once you've formulated a definition that readers will accept—a demanding task in itself—you might need to look at your particular subject to see if it fits your general definition. It should provide evidence of one of the following:

- It is a clear example of the class defined.

- It clearly falls outside the defined class.

- It falls between two closely related classes or fulfills some conditions of the defined class but not others.

- It defies existing classes and categories and requires an entirely new definition.

How do you make this key move in an argument? Here's an example from an article by Anthony Tommasini entitled "Opera? Musical? Please Respect the Difference." Early in the piece, Tommasini argues that a key element separates the two musical forms:

> Both genres seek to combine words and music in dynamic, felicitous and, to invoke that all-purpose term, artistic ways. But in opera, music is the driving force; in musical theater, words come first.

His claim of definition (or of difference) makes sense because it clarifies aspects of the two genres.

> This explains why for centuries opera-goers have revered works written in languages they do not speak.... As long as you basically know what is going on and what is more or less being said, you can be swept away by a great opera, not just by music, but by visceral drama.

> In contrast, imagine if the exhilarating production of Cole Porter's *Anything Goes* now on Broadway ... were to play in Japan without any kind of titling technology. The wit of the musical is embedded in its lyrics.... .

But even after having found a distinction so perceptive, Tommasini (like most writers making arguments of definition) still has to acknowledge exceptions.

> Theatergoing audiences may not care much whether a show is a musical or an opera. But the best achievements in each genre ... have been from composers and writers who grounded themselves in a tradition, *even while reaching across the divide*. [emphasis added]

If evidence you've gathered while developing an argument of definition suggests that similar limitations may be necessary, don't hesitate to modify your claim. It's amazing how often seemingly cut-and-dried matters of definition become blurry—and open to compromise and accommodation—as you learn more about them. That has proved to be the case as various campuses across the country have tried to define *hate speech* or *internship*—tricky matters. And even the Supreme Court has never said exactly what *pornography* is. Just when matters seem to be settled, new legal twists develop. Should virtual child pornography created with software be illegal, as is the real thing? Or is a virtual image—even a lewd one—an artistic expression that is protected (as other works of art are) by the First Amendment?

Considering Design and Visuals

In thinking about how to present your argument of definition, you may find a simple visual helpful, such as the Venn diagram on p. 336 from Wikimedia Commons that defines *sustainability* as the place where our society and its economy intersect with the environment. Such a visual might even suggest a structure for an oral presentation.

Remember too that visuals like photographs, charts, and graphs can also help you make your case. Such items might demonstrate that the conditions for a definition have been met—as the widely circulated and horrific photographs from Abu Ghraib prison in Iraq helped to define *torture*. Or you might create a graphic yourself to illustrate a concept you are defining, perhaps through comparison and contrast.

Finally, don't forget that basic design elements—such as boldface and italics, headings, or links in online text—can contribute to (or detract from) the credibility and persuasiveness of your argument of definition. (See Chapter 22 for more on "Visual Rhetoric.")

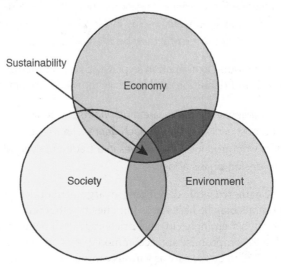

GUIDE TO WRITING AN ARGUMENT OF DEFINITION

Finding a Topic

You're entering an argument of definition when you:

- formulate a controversial or provocative definition: *The American Dream, which once meant a McMansion in a gated community, now has taken on a new definition.*

- challenge a definition: *For most Americans today, the American Dream involves not luxury but the secure pensions, cheap energy costs, and health insurance that workers in the 1950s and 1960s supposedly enjoyed.*

- try to determine whether something fits an existing definition: *Expanding opportunity is (or is not) central to the American Dream.*

- seek to broaden an existing definition or create a new definition to accommodate wider or differing perspectives: *In a world where information is easily and freely shared, it may be time to explore alternative understandings of the American Dream.*

Look for issues of definition in your everyday affairs—for instance, in the way that jobs are classified at work, that key terms are used in your academic major, that politicians characterize social issues that concern you, and so on. Be especially alert to definitional arguments that may arise when you or others deploy adjectives such as *true, real, actual,* or *genuine: a true patriot, real reform, authentic Mexican food.*

Researching Your Topic

You can research issues of definition by using the following sources:

- college dictionaries and encyclopedias

- unabridged dictionaries

- specialized reference works and handbooks, such as legal and medical dictionaries

- your textbooks (check their glossaries)

- newsgroups and blogs that focus on particular topics, especially political ones

- community or advocacy groups that are engaged in legal or social issues

- social media postings by experts you respect

Browse in your library reference room and use the electronic indexes and databases to determine how often disputed or contentious terms or phrases occur in influential online newspapers, journals, and Web sites.

When dealing with definitions, ask librarians about the most appropriate and reliable sources. For instance, to find the definition of a legal term, *Black's Law Dictionary* or a database such as FindLaw may help. Check USA.gov for how the government defines terms.

Formulating a Claim

After exploring your subject, try to formulate a thesis that lets readers know where you stand or what issues are at stake. Begin with the following types of questions:

- questions related to genus: *Is assisting in suicide a crime?*

- questions related to species: *Is marijuana a harmful addictive drug or a useful medical treatment?*

- questions related to conditions: *Must the imposition of sexual attention be both unwanted and unsolicited to be considered sexual harassment?*

- questions related to fulfillment of conditions: *Has our college kept in place traditions or policies that might constitute racial discrimination?*

- questions related to membership in a named class: *Can a story put together out of thirty-one retweets be called a novel, or even a short story?*

If you start with a thesis, it should be a complete statement that makes a claim of definition and states the reasons supporting it. You may later decide to separate the claim from its supporting reasons. But a working thesis should be a fully articulated thought that spells out all the details and qualifications: *Who? What? Where? When? How many? How regularly? How completely?*

However, since arguments of definition are often exploratory and tentative, an initial thesis (if you have one) may simply describe problems in formulating a particular definition: *What we mean by X is likely to remain unsettled until we can agree more fully about Y and Z; The key to understanding what constitutes X may lie in appreciating how different groups approach Y and Z.*

Examples of Definitional Claims

- Assisting a gravely ill person in committing suicide should not be considered *murder* when the motive for the act is to ease a person's suffering and not to benefit from the death.

- Although somewhat addictive, marijuana should not be classified as a *dangerous drug* because it damages individuals and society less than heroin or cocaine and because it helps people with life-threatening diseases live more comfortably.

- Giving college admission preference to all racial minorities can be an example of *class discrimination* because such policies may favor middle- and upper-class students who are already advantaged.

- Attempts to define the concept of *freedom* need to take into account the way the term is historically understood in cultures worldwide, not just in the countries of Western Europe and North America.

Preparing a Proposal

If your instructor asks you to prepare a proposal for your project, here's a format that may help:

State your thesis or hypothesis completely. If you're having trouble doing so, try outlining it in Toulmin terms:

Claim:

Reason(s):

Warrant(s):

Alternatively, you might describe the complications of a definitional issue you hope to explore in your project, with the thesis perhaps coming later.

- Explain why this argument of definition deserves attention. What's at stake? Why is it important for your readers to consider?

- Identify whom you hope to reach through your argument and why these readers would be interested in it. How might you involve them in the paper?

- Briefly discuss the key challenges that you anticipate in preparing your argument.

- Determine what sources you expect to consult: Web? Databases? Dictionaries? Encyclopedias? Periodicals?

- Determine what visuals to include in your definitional argument.

Considering Format and Media

Your instructor may specify that you use a particular format and/or medium. If not, ask yourself these questions to help you make a good choice:

- What format is most appropriate for your argument of definition? Does it call for an academic essay, a report, an infographic, a brochure, or something else?

- What medium is most appropriate for your argument? Would it be best delivered orally to a live audience? Presented as an audio essay or podcast? Presented in print only or in print with illustrations?

- Will you need visuals, such as moving or still images, maps, graphs, charts—and what function will they play in your argument? Make sure they are not just "added on" but are necessary components of the argument.

Thinking about Organization

Your argument of definition is likely to include some of the following parts:

- a claim involving a question of definition
- a general definition of some key concept
- a careful look at your subject in terms of that general definition
- evidence for every part of the argument, including visual evidence if appropriate
- a careful consideration of alternative views and counterarguments
- a conclusion drawing out the implications of the argument

It's impossible, however, to predict what emphasis each of those parts might receive or what the ultimate shape of an argument of definition will be. Try to account for the ways people with different points of view will likely respond to your argument. Then, consider how to address such differences civilly in the body of your argument.

Getting and Giving Response: Questions for Peer Response

Your instructor may assign you to a group for the purpose of reading and responding to each other's drafts. If not, ask for responses from serious readers or consultants at a writing center. Use the following questions to evaluate a colleague's draft. Be sure to illustrate your comments with examples; specific comments help more than general observations.

The Claim

- Is the claim clearly an issue of definition?
- Is the claim significant enough to interest readers?
- Are clear and specific criteria established for the concept being defined? Do the criteria define the term adequately? Using this definition, could most readers identify what's being defined and distinguish it from other related concepts?

Evidence for the Claim

- Is enough evidence furnished to explain or support the definition? If not, what kind of additional evidence is needed?
- Is the evidence in support of the claim simply announced, or are its significance and appropriateness analyzed? Is a more detailed discussion needed?
- Are all the conditions of the definition met in the concept being examined?

- Are any objections readers might have to the claim, criteria, evidence, or way the definition is formulated adequately addressed? Have you represented other points of view completely and fairly?

- What kinds of sources are cited? How credible and persuasive will they be to readers? What other kinds of sources might work better?

- Are all quotations introduced with appropriate signal phrases (such as "As Tyson argues, …") and blended smoothly into the writer's sentences?

- Are all visual sources labeled, introduced, and commented upon?

Organization and Style

- How are the parts of the argument organized? Is this organization effective?

- Will readers understand the relationships among the claims, supporting reasons, warrants, and evidence? If not, how might those connections be clearer? Is the function of every visual clear? Are more transitions needed? Would headings or graphic devices help?

- Are the transitions or links from point to point, sentence to sentence, and paragraph to paragraph clear and effective? If not, how could they be improved?

- Are all visuals (or other elements such as audio or video clips) carefully integrated into the text? Is each visual introduced and commented on to point out its significance? Is each visual labeled as a figure or a table and given a caption as well as a citation?

- Is the style suited to the subject? Is it too formal, casual, or technical? Can it be improved?

- Which sentences seem effective? Which ones seem weaker, and how could they be improved? Should short sentences be combined, and any longer ones be broken up?

- How effective are the paragraphs? Too short or too long? How can they be improved?

- Which words or phrases seem effective? Do any seem vague or inappropriate for the audience or the writer's purpose? Are technical or unfamiliar terms defined?

Spelling, Punctuation, Mechanics, Documentation, and Format

- Are there any errors in spelling, punctuation, capitalization, and the like?

- Is the documentation appropriate and consistent? (See Chapter 30.)

- Does the paper or project follow an appropriate format? Is it appropriately designed and attractively presented?

PROJECTS

1. Write an argument of definition about a term such as *military combatants* or *illegal alien* that has suddenly become culturally significant or recently changed in some important way. Either defend the way the term has come to be defined or raise questions about its appropriateness, offensiveness, inaccuracy, and so on. Consider words or expressions such as *terrorism, marriage equality, racist, assisted suicide, enhanced interrogation, tea partier, collateral damage, forcible rape, net neutrality*, etc.

2. Write an essay in which you compare or contrast the meaning of two related terms, explaining the differences between them by using one or more methods of definition: formal definition, operational definition, definition by example. Be clever in your choice of the initial terms: look for a pairing in which the differences might not be immediately apparent to people unfamiliar with how the terms are used in specific communities. Consider terms such as *liberal/progressive, classy/cool, lead soprano/prima donna, student athlete/jock, highbrow /intellectual*, and so on.

3. In an essay at the end of this chapter, Natasha Rodriguez explores the adjective *underprivileged*, trying to understand why this label bothers her so much. She concludes that needing financial aid should not be conflated with being disadvantaged. After reading this selection carefully, respond to Rodriguez's argument in an argument of definition of your own. Or, alternatively, explore a concept similar to "underprivileged" with the same intensity that Rodriguez brings to her project. Look for a term to define and analyze either from your major or from an area of interest to you.

4. Because arguments of definition can have such important consequences, it helps to develop one by first getting input from lots of "stakeholders," that is, from people or groups likely to be affected by any change in the way a term is defined. Working with a small group, identify a term in your school or wider community that might need a fresh formulation or a close review. It could be a familiar campus word or phrase such as *nontraditional student, diversity, scholastic dishonesty*, or *social justice*; or it may be a term that has newly entered the local environment, perhaps reflecting an issue of law enforcement, safety, transportation, health, or even entertainment. Once you have settled on a significant term, identify a full range of stakeholders. Then, through some systematic field research (interviews, questionnaires) or by examining existing documents and materials (such as library sources, Web sites, pamphlets, publications), try to understand how the term currently functions in your community. Your definitional argument will, in effect, be what you can learn about the meanings that word or phrase has today for a wide variety of people.

Two Sample Definitional Arguments

Who Are You Calling Underprivileged?

NATASHA RODRIGUEZ

Courtesy of
Natasha
Rodriguez

I have come to loathe the word "underprivileged." When I filled out my college applications, I checked off the Latino/Hispanic box whenever I was asked to give my ethnicity. My parents in turn indicated their income, hoping that we would qualify for financial aid. But while I waited for acceptances and rejections, several colleges I was considering sent me material that made me feel worthless rather than excited about attending those institutions.

The first mailing I received was a brochure that featured a photograph of African-American, Asian, and Latino teens standing around in a cluster, their faces full of laughter and joy. The title of the brochure was "Help for Underprivileged Students." At first I was confused: "Underprivileged" was not a word that I associated with myself. But there was the handout, with my name printed boldly on the surface.

The author questions the connotations of underprivileged.

The text went on to inform me that, since I was a student who had experienced an underprivileged life, I could qualify for several kinds of financial aid and scholarships. While I appreciated the intent, I was turned off by that one word—"underprivileged."

I had never been called that before. The word made me question how I saw myself in the world. Yes, I needed financial aid, and I had received generous scholarships to help me attend a private high school on the Upper East Side of New York. Surely that didn't mean that I had lived a less-privileged life than others. My upbringing had been very happy.

What does "underprivileged" actually mean? According to most dictionaries, the word refers to a person who does not enjoy the same standard of living or rights as a majority of people in a society. I don't fit that definition. Even though my family does not have a lot of money, we have always had enough to get by, and I have received an excellent education.

The author then gives a standard definition for underprivileged *and explains why she refuses the label.*

What angered me most about the label was why colleges would ever use such a term. Who wants to be called underprivileged? I'm sure that even those who have had no opportunities would not want

---

Natasha Rodriguez is a student at Sarah Lawrence College, where she edits the features section of her school newspaper, the *Phoenix.*

their social status rubbed in their faces so blatantly. People should be referred to as underprivileged only if they're the ones who are calling themselves that.

Misfortune, like beauty, is in the eye of the beholder. It's not appropriate to slap labels on people that they might not like or even agree with. Social research has found that those who are negatively labeled usually have lower self-esteem than others who are not labeled in that way. So why does the label of "underprivileged" persist?

The author examines the assumptions colleges make based on ethnicity and income.

Most colleges brag about the diversity of their students. But I don't want to be bragged about if my ethnicity is automatically associated with "underprivileged." Several colleges that had not even received information on my parents' finances just assumed that I was underprivileged because I had checked "Latino/Hispanic" on their applications.

That kind of labeling has to stop. Brochures and handouts could be titled "Help for Students in Need" rather than "Help for Underprivileged Students." I am sure that many people, myself included, are more than willing to admit that they require financial aid, and would feel fine about a college that referred to them as a student in need.

The essay concludes with the author's own self-definition.

That's a definition I can agree with. I am a student in need; I'm just not an underprivileged one.

Friending: The Changing Definition of Friendship in the Social Media Era

JOYCE XINRAN LIU

March 6, 2014

In just two months, I boosted my LinkedIn connections from 300 to almost 500. I was proud of winning the numbers game. However, recently when I was trying to request an informational interview via LinkedIn, I was depressed that less than 5% actually responded to me. I think I know most of them, but I actually don't. Or they don't think so. Maybe this is social media's fault. It creates the illusion of intimacy and closeness that doesn't actually exist. Maybe I should blame myself. I rushed to think of my social media connections as true friends that I could rely on.

I forgot the rules of friendship. Social media is a new platform for communication that expands and accelerates the way we connect and engage people, but the old rules of thumb for building relationships are still there. To understand what makes a friend a "friend" in social media, we'd better step back and think about the chemistry needed in true friendship (sans social media).

To make a true friend, we first need to get to know the person well, such that we understand what she likes and dislikes, what experiences have made her who she is today, and what her values are in life. Yet knowing someone does not guarantee a lasting friendship. For example, some people know their boss pretty well, yet they may not define their boss as a friend. In addition to knowing each other well, building friendships takes time; it's necessary for both sides to have some investment in the relationship.

Now let's get back to the world of social media and reconsider the process of making friends. Facebook, Twitter, LinkedIn, and many other social media platforms have provided tons of personal information — both ongoing and historical — about people we want to know. For example, we can gain insights into someone's social life and interests through Facebook, get up-to-the-minute status updates from Twitter, and read someone's full professional experience on LinkedIn. A five-minute search on a social media platform can make us feel that we are old friends of the person we want to make friends with. But this is only one side of the story since the person we are searching into may not feel the same way as we

---

Joyce Xinran Liu is a graduate in Integrated Marketing Communications at Northwestern University's Medill School. She posted this piece on a blog called *Vitamin IMC*, a site developed by the graduate students in the program to "educate marketers, potential students and companies about integrated marketing communications—what it is, how it's applied and how it builds profit within organizations."

do. This is often the case. A one-way connection without reciprocal engagement can never be thought of as a friendship, even on social media.

When acquaintances share their joys, complaints or even private information on social media, does it mean that they deem all of these online connections as real friends? Probably not. But why share their private information then? My argument is that they sacrifice their privacy in exchange for intimacy. Some people may want to make more friends, attract more attention, or even enhance self-esteem with the inflated intimacy they receive from friends, acquaintances and mere strangers on social media. These shared social media updates make people feel close, but it doesn't always mean they are close.

It's not social media's fault that it helps us develop a wide net of connections, yet still leaves us wanting more. We've created the myth of building strong relationships via social media. It's possible to build friendship online, but more often we need to integrate online engagement with offline interaction. Overall, social media has changed ways people interact with each other, but it has not affected the rooted norms and socialization process of making friends either online or offline. And it's time to adjust our expectations for building relationships in this new media space.

Evaluations

"We don't want to go there for coffee. Their beans aren't fair trade, the drinks are high in calories, and the stuff is *way* overpriced."

The campus storytelling project has just won a competition sponsored by NPR, and everyone involved is thrilled. Then they realize that this year all but one of the leaders of this project will graduate and that they have very few new recruits. So they put their heads together to figure out what qualities they need in new recruits that will help maintain the excellence of their project.

Orson Welles's masterpiece *Citizen Kane* is playing at the Student Union for only one more night, but the new *Captain America* is featured across the street in 3-D. Guess which movie your roomie wants to see? You intend to set her straight.

Left to right: Mario Tama/Getty Images; Jonah Willihnganz, The Stanford Storytelling Project; Hulton Archive/Getty Images

Understanding Evaluations

Evaluations are everyday arguments. By the time you leave home in the morning, you've likely made a dozen informal evaluations: You've selected dressy clothes because you have a job interview with a law firm. You've chosen low-fat yogurt and fruit over the pancakes you really love. You've queued up the perfect playlist on your iPhone for your hike to campus. In each case, you've applied criteria to a particular problem and then made a decision. That's evaluating on the fly.

Some professional evaluations require more elaborate standards, evidence, and paperwork (imagine an aircraft manufacturer certifying a new jet for passenger service), but they don't differ structurally from the simpler choices that people make all the time. People love to voice their opinions, and they always have. In fact, a mode of ancient rhetoric—called the *ceremonial* or *epideictic* (see Chapter 9)—was devoted entirely to speeches of praise and blame.

Today, rituals of praise and blame are a significant part of American life. Adults who would choke at the notion of debating causal or definitional claims will happily spend hours appraising the Oakland Raiders, Boston Red Sox, or Tampa Bay Rays. Other evaluative spectacles in our culture include awards shows, beauty pageants, most-valuable-player presentations, lists of best-dressed or worst-dressed celebrities, "sexiest people" magazine covers, literary prizes, political opinion polls, consumer product magazines, and—the ultimate formal public gesture of evaluation—elections. Indeed, making evaluations is a form of entertainment in America and generates big audiences (think of *The Voice*) and revenues.

FIGURE 18.1 Arguments about sports are usually evaluations of some kind. Cal Sport Media via AP Images

RESPOND

The last ten years have seen a proliferation of "reality" talent shows —*Dancing with the Stars, So You Think You Can Dance, American* (or *Canadian* or *Australian* or many other) *Idol, America's Got Talent, The Voice,* and so on. Write a short opinion piece assessing the merits of a particular "talent" show. What should a proper event of this kind accomplish? Does the event you're reviewing do so?

Criteria of Evaluation

Arguments of evaluation can produce simple rankings and winners or can lead to profound decisions about our lives, but they always involve standards. The particular standards we establish for judging anything — whether an idea, a work of art, a person, or a product — are called **criteria of evaluation**. Sometimes criteria are self-evident: a car that gets fifteen miles per gallon is a gas hog, and a piece of fish that smells even a little off shouldn't be eaten. But criteria get complicated when a subject is abstract: *What features make a song a classic? What constitutes a fair wage? How do we measure a successful foreign policy or college career?* Struggling to identify such difficult criteria of evaluation can lead to important insights into your values, motives, and preferences.

Why make such a big deal about criteria when many acts of evaluation seem effortless? We should be suspicious of our judgments especially when we make them casually. It's irresponsible simply to think that spontaneous and uninformed quips should carry the same weight as well-informed and well-reasoned opinions. Serious evaluations always require reflection, and when we look deeply into our judgments, we sometimes discover important questions that typically go unasked, many prefaced by *why*:

- You challenge the grade you received in a course, but you don't question the practice of grading.

- You argue passionately that a Republican Congress is better for America than a Democratic alternative, but you fail to ask why voters get only two choices.

- You argue that buying a hybrid car makes more sense than keeping an SUV, but you don't ask whether taking alternative forms of transportation (like the bus or a bike) makes the most sense of all.

Push an argument of evaluation hard enough and even simple judgments become challenging and intriguing.

In fact, for many writers, grappling with criteria is the toughest step in producing an evaluation. When you offer an opinion about a topic you know reasonably well, you want readers to learn something from your judgment. So you need time to think about and then justify the criteria for your opinion, whatever the subject.

Do you think, for instance, that you could explain what (if anything) makes a veggie burger good? Though many people have eaten veggie burgers, they probably haven't spent much time thinking about them. But it wouldn't be enough to claim merely that a proper one should be juicy or tasty—such trite claims are not even interesting. The following criteria offered on the *Cook's Illustrated* Web site show what happens when experts give the issue a closer look:

> We wanted to create veggie burgers that even meat eaters would love. We didn't want them to taste like hamburgers, but we did want them to act like hamburgers, *having a modicum of chew, a harmonious blend of savory ingredients, and the ability to go from grill to bun without falling apart.* [emphasis added]
>
> —*Cook's Illustrated*

After a lot of experimenting, *Cook's Illustrated* came up with a recipe that met these criteria.

Criteria of evaluation aren't static, either. They differ according to time and audience. Much market research, for example, is designed to find out what particular consumers want now and may want in the future—what their criteria are for buying a product. In good times, people may demand homes with soaring entryways, lots of space, and premium appliances. In tougher times, they may care more about efficient use of space, quality insulation, and energy-efficient stoves and dishwashers. Shifts in values, attitudes, and criteria happen all the time.

FIGURE 18.2 What criteria of evaluation are embedded in this visual argument? © Ildi Papp/age fotostock

RESPOND

Choose one item from the following list that you understand well enough to evaluate. Develop several criteria of evaluation that you could defend to distinguish excellence from mediocrity in the area. Then choose an item that you don't know much about and explain the research you might do to discover reasonable criteria of evaluation for it.

smartwatches	U.S. vice presidents
NFL quarterbacks	organic vegetables
social networking sites	all-electric cars
TV journalists	spoken word poetry
video games	athletic shoes
graphic narratives	country music bands
Navajo rugs	sci-fi films

Characterizing Evaluation

One way of understanding evaluative arguments is to consider the types of evidence they use. A distinction explored in Chapter 12 between hard evidence and constructed arguments based on reason is helpful here: we defined **hard evidence** as facts, statistics, testimony, and other kinds of arguments that can be measured, recorded, or even found—the so-called smoking gun in a criminal investigation. We defined constructed arguments based on reason as those that are shaped by language and various kinds of logic.

We can talk about arguments of evaluation the same way, looking at some as quantitative and others as qualitative. **Quantitative arguments** of evaluation rely on criteria that can be measured, counted, or demonstrated in some mechanical fashion (something is taller, faster, smoother, quieter, or more powerful than something else). In contrast, **qualitative arguments** rely on criteria that must be explained through language and media, relying on such matters as values, traditions, and emotions (something is more ethical, more beneficial, more handsome, or more noble than something else). A claim of evaluation might be supported by arguments of both sorts.

Quantitative Evaluations

At first glance, quantitative evaluations seem to hold all the cards, especially in a society as enamored of science and technology as our own is. Making judgments should be easy if all it involves is measuring and counting—and in some cases, that's the way things work out. *Who's the tallest or heaviest or loudest person in your class?* If your classmates allow themselves to be measured, you could find out easily enough, using the right equipment and internationally sanctioned standards of measurement—the meter, the kilo, or the decibel.

But what if you were to ask, *Who's the smartest person in class?* You could answer this more complex question quantitatively, using IQ tests or college entrance examinations that report results numerically. In fact, almost all college-bound students in the United States submit to this kind of evaluation, taking either the SAT or the ACT to demonstrate their verbal and mathematical prowess. Such measures are widely accepted by educators and institutions, but they are also vigorously challenged. What do they actually measure? They predict likely academic success only in college, which is one kind of intelligence.

Quantitative measures of evaluation can be enormously useful, but even the most objective measures have limits. They've been devised by fallible people who look at the world from their own inevitably limited perspectives.

Qualitative Evaluations

Many issues of evaluation that are closest to people's hearts aren't subject to quantification. *What makes a movie great?* If you suggested a quantitative measure like length, your friends would probably hoot, "Get serious!" But what about box-office receipts, adjusted for inflation? Would films that made the most money—an easily quantifiable measure—be the "best pictures"? That select group would include movies such as *Star Wars, The Sound of Music, Gone with the Wind, Titanic, Avatar, and E.T.* An interesting group of films—but the best?

To define the criteria for "great movie," you'd more likely look for the standards and evidence that serious critics explore in their arguments, abstract or complicated issues such as their societal impact, cinematic technique, dramatic structures, intelligent casting, and so on. Most of these markers of quality could be defined and identified with some precision but not measured or counted. You'd also have to make your case rhetorically, convincing the audience to accept the markers of quality you are offering and yet appreciating that they might not. A movie reviewer making qualitative judgments might spend as much time defending criteria of evaluation as providing evidence that these standards are present in a particular film. But putting those standards into action can be what makes a review something worth reading. Consider how Roger Ebert, in writing about *Toy Story*, the first all-computer-made feature film, teaches his readers how to find evidence of quality in a great movie:

> *Toy Story* creates a universe out of a couple of kids' bedrooms, a gas station, and a stretch of suburban highway. Its heroes are toys, which come to life when nobody is watching. Its conflict is between an old-fashioned cowboy who has always been a little boy's favorite toy, and the new space ranger who may replace him. The villain is the mean kid next door who takes toys apart

and puts them back together again in macabre combinations. And the result is a visionary roller-coaster ride of a movie.

For the kids in the audience, a movie like this will work because it tells a fun story, contains a lot of humor, and is exciting to watch. Older viewers may be even more absorbed, because *Toy Story*, the first feature made entirely by computer, achieves a three-dimensional reality and freedom of movement that is liberating and new. The more you know about how the movie was made, the more you respect it.

FIGURE 18.3 Web sites such as Netflix and Rotten Tomatoes offer recommendations for films based on users' past selections and the ratings of other users and critics. Sometimes those judgments are at odds. Then whom do you trust? © Denis ALLARD/ REA/Redux

RESPOND

For examples of powerful evaluation arguments, search the Web or your library for eulogies or obituaries of famous, recently deceased individuals. Try to locate at least one such item, and then analyze the types of claims it makes about the accomplishments of the deceased. What types of criteria of evaluation hold the obituary or eulogy together? Why should we respect or admire the person?

Developing an Evaluative Argument

Developing an argument of evaluation can seem like a simple process, especially if you already know what your claim is likely to be. To continue the movie theme for one more example:

> *Citizen Kane* is the finest film ever made by an American director.

Having established a claim, you would then explore the implications of your belief, drawing out the reasons, warrants, and evidence that might support it:

Claim	*Citizen Kane* is the finest film ever made by an American director ...
Reason	... because it revolutionizes the way we see the world.
Warrant	Great films change viewers in fundamental ways.
Evidence	Shot after shot, *Citizen Kane* presents the life of its protagonist through cinematic images that viewers can never forget.

The warrant here is, in effect, an implied statement of criteria—in this case, the quality that defines "great film" for the writer. It may be important for the writer to share that assumption with readers and perhaps to identify other great films that similarly make viewers appreciate new perspectives.

As you can see, in developing an evaluative argument, you'll want to pay special attention to criteria, claims, and evidence.

Formulating Criteria

Although even casual evaluations (*The band sucks!*) might be traced to reasonable criteria, most people don't defend their positions until they are challenged (*Oh yeah?*). Similarly, writers who address readers with whom they share core values rarely discuss their criteria in great detail. A film critic like the late Roger Ebert (see p. 352) isn't expected to restate all his principles every time he writes a movie review. Ebert assumes that his readers will—over time—come to appreciate his standards. Still, criteria can make or break a piece.

So spend time developing your criteria of evaluation. What exactly makes a shortstop an all-star? Why is a standardized test an unreliable measure of intelligence? Fundamentally, what distinguishes an inspired rapper from a run-of-the-mill one? List the possibilities and then pare them down to the essentials. If you offer vague, dull, or unsupportable principles, expect to be challenged.

You're most likely to be vague about your beliefs when you haven't thought (or read) enough about your subject. Push yourself at least as far as you imagine readers will. Anticipate readers looking over your shoulder, asking difficult questions. Say, for example, that you intend to argue that anyone who wants to stay on the cutting edge of personal technology will obviously want Apple's latest iPad because it does so many amazing things. But what does that mean exactly? What makes the device "amazing"? Is it that it gives access to email and the Web, has a high-resolution screen, offers an astonishing number of apps, and makes a good e-reader? These are particular features of the device. But can you identify a more fundamental quality to explain the product's appeal, such as an iPad user's experience, enjoyment, or feeling of productivity? You'll often want to raise your evaluation to a higher level of generality like this so that your appraisal of a product, book, performance, or political figure works as a coherent argument, and not just as a list of random observations.

Be certain, too, that your criteria of evaluation apply to more than just your topic of the moment. Your standards should make sense on their own merits and apply across the board. If you tailor your criteria to get the outcome you want, you are doing what is called "special pleading." You might be pleased when you prove that the home team is awesome, but it won't take skeptics long to figure out how you've cooked the books.

RESPOND

Local news and entertainment magazines often publish "best of" issues or articles that catalog their readers' and editors' favorites in such categories as "best place to go on a first date," "best ice cream sundae," and "best dentist." Sometimes the categories are specific: "best places to say 'I was retro before retro was cool'" or "best movie theater seats." Imagine that you're the editor of your own local magazine and that you want to put out a "best of" issue tailored to your hometown. Develop ten categories for evaluation. For each category, list the evaluative criteria that you would use to make your judgment. Next, consider that because your criteria are warrants, they're especially tied to audience. (The criteria for "best dentist," for example, might be tailored to people whose major concern is avoiding pain, to those whose children will be regular patients, or to those who want the cheapest possible dental care.) For several of the evaluative categories, imagine that you have to justify your judgments to a completely different audience. Write a new set of criteria for that audience.

Making Claims

In evaluations, claims can be stated directly or, more rarely, strongly implied. For most writers, strong statements followed by reasonable qualifications work best. Consider the differences between the following three claims and how much greater the burden of proof is for the first claim:

> Jessica Williams is the funniest "correspondent" ever on *The Daily Show*.

> Jessica Williams has emerged as one of the funniest of *The Daily Show's* "correspondents."

> Jessica Williams may come to be regarded as one of the funniest and most successful of the "correspondents" on *The Daily Show*.

FIGURE 18.4 The funniest of all? Jessica Williams reporting on *The Daily Show*.

Here's a second set of examples demonstrating the same principle, that qualifications generally make a claim of evaluation easier to deal with and smarter:

> The Common Core Standards movement sure is a dumb idea.

> The Common Core Standards movement in educational reform is likely to do more harm than good.

> While laudable in their intentions to raise standards and improve student learning, the Common Core Standards adopted throughout the United States continue to put so high a premium on testing that they may well undermine the goals they seek to achieve.

The point of qualifying a statement isn't to make evaluative claims bland but to make them responsible and reasonable. Consider how Reagan Tankersley uses the criticisms of a musical genre he enjoys to frame a claim he makes in its defense:

> Structurally, dubstep is a simple musical form, with formulaic progressions and beats, something that gives a musically tuned ear little to grasp or analyze.

For this reason, a majority of traditionally trained musicians find the genre to be a waste of time. These people have a legitimate position.... However, I hold that it is the simplicity of dubstep that makes it special: the primal nature of the song is what digs so deeply into fans. It accesses the most primitive area in our brains that connects to the uniquely human love of music.

—Reagan Tankersley, "Dubstep: Why People Dance"

Tankersley doesn't pretend that dubstep is something it's not, nor does he expect his argument to win over traditionally minded critics. Yet he still makes a claim worth considering.

FIGURE 18.5 Dubstep DJs Benga, Artwork, and Skream of Magnetic Man perform. Chiaki Nozu/Wire Image/Getty Images

One tip: Nothing adds more depth to an opinion than letting others challenge it. When you can, use the resources of the Internet or local discussion boards to get responses to your opinions or topic proposals. It can be eye-opening to realize how strongly people react to ideas or points of view that you regard as perfectly normal. Share your claim and then, when you're ready, your first draft with friends and classmates, asking them to identify places where your ideas need additional support, either in the discussion of criteria or in the presentation of evidence.

Presenting Evidence

Generally, the more evidence in an evaluation the better, provided that the evidence is relevant. For example, in evaluating the performance of two laptops, the speed of their processors would be essential; the quality of their keyboards or the availability of service might be less crucial yet still worth mentioning. But you have to decide how much detail your readers want in your argument. For technical subjects, you might make your basic case briefly and then attach additional supporting documents at the end—tables, graphs, charts—for those who want more data.

Just as important as relevance in selecting evidence is presentation. Not all pieces of evidence are equally convincing, nor should they be treated as such. Select evidence that is most likely to influence your readers, and then arrange the argument to build toward your best material. In most cases, that best material will be evidence that's specific, detailed, memorable, and derived from credible sources. The details in these paragraphs from Sean Wilsey's review of *Fun Home: A Family Tragicomic*, a graphic novel by Alison Bechdel, tell you precisely what makes the work "lush," "absorbing," and well worth reading:

> It is a pioneering work, pushing two genres (comics and memoir) in multiple new directions, with panels that combine the detail and technical proficiency of R. Crumb with a seriousness, emotional complexity, and innovation completely its own. Then there are the actual words. Generally this is where graphic narratives stumble. Very few cartoonists can also write—or, if they can, they manage only to hit a few familiar notes. But *Fun Home* quietly succeeds in telling a story, not only through well-crafted images but through words that are equally revealing and well chosen. Big words, too! In 232 pages this memoir sent me to the dictionary five separate times (to look up "bargeboard," "buss," "scutwork," "humectant," and "perseverated").
>
> A comic book for lovers of words! Bechdel's rich language and precise images combine to create a lush piece of work—a memoir where concision and detail are melded for maximum, obsessive density. She has obviously spent years getting this memoir right, and it shows. You can read *Fun Home* in a sitting, or get lost in the pictures within the pictures on its pages. The artist's work is so absorbing you feel you are living in her world.
>
> —Sean Wilsey, "The Things They Buried"

The details in this passage make the case that Alison Bechdel's novel is one that pushes both comics and memoirs in new directions.

In evaluation arguments, don't be afraid to concede a point when evidence goes contrary to the overall claim you wish to make. If you're really skillful, you can even turn a problem into an argumentative asset, as Bob Costas does in acknowledging the flaws of baseball great Mickey Mantle in the process of praising him:

> None of us, Mickey included, would want to be held to account for every moment of our lives. But how many of us could say that our best moments were as magnificent as his?
>
> —Bob Costas, "Eulogy for Mickey Mantle"

RESPOND

Take a close look at the cover of Alison Bechdel's graphic novel *Fun Home: A Family Tragicomic*. In what various ways does it make an argument of evaluation designed to make you want to read the work? Examine other books, magazines, or media packages (such as video game or software boxes) and describe any strategies they use to argue for their merit.

Fun Home: A Family Tragicomic by Alison Bechdel. Cover illustration © 2007 by Alison Bechdel.
Reprinted by permission of Houghton Mifflin Harcourt Publishing Company. All rights reserved.

Considering Design and Visuals

Visual components play a significant role in many arguments of evaluation, especially those based on quantitative information. As soon as numbers are involved in supporting a claim, think about ways to arrange them in tables, charts, graphs, or infographics to make the information more accessible to readers. Visual elements are especially helpful when comparing items. Indeed, a visual spread like the one in the federal government's comparison of electric and hybrid cars (see p. 360) becomes an argument in itself about the vehicles the government has analyzed for fuel economy. The facts seem to speak for themselves because they are presented with care and deliberation. In the same way, you will want to make sure that you use similar care when using visuals to inform and persuade readers.

But don't ignore other basic design features of a text—such as headings for the different criteria you're using or, in online evaluations, links to material related to your subject.

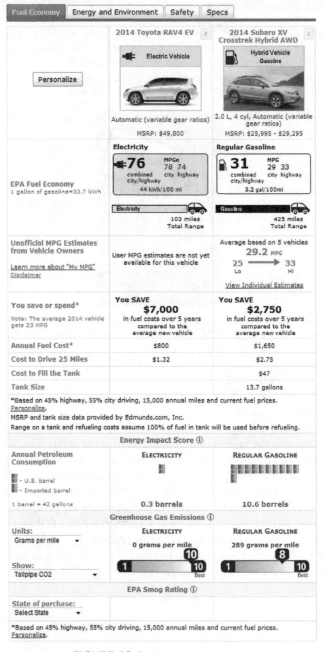

FIGURE 18.6 U.S. Department of Energy

GUIDE TO WRITING AN EVALUATION

Finding a Topic

You're entering an argument of evaluation when you:

- make a judgment about quality: Citizen Kane *is probably the finest film ever made by an American director.*

- challenge such a judgment: Citizen Kane *is vastly overrated by most film critics.*

- construct a ranking or comparison: Citizen Kane *is a more intellectually challenging movie than* Casablanca.

- explore criteria that might be used in making evaluative judgments: *Criteria for judging films are evolving as the production and audiences of films become ever more international.*

Issues of evaluation crop up everywhere—in the judgments you make about public figures or policies; in the choices you make about instructors and courses; in the recommendations you offer about books, films, or television programs; in the preferences you exercise in choosing products, activities, or charities. Evaluations typically use terms that indicate value or rank—*good/bad, effective/ineffective, best/worst, competent/incompetent, successful/unsuccessful.* When you can choose a topic for an evaluation, consider writing about something on which others regularly ask your opinion or advice.

Researching Your Topic

You can research issues of evaluation by using the following sources:

- journals, reviews, and magazines (for current political and social issues)

- books (for assessing judgments about history, policy, etc.)

- biographies (for assessing people)

- research reports and scientific studies

- books, magazines, and Web sites for consumers

- periodicals and Web sites that cover entertainment and sports

- blogs and social media sites that explore current topics

Surveys and polls can be useful in uncovering public attitudes: *What kinds of movies are young people seeing today? Who are the most admired people in the country? What activities or businesses are thriving or waning?* You'll discover that Web sites, newsgroups, and blogs thrive on evaluation. (Ever receive an invitation to "like" something on social media?) Browse these public forums for ideas, and, when possible, explore your own topic ideas there. But remember that all sources need to be evaluated themselves; examine each source carefully, making sure that it is legitimate and credible.

Formulating a Claim

After exploring your subject, try to draw up a full and specific claim that lets readers know where you stand and on what criteria you'll base your judgments. Come up with a thesis that's challenging enough to attract readers' attention. In developing a thesis, you might begin with questions like these:

- What exactly is my opinion? Where do I stand?

- Can I make my judgment more clear-cut?

- Do I need to narrow or qualify my claim?

- By what standards will I make my judgment?

- Will readers accept my criteria, or will I have to defend them, too? What criteria might others offer?

- What evidence or major reasons can I offer in support of my evaluation?

For a conventional evaluation, your thesis should be a complete statement. In one sentence, make a claim of evaluation and state the reasons that support it. Be sure your claim is specific. Anticipate the questions readers might have: *Who? What? Where? Under what conditions? With what exceptions? In all cases?* Don't expect readers to guess where you stand.

For a more exploratory argument, you might begin (and even end) with questions about the process of evaluation itself. *What are the qualities we seek — or ought to — in our political leaders? What does it say about our cultural values when we find so many viewers entertained by so-called reality shows on television? What might be the criteria for collegiate athletic programs consistent with the values of higher education?* Projects that explore topics like these might not begin with straightforward theses or have the intention to persuade readers.

Examples of Evaluative Claims

- Though they may never receive Oscars for their work, Tom Cruise and Keanu Reeves deserve credit as actors who have succeeded in a wider range of film roles than most of their contemporaries.

- People are returning to cities because they find life there more civilized than in the suburbs.

- Lena Dunham's writing and acting on *Girls* is the most honest presentation of the lives of twentysomething women today.

- Jimmy Carter has been highly praised for his work as a former president of the United States, but history may show that even his much-derided term in office laid the groundwork for the foreign policy and economic successes now attributed to later administrations.

- Young adults today are shying away from diving into the housing market because they no longer believe that homeownership is a key element in economic success.

Preparing a Proposal

If your instructor asks you to prepare a proposal for your project, here's a format that may help:

State your thesis completely. If you're having trouble doing so, try outlining it in Toulmin terms:

Claim:

Reason(s):

Warrant(s):

Alternatively, you might describe your intention to explore a particular question of evaluation in your project, with the thesis perhaps coming later.

- Explain why this issue deserves attention. What's at stake?

- Identify whom you hope to reach through your argument and why these readers would be interested in it.

- Briefly discuss the key challenges you anticipate in preparing your argument.

- Determine what research strategies you'll use. What sources do you expect to consult?

Considering Format and Media

Your instructor may specify that you use a particular format and/or medium. If not, ask yourself these questions to help you make a good choice:

- What format is most appropriate for your argument of evaluation? Does it call for an academic essay, a report, an infographic, a brochure, or something else?

- What medium is most appropriate for your argument? Would it be best delivered orally to a live audience? Presented as an audio essay or podcast? Presented in print only or in print with illustrations?

- Will you need visuals, such as moving or still images, maps, graphs, charts—and what function will they play in your argument? Make sure they are not just "added on" but are necessary components of the argument.

Thinking about Organization

Your evaluation will likely include elements such as the following:

- an evaluative claim that makes a judgment about a person, idea, or object

- the criterion or criteria by which you'll measure your subject

- an explanation or justification of the criteria (if necessary)

- evidence that the particular subject meets or falls short of the stated criteria

- consideration of alternative views and counterarguments

All these elements may be present in arguments of evaluation, but they won't follow a specific order. In addition, you'll often need an opening paragraph to explain what you're evaluating and why. Tell readers why they should care about your subject and take your opinion seriously.

Getting and Giving Response: Questions for Peer Response

Your instructor may assign you to a group for the purpose of reading and responding to each other's drafts. If not, ask for responses from serious readers or consultants at a writing center. Use the following questions to evaluate a colleague's draft. Be sure to illustrate your comments with examples; specific comments help more than general observations.

The Claim

- Is the claim an argument of evaluation? Does it make a judgment about something?

- Does the claim establish clearly what's being evaluated?

- Is the claim too sweeping? Does it need to be qualified?

- Will the criteria used in the evaluation be clear to readers? Do the criteria need to be defined more precisely?

- Are the criteria appropriate ones to use for this evaluation? Are they controversial? Should they be defended?

Evidence for the Claim

- Is enough evidence provided to show that what's being evaluated meets the established criteria? If not, what additional evidence is needed?

- Is the evidence in support of the claim simply announced, or are its significance and appropriateness analyzed? Is more detailed discussion needed?

- Are any objections readers might have to the claim, criteria, or evidence adequately addressed?

- What kinds of sources are cited? How credible and persuasive will they be to readers? What other kinds of sources might work better?

- Are all quotations introduced with appropriate signal phrases (such as "As Tyson argues, ...") and blended smoothly into the writer's sentences?

- Are all visual sources labeled, introduced, and commented upon?

Organization and Style

- How are the parts of the argument organized? Is this organization effective?

- Will readers understand the relationships among the claims, supporting reasons, warrants, and evidence? If not, how might those connections be clearer? Is the function of every visual clear? Are more transitions needed? Would headings or graphic devices help?

- Are the transitions or links from point to point, sentence to sentence, and paragraph to paragraph clear and effective? If not, how could they be improved?

- Are all visuals carefully integrated into the text? Is each visual introduced and commented on to point out its significance? Is each visual labeled as a figure or a table and given a caption as well as a citation?

- Is the style suited to the subject? Is it too formal, casual, or technical? Can it be improved?

- Which sentences seem effective? Which ones seem weaker, and how could they be improved? Should short sentences be combined, and any longer ones be broken up?

- How effective are the paragraphs? Too short or too long? How can they be improved?

- Which words or phrases seem effective? Do any seem vague or inappropriate for the audience or the writer's purpose? Are technical or unfamiliar terms defined?

Spelling, Punctuation, Mechanics, Documentation, and Format

- Are there any errors in spelling, punctuation, capitalization, and the like?

- Is the documentation appropriate and consistent? (See Chapter 30.)

- Does the paper or project follow an appropriate format? Is it appropriately designed and attractively presented?

PROJECTS

1. What kinds of reviews or evaluations do you consult most often or read regularly—those of TV shows, sports teams, video games, fashions, fishing gear, political figures? Try composing an argument of evaluation in your favorite genre: make and defend a claim about the quality of some object, item, work, or person within your area of interest or special knowledge. Let the paper demonstrate an expertise you have gained by your reading. If it helps, model your evaluation upon the work of a reviewer or expert you particularly respect.

2. Prepare a project in which you challenge what you regard as a wrong-headed evaluation, providing sound reasons and solid evidence for challenging this existing and perhaps commonly held view. Maybe you believe that a classic novel you had to read in high school is overrated or that people who criticize video games really don't understand them. Explain why the topic of your evaluation needs to be reconsidered and provide reasons, evidence, and, if necessary, different criteria of evaluation for doing so. For an example of this type of evaluation, see Sean Kamperman's "The Wikipedia Game" on pp. 367–370.

3. Write an evaluation in which you compare or assess the contributions or achievements of two or three notable people working within the same field or occupation. They may be educators, entrepreneurs, artists, legislators, editorial cartoonists, fashion designers, programmers, athletes—you name it. While your first instinct might be to rank these individuals and pick a "winner," this evaluation will work just as well if you can help readers appreciate the different paths by which your subjects have achieved distinction.

4. Within this chapter, the authors claim that criteria of evaluation can change depending on times and circumstances: "In good times, people may demand homes with soaring entryways, lots of space, and premium appliances. In tougher times, they may care more about efficient use of space, quality insulation, and energy-efficient stoves and dishwashers." Working in a group, discuss several scenarios of change and then explore how those circumstances could alter the way we evaluate particular objects, activities, or productions. For example, what impact might global warming have upon the way we determine desirable places to live or vacation? How might a continued economic downturn change the criteria by which we judge successful careers or good educational paths for our children? If people across the globe continue to put on weight, how might standards of personal beauty or fashion alter? If government institutions continue to fall in public esteem, how might we modify our expectations for elected officials? Following the discussion, write a paper or prepare a project in which you explore how one scenario for change might revise customary values and standards of evaluation.

The Wikipedia Game: Boring, Pointless, or Neither?

SEAN KAMPERMAN

When most people think about Wikipedia — the self-styled "free, Web-based, collaborative, multilingual encyclopedia project" — they are likely reminded of the preliminary research they did for that term paper on post-structuralism, or of the idle minutes they may've spent exploring an interesting topic just for the heck of it — the neuroanatomy of purple-striped jellyfish, for example, or *Jersey Shore*. First and foremost a layman's tool, Wikipedia has struggled to find legitimacy alongside more reputable reference sources such as *Encyclopaedia Britannica*, even in spite of the outstanding quality of many of its entries. But fortunately for the makers of the Free Encyclopedia — and for the rest of us — Wikipedia's usefulness goes far beyond its intended "encyclopedic" purpose. Under the right circumstances, it can be as much a source of entertainment as one of knowledge and self-improvement.

Opening paragraph provides a context and a subtle evaluative thesis: "Wikipedia's usefulness goes far beyond its intended 'encyclopedic' purpose."

A prime example of this fact is a phenomenon identified as the Wikipedia game — or, as it's now known to users of Apple and Android smart phones, "WikiHunt." WikiHunt is a simple game whose rules draw upon the unique architectural features of wikis, in that players perform "moves" by following the links that connect one Wikipedia entry to another. Driven by cultural conditions of dilettantism and the spurts of creativity that tend to come on in times of extreme boredom, dozens if not hundreds of Wikipedia users in high school computer labs, college dormitories, and professional workspaces around the globe have "discovered" the game on their own. Some have even gone so far as to claim sole proprietorship — as in the case of two of my friends, who swear they invented the game while sitting through a lecture on academic dishonesty. Questions of original authorship aside, the Wikipedia game would

WikiHunt is introduced as a cultural phenomenon.

Sean Kamperman wrote "The Wikipedia Game: Boring, Pointless, or Neither?" in spring 2010 for a lower-division course on rhetoric and media at the University of Texas at Austin. In his topic proposal he briefly described Wikipedia games familiar to many students and then indicated what he intended to explore: "A lot of scholars have been very critical of Wikipedia — some going so far as to discourage its use altogether, even for the purpose of gathering background info. Does the fact that games like these use Wikipedia detract from their educational value? Or do the games in some way rebut these criticisms, demonstrating that the practical uses of user-generated online encyclopedias go beyond traditional research and, by extension, considerations of factual correctness?" His paper is the answer to those questions.

appear to be a bona fide grassroots phenomenon — and one well worth examining if we consider its possible implications for learning and education.

Understanding that not every reader will know WikiHunt, Kamperman offers a detailed explanation.

If you've never played the Wikipedia game, it's fun — educational — and, for the most part, free; indeed, all you'll need is one or more friends, two computers, and an Internet connection. To begin, navigate to the Wikipedia homepage and click the "Random article" link on the left-hand side of the screen. As advertised, this link will lead you and your friend to two randomly generated Wikipedia articles. The objective from here is to get from your article to your opponent's using nothing but links to other articles. These links, which appear within the text of the articles themselves, are bits of hypertext denoted in blue; click on any of them, and you'll be instantly transported to another article and another set of links. Depending on which version of the rules you're going by, either the player who finishes first or the one who gets to his or her opponent's page using the fewest number of links is the winner. Easy, right?

The paper returns to its thesis when it notes how unexpectedly hard WikiHunt is.

Not exactly. What makes the Wikipedia game hard — and coincidentally, what makes it so much fun — is the vastness of the Web site's encyclopedic content. Click the "Random article" button enough times, and you'll see a pattern emerge: the majority of articles that pop up are short ones covering extremely obscure topics, usually having to do with something related to European club soccer. Entries such as these, labeled "orphans" for their relative paucity of length and links, in fact comprise the majority of Wikipedia articles. So the chances of you or your opponent hitting the randomly-generated-article jackpot and getting a "Jesus" or an "Adolf Hitler" — two pages with tons of links — are pretty slim. Rather, the task at hand usually requires that players navigate from orphan to orphan, as was the case in a game I played just last night with my friends David and Paige. They were unlucky enough to pull up an article on the summer village of Whispering Hills, Alberta, and I was no less unfortunate to get one on "blocking," an old 3D computer animation technique that makes characters and objects look like they're moving. Between these two pages, we were supplied with a total of nineteen links — they had nine doors to choose from, whereas I had ten. That's not a lot to work with. As you can probably surmise, games like this one take more than a few idle minutes — not to mention a heck of a lot of brainpower and spontaneous strategizing.

Indeed, what makes the Wikipedia game interesting is that it welcomes comparison between the players' respective strategies and methods for getting from point A to point B, highlighting differences between their thought processes and respective knowledge sets. To elaborate using the aforementioned example, I initially knew nothing about either Whispering Hills, Alberta, or "Blocking (animation)." What I did know, however, was that in order to get to Canada, I'd have to go through the good old U.S. of A. So I clicked a link at the bottom of the page entitled "Categories: animation techniques," and from there looked for a well-known technique that I knew to be associated with an American software company. Selecting "PowerPoint animation," I was led from there to the article on Microsoft—which, thanks to the company's late '90s monopolistic indiscretions, furnished me with a link to the U.S. Department of Justice. Five clicks later and I was in Alberta, looking for a passageway to Whispering Hills, one of the province's smallest, obscurest villages. I finally found it in a series of lists on communities in Alberta—but not before my opponents beat me to the punch and got to my page on "blocking" first. David, a computer science major, had taken a different approach to clinch the win; rather than drawing upon his knowledge of a macroscopic, big-picture subject like geography, he skipped from the article on Canada to a page entitled "Canadian industrial research and development organizations," from which he quickly bored through twelve articles on various topics in the computer sciences before falling on "Blocking (animation)." In his case, specialized knowledge was the key to winning.

Kamperman uses his own experience to show precisely how WikiHunt tracks users' processes of thought and "knowledge sets."

But did David and Paige really win? Perhaps—but in the wide world of the Wikipedia game, there are few hard-and-fast rules to go by. Whereas my opponents got to their destination quicker than I, my carefully planned journey down the funnel from big ("United States") to small ("List of summer villages in Alberta") got me to Whispering Hills using two fewer links than they. So in this example, one sees not a clear-cut lesson on how to win the game, but rather a study in contrasting styles. A player can rely on specialized knowledge, linking quickly to familiar domains and narrowing the possibilities from there; or, she/he may choose to take a slower, more methodical approach, employing abstract, top-down reasoning skills to systematically sift through broader categories of information. Ultimately, victory is possible in either case.

Its more casual, entertaining uses aside, Wikipedia gets a bad rap, especially in the classroom. Too many college professors and high school English teachers have simply written it off, some even going so far as to expressly forbid their students from using it while at school. These stances and attitudes are understandable. Teaching students how to find good sources and properly credit them is hard enough without the competing influence of the Wikipedia community, whose definition of an acceptably accurate source seems to extend not only to professionally or academically vetted articles, but to blogs as well, some obviously plagiarized. But to deny Wikipedia a place in the classroom is to deny both students and teachers alike the valuable experience of playing a game that shows us not only what we know, but how we know — how our brains work when posed with the everyday challenge of having to connect ostensibly unrelated pieces of information, and furthermore, how they work differently in that respect.

Knowledge building is a connective or associative process, as the minds behind Wikipedia well know. A casual perusal of any Wikipedia article reveals reams and reams of blue hypertext — bits of text that, when set in isolation, roughly correspond to discrete categories of information about the world. In a sense, the visual rhetoric of Wikipedia invokes the verbal rhetoric of exploration, prompting intrepid Web-using truth seekers to go sailing through a bright blue sea of information that is exciting by virtue of its seeming limitlessness. It should comfort teachers to know that, in quickly navigating through linked knowledge categories to reach their respective destinations, Wikipedia gamers aren't relying too much on their understanding of the articles themselves; rather, what they're relying on is their ability to understand relationships.

The fact that so many people have independently found the fun at the heart of Wikipedia should be a heads-up. The Wikipedia game is a grassroots technological innovation that sheds new light on what it means to know — and, perhaps more importantly, one that reminds us that, yes, learning can be fun. It isn't too hard to imagine versions of the game that could be played by kids in school, and how teachers could then use the game to learn more about the stuff of their trade — namely, learning and how it works. So the next time you hear a friend, teacher, or coworker dismiss the Free Encyclopedia as "unreliable" or "unacademic," do knowledge a favor and challenge them to the following:

"Villa of Livia" to "List of Montreal Expos broadcasters" …

… no click-backs …

… twenty links or less.

Go.

Acknowledging reservations about Wikipedia, the paper asserts that WikiHunt shows players "how we know."

Argues that WikiHunt is about learning relationships between ideas.

Defends Wikipedia as supporting a game that proves to be about "learning and how it works."

My Awkward Week with Google Glass

HAYLEY TSUKAYAMA

The Washington
Post/Getty
Images

April 29, 2014

It's a Wednesday night, and I'm turning heads on the sidewalk. People are slowing halfway down the block as I approach. They're whispering about me as I walk through the room. Strangers are watching me, sometimes even stopping me on the street.

Why? Because I'm wearing Google Glass. And I hate it.

I shouldn't feel this way. I like new technology — I've been a tech reporter at the *Washington Post* for more than three years. And I admire the vision of technology that Google promises Glass can offer: a device that lets you keep track of e-mails, texts and other messages in a seamless way — all through a screen that's perched just over your right eye.

Headed into a week with Glass, on loan from a co-worker, I was prepared to review a buggy product. Glass, after all, is still in testing, and has only been released to developers, media and just a handful of "normal" people who were willing to spend $1,500 on an untested product. I expected tension headaches from constantly trying to focus on a floating screen above my line of vision. (I got only one headache, for what it's worth.) I even prepared myself to be comfortable talking aloud to the product in public because you can control Glass through voice commands.

What I wasn't prepared for was the attention I got. Sporting Glass put me among only a handful of people in Washington, and that meant getting a lot of looks. Most of it was good attention from curious people, but it still made me miserable. For wallflowers like me, wearing something that draws constant attention is more or less my personal idea of hell.

I've heard just about every privacy concern raised about Glass, but, as the one wearing the device, I wasn't expecting that the privacy most invaded would be my own. That type of anxiety should lessen over time, particularly as Google works with designer labels such as Luxottica's Oakley and Ray-Ban to make prettier models. But anyone who opts to buy Glass should be ready and willing to become a constant topic of conversation and to answer questions from strangers. Wearing Google Glass in public is like wearing a sandwich-board that says "Talk to me!" And, given the rare but highly publicized fights, robberies and other major incidents some Glass users have experienced, I was a little wary about wearing the device in public.

In the name of fairness, though, I did wear them—nearly everywhere: to work, to the grocery store, out with friends, even to choir rehearsal. Here's a sample of what I heard (or overheard) from friends and strangers in the week I spent with Glass:

"Is she wearing Google Glass?" "Is that what I think that is?" "Are you recording, like, right now?" "You look ridiculous."

Or, my personal favorite, delivered deadpan, from a friend: "Oh, *Hayley*."

But beyond the personal privacy issues, I found that Google Glass is an intriguing device that has a lot of flaws. After more than two years in development, the number of remaining technical bugs is surprising.

On the hardware side, the problems ranged from the device becoming too warm—sometimes after just 10 minutes of use—to needing to be charged multiple times a day. The sensors on the device were far from perfect, and there were many times when I had to re-tap, re-swipe or (and maybe this was the worst part) jerk my head up repeatedly to wake up the device when it went dormant. I probably reset the device at least half a dozen times in the course of normal use because it wouldn't respond to my frantic taps, or refused to connect to my smartphone even when there were no other network problems.

Glass works better with Google's Android phones (in my case, an HTC One M8 on loan from HTC) than with the iPhone, if only because the integration between the Google systems is much smoother. As for software, developers have been smart about designing Glass apps to minimize the amount of data bombarding users. Big names such as Facebook, Twitter and CNN provide a strong app core for Glass. The CNN app, for example, will let you see headlines for top stories, or by subject, and serves headlines, photos and short video.

There are other apps that would be nice to have, however, particularly more photo apps to take advantage of the point-of-view vantage you get with the device.

The iPhone experience with Glass is improving. In fact, Google added a feature allowing Glass users to see iPhone text notifications during the week I wore the device. And some functions of Glass, such as the ability to project what a Glass user sees to a paired phone, were fantastic and useful in ways I didn't anticipate.

But though I tried, very hard, to make Glass a part of my life, I simply didn't feel comfortable with the screen hovering just out of my line of sight. I didn't get any direct challenges about filming others without their permission—not that I ever did film people without permission—but nearly every person who questioned me about Glass asked if I was filming.

What struck me most, however, was what happened when I let others try on the device, giving me a glimpse of how I appeared when I was wearing Glass: a conversation partner who was like a dinner guest who keeps looking at the door, as if to check if there's another person in the room they'd rather be talking to. Think of every person wearing earbuds or a Bluetooth headset who has annoyed you for the same reason. Now multiply it by a factor of 10.

All of which goes against what Glass is supposedly all about: the idea that you can avoid those awkward moments when you try to sneak a peek at your smartphone, which is always much more obvious than you think.

After a few earnest days of trying to make the thing work, I stopped trying to force the issue and used it as I would in real life—in situations when I needed to watch something hands-free, or when I wasn't required to actively engage with other people. In those cases, Glass worked as promised. It delivered updates to keep me informed without overwhelming me and acted as a useful second screen to my smartphone.

But that also meant that, more often than not, Glass ended up perched on the top of my head—the way you wear your sunglasses indoors—or discreetly tucked into my bag, in order to keep it from being the only subject of conversation.

Would I buy Google Glass? Not now, especially with that $1,500 price tag. The device has a lot of evolving to do before it's ready for the world. The world has some evolving to do before it's ready for Glass, too.

Causal Arguments

In spite of the fact that they have thrived for over fifty million years, around nine years ago colonies of bees started dying ... and dying. Are pesticides the cause? Or perhaps it's the move agriculture has made from planting cover crops like alfalfa and clover that create natural fertilizers to using synthetic fertilizers that cater to crop monocultures but leave no food support for bees? Scientists believe a combination of these factors account for the current loss of bees.

Small business owners and big companies alike still seem reluctant to hire new employees. Is it because of complex government regulations, continuing uncertainties about health care costs, worries about debt, improvements in productivity—or all of the above? People needing jobs want to know.

Most state governments use high taxes to discourage the use of tobacco products. But when anti-smoking campaigns and graphic warning labels convince people to quit smoking, tax revenues decline, reducing support for health and education programs. Will raising taxes even higher restore that lost revenue?

Left to right: c. byatt-norman/Shutterstock; Robyn Beck/AFP/Getty Images; AP Photo/Jeff Roberson

Understanding Causal Arguments

Americans seem to be getting fatter, so fat in fact that we hear often about the "obesity crisis" in the United States. But what is behind this rise in weight? Rachel Berl, writing for *U.S. News and World Report*, points to unhealthy foods and a sedentary lifestyle:

> "There is no single, simple answer to explain the obesity patterns" in America, says Walter Willett, who chairs the department of nutrition at the Harvard School of Public Health. "Part of this is due to lower incomes and education, which result in purchases of cheap foods that are high in refined starch and sugar. More deeply, this also reflects lower public investment in education, public transportation, and recreational facilities," he says. The bottom line: cheap, unhealthy foods mixed with a sedentary lifestyle have made obesity the new normal in America. And that makes it even harder to change, Willett says.
>
> —Rachel Pomerance Berl

Many others agree that as processed fast food and other things such as colas have gotten more and more affordable, consumption of them has gone up, along with weight. But others offer different theories for the rise in obesity.

Whatever the reasons for our increased weight, the consequences can be measured by everything from the width of airliner seats to the rise of diabetes in the general population. Many explanations are offered by scientists, social critics, and health gurus, and some are refuted. Figuring out what's going on is a national concern—and an important exercise in cause-and-effect argument.

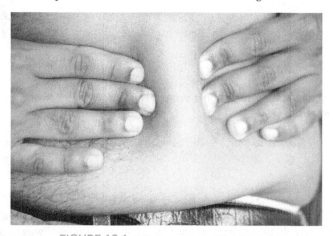

FIGURE 19.1   © Bartomeu Amengual/age fotostock

Causal arguments—from the causes of poverty in rural communities to the consequences of ocean pollution around the globe—are at the heart of many major policy decisions, both national and international. But arguments about causes and effects also inform many choices that people make every day. Suppose that you need to petition for a grade change because you were unable to turn in a final project on time. You'd probably enumerate the reasons for your failure—the death of your cat, followed by an attack of the hives, followed by a crash of your computer—hoping that an associate dean reading the petition might see these explanations as tragic enough to change your grade. In identifying the causes of the situation, you're implicitly arguing that the effect (your failure to submit the project on time) should be considered in a new light. Unfortunately, the administrator might accuse you of faulty causality (see p. 228) and judge that failure to complete the project is due more to your procrastination than to the reasons you offer.

Causal arguments exist in many forms and frequently appear as part of other arguments (such as evaluations or proposals). It may help focus your work on causal arguments to separate them into three major categories:

Arguments that state a cause and then examine its effects

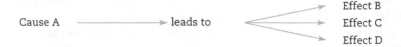

Arguments that state an effect and then trace the effect back to its causes

Arguments that move through a series of links: A causes B, which leads to C and perhaps to D

Cause A ➤ leads to Cause B ➤ leads to Cause C ➤ leads to Effect D

Arguments That State a Cause and Then Examine Its Effects

What would happen if Congress suddenly came together and passed immigration reform that gave millions of people in the United States a legal pathway to citizenship? Before such legislation could be enacted, the possible effects of this "cause" would have to be examined in detail and argued intensely. Groups on various sides of this hot-button issue are actually doing so now, and the sides present very different scenarios. In this debate, you'd be successful if you could convincingly describe the consequences of such a change. Alternatively, you could challenge the causal explanations made by people you don't agree with. But speculation about causes and effects is always risky because life is complicated.

Consider the following passage from researcher Gail Tverberg's blog *Our Finite World*, from 2011, describing possible consequences of the commitment to increase the production of ethanol from corn:

> At the time the decision was made to expand corn ethanol production, we seemed to have an excess of arable land, and corn prices were low. Using some corn for ethanol looked like it would help farmers, and also help increase fuel for our vehicles. There was also a belief that cellulosic ethanol production might be right around the corner, and could substitute, so there would not be as much pressure on food supplies.
>
> Now the situation has changed. Food prices are much higher, and the number of people around the world with inadequate food supply is increasing. The ethanol we are using for our cars is much more in direct competition with the food people around the world are using, and the situation may very well get worse, if there are crop failures.
>
> —Gail Tverberg, *Our Finite World*

FIGURE 19.2 Paresh Nath, cartoonist for India's *National Herald*, personifies the causes for a world food crisis in this item from March 2011. © Paresh Nath, Cagle Cartoons, Inc.

Note that the researcher here begins by pointing out the cause-effect relationship that the government was hoping for and then points to the potential effects of that policy when circumstances change. As it turns out, using corn for fuel did have many unintended consequences, for example, inflating the price not only of corn but of wheat and soybeans as well, leading to food shortages and even food riots around the globe.

Arguments That State an Effect and Then Trace the Effect Back to Its Causes

This type of argument might begin with a specific effect (a catastrophic drop in sales of music CDs) and then trace it to its most likely causes (the introduction of MP3 technology, new modes of music distribution, a preference for single song purchases). Or you might examine the reasons that music executives offer for their industry's dip and decide whether their causal analyses pass muster.

Like other kinds of causal arguments, those tracing effects to a cause can have far-reaching significance. In 1962, for example, the scientist Rachel Carson seized the attention of millions with a famous causal argument about the effects that the overuse of chemical pesticides might have on the environment. Here's an excerpt from the beginning of her book-length study of this subject. Note how she begins with the effects before saying she'll go on to explore the causes:

> [A] strange blight crept over the area and everything began to change. Some evil spell had settled on the community: mysterious maladies swept the flocks of chickens; the cattle and sheep sickened and died. Everywhere was a shadow of death. The farmers spoke of much illness among their families… . There had been several sudden and unexplained deaths, not only among adults but even among children, who would be stricken suddenly while at play and die within a few hours. The roadsides, once so attractive, were now lined with browned and withered vegetation as though swept by fire. These, too, were silent, deserted by all living things. Even the streams were now lifeless. Anglers no longer visited them, for all the fish had died.
>
> In the gutters under the eaves and between the shingles of the roofs, a white granular powder still showed a few patches; some weeks before it had fallen like snow upon the roofs and lawns, the fields and streams. No witchcraft, no enemy action had silenced the rebirth of new life in this stricken world. The people had done it themselves… . What has silenced the voices of spring in countless towns in America? This book is an attempt to explain.
>
> —Rachel Carson, *Silent Spring*

Today, one could easily write a causal argument of the first type about *Silent Spring* and the environmental movement that it spawned.

Arguments That Move through a Series of Links: A Causes B, Which Leads to C and Perhaps to D

In an environmental science class, for example, you might decide to argue that, despite reductions in acid rain, tightened national regulations regarding smokestack emissions from utility plants are still needed for the following reasons:

1. Emissions from utility plants in the Midwest still cause significant levels of acid rain in the eastern United States.

2. Acid rain threatens trees and other vegetation in eastern forests.

3. Powerful lobbyists have prevented midwestern states from passing strict laws to control emissions from these plants.

4. As a result, acid rain will destroy most eastern forests by 2030.

In this case, the first link is that emissions cause acid rain; the second, that acid rain causes destruction in eastern forests; and the third, that states have not acted to break the cause-and-effect relationship that is established by the first two points. These links set the scene for the fourth link, which ties the previous points together to argue from effect: unless X, then Y.

RESPOND

The causes of some of the following events and phenomena are well known and frequently discussed. But do you understand these causes well enough to spell them out to someone else? Working in a group, see how well (and in how much detail) you can explain each of the following events or phenomena. Which explanations are relatively clear, and which seem more open to debate?

earthquakes/tsunamis

popularity of Lady Gaga or Taylor Swift or the band Wolf Alice

Cold War

Edward Snowden's leak of CIA documents

Ebola crisis in western Africa

popularity of the *Transformers* films

swelling caused by a bee sting

sharp rise in cases of autism or asthma

climate change

Characterizing Causal Arguments

Causal arguments tend to share several characteristics.

They Are Often Part of Other Arguments.

Many stand-alone causal arguments address questions that are fundamental to our well-being: *Why are juvenile asthma and diabetes increasing so dramatically in the United States? What are the causes of the rise in cases of malaria in Africa, and what can we do to counter this rise? What will happen to Europe if its birthrate continues to decline?*

But causal analyses often work to support other arguments—especially proposals. For example, a proposal to limit the time that children spend playing video games might first draw on a causal analysis to establish that playing video games can have bad results—such as violent behavior, short attention spans, and decreased social skills. The causal analysis provides a rationale that motivates the proposal. In this way, causal analyses can be useful in establishing good reasons for arguments in general.

They Are Almost Always Complex.

The complexity of most causal relationships makes it difficult to establish causes and effects. For example, in 2011 researchers at Northwestern University reported a startling correlation: youths who participated in church activities were far more likely to grow into obese adults than their counterparts who were not engaged in religious activities. How does one even begin to explain such a peculiar and unexpected finding? Too many church socials? Unhealthy food at potluck meals? More regular social engagement? Perhaps.

Or consider the complexity of analyzing the causes of food poisoning when they strike large populations: in 2008, investigators spent months trying to discover whether tomatoes, cilantro, or jalapeño peppers were the cause of a nationwide outbreak of salmonella. More than seventeen states were affected. But despite such challenges, whenever it is possible to demonstrate convincing causal connections between X and Y, we gain important knowledge and powerful arguments. That's why, for example, great effort went into establishing an indisputable link between smoking and lung cancer. Once proven, decisive legal action could finally be taken to warn smokers.

They Are Often Definition Based.

One reason that causal arguments are complex is that they often depend on careful definitions. Recent figures from the U.S. Department of Education, for example, show that the number of high school dropouts is rising and that this rise has caused an increase in youth unemployment. But exactly how does the study define *dropout*? A closer look may suggest that some students (perhaps a lot) who drop out later "drop back in" and complete high school or that some who drop out become successful entrepreneurs or business owners. Further, how does the study define *employment*? Until you can provide definitions for all key terms in a causal claim, you should proceed cautiously with your argument.

"The rise in unemployment, however, which was somewhat offset by an expanding job market, was countered by an upturn in part-time dropouts, which, in turn, was diminished by seasonal factors, the anticipated summer slump, and, over-all, a small but perceptible rise in actual employment."

FIGURE 19.3 Causal arguments can also be confusing.

© Ed Arno/The New Yorker Collection/The Cartoon Bank

They Usually Yield Probable Rather Than Absolute Conclusions.

Because causal relationships are almost always complex or subtle, they seldom can yield more than a high degree of probability. Consequently, they are almost always subject to criticism or open to charges of false causality. (We all know smokers who defy the odds to live long, cancer-free lives.) Scientists in particular are wary when making causal claims.

Even after an event, proving precisely what caused it can be hard. During the student riots of the late 1960s, for example, a commission was charged with determining the causes of riots on a particular campus. After two years of work and almost a thousand pages of evidence and reports, the commission was unable to pinpoint anything but a broad network of contributing causes and related conditions. And how many years is it likely to take to unravel all the factors responsible for the extended recession and economic decline in the United States that began in 2008? After all, serious scholars are still arguing about the forces responsible for the Great Depression of 1929.

To demonstrate that X caused Y, you must find the strongest possible evidence and subject it to the toughest scrutiny. But a causal argument doesn't fail just because you can't find a single compelling cause. In fact, causal arguments are often most effective when they help readers appreciate how tangled our lives and landscapes really are.

Developing Causal Arguments

Exploring Possible Claims

To begin creating a strong causal claim, try listing some of the effects—events or phenomena—that you'd like to know the causes of:

- Why do college tuition costs routinely outstrip the rate of inflation?
- What's really behind the slow pace of development of alternative energy sources?
- Why are almost all the mothers in animated movies either dead to begin with or quickly killed off?
- Why is same-sex marriage more acceptable to American society than it was a decade ago?
- Why do so few younger Americans vote, even in major elections?

Or try moving in the opposite direction, listing some phenomena or causes you're interested in and then hypothesizing what kinds of effects they may produce:

- How will the growing popularity of e-readers change our relationships to books?
- What will happen as the result of efforts to repeal the Affordable Health Care Act?
- What will be the consequences if more liberal (or conservative) judges are appointed to the U.S. Supreme Court?
- What will happen as China and India become dominant industrialized nations?

Read a little about the causal issues that interest you most, and then try them out on friends and colleagues. They might suggest ways to refocus or clarify what you want to do or offer leads to finding information about your subject. After some initial research, map out the causal relationship you want to explore in simple form:

X might cause (or might be caused by) **Y** for the following reasons:

1.

2.

3. (add more as needed)

Such a statement should be tentative because writing a causal argument should be an exercise in which you uncover facts, not assume them to be true. Often, your early assumptions (*Tuition was raised to renovate the stadium*) might be undermined by the facts you later discover (*Tuition doesn't fund the construction or maintenance of campus buildings*).

You might even decide to write a wildly exaggerated or parodic causal argument for humorous purposes. Humorist Dave Barry does this when he explains the causes of El Niño and other weather phenomena: "So we see that the true cause of bad weather, contrary to what they have been claiming all these years, is TV weather forecasters, who have also single-handedly destroyed the ozone layer via overuse of hair spray." Most of the causal reasoning you do, however, will take a serious approach to subjects that you, your family, and your friends care about.

RESPOND

Working with a group, write a big *Why?* on a sheet of paper or computer screen, and then generate a list of *why* questions. Don't be too critical of the initial list:

Why

—*do people laugh?*

—*do swans mate for life?*

—*do college students binge drink?*

—*do teenagers drive fast?*

—*do babies cry?*

—*do politicians take risks on social media?*

Generate as lengthy a list as you can in fifteen minutes. Then decide which of the questions might make plausible starting points for intriguing causal arguments.

© Bill Coster/age fotostock

Defining the Causal Relationships

In developing a causal claim, you can examine the various types of causes and effects in play in a given argument and define their relationship. Begin by listing all the plausible causes or effects you need to consider. Then decide which are the most important for you to analyze or the easiest to defend or critique. The following chart on "Causes" may help you to appreciate some important terms and relationships. Even the most everyday causal analysis can draw on such distinctions among reasons and causes. What persuaded you, for instance, to choose the college you decided to attend? *Proximate* reasons might be the location of the school or the college's curriculum in your areas of interest. But what are the *necessary* reasons—the ones without which your choice of that college could not occur? Adequate financial support? Good test scores and academic record? The expectations of a parent?

TYPE OF CAUSES	WHAT IT IS OR DOES	WHAT IT LOOKS LIKE
Sufficient cause	Enough for something to occur on its own	Lack of oxygen is sufficient to cause death Cheating on an exam is sufficient to fail a course
Necessary cause	Required for something to occur (but in combination with other factors)	Fuel is necessary for fire Capital is necessary for economic growth
Precipitating cause	Brings on a change	Protest march ignites a strike by workers Plane flies into strong thunderstorms
Proximate cause	Immediately present or visible cause of action	Strike causes company to declare bankruptcy Powerful wind shear causes plane to crash
Remote cause	Indirect or underlying explanation for action	Company was losing money on bad designs and inept manufacturing Wind shear warning failed to sound in cockpit
Reciprocal causes	One factor leads to a second, which reinforces the first, creating a cycle	Lack of good schools leads to poverty, which further weakens education, which leads to even fewer opportunities . . .

Once you've identified a causal claim, you can draw out the reasons, warrants, and evidence that can support it most effectively:

Claim	Certain career patterns cause women to be paid less than men.
Reason	Women's career patterns differ from men's.
Warrant	Successful careers are made during the period between ages twenty-five and thirty-five.
Evidence	Women often drop out of or reduce work during the decade between ages twenty-five and thirty-five to raise families.

Claim	Lack of community and alumni support caused the football coach to lose his job.
Reason	Ticket sales and alumni support have declined for three seasons in a row despite a respectable team record.
Warrant	Winning over fans is as important as winning games for college coaches in smaller athletic programs.
Evidence	Over the last ten years, coaches at several programs have been sacked because of declining support and revenues.

RESPOND

Here's a schematic causal analysis of one event, exploring the difference among precipitating, necessary, and sufficient causes. Critique and revise the analysis as you see fit. Then create another of your own, beginning with a different event, phenomenon, incident, fad, or effect.

Event: Traffic fatality at an intersection

Precipitating cause: A pickup truck that runs a red light, totals a Prius, and injures its driver

Necessary cause: Two drivers who are navigating Friday rush-hour traffic (if no driving, then no accident)

Sufficient cause: A truck driver who is distracted by a cell-phone conversation

Supporting Your Point

In drafting your causal argument, you'll want to do the following:

- Show that the causes and effects you've suggested are highly probable and backed by evidence, or show what's wrong with the faulty causal reasoning you may be critiquing.

- Assess any links between causal relationships (what leads to or follows from what).

- Show that your explanations of any causal chains are accurate, or identify where links in a causal chain break down.

- Show that plausible cause-and-effect explanations haven't been ignored or that the possibility of multiple causes or effects has been considered.

In other words, you will need to examine your subject carefully and find appropriate ways to support your claims. There are different ways to accomplish that goal.

For example, in studying effects that are physical (as they would be with diseases or climate conditions), you can offer and test *hypotheses*, or theories about possible causes. That means researching such topics thoroughly because you'll need to draw upon authorities and research articles for your explanations and evidence. (See Chapter 25, "Academic Arguments," and Chapter 26, "Finding Evidence.") Don't be surprised if you find yourself debating which among conflicting authorities make the most plausible causal or explanatory arguments. Your achievement as a writer may be simply that you present these differences in an essay, leaving it to readers to make judgments of their own—as John Tierney does in "Can a Playground Be Too Safe?" at the end of this chapter (see p. 399).

But not all the evidence in compelling causal arguments needs to be strictly scientific or scholarly. Many causal arguments rely on **ethnographic observations**—the systematic study of ordinary people in their daily routines. How would you explain, for example, why some people step aside when they encounter someone head-on and others do not? In an argument that attempts to account for such behavior, investigators Frank Willis, Joseph Gier, and David Smith observed "1,038 displacements involving 3,141 persons" at a Kansas City shopping mall. In results that surprised the investigators, "gallantry" seemed to play a significant role in causing people to step aside for one another—more so than other causes that the investigators had anticipated (such as deferring to someone who's physically stronger or higher in status). Doubtless you've read of other such studies, perhaps in psychology courses. You may even decide to do a little fieldwork on your own—which raises the possibility of using personal experiences in support of a causal argument.

Indeed, people's experiences generally lead them to draw causal conclusions about things they know well. Personal experience can also help build your credibility as a writer, gain the empathy of listeners, and thus support a causal claim. Although one person's experiences cannot ordinarily be universalized, they can still argue eloquently for causal relationships. Listen to Sara Barbour, a recent graduate of Columbia University, as she draws upon her own carefully described experiences to bemoan what may happen when e-readers finally displace printed books:

> In eliminating a book's physical existence, something crucial is lost forever. Trapped in a Kindle, the story remains but the book can no longer be scribbled in, hoarded, burned, given, or received. We may be able to read it, but we can't share it with others in the same way, and its ability to connect us to people, places, and ideas is that much less powerful.
>
> I know the Kindle will eventually carry the day—an electronic reader means no more embarrassing coffee stains, no more library holds and renewals, no

more frantic flipping through pages for a lost quote, or going to three book-stores in one afternoon to track down an evasive title. Who am I to advo-cate the doom of millions of trees when the swipe of a finger can deliver all 838 pages of *Middlemarch* into my waiting hands?

But once we all power up our Kindles something will be gone, a kind of lan-guage. Books communicate with us as readers—but as important, we com-municate with each other through books themselves. When that connection is lost, the experience of reading—and our lives—will be forever altered.

—Sara Barbour, "Kindle vs. Books: The Dead Trees Society,"
Los Angeles Times, June 17, 2011

All these strategies—testing hypotheses, presenting experimental evidence, and offering personal experience—can help you support a causal argument or under-mine a causal claim you regard as faulty.

RESPOND

One of the fallacies of argument discussed in Chapter 13 is the *post hoc, ergo propter hoc* ("after this, therefore because of this") fallacy. Causal arguments are particularly prone to this kind of fallacious reasoning, in which a writer asserts a causal relationship between two entirely unconnected events. When Angelina Jolie gave birth to twins in 2008, for instance, the stock market rallied by nearly six hundred points, but it would be difficult to argue that either event is related to the other.

Because causal arguments can easily fall prey to this fallacy, you might find it instructive to create and defend an absurd connection of this kind. Begin by asserting a causal link between two events or phenomena that likely have no relationship: *The enormous popularity of* Doctor Who *is partially due to global warming*. Then spend a page or so spinning out an imaginative argument to defend the claim. It's OK to have fun with this exercise, but see how convincing you can be at generating plausibly implausible arguments.

Considering Design and Visuals

You may find that the best way to illustrate a causal relationship is to present it visu-ally. Even a simple bar graph or chart can demonstrate a relationship between two variables that might be related to a specific cause, like the one above showing the dramatic effects of lowered birthrates. The report that uses this figure explores the effects that such a change would have on the economies of the world.

The comparative size of successive generations across time when fertility is constant at 1.3 births per woman

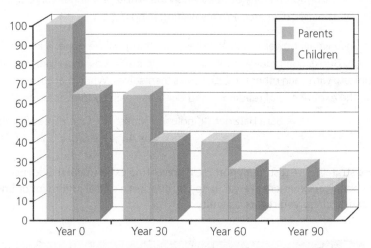

FIGURE 19.4 A simple graph can provide dramatic evidence for a causal claim—in this case, the effect of reduced fertility rates on a population.
Data from Statistics Bureau, MIC; Ministry of Health, Labour and Welfare

Or you may decide that the most dramatic way to present important causal information about a single issue or problem is via an infographic, cartoon, or public service announcement. Our arresting example on the next page is part of a campaign by People for the Ethical Treatment of Animals (PETA). An organization that advocates for animal rights, PETA promotes campaigns that typically try to sway people to adopt vegetarian diets by depicting the practices of the agriculture industry as cruel. (Many of us have also seen their celebrity anti-fur campaigns; see p. 246 for one example.) Their "Meat's Not Green!" campaign, however, attempts to reach an audience that might not buy into the animal rights argument. Instead, it appeals to people who have environmentalist beliefs by presenting data that claims a causal link between animal farming and environmental destruction. How much of this data surprises you?

FIGURE 19.5 PETA's ad campaign expands its focus to environmentalists by explaining through causal links why they should consider vegetarian diets.
Courtesy of People for the Ethical Treatment of Animals; peta.org

GUIDE TO WRITING A CAUSAL ARGUMENT

Finding a Topic

You're entering a causal argument when you:

- state a cause and then examine its effects: *The ongoing economic downturn has led more people to return to college to enhance their job market credentials.*

- describe an effect and trace it back to its causes: *There has been a recent surge in the hiring of part-time contract workers, likely due to the reluctance of businesses to hire permanent employees who would be subject to new health care regulations.*

- trace a string of causes to figure out why something happened: *The housing and financial markets collapsed in 2008 after government mandates to encourage home-ownership led banks to invent questionable financial schemes in order to offer sub-prime mortgages to borrowers who bought homes they could not afford with loans they could not pay back.*

- explore plausible consequences (intended or not) of a particular action, policy, or change: *The ban on incandescent lightbulbs may draw more attention to climate change than any previous government action.*

Spend time brainstorming possibilities for causal arguments. Many public issues lend themselves to causal analysis and argument: browse the homepage of a newspaper or news source on any given day to discover plausible topics. Consider topics that grow from your own experiences.

It's fair game, too, to question the accuracy or adequacy of existing arguments about causality. You can write a strong paper by raising doubts about the facts or assumptions that others have made and perhaps offering a better causal explanation on your own.

Researching Your Topic

Causal arguments will lead you to many different resources:

- current news media — especially magazines and newspapers (online or in print)

- online databases

- scholarly journals

- books written on your subject (here you can do a keyword search, either in your library or online)

- blogs, Web sites, or social networking sites

In addition, why not carry out some field research? Conduct interviews with appropriate authorities on your subject, create a questionnaire aimed at establishing a range of opinions on your subject, or arrange a discussion forum among people with a stake in the issue. The information you get from interviews, questionnaires, or open-ended dialogue might provide ideas to enrich your argument or evidence to back up your claims.

Formulating a Claim

For a conventional causal analysis, try to formulate a claim that lets readers know where you stand on some issue involving causes and effects. First, identify the kind of causal argument that you expect to make (see pp. 375–379 for a review of these kinds of arguments) or decide whether you intend, instead, to debunk an existing cause-and-effect claim. Then explore your relationship to the claim. What do you know about the subject and its causes and effects? Why do you favor (or disagree with) the claim? What significant reasons can you offer in support of your position?

End this process by formulating a thesis—a complete sentence that says, in effect, *A causes (or does not cause or is caused by) B*, followed by a summary of the reasons supporting this causal relationship. Make your thesis as specific as possible and be sure that it's sufficiently controversial or intriguing to hold a reader's interest. Of course, feel free to revise any such claim as you learn more about a subject.

For causal topics that are more open-ended and exploratory, you may not want to take a strong position, particularly at the outset. Instead, your argument might simply present a variety of reasonable (and possibly competing) explanations and scenarios.

Examples of Causal Claims

- Right-to-carry gun laws have led to increased rates of crime in states that have approved such legislation.

- Sophisticated use of social media is now a must for any political candidate who hopes to win.

- Grade inflation is lowering the value of a college education.

- The proliferation of images in film, television, and computer-generated texts is changing the way we read and use information.

- Experts don't yet agree on the long-term impact that sophisticated use of social media will have on American political campaigns, though some effects are already evident.

Preparing a Proposal

If your instructor asks you to prepare a proposal for your project, here's a format that may help:

State your thesis completely. If you're having trouble doing so, try outlining it in Toulmin terms:

Claim:

Reason(s):

Warrant(s):

Alternatively, you might indicate an intention to explore a particular causal question in your project, with the thesis perhaps coming later.

- Explain why this issue deserves attention. What's at stake?

- Identify whom you hope to reach through your argument and why this group of readers would be interested in it.

- Briefly discuss the key challenges you anticipate in preparing your argument.

- Determine what research strategies you'll use. What sources do you expect to consult?

- Briefly identify and explore the major stakeholders in your argument and what alternative perspectives you may need to consider as you formulate your argument.

Considering Format and Media

Your instructor may specify that you use a particular format and/or medium. If not, ask yourself these questions to help you make a good choice:

- What format is most appropriate for your causal argument? Does it call for an academic essay, a report, an infographic, a brochure, or something else?

- What medium is most appropriate for your argument? Would it be best delivered orally to a live audience? Presented as an audio essay or podcast? Presented in print only or in print with illustrations?

- Will you need visuals, such as moving or still images, maps, graphs, charts—and what function will they play in your argument? Make sure they are not just "added on" but are necessary components of the argument.

Thinking about Organization

Your causal argument will likely include elements such as the following:

- a specific causal claim somewhere in the paper — or the identification of a significant causal issue

- an explanation of the claim's significance or importance

- evidence sufficient to support each cause or effect — or, in an argument based on a series of causal links, evidence to support the relationships among the links

- a consideration of other plausible causes and effects, and evidence that you have thought carefully about these alternatives before offering your own ideas

Getting and Giving Response: Questions for Peer Response

Your instructor may assign you to a group for the purpose of reading and responding to each other's drafts. If not, ask for responses from serious readers or consultants at a writing center. Use the following questions to evaluate a colleague's draft. Be sure to illustrate your comments with examples; specific comments help more than general observations.

The Claim

- Does the claim state a causal argument?

- Does the claim identify clearly what causes and effects are being examined?

- What about the claim will make it appeal to readers?

- Is the claim too sweeping? Does it need to be qualified? How might it be narrowed and focused?

- How strong is the relationship between the claim and the reasons given to support it? How could that relationship be made more explicit?

Evidence for the Claim

- What's the strongest evidence offered for the claim? What, if any, evidence needs to be strengthened?

- Is enough evidence offered to show that these causes are responsible for the identified effect, that these effects result from the identified cause, or that a series of causes and effects are linked? If not, what additional evidence is needed? What kinds of sources might provide this evidence?

- How credible will the sources be to potential readers? What other sources might be more persuasive?

- Is evidence in support of the claim analyzed logically? Is more discussion needed?

- Have alternative causes and effects been considered? Have objections to the claim been carefully considered and presented fairly? Have these objections been discussed?

Organization and Style

- How are the parts of the argument organized? Is this organization effective?

- Will readers understand the relationships among the claims, supporting reasons, warrants, and evidence? If not, how might those connections be clearer? Is the function of every visual clear? Are more transitions needed? Would headings or graphic devices help?

- Are the transitions or links from point to point, sentence to sentence, and paragraph to paragraph clear and effective? If not, how could they be improved?

- Are all visuals (or other elements such as audio or video clips) carefully integrated into the text? Is each visual introduced and commented on to point out its significance? Is each visual labeled as a figure or a table and given a caption as well as a citation?

- Is the style suited to the subject? Is it too formal, casual, or technical? Can it be improved?

- Which sentences seem effective? Which ones seem weaker, and how could they be improved? Should short sentences be combined, and any longer ones be broken up?

- How effective are the paragraphs? Too short or too long? How can they be improved?

- Which words or phrases seem effective? Do any seem vague or inappropriate for the audience or the writer's purpose? Are technical or unfamiliar terms defined?

Spelling, Punctuation, Mechanics, Documentation, and Format

- Are there any errors in spelling, punctuation, capitalization, and the like?

- Is the documentation appropriate and consistent? (See Chapter 30.)

- Does the paper or project follow an appropriate format? Is it appropriately designed and attractively presented?

PROJECTS

1. Develop an argument exploring one of the cause-and-effect topics mentioned in this chapter. Just a few of those topics are listed below:

    Disappearance of honeybees in the United States

    Causes of long-term unemployment or declining job markets

    Using the tax code to discourage/encourage specific behaviors (i.e., smoking, eating unhealthy foods, hiring more workers)

    Increasing numbers of obese children and/or adults

    Ramifications of increasing amounts of time spent on social media sites

    Results of failing to pass immigration reform legislation

    Repercussions of U.S. ethanol policy

    What is lost/gained as paper books disappear

2. Write a causal argument about a subject you know well, even if the topic does not strike you as particularly "academic": *What accounts for the popularity of The Hunger Games trilogy? What are the likely consequences of students living more of their lives via social media? How are video games changing the way students you know learn? Why do women love shoes?* In this argument, be sure to separate precipitating or proximate causes from sufficient or necessary ones. In other words, do a deep and revealing causal analysis about your subject, giving readers new insights.

3. John Tierney's essay "Can a Playground Be Too Safe?" (see p. 399) explores some unintended consequences of noble-minded efforts in recent decades to make children's playgrounds safer. After reading the Tierney piece, list any comparable situations you know of where unintended consequences may have undermined the good (or maybe even bad?) intentions of those who took action or implemented some change. Choose the most intriguing situation, do the necessary research, and write a causal argument about it.

4. Raven Jiang's "Dota 2: The Face of Professional Gaming" (see p. 396) argues that crowdfunding and netstreaming are two major causes in the rise of big-money professional gaming, which he sees as a phenomenon that is here to stay ("Watch out NFL, America's sport is about to change"). In a project of your own, describe the causes that have led to a particular effect on your campus or in your community or place of work. You may point out, as Jiang does, both advantages and disadvantages of the change brought about by the causes you analyze.

Two Sample Causal Arguments

Dota 2: The Face of Professional Gaming

RAVEN JIANG

August 5, 2014

The introductory paragraph presents the "effect": a huge rise in professional online gaming.

Just over a week ago, history was made when a team of five young Chinese men left Seattle with $5 million in winnings. The game they were playing was not poker but "Dota 2," a multiplayer online game made by the Bellevue-based gaming company Valve. This year's annual "Dota 2" Internationals tournament, the fourth one since its creation, presented the largest prize pool ever seen in professional gaming — a total of $10.9 million. ESPN covered the matches and it seemed like every media outlet was trying to get in on the story, if only as a human interest piece. There is a sense that we are entering new uncharted territories.

A causal claim is stated.

Since the early 2000s, much has been written and said about the slow but steady rise of professional video gaming. What happened this month at Seattle is a coming-of-age story that we are all familiar with, but it is also so much more. A confluence of factors had brought the 2014 "Dota 2" Internationals into the mainstream consciousness and they represent an interesting microcosm of the technological forces that are shaping our future, gaming and otherwise.

The first cause is introduced: crowdfunding.

Kickstarter brought the idea of crowdfunding into our daily lives, but Valve made it addictive with "Dota 2." Unlike past video gaming tournaments that relied solely on sponsorships for prize money, which were often the first thing on the chopping boards when it came to corporate budget cuts, the Internationals were almost entirely crowdfunded via in-game item purchases by online players.

The benefits of crowdfunding are stated.

In the weeks leading up to the event, fans could purchase tournament-related in-game items to contribute to the prize pool and to eventually earn vanity visual effects that they could show off in-game on their characters. And just like a Kickstarter campaign, there was a counter tracking the amount raised, with final rewards that fans earn determined by the final total — think Kickstarter fundraising goals. For example, the reward for hitting $3.5 million this time was access to special chat emoticons. In this way, much

Raven Jiang is an undergraduate at Stanford University, studying computer science. His piece was first published in the Stanford Daily, a student-produced newspaper founded in 1892.

like purchasing swag at an indie concert, fans not only contribute to the prize pool but feel like they get something back in return.

So, fans pay both to support the goal of having a more exciting tournament with bigger stakes and to gain personal items; Valve takes a cut as profits and professional Dota players get to make a career out of their passion. As Michael Scott once said, this is a win-win-win outcome. The final prize pool of $10.9 million was more than three times that of last year. To put that into perspective, the second placing team this year won more money than last year's winning team. That's a growth rate that would make Bernie Madoff jealous.

The author points out benefits to the winners as well as the viewers.

The successful use of crowdfunding by Valve is a great example of the value of crowdfunding as a whole. The reason why corporate sponsorships have historically been unreliable is because they are a poor indirect proxy for consumer demand. Much like the homemade gadgets that find their audience on Kickstarter, Valve is tapping into an underserved demand by getting the consumers to directly pay for the cost of production.

The other major force behind the modern "Dota 2" juggernaut is live game streaming. YouTube brought us video sharing and Netflix brought us the Internet's take on cable TV, but online gaming is helping to turn a very different form of visual entertainment into its own industry. Just like the Super Bowl, we now have the huge events that draw millions of viewers in the likes of the Internationals. But beyond that familiar format, there is also a burgeoning cottage industry of individual gamers who stream their gaming sessions live online and make money off of advertising and product placements. A popular full-time game streamer can take home a six-digit income doing what his parents say will never amount to much, probably right in their basement.

The second major cause is presented to support the claim.

The prevalence of game streaming has created the interesting situation in which many fans of popular online games seldom ever actually feel the need to play them, because watching is so much less stressful, less time-consuming, and more readily accessible. In some sense, "Dota 2," a game notorious for its complex game mechanics, can probably thank the rise of stream watching for the success of its annual championship events, because let's face it: If every sports fan had to be able to play the game in order to understand and enjoy watching it, then college football would be bankrupt. With the professionalization of online gaming that parallels the paths taken by its traditional counterparts, it is no wonder

Google recently decided to fork out a cool billion dollars to acquire the major game streaming site Twitch.tv.

The point is that online gaming is going to be a big deal. And it is a big deal not just because video gaming is becoming big money, but because its rise is symbolic of the same technological shifts that are changing all other aspects of our lives.

The future is already here in South Korea, where professional "Starcraft" gamers are literally national celebrities. Significant milestones like the recent "Dota 2" Internationals suggest that the U.S. is on its way there. Watching the live stream of the Internationals with its extremely professional production value, the seasoned commentators throwing team and player stats at each other and the incredible amount of skill and concentration exhibited by the competitors, an alien visitor from Alpha Centauri would be hard-pressed to say what exactly differentiates "Dota 2" from sports. (I suppose there has not been any accusation of steroid abuse. Yet.)

That said, it is not all rainbows and unicorns. There is a general feeling that this year's matches at the Internationals have not been as exciting and eventful as last year's. Perhaps the unprecedented prize pool this year was causing players to be more risk-averse, leading to fewer clutch plays and comebacks from behind. Both of the teams in the final were also Chinese, who are known for being more methodological both in play style and training processes. The old fan favorite Na'Vi, the Eastern European past championship winners known for their dramatic comebacks and eccentric play styles, did not manage to get into the final four this year. Still, even if "Dota 2" does falter, it has already pushed the boundaries for professional gaming and paved the way for the future.

Watch out NFL, America's sport is about to change.

The author gives proof that online video gaming is already big time in South Korea and the United States.

The downsides of the dramatic rise in online gaming are presented.

The concluding sentence assures readers that even if Dota 2 itself fails, what it represents has already had a major impact on the future of gaming.

Can a Playground Be Too Safe?

JOHN TIERNEY

FIGURE 19.6 A childhood relic: jungle gyms, like this one in Riverside Park in Manhattan, have disappeared from most American playgrounds in recent decades. © Dith Pran/The New York Times/Redux

When seesaws and tall slides and other perils were disappearing from New York's playgrounds, Henry Stern drew a line in the sandbox. As the city's parks commissioner in the 1990s, he issued an edict concerning the ten-foot-high jungle gym near his childhood home in northern Manhattan.

"I grew up on the monkey bars in Fort Tryon Park, and I never forgot how good it felt to get to the top of them," Mr. Stern said. "I didn't want to see that playground bowdlerized. I said that as long as I was parks commissioner, those monkey bars were going to stay."

His philosophy seemed reactionary at the time, but today it's shared by some researchers who question the value of safety-first playgrounds. Even if children do suffer fewer physical injuries — and the evidence for that is debatable — the

John Tierney is a journalist and coauthor of the book *Willpower: Rediscovering the Greatest Human Strength* (2011). He writes the science column "Findings" for the *New York Times*, where this piece was originally published on July 18, 2011. You will note that, as a journalist, Tierney cites sources without documenting them formally. An academic version of this argument might offer both in-text citations and a list of sources at the end.

critics say that these playgrounds may stunt emotional development, leaving children with anxieties and fears that are ultimately worse than a broken bone.

"Children need to encounter risks and overcome fears on the playground," said Ellen Sandseter, a professor of psychology at Queen Maud University in Norway. "I think monkey bars and tall slides are great. As playgrounds become more and more boring, these are some of the few features that still can give children thrilling experiences with heights and high speed."

After observing children on playgrounds in Norway, England, and Australia, Dr. Sandseter identified six categories of risky play: exploring heights, experiencing high speed, handling dangerous tools, being near dangerous elements (like water or fire), rough-and-tumble play (like wrestling), and wandering alone away from adult supervision. The most common is climbing heights.

"Climbing equipment needs to be high enough, or else it will be too boring in the long run," Dr. Sandseter said. "Children approach thrills and risks in a progressive manner, and very few children would try to climb to the highest point for the first time they climb. The best thing is to let children encounter these challenges from an early age, and they will then progressively learn to master them through their play over the years."

Sometimes, of course, their mastery fails, and falls are the common form of playground injury. But these rarely cause permanent damage, either physically or emotionally. While some psychologists — and many parents — have worried that a child who suffered a bad fall would develop a fear of heights, studies have shown the opposite pattern: A child who's hurt in a fall before the age of nine is less likely as a teenager to have a fear of heights.

By gradually exposing themselves to more and more dangers on the playground, children are using the same habituation techniques developed by therapists to help adults conquer phobias, according to Dr. Sandseter and a fellow psychologist, Leif Kennair, of the Norwegian University for Science and Technology.

"Risky play mirrors effective cognitive behavioral therapy of anxiety," they write in the journal *Evolutionary Psychology*, concluding that this "anti-phobic effect" helps explain the evolution of children's fondness for thrill-seeking. While a youthful zest for exploring heights might not seem adaptive — why would natural selection favor children who risk death before they have a chance to reproduce? — the dangers seemed to be outweighed by the benefits of conquering fear and developing a sense of mastery.

"Paradoxically," the psychologists write, "we posit that our fear of children being harmed by mostly harmless injuries may result in more fearful children and increased levels of psychopathology."

The old tall jungle gyms and slides disappeared from most American playgrounds across the country in recent decades because of parental concerns, federal guidelines, new safety standards set by manufacturers and—the most frequently cited factor—fear of lawsuits.

Shorter equipment with enclosed platforms was introduced, and the old pavement was replaced with rubber, wood chips, or other materials designed for softer landings. These innovations undoubtedly prevented some injuries, but some experts question their overall value.

"There is no clear evidence that playground safety measures have lowered the average risk on playgrounds," said David Ball, a professor of risk management at Middlesex University in London. He noted that the risk of some injuries, like long fractures of the arm, actually increased after the introduction of softer surfaces on playgrounds in Britain and Australia.

"This sounds counterintuitive, but it shouldn't, because it is a common phenomenon," Dr. Ball said. "If children and parents believe they are in an environment which is safer than it actually is, they will take more risks. An argument against softer surfacing is that children think it is safe, but because they don't understand its properties, they overrate its performance."

Reducing the height of playground equipment may help toddlers, but it can produce unintended consequences among bigger children. "Older children are discouraged from taking healthy exercise on playgrounds because they have been designed with the safety of the very young in mind," Dr. Ball said. "Therefore, they may play in more dangerous places, or not at all."

Fear of litigation led New York City officials to remove seesaws, merry-go-rounds, and the ropes that young Tarzans used to swing from one platform to another. Letting children swing on tires became taboo because of fears that the heavy swings could bang into a child.

"What happens in America is defined by tort lawyers, and unfortunately that limits some of the adventure playgrounds," said Adrian Benepe, the current parks commissioner. But while he misses the Tarzan ropes, he's glad that the litigation rate has declined, and he's not nostalgic for asphalt pavement.

"I think safety surfaces are a godsend," he said. "I suspect that parents who have to deal with concussions and broken arms wouldn't agree that playgrounds have become too safe." The ultra-safe enclosed platforms of the 1980s and 1990s may have been an overreaction, Mr. Benepe said, but lately there have been more creative alternatives.

"The good news is that manufacturers have brought out new versions of the old toys," he said. "Because of height limitations, no one's building the old monkey bars anymore, but kids can go up smaller climbing walls and rope nets and artificial rocks."

Still, sometimes there's nothing quite like being ten feet off the ground, as a new generation was discovering the other afternoon at Fort Tryon Park. A soft rubber surface carpeted the pavement, but the jungle gym of Mr. Stern's youth was still there. It was the prime destination for many children, including those who'd never seen one before, like Nayelis Serrano, a ten-year-old from the South Bronx who was visiting her cousin.

When she got halfway up, at the third level of bars, she paused, as if that was high enough. Then, after a consultation with her mother, she continued to the top, the fifth level, and descended to recount her triumph.

"I was scared at first," she explained. "But my mother said if you don't try, you'll never know if you could do it. So I took a chance and kept going. At the top I felt very proud." As she headed back for another climb, her mother, Orkidia Rojas, looked on from a bench and considered the pros and cons of this unfamiliar equipment.

"It's fun," she said. "I'd like to see it in our playground. Why not? It's kind of dangerous, I know, but if you just think about danger you're never going to get ahead in life."

CHAPTER

20

Proposals

A student looking forward to spring break proposes to two friends that they join a group that will spend the vacation helping to build a school in a Haitian village.

The members of a club for undergrad business majors talk about their common need to create informative, appealing, interactive résumés. After much talk, three members suggest that the club develop a résumé app especially for business majors looking for a first job.

A project team at a large architectural firm works for three months developing a response to an RFP (request for proposal) to convert a university library into a digital learning center.

Left to right: © Florian Kopp/agefotostock.com; spaxiax/Shutterstock; AP Photo/Eric Gay

Understanding and Categorizing Proposals

We live in an era of big proposals—complex programs for health care reform, bold dreams to privatize space exploration, multibillion-dollar designs for high-speed rail systems, ceaseless calls to improve education, and so many other such ideas brought down to earth by sobering proposals for budget reform and deficit reduction. As a result, there's often more talk than action because persuading people (or legislatures) to do something—or *anything!*—is always hard. But that's what *proposal arguments* do: they provide thoughtful reasons for supporting or sometimes resisting change.

Such arguments, whether national or local, formal or casual, are important not only on the national scene but also in all of our lives. How many proposals do you make or respond to in one day? A neighbor might suggest that you volunteer to help clean up an urban creek bed; a campus group might demand that students get better seats at football games; a supervisor might ask for ideas to improve customer satisfaction at a restaurant; you might offer an ad agency reasons to hire you as a summer intern—or propose to a friend that you take in the latest zombie film. In each case, the proposal implies that some action should take place and suggests that there are sound reasons why it should.

FIGURE 20.1 This cartoon, by Steve Breen, suggests that high-speed rail proposals are going to run into a major obstacle in California.

By permission of Steve Breen and Creators Syndicate, Inc.

In their simplest form, proposal arguments look something like this:

A should do B because of C.

```
├─────────── A ───────────┤ ├───────────── B ─────────────┤
Our student government should endorse the Academic Bill of Rights
├───────────────────────── C ─────────────────────────────┤
```
because students should not be punished in their courses for their personal political views.

Proposals come at us so routinely that it's not surprising that they cover a dizzyingly wide range of possibilities. So it may help to think of proposal arguments as divided roughly into two kinds—those that focus on specific practices and those that focus on broad matters of policy. Here are several examples of each kind:

Proposals about Practices

- The college should allow students to pay tuition on a month-by-month basis.

- Commercial hotels should stop opposing competitors like Airbnb.

- College athletes should be paid for the services they provide.

Proposals about Policies

- The college should adopt a policy guaranteeing that students in all majors can graduate in four years.

- The United Nations should make saving the oceans from pollution a global priority.

- Major Silicon Valley firms should routinely reveal the demographic makeup of their workforces.

RESPOND

People write proposal arguments to solve problems and to change the way things are. But problems aren't always obvious: what troubles some people might be no big deal to others. To get an idea of the range of problems people face on your campus (some of which you may not even have thought of as problems), divide into groups, and brainstorm about things that annoy you on and around campus, including wastefulness in the cafeterias, 8:00 a.m. classes, and long lines for football or concert tickets. Ask each group to aim for at least a dozen gripes. Then choose three problems, and as a group, discuss how you'd prepare a proposal to deal with them.

Characterizing Proposals

Proposals have three main characteristics:

1. They call for change, often in response to a problem.

2. They focus on the future.

3. They center on the audience.

Proposals always call for some kind of action. They aim at getting something done—or sometimes at *preventing* something from being done. Proposals marshal evidence and arguments to persuade people to choose a course of action: *Let's build a completely green house. Let's oppose the latest Supreme Court ruling on Internet privacy. Let's create a campus organization for first-generation college students. Let's ban drones from campus airspace, especially at sporting events.* But you know the old saying, "You can lead a horse to water, but you can't make it drink." It's usually easier to *convince* audiences what a good course of action is than to *persuade* them to take it (or pay for it). Even if you present a cogent proposal, you may still have work to do.

Proposal arguments must appeal to more than good sense. Ethos matters, too. It helps if a writer suggesting a change carries a certain gravitas earned by experience or supported by knowledge and research. If your word and credentials carry weight, then an audience is more likely to listen to your proposal. So when the commanders of three *Apollo* moon missions, Neil Armstrong, James Lovell, and Eugene Cernan, wrote an open letter to President Obama expressing their dismay at his administration's decision to cancel NASA's plans for advanced spacecraft and new lunar missions, they won a wide audience:

> For The United States, the leading space faring nation for nearly half a century, to be without carriage to low Earth orbit and with no human exploration capability to go beyond Earth orbit for an indeterminate time into the future, destines our nation to become one of second or even third rate stature. While the President's plan envisages humans traveling away from Earth and perhaps toward Mars at some time in the future, the lack of developed rockets and spacecraft will assure that ability will not be available for many years.

> Without the skill and experience that actual spacecraft operation provides, the USA is far too likely to be on a long downhill slide to mediocrity. America must decide if it wishes to remain a leader in space. If it does, we should institute a program which will give us the very best chance of achieving that goal.

But even their considerable ethos was not enough to carry the day with the space agency and the man who made the decision.

FIGURE 20.2 All that remains of the American space program?

Michael Williamson/The Washington Post/Getty Images

Yet, as the space program example obviously demonstrates, proposal arguments focus on the future—what people, institutions, or governments should do over the upcoming weeks, months, or, in the NASA moon-mission example, decades. This orientation toward the future presents special challenges, since few of us have crystal balls. Proposal arguments must therefore offer the best evidence available to suggest that actions we recommend will achieve what they promise.

In May 2014, Senator Elizabeth Warren introduced legislation aimed at reducing student loan debt, in part by allowing for refinancing. In an interview in *Rolling Stone*, Senator Warren explained:

> Homeowners refinance their loans when interest rates go down. Businesses refinance their loans. But right now, there's no way for students to be able to do that. I've proposed that we reduce the interest rate on the outstanding loan debt to the same rate Republicans and Democrats came together last year to set on new loans [3.86 percent]. For millions of borrowers, that would cut interest rates in half or more.

Yet Warren's proposal soon came under fire, particularly from senators who argued that the proposed bill did little to reduce borrowing or lower the cost of higher education. So despite the concerns of bankers and economists that the $1.1 trillion student loan debt is dampening the national economy, the bill was turned aside on June 11, 2014.

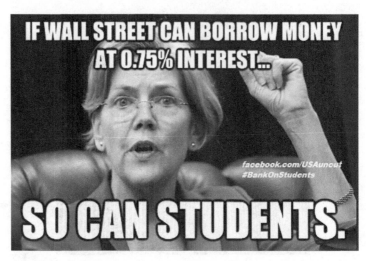

FIGURE 20.3 http://www.ClassWarfareExists.com

Which raises the matter of audiences, and we are left asking whether Senator Warren's bill spoke equally well to students, parents, bankers, and members of Congress. Some of those audiences failed to be convinced.

Some proposals are tailored to general audiences; consequently, they avoid technical language, make straightforward and relatively simple points, and sometimes use charts, graphs, and tables to make data comprehensible. You can find such arguments, for example, in newspaper editorials, letters to the editor, and political documents like Senator Warren's proposed legislation. And such appeals to a broad group make sense when a proposal—say, to finance new toll roads or build an art museum—must surf on waves of community support and financing.

But often proposals need to win the approval of specific groups or individuals (such as financiers, developers, public officials, and legislators) who have the power to make change actually happen. Such arguments will usually be more technical, detailed, and comprehensive than those aimed at the general public because people directly involved with an issue have a stake in it. They may be affected by it themselves and thus have in-depth knowledge of the subject. Or they may be responsible for implementing the proposal. You can expect them to have specific questions about it and, possibly, formidable objections. So identifying your potential audiences is critical to the success of any proposal. On your own campus, for example, a plan to alter admissions policies might be directed both to students in general and (perhaps in a different form) to the university president, members of the faculty council, and admissions officers.

FIGURE 20.4 Proposals have to take audience values into account. Shooting deer, even when they're munching on garden flowers, is unacceptable to most suburbanites. Ron Sanford/Science Source®/Photo Researchers

An effective proposal also has to be compatible with the values of the audience. Some ideas may make good sense but cannot be enacted. For example, many American towns and cities have a problem with expanding deer populations. Without natural predators, the deer are moving closer to homes, dining on gardens and shrubbery, and endangering traffic. Yet one obvious and feasible solution—culling the herds through hunting—is usually not saleable to communities (perhaps too many people remember *Bambi*).

RESPOND

Work in a group to identify about half a dozen problems on your campus or in the local community, looking for a wide range of issues. (Don't focus on problems in individual classes.) Once you have settled on these issues, then use various resources—the Web, the phone book (if you can find one), a campus directory—to locate specific people, groups, or offices whom you might address or influence to deal with the issues you have identified.

Developing Proposals

In developing a proposal, you will have to do some or all of the following:

- Define a problem that needs a solution or describe a need that is not currently addressed.
- Make a strong claim that addresses the problem or need. Your solution should be an action directed at the future.
- Show why your proposal will fix the problem or address the need.
- Demonstrate that your proposal is feasible.

This might sound easy, but writing a proposal argument can be a process of discovery. At the outset, you think you know exactly what ought to be done, but by the end, you may see (and even recommend) other options.

Defining a Need or Problem

To make a proposal, first establish that a need or problem exists. You'll typically dramatize the problem that you intend to fix at the beginning of your project and then lead up to a specific claim. But in some cases, you could put the need or problem right after your claim as the major reason for adopting the proposal:

> Let's ban cell phones on campus now. Why? Because we've become a school of walking zombies. No one speaks to or even acknowledges the people they meet or pass on campus. Half of our students are so busy chattering to people that they don't participate in the community around them.

How can you make readers care about the problem you hope to address? Following are some strategies:

- Paint a vivid picture of the need or problem.
- Show how the need or problem affects people, both those in the immediate audience and the general public as well.
- Underscore why the need or problem is significant and pressing.
- Explain why previous attempts to address the issue may have failed.

For example, in proposing that the military draft be restored in the United States or that all young men and women give two years to national service (a tough sell!), you might begin by drawing a picture of a younger generation that is self-absorbed, demands instant gratification, and doesn't understand what it means to participate as a full member of society. Or you might note how many young people today fail to develop the life skills they need to strike out on their own. Or like congressional representative Charles Rangel (D-New York), who regularly proposes a Universal National Service Act, you could define the issue as a matter of fairness, arguing that the current all-volunteer army shifts the burden of national service to a small and unrepresentative sample of the American population. Speaking on CNN on January 26, 2013, Rangel said:

> Since we replaced the compulsory military draft with an all-volunteer force in 1973, our nation has been making decisions about wars without worry over who fights them. I sincerely believe that reinstating the draft would compel the American public to have a stake in the wars we fight as a nation. That is why I wrote the Universal National Service Act, known as the "draft" bill, which requires all men and women between ages 18 and 25 to give two years of service in any capacity that promotes our national defense.

Of course, you would want to cite authorities and statistics to prove that any problem you're diagnosing is real and that it touches your likely audience. Then readers *may* be ready to hear your proposal.

In describing a problem that your proposal argument intends to solve, be sure to review earlier attempts to fix it. Many issues have a long history that you can't afford to ignore (or be ignorant of). Understand too that some problems seem to grow worse every time someone tinkers with them. You might pause before proposing any new attempt to reform the current system of financing federal election campaigns when you discover that previous reforms have resulted in more bureaucracy, more restrictions on political expression, and more unregulated money flowing into the system. *"Enough is enough"* can be a potent argument when faced with such a mess.

FIGURE 20.5 File this cartoon under "anticipate objections to your proposal."
© Mike Keefe/Cagle Cartoons, Inc.

RESPOND

If you review "Let's Charge Politicians for Wasting Our Time" at the end of this chapter, a brief proposal by political and culture writer/blogger Virginia Postrel, you'll see that she spends quite a bit of time pointing out the irritation caused by unwanted political robocalls to her landline, even though she recognizes that such calls are illegal on cell phones. Does this focus on the landline take away from her proposal that the politicians should have to pay a fee for such calls as well as for unsolicited email messages they send, a proposal also put forward by technology guru Esther Dyson? Would you advise her to revise her argument—and if so, how?

Making a Strong and Clear Claim

After you've described and analyzed a problem, you're prepared to offer a fix. Begin with your claim (a proposal of what X or Y should do), followed by the reason(s) that X or Y should act and the effects of adopting the proposal:

Claim	Communities should encourage the development of charter schools.
Reason	Charter schools are not burdened by the bureaucracy that is associated with most public schooling.
Effects	Instituting such schools will bring more effective education to communities and offer an incentive to the public schools to improve their programs.

Having established a claim, you can explore its implications by drawing out the reasons, warrants, and evidence that can support it most effectively:

Claim	In light of a recent U.S. Supreme Court decision that ruled that federal drug laws cannot be used to prosecute doctors who prescribe drugs for use in suicide, our state should immediately pass a bill legalizing physician-assisted suicide for patients who are terminally ill.
Reason	Physician-assisted suicide can relieve the suffering of those who are terminally ill and will die soon.
Warrant	The relief of suffering is desirable.
Evidence	Oregon voters have twice approved the state's Death with Dignity Act, which has been in effect since 1997, and to date the suicide rate has not risen sharply, nor have doctors given out a large number of prescriptions for death-inducing drugs. Several other states are considering ballot initiatives in favor of doctor-assisted suicide.

The *reason* sets up the need for the proposal, whereas the *warrant* and *evidence* demonstrate that the proposal is just and could meet its objective. Your actual argument would develop each point in detail.

RESPOND

For each problem and solution below, make a list of readers' likely objections to the solution offered. Then propose a solution of your own, and explain why you think it's more workable than the original.

Problem	Future deficits in the Social Security system
Solution	Raise the age of retirement to seventy-two.

Problem	Severe grade inflation in college courses
Solution	Require a prescribed distribution of grades in every class: 10% A; 20% B; 40% C; 20% D; 10% F.

Problem	Increasing rates of obesity in the general population
Solution	Ban the sale of high-fat sandwiches and entrees in fast-food restaurants.

Problem	Inattentive driving because drivers are texting
Solution	Institute a one-year mandatory prison sentence for the first offense.

Problem	Increase in sexual assaults on and around campus
Solution	Establish a 10:00 p.m. curfew on weekends.

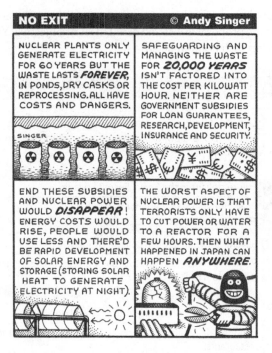

FIGURE 20.6 A proposal argument in four panels. You might compare this argument with Taylor Pearson's "Why You Should Fear Your Toaster More Than Nuclear Power" in **Chapter 16**. © Andy Singer/Cagle Cartoons, Inc.

Showing That the Proposal Addresses the Need or Problem

An important but tricky part of making a successful proposal lies in relating the claim to the need or problem that it addresses. Facts and probability are your best allies. Take the time to show precisely how your solution will fix a problem or at least improve upon the current situation. Sometimes an emotional appeal is fair play, too. Here's former NBA player John Amaechi using that approach when he asks super-star Kobe Bryant of the L.A. Lakers not to appeal a $100,000 penalty he received for hurling an antigay slur at a referee:

> Kobe, stop fighting the fine. You spoke ill-advised words that shot out like bullets, and if the emails I received from straight and gay young people and sports fans in Los Angeles alone are anything to go by, you did serious damage with your outburst.

FIGURE 20.7 Left: John Amaechi; right: Kobe Bryant.
Left: Chris Goodney/Bloomberg News/Getty Images; right: © Lucy Nicholson/Reuters/LANDOV

A young man from a Los Angeles public school emailed me. You are his idol. He is playing up, on the varsity team, he has your posters all over his room, and he hopes one day to play in college and then in the NBA with you. He used to fall asleep with images of passing you the ball to sink a game-winning shot. He watched every game you played this season on television, but this week he feels less safe and less positive about himself because he stared adoringly into your face as you said the word that haunts him in school every single day.

Kobe, stop fighting the fine. Use that money and your influence to set a new tone that tells sports fans, boys, men, and the society that looks up to you that the word you said in anger is not OK, not ever. Too many athletes take the trappings of their hard-earned success and leave no tangible legacy apart from "that shot" or "that special game."

—John Amaechi, "A Gay Former NBA Player Responds to Kobe Bryant"

The paragraph describing the reaction of the schoolboy provides just the tie that Amaechi needs between his proposal and the problem it would address. The story also gives his argument more power.

Alternatively, if you oppose an idea, these strategies work just as well in reverse: if a proposal doesn't fix a problem, you have to show exactly why. Here are a few paragraphs from an editorial posting by Doug Bandow for *Forbes* in which he refutes a proposal for reinstating military conscription:

All told, shifting to conscription would significantly weaken the military. New "accessions," as the military calls them, would be less bright, less well educated, and less positively motivated. They would be less likely to stay in uniform, resulting in a less experienced force. The armed forces would be less effective in combat, thereby costing America more lives while achieving fewer foreign policy objectives.

Why take such a step?

One argument, most recently articulated by Thomas Ricks of the Center for a New American Security, is that a draft would save "the government money." That's a poor reason to impress people into service.

First, conscription doesn't save much cash. It costs money to manage and enforce a draft—history demonstrates that not every inductee would go quietly. Conscripts serve shorter terms and reenlist less frequently, increasing turnover, which is expensive. And unless the government instituted a Czarist lifetime draft, everyone beyond the first ranks would continue to expect to be paid.

Second, conscription shifts rather than reduces costs. Ricks suggested that draftees should "perform tasks currently outsourced at great cost to the Pentagon: paperwork, painting barracks, mowing lawns, driving generals around." Better to make people do grunt work than to pay them to do it? Force poorer young people into uniform in order to save richer old people tax dollars. Ricks believes that is a good reason to jail people for refusing to do as the government demands?

The government could save money in the same way by drafting FBI agents, postal workers, Medicare doctors, and congressmen. Nothing warrants letting old politicians force young adults to pay for Washington's profligacy. Moreover, by keeping some people who want to serve out while forcing others who don't want to serve in—creating a veritable evasion industry along the way—conscription would raise total social costs. It would be a bad bargain by any measure.

—Doug Bandow, "A New Military Draft Would Revive a Very Bad Old Idea"

Finally, if your own experience backs up your claim or demonstrates the need or problem that your proposal aims to address, then consider using it to develop your proposal (as John Amaechi does in addressing his proposal to Kobe Bryant). Consider the following questions in deciding when to include your own experiences in showing that a proposal is needed or will in fact do what it claims:

- Is your experience directly related to the need or problem that you seek to address or to your proposal about it?

- Will your experience be appropriate and speak convincingly to the audience? Will the audience immediately understand its significance, or will it require explanation?

- Does your personal experience fit logically with the other reasons that you're using to support your claim?

Be careful. If a proposal seems crafted to serve mainly your own interests, you won't get far.

Showing That the Proposal Is Feasible

To be effective, proposals must be *feasible*—that is, the action proposed can be carried out in a reasonable way. Demonstrating feasibility calls on you to present evidence—from similar cases, from personal experience, from observational data, from interview or survey data, from Internet research, or from any other sources—showing that what you propose can indeed be done with the resources available. "Resources available" is key: if the proposal calls for funds, personnel, or skills beyond reach or reason, your audience is unlikely to accept it. When that's the case, it's time to reassess your proposal, modify it, and test any new ideas against these revised criteria. This is also when you can reconsider proposals that others might suggest are better, more effective, or more workable than yours. There's no shame in admitting that you may have been wrong. When drafting a proposal, ask friends to think of counterproposals. If your own proposal can stand up to such challenges, it's likely a strong one.

Considering Design and Visuals

Because proposals often address specific audiences, they can take a number of forms—a letter, a memo, a Web page, a feasibility report, an infographic, a brochure, a prospectus, or even an editorial cartoon (see Andy Singer's "No Exit" item on p. 414). Each form has different design requirements. Indeed, the design may add powerfully to—or detract significantly from—the effectiveness of the proposal. Typically, though, proposals are heavy in photographs, tables, graphs, comparison charts, and maps, all designed to help readers understand the nature of a problem and how to solve it. Needless to say, any visual items should be handsomely presented: they contribute to your ethos.

Lengthy reports also usually need headings—or, in an oral report, slides—that clearly identify the various stages of the presentation. Those headings, which will vary, would include items such as Introduction, Nature of the Problem, Current Approaches or Previous Solutions, Proposal/Recommendations, Advantages, Counterarguments, Feasibility, Implementation, and so on. So before you produce a final copy of any proposal, be sure its design enhances its persuasiveness.

A related issue to consider is whether a graphic image might help readers understand key elements of the proposal—what the challenge is, why it demands action, and what exactly you're suggesting—and help make the idea more attractive. That strategy is routinely used in professional proposals by architects, engineers, and government agencies.

For example, the artist rendering below shows the Bionic Arch, a proposed skyscraper in Taiwan designed by architect Vincent Callebaut. As a proposal, this one stands out because it not only suggests an addition to the city skyline, but it also offers architectural innovations to make the structure more environmentally friendly. If you look closely, you'll notice that each floor of the building includes suspended "sky gardens" that, according to the proposal, will help solve the problem of city smog by siphoning away toxic fumes. According to Callebaut, "The skyscraper reduces our ecological footprint in the urban area. It respects the environment and gives a new symbiotic ecosystem for the biodiversity of Taiwan. The Bionic Arch is the new icon of sustainable development." Who wouldn't support a building that looked great *and* helped clean the air?

FIGURE 20.8 The Bionic Arch proposes to do more than add retail and office space. AP/Wide World Photos

GUIDE TO WRITING A PROPOSAL

Finding a Topic or Identifying a Problem

You're entering a proposal argument when you:

- make a claim that supports a change in practice: *Bottled water should carry a warning label describing the environmental impact of plastic.*

- make a claim that supports a change in policy: *Government workers, especially legislators and administrative officials, should never be exempt from laws or programs imposed on other citizens.*

- make a claim that resists suggested changes in practice or policy: *The surest way to guarantee that HOV lanes on freeways improve traffic flow is not to build any.*

- explore options for addressing existing issues or investigate opportunities for change: *Urban planners need to examine the long-term impact digital technologies may have on transportation, work habits, housing patterns, power usage, and entertainment opportunities in cities of the future.*

Since your everyday experience often calls on you to consider problems and to make proposals, begin your brainstorming for topics with practical topics related to your life, education, major, or job. Or make an informal list of proposals that you would like to explore in broader academic or cultural areas—problems you see in your field or in the society around you. Or do some freewriting on a subject of political concern, and see if it leads to a call for action.

Researching Your Topic

For many proposals, you can begin your research by consulting the following types of sources:

- newspapers, magazines, reviews, and journals (online and print)

- television or radio news reports

- online databases

- government documents and reports

- Web sites, blogs, social networking sites, listservs, or newsgroups

- books

- experts in the field, some of whom might be right on your campus

Consider doing some field research, if appropriate — a survey of student opinions on Internet accessibility, for example, or interviews with people who have experienced the problem you are trying to fix.

Finally, remember that your proposal's success can depend on the credibility of the sources you use to support it, so evaluate each source carefully (see Chapter 27).

Formulating a Claim

As you think about and explore your topic, begin formulating a claim about it. To do so, come up with a clear thesis that makes a proposal and states the reasons that this proposal should be adopted. To start formulating a claim, explore and respond to the following questions:

- What do I know about the proposal that I'm making?

- What reasons can I offer to support my proposal?

- What evidence do I have that implementing my proposal will lead to the results I want?

Rather than make a specific proposal, you may sometimes want to explore the range of possibilities for addressing a particular situation or circumstance. In that case, a set of open-ended questions might be a more productive starting point than a focused thesis, suggesting, for instance, what goals any plausible proposal might have to meet.

Examples of Proposal Claims

- Because lowering the amount of fuel required to be blended with ethanol would lower greenhouse gas emissions by millions of tons and decrease land use that is releasing unhealthy amounts of carbon into the atmosphere, the EPA proposal to reduce ethanol produced from corn should be adopted.

- Every home should be equipped with a well-stocked emergency kit that can sustain inhabitants for at least three days in a natural disaster.

- Congress should repeal the Copyright Extension Act, since it disrupts the balance between incentives for creators and the right of the public to information as set forth in the U.S. Constitution.

- To simplify the lives of consumers and eliminate redundant products, industries that manufacture rechargeable batteries should agree on a design for a universal power adapter.

- People from different economic classes, age groups, political philosophies, and power groups (government, Main Street, Wall Street) all have a stake in reforming current budget and tax policies. But how do we get them to speak and to listen to each other? That is the challenge we face if we hope to solve our national economic problems.

Preparing a Proposal

If your instructor asks you to prepare a proposal for your project, here's a format that may help:

> State the thesis of your proposal completely. If you're having trouble doing so, try outlining it in Toulmin terms:
>
> Claim:
>
> Reason(s):
>
> Warrant(s):
>
> Alternatively, you might describe your intention to explore a particular problem in your project, with the actual proposal (and thesis) coming later.

- Explain why this issue deserves attention. What's at stake?

- Identify and describe those readers whom you hope to reach with your proposal. Why is this group of readers appropriate? Can you identify individuals who can actually fix a problem?

- Briefly discuss the major difficulties that you foresee for your proposal. How will you demonstrate that the action you propose is necessary and workable? Persuade the audience to act? Pay for the proposal?

- Determine what research strategies you'll use. What sources do you expect to consult?

Considering Format and Media

Your instructor may specify that you use a particular format and/or medium. If not, ask yourself these questions to help you make a good choice:

- What format is most appropriate for your proposal? Does it call for an academic essay, a report, an infographic, a brochure, or something else?

- What medium is most appropriate for your argument? Would it be best delivered orally to a live audience? Presented as an audio essay or podcast? Presented in print only or in print with illustrations?

- Will you need visuals, such as moving or still images, maps, graphs, charts—and what function will they play in your argument? Make sure they are not just "added on" but are necessary components of the argument.

Thinking about Organization

Proposals can take many different forms but generally include the following elements:

- a description of the problem you intend to address or the state of affairs that leads you to propose the action

- a strong and specific proposal, identifying the key reasons for taking the proposed action and the effects that taking this action will have

- a clear connection between the proposal and a significant need or problem

- a demonstration of ways in which the proposal addresses the need

- evidence that the proposal will achieve the desired outcome

- a consideration of alternative ways to achieve the desired outcome and a discussion of why these may not be feasible

- a demonstration that the proposal is feasible and an explanation of how it may be implemented

Getting and Giving Response: Questions for Peer Response

Your instructor may assign you to a group for the purpose of reading and responding to each other's drafts. If not, ask for responses from serious readers or consultants at a writing center. Use the following questions to evaluate a colleague's draft. Since specific comments help more than general observations, be sure to illustrate your comments with examples. Some of the questions below assume a conventional, thesis-driven project, but more exploratory, open-ended proposal arguments also need to be clearly phrased, organized, and supported with evidence.

The Claim

- Does the claim clearly call for action? Is the proposal as clear and specific as possible? Is it realistic or possible to accomplish?

- Is the proposal too sweeping? Does it need to be qualified? If so, how?

- Does the proposal clearly address the problem that it intends to solve? If not, how could the connection be strengthened?

- Is the claim likely to get the audience to act rather than just to agree? If not, how could it be revised to do so?

Evidence for the Claim

- Is enough evidence furnished to get the audience to support the proposal? If not, what kind of additional evidence is needed? Does any of the evidence provided seem inappropriate or otherwise ineffective? Why?

- Is the evidence in support of the claim simply announced, or are its significance and appropriateness analyzed? Is a more detailed discussion needed?

- Are objections that readers might have to the claim or evidence adequately and fairly addressed?

- What kinds of sources are cited? How credible and persuasive will they be to readers? What other kinds of sources might work better?

- Are all quotations introduced with appropriate signal phrases (such as "As Tyson argues, …") and blended smoothly into the writer's sentences?

- Are all visual sources labeled, introduced, and commented upon?

Organization and Style

- How are the parts of the argument organized? Is this organization effective?

- Will readers understand the relationships among the claims, supporting reasons, warrants, and evidence? If not, how might those connections be clearer? Is the function of every visual clear? Are more transitions needed? Would headings or graphic devices help?

- Are the transitions or links from point to point, sentence to sentence, and paragraph to paragraph clear and effective? If not, how could they be improved?

- Are all visuals carefully integrated into the text? Is each visual introduced and commented on to point out its significance? Is each visual labeled as a figure or a table and given a caption as well as a citation?

- Is the style suited to the subject? Is it too formal, casual, or technical? Can it be improved?

- Which sentences seem effective? Which ones seem weaker, and how could they be improved? Should short sentences be combined, and any longer ones be broken up?

- How effective are the paragraphs? Too short or too long? How can they be improved?

- Which words or phrases seem effective? Do any seem vague or inappropriate for the audience or the writer's purpose? Are technical or unfamiliar terms defined?

Spelling, Punctuation, Mechanics, Documentation, and Format

- Are there any errors in spelling, punctuation, capitalization, and the like?

- Is the documentation appropriate and consistent? (See Chapter 30.)

- Does the paper or project follow an appropriate format? Is it appropriately designed and attractively presented?

PROJECTS

1. Identify a proposal currently in the news or one advocated unrelentingly by the media that you *really* don't like. It may be a political initiative, a cultural innovation, a transportation alternative, or a lifestyle change. Spend time studying the idea more carefully than you have before. And then compose a proposal argument based on your deeper understanding of the proposal. You may still explain why you think it's a bad idea. Or you may endorse it, using your new information and your interesting perspective as a former dissenter.

2. The uses and abuses of technology and media—from smartphones and smartwatches to social networks—seem to be on everyone's mind. Write a proposal argument about some pressing dilemma caused by the digital screens that are changing (ruining?) our lives. You might want to explain how to bring traditional instructors into the digital age or establish etiquette for people who walk in traffic using handheld electronic devices. Or maybe you want to keep parents off of social networks. Or maybe you have a great idea for separating professional and private lives online. Make your proposal in some pertinent medium: print op-ed, cartoon, photo essay, infographic, set of PowerPoint or Prezi slides, podcast.

3. Write a proposal to yourself diagnosing some minor issue you would like to address, odd behavior you'd like to change, or obsession you'd like to curb. Explore the reasons behind your mania and the problems it causes you and others. Then come up with a plausible proposal to resolve the issue and prove that you can do it. Make the paper hilarious.

4. Working in a group initially, come up with a list of problems—local, national, or international—that seem just about insoluble, from persuading nations to cut down on their CO_2 emissions to figuring out how to keep tuition costs in check. After some discussion, focus on just one or two of these matters and then discuss not the issues themselves but the general reasons that the problems have proven intractable. What exactly keeps people from agreeing on solutions? Are some people content with the status quo? Do some groups profit from the current arrangements? Are alternatives to the status quo just too costly or not feasible for other reasons? Do people find change uncomfortable? Following the discussion, work alone or collaboratively on an argument that examines the general issue of *change*: What makes it possible in any given case? What makes it difficult? Use the problems you have discussed as examples to illustrate your argument. Your challenge as a writer may be to make such an open-ended discussion interesting to general readers.

Two Sample Proposals

A Call to Improve Campus Accessibility

MANASI DESHPANDE

Courtesy of
Manasi
Deshpande

The paper
opens with
a personal
example and
dramatizes
the issue
of campus
accessibility.

Both problem
and solution
are previewed
here, with more
details provided
in subsequent
sections of the
paper.

The
introduction's
final paragraph
summarizes the
argument.

The author's
fieldwork
(mainly
interviews)
enhances her
authority and
credibility.

Introduction

Wes Holloway, a sophomore at the University of Texas at Austin (UT), never considered the issue of campus accessibility during his first year on campus. But when an injury his freshman year left him wheelchair-bound, he was astonished to realize that he faced an unexpected challenge: maneuvering around the UT campus. Hills that he had effortlessly traversed became mountains; doors that he had easily opened became anvils; and streets that he had mindlessly crossed became treacherous terrain. Says Wes: "I didn't think about accessibility until I had to deal with it, and I think most people are the same way."

For the ambulatory individual, access for the mobility impaired on the UT campus is easy to overlook. Automatic door entrances and bathrooms with the universal handicapped symbol make the campus seem sufficiently accessible. But for many students and faculty at UT, including me, maneuvering the UT campus in a wheelchair is a daily experience of stress and frustration. Although the University has made a concerted and continuing effort to improve access, students and faculty with physical disabilities still suffer from discriminatory hardship, unequal opportunity to succeed, and lack of independence.

The University must make campus accessibility a higher priority and take more seriously the hardship that the campus at present imposes on people with mobility impairments. Better accessibility would also benefit the numerous students and faculty with temporary disabilities and help the University recruit a more diverse body of students and faculty.

Assessment of Current Efforts

The current state of campus accessibility leaves substantial room for improvement. There are approximately 150 academic and

Manasi Deshpande wrote a longer version of this essay for a course preparing her to work as a consultant in the writing center at the University of Texas at Austin. We have edited it to emphasize the structure of her complex proposal. Note, too, how she reaches out to a general audience to make an argument that might seem to have a narrow constituency. This essay is documented using MLA style.

administrative buildings on campus (Grant). Eduardo Gardea, intern architect at the Physical Plant, estimates that only about nineteen buildings comply fully with the Americans with Disabilities Act (ADA). According to Penny Seay, PhD, director of the Center for Disability Studies at UT Austin, the ADA in theory "requires every building on campus to be accessible." However, as Bill Throop, associate director of the Physical Plant, explains, there is "no legal deadline to make the entire campus accessible"; neither the ADA nor any other law mandates that certain buildings be made compliant by a certain time. Though not bound by specific legal obligation, the University should strive to fulfill the spirit of the law and recognize campus accessibility as a pressing moral obligation.

The Benefits of Change

Benefits for People with Permanent Mobility Impairments

Improving campus accessibility would significantly enhance the quality of life of students and faculty with mobility impairments. The campus at present poses discriminatory hardship on these individuals by making daily activities such as getting to class and using the bathroom unreasonably difficult. Before Wes Holloway leaves home, he must plan his route carefully to avoid hills, use ramps that are easy to maneuver, and enter the side of the building with the accessible entrance. As he goes to class, Wes must go out of his way to avoid poorly paved sidewalks and roads. Sometimes he cannot avoid them and must take an uncomfortable and bumpy ride across potholes and uneven pavement. If his destination does not have an automatic door, he must wait for someone to open the door for him because it is too heavy for him to open himself. To get into Burdine Hall, he has to ask a stranger to push him through the heavy narrow doors because his fingers would get crushed if he pushed himself. Once in the classroom, Wes must find a suitable place to sit, often far away from his classmates because stairs block him from the center of the room.

Other members of the UT community with mobility impairments suffer the same daily hardships as Wes. According to Mike Gerhardt, student affairs administrator of Services for Students with Disabilities (SSD), approximately eighty students with physical disabilities, including twenty to twenty-five students using wheelchairs, are registered with SSD. However, the actual number of students with mobility impairments is probably higher because some

The paper uses several layers of headings to organize its diverse materials.

The author outlines the challenges faced by a student with mobility impairment.

Accessibility issues are given a human face with examples of the problems that mobility-impaired people face on campus.

students choose not to seek services from SSD. The current state of campus accessibility discriminates against all individuals with physical disabilities in the unnecessary hardship it imposes and in the ways it denies them independence.

Benefits for People with Temporary Mobility Impairments

The author broadens the appeal of her proposal by showing how improved accessibility will benefit everyone on campus.

In addition to helping the few members of the UT campus with permanent mobility impairments, a faster rate of accessibility improvement would also benefit the much larger population of people with temporary physical disabilities. Many students and faculty will become temporarily disabled from injury at some point during their time at the University. They will encounter difficulties similar to those facing people with permanent disabilities, including finding accessible entrances, opening doors without automatic entrances, and finding convenient classroom seating. And, according to Dr. Jennifer Maedgen, assistant dean of students and director of SSD, about 5 to 10 percent of the approximately one thousand students registered with SSD at any given time have temporary disabilities. By improving campus accessibility, the University would in fact reach out to all of its members, even those who have never considered the possibility of mobility impairment or the state of campus accessibility.

Numbers provide hard evidence for an important claim.

Benefits for the University

The author offers a new but related argument: enhanced accessibility could bolster recruitment efforts.

Better accessibility would also benefit the University as a whole by increasing recruitment of handicapped individuals and thus promoting a more diverse campus. When prospective students and faculty with disabilities visit the University, they might decide not to join the UT community because of poor access. On average, about one thousand students, or 2 percent of the student population, are registered with SSD. Mike Gerhardt reports that SSD would have about 1,500 to 3,000 registered students if the University reflected the community at large with respect to disability. These numbers suggest that the University can recruit more students with disabilities by taking steps to ensure that they have an equal opportunity to succeed.

The paper briefly notes possible objections to the proposal.

Counterarguments

Arguments against devoting more effort and resources to campus accessibility have some validity but ultimately prove inadequate.

Some argue that accelerating the rate of accessibility improvements and creating more efficient services require too much spending on too few people. However, this spending actually enhances the expected quality of life of all UT community members rather than just the few with permanent physical disabilities. Unforeseen injury can leave anyone with a permanent or temporary disability at any time. In making decisions about campus accessibility, administrators must realize that having a disability is not a choice and that bad luck does not discriminate. They should consider how their decisions would affect their campus experience if they became disabled. Despite the additional cost, the University should make accessibility a priority and accommodate more accessibility projects in its budget.

Recommendations
Foster Empathy and Understanding for Long-Term Planning

The University should make campus accessibility a higher priority and work toward a campus that not only fulfills legal requirements but also provides a user-friendly environment for the mobility impaired. It is difficult for the ambulatory person to empathize with the difficulties faced by these individuals. Recognizing this problem, the University should require the administrators who allocate money to ADA projects to use wheelchairs around the campus once a year. Administrators must realize that people with physical disabilities are not a small, distant, irrelevant group; anyone can join their ranks at any time. Administrators should ask themselves if they would find the current state of campus accessibility acceptable if an injury forced them to use a wheelchair on a permanent basis.

After establishing a case for enhanced campus accessibility, the author offers specific suggestions for action.

In addition, the University should actively seek student input for long-term improvements to accessibility. The University is in the process of creating the ADA Accessibility Committee, which, according to the office of the Dean of Students' Web site, will "address institutionwide, systemic issues that fall under the scope of the Americans with Disabilities Act." Students should play a prominent and powerful role in this new ADA Accessibility Committee. The Committee should select its student representatives carefully to make sure that they are driven individuals committed to working for progress and representing the interests of students with disabilities. The University should consider making Committee positions paid so that student representatives can devote sufficient time to their responsibilities.

Improve Services for the Mobility Impaired

The University should also work toward creating more useful, transparent, and approachable services for its members with physical disabilities by making better use of online technology and helping students take control of their own experiences.

First, SSD can make its Web site more useful by updating it frequently with detailed information on construction sites that will affect accessible routes. The site should delineate alternative accessible routes and approximate the extra time required to use the detour. This information would help people with mobility impairments to plan ahead and avoid delays, mitigating the stress of maneuvering around construction sites.

The University should also develop software for an interactive campus map. The software would work like MapQuest or Google Maps but would provide detailed descriptions of accessible routes on campus from one building to another. It would be updated frequently with new ADA improvements and information on construction sites that impede accessible routes.

Since usefulness of services is most important for students during their first encounters with the campus, SSD should hold one-on-one orientations for new students with mobility impairments. SSD should inform students in both oral and written format of their rights and responsibilities and make them aware of problems that they will encounter on the campus. Beyond making services more useful, these orientations would give students the impression of University services as open and responsive, encouraging students to report problems that they encounter and assume the responsibility of self-advocacy.

As a continuing resource for people with physical disabilities, the SSD Web site should include an anonymous forum for both general questions and specific complaints and needs. Many times, students notice problems but do not report them because they find visiting or calling SSD time-consuming or because they do not wish to be a burden. The anonymity and immediate feedback provided by the forum would allow for more freedom of expression and provide students an easier way to solve the problems they face.

Services for the mobility impaired should also increase their transparency by advertising current accessibility projects on their Web sites. The University should give its members with mobility impairments a clearer idea of its efforts to improve campus accessibility. Detailed online descriptions of ADA projects, including the cost of each project, would affirm its resolve to create a better environment for its members with physical disabilities.

Conclusion

Although the University has made progress in accessibility improvements on an old campus, it must take bolder steps to improve the experience of its members with mobility impairments. At present, people with permanent mobility impairments face unreasonable hardship, unequal opportunity to succeed, and lack of independence. To enhance the quality of life of all of its members and increase recruitment of disabled individuals, the University should focus its resources on increasing the rate of accessibility improvements and improving the quality of its services for the mobility impaired.

The writer reiterates her full proposal.

As a public institution, the University has an obligation to make the campus more inclusive and serve as an example for disability rights. With careful planning and a genuine desire to respond to special needs, practical and cost-effective changes to the University campus can significantly improve the quality of life of many of its members and prove beneficial to the future of the University as a whole.

Works Cited

Gardea, Eduardo. Personal interview. 24 Mar. 2005.

Gerhardt, Michael. Personal interview. 8 Apr. 2005.

Grant, Angela. "Making Campus More Accessible." *Daily Texan Online*. 14 Oct. 2003. Web. 1 Mar. 2005.

Holloway, Wesley Reed. Personal interview. 5 Mar. 2005.

Maedgen, Jennifer. Personal interview. 25 Mar. 2005.

Office of the Dean of Students, University of Texas at Austin. "ADA Student Forum." 6 Apr. 2005. Web. 23 Apr. 2005.

Seay, Penny. Personal interview. 11 Mar. 2005.

Throop, William. Personal interview. 6 Apr. 2005.

Let's Charge Politicians for Wasting Our Time

VIRGINIA POSTREL

There's an election today here in California, and that means my landline at home is ringing constantly with robocalls from assorted public figures whose recorded voices urge me to get out and vote for their favorite candidates. One called the other day while I was conducting an interview on the mobile phone I use for most purposes. I didn't answer, but it interrupted the flow of the conversation. Yesterday I picked up the receiver to find five voice mails, all from recorded political voices (including two identical messages from the same sheriff candidate).

Our phone number is on the National Do Not Call Registry, but those rules for telemarketers don't apply to political campaigns. The folks who make the laws aren't about to do away with a technique that works.

Political robocalls are illegal to mobile phones but OK to most landlines, as long as they meet disclosure requirements. Everyone I know hates such calls, and even political consultants know they're a problem. "Some voters get turned off by too many robocalls," cautions a political-strategy website. The cumulative annoyance, it warns, means that voters may resent yours even if they're rare. Yep.

Recorded, automatically dialed messages arguably constitute a legitimate and potentially important form of political speech. If I weren't so annoyed, I might actually like to know who's endorsing whom for sheriff. But it's ridiculous that the only way to limit the onslaught is to pay someone $24.99 to tell organizations, who may or may not listen, that I don't want them bothering me.

Here's a better idea: You should be able to set a charge for calling you. Every number that isn't on your "free" list would automatically be assessed a fee. The phone company would get a percentage of the revenue, and you'd be able to adjust the fee to different levels at different times of the day or for different seasons. (The nearer the election, the higher I'd make my charge.) If candidates really think it's valuable to call me, they should be willing to pay. Otherwise, they're just forcing me to subsidize their political efforts with my time and attention.

Technology investor Esther Dyson has for years been pushing a similar idea for e-mail. Unsolicited phone calls are much more annoying, and the technological challenges of "reversing the charges" should be much easier. Although you can't track down the true scamsters who break the do-not-call law and peddle fraudulent schemes from phony numbers, the politicians and charities that pester us for support aren't trying to hide. They're just trying to get something scarce and precious — our time and attention — for free.

Virginia Postrel posted this column on the Bloomberg View on June 3, 2014. She has also written for *Forbes*, the *Wall Street Journal*, the *New York Times*, and the *Atlantic*.

CHAPTER
21

Style in Arguments

The images below all reflect the notable styles of musicians from different times and musical traditions: Yo-Yo Ma, Count Basie, Kiss, and Rihanna. One could argue that these performers craft images to define their stage personalities, but how they present themselves also reflects the music they play and the audiences they perform for. Imagine Yo-Yo Ma appearing in Kiss makeup at Carnegie Hall. It doesn't work.

Writers, too, like to think of themselves as creating styles that express their ethos and life experiences—and they do. But in persuasive situations, style is also a matter of the specific choices they make—strategically and self-consciously—to influence audiences.

So it's not surprising that writers adapt their voices to a range of rhetorical situations, from very formal to very casual. At the formal and professional end of the scale, consider the opening paragraph of a dissent by Justice Sonia Sotomayor to a Supreme Court decision affecting affirmative action in Michigan public universities. Writing doesn't get much more consequential than this, and that earnestness is reflected in the justice's sober, authoritative, but utterly clear style:

All photos © Photofest, Inc.

We are fortunate to live in a democratic society. But without checks, democratically approved legislation can oppress minority groups. For that reason, our Constitution places limits on what a majority of the people may do. This case implicates one such limit: the guarantee of equal protection of the laws. Although that guarantee is traditionally understood to prohibit intentional discrimination under existing laws, equal protection does not end there. Another fundamental strand of our equal protection jurisprudence focuses on process, securing to all citizens the right to participate meaningfully and equally in self-government. That right is the bedrock of our democracy, for it preserves all other rights.

—Sonia Sotomayor, dissenting opinion, April 22, 2014

Contrast this formal style (perhaps the equivalent of Yo-Yo Ma's tuxedo?) to the more personal language Alexis C. Madrigal uses in an article for *the Atlantic* to argue that we are finally tiring of the relentless "stream" of information pouring down on us via social media. His subject is serious and his readers are too, but Madrigal employs a rougher style to express the resentment of people he sees as victimized by a once-promising technology that trivializes everything:

Nowadays, I think all kinds of people see and feel the tradeoffs of the stream, when they pull their thumbs down at the top of their screens to receive a new update from their social apps.

It is too damn hard to keep up. And most of what's out there is crap.

When the half-life of a post is half a day or less, how much time can media makers put into something? When the time a reader spends on a story is (on the high end) two minutes, how much time should media makers put into something?

—Alexis C. Madrigal, "2013: The Year 'the Stream' Crested"

Just a paragraph later, Madrigal again tunes his style to accommodate both high and low notes (maybe riffing like Count Basie?). First, he alludes to one of the toughest novels of the twentieth century, and then he chooses sentence structures—a fragment followed by two very short, emphatic, not-quite-parallel clauses—to mark the contrast between the formidable book and social media:

I am not joking when I say: it is easier to read *Ulysses* than it is to read the Internet. Because at least *Ulysses* has an end, an edge. *Ulysses* can be finished. The Internet is never finished.

Far more casual in subject matter and style is a blog item by Huffington Post book editor Claire Fallon, arguing (tongue-in-cheek) that Shakespeare's Romeo is one of those literary figures readers just love to hate. The range of Fallon's vocabulary choices—from "most romantic dude" to "penchant for wallowing"—suggests the (Rihanna-like?) playfulness of the exercise. Style is obviously a big part of Fallon's game:

> Romeo, Romeo, wherefore art thou such a wishy-washy doofus? Shakespeare himself would likely be baffled by the elevation of Romeo to the position of "most romantic dude in literature"—he spends his first scene in the play insisting he's heartbroken over a girl he goes on to completely forget about the second he catches a glimpse of Juliet! Poor Rosaline (or rather, nice bullet-dodging, Rosaline). Romeo's apparent penchant for wallowing in the romantic misery of unrequited love finds a new target in naive Juliet, who then dies for a guy who probably would have forgotten about her as soon as their honeymoon ended. Yes, Romeo is self-absorbed, fickle, and rather whiny, but we clearly love him anyway.
>
> —Claire Fallon, "11 Unlikeable Classical Book Characters We Love to Hate"

As you might guess from these examples, style always involves making choices about language across a wide range of situations. Style can be public or personal, conventional or creative, and everything in between. When you write, you'll find that you have innumerable tools and options for expressing yourself exactly as you need to. This chapter introduces you to some of them.

Style and Word Choice

Words matter—and those you choose will define the style of your arguments.

For most academic arguments, what is called formal or professional style is appropriate. Such language sounds weighty because it usually is. It is not shy about employing highbrow terms, conventional vocabulary, or technical language because that's what readers of academic journals or serious magazines and newspapers expect. Formal writing typically avoids contractions, phrases that mimic speech, and sometimes even the pronoun *I*. But what may be most remarkable about the style is how little it draws attention to itself—and that's usually deliberate. Here's a levelheaded paragraph from *the Economist* arguing that digital education may yet have a huge impact on colleges and universities:

> So demand for education will grow. Who will meet it? Universities face a new competitor in the form of massive open online courses, or MOOCs. These digitally-delivered courses, which teach students via the web or tablet apps, have big advantages over their established rivals. With low startup costs and powerful economies of scale, online courses dramatically lower the price of learning and widen access to it, by removing the need for students to be taught at set times or places. The low cost of providing courses—creating a new one costs about $70,000—means they can be sold cheaply, or even given away. Clayton Christensen of Harvard Business School considers MOOCs a potent "disruptive technology" that will kill off many inefficient universities. "Fifteen years from now more than half of the universities [in America] will be in bankruptcy," he predicted last year.
>
> — "The Future of Universities: The Digital Degree"

The editors assume that readers of *the Economist* will understand technical terms such as "startup costs" and "economies of scale," though they do pause to explain "MOOCs"—a much-hyped innovation yet to catch on. Even as it delivers what seems like bad news for universities, the paragraph is efficient and cool in tone—modeling a style you'll often use in academic projects.

Colloquial words and phrases, *slang*, and even first- and second-person pronouns (*I, me, we, you*) can create relationships with audiences that feel much more intimate. When you use everyday language in arguments, readers are more likely to identify with you personally and, possibly, with the ideas you represent or advocate. In effect, such vocabulary choices lessen the distance between you and readers.

Admittedly, some colloquial terms simply bewilder readers not tuned in to them. A movie review in *Rolling Stone* or a music review in *Spin* might leave your parents (or some authors) scratching their heads. Jon Dolan, for example, has this to say about Drake's song "Draft Day":

> Drake's latest statement-of-Drakeness casually big-ups his sports bros Johnny Manziel and Andrew Wiggins over a dreamy sample of Lauryn Hill's "Doo Wop (That Thing)," then drops a little Jennifer Lawrence fan fic: "On some Hunger Games sh–t/I would die for my district." It's baller brio with a characteristic light touch. May the odds be ever in your favor, son!
>
> —Jon Dolan, *Rolling Stone*, "Drake, 'Draft Day' "

Huh, we say. But you probably get it.

Be alert, too, to the use of *jargon*, the special vocabulary of members of a profession, trade, or field. Although jargon serves as shorthand for experts, it can alienate readers who don't recognize technical words or acronyms.

Another verbal key to an argument's style is its control of **connotation**, the associations that surround many words. Consider the straightforward connotative differences among the following three statements:

> Students from the Labor Action Committee (LAC) carried out a hunger strike to call attention to the below-minimum wages that are being paid to campus temporary workers, saying, "The university must pay a living wage to all its workers."

> Left-wing agitators and radicals tried to use self-induced starvation to stampede the university into caving in to their demands.

> Champions of human rights put their bodies on the line to protest the university's tightfisted policy of paying temporary workers scandalously low wages.

The style of the first sentence is the most neutral, presenting facts and offering a quotation from one of the students. The second sentence uses loaded terms like "agitators," "radicals," and "stampede" to create a negative image of this event, while the final sentence uses other loaded words to create a positive view. As these examples demonstrate, the words you choose can change everything about a sentence.

But now watch how author Sherman Alexie, in an essay about Jason Collins, the first openly gay NBA star (see p. 249) makes the connotations surrounding three colloquial terms all meaning "beautiful" key to a controversial claim he intends to put forward:

> Cut. Shredded. Jacked. Those are violent straight-boy adjectives that mean "beautiful." But we straight boys aren't supposed to think of other men as beautiful. We're supposed to think of the most physically gifted men as warrior soldiers, as dangerous demigods.

> And there's the rub: When we're talking about professional athletes, we are mostly talking about males passionately admiring the physical attributes and abilities of other males. It might not be homosexual, but it certainly is homoerotic.

Here, words actually *become* the argument.

RESPOND

Review the excerpts in this section and choose one or two words or phrases that you think are admirably selected or unusually interesting choices. Then explore the meanings and possibly the connotations of the word or words in a nicely developed paragraph or two.

Sentence Structure and Argument

Writers of effective arguments know that "variety is the spice of life" when it comes to stylish sentences. A strategy as simple as *varying sentence length* can keep readers attentive and interested. For instance, the paragraph from *the Economist* in the preceding section (p. 438) has sentences as short as four words and as lengthy as thirty-six. Its authors almost certainly didn't pause as they wrote and think, hmm, we need a little variation here. Instead, as experienced writers, they simply made sure that their sentences complemented the flow of their ideas and also kept readers engaged.

Sentences, you see, offer you more options and special effects than you can ever exhaust. To pull examples from selections earlier in this chapter, just consider how dramatic, punchy, or even comic short sentences can be:

> The Internet is never finished. —Alexis C. Madrigal

> May the odds be ever in your favor, son! —Jon Dolan

Longer sentences can explain ideas, build drama, or sweep readers along:

> With low startup costs and powerful economies of scale, online courses dramatically lower the price of learning and widen access to it, by removing the need for students to be taught at set times or places.
>
> — *The Economist*

Meanwhile, sentences of medium length handle just about any task assigned without a fuss. They are whatever you need them to be: serviceable, discrete, thoughtful, playful. And they pair up nicely with companions:

> But without checks, democratically approved legislation can oppress minority groups. For that reason, our Constitution places limits on what a majority of the people may do.
>
> —Sonia Sotomayor

Balanced or parallel sentences, in which clauses or phrases are deliberately matched, as highlighted in the following examples, draw attention to ideas and relationships:

> *Ulysses* can be finished. The Internet is never finished.
>
> —Alexis C. Madrigal

> When we're talking about professional athletes, we are mostly talking about males passionately admiring the physical attributes and abilities of other males. It might not be homosexual, but it certainly is homoerotic.
>
> —Sherman Alexie

Sentences with especially complicated structures or interruptions make you pay attention to their motions and, therefore, their ideas:

> The low cost of providing courses—creating a new one costs about $70,00—means they can be sold cheaply, or even given away.
>
> — *The Economist*

> Drake's latest statement-of-Drakeness casually big-ups his sports bros Johnny Manziel and Andrew Wiggins over a dreamy sample of Lauryn Hill's "Doo Wop (That Thing)," then drops a little Jennifer Lawrence fan fic: "On some *Hunger Games* sh–t/I would die for my district."
>
> —Jon Dolan

Even sentence fragments—which don't meet all the requirements for full sentence status—have their place when used for a specific effect:

> Because at least *Ulysses* has an end, an edge. —Alexis C. Madrigal

> Poor Rosaline (or rather, nice bullet-dodging, Rosaline). —Claire Fallon

> Cut. Shredded. Jacked. —Sherman Alexie

You see, then, that there's *much* more to the rhetoric of sentences than just choosing subjects, verbs, and objects—and far more than we can explain in one section. But you can learn a lot about the power of sentences simply by observing how the writers you admire engineer them—and maybe imitating some of those sentences yourself. You might also make it a habit to read and re-read your own sentences aloud (or in your head) as you compose them to gauge whether words and phrases are meshing with your ideas. And then tinker, tinker, tinker — until the sentences feel right.

RESPOND

Working with a classmate, first find a paragraph you both admire, perhaps in one of the selections in Part 3 of this book. Then, individually write paragraphs of your own that imitate the sentences within it — making sure that both these new items are on subjects different from that of the original paragraph. When you are done, compare your paragraphs and pick out a few sentences you think are especially effective.

Punctuation and Argument

In a memorable comment, actor and director Clint Eastwood said, "You can show a lot with a look…. It's punctuation." He's certainly right about punctuation's effect, and it is important that as you read and write arguments, you consider punctuation closely.

Eastwood may have been talking about the dramatic effect of end punctuation: the finality of periods; the tentativeness of ellipses (…); the query, disbelief, or uncertainty in question marks; or the jolt in the now-appearing-almost-everywhere exclamation point! Yet even exclamations can help create tone if used strategically. In an argument about the treatment of prisoners at Guantánamo, consider how Jane Mayer evokes the sense of desperation in some of the suspected terrorists:

> As we reached the end of the cell-block, hysterical shouts, in broken English, erupted from a caged exercise area nearby. "Come here!" a man screamed. "See here! They are liars! … No sleep!" he yelled. "No food! No medicine! No doctor! Everybody sick here!"
>
> —Jane Mayer, "The Experiment"

Punctuation that works within sentences can also do much to enhance meaning and style. The *semicolon*, for instance, marks a pause that is stronger than a comma but not as strong as a period. Semicolons function like "plus signs"; used correctly, they join items that are alike in structure, conveying a sense of balance, similarity, or even contrast. Do you recall Nathaniel Stein's parody of grading standards at Harvard University (see p. 248)? Watch as he uses a semicolon to enhance the humor in his description of what an A+ paper achieves:

> Nearly every single word in the paper is spelled correctly; those that are not can be reasoned out phonetically within minutes.
>
> —Nathaniel Stein, "Leaked! Harvard's Grading Rubric"

FIGURE 21.1 "You can show a lot with a look.... It's punctuation." © Photofest, Inc.

In many situations, however, semicolons, with their emphasis on symmetry and balance, can feel stodgy, formal, and maybe even old-fashioned, and lots of writers avoid them, perhaps because they are very difficult to get right. Check a writing handbook before you get too friendly with semicolons.

Much easier to manage are colons, which function like pointers within sentences: they say *pay attention to this*. Philip Womack's London *Telegraph* review of *Harry Potter and the Deathly Hallows, Part 2* demonstrates how a colon enables a writer to introduce a lengthy illustration clearly and elegantly:

> The first scene of David Yates's film picks up where his previous installment left off: with a shot of the dark lord Voldemort's noseless face in triumph as he steals the most powerful magic wand in the world from the tomb of Harry's protector, Professor Dumbledore.
>
> —Philip Womack

And Paul Krugman shows how to use a colon to catch a reader's attention:

> Recently two research teams, working independently and using different methods, reached an alarming conclusion: The West Antarctic ice sheet is doomed.
>
> —Paul Krugman, "Point of No Return"

Colons can serve as lead-ins for complete sentences, complex phrases, or even single words. As such, they are versatile and potentially dramatic pieces of punctuation.

Like colons, dashes help readers focus on important, sometimes additional details. But they have even greater flexibility since they can be used singly or in pairs. Alone, dashes function much like colons to add information. Here's Eugene Washington commenting pessimistically on a political situation in Iraq, using a single dash to extend his thoughts:

> The aim of U.S. policy at this point should be minimizing the calamity, not chasing rainbows of a unified, democratic, pluralistic Iraq—which, sadly, is something the power brokers in Iraq do not want.
>
> —Eugene Robinson, "The 'Ungrateful Volcano' of Iraq"

And here are paired dashes used to insert such information in the opening of the Philip Womack review of *Deathly Hallows 2* cited earlier:

> *Harry Potter and the Deathly Hallows, Part 2*—the eighth and final film in the blockbusting series—begins with our teenage heroes fighting for their lives, and for their entire world.

And finally, notice how in an essay about President Obama's second term, writer Peggy Noonan surrounds a single word with dashes to emphasize it:

> All this is weird, unprecedented. The president shows no sign— none—of being overwhelmingly concerned and anxious at his predicaments or challenges.
>
> —Peggy Noonan, "The Daydream and the Nightmare"

As these examples illustrate, punctuation often enhances the rhythm of an argument. Take a look at how Maya Angelou uses a dash along with another punctuation mark—ellipsis points—to create a pause or hesitation, in this case one that builds anticipation:

> Then the voice, husky and familiar, came to wash over us— "The winnah, and still heavyweight champeen of the world … Joe Louis."
>
> —Maya Angelou, "Champion of the World"

RESPOND

Try writing a brief movie review for your campus newspaper, experimenting with punctuation as one way to create an effective style. See if using a series of questions might have a strong effect, whether exclamation points would add or detract from the message you want to send, and so on. When you've finished the review, compare it to one written by a classmate, and look for similarities and differences in your choices of punctuation.

Special Effects: Figurative Language

You don't have to look hard to find examples of figurative language adding style to arguments. When a writing teacher suggests you take a weed whacker to your prose, she's using a figure of speech (in this case, a *metaphor*) to suggest you cut the wordiness. To indicate how little he trusts the testimony of John Koskinen, head of the Internal Revenue Service, political pundit Michael Gerson takes the metaphor of a "witch hunt" and flips it on the bureaucrat, relying on readers to recognize an *allusion* to Shakespeare's *Macbeth*:

> Democrats were left to complain about a Republican "witch hunt"—while Koskinen set up a caldron, added some eye of newt and toe of frog and hailed the Thane of Cawdor.
>
> —Michael Gerson, "An Arrogant and Lawless IRS"

FIGURE 21.2 John Koskinen Alex Wong/Getty Images

Figurative language like this—indispensable to writers—dramatizes ideas, either by clarifying or enhancing the thoughts themselves or by framing them in language that makes them stand out. As a result, figurative language makes arguments attractive, memorable, and powerful. An apt simile, a timely rhetorical question, or a wicked understatement might do a better job bringing an argument home than whole paragraphs of evidence.

Figures of speech are usually classified into two main types: **tropes**, which involve a change in the ordinary meaning of a word or phrase; and **schemes**, which involve a special arrangement of words. Here is a brief alphabetical listing—with examples—of some of the most familiar kinds.

Tropes

To create tropes, you often have to think of one idea or claim in relationship to others. Some of the most powerful—one might even say *inevitable*—tropes involve making purposeful comparisons between ideas: analogies, metaphors, and similes. Other tropes such as irony, signifying, and understatement are tools for expressing attitudes toward ideas: you might use them to shape the way you want your audience to think about a claim that you or someone else has made.

Allusion

An **allusion** is a connection that illuminates one situation by comparing it to another similar but usually more famous one, often with historical or literary connections. Allusions work with events, people, or concepts—expanding and enlarging them so readers better appreciate their significance. For example, a person who makes a career-ending blunder might be said to have met her *Waterloo*, the famous battle that terminated Napoleon's ambitions. Similarly, every impropriety in Washington brings up mentions of *Watergate*, the only scandal to lead to a presidential resignation; any daring venture becomes a *moon shot*, paralleling the ambitious program that led to a lunar landing in 1969. Using allusions can be tricky: they work only if readers get the connection. But when they do, they can pack a wallop. When on **p. 445** Michael Gerson mentions "eye of newt" and "toe of frog" in the same breath as IRS chief John Koskinen, he knows what fans of *Macbeth* are thinking. But other readers might be left clueless.

Analogy

Analogies compare two things, often point by point, either to show similarity or to suggest that if two concepts, phenomena, events, or even people are alike in one way, they are probably alike in other ways as well. Often extended in length, analogies can clarify or emphasize points of comparison, thereby supporting particular claims.

Here's the first paragraph of an essay in which a writer who is also a runner thinks deeply about the analogies between the two tough activities:

When people ask me what running and writing have in common, I tend to look at the ground and say it might have something to do with discipline: You do both of those things when you don't feel like it, and make them part of your regular routine. You know some days will be harder than others, and on some you won't hit your mark and will want to quit. But you don't. You force yourself into a practice; the practice becomes habit and then simply part of your identity. A surprising amount of success, as Woody Allen once said, comes from just showing up.

—Rachel Toor, "What Writing and Running Have in Common"

To be effective, an analogy has to make a good point and hold up to scrutiny. If it doesn't, it can be criticized as a faulty analogy, a fallacy of argument (see p. 232).

Antonomasia

Antonomasia is an intriguing trope that simply involves substituting a descriptive phrase for a proper name. It is probably most familiar to you from sports or entertainment figures: "His Airness" still means Michael Jordan; Aretha Franklin remains "The Queen of Soul," jazz singer Mel Torme was "The Velvet Fog," and Superman, of course, is "The Man of Steel." In politics, antonomasia is sometimes used neutrally (Ronald Reagan as "The Gipper"), sometimes as a backhanded compliment (Margaret Thatcher as "The Iron Lady"), and occasionally as a crude and sexist put-down (Sarah Palin as "Caribou Barbie"). As you well know if you have one, nicknames can pack potent arguments into just one phrase.

FIGURE 21.3 This cartoon draws a number of suggestive analogies (and one potent allusion) in the way it depicts the pope and personifies "economic inequality." © John Cole/Cagle Cartoons, Inc.

Hyperbole

Hyperbole is the use of overstatement for special effect, a kind of fireworks in prose. The tabloid gossip magazines that scream at you in the checkout line survive by hyperbole. Everyone has seen these overstated arguments and perhaps marveled at the way they sell.

Hyperbole can, however, serve both writers and audiences when very strong opinions need to be registered. One senses exasperation in the no-holds-barred opening of Rex Reed's review of the film *Tammy*—the paragraph ripples with hyperbole and other tropes:

> The good news is that *Tammy* is not a crappy remake of the 1957 *Tammy* movie with Debbie Reynolds that spawned three sequels and a TV comedy series. The bad news is that this one is much worse. It's a desperate and brainless vehicle for Melissa McCarthy, which she wrote herself, with her husband, Ben Falcone, who also directed, with all the efficiency and verve of an abandoned Volkswagen on the Jersey Turnpike. There isn't a single shred of evidence that either of them has one iota of talent in the world of filmmaking. *Tammy* is not just a celebration of everything vulgar and stupid in the dumbing down of American movies. It's a rambling, pointless and labored attempt to cash in on Ms. McCarthy's fan base without respect for any audience with a collective IQ of 10. And it's about as funny as a liver transplant.
>
> —Rex Reed, "Melissa McCarthy Gives 'Tammy' Her All, but It's Nowhere Near Enough"

Can you tell that Reed did not like the film?

Irony

Irony is a complex trope in which words convey meanings that are in tension with or even opposite to their literal meanings. Readers who catch the irony realize that a writer is asking them (or someone else) to think about all the potential connotations in their language. One of the most famous uses of satiric irony in literature occurs in Shakespeare's *Julius Caesar* when Antony punctuates his condemnation of Caesar's assassins with the repeated word "honourable." He begins by admitting, "So are they all, honourable men" but ends railing against "the honourable men / Whose daggers have stabb'd Caesar." Within just a few lines, Antony's funeral speech has altered the meaning of the term.

In popular culture, irony often takes a humorous bent in publications such as the *Onion* and the appropriately named *Ironic Times*. Yet even serious critics of society and politics use satiric devices to undercut celebrities and politicians, particularly when such powerful figures ignore the irony in their own positions. After

Hillary Clinton argued that Americans don't regard her and her husband as part of the country's problem with income inequality "because we pay ordinary income tax … and we've done it through dint of hard work," *Washington Post* columnist and fellow liberal Ruth Marcus offered advice rich in sarcasm and irony:

> And for goodness' sake—*truly well-off? hard work?* You are truly well-off by anyone's definition of the term. And hard work is the guys tearing up my roof right now. It's not flying by private jet to pick up a check for $200,000 to stand at a podium for an hour… .
>
> —Ruth Marcus, "Hillary Clinton's Money Woes"

Metaphor

A bedrock of our language, **metaphor** creates or implies a comparison between two things, illuminating something unfamiliar by correlating it to something we usually know much better. For example, to explain the complicated structure of DNA, scientists Watson and Crick famously used items people would likely recognize: a helix (spiral) and a zipper. Metaphors can clarify and enliven arguments. In the following passage, novelist and poet Benjamin Sáenz uses several metaphors (highlighted) to describe his relationship to the southern border of the United States:

> It seems obvious to me now that I remained always a son of the border, a boy never quite comfortable in an American skin, and certainly not comfortable in a Mexican one. My entire life, I have lived in a liminal space, and that space has both defined and confined me. That liminal space wrote and invented me. It has been my prison, and it has also been my only piece of sky.
>
> —Benjamin Sáenz, "Notes from Another Country"

In another example from Andrew Sullivan's blog, he quotes an 1896 issue of *Munsey's Magazine* that uses a metaphor to explain what, at that time, the bicycle meant to women and to clarify the new freedom it gave women who weren't accustomed to being able to ride around on their own:

> To men, the bicycle in the beginning was merely a new toy, another machine added to the long list of devices they knew in their work and play. To women, it was a steed upon which they rode into a new world.

FIGURE 21.4 It's not just a street; it's a metonym! Martin Lehmann/Shutterstock

Metonymy

Metonymy is a rhetorical trope in which a writer uses a particular object to stand for a general concept. You'll recognize the move immediately in the expression "The *pen* is mightier than the *sword*" — which obviously is not about Bics and sabers. Metonyms are vivid and concrete ways of compacting big concepts into expressive packages for argument: the term *Wall Street* can embody the nation's whole complicated banking and investment system, while all the offices and officials of the U.S. military become the *Pentagon*. You can quickly think of dozens of expressions that represent larger, more complex concepts: *Nashville, Hollywood, Big Oil, the Press, the Oval Office*, even perhaps *the electorate*.

Oxymoron

Oxymoron is a rhetorical trope that states a paradox or contradiction. John Milton created a classic example when he described Hell as a place of "darkness visible." We may be less poetic today, but we nevertheless appreciate the creativity (or arrogance) in expressions such as *light beer, sports utility vehicle, expressway gridlock*, or *negative economic growth*. You might not have much cause to use this figure in your writing, but you'll get credit for noting and commenting on oxymoronic ideas or behaviors.

Rhetorical Question

Rhetorical questions, which we use frequently, are questions posed by a speaker or writer that don't really require answers. Instead, an answer is implied or unimportant. When you say "Who cares?" or "What difference does it make?" you're using such questions.

Rhetorical questions show up in arguments for many reasons, most often perhaps to direct readers' attention to the issues a writer intends to explore. For example, Erin Biba asks a provocative, open-ended rhetorical question in her analysis of Facebook "friending":

> So if we're spending most of our time online talking to people we don't even know, how deep can the conversation ever get?
>
> —Erin Biba, "Friendship Has Its Limits"

Signifying

Signifying, in which a speaker or writer cleverly and often humorously needles another person, is a distinctive trope found extensively in African American English. In the following passage, two African American men (Grave Digger and Coffin Ed) signify on their white supervisor (Anderson), who has ordered them to discover the originators of a riot:

> "I take it you've discovered who started the riot," Anderson said.
>
> "We knew who he was all along," Grave Digger said.
>
> "It's just nothing we can do to him," Coffin Ed echoed.
>
> "Why not, for God's sake?"
>
> "He's dead," Coffin Ed said.
>
> "Who?"
>
> "Lincoln," Grave Digger said.
>
> "He hadn't ought to have freed us if he didn't want to make provisions to feed us," Coffin Ed said. "Anyone could have told him that."
>
> —Chester Himes, *Hot Day, Hot Night*

Coffin Ed and Grave Digger demonstrate the major characteristics of effective signifying—indirection, ironic humor, fluid rhythm, and a surprising twist at the end. Rather than insulting Anderson directly by pointing out that he's asked a dumb question, they criticize the question indirectly by ultimately blaming a white man for the riot (and not just any white man, but one they're supposed to revere). This twist leaves the supervisor speechless, teaching him something and giving Grave Digger and Coffin Ed the last word—and last laugh.

Take a look at the example of signifying from a *Boondocks* cartoon (see **below**). Note how Huey seems to be sympathizing with Jazmine and then, in two surprising twists, reveals that he has been needling her all along.

FIGURE 21.5 In these *Boondocks* strips, Huey signifies on Jazmine, using indirection, ironic humor, and two surprising twists. © THE BOONDOCKS © 1999 Aaron McGruder. Dist. by UNIVERSAL UCLICK. Reprinted with permission. All rights reserved.

Simile

A **simile** uses *like* or *as* to compare two things. Here's a simile from an essay on cosmology from the *New York Times*:

> Through his general theory of relativity, Einstein found that space, and time too, can bend, twist, and warp, responding much as a trampolin does to a jumping child.
>
> —Brian Greene, "Darkness on the Edge of the Universe"

And here is a series of similes, from an excerpt of a *Wired* magazine review of a new magazine for women:

> Women's magazines occupy a special niche in the cluttered infoscape of modern media. Ask any *Vogue* junkie: no girl-themed Web site or CNN segment on women's health can replace the guilty pleasure of slipping a glossy fashion rag into your shopping cart. Smooth as a pint of chocolate Häagen-Dazs,

feckless as a thousand-dollar slip dress, women's magazines wrap culture, trends, health, and trash in a single, decadent package. But like the diet dessert recipes they print, these slick publications can leave a bad taste in your mouth.

—Tiffany Lee Brown, "En Vogue"

Here, three similes—*smooth as a pint of chocolate Häagen-Dazs* and *feckless as a thousand-dollar slip dress* in the third sentence, and *like the diet dessert recipes* in the fourth—add to the image of women's magazines as a mishmash of "trash" and "trends."

Understatement

Understatement uses a quiet message to make its point. In her memoir, Rosa Parks—the civil rights activist who made history in 1955 by refusing to give up her bus seat to a white passenger—uses understatement so often that it becomes a hallmark of her style. She refers to her lifelong efforts to advance civil rights as just a small way of "carrying on."

Understatement can be particularly effective in arguments that might seem to call for its opposite. Outraged that New York's Metropolitan Opera has decided to stage *The Death of Klinghoffer*, a work depicting the murder by terrorists of a wheelchair-bound Jewish passenger on a cruise ship in 1985, writer Eve Epstein in particular points to an aria in which a terrorist named Rambo blames all the world's problems on Jews, and then, following an evocative dash, she makes a quiet observation:

Rambo's aria echoes the views of *Der Stürmer*, Julius Streicher's Nazi newspaper, without a hint of irony or condemnation. The leitmotif of the morally and physically crippled Jew who should be disposed of has been heard before—and it did not end well.

—Eve Epstein, "The Met's Staging of *Klinghoffer* Should Be Scrapped"

"It did not end well" alludes, of course, to the Holocaust.

RESPOND

Use online sources (such as American Rhetoric's Top 100 Speeches at **americanrhetoric. com/top100speechesall.html**) to find the text of an es-say or a speech by someone who uses figures of speech liberally. Pick a paragraph that is rich in figures and rewrite it, eliminating every bit of figurative language. Then read the original and your revised version aloud to your class. Can you imagine a rhetorical situation in which your pared-down version would be more appropriate?

Schemes

Schemes are rhetorical figures that manipulate the actual word order of phrases, sentences, or paragraphs to achieve specific affects, adding stylistic power or "zing" to arguments. The variety of such devices is beyond the scope of this work. Following are schemes that you're likely to see most often, again in alphabetical order.

Anaphora

Anaphora, or effective repetition, can act like a drumbeat in an argument, bringing the point home. Sometimes an anaphora can be quite obvious, especially when the repeated expressions occur at the beginning of a series of sentences or clauses. Here is President Lyndon Johnson urging Congress in 1965 to pass voting rights legislation:

> There is no constitutional issue here. The command of the Constitution is plain.
>
> There is no moral issue. It is wrong—deadly wrong—to deny any of your fellow Americans the right to vote in this country.
>
> There is no issue of States rights or national rights. There is only the struggle for human rights.
>
> I have not the slightest doubt what will be your answer.

Repetitions can occur within sentences or paragraphs as well. Here, in an argument about the future of Chicago, Lerone Bennett Jr. uses repetition to link Chicago to innovation and creativity:

> [Chicago]'s the place where organized Black history was born, where gospel music was born, where jazz and the blues were reborn, where the Beatles and the Rolling Stones went up to the mountaintop to get the new musical commandments from Chuck Berry and the rock'n'roll apostles. —Lerone Bennett Jr. "Blacks in Chicago"

Antithesis

Antithesis is the use of parallel words or sentence structures to highlight contrasts or opposition:

> Marriage has many pains, but celibacy has no pleasures.
>
> —Samuel Johnson
>
> Those who kill people are called murderers; those who kill animals, sportsmen.

Inverted Word Order

Inverted word order is a comparatively rare scheme in which the parts of a sentence or clause are not in the usual subject-verb-object order. It can help make arguments particularly memorable:

> Into this grey lake plopped the thought, I know this man, don't I?
>
> —Doris Lessing

> Hard to see, the dark side is. —Yoda

Parallelism

Parallelism involves the use of grammatically similar phrases or clauses for special effect. Among the most common of rhetorical effects, parallelism can be used to underscore the relationships between ideas in phrases, clauses, complete sentences, or even paragraphs. You probably recognize the famous parallel clauses that open Charles Dickens's *A Tale of Two Cities*:

> It was the best of times,
>
> it was the worst of times …

The author's paralleled clauses and sentences go on and on through more than a half-dozen pairings, their rhythm unforgettable. Or consider how this unattributed line from the 2008 presidential campaign season resonates because of its elaborate and sequential parallel structure:

> Rosa sat so that Martin could walk. Martin walked so that Obama could run. Obama ran so that our children could fly.

RESPOND

Identify the figurative language used in the following slogans. Note that some slogans may use more than one device.

"A day without orange juice is like a day without sunshine." (Florida Orange Juice)

"Open happiness." (Coca-Cola)

"Be all that you can be." (U.S. Army)

"Breakfast of champions." (Wheaties)

"America runs on Dunkin'." (Dunkin' Donuts)

"Like a rock." (Chevrolet trucks)

CULTURAL CONTEXTS FOR ARGUMENT

Levels of Formality and Other Issues of Style

At least one important style question needs to be asked when arguing across cultures: what level of formality is most appropriate? In the United States, a fairly informal style is often acceptable and even appreciated. Many cultures, however, tend to value formality. If in doubt, err on the side of formality:

- Take care to use proper titles as appropriate (*Ms., Mr., Dr.,* and so on).

- Don't use first names unless you've been invited to do so.

- Steer clear of slang and jargon. When you're communicating with members of other cultures, slang may not be understood, or it may be seen as disrespectful.

- Avoid potentially puzzling pop cultural allusions, such as sports analogies or musical references.

When arguing across cultures or languages, another stylistic issue might be clarity. When communicating with people whose native languages are different from your own, analogies and similes almost always aid in understanding. Likening something unknown to something familiar can help make your argument forceful — and understandable.

CHAPTER
22

Visual Rhetoric

T o commemorate the two hundredth anniversary of "The Star-Spangled Banner," its lyrics composed by Francis Scott Key in September 1814 following the failed British bombardment of Fort McHenry outside Baltimore, the Smithsonian Institution asked a group of artists to reflect on what the American flag means today. Most of the artists expressed their ideas and opinions visually, through paintings, photographs, montages, sculptures, films, even a graphic "fantasy." Three of their items are reproduced above: left to right, a steel-and-aluminum flag by architect Daniel Libeskind; a figure in acrylic and watercolor by Anita Kunz; and a photo collage by graphic designer David Carson. Even so small a sampling of visual rhetoric underscores what you doubtless already know: images tease our imaginations, provoke responses from viewers, and, yes, make arguments. They have clout.

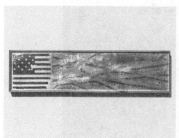  

The Power of Visual Arguments

Even in everyday situations, images—from T-shirts to billboards to animated films and computer screens—influence us. Media analyst Kevin Kelly ponders the role screens and their images now play in our lives:

> Everywhere we look, we see screens. The other day I watched clips from a movie as I pumped gas into my car. The other night I saw a movie on the backseat of a plane. We will watch anywhere. Screens playing video pop up in the most unexpected places—like ATM machines and supermarket checkout lines and tiny phones; some movie fans watch entire films in between calls. These ever-present screens have created an audience for very short moving pictures, as brief as three minutes, while cheap digital creation tools have empowered a new generation of filmmakers, who are rapidly filling up those screens. We are headed toward screen ubiquity.
>
> —Kevin Kelly, "Becoming Screen Literate"

Of course, visual arguments weren't invented by YouTube, and their power isn't novel either. The pharaohs of Egypt lined the banks of the Nile River with statues of themselves to assert their authority, and there is no shortage of monumental effigies in Washington, D.C., today.

FIGURE 22.1 Not only the high and mighty: sculpture of a Great Depression–era breadline at the Franklin Delano Roosevelt Memorial in Washington, D.C. © Mel Longhurst/Photoshot

Still, the ease with which all of us make and share images *is* unprecedented: people are uploading a billion shots a *day* to Snapchat, a photo-messaging application that deletes items after only a brief viewing. And most of us have easily adjusted to instantaneous multichannel, multimedia connectivity (see Chapter 24). We expect it to be seamless too. The prophet of this era was Marshall McLuhan, who nearly fifty years ago proclaimed that "the medium is the massage," with the play on *message* and *massage* intentional. As McLuhan says, "We shape our tools and afterwards our tools shape us…. . All media works us over completely."

RESPOND

Find an advertisement, either print or digital, that uses both verbal and visual elements. Analyze its argument first by pointing out the claims the ad makes (or implies) and then by identifying the ways it supports them verbally and/or visually. (If it helps, go over the questions about multimedia texts offered in Chapter 24 on pp. 491–493.) Then switch ads with a classmate and discuss his/her analysis. Compare your responses to the two ads. If they're different—and they probably will be—how might you account for the differences?

Using Visuals in Your Own Arguments

Given the power of images, it's only natural that you would use them in your own composing. In fact, many college instructors now expect papers for their courses to be posted to the Web, where digital photos, videos, and design elements are native. Other instructors invite or even require students to do multimedia reports or to use videos, photo collages, cartoons, or other media to make arguments—an assignment not unlike that given to the artists in the Smithsonian's "Star-Spangled Banner" project. If using visual media still strikes you as odd in academic settings, just consider that such arguments can have all the reach and versatility of more conventional verbal appeals to pathos, ethos, and logos. Often even more.

Using Images and Visual Design to Create Pathos

Many advertisements, YouTube videos, political posters, rallies, marches, and even church services use visual images to trigger emotions. You can't flip through a magazine, watch a video, or browse the Web without being cajoled or seduced by figures or design elements of all kinds—most of them fashioned in some way to attract your eye and attention.

Technology has also made it incredibly easy for you to create on-the-spot photographs and videos that you can use for making arguments of your own. With a GoPro camera strapped to your head, you could document transportation problems in and around campus and then present your visual evidence in a paper or an oral report. You don't have to be a professional these days to produce poignant, stirring, or even satirical visual texts.

Yet just because images are powerful doesn't mean they always work. When you compose visually, you have to be certain to generate impressions that support your arguments, not weigh against them.

Shape Visuals to Convey Appropriate Feelings

To appeal visually to your readers' emotions, think first of the goal of your writing: you want every image or use of multimedia to advance that purpose. Consider, for a moment, the iconic *Apollo 8* "earthrise" photograph of our planet hanging above the horizon of the moon. You could adapt this image to introduce an appeal for additional investment in the space program. Or it might become part of an argument about the need to preserve frail natural environments, or a stirring appeal against nationalism: *From space, we are one world.* Any of these claims might be supported successfully without the image, but the photograph — like most visuals — will probably touch members of your audience more strongly than words alone could.

FIGURE 22.2 Still striking almost fifty years later, this 1968 *Apollo 8* photograph of the earth shining over the moon can support many kinds of arguments. NASA

Consider Emotional Responses to Color

As the "earthrise" photo demonstrates, color can have great power too: the beautiful blue earth floating in deep black space carries a message of its own. Indeed, our response to color is part of our biological and cultural makeup. So it makes sense to consider what shades are especially effective with the kinds of arguments you're making, whether they occur in images themselves or in elements such as headings, fonts, backgrounds, screens, banners and so on. And remember that a black-and-white image can also be a memorable design choice.

In most situations, let your selection of colors be guided by your own good taste, by designs you admire, or by the advice of friends or helpful professionals. Some design and presentation software will even help you choose colors by offering dependable "default" shades or an array of pre-existing designs and compatible colors (for example, of presentation slides). To be emotionally effective, the colors you choose for a design should follow certain commonsense principles. If you're using background colors on a political poster, Web site, or slide, the contrast between words and background should be vivid enough to make reading easy. For example, white letters on a yellow background are not usually legible. Similarly, bright background colors should be avoided for long documents because reading is easiest with dark letters against a light or white background. Avoid complex patterns; even though they might look interesting and be easy to create, they often interfere with other more important elements of a presentation.

When you use visuals in your college projects, test them on prospective readers. That's what professionals do because they appreciate how delicate the choices of visual and multimedia texts can be. These responses will help you analyze your own arguments and improve your success with them.

FIGURE 22.3 Eve Arnold took this powerful black-and-white photograph in 1958 at a party in Virginia for students being introduced to mixed-race schools. How might a full-color image have changed the impact of the scene? © Eve Arnold/Magnum Photos

Using Images to Establish Ethos

If you are on Facebook, LinkedIn, or other social networking sites, you no doubt chose photographs for those sites with an eye to creating a sense of who you are, what you value, and how you wish to be perceived. You fashioned a self-image. So it shouldn't come as a surprise that you can boost your credibility as a writer by using visual design strategically: we know one person whose Facebook presentation of images and media so impressed a prospective employer that she got a job on the spot. So whether you are using photographs, videos, or other media on your personal pages or in your college work, it pays to attend to how they construct your ethos.

FIGURE 22.4 How does a photograph like this 1999 Bruce Davidson shot of President Bill Clinton shape your sense of Clinton's ethos? Based on this image alone, what words might you use to describe Clinton as a *politician*? © Bruce Davidson/Magnum Photos

Understand How Images Enhance Credibility and Authority

You might have noticed that just about every company, organization, institution, government agency, or club now sports a logo or an emblem. Whether it's the Red Cross, the Canadian Olympic Committee, or perhaps the school you attend, such groups use carefully crafted images to signal their authority and trustworthiness. An emblem or a logo can also carry a wealth of cultural and historical implications. That's why university Web sites typically include the seal of the institution somewhere on the homepage (and always on its letterhead) or why the president of the United States travels with a presidential seal to hang on the speaker's podium.

Though you probably don't have a personal logo or trademark, your personal ethos functions the same way when you make an argument. You can establish it by offering visual evidence of your knowledge or competence. In an essay on safety issues in competitive biking, you might include a photo of yourself in a key race, embed a video showing how often serious accidents occur, or include an audio file of an interview with an injured biker. The photo proves that you have personal experience with biking, while the video and audio files show that you have done research and know your subject well, thus helping to affirm your credibility.

Predictably, your choice of *medium* also says something important about you. Making an appeal on a Web site sends signals about your technical skills, contemporary orientation, and personality. So if you direct people to a Facebook or Flickr page, be sure that any materials there present you favorably. Be just as careful in a classroom that any handouts or slides you use for an oral report demonstrate your competence. And remember that you don't always have to be high-tech to be effective: when reporting on a children's story that you're writing, the most sensible medium of presentation might be cardboard and paper made into an oversized book and illustrated by hand.

You demonstrate your ethos simply by showing an awareness of the basic design conventions for any kind of writing you're doing. It's no accident that lab reports for science courses are sober and unembellished. Visually, they reinforce the professional ethos of scientific work. The same is true of a college research paper. So whether you're composing a term paper, a résumé, a film, an animated comic, or a Web site, look for successful models and follow their design cues.

FIGURE 22.5 Take a look at these three government logos, each of which intends to convey credibility, authority, and maybe more. Do they accomplish their goals? Why or why not? Left to right: NASA; Courtesy Internal Revenue Service; Courtesy Environmental Protection Agency

Consider How Details of Design Reflect Your Ethos

As we have just suggested, almost every design element you use in a paper or project sends signals about character and ethos. You might resent the tediousness of placing page numbers in the appropriate corner, aligning long quotations just so, and putting footnotes in the right place, but these details prove that you are paying attention. Gestures as simple as writing on official stationery (if, for example, you are representing a club or campus organization) or dressing up for an oral presentation matter too: suddenly you seem more mature and competent.

Even the type fonts that you select for a document can mark you as warm and inviting or as efficient and contemporary. The warm and inviting fonts often belong to a family called *serif*. The serifs are those little flourishes at the ends of the strokes that make the fonts seem handcrafted and artful:

warm and inviting (Bookman Old Style)

warm and inviting (Times New Roman)

warm and inviting (Georgia)

Cleaner, modern fonts go without those little flourishes and are called *sans serif*. These fonts are cooler, simpler, and, some argue, more readable on a computer screen (depending on screen resolution):

efficient and contemporary (Helvetica)

efficient and contemporary (Verdana)

efficient and contemporary (Comic Sans MS)

Other typographic elements send messages as well. The size of type can make a difference. If your text or headings are in boldface and too large, you'll seem to be shouting:

LOSE WEIGHT! PAY NOTHING!*

Tiny type, on the other hand, might make you seem evasive:

*Excludes the costs of enrollment and required meal purchases. Minimum contract: 12 months.

Finally, don't ignore the signals you send through your choice of *illustrations* and *photographs* themselves. Images communicate your preferences, sensitivities, and inclusiveness—sometimes inadvertently. Conference planners, for example, are careful to create brochures that represent all participants, and they make sure that the brochure photos don't show only women, only men, or only members of one racial or ethnic group.

RESPOND

Choose a project or an essay you have written recently and examine it for how well *visually* it establishes your credibility and how well it is designed. Ask a classmate or friend to look at it and describe the ethos you convey through the item. Then go back to the drawing board with a memo to yourself about how you might use images or media to improve it.

FIGURE 22.6 Who's missing in this picture of senior advisers to the president taken in December 2012? The *New York Times*, which published the item, pointed out that, if you looked very closely, you could see Valerie Jarrett's leg. The White House, photo by Pete Souza

Using Visual Images to Support Logos

Not that long ago, media critics ridiculed the colorful charts and graphs in newspapers like *USA Today*. Now, comparable features appear in even the most traditional publications because they work: they convey information efficiently *and* persuasively. We now expect evidence to be presented graphically and have learned to use and interact with multiple streams of data and information.

Organize Information Visually

Graphic presentation calls for design that enables readers and viewers to look at an item and understand what it does. A brilliant, much-copied ex-ample of such an intuitive design is a seat adjuster invented many years ago by Mercedes-Benz (see photo below). It's shaped like a tiny seat. Push any element of the control, and the real seat moves in that direction—back and forth, up and down. No instructions are necessary.

FIGURE 22.7 Mercedes-Benz's seat adjuster © Ron Kimball/Kimball Stock

Good visual design can work the same way in an argument by conveying evidence, data, and other information without elaborate instructions. Titles, headings, subheadings, enlarged quotations, running heads, and boxes are some common visual signals:

- Use headings to guide your readers through your print or electronic document. For long and complex pieces, use subheadings as well, and make sure they are parallel.

- Use type font, size, and color to show related information among headings.

- Arrange headings or text on a page to enforce relationships among comparable items, ideas, or bits of evidence.

- Use a list or a box to set off material for emphasis or to show that it differs from the rest of the presentation. You can also use shading, color, and typography for emphasis.

- Place your images and illustrations strategically. What you position front and center will appear more important than items in less conspicuous places. Images of comparable size will be treated as equally important.

Remember, too, that design principles evolve and change from medium to medium. A printed text or presentation slide, for example, ordinarily works best when its elements are easy to read, simply organized, and surrounded by restful white space. But some electronic texts thrive on visual clutter, packing a grab bag of data into a limited space (See the "infographic of Infographics" on p. 467.) Look closely, though, and you'll probably find the logic in these designs.

Use Visuals to Convey Data Efficiently

Words are capable of great precision and subtlety, but some information is conveyed far more effectively by charts, graphs, drawings, maps, or photos—as several items in Chapter 12 illustrate. When making an argument, especially to a large group, consider what information might be more persuasive and memorable in nonverbal form.

A *pie chart* is an effective way of comparing parts to the whole. You might use a pie chart to illustrate the ethnic composition of your school, the percentage of taxes paid by people at different income levels, or the consumption of energy by different nations. Pie charts depict such information memorably.

A *graph* is an efficient device for comparing items over time or according to other variables. You could use a graph to trace the rise and fall of test scores over several decades, to show college enrollment by sex, race, and Hispanic origin, or to track bicycle usage in the United States, as in the bar graph on p. 468.

Diagrams or *drawings* are useful for attracting attention to details. Use drawings to illustrate complex physical processes or designs of all sorts. After the 2001 attack on the World Trade Center, for example, engineers prepared drawings and diagrams to help citizens understand precisely what led to the total collapse of the buildings.

You can use *maps* to illustrate location and spatial relationships—something as simple as the distribution of office space in your student union or as complex as poverty in the United States, as in the map on p. 468. In fact, scholars in many fields now use geographic information system (GIS) technology to merge maps with databases in all fields to offer new kinds of arguments about everything from traffic patterns and health care trends to character movements in literary works. Plotting data this way yields information far different from what might be offered in words alone. You can find more about GIS applications online.

Timelines allow you to represent the passage of time graphically, and online tools like Dipity can help you create them for insertion into your documents. Similarly, Web pages can make for valuable illustrations. Programs like ShrinkTheWeb let you create snapshots of Web sites that can then be inserted easily into your writing. And when you want to combine a variety of graphs, charts, and other texts into a single visual argument, you might create an *infographic* using software such as Google Public Data Explorer, Many Eyes, StatPlanet, and Wordle.

Follow Professional Guidelines for Presenting Visuals

Charts, graphs, tables, illustrations, timelines, snapshots of Web sites, and video clips play such an important role in many fields that professional groups have come up with guidelines for labeling and formatting these items. You need to become familiar with those conventions as you advance in a field. A guide such as the *Publication Manual of the American Psychological Association* (6th edition) or the *MLA Handbook for Writers of Research Papers* (7th edition) describes these rules in detail. See also Chapter 23, "Presenting Arguments."

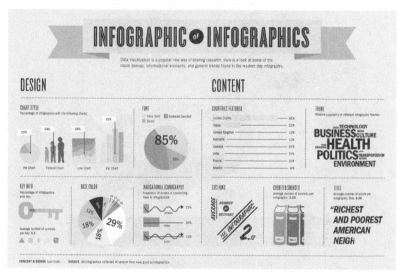

FIGURE 22.8   © Ivan Cash, CashStudios.com

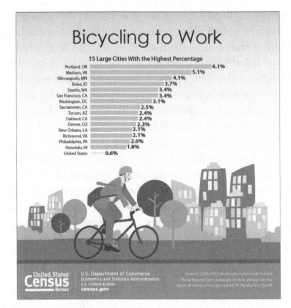

FIGURE 22.9 U.S. Census Bureau

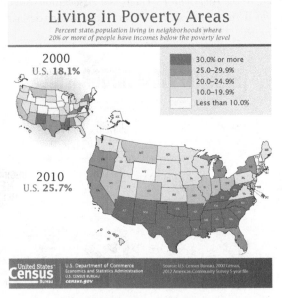

FIGURE 22.10 U.S. Census Bureau

Remember to Check for Copyrighted Material

You also must be careful to respect copyright rules when using visual items that were created by someone else. If you do introduce any borrowed items into academic work, be careful to document them fully. It's relatively easy these days to download visual texts of all kinds from the Web. Some of these items — such as clip art or government documents — may be in the *public domain*, meaning that you're free to use them without requesting permission or paying a royalty. But other visual texts may require permission, especially if you intend to publish your work or use the item commercially. Remember: anything you place on a Web site is considered "published." (See Chapter 29 for more on intellectual property and fair use.)

Presenting Arguments

For many arguments you make in college, the format you've used since grade school is still a sensible choice—a traditional paper with double spacing, correct margins, MLA- or APA-style notes, and so on. Printed texts like these offer a methodical way to explain abstract ideas or to set down complicated chains of reasoning. Even spruced up with images or presented online (to enable color, media, and Web links), such conventional arguments—whether configured as essays, newsletters, or brochures—are cheap to create and easy to reproduce and share. You will find examples of printed texts throughout this book and especially in **Part 5** on "Research and Arguments."

But print isn't your only medium for advancing arguments. Sometimes, you'll need to make a case orally, drawing on the visual or multimedia strategies discussed in previous chapters. Like Lawrence Lessig above, speaking about Internet gambling, you might need slides and Web tools to back up points in a lecture; or like Josette Sheeran, a panelist at a conference on world food security, you may find yourself engaged in serious discussions; or maybe like fellow student George Chidiac, you just need to deliver a first-rate oral report in class. Knowing how to speak eloquently to a point is a basic rhetorical skill.

Left to right: AP Photo/Paul Chiasson, CP; AP Photo/Andrew Medichini; Courtesy of George Chidiac

Class and Public Discussions

No doubt you find yourself arguing all the time at school, maybe over a poem with a classmate in an English course or perhaps with a teaching assistant whose interpretation of economic trends you're sure is flat wrong. Or maybe you spoke up at a campus meeting against the administration's enforcement of "free speech zones" — *or wish you had*. The fact is, lots of people are shy about joining class discussions or public debates, even those that interest them. They find such occasions intimidating. Perhaps they don't want to tip their hands, or fear they know too little about a subject, or simply don't like the give-and-take of spirited debate.

You can improve your participation in such situations by observing both effective and ineffective speakers. Watch how the participants who enliven a discussion stay on topic, add new information or ideas, and pay attention to all members of the group. Notice, too, that less successful speakers often can't stop talking, somehow make all discussions about themselves, or just play the smart aleck when they don't know much about a topic. Surely, you can do better.

You can start just by joining in on conversations whenever you can. If speaking is a problem, take it slow at first — a comment or two, something as simple as "That's a really good idea!" or "I wonder how accurate this data is?" The more that you hear your own voice in discussions, the more comfortable you'll be offering your opinions in detail. Here are some more tips:

- Do the required reading in a class so that you know what you're talking about. That alone will give you a leg up in most groups.

- Listen carefully and purposefully, and jot down important points.

- Speak briefly to the point under discussion so that your comments are relevant. Don't do all the talking.

- Ask questions about issues that bother you: others probably have the same thoughts.

- Occasionally, summarize points that have already been made to make sure that everyone is "on the same page." Keep the summary brief.

- Respond to questions or comments by others in specific rather than vague terms.

- Try to learn the names of people in a discussion, and then use them.

- When you're already a player in a discussion, invite others to join in.

CULTURAL CONTEXTS FOR ARGUMENT

Speaking Up in Class

Speaking up in class is viewed as inappropriate or even rude in some cultures. In the United States and Canada, however, doing so is ex-pected and encouraged. Some instructors even assign credit for such class participation.

Preparing a Presentation

Sooner or later, you'll be asked to deliver a presentation in a college class. That's because the ability to explain material clearly to an audience is a skill much admired by potential employers. Unfortunately, instructors sometimes give little practical advice about how to hone that talent, which is not a natural gift for most people. While it's hard to generalize here, capable presenters attribute their success to the following strategies and perceptions:

- They make sure they know their subjects thoroughly.
- They pay attention to the values, ideas, and needs of their listeners.
- They use patterns and styles that make their spoken arguments easy to follow.
- They realize that oral arguments are interactive. (Live audiences can argue back!)
- They appreciate that most oral presentations involve visuals, and they plan accordingly. (We'll address multimedia presentations in the next chapter.)
- They practice, practice—and then practice some more.

We suggest a few additional moves for when you are specifically required to make a formal argument or presentation in class (or on the job): assess the rhetorical situation you face, nail down the details of the presentation, fashion a script or plan, choose media to fit your subject, and then deliver a good show.

Assess the Rhetorical Situation

Whether asked to make a formal oral report in class, to speak to the general public, or to join a panel discussion, ask yourself the same questions about rhetorical choices that you face whenever you make an argument.

Understanding Purpose. Figure out the major purpose of the assignment or situation. Is it to inform and enlighten your audience? To convince or persuade them? To explore a concept or principle? To stimulate discussion? To encourage a decision? Something else? Very important in school, will you be speaking to share your expertise or to prove that you have it (as you might in a class report)?

Assessing the Audience. Determine who will be listening to your talk. Just an instructor and classmates? Interested observers at a public meeting? People who know more about the subject than you do—or less? Or will you be a peer of the audience members—typically, a classmate? What mix of age groups, of gender, of political affiliation, of rank, etc., will be in the group? What expectations will listeners bring to the talk, and what opinions are they likely to hold? Will this audience be invited to ask questions after the event?

Deciding on Content. What exactly is the topic for the presentation? What is its general scope? Are you expected to make a narrow and specific argument drawn from a research assignment? Are you expected to argue facts, definitions, causes and effects? Will you be offering an evaluation or perhaps a proposal? What degree of detail is necessary, and how much evidence should you provide for your claims?

Choosing Structure and Style. Will your instructor or audience expect a specific type of report? What "parts" must your presentation include: introduction, background information, thesis, evidence, refutation, discussion, conclusion? Can you model the talk after other reports you have heard or public events you have attended? Can you modify a conventional presentation to suit your topic better? Will the audience expect a serious presentation in academic style or can you be friendly and colloquial, perhaps even funny? Crucially, by what standards is your report likely to be assessed or graded?

FIGURE 23.1 Here's a live audience watching an HD broadcast of a performance inside the opera house right in front of them. Probably a grumpy group. Lonely Planet/Getty Images

Following are three excerpts from a detailed, three-page outline that sophomore George Chidiac worked up on his own to prepare for a fifteen-minute oral report on Thomas More's "Petition for Free Speech" (1523)—an important document on the path to establishing free speech as a natural right. Chidiac's outline of rhetorical issues and concerns prepped him well enough to deliver the entire report without notes. His thesis is highlighted, but also notice the question Chidiac asks at the very end: *So what?* He recognizes an obligation to explain why his report should matter to his audience.

Oral Report Outline

Requirements:

10 minutes

Share what I've learned in my research

Help colleagues appreciate the research I've done

Introduction

Introduce myself

Agenda—subject of presentation

> Define free speech: the right to express any opinions without censorship or restraint

Set the stage and present a dilemma

> <u>Stage:</u> From history of free speech, we are going to micro-focus to Renaissance, to 16th-century England, to April 18, 1523, in the House of Commons where I want to share insight on a pivotal point in the advancement of free speech in a political context.

> <u>Dilemma:</u> The king called all his advisers and those able to enact legislation to raise funds to go to war. You are the intermediary between the main legislative body and the king. You have three obligations: one to truth, one to the king, and one to the body you're representing. The king wants money, the legislative body cannot object, and you want truth and the best outcome to win out. How do you *reconcile* this?

What

What's my message? What's the focal point of my presentation?

> I want to provide a snapshot in time of the evolution of free speech.

> Thomas More, in his *Petition for Free Speech*, incrementally advanced free speech as a duty and a right.

Who

Who made this happen? Who was involved?

> Thomas More

>> Brief bio: Before he became Speaker → Chancellor of England, friend of King Henry VIII, theologian, poet, father

Henry VIII

William Roper (minor role)

    Brief bio: son-in-law and chief biographer

* * *

Why

Why was More's Petition "successful"? Why did Henry VIII accept the petition?

    Henry VIII's character

        Humanist—or wished to subscribe to humanist principles

        Resembled More

            Rediscovery and reevaluation of classical civilization and application into modern intellectual and social culture

            Spirit of *amicitia*—friendship with counsel—constancy, mutual loyalty, and concern for justice where the crux was "freedom of speech"

    Parliamentary expectations

        Relationship between king and Parliament

            Still a matter of license, not true freedom—sufferance

            Members of Parliament acting in goodwill

            By accepting the petition, Henry acknowledged that while not all parliamentary speech should be *permitted*, not all speech critical of monarchy is *slanderous*

    Oncoming war

* * *

SO WHAT?

What do I want my colleagues to take with them? Big lesson?

    Freedom of speech we have today wasn't always enjoyed.

Nail Down the Specific Details

Big-picture rhetorical considerations are obviously important in an oral report, but so are the details. Pay attention to exactly how much time you have to prepare for an event, a lecture, or a panel session, and how long the actual presentation should be: *never* infringe on the time of other speakers. Determine what visual aids, slides, or handouts might make the presentation successful. Will you need an overhead projector, a flip chart, a whiteboard? Decide whether presentation software, such as PowerPoint, Keynote, or Prezi, will help you make a stronger report. Then figure out where to acquire the equipment as well as the expertise to use it. If you run into problems, especially with classroom reports, consider low-tech alternatives. Sometimes, speaking clearly or sharing effective handouts works better than a plodding slideshow.

If possible, check out where your presentation will take place. In a classroom with fixed chairs? A lecture or assembly hall? An informal sitting area? Will you have a lectern? Other equipment? Will you sit or stand? Remain in one place or move around? What will the lighting be, and can you adjust it? Take nothing for granted, and if you plan to use media equipment, be ready with a backup strategy if a projector bulb dies or a Web site won't load.

Not infrequently, oral presentations are group efforts. When that's the case, plan and practice accordingly. The work should be divvied up according to the strengths of the participants: you will need to work out who speaks when, who handles the equipment, who takes the questions, and so on.

Fashion a Script Designed to Be Heard by an Audience

Unless you are presenting a formal lecture (pretty rare in college), most oral presentations are delivered from notes. But even if you do deliver a live presentation from a printed text, be sure to compose a script that is designed to be *heard* rather than *read*. Such a text—whether in the form of note cards, an overhead list, or a fully written-out paper—should feature a strong introduction and conclusion, an unambiguous structure with helpful transitions and signposts, concrete diction, and straightforward syntax.

Strong Introductions and Conclusions. Like readers, listeners remember beginnings and endings best. Work hard, therefore, to make these elements of your spoken argument memorable and personable. Consider including a provocative or puzzling statement, opinion, or question; a memorable anecdote; a powerful quotation; or a strong visual image. If you can connect your report directly to the interests or experiences of your listeners in the introduction or conclusion, then do so.

Be sure that your introduction clearly explains what your presentation will cover, what your focus will be, and perhaps even how the presentation will be arranged. Give listeners a mental map of where you are taking them. If you are using presentation software, a bare-bones outline sometimes makes sense, especially when the argument is a straightforward academic presentation: thesis + evidence.

The conclusion should drive home and reinforce your main point. You can summarize the key arguments you have made (again, a simple slide could do some of the work), but you don't want to end with just a rehash, especially when the presentation is short. Instead, conclude by underscoring the *implications* of your report: what do you want your audience to be thinking and feeling at the end?

Clear Structures and Signposts. For a spoken argument, you want your organizational structure to be crystal clear. So make sure that you have a sharply delineated beginning, middle, and end and share the structure with listeners. You can do that by remembering to pause between major points of your presentation and to offer *signposts* marking your movement from one topic to the next. They can be transitions as obvious as *next, on the contrary,* or *finally*. Such words act as memory points in your spoken argument and thus should be explicit and concrete: *The second crisis point in the breakup of the Soviet Union occurred hard on the heels of the first,* rather than just *The breakup of the Soviet Union led to another crisis.* You can also keep listeners on track by repeating key words and concepts and by using unambiguous topic sentences to introduce each new idea. These transitions can also be highlighted as you come to them on a whiteboard or on presentation slides.

Straightforward Syntax and Concrete Diction. Avoid long, complicated sentences in an oral report and use straightforward syntax (subject-verb-object, for instance, rather than an inversion of that order). Remember, too, that listeners can grasp concrete verbs and nouns more easily than they can mentally process a steady stream of abstractions. When you need to deal with abstract ideas, illustrate them with concrete examples.

Take a look at the following text that student Ben McCorkle wrote about *The Simpsons,* first as he prepared it for an essay and then as he adapted it for a live oral and multimedia presentation:

Print Version

The Simpson family has occasionally been described as a *nuclear* family, which obviously has a double meaning: first, the family consists of two parents and three children, and, second, Homer works at a nuclear power plant with very relaxed safety codes. The overused label "dysfunctional," when applied to the Simpsons, suddenly takes on new meaning. Every episode seems to include a scene in which son Bart is being choked by his father, the baby is being neglected, or Homer is sitting in a drunken stupor transfixed by the television screen. The comedy in these scenes comes from the exaggeration of commonplace household events (although some talk shows and news programs would have us believe that these exaggerations are not confined to the madcap world of cartoons).

—Ben McCorkle, "*The Simpsons*: A Mirror of Society"

Oral Version (with a visual illustration)

What does it mean to describe the Simpsons as a *nuclear* family? Clearly, a double meaning is at work. First, the Simpsons fit the dictionary meaning—a family unit consisting of two parents and some children. The second meaning, however, packs more of a punch. You see, Homer works at a nuclear power plant [pause here] with *very* relaxed safety codes!

Still another overused family label describes the Simpsons. Did everyone guess I was going to say *dysfunctional*? And like *nuclear*, when it comes to the Simpsons, *dysfunctional* takes on a whole new meaning.

Remember the scene when Bart is being choked by his father?

How about the many times the baby is being neglected?

Or the classic view—Homer sitting in a stupor transfixed by the TV screen!

My point here is that the comedy in these scenes often comes from double meanings—and from a lot of exaggeration of everyday household events.

Note that the second version presents the same information as the first, but this time it's written to be *heard*. The revision uses simpler syntax, so the argument is easy to listen to, and employs signposts, repetition, a list, and italicized words to prompt the speaker to give special emphasis where needed.

FIGURE 23.2 Homer Simpson in a typical pose © Photofest, Inc.

RESPOND

Take three or four paragraphs from an essay that you've recently written. Then, following the guidelines in this chapter, rewrite the passage to be heard by a live audience. Finally, make a list of every change that you made.

Repetition, Parallelism, and Climactic Order. Whether they're used alone or in combination, repetition, parallelism, and climactic order are especially appropriate for spoken arguments that sound a call to arms or that seek to rouse the emotions of an audience. Perhaps no person in the twentieth century used them more effectively than Martin Luther King Jr., whose sermons and speeches helped to spearhead the civil rights movement. Standing on the steps of the Lincoln Memorial in Washington, D.C., on August 23, 1963, with hundreds of thousands of marchers before him, King called on the nation to make good on the "promissory note" represented by the Emancipation Proclamation.

Look at the way that King uses repetition, parallelism, and climactic order in the following paragraph to invoke a nation to action:

> It is obvious today that America has defaulted on this promissory note insofar as her citizens of color are concerned. Instead of honoring this sacred obligation, America has given the Negro people a bad *check* which has come back marked *"insufficient funds."* But *we* refuse to believe that the bank of justice is bankrupt. *We* refuse to believe that there are *insufficient funds* in the great vaults of opportunity of this nation. So *we have come* to cash this *check*—a *check* that will give us upon demand the riches of freedom and the security of justice. *We have also come* to this hallowed spot to remind America of the fierce urgency of now. There is no time to engage in the luxury of cooling off or to take the tranquillizing drug of gradualism. *Now* is the time *to rise* from the dark and desolate valley of segregation to the sunlit path of racial justice. *Now* is the time *to open* the doors of opportunity to all of God's children. *Now* is the time *to lift* our nation from the quicksands of racial injustice to the solid rock of brotherhood.
>
> —Martin Luther King Jr., "I Have a Dream" (emphasis added)

The italicized words highlight the way that King uses repetition to drum home his theme and a series of powerful verb phrases (*to rise, to open, to lift*) to build to a strong climax. These stylistic choices, together with the vivid image of the "bad check," help to make King's speech powerful, persuasive—and memorable.

You don't have to be as highly skilled as King to take advantage of the power of repetition and parallelism. Simply repeating a key word in your argument can impress it on your audience, as can arranging parts of sentences or items in a list in parallel order.

Choose Media to Fit Your Subject

Visual materials—charts, graphs, posters, and presentation slides—are major tools for conveying your message and supporting your claims. People are so accustomed to visual (and aural) texts that they genuinely expect to see them in most oral reports. And, in many cases, a picture, video, or graph can truly be worth a thousand words. (For more about visual argument, see Chapter 22.)

Successful Use of Visuals. Be certain that any visuals that you use are large enough to be seen by all members of your audience. If you use slides or overhead projections, the information on each frame should be simple, clear, and easy to process. For slides, use 24-point type for major headings, 18 point for subheadings, and at least 14 point for other text. Remember, too, to limit the number of words per slide. The same rules of clarity and simplicity hold true for posters, flip charts, and whiteboards. (Note that if your presentation is based on source materials—either text or images—remember to include a slide that lists all those sources at the end of the presentation.)

Use presentation software to furnish an overview for a report or lecture and to give visual information and signposts to listeners. Audiences will be grateful to see the people you are discussing, the key data points you are addressing, the movement of your argument as it develops. But if you've watched many oral presentations, you're sure to have seen some bad ones. Perhaps nothing is deadlier than a speaker who stands up and just reads from each screen. Do this and you'll just put people to sleep. Also remember not to turn your back on your audience when you refer to these visuals. And if you prepare supplementary materials (such as bibliographies or other handouts), don't distribute them until the audience actually needs them, or wait until the end of the presentation so that they don't distract listeners from your spoken arguments. (For advice on creating multimedia arguments, see Chapter 24.)

The best way to test the effectiveness of any images, slides, or other visuals is to try them out on friends, family members, classmates, or roommates. If they don't get the meaning of the visuals right away, revise and try again.

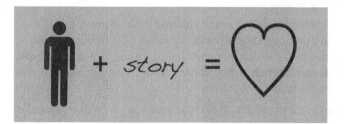

FIGURE 23.3 Four simple and evocative slides from a presentation entitled "We Learn through Stories." Imagine the commentary that might accompany them. *Photo:* Fotovika/Shutterstock; *Diagrams:* Darren Kuropatwa; Robot designed by Simon Child from the Noun Project-Creative Commons—Attribution (CC BY 3.0)

Accommodations for Everyone. Remember that visuals and accompanying media tools can help make your presentation accessible but that some members of your audience may not be able to see your presentation or may have trouble seeing or hearing them. Here are a few key rules to remember:

- Use words to describe projected images. Something as simple as "That's Eleanor Roosevelt in 1944" can help even sight-impaired audience members appreciate what's on a screen.

- If you use video, take the time to label sounds that might not be audible to audience members who are hearing impaired. (Be sure your equipment is caption capable and use the captions; they can be helpful to everyone when audio quality is poor.)

- For a lecture, consider providing a written handout that summarizes your argument or putting the text on an overhead projector — for those who learn better by reading *and* listening.

Deliver a Good Show

In spite of your best preparation, you may feel some anxiety before a live presentation. This is natural. (According to one Gallup poll, Americans often identify public speaking as a major fear — scarier than possible attacks from outer space.) Experienced speakers say that they have strategies for dealing with anxiety, and even suggest that a little nervousness — and its accompanying adrenaline — can work to a speaker's advantage.

The most effective strategy seems to be simply knowing your topic and material thoroughly. Confidence in your own knowledge goes a long way toward making you an eloquent speaker. In addition to being well prepared, you may want to try some of the following strategies:

- Practice a number of times, running through every part of the presentation. Leave nothing out, even audio or video clips. Work with the equipment you intend to use so that you are familiar with it. It also may help to visualize your presentation, imagining the scene in your mind as you run through your materials.

- Time your presentation to make sure you stay within your allotted slot.

- Tape yourself (video, if possible) at least once so that you can listen to your voice. Tone of voice and body language can dispose audiences for — or against — speakers. For most oral arguments, you want to develop a tone that conveys commitment to your position as well as respect for your audience.

- Think about how you'll dress for your presentation, remembering that audience members notice how a speaker looks. Dressing for a presentation depends on what's appropriate for your topic, audience, and setting, but experienced speakers choose clothes that are comfortable, allow easy movement, and aren't overly casual. Dressing up indicates that you take pride in your appearance, have confidence in your argument, and respect your audience. (Notice George Chidiac's bow tie on **p. 470**.)

- Get some rest before the presentation, and avoid consuming too much caffeine.

- Relax! Consider doing some deep-breathing exercises. Then pause just before you begin, concentrating on your opening lines.

- Maintain eye contact with members of your audience. Speak to them, not to your text or to the floor.

- Interact with the audience whenever possible; doing so will often help you relax and even have some fun.

- Most speakers make a stronger impression standing than sitting, so stand if you have that option. Moving around a bit may help you maintain good eye contact.

- Remember to allow time for audience responses and questions. Keep your answers brief so that others may join the conversation.

- Finally, at the very end of your presentation, thank the audience for its attention to your arguments.

A Note about Webcasts: Live Presentations over the Web

This discussion of live oral presentations has assumed that you'll be speaking before an audience in the same room with you. Increasingly, though—especially in business, industry, and science—the presentations you make will be live, but you won't occupy the same physical space as the audience. Instead, you might be in front of a camera that will capture your voice and image and relay them via the Web to attendees who might be anywhere in the world. In another type of Webcast, participants can see only your slides or the software that you're demonstrating, using a screen-capture relay without cameras: you're not visible but still speaking live.

In either case, most of the strategies that work well for oral presentations with an in-house audience will continue to serve in Webcast environments. But there are some significant differences:

- Practice is even more important in Webcasts, since you need to be able to access online any slides, documents, video clips, names, dates, and sources that you provide during the Webcast.

- Because you can't make eye contact with audience members, it's important to remember to look into the camera (if you are using one), at least from time to time. If you're using a stationary Webcam, perhaps one mounted on your computer, practice standing or sitting without moving out of the frame and yet without looking stiff.

- Even though your audience may not be visible to you, assume that if you're on camera, the Web-based audience can see you. If you slouch, they'll notice. Assume too that your microphone is always live. Don't mutter under your breath, for example, when someone else is speaking or asking a question.

RESPOND

Attend a presentation on your campus, and observe the speaker's delivery. Note the strategies that the speaker uses to capture and hold your attention (or not). What signpost language and other guides to listening can you detect? How well are visuals integrated into the presentation? What aspects of the speaker's tone, dress, eye contact, and movement affect your understanding and your appreciation (or lack of it)? What's most memorable about the presentation, and why? Finally, write up an analysis of this presentation's effectiveness.

CHAPTER
24

Multimedia Arguments

The very first paragraph in Chapter 9 features a tweet by Michelle Obama focusing on political kidnapping in Nigeria. And elsewhere in the book, we draw on examples from a wide range of media and genres, including online news sources, blog posts and comments, editorial cartoons, ads, maps, infographics, bumper stickers, even a selfie—and of the pope, no less. In one way or another, all of these items illustrate principles of persuasion. And while much of this book is about more conventional forms of argument—essays, extended articles, and academic papers—the fact is that many arguments are now shaped, distributed, and connected in ways that no one imagined a generation ago.

Online sources used daily such as *Gawker* and *Huffington Post* and social networks such as Facebook and Twitter have virtually redefined the nature of influence and persuasion. The cascade of information you take for granted, the 24-hour news cycle, the incessant connectivity of screens simply amazes anyone old enough to remember when newspapers were flung on doorsteps by kids on bicycles. More to the point here: all this online and onscreen activity is rhetorical in both its aims and its methods. We want to spend a chapter exploring new media, teasing out some connections between traditional modes of persuasion and those currently reshaping our social and political lives.

Left to right: Iain Masterton/age fotostock/Superstock; imageBROKER/Superstock; Yoko Aziz/Superstock

Old Media Transformed by New Media

Civic arguments and opinions used to be delivered orally, typically in speeches, debates, and dialogues and often at public forums. Later, especially after the development of printing, they arrived via paper, and then through other media such as film and over-the-air broadcasting. Some of these traditional channels of communication were actual physical objects distributed one by one: books, journals, newspapers, fliers, photographs. Other "old media" such as movies, TV news, or radio shows were more like performances that could not be distributed or shared readily, at least not until audio- and videotape became cheap. Yet these media were all-powerful, handy, and relatively inexpensive shapers of opinion: books and serious magazines appealed to readers accustomed to intellectual challenges; well-staffed newspapers provided professional (if sometimes sensational) coverage of local and world affairs; nightly, the three national TV networks reached large and relatively undistracted audiences, establishing some degree of cultural consensus.

At least that's the romantic side of old media. We all recognize today the remarkable limitations of paper books and journals or celluloid film and print photographs. But we didn't appreciate quite how clumsy, hard to locate, hard to distribute, hard to search, and hard to archive analog objects could be until they went digital.

FIGURE 24.1 NBA superstar LeBron James chose a traditional genre to announce his return to the Cleveland Cavaliers in 2014, explaining, "I'm doing this essay because I want an opportunity to explain myself *uninterrupted*" (emphasis added). Of course, his essay appeared online at SportsIllustrated.com. Walter Iooss Jr./Sports Illustrated/Contour by Getty Images; Graphics: si.com

Fortunately, to one degree or another, electronic media have made peace with all these genres and formats and transformed them—though almost always with some compromises. Books on e-readers have become like ancient scrolls again, handy for sequential reading, but not so great for moving back and forth or browsing. Magazine articles or newspaper editorials (when not blocked by paywalls) can be found instantly online (or in databases), complete with updates and corrections, links that help establish their context, and, usually, lots and lots of comments. The downside? Lots and lots of inane, offensive, and bitter comments. And of course films and music are now accessible everywhere. You can experience *Lawrence of Arabia*—with its awesome horizons and desert landscapes—on your iPhone while in line at McDonald's. Or maybe you can't.

The bigger point is that the serious, attentive, and carefully researched arguments that represent the best of old media are in no danger of disappearing. Books, research articles, and serious pieces of journalism are still being ground out—and read attentively—in the new media world because they play an essential role there. They provide the logos (see Chapter 12) for innumerable Web sites and Web 2.0 networks, the full-bodied arguments, research studies, and no-nonsense science propping up all those links in tighter, punchier new media features. They give clout and credibility to the quick blog post, the Facebook status, even the trending Twitter hashtag.

FIGURE 24.2 The ubiquitous hashtag is liable to turn up anywhere. knape/Getty Images

New Content in New Media

As you well know, new media represent a vast array of interconnected, electronic platforms where ideas and arguments (and a great deal else) can be introduced and shared. In these "environments," the content is almost anything that can be delivered digitally—words, pictures, movement, and sounds. Perhaps the first Web capability that writers and thinkers appreciated was the distribution of traditional printed texts via online databases; it made possible huge advances in speed, accuracy, and efficiency. (Consider, for a moment, the professional databases in every field and discipline that are available through your school library.)

Online content quickly evolved once it became apparent that just about anyone could create a Web site—and they did. Soon valuable sites emerged, covering every imaginable topic, many of them focusing on serious social and political concerns. Today, such blogs range from those that collect short items and links to promote a topic or point of view (*Instapundit, The Daily Kos*) to slick, full-featured magazines with original content and extensive commentary (*Salon, Gawker*). Social, political, and cultural sites such as Slate, Drudge, and Politico have become powerful shapers of opinion by showcasing a wide variety of writers and arguments. Right from the beginning, blogs demonstrated that interactive online sites could create virtual communities and audiences, enabling people (sometimes acting as citizen journalists) to find allies for their causes and concerns.

FIGURE 24.3 "Like" is easy; contributing is hard.
(See **Chapter 9** on the difference between convincing and persuading.)

Enter Web 2.0 social media and the wildly diverse worlds they now represent. Consider the vast difference among platforms and environments such as Facebook, YouTube, Reddit, Flickr, Pinterest, Yelp, and, of course, Twitter. Reviews on Yelp are by nature evaluative arguments, and many Facebook postings have a persuasive bent, though they may not go much beyond observations, claims, or complaints supported by links or images. Both services are hugely influential because of their vast reach, as is Twitter—despite (or, maybe, *because of*) its 140-character limit. Indeed, the frameworks of these self-selected environments encourage posting and, to varying degrees, opinion making and sharing. And what gets posted in social media? Everything allowed—especially stuff already available in digital form on other online sites: cool pictures, funny people and pets, outrageous videos, trendy performers, and, yes, lots of links to serious talk about politics, culture, and social issues.

New Audiences in New Media

When it comes to making arguments, perhaps the most innovative aspect of new media is its ability to summon audiences. Since ancient times (see p. 172), rhetoricians have emphasized the need to frame arguments to influence people, but new media and social networks now create places for specific audiences to emerge and make the arguments themselves, assembling them in bits and pieces, one comment or supporting link at a time. Audiences muster around sites that represent their perspectives on politics or mirror their social conditions and interests.

It seems natural. Democrats engage with different blog sites than do Libertarians; champions of immigration or gun rights advocates have their favored places too. Within social networks themselves, supporters of causes can join existing activist communities or create new alliances among people with compatible views. And then all those individuals contribute to the never-ending newsfeeds: links, favorite books and authors, preferred images or slogans, illustrative videos, and so on. They stir the pot and generate still more energy, concern, and emotion. It can be very exciting or begin to sound like an echo chamber. But activity within virtual communities itself is potent and powerful. Some have attributed President Obama's second-term electoral victory, in part, to the buzz his campaign generated within social media. These days, assembling an audience may be just as important as making or winning arguments.

FIGURE 24.4 Here's what Twitter's audience looked like when the government of Turkey tried to ban the service. Adem Altam/Getty Images

That principle may help account for the Twitter phenomenon. There, celebrities and political figures alike, for a wide variety of reasons, attract "followers" cued into their occasional 140-character musings (Hillary Clinton: 1.6M followers; Pope Francis: 4.2M; Taylor Swift: 40M+). In some respects, "following" becomes a measure of ethos, the trust and connection people have in the person offering a point of view (see Chapter 11). Sometimes that ethos is largely just about media fame, but in other cases it may measure genuine influence that public figures have earned by virtue of their ideas or opinions. People who sign on as their followers signal their willingness to listen to their Twitter commentary — ideas they probably agree with already.

But logos would seem to have little chance of emerging in a platform like Twitter: can you do much more than make a bare claim or two in the few words and symbols allowed? That's where hashtags come in. Hashtags are words prefixed with a # sign in a Twitter posting to identify a topic and place around which an audience may gather. It provides a way of linking related comments within the vast environment or, just as important, drawing audiences to specific ideas. This is the point, for instance, of Mrs. Obama holding up a card with the #BringBackOurGirls hashtag (see p. 155) — using her ethos to attract an even larger audience to the issue she and many others support. So, once again, the audience in new media becomes a tangible object — its political power evident in the sheer number of people weighing in on controversies, expressing their sentiments succinctly, but also accumulating a sense of direction, solidarity, and gravity. It's also why political journalists or print publications now routinely identify trending hashtags in their reporting or even direct audiences to Twitter to track breaking stories or social movements as they unfold there.

It's a kind of suasion Aristotle could not have imagined.

FIGURE 24.5 No comment necessary. © Andy Singer/Cagle Cartoons, Inc.

Analyzing Multimedia Arguments

As the previous section suggests, a multimedia argument can be complex. But you can figure it out by giving careful attention to its key components: the creators and distributors; the medium it uses; the viewers and readers it hopes to reach; its content and purpose; its design. Following are some questions to ask when you want to understand the rhetorical strategies in arguments and interactions you encounter in social media or on blogs, Web sites, or other nontraditional media. It's worth noting that the questions here don't differ entirely from those you might ask about books, journal articles, news stories, or print ads when composing a rhetorical analysis (see Chapter 14).

Questions about Creators and Distributors

- Who is responsible for this multimedia text? Did someone else distribute, repurpose, or retweet the item?

- What can you find out about these people and any other work they might have done?

- What does the creator's attitude seem to be toward the content: serious, ironic, emotionally charged, satiric, comic? What is the attitude of the distributor, if different from the creator?

- What do the creator and the distributor expect the effects of the text or posting to be? Do they share the same intentions? (Consider, for example, that someone might post an item in order to mock or criticize it.)

Questions about the Medium

- Which media are used by this text? Images only? Words and images? Sound, video, animation, graphs, charts? Does the site or environment where the text appears suggest a metaphor: photo album, pin-up board, message board, chat room?

- In what ways is this text or its online environment interactive? Who can contribute to or comment on it? Where can an item be sent or redirected? How did it get to where you encountered it?

- How do various texts work together in the site? Do they make arguments? Accumulate evidence? Provide readers with examples and illustrations?

- What effect does the medium have on messages or items within it? How would a message, text, or item be altered if different media were used?

- Do claims or arguments play an explicit role in the medium? How are they presented, clarified, reinforced, connected, constrained, or commented upon?

Questions about Audience and Viewers

- What are the likely audiences for the text or medium? How are people invited into the text or site? Who might avoid the experience?

- How does the audience participate in the site or platform? Does the audience respond to content, create it, or something else? What audience interactions or connections occur there? Can participants interact with each other?

- How does the text or media site evoke or reward participation? Are audience members texted or emailed about events or interactions in the site?

Questions about Content and Purpose

- What purpose does the multimedia text achieve? What is it designed to convey?

- What social, cultural, or political values does the text or site support? Cultural interaction? Power? Resistance? Freedom?

- Does the text, alone or in reaction to others, reinforce these values or question them? Does the text constitute an argument in itself or contribute to another claim in some way — as an illustration, example, exception, metaphor, analogy?

- What emotions does the multimedia site or text evoke? Are these the emotions that it intends to raise? How does it do it?

Questions about Design

- How does the site present itself? What draws you to it? How easy is the environment to sign up for, learn, or use?

- How is the multimedia text or environment structured? Does the structure enhance its purpose or functionality? If it presents data, is the information easy to understand? (See also Chapter 22, "Visual Rhetoric.")

- How are arguments, concepts, or ideas presented or framed within the text or environment? How are ideas identified? How are they amplified or connected to other supporting texts and ideas?

- What details are emphasized in the text or media environment? What details are omitted or de-emphasized? To what effect? Is anything down-played, ambiguous, confusing, distracting, or obviously omitted? Why?

- What, if anything, is surprising about the design of the text or environment? What do you think is the purpose of that surprise?

- How are you directed to move within the text or site? Are you encouraged to read further? Click on links? Contribute links and information?

RESPOND

Using the discussion of multimedia arguments in this chapter and the questions about multimedia texts and platforms above, find a multimedia text that makes an intriguing argument or a social media platform where you sometimes encounter debates about political and social issues. Then write a brief rhetorical analysis of the text or the site, focusing more on the way the messages are conveyed than on the messages that are in play.

FIGURE 24.6 This is the central image on the homepage of Wikipedia, a collaborative nonprofit encyclopedia project. Since its launch (as Nupedia) in 2000, Wikipedia has grown to include 31 million articles in 285 languages (4.5 million articles in English), all of them authored by volunteers around the world. This central image acts as a logo, a portal to access the site's content, and, in a way, a mission statement for the organization. How does your eye construct this logo? What do you notice first, and how do your eyes move around the page? Do the parts make sense when you put them together? Creative Commons

Making Multimedia Arguments

Though you have likely been active in new media platforms for quite some time — browsing Web sites, checking Facebook, sending text messages, following "Texas Humor" on Twitter — you may not have thought of these activities as rhetorical. But they certainly can be, especially those that might have classroom or extracurricular connections. Here we discuss just a few such situations. In other chapters in this section, we talk in more detail about visual rhetoric (often a component in new media) and oral presentations, which now almost always have a digital component.

Web Sites

It's likely you have already created Web sites for a class or for an organization to which you belong. In planning any Web site, pay careful attention to your rhetorical situation (see Chapter 9)—the purpose of your site, its intended audience, and the overall impression that you want to make. To get started, you may want to study several sites that you admire, looking for effective design ideas or ways of organizing navigation and information. Creating a map or storyboard for your site will help you to think through the links from page to page.

Experienced Web designers such as Robin Williams cite several important principles for Web-based presentations. The first of these is *contrast*, which is achieved through the use of color, icons, boldface, and so on; contrast helps guide readers through the site (see also Chapter 22). The second principle, *proximity*, calls on you to keep together the parts of a page that are closely related, again for ease of reading. *Repetition* means using a consistent design throughout the site for the elements (such as headings and links) that help readers move smoothly through the environment. Finally, designers concentrate on an *overall impression* or mood for the site, which means that the colors and visuals on the pages should help to create that impression rather than challenge or undermine it.

Here are some additional tips that may help you design your site:

- The homepage should be informative, eye-catching, and inviting (see Chapter 22)—especially when making an argument. Use titles and illustrations to make clear what the site is about.

- Think carefully about two parts of every page—the navigation area (menus or links) and the content areas. You want to make these two areas distinct from one another. And make sure you *have* a navigation area for every page, including links to the key sections of the site and a link back to the homepage. Ease of navigation is one key to a successful Web site.

- Either choose a design template that is provided by Web-writing tools or create a template of your own that ensures that the elements of each page are consistent.

- Consider how to balance claims and evidence on a page. Claims might be connected to supporting links, or they can be enhanced by images or videos that dramatize a position you want to champion.

- Remember to include Web contact information on every page, but not your personal address or phone number.

Videos

When is a video the best medium for delivering a message? Given the ease with which competent digital films can be produced, the answer is certainly more often than ever before. You will see videos routinely now, for example, on college and university sites, showcasing distinguished students and faculty or explaining programs. It is an effective way to enhance the ethos of a group or institution. Videos can also document public events or show how to do practical things such as registering to vote or navigating an unfamiliar campus. So whenever a video fits well with the purpose of the message, consider creating one.

You can, of course, shoot a video with your smartphone. But more sophisticated software might be needed to edit your film and get it ready for prime time: iMovie, Movie Maker, Blender (for animation) or Animoto, Camtasia, and Soundslides (for combining media such as digital video, photos, music, and text).

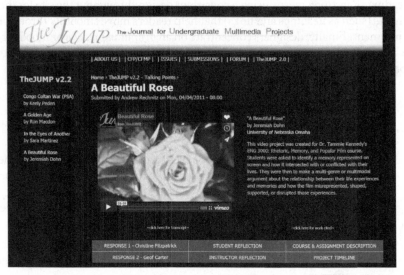

FIGURE 24.7 Here is an example of a video entitled "A Beautiful Rose," created by Jeremiah Dohn for a class assignment and subsequently accepted by the online journal *The Jump.* The Journal for Undergraduate Multimedia Projects

Wikis

To make working on group projects easier, many classes use wikis, which are Web-based sites that enable writers to collaborate in the creation of a single project or database. The most famous group effort of this kind is, of course, Wikipedia, but software such as DokuWiki, MediaWiki, or Tiki Wiki helps people to manage similar, if less ambitious, efforts of their own, whether it be exploring questions raised in academic courses or examining and supporting needs within a community. Wiki projects can be argumentative in themselves, or they might furnish raw data and evidence for subsequent projects.

If asked to participate in a wiki, you should, naturally, learn how to use the assigned software and follow course or project guidelines for entering and documenting the material you contribute. Just as you will expect your colleagues to use reliable sources or make accurate observations, they will depend on you to do your part in shaping the project. Within the wiki, participants will be able to draw upon each other's strengths and, ideally, to compensate for any weaknesses. So take your responsibilities seriously.

Blogs

Perhaps no Web texts have been more instrumental in advancing political, social, and cultural issues than blogs, which are now too numerous to count. Blogs open an ideal space for building interactive communities, engaging in arguments, and giving voice to views and opinions of ordinary citizens. Today, just about all major news media, including the most prestigious newspapers and journals, feature the functionality of blogs or sponsor blogs themselves as part of their electronic versions.

Like everything else, blogs have downsides: they are idiosyncratic, can be self-indulgent and egoistic, and can distort issues by spreading misinformation *very* quickly. If you're a fan of blogs, be sure to read carefully, remembering that information on blogs hasn't been critically reviewed in the way that traditional print sources edit their stories. But also remember that blogs have reported many instances of the mainstream news sources failing to live up to their own standards.

Activist blogs of all kinds get plenty of attention, and you can easily join in on the conversation there, sharing your arguments in the comments section. If you do blog yourself, or comment on others' postings, remember to follow commonsense good manners: be respectful and think carefully about what you are saying and about the impression you want to leave with those who read you. Blogging software, in case you want to open shop yourself, includes Blogger, Tumblr, and WordPress.

Social Media

You likely know a great deal already about the strengths and weaknesses of social media such as Facebook, Twitter, Snapchat, Pinterest, or whatever platforms you use—especially their remarkable ability to absorb big chunks of time.

But do consider how these media may be influencing your political and cultural views, and pay attention to how arguments there are made, supported, and connected. Think about how people with similar views come together in social media and perhaps what role these platforms now play in shaping current social and political activism. What audience roles have you assumed, what causes do you follow or champion, what ethos have you fashioned for yourself in these environments?

Then consider opportunities for using these platforms in your academic work. Social media provide tools for connecting with experts in a field, collaborating on projects with classmates, or sharing your insights with people around the world. Twitter will keep you up-to-date on news and events in almost every field and discipline. And platforms like Facebook or Kickstarter can help you find people who share your ideas and are even willing to support them financially. Social media offer potent (if occasionally risky) tools for expanding all the worlds you live in—including the academic one.

RESPOND

Go to a blog that you admire or consult frequently. Then answer the following questions:

Why is a blog—a digital presentation—the best way to present this material?

What advantages over a print text or a live oral and multimedia presentation does the blog have?

How could you "translate" the argument(s) of this site into print format, oral format, or social media platform? What might be gained or lost in the process?

part 5

Research and Arguments

CHAPTER
25

Academic Arguments

Much of the writing you will do in college (and some of what you will no doubt do later in your professional work) is generally referred to as *academic discourse* or *academic argument*. Although this kind of writing has many distinctive features, in general it shares these characteristics:

- It is based on research and uses evidence that can be documented.
- It is written for a professional, academic, or school audience likely to know something about its topic.
- It makes a clear and compelling point in a fairly formal, clear, and sometimes technical style.
- It follows agreed-upon conventions of format, usage, and punctuation.
- It is documented, using some professional citation style.

Academic writing is serious work, the kind you are expected to do whenever you are assigned a term essay, research paper, or capstone project. Manasi Deshpande's proposal "A Call to Improve Campus Accessibility" in Chapter 20 is an example of an academic argument of the kind you may write in college. You will find other examples of such work throughout this book.

Left to right: Imaginechina via AP Images; AP/Invision/Charles Sykes; © Javier Larrea/age fotostock

Understanding What Academic Argument Is

Academic argument covers a wide range of writing, but its hallmarks are an appeal to reason and a faith in research. As a consequence, such arguments cannot be composed quickly, casually, or off the top of one's head. They require careful reading, accurate reporting, and a conscientious commitment to truth. But academic pieces do not tune out all appeals to ethos or emotion: today, we know that these arguments often convey power and authority through their impressive lists of sources and their immediacy. But an academic argument crumbles if its facts are skewed or its content proves to be unreliable.

Look, for example, how systematically Susannah Fox and Lee Rainie, director and codirector of the Pew Internet Project, present facts and evidence in arguing that the Internet has been, overall, a big plus for society and individuals alike.

> [Today,] 87% of American adults now use the Internet, with near-saturation usage among those living in households earning $75,000 or more (99%), young adults ages 18–29 (97%), and those with college degrees (97%). Fully 68% of adults connect to the Internet with mobile devices like smartphones or tablet computers.
>
> The adoption of related technologies has also been extraordinary: Over the course of Pew Research Center polling, adult ownership of cell phones has risen from 53% in our first survey in 2000 to 90% now. Ownership of smartphones has grown from 35% when we first asked in 2011 to 58% now.
>
> Impact: Asked for their overall judgment about the impact of the Internet, toting up all the pluses and minuses of connected life, the public's verdict is overwhelmingly positive: 90% of Internet users say the Internet has been a good thing for them personally and only 6% say it has been a bad thing, while 3% volunteer that it has been some of both. 76% of Internet users say the Internet has been a good thing for society, while 15% say it has been a bad thing and 8% say it has been equally good and bad.
>
> —Susannah Fox and Lee Rainie, "The Web at 25 in the U.S."

Note, too, that these writers draw their material from research and polls conducted by the Pew Research Center, a well-known and respected organization. Chances are you immediately recognize that this paragraph is an example of a researched academic argument.

You can also identify academic argument by the way it addresses its audiences. Some academic writing is clearly aimed at specialists in a field who are familiar with both the subject and the terminology that surrounds it. As a result, the researchers make few concessions to general readers unlikely to encounter or appreciate their work. You see that single-mindedness in this abstract of an article about migraine headaches in a scientific journal: it quickly becomes unreadable to nonspecialists.

Abstract

Migraine is a complex, disabling disorder of the brain that manifests itself as attacks of often severe, throbbing head pain with sensory sensitivity to light, sound and head movement. There is a clear familial tendency to migraine, which has been well defined in a rare autosomal dominant form of familial hemiplegic migraine (FHM). FHM mutations so far identified include those in CACNA1A (P/Q voltage-gated Ca(2+) channel), ATP1A2 (N(+)-K(+)-ATPase) and SCN1A (Na(+) channel) genes. Physiological studies in humans and studies of the experimental correlate—cortical spreading depression (CSD)—provide understanding of aura, and have explored in recent years the effect of migraine preventives in CSD....

—Peter J. Goadsby, "Recent Advances in Understanding
Migraine Mechanisms, Molecules, and Therapeutics,"
Trends in Molecular Medicine (January 2007)

Yet this very article might later provide data for a more accessible argument in a magazine such as *Scientific American*, which addresses a broader (though no less serious) readership. Here's a selection from an article on migraine headaches from that more widely read journal (see also the infographic on **p. 504**):

At the moment, only a few drugs can prevent migraine. All of them were developed for other diseases, including hypertension, depression and epilepsy. Because they are not specific to migraine, it will come as no surprise that they work in only 50 percent of patients—and, in them, only 50 percent of the time—and induce a range of side effects, some potentially serious.

Recent research on the mechanism of these antihypertensive, antiepileptic and antidepressant drugs has demonstrated that one of their effects is to inhibit cortical spreading depression. The drugs' ability to prevent migraine with and without aura therefore supports the school of thought that cortical spreading depression contributes to both kinds of attacks. Using this observation as a starting point, investigators have come up with novel drugs that specifically inhibit cortical spreading depression. Those drugs are now being tested in migraine sufferers with and without aura. They work by preventing gap junctions, a form of ion channel, from opening, thereby halting the flow of calcium between brain cells.

—David W. Dodick and J. Jay Gargus,
"Why Migraines Strike," *Scientific American* (August 2008)

Such writing still requires attention, but it delivers important and comprehensible information to any reader seriously interested in the subject and the latest research on it.

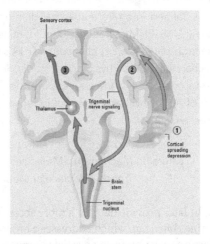

FIGURE 25.1 Infographic: The Root of Migraine Pain © Tolpa Studios, Inc.

Even when academic writing is less technical and demanding, its style will retain a degree of formality. In academic arguments, the focus is on the subject or topic rather than the authors, the tone is straightforward, the language is largely unadorned, and all the *i*'s are dotted and *t*'s crossed. Here's an abstract for an academic paper written by a scholar of communications on the Burning Man phenomenon, demonstrating those qualities:

Every August for more than a decade, thousands of information technologists and other knowledge workers have trekked out into a barren stretch of alkali desert and built a temporary city devoted to art, technology, and communal living: Burning Man. Drawing on extensive archival research, participant observation, and interviews, this paper explores the ways that Burning Man's bohemian ethos supports new forms of production emerging in Silicon Valley and especially at Google. It shows how elements of the Burning Man world—including the building of a socio-technical commons, participation in project-based artistic labor, and the fusion of social and professional interaction—help shape and legitimate the collaborative manufacturing processes driving the growth of Google and other firms. The paper thus develops the notion that Burning Man serves as a key cultural infrastructure for the Bay Area's new media industries.

—Fred Turner, "Burning Man at Google:
A Cultural Infrastructure for New Media Production"

You might imagine a different and far livelier way to tell a story about the annual Burning Man gathering in Nevada, but this piece respects the conventions of its academic field.

FIGURE 25.2 A scene from Burning Man Mike Nelson/AFP/Getty Images

Another way you likely identify academic writing—especially in term papers or research projects—is by the way it draws upon sources and builds arguments from research done by experts and reported in journal articles and books. Using an even-handed tone and dealing with all points of view fairly, such writing brings together multiple voices and intriguing ideas. You can see these moves in just one paragraph from a heavily documented student essay examining the comedy of Chris Rock:

The breadth of passionate debate that [Chris] Rock's comedy elicits from intellectuals is evidence enough that he is advancing discussion of the foibles of black America, but Rock continually insists that he has no political aims: "Really, really at the end of the day, the only important thing is being funny. I don't go out of my way to be political" (qtd. in Bogosian 58). His unwillingness

to view himself as a black leader triggers Justin Driver to say, "[Rock] wants
to be caustic and he wants to be loved" (32). Even supporters wistfully sigh,
"One wishes Rock would own up to the fact that he's a damned astute social
critic" (Kamp 7).

—Jack Chung, "The Burden of Laughter:
Chris Rock Fights Ignorance His Way"

Readers can quickly tell that author Jack Chung has read widely and thought carefully about how to support his argument.

As you can see even from these brief examples, academic arguments cover a
broad range of topics and appear in a variety of media—as a brief note in a journal
like *Nature*, for example, a poster session at a conference on linguistics, a short paper
in *Physical Review Letters*, a full research report in microbiology, or an undergraduate honors thesis in history. What do all these projects have in common? One professor we know defines academic argument as "carefully structured research," and that
seems to us to be a pretty good definition.

Conventions in Academic Argument Are Not Static.

Far from it. In fact, the rise of new technologies and the role that blogs, wikis, social
media sites, and other digital discourses play in all our lives are affecting academic
writing as well. Thus, scholars today are pushing the envelope of traditional academic writing in some fields. Physicians, for example, are using narrative (rather
than charts) more often in medicine to communicate effectively with other medical
personnel. Professional journals now sometimes feature serious scholarly work in
new formats—such as comics (as in legal scholar Jamie Boyle's work on intellectual property, or Nick Sousanis's Columbia University PhD dissertation, which
is entirely in comic form). And student writers are increasingly producing serious
academic arguments using a wide variety of modalities, including sound, still and
moving images, and more.

Developing an Academic Argument

In your first years of college, the academic arguments you make will probably include
the features and qualities we've discussed above—and which you see demonstrated
in the sample academic arguments at the end of this chapter. In addition, you can
make a strong academic argument by following some time-tested techniques.

Choose a topic you want to explore in depth. Unless you are assigned a
topic (and remember that even assigned topics can be tweaked to match your interests), look for a subject that intrigues you—one you *want* to learn more about. One of
the hardest parts of producing an academic argument is finding a topic narrow
enough to be manageable in the time you have to work on it but also rich enough to

sustain your interest over the same period. Talk with friends about possible topics and explain to them why you'd like to pursue research on this issue. Look through your Twitter feeds and social network postings to identify themes or topics that leap out as compelling. Browse through books and articles that interest you, make a list of potential subjects, and then zero in on one or two top choices.

Get to know the conversation surrounding your topic. Once you've chosen a topic, expect to do even more reading and browsing—a lot more. Familiarize yourself with what's been said about your subject and especially with the controversies that currently surround it. Where do scholars agree, and where do they disagree? What key issues seem to be at stake? You can start by exploring the Internet, using key terms that are associated with your topic. But you may be better off searching the more specialized databases at your library with the assistance of a librarian who can help you narrow your search and make it more efficient. Library databases will also give you access to materials not available via Google or other online search engines—including, for example, full-text versions of journal articles. For much more on identifying appropriate sources, see Chapter 26, "Finding Evidence."

Assess what you know and what you need to know. As you read about your topic and discuss it with others, keep notes on what you have learned, including what you already know about it. Such notes should soon reveal where the gaps are in your knowledge. For instance, you may discover a need to learn about legal issues and thus end up doing research in a law school library. Or perhaps talking with experts about your topic might be helpful. Instructors on your campus may have the knowledge you need, so explore your school's Web site to find faculty or staff to talk with. Make an appointment to visit them during office hours and bring the sorts of questions to your meeting that show you've done basic work on the subject. And remember that experts are now only a click away: a student we know, working on Internet privacy concerns, wrote a brief message to one of the top scholars in the field asking for help with two particular questions—and got a response within two days!

Come up with a claim about your topic. The chapters in Part 3, "Writing Arguments," offer instruction in formulating thesis statements, which most academic arguments must have. Chapters 16–20, in particular, explain how to craft claims tailored to individual projects ranging from arguments of fact to proposals. Remember here, though, that good claims are controversial. After all, you don't want to debate something that everyone already agrees upon or accepts.

In addition, your claim needs to say something consequential about that important or controversial topic and be supported with strong evidence and good reasons (see Chapter 26). Here, for example, is the claim that student Charlotte Geaghan-Breiner makes after observing the alienation of today's children from the natural world and arguing for the redesign of schoolyards that invite children to interact with nature: "As a formative geography of childhood, the schoolyard serves as the perfect place to address nature deficit disorder." Charlotte develops her claim and supports it with evidence about the physical, psychological, academic, and social benefits of interacting with the natural world. She includes images illustrating the contrast between traditional schoolyards and "biophilic," or nature-oriented, schoolyards and establishes guidelines for creating natural play landscapes. (See Charlotte's complete essay, reprinted at the end of this chapter.)

Consider your rhetorical stance and purpose. Once you have a claim, ask yourself where you stand with respect to your topic and how you want to represent yourself to those reading your argument:

- You may take the stance of a reporter: you review what has been said about the topic; analyze and evaluate contributions to the conversation surrounding it; synthesize the most important strands of that conversation; and finally draw conclusions based on them.

- You may see yourself primarily as a critic: you intend to point out the problems and mistakes associated with some view of your topic.

- You may prefer the role of an advocate: you present research that strongly supports a particular view on your topic.

Whatever your perspective, remember that in academic arguments you want to come across as fair and evenhanded, especially when you play the advocate. Your stance will always be closely tied to your purpose, which in most of your college writing will be at least twofold: to do the best job in fulfilling an assignment for a course and to support the claim you are making to the fullest extent possible. Luckily, these two purposes work well together.

Think about your audience(s). Here again, you will often find that you have at least two audiences—and maybe more. First, you will be writing to your instructor, so take careful notes when the assignment is given and, if possible, set up a conference to nail down your teacher's expectations: what will it take to convince this audience that you have done a terrific job of writing an academic argument? Beyond your instructor, you should also think of your classmates as an audience—informed, intelligent peers who will be interested in what you have to say. Again, what do you know about these readers, and what will they expect from your project?

Finally, consider yet another important audience—people who are already discussing your topic. These will include the authors whose work you have read and the larger academic community of which they are now a part. If your work appears online or in some other medium, you will reach more people than you initially expect, and most if not all of them will be unknown to you. As a result, you need to think carefully about the various ways your argument could be read—or misread—and plan accordingly.

Concentrate on the material you are gathering. Any academic argument is only as good as the evidence it presents to support its claims. Give each major piece of evidence (say, a lengthy article that addresses your subject directly) careful scrutiny:

- Summarize its main points.
- Analyze how those points are pertinent.
- Evaluate the quality of the supporting evidence.
- Synthesize the results of your analysis and evaluation.
- Summarize what you think about the article.

In other words, test each piece of evidence and then decide which to keep—and which to throw out. But do not gather only materials that favor your take on the topic. You want, instead, to look at all legitimate perspectives on your claim, and in doing so, you may even change your mind. That's what good research for an academic argument can do: remember the "conscientious commitment to truth" we mentioned earlier? Keep yourself open to discovery and change. (See Chapter 27, "Evaluating Sources," and Chapter 28, "Using Sources.")

Give visual and nonprint materials the same scrutiny you would to print sources, since these days you will likely be gathering or creating such materials in many fields. Remember that the graphic representation of data always involves an interpretation of that material: numbers can lie and pictures distort. (For more information on evaluating visuals, see Chapter 22.) In addition, infographics today often make complex academic arguments in a visual form. (See p. 306 for one such example.)

Take special care with documentation. As you gather materials for your academic argument, record where you found each source so that you can cite it accurately. For print sources, develop a working bibliography either on your computer or in a notebook you can carry with you. For each book, write the name of the author, the title of the book, the city of publication, the publisher, the date of publication, and the place that you found it (the section of the library, for example, and the call number for the book). For each print article, write the name of the author, the title of the article, the title of the periodical, and the volume, issue, publication date, and exact page numbers. Include any other information you may later need in preparing a works cited list or references list.

For electronic sources, keep a careful record of the information you'll need in a works cited list or references list. Write the author and title information, the name of the database or other online site where you found the source, the full URL, the date the document was first produced, the date it was published on the Web or most recently updated, and the date you accessed and examined it. The simplest way to ensure that you have this information is to print a copy of the source, highlight source information, and write down any other pertinent information.

Remember, too, that different academic fields use different systems of documentation, so if your instructor has not recommended a style of documentation to you, ask in class about it. Scholars have developed these systems over long periods of time to make research in an area reliable and routine. Using documentation responsibly shows that you understand the conventions of your field or major and that you have paid your dues, thereby establishing your position as a member of the academic community. (For more detailed information, see Chapter 30, "Documenting Sources.")

Think about organization. As you review the research materials you have gathered, you are actually beginning the work of drafting and designing your project. Study the way those materials are organized, especially any from professional journals, whether print or digital. You may need to include in your own argument some of the sections or features you find in professional research:

- Does the article open with an abstract, summarizing its content?
- Does the article give any information about the author or authors and their credentials?
- Is there a formal introduction to the subject or a clear statement of a thesis or hypothesis?
- Does the article begin with a "review of literature," summarizing recent research on its topic?
- Does the piece describe its methods of research?
- How does the article report its results and findings?
- Does the article use charts and graphs or other visuals to report data?
- Does the piece use headings and subheadings?
- How does the work summarize its findings or how does it make recommendations?
- Does the essay offer a list of works cited or references?

Anticipate some variance in the way materials are presented from one academic field to another.

As you organize your own project, check with your instructor to see if there is a recommended pattern for you to follow. If not, create a scratch outline or storyboard to describe how your essay will proceed. In reviewing your evidence, decide which pieces support specific points in the argument. Then try to position your strongest pieces of evidence in key places — near the beginning of paragraphs, at the end of the introduction, or toward a powerful conclusion. In addition, strive to achieve a balance between, on the one hand, your own words and argument and, on the other hand, the sources that you use or quote in support of the argument. The sources of evidence are important supports, but they shouldn't overpower the structure of your argument itself. Finally, remember that your organization needs to take into account the placement of visuals—charts, tables, photographs, and so on. (For specific advice on structuring arguments, review the "Thinking about Organization" sections in the "Guides to Writing" for Chapters 16–20.)

Consider style and tone. Most academic argument adopts the voice of a reasonable, fair-minded, and careful thinker who is interested in coming as close to the truth about a topic as possible. A style that achieves that tone may have some of the following features:

- It strives for clarity and directness, though it may use jargon appropriate to a particular field.
- It favors denotative rather than connotative language.
- It is usually impersonal, using first person (*I*) sparingly.
- In some fields, it may use the passive voice routinely.
- It uses technical language, symbols, and abbreviations for efficiency.
- It avoids colloquialisms, slang, and sometimes even contractions.

The examples at the end of this chapter demonstrate traditional academic style, though there is, as always, a range of possibilities in its manner of expression.

Consider genre, design, and visuals. Most college academic arguments look more like articles in professional journals than like those one might find in a glossier periodical like *Scientific American*—that is, they are still usually black on white, use a traditional font size and type (like 11-point Times New Roman), and lack any conscious design other than inserted tables or figures. But such conventions are changing.

Indeed, student writers today can go well beyond print, creating digital documents that integrate a variety of media and array data in strikingly original ways. But always consider what genres best suit your topic, purpose, and audience and then act accordingly. As you think about the design possibilities for your academic argument, you may want to consult your instructor—and to test your ideas and innovations on friends or classmates.

In choosing visuals to include in your argument, be sure each one makes a strong contribution to your message and is appropriate and fair to your topic and your audience. Treat visuals as you would any other sources and integrate them into your text. Like quotations, paraphrases, and summaries, visuals need to be introduced and commented on in some way. In addition, label and number ("Figure 1," "Table 2," and so on) each visual, provide a caption that includes source information and describes the visual, and cite the source in your references page or works cited list. Even if you create a visual (such as a bar graph) by using information from a source (the results, say, of a Gallup poll), you must cite the source. If you use a photograph you took yourself, cite it as a personal photograph.

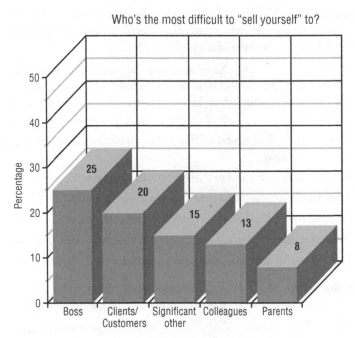

FIGURE 25.3 This bar chart, based on data from a Sandler Training survey of 1,053 adults, would be listed in your works cited or references under the authors' names.

Data from Sandler Training survey of 1,053 adults.

Reflect on your draft and get responses. As with any important piece of writing, an academic argument calls for careful reflection on your draft. You may want to do a "reverse outline" to test whether a reader can pull a logical and consistent pattern out of the paragraphs or sections you have written. In addition, you can also judge the effectiveness of your overall argument, assessing what each paragraph contributes and what may be missing. Turning a critical eye to your own work at the draft stage can save much grief in the long run. Be sure to get some response from classmates and friends too: come up with a set of questions to ask them about your draft and push them for honest responses. Find out what in your draft is confusing or unclear to others, what needs further evidence, and so on.

Edit and proofread your text. Proofread an academic argument at least three times. First review it for ideas, making sure that all your main points and supporting evidence make sense and fit nicely together. Give special attention to transitions and paragraph structure and the way you have arranged information, positioned headings, and captioned graphic items. Make sure the big picture is in focus.

Then read the text word by word to check spelling, punctuation, quotation marks, apostrophes, abbreviations—in short, all the details that can go wrong simply because of a slip in attention. To keep their focus at this level, some readers will even read an entire text backwards. Notice too where your computer's spelling and grammar checkers may be underlining particular words and phrases. Don't ignore these clear signals.

Finally, check that every source mentioned in the academic argument appears in the works cited or references list and that every citation is correct. This is also the time to make any final touchups to your overall design. Remember that how the document looks is part of what establishes its credibility.

RESPOND

1. Look closely at the following five passages, each of which is from an opening of a published work, and decide which ones provide examples of academic argument. How would you describe each one, and what are its key features? Which is the most formal and academic? Which is the least? How might you revise them to make them more—or less—academic?

> During the Old Stone Age, between thirty-seven thousand and eleven thousand years ago, some of the most remarkable art ever conceived was etched or painted on the walls of caves in southern France and northern Spain. After a visit to Lascaux, in the Dordogne, which was discovered in 1940, Picasso reportedly said to his guide, "They've invented everything." What those first artists invented was a language of signs for which there will never be a Rosetta stone; perspective, a technique that was not rediscovered until the Athenian Golden Age; and a bestiary of such vitality and finesse that, by the flicker of torchlight, the animals seem to surge from the walls, and move across them like figures in a magic-lantern show (in that sense, the artists invented animation). They also thought up the grease lamp—a lump of fat, with a plant wick, placed in a hollow stone—to light their workplace; scaffolds to reach high places; the principles of stenciling and Pointillism; powdered colors, brushes, and stumping cloths; and, more to the point of Picasso's insight, the very concept of an image. A true artist reimagines that concept with every blank canvas—but not from a void.
>
> —Judith Thurman, "First Impressions," *The New Yorker*

> I stepped over the curb and into the street to hitchhike. At the age of ten I'd put some pretty serious mileage on my thumb. And I knew how it was done. Hold your thumb up, not down by your hip as though you didn't much give a damn whether you got a ride or not. Always hitch at a place where a driver could pull out of traffic and give you time to get in without risking somebody tailgating him.
>
> —Harry Crews, "On Hitchhiking," *Harper's*

Coral reef ecosystems are essential marine environments around the world. Host to thousands (and perhaps millions) of diverse organisms, they are also vital to the economic well-being of an estimated 0.5 billion people, or 8% of the world's population who live on tropical coasts (Hoegh-Guldberg 1999). Income from tourism and fishing industries, for instance, is essential to the economic prosperity of many countries, and the various plant and animal species present in reef ecosystems are sources for different natural products and medicines. The degradation of coral reefs can therefore have a devastating impact on coastal populations, and it is estimated that between 50% and 70% of all reefs around the world are currently threatened (Hoegh-Guldberg). Anthropogenic influences are cited as the major cause of this degradation, including sewage, sedimentation, direct trampling of reefs, over-fishing of herbivorous fish, and even global warming (Umezawa et al. 2002; Jones et al. 2001; Smith et al. 2001).

—Elizabeth Derse, "Identifying the Sources of Nitrogen to Hanalei Bay, Kauai, Utilizing the Nitrogen Isotope Signature of Macroalgae," *Stanford Undergraduate Research Journal*

While there's a good deal known about invertebrate neurobiology, these facts alone haven't settled questions of their sentience. On the one hand, invertebrates lack a cortex, amygdala, as well as many of the other major brain structures routinely implicated in human emotion. And unsurprisingly, their nervous systems are quite minimalist compared to ours: we have roughly a hundred thousand bee brains worth of neurons in our heads. On the other hand, some invertebrates, including insects, do possess the rudiments of our stress response system. So the question is still on the table: do they experience emotion in a way that we would recognize, or just react to the world with a set of glorified reflexes?

—Jason Castro, "Do Bees Have Feelings?" *Scientific American*

Bambi's mother, shot. Nemo's mother, eaten by a barracuda. Lilo's mother, killed in a car crash. Koda's mother in *Brother Bear*, speared. Po's mother in *Kung Fu Panda 2*, done in by a power-crazed peacock. Ariel's mother in the third *Little Mermaid*, crushed by a pirate ship. Human baby's mother in *Ice Age*, chased by a saber-toothed tiger over a waterfall…. The mothers in these movies are either gone or useless. And the father figures? To die for!

—Sarah Boxer, "Why Are All the Cartoon Mothers Dead?" *The Atlantic*

2. Working with another student in your class, find examples from two or three different fields of academic arguments that strike you as being well written and effective. Spend some time looking closely at them. Do they exemplify the key features of academic arguments discussed in this chapter? What other features do they use? How are they organized? What kind of tone do the writers use? What use do they make of visuals? Draw up a brief report on your findings (a list will do), and bring it to class for discussion.

3. Read the following three paragraphs, and then list changes that the writer might make to convert them into an academic argument:

> The book—the physical paper book—is being circled by a shoal of sharks, with sales down 9 percent this year alone. It's being chewed by the e-book. It's being gored by the death of the bookshop and the library. And most importantly, the mental space it occupied is being eroded by the thousand Weapons of Mass Distraction that surround us all. It's hard to admit, but we all sense it: it is becoming almost physically harder to read books.
>
> In his gorgeous little book *The Lost Art of Reading—Why Books Matter in a Distracted Time*, the critic David Ulin admits to a strange feeling. All his life, he had taken reading as for granted as eating—but then, a few years ago, he "became aware, in an apartment full of books, that I could no longer find within myself the quiet necessary to read." He would sit down to do it at night, as he always had, and read a few paragraphs, then find his mind was wandering, imploring him to check his email, or Twitter, or Facebook. "What I'm struggling with," he writes, "is the encroachment of the buzz, the sense that there's something out there that merits my attention."
>
> I think most of us have this sense today, if we are honest. If you read a book with your laptop thrumming on the other side of the room, it can be like trying to read in the middle of a party, where everyone is shouting to each other. To read, you need to slow down. You need mental silence except for the words. That's getting harder to find.
>
> —Johann Hari, "How to Survive the Age of Distraction"

4. Choose two pieces of your college writing, and examine them closely. Are they examples of strong academic writing? How do they use the key features that this chapter identifies as characteristic of academic arguments? How do they use and document sources? What kind of tone do you establish in each? After studying the examples in this chapter, what might you change about these pieces of writing, and why?

5. Go to a blog that you follow, or check out one on the *Huffington Post* or *Ricochet*. Spend some time reading the articles or postings on the blog, and look for ones that you think are the best written and the most interesting. What features or characteristics of academic argument do they use, and which ones do they avoid?

Where the Wild Things Should Be: Healing Nature Deficit Disorder through the Schoolyard

CHARLOTTE GEAGHAN-BREINER

Title begins with a reference many readers will recognize (Sendak) and then points to the direction the argument will take.

The developed world deprives children of a basic and inalienable right: unstructured outdoor play. Children today have substantially less access to nature, less free range, and less time for independent play than previous generations had. Experts in a wide variety of fields cite the rise of technology, urbanization, parental over-scheduling, fears of stranger-danger, and increased traffic as culprits. In 2005 journalist Richard Louv articulated the causes and consequences of children's alienation from nature, dubbing it "nature deficit disorder." Louv is not alone in claiming that the widening divide between children and nature has distressing health repercussions, from obesity and attention disorders to depression and decreased cognitive functioning. The dialogue surrounding nature deficit disorder deserves the attention and action of educators, health professionals, parents, developers, environmentalists, and conservationists alike.

Background information introduces a claim that states an effect and traces it back to its various causes.

Considerable evidence supports the claim.

The most practical solution to this staggering rift between children and nature involves the schoolyard. The schoolyard habitat movement, which promotes the "greening" of school grounds, is quickly gaining international recognition and legitimacy. A host of organizations, including the National Wildlife Federation, the American Forest Foundation, and the Council for Environmental Education, as well as their international counterparts, have committed themselves to this cause. However, while many recognize the need for "greened school grounds," not many describe such landscapes beyond using adjectives such as "lush," "green," and "natural." The literature thus lacks a coherent research-based proposal that both asserts the power of "natural" school grounds *and* delineates what such grounds might look like.

Presents a solution to the problem and foreshadows full thesis

The author identifies a weakness in the proposed solution.

My research strives to fill in this gap. I advocate for the schoolyard as the perfect place to address nature deficit disorder, demonstrate the benefits of greened schoolyards, and establish the tenets

Ending paragraph of the introduction presents the full thesis and outlines the entire essay.

Charlotte Geaghan-Breiner wrote this academic argument for her first-year writing class at Stanford University.

of natural schoolyard design in order to further the movement and inspire future action.

Asphalt Deserts: The State of the Schoolyard Today

As a formative geography of childhood, the schoolyard serves as the perfect place to address nature deficit disorder. Historian Peter Stearns argues that modern childhood was transformed when schooling replaced work as the child's main social function (1041). In this contemporary context, the schoolyard emerges as a critical setting for children's learning and play. Furthermore, as parental traffic and safety concerns increasingly constrain children's free range outside of school, the schoolyard remains a safe haven, a protected outdoor space just for children.

Despite the schoolyard's major significance in children's lives, the vast majority of schoolyards fail to meet children's needs. An outdated theoretical framework is partially to blame. In his 1890 *Principles of Psychology*, psychologist Herbert Spencer championed the "surplus energy theory": play's primary function, according to Spencer, was to burn off extra energy (White). Play, however, contributes to the social, cognitive, emotional, and physical growth of the child (Hart 136); "[l]etting off steam" is only one of play's myriad functions. Spencer's theory thus constitutes a serious oversimplification, but it still continues to inform the design of children's play areas.

Most US playgrounds conform to an equipment-based model constructed implicitly on Spencer's surplus energy theory (Frost and Klein 2). The sports fields, asphalt courts, swing sets, and jungle gyms common to schoolyards relegate nature to the sidelines and prioritize gross motor play at the expense of dramatic play or exploration. An eight-year-old in England says it best: "The space outside feels boring. There's nothing to do. You get bored with just a square of tarmac" (Titman 42). Such an environment does not afford children the chance to graduate to new, more complex challenges as they develop. While play equipment still deserves a spot in the schoolyard, equipment-*dominated* playscapes leave the growing child bereft of stimulating interactions with the environment.

Also to blame for the failure of school grounds to meet children's needs are educators' and developers' adult-centric aims. Most urban schoolyards are sterile environments with low biodiversity (see fig. 1). While concrete, asphalt, and synthetic turf may be easier to maintain and supervise, they exacerbate the "extinction of

---

Author uses subheads to help guide readers through the argument.

Explains why it's valuable to focus on the schoolyard

Quotations by children provide evidence to support the claim and bring in a personal touch. Note that the writer is following MLA style for in-text citations.

Presents reasons why schoolyards continue to be poorly designed

experience," a term that Pyle has used to describe the disappearance of children's embodied, intuitive experiences in nature. Asphalt deserts are major instigators of this "cycle of impoverishment" (Pyle 312). Loss of biodiversity begets environmental apathy, which in turn allows the process of extinction to persist. Furthermore, adults' preference for manicured, landscaped grounds does little to enhance children's creative outdoor play. Instead of rich, stimulating play environments for children, such highly ordered schoolyards are constructed with adults' convenience in mind.

The Greener, the Better: The Benefits of Greened School Grounds

Author cites research that discusses the health benefits of interacting with nature.

A great body of research documents the physiological, cognitive, psychological, and social benefits of contact with nature. Health experts champion outdoor play as an antidote to two major trends in children of the developed world: the Attention Deficit Disorder and obesity epidemics. A 2001 study by Taylor, Kuo, and Sullivan indicates that green play settings decrease the severity of symptoms in children with ADD. They also combat inactivity in children by diversifying the "play repertoire" and providing for a wider range of physical activity than traditional playgrounds. In the war against childhood obesity, health advocates must add the natural schoolyard to their arsenal.

Note that the figure is introduced in the text and has a caption.

Fig. 1: *Addison Elementary in Palo Alto, CA, conforms to the traditional playground model, dominated by synthetic landcover and equipment.* Photo by Charlotte Geaghan-Breiner

The schoolyard also has the ability to influence the way children play. Instead of being prescribed a play structure with a clear purpose (e.g., a swing set), children in natural schoolyards must discover the affordances of their environment—they must imagine what could be. In general, children exhibit more prosocial behavior and higher levels of inclusion in the natural schoolyard (Dyment 31). A 2006 questionnaire-based study of a greening initiative in Toronto found that the naturalization of the school grounds yielded a decrease in aggressive actions and disciplinary problems and a corresponding increase in civility and cooperation (Dyment 28). The greened schoolyard offers benefits beyond physical and mental health; it shapes the character and quality of children's play interactions.

Social benefits of interacting with nature

The schoolyard also has the potential to shape the relationship between children and the natural world. In the essay "Eden in a Vacant Lot," Pyle laments the loss of vacant lots and undeveloped spaces in which children can play and develop intimacy with the land. However, Pyle overlooks the geography of schoolyards, which can serve as enclaves of nature in an increasingly urbanized and developed world. Research has shown that school ground naturalization fosters nature literacy and intimacy just as Pyle's vacant lots do. For instance, a school ground greening program in Toronto dramatically enhanced children's environmental awareness, sense of stewardship, and curiosity about their local ecosystem (Dyment 37). When integrated with nature, the schoolyard can mitigate the effects of nature deficit disorder and reawaken children's innate biophilia, or love of nature.

Biophilic Design: Establishing the Tenets of Natural Schoolyard Design

The need for naturalized schoolyards is urgent. But how might theory actually translate into reality? Here I will propose four principles of biophilic schoolyard design, or landscaping that aims to integrate nature and natural systems into the man-made geography of the schoolyard.

The author establishes four guidelines for redesigning schoolyards.

The first is biodiversity. Schools should strive to incorporate a wide range of greenery and wildlife on their grounds (see fig. 2). Native plants should figure prominently so as to inspire children's interest in their local habitats. Inclusion of wildlife in school grounds can foster meaningful interactions with other species. Certain plants and flowers, for example, attract birds, butterflies, and other insects; aquatic areas can house fish, frogs, tadpoles, and pond bugs. School pets and small-scale farms also serve to teach children important lessons about responsibility, respect, and compassion for animals. Biodiversity, the most vital feature of biophilic design, transforms former "asphalt deserts" into realms teeming with life.

The second principle that schoolyard designers should keep in mind is sensory stimulation. The greater the degree of sensory richness in an environment, the more opportunities it affords the child to imagine, learn, and discover. School grounds should feature a range of colors, textures, sounds, fragrances, and in the case of the garden, tastes. Such sensory diversity almost always accompanies natural environments, unlike concrete, which affords comparatively little sensory stimulation.

Diversity of topography constitutes another dimension of a greened schoolyard (Fjortoft and Sageie 83). The best school grounds afford children a range of places to climb, tunnel, frolic, and sit. Natural elements function as "play equipment": children can sit on stumps, jump over logs, swing on trees, roll down grassy mounds, and climb on boulders. The playscape should also offer nooks and crannies for children to seek shelter and refuge. While asphalt lots and play structures are still fun for children, they should not dominate the school grounds (see fig. 3).

A figure illustrates a specific point about play structures.

Fig. 2: *A seating area at Ohlone School in Palo Alto, CA, features a healthy range of plant species.* Photo by Charlotte Geaghan-Breiner

Fig. 3: Peninsula School in Menlo Park, CA, has integrated traditional equipment, such as a playhouse and slide, into the natural setting. Photo by Charlotte Geaghan-Breiner

Last but not least, naturalized schoolyards must embody the theory of loose parts proposed by architect Simon Nicholson. "In any environment," he writes, "both the degree of inventiveness and the possibility of discovery are directly proportional to the number and kinds of variables in it" (qtd. in Louv 87). Loose parts — sand, water, leaves, nuts, seeds, rocks, and sticks — are abundant in the natural world. The detachability of loose parts makes them ideal for children's construction projects. While some might worry about the possible hazards of loose parts, conventional play equipment is far from safe: more than 200,000 of children's emergency room visits every year in the United States are linked to these built structures (Frost 217). When integrated into the schoolyard through naturalization, loose parts offer the child the chance to gain ever-increasing mastery of the environment.

The four tenets proposed provide a concrete basis for the application of biophilic design to the schoolyard. Such design also requires a frame-shift away from adult preferences for well-manicured grounds and towards children's needs for wilder spaces that can be constructed, manipulated, and changed through play (Lester and Maudsley 67; White and Stoecklin). Schoolyards designed according to the precepts of biodiversity, sensory stimulation, diversity of topography, and loose parts will go a long way in healing the rift between children and nature, a rift that adult-centric design only widens.

Grounds for Change

Author restates her claim.

In conclusion, I have shown that natural schoolyard design can heal nature deficit disorder by restoring free outdoor play to children's lives in the developed world. Successful biophilic schoolyards challenge the conventional notion that natural and man-made landscapes are mutually exclusive. Human-designed environments, and especially those for children, should strive to integrate nature into the landscape. All schools should be designed with the four tenets of natural schoolyard design in mind.

Offers examples of successful biophilic schoolyard design

Though such sweeping change may seem impractical given limitations on school budgets, greening initiatives that use natural elements, minimal equipment, and volunteer work can be remarkably cost-effective. Peninsula School in Menlo Park, California, has minimized maintenance costs through the inclusion of hardy native species; it is essentially "designed for neglect" (Dyment 44). Gardens and small-scale school farms can also become their own source of funding, as they have for Ohlone Elementary School in Palo Alto, California. Ultimately, the cognitive, psychological, physiological, and social benefits of natural school grounds are priceless. In the words of author Richard Louv, "School isn't supposed to be a polite form of incarceration, but a portal to the wider world" (Louv 226). With this in mind, let the schoolyard restore to children their exquisite intimacy with nature: their inheritance, their right.

Works Cited

Dyment, Janet. "Gaining Ground: The Power and Potential of School Ground Greening in the Toronto District School Board." Evergreen, 2006. Web. 8 May 2012.

Fjortoft, Ingunn, and Jostein Sageie. "The Natural Environment as a Playground for Children." *Landscape and Urban Planning* 48.1/2 (2000): 83–97. Web. 28 May 2012.

Frost, Joe L. *Play and Playscapes*. Albany, NY: Delmar, 1992. Print.

Frost, Joe L., and Barry L. Klein. *Children's Play and Playgrounds*. Boston: Allyn and Bacon, 1979. Print.

Hart, Roger. "Containing Children: Some Lessons on Planning for Play from New York City." *Environment and Urbanization* 14.2 (2002): 135–48. Web. 28 May 2012.

Lester, Stuart, and Martin Maudsley. *Play, Naturally: A Review of Children's Natural Play*. London: Play England, National Children's Bureau, 2007. Print.

Louv, Richard. *Last Child in the Woods: Saving Our Children from Nature-Deficit Disorder*. Chapel Hill, NC: Algonquin of Chapel Hill, 2005. Print.

Nicholson, S. "How Not to Cheat Children: The Theory of Loose Parts." *Landscape Architecture* 62 (1971): 30–35. *Children, Youth, and Environments*. Web. 28 May 2012.

Pyle, Robert M. "Eden in a Vacant Lot: Special Places, Species, and Kids in the Neighborhood of Life." *Children and Nature: Psychological, Sociocultural, and Evolutionary Investigations*. Ed. Peter H. Kahn and Stephen R. Kellert. Cambridge, MA: MIT, 2002. 305–27. Print.

Stearns, Peter N. "Conclusion: Change, Globalization and Childhood." *Journal of Social History* 38.4 (2005): 1041–46. Print.

Taylor, Andrea F., Frances E. Kuo, and William C. Sullivan. "Coping with ADD: The Surprising Connection to Green Play Settings." *Environment and Behavior* 33.1 (2001): 54–77. Print.

Titman, Wendy. *Special Places; Special People: The Hidden Curriculum of Schoolgrounds*. Surrey, England: World Wide Fund for Nature, 1994. Web. 8 May 2012.

White, Randy. "Young Children's Relationship with Nature: Its Importance to Children's Development & the Earth's Future." *Taproot* 16.2 (2006). *White Hutchinson Leisure and Learning Group*. Web. 28 May 2012.

White, Randy, and Vicki Stoecklin. "Children's Outdoor Play & Learning Environments: Returning to Nature." *Early Childhood News Mar. 1998. White Hutchinson Leisure and Learning Group*. Web. 28 May 2012.

GrAI/Shutterstock

China: The Prizes and Pitfalls of Progress

LAN XUE

Abstract

Pushes to globalize science must not threaten local innovations in developing countries, argues Lan Xue.

Developing countries such as China and India have emerged both as significant players in the production of high-tech products and as important contributors to the production of ideas and global knowledge. China's rapid ascent as a broker rather than simply a consumer of ideas and innovation has made those in the "developed" world anxious. A 2007 report by UK think tank Demos says that "U.S. and European pre-eminence in science-based innovation cannot be taken for granted. The centre of gravity for innovation is starting to shift from west to east."[1]

This article was written by Lan Xue, a faculty member in the School of Public Policy and Management and the director of the China Institute for Science and Technology Policy, both at Tsinghua University in Beijing, China. It was published in the online edition of *Nature* in July 2008.

But the rapid increase in research and development spending in China—of the order of 20% per year since 1999—does not guarantee a place as an innovation leader. Participation in global science in developing countries such as China is certainly good news for the global scientific community. It offers new opportunities for collaboration, fresh perspectives, and a new market for ideas. It also presents serious challenges for the management of innovation in those countries. A major discovery in the lab does not guarantee a star product in the market. And for a country in development, the application of knowledge in productive activities and the related social transformations are probably more important than the production of the knowledge itself. By gumming the works in information dissemination, by misplacing priorities, and by disavowing research that, although valuable, doesn't fit the tenets of modern Western science, developing countries may falter in their efforts to become innovation leaders.

Vicious Circle

China's scientific publications (measured by articles recorded in the Web of Science) in 1994 were around 10,000, accounting for a little more than 1% of the world total. By 2006, the publications from China rose to more than 70,000, increasing sevenfold in 12 years and accounting for almost 6% of the world total (see graph, next page). In certain technical areas, the growth has been more dramatic. China has been among the leading countries in nanotechnology research, for example, producing a volume of publications second only to that of the United States.

The publish-or-perish mentality that has arisen in China, with its focus on Western journals, has unintended implications that threaten to obviate the roughly 8,000 national scientific journals published in Chinese. Scientists in developing countries such as China and India pride themselves on publishing articles in journals listed in the Science Citation Index (SCI) and the Social Science Citation Index (SSCI) lists. In some top-tier research institutions in China, SCI journals have become the required outlet for research.

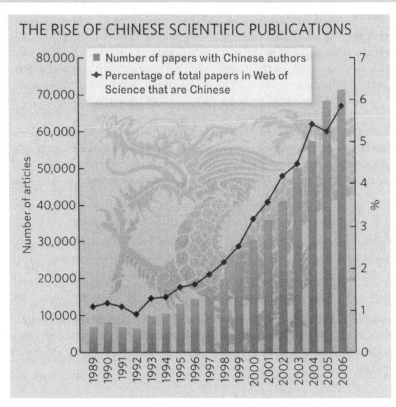

THE RISE OF CHINESE SCIENTIFIC PUBLICATIONS

Nature Publishing Group. Illustration by D. Parkins.

A biologist who recently returned to China from the United States was told by her colleague at the research institute in the prestigious Chinese Academy of Sciences (CAS) that publications in Chinese journals don't really count toward tenure or promotion. Moreover, the institute values only those SCI journals with high impact factors. Unfortunately, the overwhelming majority of the journals in SCI and SSCI lists are published in developed countries in English or other European languages. The language requirement and the high costs of these journals mean that few researchers in China will have regular access to the content. Thus as China spends more and publishes more, the results will become harder to find for Chinese users. This trend could have a devastating impact on the local scientific publications and hurt China's ability to apply newly developed knowledge in an economically useful way.

Several members of the CAS expressed their concerns on this issue recently at the 14th CAS conference in Beijing. According to Molin Ge, a theoretical physicist at the Chern Institute of Mathematics, Nankai University, Tianjin, as more high-quality submissions are sent to overseas journals, the quality of submissions to local Chinese journals declines, which lowers the impact of the local Chinese journals. This becomes a vicious circle because the lower the impact, the less likely these local journals are to get high-quality submissions.[2]

Setting Agendas

Research priorities in developing countries may be very different from those in developed nations, but as science becomes more globalized, so too do priorities. At the national level, developing countries' research priorities increasingly resemble those of the developed nations, partly as a result of international competitive pressures. For example, after the United States announced its National Nanotechnology Initiative (NNI) in 2001, Japan and nations in Europe followed suit, as did South Korea, China, India, and Singapore. According to a 2004 report by the European Union,[3] public investment in nanotechnology had increased from €400 million (U.S. $630 million) in 1997 to more than €3 billion in 2004.

Part of the pressure to jump on the international bandwagon comes from researchers themselves. Scientists in the developing world maintain communications with those elsewhere. It is only natural that they want to share the attention that their colleagues in the developed Western world and Japan are receiving by pursuing the same hot topics. The research is exciting, fast-moving, and often easier to publish. At the same time, there are many other crucial challenges to be met in developing countries. For example, public health, water and food security, and environmental protection all beg for attention and resources. If people perceive these research areas as less intellectually challenging and rewarding, the issues will fail to receive the resources, support, and recognition they require. Without better agenda-setting practices, the scientific community will continue to face stinging criticism. It can send a satellite to Mars but not solve the most basic problems that threaten millions of lives in the developing world.

The introduction of Western scientific ideals to the developing world can generate an environment that is hostile to the indigenous research that prima facie does not fit those ideals. The confrontation between Western medicine and traditional Chinese medicine dates back to the early days of the twentieth century when Western medicine was first introduced in China. The debate reached a peak last year when a famous actress, Xiaoxu Chen, died from breast cancer. She allegedly insisted on treatment by Chinese traditional medicine, raising the hackles of some who claimed it to be worthless. Many Chinese still support traditional medicine and say that the dominance of Western medicine risks endangering China's scientific and cultural legacy.

A similar row erupted around earthquake prediction. In the 1960s and 1970s, China set up a network of popular earthquake-prediction stations, using simple instruments and local knowledge. For the most part, the network was decommissioned as China built the modern earthquake-monitoring system run by the China Earthquake Administration. When the system failed to predict the recent Sichuan earthquake, several people claimed that non-mainstream approaches had predicted its imminence. Scientists in the agency have tended to brush off such unofficial and individual predictions. To many this seems arrogant and bureaucratic.

It would be foolish and impossible to stop the globalization of science. There are tremendous benefits to science enterprises in different countries being integrated into a global whole. One should never think of turning back the clock. At the same time, it is possible to take some practical steps to minimize the harmful effects of this trend on local innovation.

Prioritizing for the People

First of all, there is a need to re-examine the governance of global science in recognition of the changing international geography of science. Many international norms and standards should be more open and accommodating to the changing environment in developing countries. For example, there is a need to re-evaluate the SCI and SSCI list of journals to include quality journals in the developing countries. In the long run, the relevant scientific community could also think about establishing an international panel to make decisions on the selection of journals for these indices, given their important influence. The recent move by Thomson Reuters, the parent company of ISI, to expand its coverage of the SCI list by adding 700 regional academic journals is a step in the right direction.[4]

English has become the de facto global language of science. Developing countries should invest in public institutions to provide translation services so that global scientific progress can be disseminated quickly. Developing countries can learn from Japan, a world leader in collecting scientific information and making it available to the public in the local language. At the same time, there should also be international institutions to provide similar services to the global science community so that "results and the knowledge generated through research should be freely accessible to all," as advocated by Nobel Laureates John Sulston and Joseph Stiglitz.[5]

When setting agendas, governments in developing countries must be careful in allocating their resources for science to achieve a balance between following the science frontier globally and addressing crucial domestic needs. A balance should also be struck between generating knowledge and disseminating and using knowledge. In addition, the global science community has a responsibility to help those developing countries that do not have adequate resources to solve problems themselves.

Finally, special efforts should be made to differentiate between pseudoscience and genuine scientific research. For the latter, one should tolerate or even encourage such indigenous research efforts in developing countries even if they do not fit the recognized international science paradigm. After all, the real advantage of a globalized scientific enterprise is not just doing the same research at a global scale, but doing new and exciting research in an enriched fashion.

Notes

1. Charles Leadbeater and James Wilsdon, *The Atlas of Ideas: How Asian Innovation Can Benefit Us All* (Demos, 2007).
2. Y. Xie et al., "Good Submissions Went Overseas—Chinese S&T Journals Could Not Keep Up with Their Overseas Peers," *Chinese Youth Daily*, June 25, 2008.
3. http://ec.europa.eu/nanotechnology/pdf/nano_com_en_new.pdf
4. http://scientific.thomsonreuters.com/press/2008/8455931/
5. Joseph Stiglitz and John Sulston, "Science is Being Held Back by Outdated Laws," *The Times*, July 5, 2008.

Finding Evidence

In making and supporting claims for academic arguments, writers use all kinds of evidence: data from journal articles; scholarly books; records from archives; blogs, wikis, social media sites, and other digital sources; personal observations and fieldwork; surveys; and even DNA. But such evidence doesn't exist in a vacuum. Instead, the quality of evidence—how and when it was collected, by whom, and for what purposes—may become part of the argument itself. Evidence may be persuasive in one time and place but not in another; it may convince one kind of audience but not another; it may work with one type of argument but not with the kind you are writing. The point is that finding "good" evidence for a research project is rarely a simple matter.

Left to right: © Wavebreakmedia, Ltd./age fotostock; www.CartoonStock.com; © Zoonar M Kang/age fotostock

Considering the Rhetorical Situation

To be most persuasive, evidence should match the time and place in which you make your argument — that is to say, your rhetorical situation. For example, arguing that government officials in the twenty-first century should use the same policies to deal with economic troubles that were employed in the middle of the twentieth might not be convincing on its own. After all, almost every aspect of the world economy has changed in the past fifty years. In the same way, a writer may achieve excellent results by citing a detailed survey of local teenagers as evidence for education reform in her small rural hometown, but she may have less success using the same evidence to argue for similar reforms in a large inner-city community.

College writers also need to consider the fields that they're working in. In disciplines such as experimental psychology or economics, **quantitative data** — the sort that can be observed and counted — may be the best evidence. In many historical, literary, or philosophical studies, however, the same kind of data may be less appropriate or persuasive, or even impossible to come by. As you become more familiar with a discipline, you'll gain a sense of what it takes to support a claim. The following questions will help you understand the rhetorical situation of a particular field:

- What kinds of data are preferred as evidence? How are such data gathered and presented?

- How are definitions, causal analyses, evaluations, analogies, and examples used as evidence?

- How does the field use firsthand and secondhand sources as evidence? What kinds of data are favored?

- How are statistics or other numerical information used and presented as evidence? Are tables, charts, or graphs commonly used? How much weight do they carry?

- What or who counts as an authority in this field? How are the credentials of authorities established?

- What weight do writers in the field give to **precedence** — that is, to examples of similar actions or decisions made in the past?

- Is personal experience allowed as evidence? When?

- How are quotations used as part of evidence?

- How are still or moving images or sound(s) used as part of evidence, and how closely are they related to the verbal parts of the argument being presented?

As these questions suggest, evidence may not always travel well from one field to another. Nor does it always travel easily from culture to culture. Differing notions of evidence can lead to arguments that go nowhere fast. For instance, when Italian journalist Oriana Fallaci interviewed Ayatollah Khomeini, Iran's supreme leader, in 1979, she argued in a way that's common in North American and Western European cultures: she presented claims that she considered to be adequately backed up with facts ("Iran denies freedom to people.... Many people have been put in prison and even executed, just for speaking out in opposition"). In response, Khomeini relied on very different kinds of evidence — analogies ("Just as a finger with gangrene should be cut off so that it will not destroy the whole body, so should people who corrupt others be pulled out like weeds so they will not infect the whole field") and, above all, the authority of the Qur'an. Partly because of these differing beliefs about what counts as evidence, the interview ended unsuccessfully.

FIGURE 26.1 The need for evidence depends a lot on the rhetorical situation.

© Mick Stevens/The New Yorker Collection/The Cartoon Bank

CULTURAL CONTEXTS FOR ARGUMENT

The Rhetorical Situation

To take another example, a *Harvard Business Review* blog post from December 4, 2013, on "How to Argue across Cultures" recounts the story of a Western business-person who was selling bicycles produced in China to a buyer in Germany. When the business owner went to pick up the bicycles, he noticed that they rattled. In considering how to bring up this defect with the Chinese supplier, the businessper-son could have confronted him directly, relying on physical evidence to support his claim. He rejected this form of evidence, however, because he knew that such a confrontation would result in loss of face for the supplier and very likely lead to an undesirable outcome. So instead, he suggested that he and the Chinese supplier take a couple of bikes out for a ride, during which the bikes rattled away. At the end of the ride, the Western businessperson quietly mentioned that he "thought his bike had rattled" and then departed, leaving the Chinese supplier to consider his subtle presentation of evidence. And it worked: when the Germans received the bicycle delivery, the rattle had been repaired.

It's always good to remember, then, that when arguing across cultural divides, whether international or more local, you need to think carefully about how you're accustomed to using evidence — and about what counts as evidence to other people (without surrendering your own intellectual principles).

Using Data and Evidence from Research Sources

The evidence you will use in most academic arguments — books, articles, videos, documents, photographs and other images — will likely come from sources you locate in libraries, in databases, or online. How well you can navigate these complex territories will determine the success of many of your academic and professional projects. Research suggests that most students overestimate their ability to manage these tools and, perhaps more important, don't seek the help they need to find the best materials for their projects. We can't cover all the nuances of doing academic research here, but we can at least point you in the right directions.

Explore library resources: printed works and databases. Your college library has printed materials (books, periodicals, reference works) as well as termi-nals that provide access to its electronic catalogs, other libraries' catalogs via the Internet, and numerous proprietary databases (such as *Academic Search Complete, Academic OneFile, JSTOR*) not available publicly on the Web. Crucially, libraries also have librarians whose job it is to guide you through these resources, help you identify reputable materials, and show you how to search for materials efficiently.

The best way to begin a serious academic argument then is often with a trip to the library or a discussion with your professor or librarian. Also be certain that you know your way around the library. If not, ask the staff there to help you locate the following tools: general and specialized encyclopedias; biographical resources; almanacs, yearbooks, and atlases; book and periodical indexes; specialized indexes and abstracts; the circulation computer or library catalog; special collections; audio, video, and art collections; and the interlibrary loan office.

At the outset of a project, determine what kinds of sources you will need to support your project. (You might also review your assignment to see whether you're required to consult different kinds of sources.) If you'll use print sources, find out whether they're readily available in your library or whether you must make special arrangements (such as an interlibrary loan) to acquire them. For example, your argument for a senior thesis might benefit from material available mostly in old newspapers and magazines: access to them might require time and ingenuity. If you need to locate other nonprint sources (such as audiotapes, videotapes, artwork, or photos), find out where those are kept and whether you need special permission to examine them.

Most academic resources, however, will be on the shelves or available electronically through databases. Here's when it's important to understand the distinction between library databases and the Internet/Web. Your library's computers hold important resources that aren't on the Web or aren't available to you except through the library's system. The most important of these resources is the library's catalog of its holdings (mostly books), but college libraries also pay to subscribe to *scholarly databases*—for example, guides to journal and magazine articles, the *Academic Search Complete* database (which holds the largest collection of multidisciplinary journals), the *LexisNexis* database of news stories and legal cases, and compilations of statistics—that you can use for free.

You should consult these electronic sources through your college library, perhaps even before turning to the Web. But using these professional databases isn't always easy or intuitive, even when you can reach them on your own computer. You likely need to learn how to focus and narrow your searches (by date, field, types of material, and so on) so that you don't generate unmanageable lists of irrelevant items. That's when librarians or your instructor can help, so ask them for assistance. They expect your questions.

For example, librarians can draw your attention to the distinction between subject headings and keywords. The Library of Congress Subject Headings (LCSH) are standardized words and phrases that are used to classify the subject matter of books and articles. Library catalogs and databases usually use the LCSH headings to index their contents by author, title, publication date, and subject headings. When you do a subject search of the library's catalog, you need to use the exact wording of the LCSH headings. On the other hand, searches with *keywords* use the computer's ability to look for any term in any field of the electronic record. So keyword searching is less restrictive, but you'll have to think hard about your search terms to get usable results and to learn how to limit or expand your search.

Determine, too, early on, how current your sources need to be. If you must investigate the latest findings about, say, a new treatment for malaria, check very recent periodicals, medical journals, and the Web. If you want broader, more detailed coverage and background information, look for scholarly books. If your argument deals with a specific time period, newspapers, magazines, and books written during that period may be your best assets.

How many sources should you consult for an academic argument? Expect to look over many more sources than you'll end up using, and be sure to cover all major perspectives on your subject. Read enough sources to feel comfortable discussing it with someone with more knowledge than you. You don't have to be an expert, but your readers should sense that you are well informed.

Explore online resources. Chances are your first instinct when you need to find information is to do a quick keyword search on the Web, which in many instances will take you to a source in Wikipedia, the free encyclopedia launched by Jimmy Wales in 2001. For years, many teachers and institutions argued that the information on Wikipedia was suspect and could not be used as a reliable source. Times have changed, however, and many serious research efforts now include a stop at Wikipedia. As always, however, let the buyer beware: you need to verify the credibility of all of your sources! If you intend to support a serious academic argument, remember to approach the Web carefully and professionally.

Like the catalogs and databases in your college library, the Internet offers two ways to search for sources related to an argument—one using subject categories and one using keywords. A subject directory organized by categories (such as you might find at About.com) allows you to choose a broad category like "entertainment" or "science," and then click on increasingly narrow categories like "movies" or "astronomy," and then "thrillers" or "the solar system," until you reach a point where you're given a list of Web sites or the opportunity to do a keyword search.

With the second kind of Internet search option, a search engine, you start right off with a keyword search—filling in a blank, for example, on Google's homepage. Because the Internet contains vastly more material than even the largest library catalog or database, exploring it with a search engine requires careful choices and combinations of keywords. For an argument about the fate of the antihero in contemporary films, for example, you might find that *film* and *hero* produce far too many possible matches, or hits. You might further narrow the search by adding a third keyword—say, *American* or *current*. In doing such searches, you'll need to observe the search logic that is followed by a particular database. Using *and* between keywords (*movies and heroes*) usually indicates that both terms must appear in a file for it to be called up. Using *or* between keywords usually instructs the computer to locate every file in which either one word or the other shows up, and using *not* tells the computer to exclude files containing a particular word from the search results (*movies not heroes*).

More crucial with a tool like Google is to discover how the resources of the site itself can refine your choice or direct you to works better suited to academic argument. When you search for any term, you can click "Advanced Search" at the bottom of the results page and bring up a full screen of options to narrow your search in important ways.

But that's not the end of your choices. With an *academic* argument, you might want to explore your topic in either Google Books or Google Scholar. Both resources send you to the level of materials you might need for a term paper or professional project. And Google offers other options as well: it can direct you to images, photographs, blogs, and so on. The lesson is simple. If your current Web searches typically involve no more than using the first box that a search engine offers, you aren't close to using all the power available to you. Explore that tool you use all the time and see what it can really do.

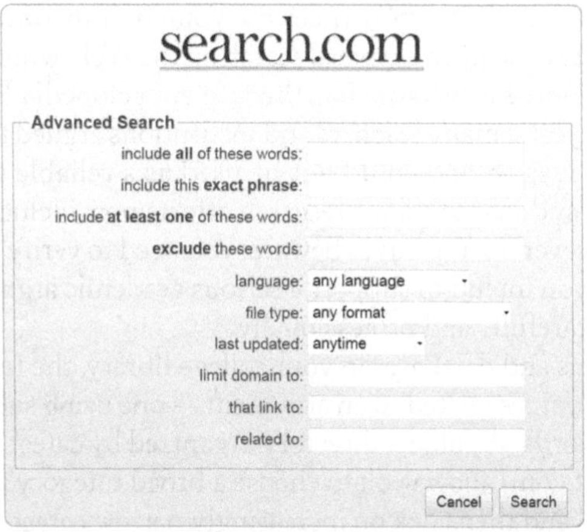

FIGURE 26.2 Most search engines offer many kinds of research tools like this "Advanced Search" page from search.com. Explore them from the "More" and "Even More" menus on search pages.

SEARCHING ONLINE OR IN DATABASES

- Don't rely on simple Web searches only.
- Find library databases targeted to your subject.
- Use advanced search techniques to focus your search.
- Learn the difference between *subject heading* and *keyword* searches.
- Understand the differences between academic and popular sources.
- Admit when you don't know how to find material—you won't be alone!
- *Routinely* ask for help from librarians and instructors.

Collecting Data on Your Own

Not all your supporting materials for an academic argument must come from print or online sources. You can present research that you have carried out or been closely involved with; this kind of research usually requires that you collect and examine data. Here, we discuss the kinds of firsthand research that student writers do most often.

Perform experiments. Academic arguments can be supported by evidence you gather through experiments. In the sciences, data from experiments conducted under rigorously controlled conditions is highly valued. For other kinds of writing, more informal experiments may be acceptable, especially if they're intended to provide only part of the support for an argument.

If you want to argue, for instance, that the recipes in *Bon Appétit* magazine are impossibly tedious to follow and take far more time than the average person wishes to spend preparing food, you might ask five or six people to conduct an experiment—following two recipes from a recent issue and recording and timing every step. The evidence that you gather from this informal experiment could provide some concrete support—by way of specific examples—for your contention.

But such experiments should be taken with a grain of salt (maybe organic in this case). They may not be effective with certain audiences. And if your experiments can easily be attacked as skewed or sloppily done ("The people you asked to make these recipes couldn't cook a Pop-Tart"), then they may do more harm than good.

Make observations. "What," you may wonder, "could be easier than observing something?" You just choose a subject, look at it closely, and record what you see and hear. But trained observers say that recording an observation accurately requires intense concentration and mental agility. If observing were easy, all eyewitnesses would provide reliable stories. Yet experience shows that when several people observe the same phenomenon, they generally offer different, sometimes even contradictory, accounts of those observations.

Before you begin an observation yourself, decide exactly what you want to find out, and anticipate what you're likely to see. Do you want to observe an action that is repeated by many people—perhaps how people behave at the checkout line in a grocery store? Or maybe you want to study a sequence of actions—for instance, the stages involved in student registration, which you want to argue is far too complicated. Or maybe you are motivated to examine the interactions of a notoriously contentious campus group. Once you have a clear sense of what you'll analyze and what questions you'll try to answer through the observation, use the following guidelines to achieve the best results:

- Make sure that the observation relates directly to your claim.

- Brainstorm about what you're looking for, but don't be rigidly bound to your expectations.

- Develop an appropriate system for collecting data. Consider using a split notebook page or screen: on one side, record the minute details of your observations; on the other, record your thoughts or impressions.

- Be aware that the way you record data will affect the outcome, if only in respect to what you decide to include in your observational notes and what you leave out.

- Record the precise date, time, and place of the observation(s).

You may be asked to prepare systematic observations in various science courses, including anthropology or psychology, where you would follow a methodology and receive precise directions. But observation can play a role in other kinds of arguments and use various media: a photo essay, for example, might serve as an academic argument in some situations.

Conduct interviews. Some evidence is best obtained through direct interviews. If you can talk with an expert — in person, on the phone, or online — you might obtain information you couldn't have gotten through any other type of research. In addition to an expert opinion, you might ask for firsthand accounts, biographical information, or suggestions of other places to look or other people to consult. The following guidelines will help you conduct effective interviews:

- Determine the exact purpose of the interview, and be sure it's directly related to your claim.

- Set up the interview well in advance. Specify how long it'll take, and if you wish to record the session, ask permission to do so.

- Prepare a written list of both factual and open-ended questions. (Brainstorming with friends can help you come up with good questions.) Leave plenty of space for notes after each question. If the interview proceeds in a direction that you hadn't expected but that seems promising, don't feel that you have to cover every one of your questions.

- Record the subject's full name and title, as well as the date, time, and place of the interview.

- Be sure to thank those people whom you interview, either in person or with a follow-up letter or email message.

A serious interview can be eye-opening when the questions get a subject to reveal important experiences or demonstrate his or her knowledge or wisdom.

Use questionnaires to conduct surveys. Surveys usually require the use of questionnaires. Questions should be clear, easy to understand, and designed so that respondents' answers can be easily analyzed. Questions that ask respondents to say "yes" or "no" or to rank items on a scale (1 to 5, for example, or "most helpful" to "least helpful") are particularly easy to tabulate. Because tabulation can take time and effort, limit the number of questions you ask. Note also that people often resent being asked to answer more than about twenty questions, especially online.

Here are some other guidelines to help you prepare for and carry out a survey:

- Ask your instructor if your college or university requires that you get approval from the local Institutional Review Board (IRB) to conduct survey research. Many schools waive this requirement if students are doing such research as part of a required course, but you should check to make sure. Securing IRB permission usually requires filling out a series of online forms, submitting all of your questions for approval, and asking those you are surveying to sign a consent form saying they agree to participate in the research.

- Write out your purpose in conducting the survey, and make sure that its results will be directly related to your purpose.

- Brainstorm potential questions to include in the survey, and ask how each relates to your purpose and claim.

"Next question: I believe that life is a constant striving for balance, requiring frequent tradeoffs between morality and necessity, within a cyclic pattern of joy and sadness, forging a trail of bittersweet memories until one slips, inevitably, into the jaws of death. Agree or disagree?"

FIGURE 26.3 A key requirement of survey questions is that they be easy to understand. © George Price/The New Yorker Collection/The Cartoon Bank

- Figure out how many people you want to contact, what the demographics of your sample should be (for example, men in their twenties or an equal number of men and women), and how you plan to reach these people.

- Draft questions that are as free of bias as possible, making sure that each calls for a short, specific answer.

- Think about possible ways that respondents could misunderstand you or your questions, and revise with these points in mind.

- Test the questions on several people, and revise those questions that are ambiguous, hard to answer, or too time-consuming to answer.

- If your questionnaire is to be sent by mail or email or posted on the Web, draft a cover letter explaining your purpose and giving a clear deadline. For mail, provide an addressed, stamped return envelope.

- On the final draft of the questionnaire, leave plenty of space for answers.

- Proofread the final draft carefully. Typos will make a bad impression on those whose help you're seeking.

- After you've done your tabulations, set out your findings in clear and easily readable form, using a chart or spreadsheet if possible.

FIGURE 26.4 Wes Anderson, film's primary advocate of Twee, and *Moonrise Kingdom* Indian Paintbrush/The Kobal Collection

Draw upon personal experience. Personal experience can serve as powerful evidence when it's appropriate to the subject, to your purpose, and to the audience. If it's your only evidence, however, personal experience usually won't be sufficient to carry the argument. Your experiences may be regarded as merely "anecdotal," which is to say possibly exceptional, unrepresentative, or even unreliable. Nevertheless, personal experience can be effective for drawing in listeners or readers, as James Parker does in the following example. His full article goes on to argue that — in spite of his personal experience with it — the "Twee revolution" has some good things going for it, including an "actual moral application":

> Eight years ago or so, the alternative paper I was working for sent me out to review a couple of folk-noise-psych-indie-beardie-weirdie bands. I had a dreadful night. The bands were bad enough—"fumbling," I scratched in my notebook, "infantile"—but what really did me in was the audience. Instead of baying for the blood of these lightweights … the gathered young people—behatted, bebearded, besmiling—obliged them with patters of validating applause. I had seen it before, this fond curiosity, this acclamation of the undercooked, but never so much of it in one place: the whole event seemed to exult in its own half-bakedness. *Be as crap as you like* was the message to the performers. *The crapper, the better. We're here for you.* I tottered home, wrote a homicidally nasty nervous breakdown of a review, and decided I should take myself out of circulation for a while. No more live reviews until I calmed down. A wave of Twee—as I now realize—had just broken over my head.
>
> —James Parker, *The Atlantic*, July/August 2014, p. 36

RESPOND

1. The following is a list of general topic ideas from the Yahoo! Directory's "Issues and Causes" page. Narrow one or two of the items down to a more specific subject by using research tools in the library or online such as scholarly books, journal articles, encyclopedias, magazine pieces, and/or informational Web sites. Be prepared to explain how the particular research resources influenced your choice of a more specific subject within the general subject area. Also consider what you might have to do to turn your specific subject into a full-blown topic proposal for a research paper assignment.

Age discrimination	Poverty
Child soldiers	Racial profiling
Climate change	Solar power
Corporal punishment	Sustainable agriculture
Drinking age	Tax reform
Educational equity	Urban sprawl
Immigration reform	Video games
Media ethics and accountability	Violence in the NFL
Military use of drones	Whistleblowing
Pornography	Zoos

2. Go to your library's online catalog page and locate its list of research databases. You may find them presented in various ways: by subject, by field, by academic major, by type—even alphabetically. Try to identify three or four databases that might be helpful to you either generally in college or when working on a specific project, perhaps one you identified in the previous exercise. Then explore the library catalog to see how much you can learn about each of these resources: What fields do they report on? What kinds of data do they offer? How do they present the content of their materials (by abstract, by full text)? What years do they cover? What search strategies do they support (keyword, advanced search)? To find such information, you might look for a help menu or an "About" link on the catalog or database homepages. Write a one-paragraph description of each database you explore and, if possible, share your findings via a class discussion board, blog, or wiki.

3. What counts as evidence depends in large part on the rhetorical situation. One audience might find personal testimony compelling in a given case, whereas another might require data that only experimental studies can provide. Imagine that you want to argue that advertisements should not include demeaning representations of chimpanzees and that the use of primates in advertising should be banned. You're encouraged to find out that a number of companies such as Honda and Puma have already agreed to such a ban, so you decide to present

your argument to other companies' CEOs and advertising officials. What kind of evidence would be most compelling to this group? How would you rethink your use of evidence if you were writing for the campus newspaper, for middle-schoolers, or for animal-rights group members? What can you learn about what sort of evidence each of these groups might value—and why?

4. Finding evidence for an argument is often a discovery process. Sometimes you're concerned not only with digging up support for an already established claim but also with creating and revising tentative claims. Surveys and interviews can help you figure out what to argue, as well as provide evidence for a claim.

Interview a classmate with the goal of writing a brief proposal argument about the career that he/she should pursue. The claim should be something like *My classmate should be doing X five years from now.* Limit yourself to ten questions. Write them ahead of time, and don't deviate from them. Record the results of the interview (written notes are fine; you don't need to tape the interview). Then interview another classmate with the same goal in mind. Ask the same first question, but this time let the answer dictate the next nine questions. You still get only ten questions.

Which interview gave you more information? Which one helped you learn more about your classmate's goals? Which one better helped you develop claims about his/her future?

Evaluating Sources

A s many examples in this text have shown, the effectiveness of an argument often depends on the quality of the sources that support or prove it. You'll need to carefully evaluate and assess all your sources, including those that you gather in libraries, from other print sources, in online searches, or in your own field research.

Remember that different sources can contribute in different ways to your work. In most cases, you'll be looking for reliable sources that provide accurate information or that clearly and persuasively express opinions that might serve as evidence for a case you're making. At other times, you may be seeking material that expresses ideas or attitudes—how people are thinking and feeling at a given time. You might need to use a graphic image, a sample of avant-garde music, or a controversial YouTube clip that doesn't fit neatly into categories such as "reliable" or "accurate" yet is central to your argument. With any and all such sources and evidence, your goals are to be as knowledgeable about them and as responsible in their use as you can be and to share honestly what you learn about them with readers.

Left to right: © Bartomeu Amengual/age fotostock; © Terry Harris/Alamy; © Zoonar/pzAxe/age fotostock

"I'm *not* being a tattle-tale! —
I'm being a reliable source!"

FIGURE 27.1 Might a tattle-tale ever be a reliable source? www.Cartoonstock.com

No writer wants to be naïve in the use of source material, especially since most of the evidence that is used in arguments on public issues—even material from influential and well-known sources—comes with considerable baggage. Scientists and humanists alike have axes to grind, corporations have products to sell, politicians have issues to promote, journalists have reputations to make, publishers and media companies have readers, listeners, viewers, and advertisers to attract and to avoid offending. All of these groups produce and use information to their own benefit, and it's not (usually) a bad thing that they do so. You just have to be aware that when you take information from a given source, it will almost inevitably carry with it at least some of the preferences, assumptions, and biases—conscious or not—of the people who produce and disseminate it. Teachers and librarians are not exempted from this caution: even when we make every effort to be clear and comprehensive in reporting information, we cannot possibly see that information from every single angle. So even the most honest and open observer can deliver only a partial account of an event.

To correct for these biases, draw on as many reliable sources as you can handle when you're preparing to write. You shouldn't assume that all arguments are equally good or that all the sides in a controversy can be supported by the same weight of evidence and good reasons. But you want to avoid choosing sources so selectively that you miss essential issues and perspectives. That's easy to do when you read only sources that agree with you or when the sources that you read all seem to carry the same message. In addition, make sure that you read each source thoroughly enough that you understand its overall points: national research conducted for the Citation Project indicates that student writers often draw from the first paragraph or page of a source and then simply drop it, without seeing what the rest of the source has to say about the topic at hand.

Especially when writing on political subjects, be aware that the sources you're reading or citing almost always support particular beliefs and goals. That fact has been made apparent in recent years by bloggers—from all parts of the political spectrum—who put the traditional news media under daily scrutiny, exposing errors, biases, and omissions. Even so, these political bloggers (mostly amateur journalists, although many are professionals in their own fields) have their own agendas and so must be read with caution themselves.

FIGURE 27.2 When might a blogger actually be a reliable source— and how would you know? © Adam Zyglis/Cagel Cartoons, Inc.

Assessing Print Sources

Since you want information to be reliable and persuasive, it pays to evaluate each potential source thoroughly. The following principles can help you evaluate print sources:

- **Relevance.** Begin by asking what a particular source will add to your argument and how closely the source is related to your argumentative claim. For a book, the table of contents and the index may help you decide. For an article, look for an abstract that summarizes its content. If you can't think of a good reason for using the source, set it aside. You can almost certainly find something better.

- **Credentials of the author.** Sometimes the author's credentials are set forth in an article, in a book, or on a Web site, so be sure to look for them. Is the author an expert on the topic? To find out, you can gather information about the person on the Internet using a search engine like Yahoo! or Ask.com. Another way to learn about the credibility of an author is to search Google Groups for postings that mention the author or to check the Citation Index to find out how others refer to this author. If you see your source cited by other sources you're using, look at how they cite it and what they say about it, which could provide clues to the author's credibility.

- **Stance of the author.** What's the author's position on the issue(s) involved, and how does this stance influence the information in the source? Does the author's stance support or challenge your own views?

- **Credentials of the publisher or sponsor.** If your source is from a newspaper, is it a major one (such as the *Wall Street Journal* or the *Washington Post*) that has historical credentials in reporting, or is it a tabloid? Is it a popular magazine like *O: The Oprah Magazine* or a journal sponsored by a professional group, such as the *Journal of the American Medical Association*? If your source is a book, is the publisher one you recognize or that has its own Web site? When you don't know the reputation of a source, ask several people with more expertise: a librarian, an instructor, or a professional in the field.

- **Stance of the publisher or sponsor.** Sometimes this stance will be obvious: a magazine called *Save the Planet!* will take a pro-environmental position, whereas one called *America First!* will probably take a conservative stance. But other times, you need to read carefully between the lines to identify particular positions and see how the stance affects the message the source presents. Start by asking what the source's goals are: what does the publisher or sponsoring group want to make happen?

- **Currency.** Check the date of publication of every book and article. Recent sources are often more useful than older ones, particularly in the sciences. However, in some fields (such as history and literature), the most authoritative works may well be the older ones.

- **Accuracy.** Check to see whether the author cites any sources for the information or opinions in the article and, if so, how credible and current they are.

- **Level of specialization.** General sources can be helpful as you begin your research, but later in the project you may need the authority or currency of more specialized sources. Keep in mind that highly specialized works on your topic may be difficult for your audience to understand.

- **Audience.** Was the source written for a general readership? For specialists? For advocates or opponents?

- **Length.** Is the source long enough to provide adequate details in support of your claim?

- **Availability.** Do you have access to the source? If it isn't readily accessible, your time might be better spent looking elsewhere.

- **Omissions.** What's missing or omitted from the source? Might such exclusions affect whether or how you can use the source as evidence?

 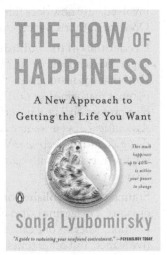

FIGURE 27.3 Note the differences between the cover of the *Journal of Abnormal Psychology* and *The How of Happiness*, a book about psychology. *Journal of Abnormal Psychology* cover reproduced with permission. Copyright © 2013 by the American Psychological Association. No further reproduction or distribution is permitted without written permission from the American Psychological Association.

Assessing Electronic Sources

You'll probably find working with digital media both exciting and frustrating, for even though these tools (the Web, social networks, Twitter, and so on) are enormously useful, they offer information of widely varying quality—and mountains and mountains of it. Because Web sources are mostly open and unregulated, careful researchers look for corroboration before accepting evidence they find online, especially if it comes from a site whose sponsor's identity is unclear.

Practicing Crap Detection

In such an environment, you must be the judge of the accuracy and trustworthiness of particular electronic sources. This is a problem all researchers face, and one that led media critic Howard Rheingold to develop a system for detecting "crap," that is, "information tainted by ignorance, inept communication, or deliberate deception." To avoid such "crap," Rheingold recommends a method of triangulation, which means finding three separate credible online sources that corroborate the point you want to make. But how do you ensure that these sources are credible? One tip Rheingold gives is to use sites like FactCheck.org to verify information, or to use the search term "whois" to find out about the author or sponsor of a site. Try googling Martin Luther King Jr., he says, and somewhere in the top ten "hits" you'll see something called "Martin Luther King, Jr.—a True Historical Examination," which sounds like it should be credible. Check by typing "whois" and the URL of the True Historical Examination, however, and you will find that it is sponsored by a group called Stormfront. Check out *that* site and you'll find that it is a white supremacist group. Hardly a fair, unbiased, and credible source.

FIGURE 27.4 *Every man [and woman] should have a built-in automatic crap detector operating inside him.*—Ernest Hemingway, during a 1954 interview with Robert Manning Alfred Eisenstadt/The Life Picture Collection/Getty Images

FIGURE 27.5 What are the kinds and levels of information available on these Web sites—a commercial site about the TV show *Stormchasers* and a federal site on tornadoes and severe weather? Left: Discovery Communications, Inc.; right: NOAA

In making judgments about online sources, then, you need to be especially mindful and to rely on the same criteria and careful thinking that you use to assess print sources. In addition, you may find the following questions helpful in evaluating online sources:

- Who has posted the document or message or created the site/medium? An individual? An interest group? A company? A government agency? For Web sites, does the URL offer any clues? Note especially the final suffix in a domain name—*.com* (commercial), *.org* (nonprofit organization), *.edu* (educational institution), *.gov* (government agency), *.mil* (military), or *.net* (network). Also note the geographical domains that indicate country of origin—as in *.ca* (Canada) or *.ar* (Argentina). Click on some links of a Web site to see if they lead to legitimate and helpful sources or organizations.

- What can you determine about the credibility of the author or sponsor? Can the information in the document or site be verified in other sources? How accurate and complete is it? On a blog, for example, look for a link that identifies the creator of the site (some blogs are managed by multiple authors).

- Who can be held accountable for the information in the document or site? How well and thoroughly does it credit its own sources? On a wiki, for example, check its editorial policies: who can add to or edit its materials?

- How current is the document or site? Be especially cautious of undated materials. Most reliable sites are refreshed or edited regularly and should list the date.

- What perspectives are represented? If only one perspective is represented, how can you balance or expand this point of view? Is it a straightforward presentation, or could it be a parody or satire?

Assessing Field Research

If you've conducted experiments, surveys, interviews, observations, or any other field research in developing and supporting an argument, make sure to review your results with a critical eye. The following questions can help you evaluate your own field research:

- Have you rechecked all data and all conclusions to make sure they're accurate and warranted?

- Have you identified the exact time, place, and participants in all your field research?

- Have you made clear what part you played in the research and how, if at all, your role could have influenced the results or findings?

- If your research involved other people, have you gotten their permission to use their words or other materials in your argument? Have you asked whether you can use their names or whether the names should be kept confidential?

- If your research involved interviews, have you thanked the person or persons you interviewed and asked them to verify the words you have attributed to them?

RESPOND

1. The chapter claims that "most of the evidence that is used in arguments on public issues ... comes with considerable baggage" (p. 545). Find an article in a journal, newspaper, or magazine that uses evidence to support a claim of some public interest. It might be a piece about new treatments for malaria, Internet privacy, dietary recommendations for schoolchildren, proposals for air-quality regulation, the rise in numbers of campus sexual assaults, and so on. Identify several specific pieces of evidence, information, or data presented in the article and then evaluate the degree to which you would accept, trust, or believe those statements. Be prepared to explain specifically why you would be inclined to trust or mistrust any claims based on the data.

2. Check out Goodreads (you can set up an account for free) and see what people there are recommending—or search for "common reading programs" or "common reading lists." Then choose one of the recommended books, preferably a work of nonfiction, and analyze it by using as many of the principles of evaluation for printed books listed in this chapter as you can without actually reading the book: Who is the author, and what are his/her credentials? Who is the publisher, and what is its reputation? What can you find out about the book's relevance and popularity: why might the book be on the list? Who is the primary audience for the book? How lengthy is it? How difficult? Finally, consider how likely it is that the book you have selected would be used in an academic paper. If you do choose a work of fiction, might the work be studied in a literature course?

3. Choose a news or information Web site that you visit routinely. Then, using the guidelines discussed in this chapter, spend some time evaluating its credibility. You might begin by comparing it with Google News or Arts & Letters Daily, two sites that have a reputation for being reliable.

CHAPTER
28

Using Sources

You may gather an impressive amount of evidence on your topic — from firsthand interviews, from careful observations, and from intensive library and online research. But until that evidence is thoroughly understood and then woven into the fabric of your own argument, it's just a stack of details. You still have to turn that data into credible information that will be persuasive to your intended audiences.

Left to right: © imageBROKER/age fotostock; kstudija/Shutterstock;
Paul Faith/PA Wire URN:9724483 (Press Association via AP Images)

Practicing Infotention

Today it's a truism to say that we are all drowning in information, that it is pouring out at us like water from a never-ending fire hose. Such a situation has its advantages: it's never been easier to locate information on any imaginable topic. But it also has distinct disadvantages: how do you identify useful and credible sources among the millions available to you, and how do you use them well once you've found them? We addressed the first of these questions in Chapter 26, "Finding Evidence." But finding good sources is only the first step. Experts on technology and information like professors Richard Lanham and Howard Rheingold point to the next challenge: managing *attention*. Lanham points out that our age of information calls on us to resist the allure of every single thing vying for our attention and to discriminate among what deserves notice and what doesn't. Building on this insight, Rheingold has coined the term "infotention," which he says "is a word I came up with to describe a mind-machine combination of brain-powered attention skills and computer-powered information filters" (Howard Rheingold, "Infotention," http://www.rheingold.com).

Practicing infotention calls for synthesizing and thinking critically about the enormous amount of information available to us from the "collective intelligence" of the Web. And while some of us can learn to be mindful while multitasking (a fighter pilot is an example Rheingold gives of those who must learn to do so), most of us are not good at it and need to train ourselves, literally, to pay attention to attention (and intention as well), to be aware of what we are doing and thinking, to take a deep breath and notice where we are directing our focus. In short, writers today need to learn to focus their attention, especially online, and learn to avoid distractions. So just how do you put all these skills together to practice infotention?

Building a Critical Mass

Throughout the chapters in Part 5, "Research and Arguments," we've stressed the need to discover as much evidence as possible in support of your claim and to read and understand it as thoroughly as you can. If you can find only one or two pieces of evidence—only one or two reasons or illustrations to back up your thesis—then you may be on unsteady ground. Although there's no definite way of saying just how much evidence is enough, you should build toward a critical mass by having several pieces of evidence all pulling in the direction of your claim. Begin by putting Rheingold's triangulation into practice: find at least three credible sources that support your point.

And remember that **circumstantial evidence** (that is, indirect evidence that *suggests* that something occurred but doesn't prove it directly) may not be enough if it is the only evidence that you have. In the infamous case of Jack the Ripper, the murderer who plagued London's East End in 1888, nothing but circumstantial evidence ever surfaced and hence no one was charged with or convicted of the crimes. In 2007, however, amateur detective Russell Edwards bought a shawl at auction—a shawl found at one of the murder sites. After consulting with a number of scientific experts and using DNA evidence, Edwards identified Jack the Ripper as Aaron Kosminski, who eventually died in an asylum.

If your evidence for a claim relies solely on circumstantial evidence, on personal experience, or on one major example, you should extend your search for additional sources and good reasons to back up your claim—or modify the argument. Your initial position may simply have been wrong.

FIGURE 28.1   © Cog Design, Ltd.

Synthesizing Information

As you gather information, you must find a way to make all the facts, ideas, points of view, and quotations you have encountered work with and for you. The process involves not only reading information and recording data carefully (paying "infotention"), but also pondering and synthesizing it — that is, figuring out how the sources you've examined come together to support your specific claims. Synthesis, a form of critical thinking highly valued by business, industry, and other institutions — especially those that reward innovation and creative thinking — is hard work. It almost always involves immersing yourself in your information or data until it feels familiar and natural to you.

At that point, you can begin to look for patterns, themes, and commonalities or striking differences among your sources. Many students use highlighters to help with this process: mark in blue all the parts of sources that mention point A; mark in green those that have to do with issue B; and so on. You are looking for connections among your sources, bringing together what they have to say about your topic in ways you can organize to help support the claim you are making.

You typically begin this process by paraphrasing or summarizing sources so that you understand exactly what they offer and which ideas are essential to your project. You also decide which, if any, sources offer materials you want to quote directly or reproduce (such as an important graph or table). Then you work to introduce such borrowed materials so that readers grasp their significance, and organize them to highlight important relationships. Throughout this review process, use "infotention" strategies by asking questions such as the following:

- Which sources help to set the context for your argument? In particular, which items present new information or give audiences an incentive for reading your work?

- Which items provide background information that is essential for anyone trying to understand your argument?

- Which items help to define, clarify, or explain key concepts of your case? How can these sources be presented or sequenced so that readers appreciate your claims as valid or, at a minimum, reasonable?

- Which of your sources might be used to illustrate technical or difficult aspects of your subject? Would it be best to summarize such technical information to make it more accessible, or would direct quotations be more authoritative and convincing?

- Which sources (or passages within sources) furnish the best support or evidence for each claim or sub-claim within your argument? Now is the time to group these together so you can decide how to arrange them most effectively.

- Which materials do the best job outlining conflicts or offering counter-arguments to claims within a project? Which sources might help you address any important objections or rebuttals?

Remember that yours should be the dominant and controlling voice in an argument. You are like the conductor of an orchestra, calling upon separate instruments to work together to create a rich and coherent sound. The least effective academic papers are those that mechanically walk through a string of sources—often just one item per paragraph—without ever getting all these authorities to talk to each other or with the author. Such papers go through the motions but don't get anywhere. You can do better.

*"Who is the fairest one of all,
and state your sources!"*

FIGURE 28.2 Backing up your claims with well-chosen sources makes almost any argument more credible. © Ed Fisher/The New Yorker Collection/The Cartoon Bank

Paraphrasing Sources You Will Use Extensively

In a **paraphrase**, you put an author's ideas—including major and minor points—into your own words and sentence structures, following the order the author has given them in the original piece. You usually paraphrase sources that you expect to use heavily in a project. But if you compose your notes well, you may be able to use much of the paraphrased material directly in your paper (with proper citation) because all of the language is your own. A competent paraphrase proves you have read material or data carefully: you demonstrate not only that you know what a source contains but also that you appreciate what it means. There's an important difference.

Here are guidelines to help you paraphrase accurately and effectively in an academic argument:

- Identify the source of the paraphrase, and comment on its significance or the authority of its author.

- Respect your sources. When paraphrasing an entire work or any lengthy section of it, cover all its main points and any essential details, following the same order the author uses. If you distort the shape of the material, your notes will be less valuable, especially if you return to them later.

- If you're paraphrasing material that extends over more than one page in the original source, note the placement of page breaks since it is highly likely that you will use only part of the paraphrase in your argument. You will need the page number to cite the specific page of material you want to cite.

- Make sure that the paraphrase is in your own words and sentence structures. If you want to include especially memorable or powerful language from the original source, enclose it in quotation marks. (See "Using Quotations Selectively and Strategically" on p. 559.)

- Keep your own comments, elaborations, or reactions separate from the paraphrase itself. Your report on the source should be clear, objective, and free of connotative language.

- Collect all the information necessary to create an in-text citation as well as an item in your works cited list or references list. For online materials, be sure you know how to recover the source later.

- Label the paraphrase with a note suggesting where and how you intend to use it in your argument.

- Recheck to make sure that the words and sentence structures are your own and that they express the author's meaning accurately.

Here is a passage from linguist David Crystal's book *Language Play*, followed by a student's paraphrase of the passage.

> Language play, the arguments suggest, will help the development of pronunciation ability through its focus on the properties of sounds and sound contrasts, such as rhyming. Playing with word endings and decoding the syntax of riddles will help the acquisition of grammar. Readiness to play with words and names, to exchange puns and to engage in nonsense talk, promotes links with semantic development. The kinds of dialogue interaction illustrated above are likely to have consequences for the development of conversational skills. And language play, by its nature, also contributes greatly to what in recent years has been called metalinguistic awareness, which is turning out to be of critical importance to the development of language skills in general and literacy skills in particular (180).

> Paraphrase of the Passage from Crystal's Book

> In *Language Play*, David Crystal argues that playing with language—creating rhymes, figuring out riddles, making puns, playing with names, using inverted words, and so on—helps children figure out a great deal, from the basics of pronunciation and grammar to how to carry on a conversation. This kind of play allows children to understand the overall concept of how language works, a concept that is key to learning to use—and read—language effectively (180).

Summarizing Sources

Unlike a paraphrase, a **summary** records just the gist of a source or a key idea—that is, only enough information to identify a point you want to emphasize. Once again, this much-shortened version of a source puts any borrowed ideas into your own words. At the research stage, summaries help you identify key points you want to make and, just as important, provide a record of what you have read. In a project itself, a summary helps readers understand the sources you are using.

Here are some guidelines to help you prepare accurate and helpful summaries:

- Identify the thesis or main point in a source and make it the heart of your summary. In a few detailed phrases or sentences, explain to yourself (and readers) what the source accomplishes.

- If your summary includes a comment on the source (as it might in the summaries used for annotated bibliographies), be sure that you won't later confuse your comments with what the source itself asserts.

- When using a summary in an argument, identify the source, state its point, and add your own comments about why the material is significant for the argument that you're making.

- Include just enough information to recount the main points you want to cite. A summary is usually much shorter than the original. When you need more information or specific details, you can return to the source itself or prepare a paraphrase.

- Use your own words in a summary and keep the language objective and denotative. If you include any language from the original source, enclose it in quotation marks.

- Collect all the information necessary to create an in-text citation as well as an item in your works cited list or references list. For online sources without page numbers, record the paragraph, screen, or section number(s) if available.

- Label the summary with a note that suggests where and how you intend to use it in your argument.

- Recheck the summary to make sure that you've captured the author's meaning accurately and that the wording is entirely your own.

Following is a summary of the David Crystal passage:

> In *Language Play*, David Crystal argues that playing with language helps children figure out how language works, a concept that is key to learning to use—and read—language effectively (180).

Notice that the summary is shorter than the paraphrase shown on p. 558.

Using Quotations Selectively and Strategically

To support your argumentative claims, you'll want to quote (that is, to reproduce an author's precise words) in at least three kinds of situations:

1. when the wording expresses a point so well that you cannot improve it or shorten it without weakening it,

2. when the author is a respected authority whose opinion supports your own ideas powerfully, and/or

3. when an author or authority challenges or seriously disagrees with others in the field.

Consider, too, that charts, graphs, and images may also function like direct quotations, providing convincing evidence for your academic argument.

In an argument, quotations from respected authorities will establish your ethos as someone who has sought out experts in the field. Just as important sometimes, direct quotations (such as a memorable phrase in your introduction or a detailed eyewitness account) may capture your readers' attention. Finally, carefully chosen quotations can broaden the appeal of your argument by drawing on emotion as well as logic, appealing to the reader's mind and heart. A student who is writing on the ethical issues of bullfighting, for example, might introduce an argument that bullfighting is not a sport by quoting Ernest Hemingway's comment that "the formal bull-fight is a tragedy, not a sport, and the bull is certain to be killed" and then accompany the quotation with an image such as the one on the next page.

The following guidelines can help you quote sources accurately and effectively:

- Quote or reproduce materials that readers will find especially convincing, purposeful, and interesting. You should have a specific reason for every quotation.

- Don't forget the double quotation marks [" "] that must surround a direct quotation in American usage. If there's a quote within a quote, it is surrounded by a pair of single quotation marks [' ']. British usage does just the opposite, and foreign languages often handle direct quotations much differently.

- When using a quotation in your argument, introduce its author(s) and follow the quotation with commentary of your own that points out its significance.

- Keep quoted material relatively brief. Quote only as much of a passage as is necessary to make your point while still accurately representing what the source actually said.

- If the quotation extends over more than one page in the original source, note the placement of page breaks in case you decide to use only part of the quotation in your argument.

- In your notes, label a quotation you intend to use with a note that tells you where you think you'll use it.

- Make sure you have all the information necessary to create an in-text citation as well as an item in your works cited list or references list.

- Copy quotations carefully, reproducing the punctuation, capitalization, and spelling exactly as they are in the original. If possible, copy the quotation from a reliable text and paste it directly into your project.

- Make sure that quoted phrases, sentences, or passages fit smoothly into your own language. Consider where to begin the quotation to make it work effectively within its surroundings or modify the words you write to work with the quoted material.

- Use square brackets if you introduce words of your own into the quotation or make changes to it ("And [more] brain research isn't going to define further the matter of 'mind'").

- Use ellipsis marks if you omit material ("And brain research isn't going to define … the matter of 'mind'").

- If you're quoting a short passage (four lines or less in MLA style; forty words or less in APA style), it should be worked into your text, enclosed by quotation marks. Longer quotations should be set off from the regular text. Begin such a quotation on a new line, indenting every line one inch or ten spaces (MLA) or a half inch or five to seven spaces (APA). Set-off quotations do not need to be enclosed in quotation marks.

- Never distort your sources or present them out of context when you quote from them. Misusing sources is a major offense in academic arguments.

FIGURE 28.3 A tragedy, not a sport? Juan Castillo/AFP/Getty Images

Framing Materials You Borrow with Signal Words and Introductions

Because source materials are crucial to the success of arguments, you need to introduce borrowed words and ideas carefully to your readers. Doing so usually calls for using a signal phrase of some kind in the sentence to introduce or frame the source. Often, a signal phrase will precede a quotation. But you need such a marker whenever you introduce borrowed material, as in the following examples:

> According to noted primatologist Jane Goodall, the more we learn about the nature of nonhuman animals, the more ethical questions we face about their use in the service of humans.

> The more we learn about the nature of nonhuman animals, the more ethical questions we face about their use in the service of humans, according to noted primatologist Jane Goodall.

> The more we learn about the nature of nonhuman animals, according to noted primatologist Jane Goodall, the more ethical questions we face about their use in the service of humans.

In each of these sentences, the signal phrase tells readers that you're drawing on the work of a person named Jane Goodall and that this person is a "noted primatologist."

Now look at an example that uses a quotation from a source in more than one sentence:

> In *Job Shift*, consultant William Bridges worries about "dejobbing and about what a future shaped by it is going to be like." Even more worrisome, Bridges argues, is the possibility that "the sense of craft and of professional vocation … will break down under the need to earn a fee" (228).

The signal verbs *worries* and *argues* add a sense of urgency to the message Bridges offers. They also suggest that the writer either agrees with—or is neutral about—Bridges's points. Other signal verbs can have a more negative slant, indicating that the point being introduced by the quotation is open to debate and that others (including the writer) might disagree with it. If the writer of the passage above had said, for instance, that Bridges *unreasonably contends* or that he *fantasizes*, these signal verbs would carry quite different connotations from those associated with *argues*.

In some cases, a signal verb may require more complex phrasing to get the writer's full meaning across:

Bridges recognizes the dangers of changes in work yet refuses to be over-come by them: "The real issue is not how to stop the change but how to provide the necessary knowledge and skills to equip people to operate suc-cessfully in this New World" (229).

As these examples illustrate, the signal verb is important because it allows you to characterize the author's or source's viewpoint as well as your own — so choose these verbs with care.

Some Frequently Used Signal Verbs

acknowledges	claims	emphasizes	remarks
admits	concludes	expresses	replies
advises	concurs	hypothesizes	reports
agrees	confirms	interprets	responds
allows	criticizes	lists	reveals
argues	declares	objects	states
asserts	disagrees	observes	suggests
believes	discusses	offers	thinks
charges	disputes	opposes	writes

Note that in APA style, these signal verbs should be in a past tense: *Blau (1992) claimed*; *Clark (2001) has concluded.*

Using Sources to Clarify and Support Your Own Argument

The best academic arguments often have the flavor of a hearty but focused intel-lectual conversation. Scholars and scientists create this impression by handling research materials strategically and selectively. Here's how some college writers use sources to achieve their own specific goals within an academic argument.

Establish context. Taylor Pearson, whose essay "Why You Should Fear Your Toaster More Than Nuclear Power" appears in Chapter 16, sets the context for his argument in the first two sentences, in which he cites a newspaper source ("Japan Nuclear Disaster Tops Scale") as representative of "headlines everywhere" warning of nuclear crises and the danger of existing nuclear plants. Assuming that these sen-tences will remind readers of other warnings and hence indicate that this is a highly fraught argument with high emotional stakes, Pearson connects those fears to his own argument by shifting, in the third sentence, into a direct rebuttal of the sources (such fears are "nothing more than media sensationalism") before stating his thesis: "We need nuclear energy. It's clean, it's efficient, it's economic, and it's probably the only thing that will enable us to quickly phase out fossil fuels." It will be up to

Pearson in the rest of the essay to explain how, even in a context of public fear, his thesis is defensible:

> For the past month or so, headlines everywhere have been warning us of the horrible crises caused by the damaged Japanese nuclear reactors. Titles like "Japan Nuclear Disaster Tops Scale" have fueled a new wave of protests against anything nuclear—namely, the construction of new nuclear plants or even the continued operation of existing plants. However, all this reignited fear of nuclear energy is nothing more than media sensationalism. We need nuclear energy. It's clean, it's efficient, it's economic, and it's probably the only thing that will enable us to quickly phase out fossil fuels.

Review the literature on a subject. You will often need to tell readers what authorities have already written about your topic, thus connecting them to your own argument. So, in a paper on the effectiveness of peer editing, Susan Wilcox does a very brief "review of the literature" on her subject, pointing to three authorities who support using the method in writing courses. She quotes from the authors and also puts some of their ideas in her own words:

> Bostock cites one advantage of peer review as "giving a sense of owner-ship of the assessment process" (1). Topping expands this view, stating that "peer assessment also involves increased time on task: thinking, comparing, contrasting, and communicating" (254). The extra time spent thinking over the assignment, especially in terms of helping someone else, can draw in the reviewer and lend greater importance to taking the process seriously, espe-cially since the reviewer knows that the classmate is relying on his advice. This also adds an extra layer of accountability for the student; his hard work—or lack thereof—will be seen by peers, not just the instructor. Cassidy notes, "[S]tudents work harder with the knowledge that they will be assessed by their peers" (509): perhaps the knowledge that peer review is coming leads to a better-quality draft to begin with.

The paragraph is straightforward and useful, giving readers an efficient overview of the subject. If they want more information, they can find it by consulting Wilcox's works cited page.

FIGURE 28.4 When using Web sources such as blogs, take special care to check authors' backgrounds and credentials. © Roz Chast/The New Yorker Collection/The Cartoon Bank

Introduce a term or define a concept. Quite often in an academic argument, you may need to define a term or explain a concept. Relying on a source may make your job easier *and* enhance your credibility. That is what Laura Pena achieves in the following paragraph, drawing upon two authorities to explain what teachers mean by a "rubric" when it comes to grading student work:

> To understand the controversy surrounding rubrics, it is best to know what a rubric is. According to Heidi Andrade, a professor at SUNY-Albany, a rubric can be defined as "a document that lists criteria and describes varying levels of quality, from excellent to poor, for a specific assignment" ("Self-Assessment" 61). Traditionally, rubrics have been used primarily as grading and evaluation tools (Kohn 12), meaning that a rubric was not used until after students handed their papers in to their teacher. The teacher would then use a rubric to evaluate the students' papers according to the criteria listed on the rubric.

Note that the first source provides the core definition while information from the second offers a detail important to understanding when and how rubrics are used—a major issue in Pena's paper. Her selection of sources here serves her thesis while also providing readers with necessary information.

Present technical material. Sources can be especially helpful, too, when material becomes technical or difficult to understand. Writing on your own, you might lack the confidence to handle the complexities of some subjects. While you should challenge yourself to learn a subject well enough to explain it in your own words, there will be times when a quotation from an expert serves both you and your readers. Here is Natalie San Luis dealing with some of the technical differences between mainstream and Black English:

> The grammatical rules of mainstream English are more concrete than those of Black English; high school students can't check out an MLA handbook on Ebonics from their school library. As with all dialects, though, there are certain characteristics of the language that most Black English scholars agree upon. According to Samy Alim, author of *Roc the Mic Right*, these characteristics are the "[h]abitual *be* [which] indicates actions that are continuing or ongoing.... Copula absence.... Stressed *been*.... *Gon* [indicating] the future tense.... *They* for possessive.... Postvocalic *-r*.... [and] *Ank* and *ang* for 'ink' and 'ing'" (115). Other scholars have identified "[a]bsence of third-person singular present-tense *s*.... Absence of possessive '*s*," repetition of pronouns, and double negatives (Rickford 111–24).

Note that using ellipses enables San Luis to cover a great deal of ground. Readers not familiar with linguistic terms may have trouble following the quotation, but remember that academic arguments often address audiences comfortable with some degree of complexity.

Develop or support a claim. Even academic audiences expect to be convinced, and one of the most important strategies for a writer is to use sources to amplify or support a claim.

Here is Manasi Deshpande, whose proposal argument appears in Chapter 20 (pp. 426–431), making the following claim: "Although the University has made a concerted and continuing effort to improve access, students and faculty with physical disabilities still suffer from discriminatory hardship, unequal opportunity to succeed, and lack of independence." See how she weaves sources together in the following paragraph to help support that claim:

> The current state of campus accessibility leaves substantial room for improvement. There are approximately 150 academic and administrative buildings on campus (Grant). Eduardo Gardea, intern architect at the Physical Plant, estimates that only about nineteen buildings comply fully with the Americans with Disabilities Act (ADA). According to Penny Seay, PhD, director of the Center for Disability Studies at UT Austin, the ADA in theory "requires every building on campus to be accessible."

Highlight differences or counterarguments. The sources you encounter in developing a project won't always agree with each other or you. In academic arguments, you don't want to hide such differences, but instead point them out honestly and let readers make judgments based upon actual claims. Here is a paragraph in which Laura Pena again presents two views on the use of rubrics as grading tools:

> Some naysayers, such as Alfie Kohn, assert that "any form of assessment that encourages students to keep asking, 'How am I doing?' is likely to change how they look at themselves and what they're learning, usually for the worse." Kohn cites a study that found that students who pay too much attention to the quality of their performance are more likely to chalk up the outcome of an assignment to factors beyond their control, such as innate ability, and are also more likely to give up quickly in the face of a difficult task (14). However, Ross and Rolheiser have found that when students are taught how to properly implement self-assessment tools in the writing process, they are more likely to put more effort and persistence into completing a difficult assignment and may develop higher self-confidence in their writing ability (sec. 2). Building self-confidence in elementary-age writers can be extremely helpful when they tackle more complicated writing endeavors in the future.

In describing Kohn as a "naysayer," Pena may tip her hand and lose some degree of objectivity. But her thesis has already signaled her support for rubrics as a grading tool, so academic readers will probably not find the connotations of the term inappropriate.

These examples suggest only a few of the ways that sources, either summarized or quoted directly, can be incorporated into an academic argument to support or enhance a writer's goals. Like these writers, you should think of sources as your copartners in developing and expressing ideas. But you are still in charge.

Avoiding "Patchwriting"

When using sources in an argument, writers—and especially those new to research-based writing—may be tempted to do what Professor Rebecca Moore Howard terms "**patchwriting**": stitching together material from Web or other sources without properly paraphrasing or summarizing and with little or no documentation. Here, for example, is a patchwork paragraph about the dangers wind turbines pose to wildlife:

> Scientists are discovering that technology with low carbon impact does not mean low environmental or social impacts. That is the case especially with wind turbines, whose long, massive fiberglass blades have been chopping

up tens of thousands of birds that fly into them, including golden eagles, red-tailed hawks, burrowing owls, and other raptors in California. Turbines are also killing bats in great numbers. The 420 wind turbines now in use across Pennsylvania killed more than 10,000 bats last year—mostly in the late summer months, according to the State Game Commission. That's an average of 25 bats per turbine per year, and the Nature Conservancy predicts as many as 2,900 turbines will be set up across the state by 2030. It's not the spinning blades that kill the bats; instead, their lungs effectively blow up from the rapid pressure drop that occurs as air flows over the turbine blades. But there's hope we may figure out solutions to these problems because, since we haven't had too many wind turbines heretofore in the country, we are learning how to manage this new technology as we go.

The paragraph reads well and is full of details. But it would be considered plagiarized (see **Chapter 29**) because it fails to identify its sources and because most of the material has simply been lifted directly from the Web. How much is actually copied? We've highlighted the borrowed material:

Scientists are discovering that technology with low carbon impact does not mean low environmental or social impacts. That is the case especially with wind turbines, whose long, massive fiberglass blades have been chopping up tens of thousands of birds that fly into them, including golden eagles, red-tailed hawks, burrowing owls, and other raptors in California. Turbines are also killing bats in great numbers. The 420 wind turbines now in use across Pennsylvania killed more than 10,000 bats last year—mostly in the late summer months, according to the State Game Commission. That's an average of 25 bats per turbine per year, and the Nature Conservancy predicts as many as 2,900 turbines will be set up across the state by 2030. It's not the spinning blades that kill the bats; instead, their lungs effectively blow up from the rapid pressure drop that occurs as air flows over the turbine blades. But there's hope we may figure out solutions to these problems because, since we haven't had too many wind turbines heretofore in the country, we are learning how to manage this new technology as we go.

But here's the point: an academic writer who has gone to the trouble of finding so much information will gain more credit and credibility just by properly identifying, paraphrasing, and quoting the sources used. The resulting paragraph is actually more impressive because it demonstrates how much reading and synthesizing the writer has actually done:

Scientists like George Ledec of the World Bank are discovering that technology with low carbon impact "does not mean low environmental or social impacts" (Tracy). That is the case especially with wind turbines. Their massive blades spinning to create pollution-free electricity are also killing thousands of valuable birds of prey, including eagles, hawks, and owls in California (Rittier). Turbines are also killing bats in great numbers (Thibodeaux). The *Pittsburgh Post-Gazette* reports that 10,000 bats a year are killed by the 420 turbines currently in Pennsylvania. According to the state game commissioner, "That's an average of 25 bats per turbine per year, and the Nature Conservancy predicts as many as 2,900 turbines will be set up across the state by 2030" (Schwartzel). It's not the spinning blades that kill the animals; instead, *DiscoveryNews* explains, "the bats' lungs effectively blow up from the rapid pressure drop that occurs as air flows over the turbine blades" (Marshall). But there's hope that scientists can develop turbines less dangerous to animals of all kinds. "We haven't had too many wind turbines heretofore in the country," David Cottingham of the Fish and Wildlife Service points out, "so we are learning about it as we go" (Tracy).

Works Cited

Marshall, Jessica. "Wind Turbines Kill Bats without Impact." *DiscoveryNews. com*. Discovery Communications, 25 Aug. 2008. Web. 11 Dec. 2011.

Rittier, John. "Wind Turbines Taking Toll on Birds of Prey." *USA Today*. Gannett, 4 Jan. 2005. Web. 10 Dec. 2011.

Schwartzel, Erich. "Pa. Wind Turbines Deadly to Bats, Costly to Farmers." *Post-Gazette.com*. PG Publishing, 17 July 2011. Web. 12 Dec. 2011.

Thibodeaux, Julie. "Bats Getting Caught in Texas Wind Turbines." *PegasusNews.com*. PanLocal Media, 9 Nov. 2011. Web. 10 Dec. 2011.

Tracy, Ryan. "Wildlife Slows Wind Power." *WallStreetJournal.com*. Dow Jones, 10 Dec. 2011. Web. 10 Dec. 2011.

RESPOND

1. Select one of the essays from Chapters 16–20 or 25. Following the guidelines in this chapter, write a paraphrase of the essay that you might use subsequently in an academic argument. Be careful to describe the essay accurately and to note on what pages specific ideas or claims are located. The language of the paraphrase should be entirely your own—though you may include direct quotations of phrases, sentences, or longer passages you would likely use in a paper. Be sure these quotations are introduced and cited in your paraphrase: *Pearson claims that nuclear power is safe, even asserting that "your toaster is far more likely to kill you than any nuclear power plant" (175).* When you are done, trade your paraphrase with a partner to get feedback on its clarity and accuracy.

2. Summarize three readings or fairly lengthy passages from Parts 2–4 of this book, following the guidelines in this chapter. Open the item with a correct MLA or APA citation for the piece (see Chapter 30). Then provide the summary itself. Follow up with a one- or two-sentence evaluation of the work describing its potential value as a source in an academic argument. In effect, you will be preparing three items that might appear in an annotated bibliography. Here's an example:

   > Pearson, Taylor. "Why You Should Fear Your Toaster More Than Nuclear Power." *Everything's an Argument.* By Andrea A. Lunsford and John J. Ruszkiewicz. 7th ed. Boston: Bedford, 2016. 174–79. Print. Argues that since the dangers of nuclear power (death, radiation, waste) are actually less than those of energy sources we rely on today, nuclear plants represent the only practical way to generate the power we need and still reduce greenhouse gases. The journalistic piece provides many interesting facts about nuclear energy, but is informally documented and so does not identify its sources in detail or include a bibliography.

3. Working with a partner, agree upon an essay that you will both read from Chapters 16–20 or 25, examining it as a potential source for a research argument. As you read it, choose about a half-dozen words, phrases, or short passages that you would likely quote if you used the essay in a paper and attach a frame or signal phrase to each quotation. Then compare the passages you selected to quote with those your partner culled from the same essay. How do your choices of quoted material create an image or ethos for the original author that differs from the one your partner has created? How do the signal phrases shape a reader's sense of the author's position? Which set of quotations best represents the author's argument? Why?

4. Select one of the essays from Chapters 16–20 or 25 to examine the different ways an author uses source materials to support claims. Begin by highlighting the signal phrases you find attached to borrowed ideas or direct quotations. How well do they introduce or frame this material? Then categorize the various ways the author actually uses particular sources. For example, look for sources that provide context for the topic, review the scholarly literature, define key concepts or terms, explain technical details, furnish evidence, or lay out contrary opinions. When you are done, write a paragraph assessing the author's handling of sources in the piece. Are the borrowed materials integrated well with the author's own thoughts? Do the sources represent an effective synthesis of ideas?

Plagiarism and Academic Integrity

I n many ways, "nothing new under the sun" is more than just a cliché. Most of what you think or write is built on what you've previously read or experienced or learned from others. Luckily, you'll seldom be called on to list every influence on your life. But you do have responsibilities in school and professional situations to acknowledge any intellectual property you've made use of when you create arguments of your own. If you don't, you may be accused of **plagiarism**—claiming as your own the words, research, or creative work of others.

What is intellectual property? It's complicated. But, for academic arguments in Western culture, it is the *expression* of ideas you find in works produced by others that you then use to advance and support your own claims. You have to document not only when you use or reproduce someone's exact words, images, music, or other creations (in whole or in part), but also when you borrow the framework others use to put ideas together in original or creative ways. Needless to say, intellectual property rights have always been contentious, but never more so than today, when new media make it remarkably easy to duplicate and share all sorts of materials. Accustomed to uploading and downloading files, cutting and pasting passages, you may be comfortable working with texts day-to-day in ways that are considered inappropriate, or even dishonest, in school. You may, for example, have patched together sources without putting them in your own words or documenting them fully, practices that will often be seen as plagiarism (see p. 567).

Left to right: © imagineasia/age fotostock; Jutta Kuss/Getty Images; Dimitri Otis/Getty Images

So it is essential that you read and understand any policies on academic integrity that your school has set down. In particular, pay attention to how those policies define, prosecute, and punish cheating, plagiarism, and collusion. Some institutions recognize a difference between intentional and unintentional plagiarism, but you don't want the honesty of anything you write to be questioned. You need to learn the rules and understand that the penalties for plagiarism are severe not only for students but for professional writers as well.

But don't panic! Many student writers today are so confused or worried about plagiarism that they shy away from using sources—or end up with a citation for almost every sentence in an essay. There's no reason to go to such extremes. As a conscientious researcher and writer, you simply need to give your best effort in letting readers know what sources you have used. Being careful in such matters will have a big payoff: when you give full credit to your sources, you enhance your ethos in academic arguments—which is why "Academic Integrity" appears in this chapter's title. Audiences will applaud you for saying thanks to those who've helped you. Crediting your sources also proves that you have done your homework: you demonstrate that you understand what others have written about the topic and encourage others to join the intellectual conversation. Finally, citing sources reminds you to think critically about how to use the evidence you've collected. Is it timely and reliable? Have you referenced authorities in a biased or overly selective way? Have you double-checked all quotations and paraphrases? Thinking through such questions helps to guarantee the integrity of your academic work.

FIGURE 29.1 The FBI has warned consumers for decades about the penalties for violating copyright. Your school no doubt has its own policies for handling such violations, including plagiarism. www.cartoonsbysheila.com

DOONESBURY   **BY GARRY TRUDEAU**

FIGURE 29.2 A Doonesbury cartoon on intellectual property pokes fun at best-selling historian and presidential biographer Stephen Ambrose, who was found to have plagiarized passages from at least twelve authors in at least six of his books—and in his doctoral dissertation. DOONESBURY © 2002 G. B. Trudeau. Reprinted with permission of UNIVERSAL UCLICK. All rights reserved.

Giving Credit

The basic principles for documenting materials are relatively simple. Give credit to all source materials you borrow by following these three steps: (1) placing quotation marks around any words you quote directly, (2) citing your sources according to the documentation style you're using, and (3) identifying all the sources you have cited in a list of references or works cited. Materials to be cited in an academic argument include all of the following:

- direct quotations
- facts that are not widely known
- arguable statements
- judgments, opinions, and claims that have been made by others
- images, statistics, charts, tables, graphs, or other illustrations that appear in any source
- collaboration—that is, the help provided by friends, colleagues, instructors, supervisors, or others

However, three important types of evidence or source material do not need to be acknowledged or documented. They are the following:

1. Common knowledge, which is a specific piece of information most readers in your intended audience will know (that Barack Obama won the 2012 presidential election, for instance)

2. Facts available from a wide variety of sources (that the Japanese bombed Pearl Harbor on December 7, 1941, for example). If, for instance, you search for a piece of information and find the same information on hundreds of different reputable Web sites, you can be pretty sure it is common knowledge.

3. Your own findings from field research (observations, interviews, experiments, or surveys you have conducted), which should be clearly presented as your own

For the actual forms to use when documenting sources, see Chapter 30.

Of course, the devil is in the details. For instance, you may be accused of plagiarism in situations like the following:

- if you don't indicate clearly the source of an idea you obviously didn't come up with on your own
- if you use a paraphrase that's too close to the original wording or sentence structure of your source material (*even* if you cite the source)
- if you leave out the parenthetical in-text reference for a quotation (*even* if you include the quotation marks themselves)

And the accusation can be made even if you didn't intend to plagiarize.

But what about all the sampling and mashups you see all the time online and in popular culture? And don't some artistic and scholarly works come close to being "mashups"? Yes and no. It's certainly fair to say, for example, that Shakespeare's plays "mash up" a lot of material from *Holinshed's Chronicles*, which he used without acknowledgment. But it's also true that Shakespeare's works are "transformative" — that is, they are made new by Shakespeare's art. Current copyright law protects such works that qualify as transformative and exempts them from copyright violations. But the issues swirling around the debate over sampling, mashups, and other uses of prior materials are far from clear, and far from over. Perhaps Jeff Shaw (in a posting that asks, "Is Mashup Music Protected by Fair Use?") sums up the current situation best:

> Lest we forget, the purpose of copyright law is to help content creators and to enhance creative expression. Fair use is an important step toward those ends, and further legislative work could solidify the step forward that fair use represents.
>
> —Jeff Shaw, "Is Mashup Music Protected by Fair Use?"

Getting Permission for and Using Copyrighted Internet Sources

When you gather information from Internet sources and use it in your own work, it's subject to the same rules that govern information gathered from other types of sources.

A growing number of online works, including books, photographs, music, and video, are published under the Creative Commons license, which often eliminates the need to request permission. These works — marked with a Creative Commons license — are made available to the public under this alternative to copyright, which grants permission to reuse or remix work under certain terms if credit is given to the work's creator.

Even if the material does not include a copyright notice or symbol ("© 2016 by Andrea A. Lunsford and John J. Ruszkiewicz," for example), it's likely to be protected by copyright laws, and you may need to request permission to use part or all of it. "Fair use" legal precedents allow writers to quote brief passages from published works without permission from the copyright holder if the use is for educational or personal, noncommercial reasons and if full credit is given to the source. For blog postings or any serious professional uses (especially online), however, you should ask permission of the copyright holder before you include any of his/her ideas, text, or images in your own argument.

If you do need to make a request for permission, here is an example:

From: sanchez.32@stanford.edu

To: litman@mindspring.com

CC: lunsford.2@stanford.edu

Subject: Request for permission

Dear Professor Litman:

I am writing to request permission to quote from your essay "Copyright, Owners' Rights and Users' Privileges on the Internet: Implied Licenses, Caching, Linking, Fair Use, and Sign-on Licenses." I want to quote some of your work as part of an article I am writing for the *Stanford Daily* to explain the complex debates over ownership on the Internet and to argue that students at my school should be participating in these debates. I will give full credit to you and will cite the URL where I first found your work (msen.com/~litman/dayton.htm).

Thank you very much for considering my request.

Raul Sanchez

Acknowledging Your Sources Accurately and Appropriately

While artists, lawyers, and institutions like the film and music industries sort out fair use laws, the bottom line in your academic work is clear: document sources accurately and fully and do not be careless about this very important procedure.

Here, for example, is the first paragraph from a print essay by Russell Platt published in the *Nation*:

Classical music in America, we are frequently told, is in its death throes: its orchestras bled dry by expensive guest soloists and greedy musicians' unions, its media presence shrinking, its prestige diminished, its educational role ignored, its big record labels dying out or merging into faceless corporate entities. We seem to have too many well-trained musicians in need of work, too many good composers going without commissions, too many concerts to offer an already satiated public.

—Russell Platt, "New World Symphony"

To cite this passage correctly in MLA documentation style, you could quote directly from it, using both quotation marks and some form of note identifying the author or source. Either of the following versions would be acceptable:

> Russell Platt has doubts about claims that classical music is "in its death throes: its orchestras bled dry by expensive guest soloists and greedy musicians unions" ("New World").

> But is classical music in the United States really "in its death throes," as some critics of the music scene suggest (Platt)?

You might also paraphrase Platt's paragraph, putting his ideas entirely in your own words but still giving him due credit by ending your remarks with a simple in-text note:

> A familiar story told by critics is that classical music faces a bleak future in the United States, with grasping soloists and unions bankrupting orchestras and classical works vanishing from radio and television, school curricula, and the labels of recording conglomerates. The public may not be willing to support all the talented musicians and composers we have today (Platt).

All of these sentences with citations would be keyed to a works cited entry at the end of the paper that would look like the following in MLA style:

> Platt, Russell. "New World Symphony." *The Nation.* The Nation, 3 Oct. 2005. Web. 15 Oct. 2015.

How might a citation go wrong? As we indicated, omitting either the quotation marks around a borrowed passage or an acknowledgment of the source is grounds for complaint. Neither of the following sentences provides enough information for a correct citation:

> But is classical music in the United States really in its death throes, as some critics of the music scene suggest, with its prestige diminished, its educational role ignored, and its big record labels dying (Platt)?

> But is classical music in the United States really in "its death throes," as some critics of the music scene suggest, with "its prestige diminished, its educational role ignored, [and] its big record labels dying"?

Just as faulty is a paraphrase such as the following, which borrows the words or ideas of the source too closely. It represents plagiarism, despite the fact that it identifies the source from which almost all the ideas—and a good many words—are borrowed:

> In "New World Symphony," Russell Platt observes that classical music is thought by many to be in bad shape in America. Its orchestras are being sucked dry by costly guest artists and insatiable unionized musicians, while its place on TV and radio is shrinking. The problem may be that we have too many well-trained musicians who need employment, too many good composers going without jobs, too many concerts for a public that prefers *The Real Housewives of Atlanta*.

Even the fresh idea not taken from Platt at the end of the paragraph doesn't alter the fact that the paraphrase is mostly a mix of Platt's original words, lightly stirred.

Acknowledging Collaboration

Writers generally acknowledge all participants in collaborative projects at the beginning of the presentation, report, or essay. In print texts, the acknowledgment is often placed in a footnote or brief prefatory note.

The seventh edition of the *MLA Handbook for Writers of Research Papers* (2009) calls attention to the growing importance of collaborative work and gives the following advice on how to deal with issues of assigning fair credit all around:

> Joint participation in research and writing is common and, in fact, encouraged in many courses and in many professions. It does not constitute plagiarism provided that credit is given for all contributions. One way to give credit, if roles were clearly demarcated or were unequal, is to state exactly who did what. Another way, especially if roles and contributions were merged and shared, is to acknowledge all concerned equally. Ask your instructor for advice if you are not certain how to acknowledge collaboration.

RESPOND

1. Define *plagiarism* in your own terms, making your definition as clear and explicit as possible. Then compare your definition with those of two or three other classmates, and write a brief report on the similarities and differences you noted in the definitions. You might research terms such as *plagiarism*, *academic honesty*, and *academic integrity* on the Web. Also be certain to check how your own school defines the words.

2. Spend fifteen or twenty minutes jotting down your ideas about intellectual property and plagiarism. Where do you stand, for example, on the issue of music file sharing? On downloading movies free of charge? Do you think these forms of intellectual property should be protected under copyright law? How do you define your own intellectual property, and in what ways and under what conditions are you willing to share it? Finally, come up with your own definition of *academic integrity*.

3. Not everyone agrees that intellectual material is property that should be protected. The slogan "information wants to be free" has been showing up in popular magazines and on the Internet for a long time, often with a call to readers to take action against protection such as data encryption and further extension of copyright.

   Using a Web search engine, look for pages where the phrase "free information" appears. Find several sites that make arguments in favor of free information, and analyze them in terms of their rhetorical appeals. What claims do the authors make? How do they appeal to their audience? What's the site's ethos, and how is it created? After you've read some arguments in favor of free information, return to this chapter's arguments about intellectual property. Which arguments do you find most persuasive? Why?

4. Although this book is concerned principally with ideas and their written expression, other forms of intellectual property are also legally protected. For example, scientific and technological developments are protectable under patent law, which differs in some significant ways from copyright law.

   Find the standards for protection under U.S. copyright law and U.S. patent law. You might begin by visiting the U.S. copyright Web site (copyright.gov). Then imagine that you're the president of a small high-tech corporation and are trying to inform your employees of the legal protections available to them and their work. Write a paragraph or two explaining the differences between copyright and patent, and suggest a policy that balances employees' rights to intellectual property with the business's needs to develop new products.

CHAPTER 30

Documenting Sources

What does documenting sources have to do with argument? First, the sources that a writer chooses form part of any argument, showing that he/she has done some research, knows what others have said about the topic, and understands how to use these items as support for a claim. Similarly, the list of works cited or references makes a statement, saying, "Look at how thoroughly this essay has been researched" or "Note how up-to-date I am!"

Writers working in digital spaces sometimes simply add hotlinks so that their readers can find their sources. If you are writing a multimodal essay that will appear on the Web, such links will be appreciated. But for now, college assignments generally call for full documentation rather than simply a link. You'll find the information you need to create in-text citations and works cited/references lists in this chapter.

Left to right: Seregram/Shutterstock; © Zero Creatives/Image/age fotostock; Iculig/Shutterstock

Documentation styles vary from discipline to discipline, with one format favored in the social sciences and another in the natural sciences, for example. Your instructor will probably assign a documentation style for you to follow. If not, you can use one of the two covered in this chapter. But note that even the choice of documentation style makes an argument in a subtle way. You'll note in the instructions that follow, for example, that the Modern Language Association (MLA) style requires putting the date of publication of a print source at or near the end of a works cited list entry, whereas the American Psychological Association (APA) style places that date near the beginning of a references list citation. Such positioning suggests that in MLA style, the author and title are of greater importance than the date for humanities scholars, while APA puts a priority on the date—and timeliness—of sources. Pay attention to such fine points of documentation style, always asking what these choices suggest about the values of scholars and researchers who use a particular system of documentation.

MLA Style

Widely used in the humanities, MLA style is fully described in the *MLA Handbook for Writers of Research Papers* (7th edition, 2009). In this discussion, we provide guidelines drawn from the *MLA Handbook* for in-text citations, notes, and entries in the list of works cited.

In-Text Citations

MLA style calls for in-text citations in the body of an argument to document sources of quotations, paraphrases, summaries, and so on. For in-text citations, use a signal phrase to introduce the material, often with the author's name (*As Geneva Smitherman explains,* …). Keep an in-text citation short, but include enough information for readers to locate the source in the list of works cited. Place the parenthetical citation as near to the relevant material as possible without disrupting the flow of the sentence, as in the following examples.

1. Author Named in a Signal Phrase

Ordinarily, use the author's name in a signal phrase to introduce the material, and cite the page number(s) in parentheses.

Ravitch chronicles how the focus in education reform has shifted toward privatizing school management rather than toward improving curriculum, teacher training, or funding (36).

2. Author Named in Parentheses

When you don't mention the author in a signal phrase, include the author's last name before the page number(s) in the parentheses.

Oil from shale in the western states, if it could be extracted, would be equivalent to six hundred billion barrels, more than all the crude so far produced in the world (McPhee 413).

3. Two or Three Authors

Use all authors' last names.

Gortner, Hebrun, and Nicolson maintain that "opinion leaders" influence other people in an organization because they are respected, not because they hold high positions (175).

4. Four or More Authors

The MLA allows you to use all authors' last names or to use only the first author's name with *et al.* (in regular type, not italicized). Although either format is acceptable when applied consistently throughout a paper, in an argument it is more fair and accurate to name all authors who contributed to the work.

> Similarly, as Goldberger, Tarule, Clinchy, and Belenky note, their new book builds on their collaborative experiences (xii).

5. Organization as Author

Give the full name of a corporate author if it's brief or a shortened form if it's long.

> Many global economists assert that the term "developing countries" is no longer a useful designation, as it ignores such countries' rapid economic growth (Gates Foundation 112).

6. Unknown Author

Use the full title of the work if it's brief or a shortened form if it's long.

> "Hype," by one analysis, is "an artificially engendered atmosphere of hysteria" ("Today's Marketplace" 51).

7. Author of Two or More Works

When you use two or more works by the same author, include the title of the work or a shortened version of it in the citation.

> Gardner presents readers with their own silliness through his description of a "pointless, ridiculous monster, crouched in the shadows, stinking of dead men, murdered children, and martyred cows" (*Grendel* 2).

8. Authors with the Same Last Name

When you use works by two or more authors with the same last name, include each author's first initial in the in-text citation.

> Public health officials agree that the potential environmental risk caused by indoor residual spraying is far lower than the potential risk of death caused by malaria-carrying mosquitoes (S. Dillon 76).

9. Multivolume Work

Note the volume number first and then the page number(s), with a colon and one space between them.

> Aristotle's "On Plants" is now available in a new translation edited by Barnes (2: 1252).

10. Literary Work

Because literary works are often available in many different editions, you need to include enough information for readers to locate the passage in any edition. For a prose work such as a novel or play, first cite the page number from the edition you used, followed by a semicolon; then indicate the part or chapter number (114; ch. 3) or act or scene in a play (42; sc. 2).

> In Ben Jonson's *Volpone,* the miserly title character addresses his treasure as "dear saint" and "the best of things" (1447; act 1).

For a poem, cite the stanza and line numbers. If the poem has only line numbers, use the word *line(s)* in the first reference (lines 33–34) and the number(s) alone in subsequent references.

> On dying, Whitman speculates, "All that goes onward and outward, nothing collapses, / And to die is different from what any one supposed, and luckier" (6.129-30).

For a verse play, omit the page number, and give only the act, scene, and line numbers, separated by periods.

> Before he takes his own life, Othello says he is "one that loved not wisely but too well" (5.2.348).

> As *Macbeth* begins, the witches greet Banquo as "Lesser than Macbeth, and greater" (1.3.65).

11. Works in an Anthology

For an essay, short story, or other short work within an anthology, use the name of the author of the work, not the editor of the anthology; but use the page number(s) from the anthology.

> In the end, if the black artist accepts any duties at all, that duty is to express the beauty of blackness (Hughes 1271).

12. Sacred Text

To cite a sacred text, such as the Qur'an or the Bible, give the title of the edition you used, the book, and the chapter and verse (or their equivalent), separated by a period. In your text, spell out the names of books. In a parenthetical reference, use an abbreviation for books with names of five or more letters (for example, *Gen.* for Genesis).

> He ignored the admonition "Pride goes before destruction, and a haughty spirit before a fall" (*New Oxford Annotated Bible*, Prov. 16.18).

13. Indirect Source

Use the abbreviation *qtd. in* to indicate that what you're quoting or paraphrasing is quoted (as part of a conversation, interview, letter, or excerpt) in the source you're using.

> As Catherine Belsey states, "to speak is to have access to the language which defines, delimits and locates power" (qtd. in Bartels 453).

14. Two or More Sources in the Same Citation

Separate the information for each source with a semicolon.

> Adefunmi was able to patch up the subsequent holes left in worship by substituting various Yoruba, Dahomean, or Fon customs made available to him through research (Brandon 115-17; Hunt 27).

15. Entire Work or One-Page Article

Include the citation in the text without any page numbers or parentheses.

> Kazuo Ishiguro's dystopian novel *Never Let Me Go* explores questions of identity and authenticity.

16. Nonprint or Electronic Source

Give enough information in a signal phrase or parenthetical citation for readers to locate the source in the list of works cited. Usually give the author or title under which you list the source. If the work isn't numbered by page but has numbered sections, parts, or paragraphs, include the name and number(s) of the section(s) you're citing. (For paragraphs, use the abbreviation *par.* or *pars.*; for section, use *sec.*; for part, use *pt.*)

In his film version of *Hamlet*, Zeffirelli highlights the sexual tension between the prince and his mother.

Zora Neale Hurston is one of the great anthropologists of the twentieth century, according to Kip Hinton (par. 2).

Describing children's language acquisition, Pinker explains that "what's innate about language is just a way of paying attention to parental speech" (qtd. in Johnson, sec. 1).

17. Visual Included in the Text

Number all figures (photos, drawings, cartoons, maps, graphs, and charts) and tables separately.

This trend is illustrated in a chart distributed by the College Board as part of its 2014 analysis of aggregate SAT data (see fig. 1).

Include a caption with enough information about the source to direct readers to the works cited entry. (For an example of an image that a student created, see the sample page from an MLA-style essay on p. 601 in this chapter.)

Explanatory and Bibliographic Notes

The MLA recommends using explanatory notes for information or commentary that doesn't readily fit into your text but is needed for clarification, further explanation, or justification. In addition, the MLA allows bibliographic notes for citing several sources for one point and for offering thanks to, information about, or evaluation of a source. Use a superscript number in your text at the end of a sentence to refer readers to the notes, which usually appear as endnotes (with the heading *Notes*, not underlined or italicized) on a separate page before the list of works cited. Indent the first line of each note five spaces, and double-space all entries.

Text with Superscript Indicating a Note

Stewart emphasizes the existence of social contacts in Hawthorne's life so that the audience will accept a different Hawthorne, one more attuned to modern times than the figure in Woodberry.[3]

Note

³Woodberry does, however, show that Hawthorne was often unsociable. He emphasizes the seclusion of Hawthorne's mother, who separated herself from her family after the death of her husband, often even taking meals alone (28). Woodberry seems to imply that Mrs. Hawthorne's isolation rubbed off on her son.

List of Works Cited

A list of works cited is an alphabetical listing of the sources you cite in your essay. The list appears on a separate page at the end of your argument, after any notes, with the heading *Works Cited* centered an inch from the top of the page; don't underline or italicize it or enclose it in quotation marks. Double-space between the heading and the first entry, and double-space the entire list. (If you're asked to list everything you've read as background—not just the sources you cite—call the list *Works Consulted.*) The first line of each entry should align on the left; subsequent lines indent one-half inch or five spaces. See p. 602 for a sample works cited page.

Print Books

The basic information for a book includes four elements, each followed by a period:

- the author's name, last name first (for a book with multiple authors, only the first author's name is inverted)
- the title and subtitle, italicized
- the publication information, including the city followed by a colon, a shortened form of the publisher's name (such as Harvard UP) followed by a comma, and the publication date
- the medium of publication (*Print*)

1. One Author

Larsen, Erik. *Dead Wake: The Last Crossing of the Lusitania.* New York: Crown, 2015. Print.

2. Two or More Authors

Jacobson, Sid, and Ernie Colón. *The 9/11 Report: A Graphic Adaptation.* New York: Hill, 2006. Print.

3. Organization as Author

American Horticultural Society. *The Fully Illustrated Plant-by-Plant Manual of Practical Techniques.* New York: American Horticultural Society and DK, 1999. Print.

4. Unknown Author

> *National Geographic Atlas of the World.* New York: Natl. Geographic, 2004.
>   Print.

5. Two or More Books by the Same Author

List the works alphabetically by title. Use three hyphens for the author's name
for the second and subsequent works by that author.

> Lorde, Audre. *A Burst of Light.* Ithaca: Firebrand, 1988. Print.

> ---. *Sister Outsider.* Trumansburg: Crossing, 1984. Print.

6. Editor

> Rorty, Amelie Oksenberg, ed. *Essays on Aristotle's Poetics.* Princeton:
>   Princeton UP, 1992. Print.

7. Author and Editor

> Shakespeare, William. *The Tempest.* Ed. Frank Kermode. London:
>   Routledge, 1994. Print.

8. Selection in an Anthology or Chapter in an Edited Book

List the author(s) of the selection or chapter; its title; the title of the book in
which the selection or chapter appears; *Ed.* and the name(s) of the editor(s); the
publication information; and the inclusive page numbers of the selection or chapter.

> Brown, Paul. " 'This thing of darkness I acknowledge mine': *The Tempest* and
>   the Discourse of Colonialism." *Political Shakespeare: Essays in Cultural
>   Materialism.* Ed. Jonathan Dollimore and Alan Sinfield. Ithaca: Cornell
>   UP, 1985. 48-71. Print.

9. Two or More Works from the Same Anthology

Include the anthology itself in the list of works cited.

> Gates, Henry Louis, Jr., and Nellie McKay, eds. *The Norton Anthology of
>   African American Literature.* New York: Norton, 1997. Print.

Then list each selection separately by its author and title, followed by a cross-reference to the anthology.

> Karenga, Maulana. "Black Art: Mute Matter Given Force and Function."
>   Gates and McKay 1973-77.

> Neal, Larry. "The Black Arts Movement." Gates and McKay 1960-72.

10. Translation
> Hietamies, Laila. *Red Moon over White Sea*. Trans. Borje Vahamaki.
>   Beaverton: Aspasia, 2000. Print.

11. Edition Other Than the First
> Lunsford, Andrea A., John J. Ruszkiewicz, and Keith Walters. *Everything's an*
>   *Argument with Readings*. 7th ed. Boston: Bedford, 2016. Print.

12. Graphic Narrative
If the words and images are created by the same person, cite a graphic narrative just as you would a book (see item 1 on p. 588).

> Bechdel, Alison. *Are You My Mother?* New York: Houghton Mifflin Harcourt,
>   2012. Print.

If the work is a collaboration, indicate the author or illustrator who is most important to your research before the title. Then list other contributors in order of their appearance on the title page. Label each person's contribution to the work.

> Stavans, Ilan, writer. *Latino USA: A Cartoon History*. Illus. Lalo Arcaraz. New
>   York: Basic, 2000. Print.

13. One Volume of a Multivolume Work
> Byron, Lord George. *Byron's Letters and Journals*. Ed. Leslie A. Marchand.
>   Vol. 2. London: Murray, 1973. Print. 12 vols.

14. Two or More Volumes of a Multivolume Work
> Byron, Lord George. *Byron's Letters and Journals*. Ed. Leslie A. Marchand. 12
>   vols. London: Murray, 1973-82. Print.

15. Preface, Foreword, Introduction, or Afterword
> Kean, Thomas H., and Lee H. Hamilton. Foreword. *The 9/11 Report: A*
>   *Graphic Adaptation*. By Sid Jacobson and Ernie Colón. New York: Hill,
>   2006. ix-x. Print.

16. Article in a Reference Work
Bierman, Paul R. "Earth." *World Book Encyclopedia*. 2015 ed. Print.

17. Book That Is Part of a Series
Include the title and number of the series after the publication information.

Moss, Beverly J. *A Community Text Arises*. Cresskill: Hampton, 2003. Print.
    Language and Social Processes Ser. 8.

18. Republication
Scott, Walter. *Kenilworth*. 1821. New York: Dodd, 1996. Print.

19. Government Document
United States. Cong. House Committee on the Judiciary. *Impeachment of
    the President. 40th Cong.*, 1st sess. H. Rept. 7. Washington: GPO, 1867.
    Print.

20. Pamphlet
An Answer to the President's Message to the Fiftieth Congress. Philadelphia:
    Manufacturers' Club of Philadelphia, 1887. Print.

21. Published Proceedings of a Conference
Edwards, Ron, ed. *Proceedings of the Third National Folklore Conference*.
    26-27 Nov. 1988. Canberra, Austral.: Australian Folk Trust, 1988. Print.

22. Title within a Title
Tavernier-Courbin, Jacqueline. *Ernest Hemingway's* A Moveable Feast: *The
    Making of Myth*. Boston: Northeastern UP, 1991. Print.

Print Periodicals

The basic entry for a periodical includes four elements, each followed by a period:

- the author's name, last name first
- the article title, in quotation marks
- the publication information, including the periodical title (italicized), the
  volume and issue numbers (if any, not italicized), the date of publication,
  and the page number(s)
- the medium of publication (*Print*)

For works with multiple authors, only the first author's name is inverted. Note that the period following the article title goes inside the closing quotation mark. Finally, note that the MLA omits *the* in titles such as *The New Yorker*.

23. Article in a Print Journal
    Give the issue number, if available.

    Anderson, Virginia. " 'The Perfect Enemy': Clinton, the Contradictions of
        Capitalism, and Slaying the Sin Within." *Rhetoric Review* 21 (2002): 384-
        400. Print.

    Radavich, David. "Man among Men: David Mamet's Homosocial Order."
        American Drama 1.1 (1991): 46-66. Print.

24. Article That Skips Pages
    Seabrook, John. "Renaissance Pears." *New Yorker* 5 Sept. 2005: 102+. Print.

25. Article in a Print Monthly Magazine
    Thompson, Derek. "The Miracle of Minneapolis." *Atlantic* March 2015: 30-32.
        Print.

26. Article in a Print Weekly Magazine
    Reed, Julia. "Hope in the Ruins." *Newsweek* 12 Sept. 2005: 58-59. Print.

27. Article in a Print Newspaper
    Friend, Tim. "Scientists Map the Mouse Genome." *USA Today* 2 Dec. 2002:
        A1. Print.

28. Editorial or Letter to the Editor
    Posner, Alan. "Colin Powell's Regret." Editorial. *New York Times* 9 Sept.
        2005: A20. Print.

29. Unsigned Article
    "Court Rejects the Sale of Medical Marijuana." *New York Times* 26 Feb.
        1998, late ed.: A21. Print.

30. Review
    Wildavsky, Ben. "Bad Educations." Rev. of *Academically Adrift: Limited
        Learning on College Campuses,* by Richard Arum and Josipa Roksa.
        Wilson Quarterly 35.2 (2011): 98-99. Print.

Digital Sources

Most of the following models are based on the MLA's guidelines for citing electronic sources in the *MLA Handbook* (7th edition, 2009), as well as on up-to-date information available at its Web site (mla.org). The MLA no longer requires the use of URLs but assumes that readers can locate a source by searching the author, title, and other publication information given in the citation. The basic MLA entry for most electronic sources should include the following elements:

- name of the author, editor, or compiler
- title of the work, document, or posting
- publication information (volume, issue, year or date). List page numbers (or *n. pag.*, not italicized, if none are listed).
- name of database, italicized
- medium of publication (*Web*, *CD-ROM*, etc.)
- date of access

31. Document from a Web Site

Begin with the author, if known, followed by the title of the work, title of the Web site, publisher or sponsor, date of publication or latest update, medium (*Web*), and the date you accessed the site.

> Stauder, Ellen Keck. "Darkness Audible." *Romantic Circle Praxis Series*. U of Maryland, 2003. Web. 28 Sept 2014.

32. Entire Web Site

Include the name of the person or group who created the site, if relevant; the title of the site, italicized, or (if there is no title) a description such as *Home page*, not italicized; the publisher or sponsor of the site; the date of publication or last update; the medium consulted (*Web*); and the date of access.

> *Kotaku*. Gawker Media, 12 Jan. 2011. Web. 30 Aug. 2014.

> Mitten, Lisa. *Native American Sites*. Lisa A. Mitten, 16 Sept. 2008. Web. 3 Dec. 2013.

33. Course, Department, or Personal Web Site

For a course Web site, include the instructor's name; the title of the site, italicized; a description of the site (such as *Course home page*, *Dept. home page*, or *Home page*—not italicized); the sponsor of the site (academic department and institution); dates of the course or last update to the page; the medium; and the date of access.

Note that the MLA spells home page as two separate words. For an academic department, list the name of the department; a description; the academic institution; the date the page was last updated (use *n.d.* for "no date," not italicized); the medium (*Web*); and the date of access.

> Dept. of English. Home page. Amherst Coll., n.d. Web. 5 Apr. 2007.

> Lunsford, Andrea A. Home page. Stanford U, 27 Mar. 2003. Web. 10 Sept. 2014.

> Lunsford, Andrea A. *Memory and Media*. Course home page. Dept. of English, Stanford U, Sept.-Dec. 2002. Web. 13 Mar. 2006.

34. Online Book

Cite an online book as you would a print book. After the print publication information (if any), give the title of the Web site or database in which the book appears, italicized; the medium (*Web*); and the date of access.

> Riis, Jacob A. *How the Other Half Lives: Studies among the Tenements of New York*. Ed. David Phillips. New York: Scribner's, 1890. *The Authentic History Center*. Web. 26 Mar. 2014.

Treat a poem, essay, or other short work within an online book as you would a part of a print book. After the print publication information (if any), give the title of the Web site or database, italicized; the medium (*Web*); and the date of access.

> Dickinson, Emily. "The Grass." *Poems: Emily Dickinson*. Boston: Roberts Brothers, 1891. *Humanities Text Initiative American Verse Project*. Web. 6 Jan. 2015.

35. Article in a Journal on the Web

For an article in an online journal, cite the same information that you would for a print journal. If the online article does not have page numbers, use *n. pag.* (not italicized). Then add the medium consulted (*Web*) and the date of access.

> Edwards, Chris. "A Wealth of Opportunity: An Undergraduate Consultant's Look into the Benefits of Working at a Writing Center." *Praxis: A Writing Center Journal* 7.2 (2010): n. pag. Web. 28 May 2011.

36. Article in a Magazine or Newspaper on the Web

For an article in an online magazine or newspaper, cite the author; the title of the article, in quotation marks; the name of the magazine or newspaper, italicized; the sponsor of the Web site; the date of publication; the medium (*Web*); and the date you accessed the article.

Broad, William J. "In Ancient Fossils, Seeds of a New Debate on Warming." *New York Times.* New York Times, 7 Nov. 2006. Web. 12 Jan. 2015.

McIntosh, Jill. "First Drive: 2013 Audi Q5 Hybrid." *Canadian Driver.* Canadian Driver Communications, 20 June 2011. Web. 15 Aug. 2011.

37. Entry in a Web Reference Work

Cite the entry as you would an entry from a print reference work (see item 16). Follow with the name of the Web site, the sponsor, the date of publication, the medium, and the date of access.

"Tour de France." *Encyclopaedia Britannica Online.* Encyclopaedia Britannica, 2006. Web. 21 May 2014.

38. Post or Comment on a Web Site

Begin with the author's name; the title of the posting, in quotation marks (if there is no title, use the description *Weblog post* or *Weblog comment*, not italicized); the name of the blog, italicized; the sponsor of the blog (use *N.p.*, not italicized, if there is no sponsor); the date of the most recent update; the medium (*Web*); and the date of access.

Marcotte, Amanda. "Rights without Perfection." *Pandagon.* N.p., 16 May 2010. Web. 16 May 2012.

39. Entry in a Wiki

Since wikis are collectively edited, do not include an author. Treat a wiki as you would a work from a Web site (see item 31). Include the title of the entry; the name of the wiki, italicized; the sponsor or publisher (use *N.p.*, not italicized, if there is no sponsor); the date of the latest update; the medium (*Web*); and the date of access.

"Fédération Internationale de Football Association." *Wikipedia.* Wikimedia Foundation, 17 June 2011. Web. 18 July 2014.

40. Posting on a Social Networking Site

To cite a posting on Facebook or another social networking site, include the writer's name, a description of the posting, the date of the posting, and the medium of delivery.

Ferguson, Sarah. Status update. 6 Mar. 2014. Facebook posting.

41. Email or Message on a Social Networking Site

Include the writer's name; the subject line, in quotation marks (for email); *Message to* (not italicized or in quotation marks) followed by the recipient's name; the date of the message; and the medium of delivery (E-mail, not italicized). Note that the MLA hyphenates *e-mail*.

Harris, Jay. "Thoughts on Impromptu State Productions." Message to the author. 16 July 2014. E-mail.

42. Tweet

Include the writer's real name, if known, with the user name (if different) in parentheses. If you don't know the real name, give just the user name. Include the entire tweet, in quotation marks. End with the date and time of the message and the medium (*Tweet*).

Andrea A. Lunsford (aalrhetorician). "Just read (again) about demise of the apostrophe. Argument getting a bit old." 27 Aug. 2014, 1:59 p.m. Tweet.

43. Work from an Online Database or a Subscription Service

For a work from an online database, list the author's name; the title of the work, in quotation marks; any print publication information; the name of the database, italicized; the medium consulted (*Web*); and the date of access.

"Bolivia: Elecciones Presidenciales de 2002." *Political Database of the Americas.* Web. 12 Nov. 2006.

Penn, Sean, and Jon Krakauer. "*Into the Wild* Script." *Internet Movie Script Database.* Web. 12 June 2011.

For a work from an online service to which your library subscribes, include the same information as for an online database. After the information about the work, give the name of the database, italicized; the medium; and the date you accessed the work.

"Breaking the Dieting Habit: Drug Therapy for Eating Disorders."
   Psychology Today Mar. 1995: 12+. *ProQuest*. Web. 30 Nov. 2014.

If you're citing an article from a subscription service to which you subscribe (such as AOL), use the following model:

Weeks, W. William. "Beyond the Ark." *Nature Conservancy* Mar.-Apr. 1999.
   America Online. Web. 30 Nov. 2008.

44. Computer Software or Video Game

Include the title, italicized; the version number (if given); publication information; and the medium. If you are citing material downloaded from a Web site, include the title and version number (if given), but instead of publication information, add the publisher or sponsor of the Web site; the date of publication; the medium (*Web*); and the date of access.

The Sims 3. Vers. 1.24. Redwood City: Electronic Arts, 2009. CD-ROM.

Web Cache Illuminator. Vers. 4.02. NorthStar Solutions, n.d. Web. 12 Nov.
   2007.

45. CD-ROM, Diskette, or Magnetic Tape

If the CD has multiple discs, insert the total number at the end of the citation.

The 1998 Grolier Multimedia Encyclopedia. Danbury: Grolier Interactive,
   1998. CD-ROM. 2 discs.

Other Sources (Including Online Versions)

46. Unpublished Dissertation

Thompson, Brian. "I'm Better Than You, and I Can Prove It: Games,
   Expertise, and the Culture of Competition." Diss. Stanford U, 2014.
   Print.

47. Published Dissertation

Baum, Bernard. *Decentralization of Authority in a Bureaucracy*. Diss. U of
   Chicago, 1959. Englewood Cliffs: Prentice, 1961. Print.

48. Article from a Microform

Sharpe, Lora. "A Quilter's Tribute." *Boston Globe* 25 Mar. 1989: 13.
   Microform. *NewsBank*: Social Relations 12 (1989): fiche 6, grids B4-6.

49. Personal, Published, or Broadcast Interview

For a personal interview, list the name of the person interviewed, the label *Personal interview* (not italicized), and the date of the interview.

> Ashdown, Audrey. Personal interview. 1 Jan. 2015.

For a published interview, list the name of the person interviewed and the title (if any), or if there is no title, use the label *Interview by [interviewer's name]* (not italicized); then add the publication information, including the medium.

> Marshall, Andrew. "The Marshall Plan." Interview by Douglas McGray. *Wired.* CondéNet, Feb. 2003. Web. 17 Mar. 2010.

> Taylor, Max. "Max Taylor on Winning." *Time* 13 Nov. 2000: 66. Print.

For a broadcast interview, list the name of the person interviewed, the label *Interview* (not italicized), and the name of the interviewer (if relevant); then list information about the program, the date of the interview, and the medium.

> Fairey, Shepard. "Spreading the Hope: Street Artist Shepard Fairey." Interview by Terry Gross. *Fresh Air.* Natl. Public Radio. WBUR, Boston. 20 Jan. 2009. Radio.

If you listened to an archived version online, after the site's sponsor (if known), add the interview date, medium (*Web*), and date of access.

> Gordon, Kim. "A 'Girl in a Band': Kim Gordon on Life after Sonic Youth." Interview by Terry Gross. *Fresh Air.* Natl. Public Radio, 4 Mar. 2015. Web. 17 Apr. 2015.

50. Letter

Treat a published letter like a work in an anthology, but include the date of the letter.

> Jacobs, Harriet. "To Amy Post." 4 Apr. 1853. *Incidents in the Life of a Slave Girl.* Ed. Jean Fagan Yellin. Cambridge: Harvard UP, 1987. 234-35. Print.

51. Film

For films, ordinarily begin with the title, followed by the director and major performers. If your essay or project focuses on a major person related to the film, such as the director, you can begin with that name or names, followed by the title and performers.

Selma. Dir. Ava DuVernay. Perf. David Oyelowo, Tom Wilkinson. Plan B
   Entertainment, 2014. Film.

Jenkins, Tamara, dir. *The Savages.* Perf. Laura Linney and Philip Seymour
   Hoffman. 2007. Fox Searchlight. Web. 4 Mar. 2008.

52. Television or Radio Program

"Baelor." *Game of Thrones.* Dir. Alan Taylor. Writ. David Benioff and D. B.
   Weiss. Perf. Sean Bean, Emilia Clarke, and Kit Harington. HBO. 9 June
   2011. Television.

Montagne, Renee. "Week in Review: The Latest on Egypt and Syria."
   Morning Edition. Natl. Public Radio. KQED, San Francisco. 23 Aug.
   2013. Radio.

53. Online Video Clip

Cite a short online video as you would a work from a Web site (see item 31).

Weber, Jan. "As We Sow, Part I: Where Are the Farmers?" *YouTube.*
   YouTube, 15 Mar. 2009. Web. 27 Sept. 2012.

54. Sound Recording

Black Rebel Motorcycle Club. "Howl." *Howl.* RCA Records, 2005. CD.

Brandon Flowers. "Crossfire." *Flamingo.* Island, 2010. MP3.

55. Work of Art or Photograph

List the artist or photographer; the work's title, italicized; the date of composition (if unknown, use *N.d.*); and the medium of composition (*Oil on canvas, Bronze,
Photograph,* etc.). Then cite the name of the museum or other location and the city.

Ulmann, Doris. *Man Leaning against a Wall.* 1930. Photograph. Smithsonian
   American Art Museum, Washington, DC.

To cite a reproduction in a book, add the publication information.

General William Palmer in Old Age. 1810. Oil on canvas. National Army
   Museum, London. *White Mughals: Love and Betrayal in Eighteenth-
   Century India.* William Dalrymple. New York: Penguin, 2002. 270. Print.

To cite artwork found online, omit the medium of composition, and after the location add the title of the database or Web site, italicized; the medium consulted (*Web*); and the date of access.

> Chagall, Marc. *The Poet with the Birds.* 1911. Minneapolis Inst. of Arts. *Artsmia.org.* Web. 6 Oct. 2003.

56. Lecture or Speech

> DeGeneres, Ellen. Baccalaureate Address. Tulane University, New Orleans, LA. 11 May 2009. Address.

57. Performance

> *Anything Goes.* By Cole Porter. Perf. Klea Blackhurst. Shubert Theatre, New Haven. 7 Oct. 2003. Performance.

58. Map or Chart

> *World Political Map (Classic).* Washington: Natl. Geographic, 2007. Print.

59. Cartoon

> Ramirez, Michael. "The Phoenix." Cartoon. *Investors.com.* Investor's Business Daily, 10 Sept. 2011. Web. 11 Sept. 2011.

60. Advertisement

> Banana Republic. Advertisement. *Wired* Sept. 2009: 13. Print.

On p. 601, note the formatting of the first page of a sample essay written in MLA style. On p. 602, you'll find a sample works cited page written for the same student essay.

Sample First Page for an Essay in MLA Style

Author name and page number in upper right corner of each page

Name, instructor, course, date aligned at left

Title centered

Figure number and caption noting the source of the photo

Lesk 1

Emily Lesk
Professor Arraéz
Electric Rhetoric
15 November 2014

Red, White, and Everywhere

America, I have a confession to make: I don't drink Coke. But don't call me a hypocrite just because I am still the proud owner of a bright red shirt that advertises it. Just call me an American. Even before setting foot in Israel three years ago, I knew exactly where I could find one. The tiny T-shirt shop in the central block of Jerusalem's Ben Yehuda Street did offer other designs, but the one with a bright white "Drink Coca-Cola Classic" written in Hebrew cursive across the chest was what drew in most of the dollar-carrying tourists. While waiting almost twenty minutes for my shirt (depicted in fig. 1), I watched nearly every customer ahead of me ask for "the Coke shirt, *todah rabah* [thank you very much]."

At the time, I never thought it strange that I wanted one, too. After having absorbed sixteen years of Coca-Cola propaganda through everything from NBC's Saturday morning cartoon lineup to the concession stand at Camden Yards (the Baltimore Orioles' ballpark), I associated the shirt with singing along to the "Just for the Taste of It" jingle and with America's favorite pastime, not with a brown fizzy beverage I refused to consume.

Fig. 1. Hebrew Coca-Cola T-shirt. Personal photograph. Despite my dislike for the beverage, I bought this Coca-Cola T-shirt in Israel.

Sample List of Works Cited for an Essay in MLA Style

Works Cited

Heading
centered

Coca-Cola Santa pin. Personal photograph by the author. 9 Nov. 2008.

Subsequent
lines of each
entry indented

"The Fabulous Fifties." *Beverage Industry* 87.6 (1996): 16. *General OneFile.*
        Web. 2 Nov. 2014.

"Fifty Years of Coca-Cola Television Advertisements." *American Memory.*
        Motion Picture, Broadcasting and Recorded Sound Division, Lib. of
        Cong. 29 Nov. 2000. Web. 5 Nov. 2014.

"Haddon Sundblom and Coca-Cola." *Thehistoryofchristmas.com.* 10
        Holidays, 2004. Web. 2 Nov. 2014.

Hebrew Coca-Cola T-shirt. Personal photograph by the author. 8 Nov.
        2014.

List is alphabet-
ized by authors'
last names (or
by title when
there is no
author)

Ikuta, Yasutoshi, ed. *'50s American Magazine Ads.* Tokyo: Graphic-Sha,
        1987. Print.

Pendergrast, Mark. *For God, Country, and Coca-Cola: The Definitive
        History of the Great American Soft Drink and the Company That
        Makes It.* 2nd ed. New York: Basic, 2000. Print.

APA Style

The Publication Manual of the American Psychological Association (6th edition, 2010) provides comprehensive advice to student and professional writers in the social sciences. Here we draw on the *Publication Manual*'s guidelines to provide an overview of APA style for in-text citations, content notes, and entries in the list of references.

In-Text Citations

APA style calls for in-text citations in the body of an argument to document sources of quotations, paraphrases, summaries, and so on. These in-text citations correspond to full bibliographic entries in the list of references at the end of the text.

1. Author Named in a Signal Phrase

Generally, give the author's name in a signal phrase to introduce the cited material, using the past tense for the signal verb. Place the date, in parentheses, immediately after the author's name. For a quotation, the page number, preceded by *p*. (not italicized), appears in parentheses after the quotation. For electronic texts or other works without page numbers, paragraph numbers may be used instead, preceded by the abbreviation *para.* For a long, set-off quotation, position the page reference in parentheses one space after the punctuation at the end of the quotation.

According to Brandon (1993), Adefunmi opposed all forms of racism and believed that black nationalism should not be a destructive force (p. 29).

As Johnson (2005) demonstrated, contemporary television dramas such as *ER* and *Lost* are not only more complex than earlier programs but "possess a quality that can only be described as subtlety and discretion" (p. 83).

2. Author Named in Parentheses

When you don't mention the author in a signal phrase, give the name and the date, separated by a comma, in parentheses at the end of the cited material.

The Sopranos has achieved a much wider viewing audience than ever expected, spawning a cookbook and several serious scholarly studies (Franklin, 2002).

3. Two Authors

Use both names in all citations. Use *and* in a signal phrase, but use an ampersand (&) in parentheses.

Associated with purity and wisdom, Obatala is the creator of human beings, whom he is said to have formed out of clay (Edwards & Mason, 1985).

4. Three to Five Authors

List all the authors' names for the first reference. In subsequent references, use just the first author's name followed by *et al.* (in regular type, not underlined or italicized).

> Lenhoff, Wang, Greenberg, and Bellugi (1997) cited tests that indicate that segments of the left brain hemisphere are not affected by Williams syndrome, whereas the right hemisphere is significantly affected (p. 1641).

> Shackelford (1999) drew on the study by Lenhoff et al. (1997).

5. Six or More Authors

Use only the first author's name and *et al.* (in regular type, not underlined or italicized) in every citation, including the first.

> As Flower et al. (2003) demonstrated, reading and writing involve both cognitive and social processes.

6. Organization as Author

If the name of an organization or a corporation is long, spell it out the first time, followed by an abbreviation in brackets. In later citations, use the abbreviation only.

First Citation	(Federal Bureau of Investigation [FBI], 2002)
Subsequent Citations	(FBI, 2002)

7. Unknown Author

Use the title or its first few words in a signal phrase or in parentheses. (In the example below, a book's title is italicized.)

> The school profiles for the county substantiate this trend (*Guide to secondary schools*, 2003).

8. Authors with the Same Last Name

If your list of references includes works by different authors with the same last name, include the authors' initials in each citation.

> G. Jones (1998) conducted the groundbreaking study of retroviruses, whereas P. Jones (2000) replicated the initial trials two years later.

9. Two or More Sources in the Same Citation

List sources by the same author chronologically by publication year. List sources by different authors in alphabetical order by the authors' last names, separated by semicolons.

> While traditional forms of argument are warlike and agonistic, alternative models do exist (Foss & Foss, 1997; Makau, 1999).

10. Specific Parts of a Source

Use abbreviations (*p.*, *pt.*, and so on) in a parenthetical citation to name the part of a work you're citing. However, *chapter* is not abbreviated.

> Pinker (2003) argued that his research yielded the opposite results (p. 6).

> Pinker (2003) argued that his research yielded the opposite results (Chapter 6).

11. Online Document

To cite a source found on the Internet, use the author's name and date as you would for a print source, and indicate the chapter or figure of the document, as appropriate. If the source's publication date is unknown, use *n.d.* ("no date"). To document a quotation, include paragraph numbers if page numbers are unavailable. If an online document has no page or paragraph numbers, provide the heading of the section and the number of the paragraph that follows.

> Werbach (2002) argued convincingly that "despite the best efforts of legislators, lawyers, and computer programmers, spam has won. Spam is killing email" (p. 1).

12. Email and Other Personal Communication

Cite any personal letters, email messages, electronic postings, telephone conversations, or personal interviews by giving the person's initial(s) and last name, the identification, and the date. Do not list email in the references list, and note that APA style uses a hyphen in the word *e-mail*.

> E. Ashdown (personal communication, March 9, 2015) supported these claims.

Content Notes

The APA recommends using content notes for material that will expand or supplement your argument but otherwise would interrupt the text. Indicate such notes in your text by inserting superscript numerals. Type the notes themselves either at the bottom of the page or on a separate page headed *Footnotes* (not italicized or in quotation marks), centered at the top of the page. Double-space all entries. Indent the first line of each note one-half inch or five spaces, and begin subsequent lines at the left margin.

Text with Superscript Indicating a Note

Data related to children's preferences in books were instrumental in designing the questionnaire.[1]

Note

[1]Rudine Sims Bishop and members of the Reading Readiness Research Group provided helpful data.

List of References

The alphabetical list of sources cited in your text is called *References*. (If your instructor asks you to list everything you've read as background — not just the sources you cite — call the list *Bibliography*.) The list of references appears on a separate page or pages at the end of your paper, with the heading *References* (not underlined, italicized, or in quotation marks) centered one inch from the top of the page. Double-space after the heading, and begin your first entry. Double-space the entire list. For print sources, APA style specifies the treatment and placement of four basic elements: author, publication date, title, and publication information. Each element is followed by a period.

- **Author:** List all authors with last name first, and use only initials for first and middle names. Separate the names of multiple authors with commas, and use an ampersand (&) before the last author's name.

- **Publication date:** Enclose the publication date in parentheses. Use only the year for books and journals; use the year, a comma, and the month or month and day for magazines and newspapers. Do not abbreviate the month. If a date is not given, put *n.d.* ("no date," not italicized) in the parentheses. Put a period after the parentheses.

- **Title:** Italicize titles and subtitles of books and periodicals. Do not enclose titles of articles in quotation marks. For books and articles, capitalize only the first word of the title and subtitle and any proper nouns or proper adjectives; also capitalize the first word following a colon. Capitalize all major words in the title of a periodical.

- **Publication information:** For a book published in the United States, list the city of publication and state abbreviation. For books published outside the United States, identify the city and country. Provide the publisher's name, dropping *Inc.*, *Co.*, or *Publishers*. If the state is already included within the publisher's name, do not include the postal abbreviation for the state. For a periodical, follow the periodical title with a comma, the volume number (italicized), the issue number (if provided) in parentheses and followed by a comma, and the inclusive page numbers of the article. For newspaper articles and for articles or chapters in books, include the abbreviation *p.* ("page") or *pp.* ("pages").

The following APA style examples appear in a "hanging indent" format, in which the first line aligns on the left and the subsequent lines indent one-half inch or five spaces.

Print Books

1. One Author

Fraser, S. (2015). *The age of acquiescence: The life and death of American resistance to organized wealth and power.* New York, NY: Little, Brown.

2. Two or More Authors

Steininger, M., Newell, J. D., & Garcia, L. (1984). *Ethical issues in psychology.* Homewood, IL: Dow Jones-Irwin.

3. Organization as Author

Use the word *Author* (not italicized) as the publisher when the organization is both the author and the publisher.

Linguistics Society of America. (2002). *Guidelines for using sign language interpreters.* Washington, DC: Author.

4. Unknown Author

National Geographic atlas of the world. (2010). Washington, DC: National Geographic Society.

5. Book Prepared by an Editor

Hardy, H. H. (Ed.). (1998). *The proper study of mankind.* New York, NY: Farrar, Straus.

6. Selection in a Book with an Editor

Villanueva, V. (1999). An introduction to social scientific discussions on class. In A. Shepard, J. McMillan, & G. Tate (Eds.), *Coming to class: Pedagogy and the social class of teachers* (pp. 262-277). Portsmouth, NH: Heinemann.

7. Translation

Pérez-Reverte, A. (2002). *The nautical chart* (M. S. Peden, Trans.). New York, NY: Harvest. (Original work published 2000)

8. Edition Other Than the First

Bok, D. (2015). *Higher education in America* (Rev. ed.). Princeton, NJ: Princeton University Press.

9. One Volume of a Multivolume Work

Will, J. S. (1921). *Protestantism in France* (Vol. 2). Toronto, Canada: University of Toronto Press.

10. Article in a Reference Work

Chernow, B., & Vattasi, G. (Eds.). (1993). Psychomimetic drug. In *The Columbia encyclopedia* (5th ed., p. 2238). New York, NY: Columbia University Press.

If no author is listed, begin with the article title, followed by the year, and the rest of the citation as shown here.

11. Republication

Sharp, C. (1978). *History of Hartlepool*. Hartlepool, United Kingdom: Hartlepool Borough Council. (Original work published 1816)

12. Graphic Narrative

If the words and images are created by the same person, cite a graphic narrative just as you would a book with one author (see item 1 on p. 607).

Bechdel, A. (2012). *Are you my mother?* New York, NY: Houghton Mifflin Harcourt.

If the work is a collaboration, indicate the author or illustrator who is most important to your research, followed by other contributors in order of their appearance on the title page. Label each person's contribution to the work.

> Stavans, I. (Writer), & Arcaraz, L. (Illustrator). (2000). *Latino USA: A cartoon history.* New York, NY: Basic.

13. Government Document

> U.S. Bureau of the Census. (2001). *Survey of women-owned business enterprises.* Washington, DC: Government Printing Office.

14. Two or More Works by the Same Author

List the works in chronological order of publication. Repeat the author's name in each entry.

> Lowin, S. (2006). *The making of a forefather: Abraham in Islamic and Jewish exegetical narratives.* Leiden, The Netherlands: Brill.

> Lowin, S. (2013). *Arabic and Hebrew love poems in Al-Andalus.* New York, NY: Routledge.

Print Periodicals

15. Article in a Journal Paginated by Volume

> Bowen, L. M. (2011). Resisting age bias in digital literacy research. *College Composition and Communication, 62,* 586-607.

16. Article in a Journal Paginated by Issue

> Carr, S. (2002). The circulation of Blair's Lectures. *Rhetoric Society Quarterly, 32*(4), 75-104.

17. Article in a Monthly Magazine

> Baker, C. (2008, September). Master of the universe. *Wired, 16*(9), 134-141.

18. Article in a Newspaper

Nagourney, A. (2002, December 16). Gore rules out running in '04. *The New York Times*, pp. A1, A8.

19. Letter to the Editor or Editorial

Erbeta, R. (2008, December). Swiftboating George [Letter to the editor]. *Smithsonian, 39*(9), 10.

20. Unsigned Article

Guidelines issued on assisted suicide. (1998, March 4). *The New York Times*, p. A15.

21. Review

Avalona, A. (2008, August). [Review of the book *Weaving women's lives: Three generations in a Navajo family*, by L. Lamphere]. *New Mexico, 86*(8), 40.

22. Published Interview

Shor, I. (1997). [Interview with A. Greenbaum]. *Writing on the Edge, 8*(2), 7-20.

23. Two or More Works by the Same Author in the Same Year

List two or more works by the same author published in the same year alphabetically by title (excluding *A*, *An*, or *The*), and place lowercase letters (*a*, *b*, etc.) after the dates.

Murray, F. B. (1983a). Equilibration as cognitive conflict. *Developmental Review, 3*, 54-61.

Murray, F. B. (1983b). Learning and development through social interaction. In L. Liben (Ed.), *Piaget and the foundations of knowledge* (pp. 176-201). Hillsdale, NJ: Erlbaum.

Digital Sources

The following models are based on the *APA's Publication Manual* (6th edition). A change for handling electronic sources involves the use of a digital object identifier (DOI) when available (instead of a URL) to locate an electronic source. The DOI is a unique number assigned to an electronic text (article, book, or other item) and intended to give reliable access to it. A second change is that a date of retrieval is no longer necessary unless a source changes very frequently. The basic APA entry for most electronic sources should include the following elements:

- name of the author, editor, or compiler
- date of electronic publication or most recent update
- title of the work, document, or posting
- publication information, including the title, volume or issue number, and page numbers
- the DOI (digital object identifier) of the document, if one is available
- a URL, only if a DOI is not available, with no angle brackets and no closing punctuation

24. Web Site

To cite a whole site, give the address in a parenthetical reference. To cite a document from a Web site, include information as you would for a print document, followed by a note on its retrieval. Provide a date of retrieval only if the information is likely to change frequently.

American Psychological Association. (2013). Making stepfamilies work. Retrieved from http://www.apa.org/helpcenter/stepfamily.aspx

Mullins, B. (1995). Introduction to Robert Hass. Readings in contemporary poetry at Dia Center for the Arts. Retrieved from http://www.diacenter .org/prg/poetry/95_96/intrhass.html

25. Article from a Periodical on the Web

For an article you read online, provide either the URL of the periodical's home-page, preceded by Retrieved from (not italicized) or a DOI.

Haines, R. (2015, February 27). The problem with separate toys for boys and girls. *The Boston Globe*. Retrieved from http://www.bostonglobe.com

Lambert, N. M., Graham, S. M., & Fincham, F. D. (2009). A prototype analysis of gratitude: Varieties of gratitude experiences. *Personality and Social Psychology Bulletin, 35*, 1193-1207. doi:10.1177/0146167209338071

26. Article or Abstract from a Database

For an article you find on a database, provide a DOI if one is available. If the online article does not have a DOI, locate the homepage for the journal in which the article appears and provide that URL. You need not identify the database you have used.

> Strully, K. (2014). Racially and ethnically diverse schools and adolescent romantic relationships. *American Journal of Sociology, 120*(3), 750-757. doi:10.1086/679190

> Hayhoe, G. (2001). The long and winding road: Technology's future. *Technical Communication, 48*(2), 133-145. Retrieved from techcomm.stc.org

27. Software or Computer Program

> OS X Lion (Version 10.7) [Computer operating system]. (2011). Cupertino, CA: Apple.

28. Online Government Document

Cite an online government document as you would a printed government work, adding the URL. Note that the APA spells website as one word.

> Finn, J. D. (1998, April). *Class size and students at risk: What is known? What is next?* Retrieved from United States Department of Education website: http://www.ed.gov/pubs/ClassSize/title.html

29. Entry in a Web Reference Work

Cite the entry as you would an entry from a print reference work (see item 10). Follow with the date of publication, the name of the Web site, and the URL.

> Tour de France. (2006). In *Encyclopaedia Britannica Online.* Retrieved from http://www.britannica.com/EBchecked/topic/600732/Tour-de-France

30. Posting or Comment on a Web Site

Begin with the author's name; the date of the most recent update; the title of the posting (if there is no title, use the description *Blog post* or *Blog comment*, not italicized); the name of the blog, italicized, and the URL.

> Marcotte, A. (2012). Rights without perfection. *Pandagon.* Retrieved from http://www.rawstory.com/rs/2010/05/pandagon-rights_without_ perfection/

31. Entry in a Wiki

Since wikis are collectively edited, do not include an author. Include the title of the entry; the date of the latest update; the name of the wiki, italicized; and the URL of the source.

> Fédération Internationale de Football Association. (2014). In *Wikipedia*.
>   Retrieved May 11, 2014 from http://en.wikipedia.org/wiki/FIFA

32. Posting on a Social Networking Site

To cite a posting on Facebook or another social networking site, include the writer's name, the date of the post, a description of the item in brackets, and the URL of the source.

> Ferguson, S. (2014, March 6). Status update [Facebook post]. Retrieved from
>   https://www.facebook.com/sarah.ferguson?fref=nf

33. Posting on a Public Facebook Page

When citing a posting on a public Facebook page or another social networking site that is visible to anyone, include the writer's name as it appears in the post. Give a few words from the post, and add an identifying label. Include the date you retrieved the post and the URL for the public page. Do not include a page on the list of references if your readers will not be able to access the source; instead, cite it as a personal communication in the text.

> American Psychological Association (2014, April 24). Why do many
>   people do their best thinking while walking? [Facebook post].
>   Retrieved April 24, 2014, from https://www.facebook.com/
>   AmericanPsychologicalAssociation

34. Tweet

Include the writer's Twitter handle; the date of the tweet; the entire text of the tweet with no end punctuation, followed by *Tweet* in brackets; the words *Retrieved from*; and the full Twitter account URL with no end punctuation.

> Aalrhetorician. (2014, August 27). Just read (again) about demise of the
>   apostrophe. Argument getting a bit old [Tweet]. Retrieved from https://
>   twitter.com/aalrhetorician

35. Newsgroup Posting

Include the author's name, the date and subject line of the posting, and the name of the newsgroup.

> Wittenberg, E. (2001, July 11). Gender and the Internet [Msg 4]. Retrieved
>   from news://comp.edu.composition

36. Email Message or Synchronous Communication

Because the APA stresses that any sources cited in your list of references must be retrievable by your readers, you shouldn't include entries for email messages or synchronous communications (MOOs, MUDs); instead, cite these sources in your text as forms of personal communication (see item 12 on p. 605). And remember that you shouldn't quote from other people's email without asking their permission to do so.

Other Sources

37. Technical or Research Reports and Working Papers

Kinley-Horn and Associates. (2011). *ADOT bicycle safety action plan* (Working Paper No. 3). Phoenix: Arizona Department of Transportation.

38. Unpublished Paper Presented at a Meeting or Symposium

Welch, K. (2002, March). *Electric rhetoric and screen literacy.* Paper presented at the meeting of the Conference on College Composition and Communication, Chicago, IL.

39. Unpublished Dissertation

Seward, D. E. (2008). *Civil voice in Elizabethan parliamentary oratory: The rhetoric and composition of speeches delivered at Westminster in 1566* (Unpublished doctoral dissertation). University of Texas at Austin, Austin, TX.

40. Poster Session

Mensching, G. (2002, May). *A simple, effective one-shot for disinterested students.* Poster session presented at the National LOEX Library Instruction Conference, Ann Arbor, MI.

41. Motion Picture, Video, or DVD

Bigelow, K. (Director). (2009). *The hurt locker* [Motion picture]. United States: Summit Entertainment.

42. Television Program, Single Episode

Burnett, A. (Writer), & Attias, D. (Director). (2014, March 26). The deal [Television series episode]. In J. Weisberg (Executive producer), *The Americans*. Los Angeles, CA: DreamWorks Television.

43. Online Video Clip

Weber, J. (2012). *As we sow, part I: Where are the farmers?* [Video file]. Retrieved from http://www.youtube.com/watch?v=_cdcDpMf6qE

44. Sound Recording

Begin with the writer's name, followed by the date of copyright. Give the recording date at the end of the entry (in parentheses, after the period) if it's different from the copyright date.

Ivey, A., Jr., & Sall, R. (1995). Rollin' with my homies [Recorded by Coolio]. On *Clueless* [CD]. Hollywood, CA: Capitol Records.

Sample Title Page for an Essay in APA Style

Running head (fifty charac- ters or fewer) appears flush left on first line of title page

Running Head: MOOD MUSIC   1

Page number appears flush right on first line of every page

Title, name, and affiliation centered and double-spaced

Mood Music: Music Preference and the Risk for Depression
and Suicide in Adolescents

Tawnya Redding

Oregon State University

Author Note

This paper was prepared for Psychology 480, taught by Professor
Ede.

Sample First Text Page for an Essay in APA Style

Full title centered

Mood Music: Music Preference and the Risk for Depression and Suicide in Adolescents

Paragraphs indented

Music is a significant part of American culture. Since the explosion of rock and roll in the 1950s, there has been a concern for the effects that music may have on listeners, and especially on young people. The genres most likely to come under suspicion in recent decades have included heavy metal, country, and blues. These genres have been suspected of having adverse effects on the mood and behavior of young listeners. But can music really alter the disposition and create self-destructive behaviors in listeners? And if so, which genres and aspects of those genres are responsible? The following review of the literature will establish the correlation between potentially problematic genres of music such as heavy metal and country and depression and suicide risk. First, correlational studies concerning music preference and suicide risk will be discussed, followed by a discussion of the literature concerning the possible reasons for this link. Finally, studies concerning the effects of music on mood will be discussed. Despite the link between genres such as heavy metal and country and suicide risk, previous research has been unable to establish the causal nature of this link.

Boldface headings help organize review

The Correlation Between Music and Depression and Suicide Risk

Parenthetical references follow APA style

A large portion of studies over the past two decades have focused on heavy metal and country music as the main genre culprits associated with youth suicidality and depression (Lacourse, Claes, & Villeneuve, 2001; Scheel & Westefeld, 1999; Stack & Gundlach, 1992). Stack and Gundlach (1992) examined the radio airtime devoted to country music in

Sample References List for an Essay in APA Style

References begin on new page

Heading is centered

MOOD MUSIC   9

References

Baker, F., & Bor, W. (2008). Can music preference indicate mental
    health status in young people? *Australasian Psychiatry, 16*(4),
    284-288. Retrieved from http://www3.interscience.wiley.com/
    journal/118565538/home

George, D., Stickle, K., Rachid, F., & Wopnford, A. (2007). The
    association between types of music enjoyed and cognitive, behavioral,
    and personality factors of those who listen. *Psychomusicology, 19*(2),
    32-56.

Lacourse, E., Claes, M., & Villeneuve, M. (2001). Heavy metal music
    and adolescent suicidal risk. *Journal of Youth and Adolescence, 30*(3),
    321-332.

Lai, Y. (1999). Effects of music listening on depressed women
    in Taiwan. *Issues in Mental Health Nursing, 20*, 229-246.
    doi:10.1080/016128499248637

Martin, G., Clark, M., & Pearce, C. (1993). Adolescent suicide: Music
    preference as an indicator of vulnerability. *Journal of the American
    Academy of Child and Adolescent Psychiatry, 32*, 530-535.

Scheel, K., & Westefeld, J. (1999). Heavy metal music and adolescent
    suicidality: An empirical investigation. *Adolescence, 34*(134), 253-273.

Siedliecki, S., & Good, M. (2006). Effect of music on power, pain,
    depression and disability. *Journal of Advanced Nursing, 54*(5), 553-
    562. doi:10.1111/j.1365-2648 .2006.03860

Smith, J. L., & Noon, J. (1998). Objective measurement of mood change
    induced by contemporary music. *Journal of Psychiatric & Mental
    Health Nursing, 5*, 403-408.

RESPOND

1. The MLA and APA styles differ in several important ways, both for in-text citations and for lists of sources. You've probably noticed a few: the APA uses lowercase letters for most words in titles and lists the publication date right after the author's name, whereas the MLA capitalizes most words and puts the publication date at the end of the works cited entry. More interesting than the details, though, is the reasoning behind the differences. Placing the publication date near the front of a citation, for instance, reveals a special concern for that information in the APA style. Similarly, the MLA's decision to capitalize titles isn't arbitrary: that style is preferred in the humanities for a reason. Working in a group, find as many consistent differences between the MLA and APA styles as you can. Then, for each difference, speculate about the reasons these groups organize or present information in that way. The MLA and APA style manuals themselves may be of help. You might also begin by determining which academic disciplines subscribe to the APA style and which to the MLA.

2. Working with another person in your class, look for examples of the following sources: an article in a journal, a book, a film, a song, and a TV show. Then make a references page or works cited list (five entries in all), using either MLA or APA style.

part 6

Public Speaking: Getting Started

CHAPTER

31

Becoming a Public Speaker

Whether in the classroom, workplace, or community, the ability to speak confidently and convincingly before an audience is empowering. Parts 6–11 of this book offer the tools you need to create and deliver effective speeches, from presentations to fellow students to speeches delivered in virtually any setting—including those delivered online. Here you will find the basic building blocks of any good speech and acquire the skills to deliver presentations in a variety of specialized contexts—from the college classroom to the civic, business, and professional arenas. You'll also find proven techniques to build your confidence by overcoming the anxiety associated with public speaking.

Gain a Vital Life Skill

Skill in public speaking will give you an unmistakable edge Now, more than ever, public speaking has become both a vital life skill and a potent weapon in career development. Business magnate Warren Buffet passionately extols the role that public speaking has played in his success:

> Be sure to do it, whether you like it or not...do it until you get comfortable with it....Public speaking is an asset that will last you 50 or 60 years, and it's a necessary skill; and if you don't like doing it, that will also last you 50 or 60 years....Once you tackle the fear and master the skill, you can run the world. You can walk into rooms, command people, and get them to listen to you and your great ideas.[1]

Skill in public speaking will give you an unmistakable edge professionally. Recruiters of recent graduates report that what distinguishes the most sought-after candidates is not the "hard" knowledge of their majors, which employers take for granted, but the "soft" skills of superior communication, which fewer candidates display.[2] Similarly, dozens of surveys of managers and executives reveal that ability in oral and written communication is among the most important skills they look for in new hires. For example, oral

---

Chapter 31, "Becoming a Public Speaker," is taken from Dan O'Hair, Hannah Rubenstein, and Rob Stewart: *A Pocket Guide to Public Speaking*, Fifth Edition, pp. 2–8 (Chapter 1, "Becoming a Public Speaker").

communication skills consistently rank in the top spots among such critical areas as leadership, teamwork, problem-solving, analytic and technical skills, and work ethic. Survey after survey confirm the value of verbal and written communication skills to employers across the board, making the public speaking course potentially the most valuable one you can take during your undergraduate career.

Enhance Your Career as a Student

Preparing speeches calls upon numerous skills that you can apply in other college courses. As in the speech class, many courses also require that you research and write about topics, analyze audiences, outline and organize ideas, and support claims. These and other skill sets covered in this book, such as working with presentation media and controlling voice and body during delivery, are valuable in any course that includes an oral-presentation component, from English composition to engineering.

SKILLS EMPLOYERS SEEK

1. Leadership ability
2. Ability to work in a team
3. Skill in written communication
4. Problem-solving skills
5. Strong work ethic
6. Analytic/quantitative and technical skills
7. **Skill in verbal communication**
8. Initiative
9. Computer skills
10. Flexibility/adaptability

Source: National Association of Colleges and Employers, *Job Outlook 2015*, **www.naceweb.org**.

Find New Opportunities for Civic Engagement

Public speaking also offers you ways to enter the public conversation about social concerns and become a more engaged citizen. Public speaking gives you a voice that can be heard and can be counted.

Climate change, energy, government debt, immigration reform — such large civic issues require our considered judgment and action. Yet today too many of us leave it up to politicians, journalists, and other "experts" to make decisions about critical issues such as these. Not including presidential elections, only about 35 percent of people in the United States regularly vote. Of these, only 22 percent are 18 to 29 years old.[3] When we as citizens speak up in sufficient numbers, democracy functions better and change that truly reflects the will of the people occurs.

As you study public speaking, you will have the opportunity to research topics that are meaningful to you, consider alternate viewpoints, and choose a course of action.[4] You will learn to distinguish between argument that advances constructive goals and uncivil speech that serves merely to inflame and demean others. You will learn, in short, the "rules of engagement" for effective public discourse.[5] As you do, you will gain confidence in your ability to join your voice with others in pursuit of issues you care about.

The Classical Roots of Public Speaking

Originally, the practice of giving speeches was known as **rhetoric** or **oratory**. Rhetoric flourished in the Greek city-state of Athens in the fifth century B.C.E. and referred to making effective speeches, particularly those of a persuasive nature.

Athens was the site of the world's first direct democracy, and public speaking was the vehicle that allowed it to succeed. Meeting in a public square called the **agora**, Athenians routinely spoke with great skill on the issues of public policy; and their belief that citizenship demands active participation in public affairs endures in modern democracies to this day.

Greek, and later Roman, teachers divided the process of preparing a speech into five parts — *invention, arrangement, style, memory,* and *delivery* — called the **canons of rhetoric**. These parts correspond to the order in which these teachers believed a speech should be put together.

- *Invention* refers to discovering the types of evidence and arguments you will use to make your case.

- *Arrangement* is organizing the speech in ways best suited to the topic and audience.

- *Style* is the way the speaker uses language to express the speech ideas.

- *Memory* is the practice of the speech until it can be delivered artfully.

- *Delivery* is the vocal and nonverbal behavior you use when speaking.

Although founding scholars such as the great Greek rhetorician Aristotle (384–322 B.C.E.) and the Roman statesman and orator Cicero (106–43 B.C.E.) surely did not anticipate the omnipresent Prezi slide show that accompanies contemporary speeches, the speechmaking structure they bequeathed to us as the canon of rhetoric remains remarkably intact. Often identified by terms other than the original, these canons nonetheless continue to be taught in current books on public speaking, including this one.

QUICK TIP

Voice Your Ideas in a Public Forum

The Greeks called it the *agora*; the Romans the *forum*. Today, the term **public forum** denotes a variety of venues for the discussion of issues of public interest, including traditional physical spaces such as town halls as well as virtual forums streamed to listeners online. Participation in any of these forums offers an excellent opportunity to pose questions and deliver brief comments, thereby providing exposure to an audience and building confidence. To find a forum in your area, check with your school or local town government, or check online at sites such as the National Issues Forum (www.nifi.org).

Learning to Speak in Public

None of us is born knowing how to deliver a successful speech. Instead, public speaking is an acquired skill that improves with practice. It is also a skill that shares much in common with other familiar activities, such as conversing and writing, and it can be much less daunting when you realize that you can draw on expertise you already have.

Draw on Conversational Skills

In several respects, planning and delivering a speech resembles engaging in a particularly important conversation. When speaking with a friend, you automatically check to make certain you are understood and adjust your meaning accordingly. You also tend to discuss issues that are appropriate to the circumstances. When a relative stranger is involved, however, you try to get to know his or her interests and attitudes before revealing any strong opinions. These instinctive adjustments to your audience, topic, and occasion represent critical steps in creating a speech. Although public speaking requires more planning, both the conversationalist and the public speaker try to uncover the audience's interests and needs before speaking.

Draw on Skills in Composition

Preparing a speech also has much in common with writing. Both depend on having a focused sense of who the audience is.[6] Both speaking and writing often require that you research a topic, offer credible evidence, employ effective transitions, and devise persuasive appeals. The principles of organizing a speech parallel those of organizing an essay, including offering a compelling introduction, a clear thesis statement, supporting ideas, and a thoughtful conclusion.

Develop an Effective Oral Style

Although public speaking has much in common with everyday conversation and with writing, a speech is a unique form of communication characterized by an oral style of language. Spoken language is simpler, more rhythmic, more repetitious, and more interactive than either conversation or writing.[7] Effective speakers use familiar words and easy-to-follow sentences. *Repetition* in even the briefest speeches is key, and speakers routinely repeat key words and phrases to emphasize ideas and help listeners follow along.

Spoken language also is often more *interactive* and *inclusive* of the audience than written language. Audience members want to know what the speaker thinks and feels and that he or she recognizes them and relates the message to them. Speakers accomplish this by making specific references to themselves and to the audience. Yet in contrast to conversation, in order to develop an effective oral style you must practice the words you will say and the way you will say them.

Effective public speakers, engaging conversationalists, and compelling writers share an important quality: They keep their focus on offering something of value for the audience.

Demonstrate Respect for Difference

Every audience member wants to feel that the speaker has his or her particular needs and interests at heart, and to feel recognized and included in the message. To create this sense of inclusion, a public speaker must be able to address diverse audiences with sensitivity, demonstrating respect for differences in culture and identity. Striving for inclusion and adopting an audience-centered perspective will bring you closer to the goal of every public speaker — establishing a genuine connection with the audience.

Public Speaking as a Form of Communication

Public speaking is one of four categories of human communication: dyadic, small group, mass, and public speaking.

- **Dyadic communication** happens between two people, as in a conversation.

- **Small group communication** involves a small number of people who can see and speak directly with one another.

- **Mass communication** occurs between a speaker and a large audience of unknown people who usually are not present with the speaker, or who are part of such an immense crowd that there can be little or no interaction between speaker and listener. In **public speaking**, a speaker delivers a message with a specific purpose to an audience of people who are present during the delivery of the speech.

Public speaking always includes a speaker who has a reason for speaking, an audience that gives the speaker its attention, and a message that is meant to accomplish a specific purpose. Public speakers address audiences largely without interruption and take responsibility for the words and ideas being expressed.

Public Speaking as an Interactive Communication Process

In any communication event, several elements are present. These include the source, the receiver, the message, the channel, and shared meaning (see **Figure 31.1**).

The **source**, or sender, creates a message. Creating, organizing, and producing the message is called **encoding**—the process of converting thoughts into words.

The recipient of the source's message is the **receiver**, or audience; interpreting the message is called **decoding**. Audience members decode the meaning of the message selectively, based on their own experiences and attitudes. **Feedback**, the audience's response to a message, can be conveyed both verbally and nonverbally.

The **message** is the content of the communication process: thoughts and ideas put into meaningful expressions, expressed verbally and nonverbally.

The medium through which the speaker sends a message is the **channel**. If a speaker delivers a message in front of a live audience, the channel is the air through which sound waves travel. Other channels include telephone, television, and the Internet.

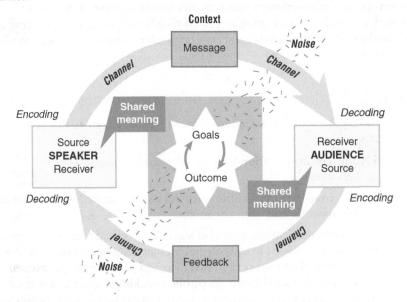

FIGURE 31.1 The Communication Process

Noise is any interference with the message. Noise can disrupt the communication process through physical sounds such as cell phones ringing and people talking or texting, through psychological distractions such as heated emotions, or through environmental interference such as a frigid room or the presence of unexpected people.

Shared meaning is the mutual understanding of a message between speaker and audience. The lowest level of shared meaning exists when the speaker has merely caught the audience's attention. As the message develops, a higher degree of shared meaning is possible. Thus listener and speaker together truly make a speech a speech—they "co-create" its meaning.

Two other factors are critical to consider when preparing and delivering a speech—context and goals. *Context* includes anything that influences the speaker, the audience, the occasion—and thus, ultimately, the speech. In classroom speeches, the context would include (among other things) recent events on campus or in the outside world, the physical setting, the order and timing of speeches, and the cultural orientations of audience members. Successful communication can never be divorced from the concerns and expectations of others.

Part of the context of any speech is the situation that created the need for it in the first place. All speeches are delivered in response to a specific **rhetorical situation**, or a circumstance calling for a public response.[8] Bearing the rhetorical situation in mind ensures that you maintain an **audience-centered perspective**—that is, that you keep the needs, values, attitudes, and wants of your listeners firmly in focus.

A clearly defined *speech purpose* or goal—what you want the audience to learn or do as a result of the speech—is a final prerequisite for an effective speech. Establishing a speech purpose early on will help you proceed through speech preparation and delivery with a clear focus in mind.

From A to Z: Overview of a Speech

Public speaking is an applied art, and every speaking opportunity, including that provided by the classroom, offers you valuable hands-on experience. To help you get started as quickly as possible, this chapter previews the steps involved in putting together any speech or presentation. Subsequent chapters expand on these steps.

Analyze the Audience

Figure 32.1 illustrates the process of preparing for a speech. The first step is to consider the audience—how their interests, needs, and opinions will influence their responses toward a given topic, speaker, and occasion. *Audience analysis* is a process of learning about audience members' attributes and motivations through techniques such as interviews and questionnaires (see Chapter 36). For a brief first speech, however, gather what information you can about the audience in the time allotted. Consider some *demographic characteristics*: ratio of males to females, age ranges, cultural background, and socioeconomic status. Take into account these characteristics as you select your topic and draft the speech, focusing on ways you can relate it meaningfully to your audience.

Select a Topic

Unless the topic is assigned, the next step is to decide what you want to speak about. First, consider the speech occasion and reason for speaking. What topics will be suitable to your audience's needs and wants in these circumstances? Within these parameters, use your own interests and expertise to guide you in selecting something to speak about (see Chapter 37 for a discussion on finding topics).

Chapter 32, "From A to Z: Overview of a Speech," is taken from Dan O'Hair, Hannah Rubenstein, and Rob Stewart: *A Pocket Guide to Public Speaking*, Fifth Edition, pp. 8–13 (Chapter 2, "From A to Z: Overview of a Speech").

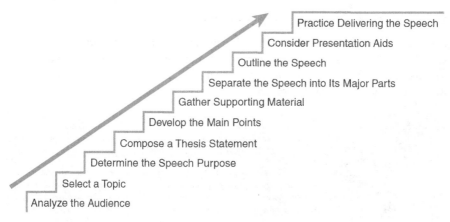

FIGURE 32.1 Steps in the Speechmaking Process

Determine the Speech Purpose

Decide what you want to accomplish with your speech. For any given topic, you should direct your speech toward one of three *general speech purposes*—to *inform*, to *persuade*, or to *mark a special occasion*. Thus you need to decide whether your goal is simply to give your audience information about the topic, to convince them to accept one position to the exclusion of other positions, or to mark a special occasion such as a wedding, a funeral, or an awards event.

Your speech should also have a *specific speech purpose*—what you want the audience to learn or do as a result of your speech. For example, if your general purpose is to inform, your specific purpose might be "to inform my audience about recent changes in federal college student loan programs." If your general purpose is to persuade, the specific purpose might be "to convince my audience that they should support improving government aid to college students."

QUICK TIP

Speak with Purpose

To ensure that the audience learns or does what you want them to as a result of your speech, keep your thesis and speech goals in sight. Write your thesis statement and general and specific speech purposes on a sticky note and place it on the edge of your computer screen. It will be an important guide in developing your speech.

Compose a Thesis Statement

Next, compose a thesis statement that clearly expresses the central idea of your speech. While the specific purpose focuses your attention on the outcome you want to achieve with the speech, the *thesis statement* concisely identifies to your audience, in a single sentence, what the speech is about:

General Purpose:	To inform
Specific Purpose:	To inform my audience about three critical steps we can take to combat identity theft and maintain identity security.
Thesis Statement:	The best ways to combat identity theft and keep yourself secure are to review your monthly financial statements, periodically check your credit report, and secure your personal information in both digital and print form.

From this point forward in the development of your speech, refer to the thesis statement often to make sure that you are on track to illustrate or prove it.

Develop the Main Points

Organize your speech around two or three *main points*. These are the primary pieces of knowledge (in an informative speech) or the key claims (in a persuasive speech). If you create a clear thesis for your speech, the main points will be easily identifiable, if not explicit:

Thesis:	The best ways to combat identity theft and keep yourself secure are to review your monthly financial statements, periodically check your credit report, and secure your personal information in both digital and print form.
	I. Review your monthly bank statements, credit card bills, and similar financial records to be certain that you are aware of all transactions.
	II. Check your consumer credit report at least twice a year.
	III. Keep your personal identifying digital and print information secure.

Gather Supporting Materials

Illustrate the main points with supporting material that clarifies, elaborates, and verifies your ideas. Supporting material potentially includes the entire world of information available to you—from personal experiences to every conceivable kind of external source. Plan to research your topic to provide evidence for your assertions and lend credibility to your message (see Chapter 39).

Separate the Speech into Its Major Parts

Every speech will have an *introduction*, a *body*, and a *conclusion*. Develop each part separately, then bring them together using transition statements (see Chapter 41). The *introduction* serves to gain the audience's attention and interest by introducing the topic and speaker and alerting the audience to your thesis (see Chapter 44). The speech *body* contains the speech's main points and subpoints, arranged to support the speech's thesis. The *conclusion* restates the speech thesis and reiterates how the main points confirm it (see Chapter 44).

Outline the Speech

An outline is a plan for arranging the elements of your speech in support of your thesis. Outlines are based on the principle of *coordination and subordination*—the logical placement of ideas relative to their importance to one another. *Coordinate points* are of equal importance and are indicated by their parallel alignment. *Subordinate points* are given less weight than the main points they support and are placed to the right of the points they support. (For a full discussion of outlining, see Chapter 43.)

Coordinate Points	I.	Main Point 1
	II.	Main Point 2
		A. Subpoint 1
		B. Subpoint 2
Subordinate Points	I.	Main Point 1
		A. First level of subordination
		1. Second level of subordination
		2. Second level of subordination
		a. Third level of subordination
		b. Third level of subordination

As your speeches become more detailed, you will need to select an appropriate *organizational pattern* (see Chapter 42). You will also need to familiarize yourself with developing both working and speaking outlines (see Chapter 43). To allow for the full development of your ideas, *working outlines* generally contain points stated in close-to-complete sentences. *Speaking outlines* are far briefer and use either short phrases or key words.

Consider Presentation Aids

As you prepare your speech, consider whether using visual, audio, or a combination of different *presentation aids* will help the audience understand points. (See Chapters 49–51.)

DEVELOPING SPEECH PARTS

Introduction

- Pique the audience's interest with a quotation, a short story, an example, or other means of gaining their attention described in Chapter 44.
- Introduce yourself and your topic.
- Preview the thesis and main points.

(Use a transition statement to signal the start of the speech body.)

Body

- Develop the main points and illustrate each one with relevant supporting material.
- Organize your ideas and evidence in a structure that suits the topic, audience, and occasion.

(Use transitions to move between main points and to the conclusion.)

Conclusion

- Review the thesis and reiterate how the main points confirm it.
- Leave the audience with something to think about.

Practice Delivering the Speech

Preparation and practice are necessary for the success of even your first speech in class. You will want to feel and appear "natural" to your listeners, an effect best achieved by rehearsing both the verbal and nonverbal **delivery** of your speech (see Chapters 47 and 48). So practice your speech often. It has been suggested that a good speech is practiced at least six times. For a four- to six-minute speech, that's only about one-half hour (figuring in restarts and pauses) of actual practice time.

QUICK TIP

Be Aware of Your Nonverbal Delivery

Audiences are highly attuned to a speaker's facial expressions, gestures, and general body movement. As you rehearse, practice smiling and otherwise animating your face in ways that feel natural to you. Audiences want to feel that you care about what you are saying, so avoid a deadpan, or blank, expression. Make eye contact with your practice audience. Doing so will make audience members feel that you recognize and respect them. Practice gestures that feel natural to you, steering clear of exaggerated movements.

Managing Speech Anxiety

Contrary to what most of us think, feeling nervous about giving a speech is not only normal but desirable. Channeled properly, nervousness can actually boost performance. The difference between seasoned public speakers and the rest of us is that the seasoned speakers know how to make their nervousness work *for* rather than *against* them. They use specific anxiety-reducing techniques, described in this chapter, to help them cope with and minimize their tension.

> I focus on the information rather than being graded. I also practice my speech a ton to really make sure I do not speak too quickly. I time myself so that I can develop an average time. This makes me more confident [in dealing] with time requirements. And, because I know that I am well prepared, I really try to just relax.
>
> —Kristen Obracay, student

Identify What Makes You Anxious

Anxiety is a state of uneasiness brought on by fear. Lacking positive public-speaking experience, feeling different from members of the audience, or feeling uneasy about being the center of attention—each of these factors can lead to the onset of **public-speaking anxiety** (PSA)—a situation-specific social anxiety that arises from anticipating giving an oral presentation.[1] Fortunately, the great majority of us can learn techniques to tame this anxiety in each of these situations and make it work for us.

Lack of Positive Experience

If you are new to public speaking or have had unpleasant experiences, anxiety about what to expect is only natural. And without positive experience to draw on, it's hard to put this anxiety into perspective. It's a bit of a vicious circle. Some people react by deciding to avoid speeches altogether, yet gaining more experience is key to overcoming speech anxiety.

Chapter 33, "Managing Speech Anxiety," is taken from Dan O'Hair, Hannah Rubenstein, and Rob Stewart: *A Pocket Guide to Public Speaking*, Fifth Edition, pp. 13–20 (Chapter 3, "Managing Speech Anxiety").

Feeling Different

The prospect of getting up in front of an audience makes many of us extrasensitive to our personal idiosyncrasies, such as a less-than-perfect haircut or an accent. We may believe that no one could possibly be interested in anything we have to say.

As inexperienced speakers, we assume that being different somehow means being inferior, which leads to anxiety. Actually, everyone is different from everyone else in many ways. However, nearly everyone experiences nervousness about giving a speech.

> I control my anxiety by mentally viewing myself as being 100 percent equal to my classmates.
>
> —Lee Morris, student

Being the Center of Attention

Certain audience behaviors—such as chatting with a neighbor or checking text messages during a presentation—can cause us as speakers to think we lost the audience's attention by doing something wrong; we wonder about our mistakes and whether others noticed these supposed flaws. Left unchecked, this kind of thinking can distract us from the speech itself, with all our attention now focused on "me." Our self-consciousness makes us feel even more conspicuous and sensitive to even the smallest faults, which increases our anxiety! Actually, an audience rarely notices anything about us that we don't want to reveal.

Pinpoint the Onset of Anxiety

Different people become anxious at different times during the speechmaking process. Depending on when it strikes, the consequences of public-speaking anxiety can include everything from procrastination to poor speech performance. But by pinpointing the onset of speech anxiety, you can manage it promptly with specific anxiety-reducing techniques.

Pre-Preparation Anxiety

Some people feel anxious the minute they know they will be giving a speech. **Pre-preparation anxiety** can be a problem when we delay planning for the speech, or when it so preoccupies us that we miss vital information necessary to fulfill the speech assignment. If this form of anxiety affects you, start very early using the stress-reducing techniques described later in this chapter.

Preparation Anxiety

For a few people, anxiety arises only when they actually begin to prepare for the speech.[2] These individuals might feel overwhelmed by the time and planning required or hit a roadblock that puts them behind schedule. Preparation pressures produce a cycle of stress, procrastination, and outright avoidance, all of which contribute to **preparation anxiety**. If you find yourself feeling anxious during this stage, immerse yourself in the speech's preparation but calm your nerves by taking short, relaxing breaks to regain your confidence and focus.

Pre-performance Anxiety

Some people experience anxiety as they rehearse their speech. This is when the reality of the situation sets in: they worry that the audience will be watching and listening only to them, feel that their ideas aren't expressed as well as they should be, or sense that preparation time is short. If this **pre-performance anxiety** is strong enough, some may even decide to stop rehearsing. If you experience heightened anxiety at this point, consider using the **anxiety stop-time technique**: Allow your anxiety to present itself for up to a few minutes until you declare time for confidence to step in so you can proceed to complete your practice.[3]

> I experience anxiety before, during, and after the speech. My "before speech" anxiety begins the night before my speech, but then I begin to look over my notecards, and I start to realize that I am ready for this speech. I practice one more time and I tell myself I am going to be fine.
>
> —Paige Mease, student

Performance Anxiety

For most people, anxiety is highest just as a speech begins.[4] **Performance anxiety** usually is most pronounced during the introduction of the speech when we are most aware of the audience's attention. Audiences we perceive as negative usually cause us to feel more anxious than those we sense are positive or neutral.[5] But experienced speakers agree that by controlling their nervousness during the introduction, the rest of the speech goes quite smoothly.

Regardless of when anxiety about a speech strikes, the important thing to remember is that you can manage the anxiety and not let it manage you—by harming your motivation, or by causing you to avoid investing the time and energy required to deliver a successful speech.

Use Proven Strategies to Build Your Confidence

A number of proven strategies exist to help you rein in your fears about public speaking, from *meditation* and *visualization* to other forms of relaxation techniques. The first step in taming speech anxiety is to have a thorough plan for each presentation.

Prepare and Practice

If you know your material and have adequately rehearsed your delivery, you're far more likely to feel confident. Once you have prepared the speech, be sure to rehearse it several times.

Modify Thoughts and Attitudes

Negative thoughts about speechmaking increase speech anxiety.[6] A positive attitude, on the other hand, actually results in lowered heart rate and reduced anxiety during the delivery of the speech.[7] As you prepare for and deliver your speech, envision it as a valuable, worthwhile, and challenging activity. Think positively about public speaking, and focus on it as an opportunity toward, not a threat to, personal growth.

> Just before a speech those feelings of anxiety undoubtedly try to sneak in. The way I keep them from taking over is to not let my mind become negative. As long as I keep positive thoughts of confidence in my head, anxiety doesn't stand a chance!
>
> —Morgan Verdery, student

QUICK TIP

Envision Your Speech as a Conversation

Rather than thinking of your speech as a formal performance where you will be judged and critiqued, try thinking of it as a kind of ordinary conversation. In this way, you will feel less threatened and more relaxed about the process.

Visualize Success

Visualization—the practice of summoning feelings and actions consistent with successful performance[8]—is a highly effective method of reducing speech anxiety.[9] The following is a script for visualizing success on a public-speaking occasion. It requires you, the speaker, to close your eyes and visualize a series of positive feelings and actions that will occur on the day of your speech.

> Close your eyes and allow your body to get comfortable in the chair in which you are sitting. Take a deep, comfortable breath and hold it...now slowly release it through your nose. Now take another deep breath and make certain that you are breathing from the diaphragm...hold it...now slowly release it and note how you feel while doing this. Now one more deep breath...hold it...and release it slowly...and begin your normal breathing pattern.

> Now begin to visualize the beginning of a day in which you are going to give an informative speech. See yourself getting up in the morning, full of energy, full of confidence, looking forward to the day's challenges. As you dress, think about how the clothes you choose make you look and feel good about yourself. As you are drive, ride, or walk to the speech setting, note how clear and confident you feel. You feel thoroughly prepared for the topic you will be presenting today.

> Now you see yourself standing or sitting in the room where you will present your speech, talking very comfortably and confidently with others in the room. The people to whom you will be presenting your speech appear to be quite friendly and are very cordial in their greetings and conversations prior to the presentation. You feel absolutely sure of your material and of your ability to present the information in a forceful, convincing, positive manner.

> Now you see yourself approaching the area from which you will present. You are feeling very good about this presentation and see yourself move eagerly forward. All of your audiovisual materials are well organized, well planned, and clearly aid your presentation.[10]

Activate the Relaxation Response

Before, during, and sometimes after a speech you may experience rapid heart rate and breathing, dry mouth, faintness, freezing-up, or other uncomfortable sensations. These physiological reactions result from the **"fight-or-flight"**

response—the body's automatic response to threatening or fear-inducing events. Research shows that you can counteract these sensations by activating a relaxation response[11] using techniques such as meditation and controlled breathing.

Briefly Meditate

You can calm yourself considerably before a presentation with this brief meditation exercise:

1. Sit comfortably in a quiet space.

2. Relax your muscles, moving from neck to shoulders to arms to back to legs.

3. Choose a word, phrase, or prayer (e.g., "Namaste," "Om," "Hail Mary, Full of Grace"). Breathe slowly and say it until you become calm (about ten to twenty minutes).

QUICK TIP

Stretch Away Stress

You can significantly lessen pre-speech jitters by stretching. A half-hour to one-hour session of whole body stretches and yoga poses, combined with deep breathing, will help discharge nervous energy.

Use Stress-Control Breathing

When you feel stressed, the center of your breathing tends to move from the abdomen to the upper chest, leaving you with a reduced supply of air. The chest and shoulders rise, and you feel out of breath. *Stress-control breathing*[12] gives you more movement in the stomach than in the chest. Try it in two stages.

Stage One

Inhale air and let your abdomen go out. Exhale air and let your abdomen go in. Do this for a while until you get into the rhythm of it.

Stage Two

As you inhale, use a soothing word such as "calm" or "relax," or use a personal mantra like this: "Inhale calm, abdomen out, exhale calm, abdomen in." Go slowly, taking about three to five seconds with each inhalation and exhalation.

Begin stress-control breathing *several days* before a speech. Then, once the occasion arrives, perform it while awaiting your turn at the podium and just before you start your speech.

> I have two ways to cope with my nervousness before I'm about to speak. I take a couple of deep breaths from my stomach; I breathe in through my nose and out through my mouth. This allows more oxygen to the brain so you can think clearly. I also calm myself down by saying, "Everything will be okay, and the world is not going to crumble before me if I mess up."
>
> Jenna Sanford, student

Use Movement to Minimize Anxiety

During delivery, you can use controlled movements with your hands and body to release nervousness. Practice natural gestures, such as holding up your index finger when stating your first main point. Think about what you want to say as you do this, instead of thinking about how you look or feel. (See Chapter 48 for tips on practicing natural gestures.) You don't have to stand perfectly still behind the podium when you deliver a speech. Walk around as you make some of your points. Movement relieves tension and helps hold the audience's attention.

QUICK TIP

Enjoy the Occasion

Most people ultimately find that giving speeches can indeed be fun. It's satisfying and empowering to influence people, and a good speech is a sure way to do this. Think of giving a speech in this way, and chances are you will find much pleasure in it.

Learn from Feedback

Speech evaluations help to identify ways to improve what you do. You can learn a lot through self-evaluation, but self-perceptions can be distorted,[13] so objective evaluations by others often are more helpful. Ultimately, all speakers rely on audience feedback to evaluate the effectiveness of their speeches.

CHECKLIST

Steps in Gaining Confidence

☐ Prepare and practice, early on and often.

☐ Modify thoughts and attitudes—think positively.

☐ Visualize success.

☐ Use stress-control breathing, meditation, and other relaxation techniques.

☐ Incorporate natural, controlled movements.

☐ Learn from the experience of public speaking and enjoy it.

CHAPTER

34

Ethical Public Speaking

W hen we have an audience's attention, we are in the unusual position of being able to influence or persuade listeners and, at times, to move them to act — for better or worse. With this power to affect the minds and hearts of others comes *responsibility* — "a charge, trust, or duty for which one is accountable."[1] Taking responsibility for your words lies at the heart of being an ethical speaker.

Ethics is the study of moral conduct. Applied to public speaking, it addresses our responsibilities when seeking influence over other people and for which there are positive and negative, or "right" and "wrong," choices of action.[2] For example, should you show a gory photograph without warning to convince audience members not to text and drive? Should you bother to check the credibility of a suspect source before offering it to the audience? Is it ethical to present only one side of an argument?

Demonstrate Competence and Character

Ethics is derived from the Greek word **ethos**, meaning "character." As Aristotle first noted, audiences listen to and trust speakers if they demonstrate *positive ethos*, or good character. Speakers in ancient Greece were regarded positively if they were well prepared, honest, and respectful toward their audience. Today, surprisingly little has changed. Modern research on **source credibility** reveals that people place their greatest trust in speakers who:

- Have a solid grasp of the subject,
- Display sound reasoning skills,
- Are honest and straightforward,
- Are genuinely interested in the welfare of their listeners.[3]

Chapter 34, "Ethical Public Speaking," is taken from Dan O'Hair, Hannah Rubenstein, and Rob Stewart: *A Pocket Guide to Public Speaking*, Fifth Edition, pp. 20–27 (Chapter 4, "Ethical Public Speaking").

Respect Your Listeners' Values

Our ethical conduct is a reflection of our **values**—our most enduring judgments or standards of what's good and bad in life, of what's important to us. Values shape our worldview[4] and form the basis on which we judge the actions of others.Conflicting values lie at the heart of many controversies that today's public speakers might address, making it difficult to speak about certain topics without challenging cherished beliefs. The United States is a country of immigrants, for example, but half of the population with only a high school education believe that immigrants threaten traditional U.S. values, while only a quarter of college-educated Americans agree.[5]

Consideration of audience members' values is an important aspect of preparing an ethical speech. As you prepare speeches on controversial topics, anticipate that audience members will hold a range of values that will differ not only from your own, but from each other's. Audience analysis is key to discovering and planning for these differences (see Chapter 36).

Contribute to Positive Public Discourse

An important measure of ethical speaking is whether it contributes something positive to **public discourse**—speech involving issues of importance to the larger community, such as whether to decriminalize marijuana or engage in a military conflict.

Perhaps the most important contribution you can make to public debates of this nature is the *advancement of constructive goals.* An ethical speech appeals to the greater good rather than narrow self-interest. It steers clear of **invective**, verbal attacks, designed to discredit and belittle those with whom you disagree. Ethical speakers avoid arguments that target a person instead of the issue at hand (ad hominem attack) or that are built upon other fallacies of reasoning.

Use Your Rights of Free Speech Responsibly

The United States vigorously protects **free speech**—defined as the right to be free from unreasonable constraints on expression[6]—thereby assuring protection both to speakers who treat the truth with respect and to those whose words are inflammatory and offensive.

Though often legally protected under the **First Amendment** (which guarantees freedoms concerning religion, expression of ideas, and rights of assembly and petition), racist, sexist, or ageist slurs, gay-bashing, and other forms of negative or hate speech clearly are unethical. **Hate speech** is any offensive communication—verbal or nonverbal—directed against people's race, ethnicity, national origin, gender, religion, sexual orientation, disability, and the like.

Be aware that even under the First Amendment, certain types of speech are not only unethical but actually illegal:

- Speech that provokes people to violence (termed "incitement" or **"fighting words"**)

- Speech that can be proved to be defamatory (termed **slander**) or potentially harmful to an individual's reputation at work or in the community

- Speech that invades a person's privacy, such as disclosing personal information about an individual that is not in the public record

How can you tell if your speech contains defamatory language? If you are talking about public figures or matters of public concern, you will not be legally liable unless it can be shown that you spoke with a **reckless disregard for the truth**—that is, if you knew that what you were saying was false but said it anyway. If your comments refer to private persons, it will be easier for them to assert a claim for defamation. You will have the burden of proving that what you said was true.

QUICK TIP

Beware the Heckler's Veto

Drowning out a speaker's message with which you disagree—called a *heckler's veto*—demonstrates disrespect both to the speaker and to fellow listeners. It robs audience members of the ability to make up their own minds about an issue and silences the free expression of ideas. Tolerance for opposing viewpoints is a necessary ingredient of an ethical—and democratic—society.

Observe Ethical Ground Rules

Ethical speech rests on a foundation of dignity and integrity. **Dignity** refers to bearing and conduct that is respectful to self and others. **Integrity** signals the speaker's incorruptibility—that he or she will avoid compromising the truth for the sake of personal expediency.[7] Speaking ethically also requires that we adhere to certain moral ground rules, or "pillars of character," including being *trustworthy, respectful, responsible, fair,* and *civic-minded.*[8]

- **Trustworthiness** is a combination of honesty and dependability. Trustworthy speakers support their points truthfully and don't offer misleading or false information.

- We demonstrate **respect** by treating audience members with civility and courtesy.[9] Respectful speakers address listeners as unique human beings, refrain from any form of personal attack, and focus on issues rather than on personalities.

- **Responsibility** means being accountable for what you say. For example, will learning about your topic in some way benefit listeners? Do you use sound evidence and reasoning? Do you offer emotional appeals because they are appropriate rather than to shore up otherwise weak arguments?

- **Fairness** refers to making a genuine effort to see all sides of an issue and acknowledging the information listeners need in order to make informed decisions.[10] Few subjects are black and white; rarely is there only one right or wrong way to view a topic.

- Being **civic-minded** means caring about your community, in word and deed. It means recognizing that things don't get better unless people volunteer their efforts to improve things. At the broadest level, being civic-minded is essential to the democratic process because democracy depends on our participation in it.

CHECKLIST

An Ethical Inventory

☐ Have you distorted any information to make your point?

☐ Have you acknowledged each of your sources?

☐ Does your speech focus on issues rather than on personalities?

☐ Have you tried to foster a sense of inclusion?

☐ Does your topic add something positive to public discourse?

☐ Have you checked your arguments for *ad hominen* attacks or other fallacies of reasoning?

☐ Is the content of your message supported by sound evidence and reasoning?

☐ Do you avoid speech that demeans those with whom you disagree?

Avoid Plagiarism

Crediting sources is a crucial aspect of any speech. **Plagiarism**—the use of other people's ideas or words without acknowledging the source—is unethical. You are obviously plagiarizing when you simply "cut and paste" material from sources into your speech and represent it as your own. But it is also plagiarism to copy material into your speech draft from a source (such as a magazine article or website) and then change and rearrange words and sentence structure here and there to make it appear as if it were your own.[11]

Orally Acknowledge Your Sources

The rule for avoiding plagiarism as a public speaker is straightforward: *Any source that requires credit in written form should be acknowledged in oral form.* These sources include direct quotations, as well as paraphrased and summarized information — any facts and statistics, ideas, opinions, or theories gathered and reported by others. For each source that requires citation, you need to include the *type of source* (magazine, book, personal interview, website, etc.), the *author or origin of the source*, the *title or a description of the source*, and the *date of the source*.

Oral presentations need not include the full bibliographic reference (i.e., full names, dates, titles, volume, and page numbers). However, you should include complete references in a bibliography or at the end of the speech outline. Rules for avoiding plagiarism apply equally to print and online sources. For specific guidelines on how to record and cite sources found on websites, see "From Source to Speech" on pp. 694–695.

One exception to sources needing citation is the use of **common knowledge** — information that is likely to be known by many people (though such information must *truly* be widely disseminated). For example, it is common knowledge that in March 2011 a massive earthquake in Japan triggered a tsunami. It is not common knowledge that the last earthquake of similar magnitude to hit Japan happened 1,200 years ago. This fact requires acknowledgment of a source — in this case, a compilation of facts published by Francie Diep in *Scientific American.*[12]

Citing Quotations, Paraphrases, and Summaries

When citing other people's ideas, you can present them in one of three ways:

- **Direct quotations** are verbatim — or word for word — presentations of statements made by someone else. Direct quotes should always be acknowledged in a speech.

- A **paraphrase** is a restatement of someone else's ideas, opinions, or theories in the speaker's own words. Because paraphrases alter the *form* but not the *substance* of another person's ideas, you must acknowledge the original source.

- A **summary** is a brief overview of someone else's ideas, opinions, or theories. While a paraphrase contains approximately the same number of words as the original source material stated in the speaker's own words, a summary condenses the same material, distilling only its essence.

Note how a speaker could paraphrase and summarize, *with credit*, the following excerpt from an article published in the *New Yorker* titled "Strange Fruit: The Rise and Fall of Açai," by John Calapinto.

Original Version:	Açai was virtually unknown outside Brazil until 10 years ago, when Ryan and Jeremy Black, two brothers from Southern California, and their friend Edmund Nichols began exporting it to the United States. Since then, the fruit has followed a cycle of popularity befitting a teenage pop singer: a Miley Cyrus–like trajectory from obscurity to hype, critical backlash, and eventual ubiquity. Embraced as a "superfruit"—a potent combination of cholesterol-reducing fats and anti-aging antioxidants—açai became one of the fastest-growing foods in history...."

Compare the original version of the excerpt to how it could be properly quoted, paraphrased, or summarized in a speech. Oral citation language is bolded for easy identification.

Direct Quotation:	**As John Calapinto states in an article titled "Strange Fruit: The Rise and Fall of Açai," published in the May 30, 2011, issue of the New Yorker,** "The fruit has followed a cycle of popularity befitting a teenage pop singer: a Miley Cyrus–like trajectory from obscurity to hype, critical backlash, and eventual ubiquity."
Oral Paraphrase:	**In an article titled "Strange Fruit: The Rise and Fall of Açai," published in the May 30, 2011, issue of the New Yorker, John Calapinto explains that** until two brothers from Southern California named Ryan and Jeremy Black, along with their friend Edmund Nichols, began exporting açai to the United States ten years ago, it was unknown here. Now, says Calapinto, açai is seen as a "superfruit" that can help with everything from lowering cholesterol to fighting aging through its antioxidant properties.
Oral Summary:	**In an article titled "Strange Fruit: The Rise and Fall of Açai," published in the May 30, 2011, issue of the New Yorker, John Calapinto says that** açai, a fruit grown in Brazil that was unknown in this country until ten years ago, is now marketed as a "superfruit" that has powerful health benefits.

For detailed directions on crediting sources in your speech, see Chapter 40, "Citing Sources in Your Speech."

Fair Use, Copyright, and Ethical Speaking

Copyright is a legal protection afforded the creators of original literary and artistic works.[13] When including copyrighted materials in your speeches, you must determine when and if you need permission to use such works.

When a work is copyrighted, you may not reproduce, distribute, or display it without the permission of the copyright holder. For any work created from 1978 to the present, a copyright is good during the author's lifetime, plus seventy years. After that, unless extended, the work falls into the *public domain*, which means anyone may reproduce it. Not subject to copyright are federal (but *not* state or local) government publications, common knowledge, and select other categories.

An exception to the prohibitions of copyright is the doctrine of **fair use**, which permits the limited use of copyrighted works without permission for the purposes of scholarship, criticism, comment, news reporting, teaching, or research.[14] This means that when preparing speeches for the classroom, you have much more latitude to use other people's creative work without seeking permission, but *with* credit in all cases, including display of the copyright symbol (©) on any copyrighted handouts or visual aids you include in your speech. Different rules apply to the professional speaker, whose use of copyrighted materials is considered part of a for-profit "performance." (For more information, see www.copyright.gov.)

Creative Commons is an organization that allows creators of works to decide how they want other people to use their copyrighted works. It offers creators six types of licenses, three of which are perhaps most relevant to students in the classroom: *attribution* (lets you use the work if you give credit the way the author requests); *noncommercial* (lets you use the work for *noncommercial purposes* only); and *no derivative works* (lets you use only verbatim—exact—versions of the work).

The rules of fair use apply equally to works licensed under Creative Commons and the laws of copyright. Student speakers may search the Creative Commons Web site for suitable materials for their speech at creativecommons.org.

Listeners and Speakers

Imagine giving a speech that no one heard. Merely considering such a circumstance points to the central role of the listener in a speech. In fact, all successful communication is two-way, including that of public speaking. It is speaker and listener together who truly make a speech possible.

Connecting with a speaker takes focus. While **hearing** is the physiological, largely passive process of perceiving sound, **listening** is the conscious act of *receiving*, constructing meaning from, and responding to spoken and nonverbal messages.[1] We can decide to tune out the speaker and ignore the message, uncritically accept or hypercritically reject whatever is said, or bring our full attention and critical faculties to bear.

Recognize That We Listen Selectively

In any given situation, no two audience members will process the information in exactly the same way. The reason lies in **selective perception** — people's perceptions are subject to their own biases and expectations, leading them to pay attention selectively to certain messages while ignoring others.[5] Several factors influence what we listen to and what we ignore:

- We pay attention to what we hold to be important.

- We pay attention to information that touches our experiences and backgrounds.

- We sort and filter new information on the basis of what we already know (e.g., we learn by analogy).

Chapter 35, "Listeners and Speakers," is taken from Dan O'Hair, Hannah Rubenstein, and Rob Stewart: *A Pocket Guide to Public Speaking*, Fifth Edition, pp. 27–32 (Chapter 5, "Listeners and Speakers").

Get Ahead by Listening

College students in the United States spend more time listening (about 24 percent) than they do on any other communication activity, such as speaking (20 percent), using the Internet (13 percent), writing (9 percent), or reading (8 percent).[2] Listening is also the number one activity employees do during the work day.[3] Managers overwhelmingly associate listening skills with competence, efficiency, and leadership potential, promoting employees who display them and hiring new entrants who possess them.[4] In both college and work arenas, skill in listening leads to success.

The principle of selective perception suggests key steps you can take in your dual roles as listener and speaker:

- As a *listener*, examine your own expectations and motivations to hear things in a certain way. Ask yourself whether you are really hearing what the speaker is saying.

- As a *speaker*, demonstrate why your topic is relevant to the audience's interest and needs. Use analogies to help the audience learn new ideas.

Anticipate Obstacles to Listening

Active listening—listening that is focused and purposeful—isn't possible under conditions that distract us. In any listening situation, including that of listening to speeches, try to identify and overcome common obstacles.

Refrain from Multitasking

You cannot actively listen well while multitasking. Activities such as checking a cell phone or calendar, finishing an assignment, or responding to a text divert our attention from the message and reduce our ability to interpret it accurately.

Work to Overcome Cultural Barriers

Differences in dialects or accents, nonverbal cues, word choices, and even physical appearance can serve as barriers to listening, but they need not if you keep your focus on the message rather than the messenger. Refrain from judging a speaker on the basis of his or her accent, appearance, or demeanor; focus instead on what is actually being said. Whenever possible, reveal your needs to him or her by asking questions.

Listening Styles and Cultural Differences

Research suggests a link between our listening styles and a culture's predominate communication style.[6] A study of young adults in the United States, Germany, and Israel[7] found distinct listening style preferences that mirrored key value preferences, or preferred states of being, of each culture. Germans tended toward action-oriented listening, Israelis displayed a content-oriented style, and Americans exhibited both people- and time-oriented styles. While preliminary in nature, and not valid as a means of stereotyping a given culture's group behavior, these findings confirm the cultural component of all forms of communication, including listening. They also point to the need to focus on intercultural understanding as you learn about your audience.

Minimize External and Internal Distractions

A *listening distraction* is anything that competes for the attention we are trying to give to something else. External distractions can originate outside of us, in the environment, while internal distractions occur with our own thoughts and feelings.

External listening distractions, such as the din of jackhammers or competing conversations, can significantly interfere with our ability to listen, so try to anticipate and plan for them. If you struggle to see or hear over noise or at a distance, arrive early and sit in the front. To reduce *internal listening distractions*, avoid daydreaming, be well rested, monitor yourself for lapses in attention, and consciously focus on listening.

Dealing with Distractions While Delivering a Speech

- ☐ *Problem:* <u>Passing distractions</u> (chatting, entry of latecomers)
  Solution: Pause until distraction recedes

- ☐ *Problem:* <u>Ongoing noise</u> (construction)
  Solution: Raise speaking volume

- ☐ *Problem:* <u>Sudden distraction</u> (collapsing chair, falling object)
  Solution: Minimize response and proceed

- ☐ *Problem:* <u>Audience interruption</u> (raised hand, prolonged comment)
  Solution: Acknowledge audience reaction and either follow up or defer response to conclusion of speech.

Guard against Scriptwriting and Defensive Listening

When we, as listeners, engage in *scriptwriting*, we focus on what we, rather than the speaker, will say next.[8] Similarly, people who engage in **defensive listening** decide either that they won't like what the speaker is going to say or that they know better. Remind yourself that effective listening precedes effective rebuttal. Try waiting for the speaker to finish before devising your own arguments.

Beware of Lazy and Overconfident Listening

Laziness and overconfidence can manifest themselves in several ways: We may expect too little from speakers, ignore important information, or display an arrogant attitude. Later, we discover we missed important information.

Practice Active Listening

Setting listening goals, listening for main ideas, and watching for nonverbal cues are practical steps you can take to become more adept at listening actively.

Set Listening Goals

Determine ahead of time what you need and expect from the listening situation:

1. **Identify your listening needs:** "I must know my classmate's thesis, purpose, main points, and type of organization in order to complete and hand in a written evaluation."

2. **Identify why listening will help you:** "I will get a better grade on the evaluation if I am able to identify and evaluate the major components of Sara's speech."

3. **Make an action statement (goal):** "I will minimize distractions, take notes, and practice the active listening steps during the speech, asking questions about anything I do not understand."

4. **Assess goal achievement:** "I did identify the components of the speech I decided to focus upon and wrote about them in class."

Listen for Main Ideas

Try these strategies to ensure that you identify and retain the speaker's main points:

- Listen for a preview of important ideas in the introduction and reiteration of them in the conclusion.

- Take notes of main points, for example, "Bipolar disorder is actually a spectrum of disorders."

- Indent supporting points under main points to indicate subordination of ideas.

QUICK TIP

Listen Responsibly

As listeners, we are ethically bound to refrain from disruptive and intimidating tactics—such as heckling, name-calling, or interrupting—that are meant to silence those with whom we disagree. If we find the arguments of others morally offensive, we are equally bound to speak up appropriately in refutation.

Evaluate Evidence and Reasoning

The ability to think critically—to evaluate claims on the basis of well-supported reasons—goes hand in hand with active listening. As you listen to speeches, use your critical faculties to do the following:

- *Evaluate the speaker's evidence.* Is it accurate? Are the sources credible?
- *Analyze the speaker's assumptions and biases.* What lies behind the speaker's assertions? Does the evidence support or contradict these assertions?
- *Assess the speaker's reasoning.* Does it betray faulty logic? Does it rely on fallacies in reasoning?
- *Consider multiple perspectives.* Is there another way to view the argument? How do other perspectives compare with the speaker's?
- *Summarize and assess the relevant facts and evidence.* How will you think or act on the basis of the evidence?

Strive for the Open and Respectful Exchange of Ideas

In contrast to *monologue*, in which we try merely to impose what we think on another person or group of people, **dialogic communication** is the open sharing of ideas in an atmosphere of respect.[9] True dialogue encourages both listener and speaker to reach conclusions together. For listeners, this means maintaining an open mind and listening with empathy.[10] For the speaker, this means approaching a speech not as an argument that must be "won," but as an opportunity to achieve understanding with audience members.

Offer Constructive and Compassionate Feedback

Follow these guidelines when evaluating the speeches of others:

- *Be honest and fair in your evaluation of the speech.* Assess the speech as a whole and remain open to ideas and beliefs that differ from your own.

- *Adjust to the speaker's style.* Each of us has a unique communication style, a way of presenting ourselves through a mix of verbal and nonverbal signals. Don't judge the content of a speaker's message by his or her style.

- *Be compassionate in your criticism.* Always start by saying something positive, and focus on the speech, not the speaker.

- *Be selective in your criticism.* Make specific rather than global statements. Rather than statements such as, "I just couldn't get into your topic," give the speaker something he or she can learn from: "I wanted more on why the housing market is falling…."

part 7

Public Speaking: Development

CHAPTER

36

Analyzing the Audience

Advertisers are shrewd analysts of people's needs and wants, extensively researching our buying habits and lifestyle choices to identify what motivates us. To engage your listeners and encourage their involvement in your message, you too must investigate your audience. **Audience analysis** is the process of gathering and analyzing information about audience members' attributes and motivations with the *explicit aim of preparing your speech in ways that will be meaningful to them*. This is the single most critical aspect of preparing for any speech.

Assuming an **audience-centered perspective** throughout the speech preparation process — from selection and treatment of the speech topic to making decisions about how you will organize, word, and deliver it — will help you prepare a presentation that your audience will want to hear.

Adapt to Audience Psychology: Who Are Your Listeners?

Audience analysis involves investigating the audience's attitudes, beliefs, and values — their *feelings and opinions* — toward the topic, toward you as the speaker, and toward the speech occasion.

Taking the measure of the audience is critical because audience members tend to evaluate information in terms of their own point of view rather than the speaker's — at least until they are convinced to take a second look.[1] You may want your audience to support a cause, but unless you know something about their perspectives on the topic, you won't be able to appeal to them effectively.

Attitudes, beliefs, and values, while intertwined, reflect distinct mental states that reveal a great deal about us. **Attitudes** are our general evaluations of people, ideas, objects, or events.[2] To evaluate something is to judge it as relatively good or bad, desirable or undesirable. People generally act in accordance with their attitudes (although the degree to which they do so depends on many factors).[3]

Chapter 36, "Analyzing the Audience," is taken from Dan O'Hair, Hannah Rubenstein, and Rob Stewart: *A Pocket Guide to Public Speaking*, Fifth Edition, pp. 34–44 (Chapter 6, "Analyzing the Audience").

Attitudes are based on **beliefs**—the ways in which people perceive reality.[4] Beliefs are our feelings about what is true or real. The less faith listeners have in the existence of something—UFOs, for instance—the less open they are to hearing about it.

Both attitudes and beliefs are shaped by **values**—our most enduring judgments about what's good in life, as shaped by our culture and our unique experiences within it. We feel our values strongly and strive to realize them.

As a rule, audience members are more interested in and pay greater attention to topics toward which they have positive attitudes and that are in keeping with their values and beliefs. The less we know about something, the more indifferent we tend to be. It is easier (though not simple) to spark interest in an indifferent audience than it is to turn negative attitudes around.

"If the Value Fits, Use It"

Evoking some combination of the audience's attitudes, beliefs, and values in the speeches you deliver will make them more personally relevant and motivating. For example, the Biodiversity Project, an organization that helps environmental groups raise public awareness, counsels speakers to appeal directly to the three foremost values their audience members hold about the environment (discovered in nationally representative surveys commissioned by the Project), offering the following as an example:

> You care about your family's health (value #1 as identified in survey) and you feel a responsibility to protect your loved ones' quality of life (value #2). The local wetland provides a sanctuary to many plants and animals. It helps clean our air and water and provides a space of beauty and serenity (value #3). All of this is about to be destroyed by irresponsible development.[5]

Gauge Listeners' Feelings toward the Topic

Consideration of the audience's attitudes (and beliefs and values) about a topic is key to offering a speech that will resonate with them (see Chapter 37). Is your topic one with which the audience is familiar, or is it new to them? Do your listeners hold positive, negative, or neutral attitudes toward the topic? Once you have this information (using tools such as interviews and questionnaires, see p. 667), adjust the speech accordingly.

If the topic is *new* to listeners,

- Start by showing why the topic is relevant to them.
- Relate the topic to familiar issues and ideas about which they already hold positive attitudes.

If listeners know *relatively little* about the topic,

- Stick to the basics and include background information.
- Steer clear of jargon, and define unclear terms.
- Repeat important points, summarizing information often.

If listeners are *negatively disposed* toward the topic,

- Focus on establishing rapport and credibility.
- Don't directly challenge listeners' attitudes; instead begin with areas of agreement.
- Discover why they have a negative bias in order to tactfully introduce the other side of the argument.
- Offer solid evidence from sources they are likely to accept.
- Give good reasons for developing a positive attitude toward the topic.[6]

If listeners hold *positive attitudes* toward the topic,

- Stimulate the audience to feel even more strongly by emphasizing the side of the argument with which they already agree.
- Tell stories with vivid language that reinforce listeners' attitudes.[7]

If listeners are a *captive audience*,

- Motivate listeners to pay attention by stressing what is most relevant to them.
- Pay close attention to the length of your speech.

Gauge Listeners' Feelings toward You as the Speaker

How audience members feel about you will also have significant bearing on their responsiveness to the message. A speaker who is well liked can gain an initial hearing even when listeners are unsure what to expect from the message itself.

To create positive audience attitudes toward you, first display the characteristics of speaker credibility (ethos) described in Chapter 34. Listeners have a natural desire to identify with the speaker and to feel that he or she shares their perceptions,[8] so establish a feeling of commonality, or **identification**, with them. Use eye contact and body movements to include the audience in your message. Sharing a personal story, emphasizing a shared role, and otherwise stressing mutual bonds all help to create identification. So, too, does the strategic use of inclusive language such as *we*, *you*, *I*, and *me* (see p. 748).

Appeal to Audience Attitudes, Beliefs, and Values

Have you...

☐ Investigated audience members' attitudes, beliefs, and values toward your topic?

☐ Assessed the audience's level of knowledge about the topic?

☐ Considered strategies to address positive, negative, and neutral responses to your speech topic?

☐ Considered appealing directly to audience members' attitudes and values in your speech?

Gauge Listeners' Feelings toward the Occasion

Depending on the circumstances calling for the speech, people will bring different sets of expectations and emotions to it. Members of a **captive audience**, who are required to hear the speaker, may be less positively disposed to the occasion than those of a **voluntary audience** who attend of their own free will. Whether planning a wedding toast or a business presentation, failure to anticipate and adjust for the audience's expectations risks alienating them.

Adapt Your Message to Audience Demographics

Demographics are the statistical characteristics of a given population. At least eight characteristics are typically considered when analyzing speech audiences: *age, ethnic and cultural background, socioeconomic status* (including *income, occupation,* and *education*), *religious and political affiliations, gender,* and *group affiliations.* Any number of other traits—for example, disability, sexual orientation, and place of residence—may be important to investigate as well.

Knowing where audience members fall in relation to audience demographics will help you identify your **target audience**—those individuals within the broader audience whom you are most likely to influence in the direction you seek. You may not be able to please everyone, but you should be able to establish a connection with your target audience.

Generational Identity and Today's Generations	
Generation	Characteristics
Traditional 1925–1945	Respect for authority and duty, disciplined, strong sense of right and wrong
Baby Boomer 1946–1964	Idealistic, devoted to career, self-actualizing, values health and wellness
Generation X 1965–1979	Seeks work-life balance, entrepreneurial, technically savvy, flexible, questions authority figures, skeptical
Generation Y/ Millennials 1980–1999	Technically savvy, optimistic, self-confident, educated, appreciative of diversity, entrepreneurial, respectful of elders, short attention spans
Generation Z 2000–	Comfortable with the highest level of technical connectivity, naturally inclined to collaborate online, boundless faith in power of technology to make things possible[9]

Age

Each age group has its own concerns, psychological drives, and motivations. People of the same generation often share a familiarity with significant individuals, local and world events, noteworthy popular culture, and so forth. Thus being aware of the **generational identity** of your audience, such as the Baby Boomers (those born between 1946 and 1964), millennials (those born between 1980 and 1999), or Generation Z (those born since 2000), allows you to develop points that are relevant to the experiences and interests of the widest possible cross section of your listeners. The table, Generational Identity and Today's Generations, lists some of the prominent characteristics and values of today's generations.

Ethnic or Cultural Background

An understanding of and sensitivity to the ethnic and cultural composition of your listeners are key factors in delivering a successful (and ethical) speech. Some audience members may have a great deal in common with you. Others may be fluent in a language other than yours and must struggle to understand you. Some members of the audience may belong to a distinct **co-culture**, or social community whose perspectives and style of communicating differ significantly from yours. All will want to feel recognized by the speaker. (See pp. 666–667.)

Socioeconomic Status

Socioeconomic status (SES) includes income, occupation, and education. Knowing roughly where an audience falls in terms of these key variables can be critical in effectively targeting your message.

Income

Income determines people's experiences on many levels. It directly affects how they are housed, clothed, and fed, and determines what they can afford. Beyond this, income has a ripple effect, influencing many other aspects of life. For example, depending on income, home ownership is either a taken-for-granted budget item or an out-of-reach dream. The same is true for any activity dependent on income. Given how pervasively income affects people's life experiences, insight into this aspect of an audience's makeup can be quite important.

Occupation

In most speech situations, the *occupation* of audience members is an important and easily identifiable demographic characteristic. Occupational interests often are tied to other areas of social concern, such as politics, the economy, education, and social reform. Personal attitudes, beliefs, and goals are also closely tied to occupational standing.

Education

Level of *education* strongly influences people's perspectives and range of abilities. Higher levels of education often lead to increased lifetime earnings, better health outcomes, and greater civic engagement.[10] Depending upon audience members' level of education, your speech may treat topics at a higher or lower level of sophistication, with fewer or more examples and illustrations.

Religion

Social and political views can be tied to religious traditions, making *religion* another key demographic variable. At least a dozen major religious traditions coexist in the United States.[11] Not all members of the same religious tradition will agree on all issues. Catholics disagree on birth control and divorce, Jews disagree on whether to recognize same-sex unions, and so forth. Awareness of an audience's general *religious orientation* can be critical when your speech touches on a topic as potentially controversial as religion itself. Capital punishment, same-sex marriage, and teaching about the origins of humankind—all are rife with religious implications.

Political Affiliation

As with religion, beware of making unwarranted assumptions about an audience's *political values and beliefs*. Some people avoid anything that smacks of politics while others enjoy a lively debate. Conservative individuals hold certain views that liberals dispute, and the chasm between far right and far left is great indeed. Unless you have prior information about the audience's political values and beliefs, you won't know where your listeners stand.

Gender

Gender is another important factor in audience analysis, if only as a reminder to avoid *gender stereotyping*. Distinct from the fixed physical characteristics of biological sex, **gender** is our social and psychological sense of ourselves as males or females.[12] Making assumptions about the preferences, abilities, and behaviors of your audience members based on their presumed gender can seriously undermine their receptivity to your message. Beyond ensuring that you treat issues of gender evenly, try to anticipate the audience members' attitudes with respect to gender and plan accordingly.

Group Affiliations

The various groups to which audience members belong—whether social, civic, work-related, or religiously or politically affiliated—reflect their interests and values and so provide insight into what they care about. Investigating the audience members' group affiliations will help you craft a message that will appeal to them.

QUICK TIP

Be Sensitive to Disability When Analyzing an Audience

One out of every five people in the United States has some sort of physical or mental disability; 14 percent of those enrolled in college and graduate school are counted as disabled.[13] Problems range from sight and hearing impairments to constraints on physical mobility and employment. Thus disability is another demographic variable to consider when analyzing an audience. Keep **persons with disabilities (PWD)** in mind when you speak, and use language and examples that afford them respect and dignity.

Adapt to Diverse Audiences

In the United States, one-third of the population, or nearly 105 million people, belong to a racial or an ethnic minority group, and 38 million people, or 13 percent, are foreign born. Nationwide, nearly 20 percent of the population speaks a language other than English in the home; two-thirds of these speak Spanish.[14] These figures suggest that audience members will hold different cultural perspectives and employ different styles of communicating that may or may not mesh with your own.

How might you prepare to speak in front of an ethnically and culturally diverse audience, including that of your classroom? In any speaking situation, your foremost concern should be to treat your listeners with dignity and to act with integrity. Since values are central to who we are, identifying those of your listeners with respect to your topic can help you to avoid ethnocentrism and deliver your message in a culturally sensitive manner.

Consider Cross-Cultural Values

People in every culture possess **cultural values** related to their personal relationships, religion, occupation, and so forth. Understanding these values can help you deliver your message sensitively. While dominant cultural values in U.S. society include *achievement and success*, *equal opportunity*, *material comfort*, and *democracy*, surveys of several Asian societies reveal such values as a *spirit of harmony*, *humility toward one's superiors*, *awe of nature*, and a *desire for prosperity*. In Mexico, *group loyalty*, *cyclical time*, and *fatalism*, among others, as cultural values.[15] Becoming familiar with differences, as well as points of sameness, in values will help you to anticipate and appeal to the values of your audience members.

Individual audience analysis is always the first step when seeking to learn about an audience. But public speakers will also benefit by sensitizing themselves to broader national differences in cultural values. Geert Hofstede's wide-ranging research reveals five major "value dimensions," or "broad preferences for one state of affairs over another," as being significant across all cultures, but in widely varying degrees. To see variations in values among fifty nations, see geert-hofstede.com.

Several other global surveys can also be extremely useful for learning about cultural values, including the *Pew Global Attitudes Project* (pewglobal.org), *Gallup World View* (worldview.gallup.com), and the World Values Survey (www.worldvaluessurvey.org).

Focus on Universal Values

As much as possible, try to determine the attitudes, beliefs, and values of audience members. At the same time, you can focus on certain values that, if not universally shared, are probably universally aspired to in the human heart. These include love, truthfulness, fairness, freedom, unity, tolerance, responsibility, and respect for life.[16]

CHECKLIST

Reviewing Your Speech in the Light of Audience Demographics

- ☐ Does your speech acknowledge potential differences in values and beliefs and address them sensitively?

- ☐ Have you reviewed your topic in light of the age range and generational identity of your listeners? Do you use examples they will recognize and find relevant?

- ☐ Have you tried to create a sense of identification between yourself and audience members?

- ☐ Are your explanations and examples at a level appropriate to the audience's sophistication and education?

- ☐ Do you make any unwarranted assumptions about the audience's political or religious values and beliefs?

- ☐ Does your topic carry religious or political overtones that are likely to stir your listeners' emotions in a negative way?

Interview and Survey Audience Members

You can discover information about your audience through personal interviews, telephone or in-person surveys, and published sources. Often, it takes just a few questions to get some idea of where audience members stand psychologically and demographically.

Conduct Interviews

Interviews, even brief ones, can reveal a lot about the audience's interests and needs. You can conduct interviews one-on-one or in a group, in person or by telephone or online. Consider interviewing a sampling of the audience, or even just one knowledgeable representative of the group that you will address. As with questionnaires (see "Survey the Audience," which follows), interviews usually consist of a mix of open- and closed-ended questions. (See Chapter 39, pp. 691–693, for more on conducting interviews.)

Survey the Audience

Surveys can be as informal as a poll of several audience members or as formal as the pre-speech distribution of a written survey, or *questionnaire*—a series of open- and closed-ended questions. **Closed-ended questions** (also called *structured questions*) elicit a small range of specific answers:

"Do you smoke cigarettes?"

Yes _____ No _____ I quit, but I smoked for _____ years.

Closed-ended questions may be either fixed-alternative or scale questions. **Fixed-alternative questions** contain a limited choice of answers, such as "Yes," "No," or "For *x* years" (as in the preceding example). **Scale questions**—also called *attitude scales*—measure the respondent's level of agreement or disagreement with specific issues:

"Flag burning should be outlawed."

1) Strongly Agree   2) Agree   3) Undecided   4) Disagree   5) Strongly Disagree

Scale questions can be used to measure how important listeners judge something to be and how frequently they engage in a particular behavior:

"How important is religion in your life?"

1) Very Important   2) Important   3) Moderately Important
4) Of Minor Importance   5) Unimportant

Open-ended questions (also called *unstructured questions*) begin with a "how," "what," "when," "where," or "why," and they are particularly useful for probing beliefs and opinions. This style of question allows respondents to elaborate as much as they wish:

"How do you feel about using the results of DNA testing to prove innocence or guilt in criminal proceedings?"

Often, it takes just a few fixed-alternative and scale questions to draw a fairly clear picture of audience members' backgrounds and attitudes and where they fall in demographic categories. You may wish to use Web-based survey software, such as SurveyMonkey or QuestionPro, to generate surveys electronically using premade templates and distribute them online.

Consult Published Sources

Organizations of all kinds publish information describing their missions, operations, and achievements. Sources include websites and related online articles, brochures, newspaper and magazine articles, and annual reports.

Although *published opinion polls* won't specifically reflect your particular listeners' responses, they too can provide valuable insight into how a representative state, national, or international sample feels about the issue in question. Consider consulting these and other polling organizations:

- Pew Research Center for the People & the Press: peoplepress.org
- National Opinion Research Center (NORC): www.norc.uchicago.edu
- Roper Center for Public Opinion Research: ropercenter.uconn.edu
- Gallup: www.gallup.com

Analyze the Speech Setting and Context

As important as analyzing the audience is assessing (and then preparing for) the setting in which you will give your speech — size of audience; location; time; length of speech; and rhetorical situation:

1. What is the physical setting of the speech — auditorium, banquet hall, classroom?

2. How will you need to position yourself and adjust your voice, with or without a microphone?

3. What is the time of event and length of the speech?

4. How many people will attend?

5. How will any equipment I plan to use in my speech, such as an LCD projector, function in the space?

6. Where will I stand or sit in relation to the audience?

7. Will I be able to interact with the listeners?

8. Who else will be speaking?

9. Are there special events or circumstances of concern to my audience that I should acknowledge?

Selecting a Topic and Purpose

One of the first tasks in preparing a speech is to select a topic and purpose for speaking that are appropriate to the audience and occasion. Unless you can clearly identify *what* you want to say and *why* you want to say it—your topic and purpose—prior to delivering a speech, you won't be able to give one that works.

Exploring Topics for Your Speech

As you explore topics, consider each one's potential appeal to the audience and its appropriateness to the rhetorical situation. Even when the topic is assigned, as often happens in the classroom and workplace, you must still decide which aspects of it best match your unique audience and speech circumstance. The "From Source to Speech: Narrowing Your Topic to Fit the Audience" later in this chapter demonstrates how you can do this.

Identify Personal Interests
Personal interests run the gamut from favorite activities and hobbies to deeply held goals and values. You can translate personal experiences into powerful topics, especially if sharing them in some way benefits the audience (see the table, Identifying Topics.) "What it's like" stories also yield captivating topics. For example, what is it like to go hang gliding in the Rocky Mountains or to be part of a medical mission team working in Uganda?

Consider Current Events and Controversial Issues
Think about events and issues that are most important to you and your audience, and consider whether you can make a difference. Be aware, however, that people rarely respond to perspectives opposed to their core values, so plan speeches on such topics carefully using audience analysis (see Chapter 36).

Chapter 37, "Selecting a Topic and Purpose," is taken from Dan O'Hair, Hannah Rubenstein, and Rob Stewart: *A Pocket Guide to Public Speaking*, Fifth Edition, pp. 44–54 (Chapter 7, "Selecting a Topic and Purpose").

Explore Topics on *CQ Researcher*

Librarians often refer students to two related publications—*CQ Researcher* (published weekly) and *CQ Global Researcher* (published monthly)—for trustworthy background information on pressing social, political, environmental, and regional issues. Available online as part of your library's electronic holdings, for each topic they include an overview and assessment of the current situation, pro/con statements from representatives of opposing positions, and bibliographies of key sources.

Survey Grassroots Issues: Engage the Community

Audience members respond with interest to local issues that may affect them directly. College students want to know why their loan rates have increased; residents want to know about local environmental issues. People are also interested in what other people in their communities are doing. Review your community's newspapers and news blogs for the local headlines.

Steer Clear of Overused and Trivial Topics

To avoid boring your classmates and instructor, stay away from tired issues, such as drunk driving and the health risks of cigarettes, as well as trite topics such as "how to change a tire." People want to hear new information and different perspectives. For ideas, consult your favorite print or online publications. Consider, too, how you can apply relevant secondary research to personal experience to form a compelling topic (see Chapter 39).

Try Brainstorming to Generate Ideas

Brainstorming is a method of spontaneously generating ideas through word association, topic mapping, or Internet browsing using search engines and directories. Brainstorming works—it is a structured and effective way to identify topic ideas in a relatively brief period of time.

To brainstorm by **word association**, write down *one* topic that might interest you and your listeners. Then jot down the first thing that comes to mind related to it. Repeat the process until you have fifteen to twenty items. Narrow the list to two or three, and then select a final topic:

cars → maintenance → engines → advantages of diesel fuels

Topic (mind) mapping is a brainstorming technique in which you lay out words in diagram form to show categorical relationships among them. Put a potential topic in the middle of a piece of paper. As related ideas come to you, write them down, as shown in Figure 37.1.

Identifying Topics

Favorite Activities

- Playing sports
- Building computers
- Fixing cars
- Designing clothes
- Reading poetry
- Playing video games
- Playing music
- Travel
- Cooking

Personal Experiences

- Travel to international destinations
- Service in the armed forces
- Volunteer work in the U.S. or abroad
- Emigrating to the U.S.
- Surviving a life-threatening disease
- Surviving disaster
- Growing up in a nontraditional family

Values

- Building a greater sense of community
- Spirituality
- Philanthropy
- Political activism
- Living a sustainable life

Goals

- Becoming a high-tech entrepreneur
- Attending graduate or professional school
- Starting a family
- Staying fit
- Learning more about one's religion

Specific Subject Interests

- Local history
- Genealogy
- U.S. or global politics
- Photography and art
- Religion
- Science

Social Problems

- Road rage
- Bullying in schools
- Gun violence
- Unemployment
- Racism
- Lack of affordable child care

Health and Nutrition

- Diets
- Exercise regimens
- Autism spectrum disorder
- Mental health benefits
- Insomnia
- Eating organic or gluten-free

Current Events

- Pending legislation
- Political races
- Climate and biodiversity
- National security
- Same-sex marriage

Grassroots Issues

- Student loan relief options
- Safer schools
- Caring for the homeless
- Drought and water conservation

New or Unusual Angles

- Unsolved crimes
- Unexplained disappearances
- Scandals
- Conspiracy theories
- Life hacks for living a more efficient life

Issues of Controversy

- Corporate personhood
- Medical marijuana
- Concealed handguns
- Veterans Affairs
- Immunizations

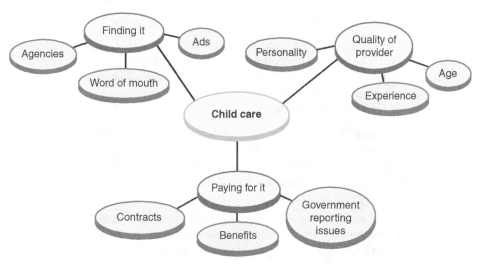

FIGURE 37.1 A Topic Map

Utilize Internet Tools

Excellent online tools for finding (and narrowing) a topic are the databases available on a library's portal, or its home page (see also p. 688). Consult general databases such as Academic OneFile (for browsing and starting the search process) and subject-specific databases such as Ethnic NewsWatch (for in-depth research on a topic). Popular Internet search engines such as Google and Bing also offer a wealth of resources to discover and narrow topics. Each search engine offers options for specialized searches within books, news, blogs, finance, images, and other sources. You can further narrow topics by limiting searches to within a range of dates (e.g., 1900–1950), to a geographic region (e.g., Europe), or to a particular language.

Identify the General Purpose of Your Speech

Once you have an idea for a topic, you'll need to refine and adapt it to your general speech purpose. The **general speech purpose** for any speech answers the question, "What is my objective in speaking on this topic to this audience on this occasion?" Public speakers typically accomplish one of three general purposes: to inform, to persuade, or to mark a special occasion.

- Do you aim primarily to educate or inform listeners about your topic? The general purpose of an **informative speech** is *to increase the audience's awareness and understanding of a topic by defining, describing, explaining, or demonstrating knowledge of the subject.*

- Is your goal to influence listeners to accept your position on a topic and perhaps to take action (e.g., "only eat wild salmon")? The general purpose of the **persuasive speech** is *to effect some degree of change in the attitudes, beliefs, values, and behaviors of audience members.*

- Are you there to mark a special occasion, such as an awards ceremony? The **special occasion speech** serves the general purpose *of entertaining, celebrating, commemorating, inspiring, or setting a social agenda,* and includes speeches of introduction, acceptance, and presentation; roasts and toasts; eulogies; and after-dinner speeches, among others.

The speech occasion itself often suggests an appropriate general speech purpose. A town activist, invited to address a civic group about installing solar panels in town buildings, may choose a *persuasive purpose* to encourage the group to get behind the effort. If invited to describe the initiative to the town finance committee, the activist may choose an *informative purpose*, in which the main goal is to help the committee understand project costs. If asked to speak at an event celebrating the project's completion, the speaker will choose a *special occasion purpose*. Addressing the same topic, the speaker selects a different general speech purpose to suit the audience and occasion.

Refine the Topic and Purpose

Once you have an idea for a topic and have established a general speech purpose, you'll need to narrow your focus to align with the nature of the occasion, audience expectations, and time constraints.

Narrow Your Topic

Just as brainstorming can be used to discover a topic, it can also be helpful in narrowing one. Using topic mapping, you can brainstorm by category (e.g., subtopic). Say your general topic is video games. Some related categories are platform (handheld, arcade), type (racing, role playing), and operating system (Linux, Macintosh, Windows).

CHECKLIST

Narrowing Your Topic

- ☐ What is my audience most likely to know about the subject?

- ☐ What do my listeners most likely want to learn?

- ☐ What aspects of the topic are most relevant to the occasion?

- ☐ Can I develop the topic using just two or three main points?

- ☐ How much can I competently research and report on in the time I am given to speak?

Form a Specific Speech Purpose

Once you've narrowed the topic, you need to refine your speech goal. You know you want to give either an informative or persuasive speech (your general purpose), but you also need to decide more specifically what you want to accomplish. The **specific speech purpose** lays out precisely what you want the audience to take away from your presentation. Ask yourself: What do you want the audience to learn/do/reconsider/agree with? Be specific about your aim, and then state it in action form, as in the following, written for an informative speech:

General Topic:	Consolidating Student Loans
Narrowed Topic:	Understanding when and why consolidating student loans makes sense
General Purpose:	To inform
Specific Speech Purpose:	To inform my audience about the factors to consider when deciding whether or not to consolidate student loans

Although the specific purpose statement need not be articulated in the actual speech, it is important to know and to keep in mind exactly what you want to accomplish.

Compose a Thesis Statement

The **thesis statement** (also called *central idea*) is the theme of the speech stated as a single, declarative sentence. It concisely expresses what the speech will attempt to demonstrate or prove. The main points, the supporting material, and the conclusion all serve to flesh out the thesis.

Both thesis and specific purpose statements describe the speech topic, but in different forms. *The specific purpose describes in action form what you want to achieve with the speech; the thesis statement concisely identifies, in a single idea, what the speech is about.* By clearly stating your speech thesis (what it's about), you set in your mind exactly what outcome you want to accomplish (the specific purpose).

The difference between the thesis and specific purpose can be clearly seen in the following examples.

Example 1

Speech Topic:	Blogs
General Speech Purpose:	To inform
Specific Speech Purpose:	To inform my audience of three benefits of keeping a blog
Thesis Statement:	Maintaining a blog provides the opportunity to practice writing, a means of networking with others who share similar interests, and the chance to develop basic website management skills.

Example 2

Speech Topic:	Service learning courses
General Speech Purpose:	To persuade
Specific Speech Purpose:	To persuade my audience that service learning courses are beneficial for gaining employment after schooling.
Thesis Statement:	To prepare for a difficult job market and enhance your résumé while making a significant difference for other people, you should take one or more service learning courses.

In an informative speech, the thesis conveys the scope of the topic, the steps associated with the topic, or the underlying elements of it. It describes what the audience will learn.

In a persuasive speech, the thesis represents what you are going to prove in the address. Notice, too, that in both examples, after you read the thesis you find yourself asking "Why?" or thinking "Prove it!" This will be accomplished by the evidence you give in the speech points (see Chapter 41).

CHECKLIST

Identifying the Speech Topic, Purpose, and Thesis

☐ Is the topic appropriate to the occasion?

☐ Will the topic appeal to my listeners' interests and needs?

☐ Will I be able to offer a fresh perspective on the topic?

☐ Have I identified the *general speech purpose*—to inform, persuade, or mark a special occasion?

☐ Have I identified what I want the audience to gain from the speech—the specific speech purpose?

☐ Have I considered how much I can competently research and then report on in the time I am given to speak?

☐ Does my thesis statement sum up in a single sentence what my speech is about?

☐ Does my thesis statement make the claim I intend to make about my topic?

FROM SOURCE TO SPEECH

Narrowing Your Topic to Fit Your Audience

How do you narrow a topic to fit the audience and the speech occasion? Consider the following case study.

A Case Study

Jenny is a member of the campus animal rights club and a student in a public speaking class. She is giving two persuasive speeches this semester: one to her public speaking class and one to the student council, as a representative of her club. For both presentations, Jenny plans to speak on the broad topic of animal rights. But she must narrow this topic considerably to fit each audience and speech occasion.

First, Jenny draws a topic map to generate ideas.

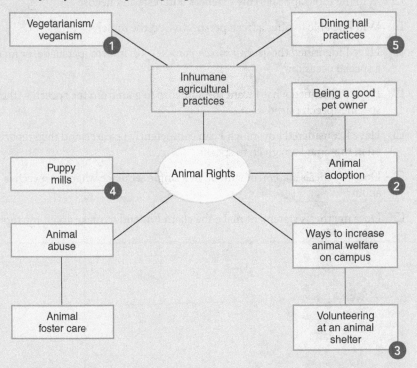

For each presentation, Jenny narrows her topic after considering her audience and the speech occasion.

Public Speaking Class (25–30 people):

- Mixed ages, races, and ethnicities, and an even mix of males and females
- Busy with classes, jobs, sports, and clubs
- Half live in campus housing, where pets are not allowed

Anderson Ross/Digital Vision/Getty Images

1 Jenny eliminates vegetarianism because she will be unlikely to change listeners' minds in a six-minute speech.

2 She eliminates animal adoption because it may not be feasible for many students.

3 Volunteering at an animal shelter is an option for all animal lovers, even those who are not allowed to have pets on campus. Jenny argues that students should donate an hour a week to a nearby shelter, so that busy students can still participate.

Student Council (8–10 people):

- Mixed demographic characteristics
- Similar interests: government, maintaining a rich campus life, an investment in ethics and the honor code, and an interest in keeping student affairs within budget

Manfred Rutz/The Image Bank/
Getty Images

4 Jenny eliminates puppy mills—though the student council may agree that the mills are harmful, they are not in a position to directly address the problem.

5 Jenny zeroes in on dining hall practices, which are directly tied to campus life. Her club's proposed resolution to use free-range eggs in the campus dining hall benefits all students and requires the support of the council—an ideal topic for this audience.

Developing Supporting Material

Good speeches contain relevant, motivating, and audience-centered **supporting material** in the form of examples, stories, testimony, facts, and statistics. Supporting material, such as you might discover in a magazine or journal article, illustrates and elaborates upon your ideas, provides the audience with evidence for your arguments, and engages them in the topic.

Offer Examples

An **example** is a typical instance of something. Without examples to illustrate the points a speaker wants to convey, listeners would get lost in a sea of abstract statements. Examples can be *brief* or *extended* and may be either *factual* or *hypothetical*.

Brief examples offer a single illustration of a point. In a speech titled "The Coming Golden Age of Medicine," Richard F. Corlin offers the following brief example to illustrate what American medicine can do:

> We often hear about the problems of the American health care delivery system, but just think what it can do. My 88-year-old father who needed a hip replacement got it—the week it was discovered that he needed it. That couldn't happen in any other country in the world.[1]

Sometimes it takes more than a brief example to effectively illustrate a point. **Extended examples** offer multifaceted illustrations of the idea, item, or event being described, thereby allowing the speaker to create a more detailed picture for the audience.

Chapter 38, "Developing Supporting Material," is taken from Dan O'Hair, Hannah Rubenstein, and Rob Stewart: *A Pocket Guide to Public Speaking*, Fifth Edition, pp. 54–60 (Chapter 8, "Developing Supporting Material").

Here, TED speaker Jonathan Drori uses an extended example to illustrate how pollen (the fertilizing element of plants) can link criminals to their crimes:

> [Pollen forensics] is being used now to track where counterfeit drugs have been made, where banknotes have come from....And murder suspects have been tracked using their clothing....Some of the people were brought to trial [for war crimes in Bosnia] because of the evidence of pollen, which showed that bodies had been buried, exhumed, and then reburied somewhere else.[2]

In some speeches, you may need to make a point about something that could happen in the future if certain events were to occur. Since it hasn't happened yet, you'll need a **hypothetical example** of what you believe the outcome might be. Republican Representative Vernon Ehlers of Michigan offered the following hypothetical example at a congressional hearing on human cloning:

> What if in the cloning process you produce someone with two heads and three arms? Are you simply going to euthanize and dispose of that person? The answer is no. We're talking about human life.[3]

Share Stories

One of the most powerful means of conveying a message and connecting with an audience is through a **story** or **narrative**. Stories help us make sense of our experiences;[4] they tell tales, both real and imaginary, relating personal experiences, folk wisdom, parables, myths, and so forth. Common to all stories are the essential elements of a plot, characters, setting, and some sort of time line.

Stories can be relatively short and simple descriptions of incidents worked into the speech, or longer accounts that constitute most of the presentation and even serve as the organizing framework for it (see narrative pattern of organization, **p. 721**). In either case, a successful story will strike an emotional connection between speaker and audience members.

In a speech on helping college students finish their degrees, Melinda French Gates offered the following brief story to illustrate the hardships many must overcome:

> Last year, we met a young man named Cornell at Central Piedmont Community College in Charlotte, North Carolina. We asked him to describe his typical day. He clocks into work at 11 P.M. When he gets off at 7 the next morning, he sleeps for an hour. In his car. Then he goes to class until 2 o'clock. "After that, " Cornell said, "I just crash."[5]

Many speakers liberally sprinkle their speeches with **anecdotes**—brief stories of interesting and often humorous incidents based on real life. The most important part of an anecdote is the *moral*—the lesson the speaker wishes to convey.[6] For example, in a speech to students at Maharishi University, comedian Jim Carrey talked about how his father's fear of being impractical led him to become an accountant instead of the comedian he wanted to be. This spurred Carrey to take another path:

> So many of us choose our path out of fear disguised as practicality....I learned many great lessons from my father, not the least of which was that you can fail at what you don't want, so you might as well take a chance on doing what you love.[7]

Draw on Testimony

Consider quoting or paraphrasing people who have an intimate knowledge of your topic. **Testimony** is firsthand findings, eyewitness accounts, and people's opinions; **expert testimony** includes findings, eyewitness accounts, or opinions from professionals trained to evaluate a given topic. **Lay testimony**, or testimony by nonexperts such as eyewitnesses, can reveal compelling firsthand information that may be unavailable to others.

Credibility plays a key role in the effectiveness of testimony, so establish the qualifications of the person whose testimony you use, and inform listeners when and where the testimony was offered:

> In testimony before the U.S. House Subcommittee on Human Rights and Wellness last week, Derek Ellerman (co-executive director of the Polaris Project) said, "Many people have little understanding of the enormity and the brutality of the sex trafficking industry in the United States...."[8]

QUICK TIP

Use a Variety of Supporting Materials

Listeners respond most favorably to a variety of supporting materials derived from multiple sources to illustrate each main point.[9] Alternating among different types of supporting material—moving from a story to a statistic, for example—will make the presentation more interesting and credible while simultaneously appealing to your audience members' different learning styles.

Provide Facts and Statistics

Most people (especially in Western society) require some type of evidence, usually in the form of facts and statistics, before they will accept someone else's claims or position.[10] **Facts** represent documented occurrences, including actual events, dates, times, people, and places. Listeners are not likely to accept your statements as factual unless you back them up with credible sources.

Use Statistics Accurately

Statistics are quantified evidence that summarizes, compares, and predicts things.

Statistics add precision to speech claims, *if* you know what the numbers actually mean and use terms that describe them accurately. Following are some basic statistical terms commonly used in speeches that include statistics.

Use Frequencies To Indicate Counts

A **frequency** is simply a count of the number of times something occurs:

> On the midterm exam there were 8 A's, 15 B's, 7 C's, 2 D's, and 1 F.

Frequencies can indicate size, describe trends, or help listeners understand comparisons between two or more categories:

- Inside the cabin, the Airbus A380 has room for at least 525 passengers — and as many as 853.[11] *(shows size)*

- According to the Centers for Disease Control (CDC), while cigarette use has declined 33 percent since 2000, the use of large cigars has increased 233 percent over this period.[12] *(describes a trend)*

- According to 2012 estimates from the U.S. Census Bureau, the total population of the state of Colorado comprised nearly 2,700,000 males and 2,600,000 females.[13] *(compares two categories)*

Use Percentages To Express Proportion

As informative as frequencies can be, the similarity or difference in magnitude between things may be more meaningfully indicated in a **percentage** — the quantified portion of a whole. Percentages help audience members easily grasp comparisons between things, such as the unemployment rate in several states:

> In May 2013, Nevada had the highest rate of unemployment, at 9.5 percent. At 3.8 percent, Nebraska had the lowest rate.[14]

Use Statistics Selectively—and Memorably

Rather than overwhelm the audience with numbers, put a few figures into context, to make your message more compelling. For example, instead of citing the actual number of persons belonging to Facebook worldwide (over 1.5 billion and counting), use a simple ratio to drive home the company's enormous reach: "Today, at least 38 percent of people in the world has a Facebook account, roughly the population of China."[15]

Because audience members cannot take the time to pause and reflect on the figures as they would with written text, consider how you can help listeners interpret the numbers you offer them, as in this example:

> As you can see, Nevada's unemployment rate is two and one-half times greater than that of Nebraska.

Use Types of Averages Accurately

An **average** describes information according to its typical characteristics. Usually we think of the average as the sum of the scores divided by the number of scores. This is the *mean*, the computed average. But there are two other kinds of averages—the *median* and the *mode*. As a matter of accuracy, in your speeches you should distinguish among these three kinds of averages.

Consider a teacher whose nine students scored 5, 19, 22, 23, 24, 26, 28, 28, and 30, with 30 points being the highest possible grade. The following illustrates how she would calculate the three types of averages:

- The **mean** score is 22.8, the *arithmetic average*, the sum of the scores divided by 9.
- The **median** score is 24, *the center-most score in a distribution* or the point above and below which 50 percent of the nine scores fall.
- The **mode** score is 28, the *most frequently occurring score* in the distribution.

The following speaker, claiming that a policy institute misrepresented the "average" tax rate for American families, illustrates how the inaccurate use of averages can deceive audience members:

> The Tax Foundation determines an *average* [*mean*] tax rate...simply by dividing all taxes paid by the total of everyone's income. For example, if four middle-income families pay $3,000, $4,000, $5,000, and $6,000, respectively, in

taxes, and one very wealthy family pays $82,000 in taxes, the *average* [*mean*] tax paid by these five families is $20,000 ($100,000 in total taxes divided by five families). But four of the five families [actually] have a tax bill equaling $6,000 or less...[Many] analysts would [more accurately] define a *median* income family—a family for whom half of all families have higher income and half have lower income—to be the "typical family."...[16]

Present Statistics Ethically

Offering listeners inaccurate statistics is unethical. Following are steps you can take to reduce the likelihood of using false or misleading statistics:

- *Use only reliable statistics.* Include statistics from the most authoritative source you can locate, and evaluate the methods used to generate the data.

- *Present statistics in context.* Inform listeners of when the data were collected and by whom, the method used to collect the data, and the scope of the research:

    > These figures represent data collected by the U.S. Department of Education during 2015 from questionnaires distributed to all public and private schools in the United States with students in at least one of grades 9–12 in the fifty states and the District of Columbia.

QUICK TIP

Avoid Cherry-Picking

Politicians are often accused of **cherry-picking**—selecting only those statistics that buttress their own arguments while ignoring competing data.[17] To present the mean when in fact one of the other averages is the better indicator of what your data represent, is an instance of cherry-picking. To be fair to audience members avoid misrepresenting the truth by offering only one-sided data. Present statistics accurately and in context, or not at all.

- *Avoid confusing statistics with "absolute truth."* Even the most recent data available will change the next time data are collected. Nor are statistics necessarily any more accurate than the human who collected them. Offer data as they appropriately represent your point, but refrain from declaring that these data are definitive.

Refer Orally to Your Sources

Clearly identify the source of your information and provide enough context (including approximate date of publication) to accurately interpret it. For guidelines on orally citing your sources, see Chapter 40, "Citing Sources in Your Speech."

CHECKLIST

Evaluating Your Research Needs

Do you need...

- ☐ Examples to illustrate, describe, or represent your ideas?

- ☐ A story or an anecdote to drive your point home?

- ☐ Firsthand findings, in the form of testimony, to illustrate your points or strengthen your argument?

- ☐ Relevant facts, or documented occurrences, to substantiate your statements?

- ☐ Statistics to demonstrate relationships?

CHAPTER
39

Finding Credible Sources in Print and Online

The search for supporting material—for the examples, facts and statistics, opinions, stories, and testimony described in Chapter 38—can be one of the most enjoyable parts of putting together a speech. It is at this stage that you can delve into your subject, sift through sources, and select relevant and audience-centered material to support your thesis and speech points. Every speech will suggest a different mix of sources, so before beginning your search, reflect on what might work best for your particular rhetorical situation.

Use a Library Portal to Access Credible Sources

Easy access to the Internet may lead you to rely heavily or even exclusively on sources you find through popular search engines such as Google and Bing. In doing so, however, you risk overlooking key sources not found through those sites and finding biased and/or false information. To circumvent this, begin your search at your school's or town's **library portal**, or electronic entry point into its holdings (e.g., the library's home page).

A key benefit of beginning your research at a library portal is the ability to access scholarly research articles and peer-reviewed journals, which contain some of the most cutting-edge and reliable research on almost any topic. Not only that, but libraries purchase access to proprietary databases and other resources that form part of the **deep Web**—the large portion of the Web that general search engines cannot access because the information is licensed and/or fee-based.

As with its shelved material, a library's e-resources are built through careful and deliberate selection. Librarians track, sort, and organize the millions of articles and book titles, both print and electronic, competing for your attention. They select only what is of value, according to well-defined standards and in consultation with faculty.[1] No such standards exist for popular Web search engines. The following table lists resources typically found on library portals.

Chapter 39, "Finding Credible Sources in Print and Online," is taken from Dan O'Hair, Hannah Rubenstein, and Rob Stewart: *A Pocket Guide to Public Speaking*, Fifth Edition, pp. 60–70 (Chapter 9, "Finding Credible Sources in Print and Online").

TYPICAL RESOURCES FOUND ON LIBRARY PORTALS

- Full text databases (newspapers, periodicals, journals)
- General reference works (dictionaries, encyclopedias, atlases, almanacs, fact books, biographical reference works, quotation resources, poetry collections)
- Books, e-books, and monographs
- Archives and special collections (collected papers, objects and images, and scholarly works unique to the institution)
- Digital collections (oral histories, letters, old newspapers, image collections, audio and video recordings)
- Video and music collections

Be a Critical Consumer of Online Information

Discerning the accuracy of open content is not always easy when you're surfing the Internet outside of a library portal. Anyone can post material on the Web and, with a little bit of design savvy, make a website look professional. Further, search engines such as Google cannot differentiate quality of information; only a human editor can do this. Each time you examine a document, especially one that has not been evaluated by credible editors, ask yourself, "Who put this information here, and why did they do so? What are the source's qualifications? Where is similar information found? When was the information posted, and is it timely?" (See "From Source to Speech: Evaluating Web Sources," pp. 694–695.)

Recognize Propaganda, Misinformation, and Disinformation

One way to judge a source's trustworthiness is to ask yourself: Is it reliable information, or is it propaganda, misinformation, or disinformation?[2] (See the table on p. 689.)

- **Information** is *data* that is presented in an understandable context. Data are raw and unprocessed facts; information makes sense of data. For example, a patient's vital signs (temperature, blood pressure, pulse, etc.) are data. Interpreting the vital signs in the context of health status is information. Information is neutral unto itself but is subject to manipulation, for purposes both good and bad. It then has the potential to become propaganda, misinformation, or disinformation.

- **Propaganda** is information represented in such a way as to provoke a desired response. The purpose of propaganda is to instill a particular attitude or emotion in order to gain support for a cause or issue. Usually presented as advertising or publicity, propaganda encourages you to think or act according to the ideological, political, or commercial perspective of the message source. Military posters that encourage enlistment are an example of propaganda.

Information, Propaganda, Misinformation, and Disinformation	
Information	Data set in a context for relevance. *Example: A fact*
Propaganda	Information represented in such a way as to provoke a desired response. *Example: An advertisement to conserve energy*
Misinformation	Something that is not true. *Example: An urban legend*
Disinformation	Deliberate falsification of information. *Example: A falsified profit-and-loss statement*

- **Misinformation** always refers to something that is not true. While propaganda may include factual information, misinformation does not. For example, in the summer of 2014, rumors circulated that the Ebola virus had mutated and become airborne when in fact it had not. One common form of misinformation on the Internet is the *urban legend* — a fabricated story passed along by unsuspecting people.

- **Disinformation**, which thrives on the Internet and elsewhere, is the deliberate falsification of information. Doctored photographs and falsified profit-and-loss statements are examples of disinformation in action.

Ethical speeches are based on sound information — on facts put into context — rather than on misinformation, propaganda, or disinformation.

Use Watchdog Sites to Check the Facts

Our most trustworthy elected officials occasionally make false assertions, and even the most reliable news sources publish errors of fact or omission. So whom should you believe — Congresswoman X's dire predictions regarding Social Security or Senator Y's rosier assessment? To check the factual accuracy of information offered by key political players and major journalistic outlets, consult these websites (bearing in mind that they too are not infallible).

- www.factcheck.org, sponsored by the Annenberg Public Policy Center
- www.politifact.com, sponsored by the *Tampa Bay Times*
- Fact Checker, a blog sponsored by the *Washington Post*

Investigate a Mix of Primary and Secondary Sources

Nearly all types of speeches can benefit from a mix of the two broad categories of supporting material: primary and secondary sources. **Primary sources** provide firsthand accounts or direct evidence of events, objects, or people (see below). **Secondary sources** provide analysis or commentary about things not directly observed or created. These include the vast world of news, commentary, analysis, and scholarship found in books, articles, and a myriad of sources other than the original (see p. 693).

A speech that contains both primary and secondary sources can be more compelling and believable than one that relies on one source type alone. The firsthand nature of a credible primary source can build trust and engage audience members emotionally. Secondary sources can help listeners put the topic in perspective. A speech on an oil spill, for example, can command more attention if it includes testimony by oil riggers and other eyewitnesses (primary sources) along with analyses of the spill from magazines and newspapers (secondary sources).

Explore Primary Sources

A primary source for a speech may be your own personal experience; a firsthand account found in letters, diaries, old newspapers, photographs, or other sources, often housed in a library's digital collection; or interviews or surveys that you conduct yourself.

Access Digital Collections

Chief among sources of primary speech materials are the many online digital collections of the world's libraries. Nearly all libraries now offer digital collections, which are generally organized by topic, material type, time period, and geographic area. Housed within these online repositories are oral histories, letters, old newspapers; photographs, prints, and paintings; and audio and video recordings.

QUICK TIP

Dazzle Them with Digital Collection Materials

Supporting material drawn from a library's digital collection can add great color and depth to speeches on many topics. A presentation on early African American actors, for example, might include a passage from a diary of a nineteenth-century actor and a photograph of him or her on stage. One way to discover a digital collection related to your topic is to enter your topic terms into a general search engine (e.g., African American actors AND digital collections).

Finding Speeches Online

Online, you can find numerous videos and audio files of speeches. These can be useful as models of speeches and primary source material.

☐ American Rhetoric (www.americanrhetoric.com) contains 5,000+ speeches.

☐ Gifts of Speech (gos.sbc.edu) features speeches by women from around the world since 1848.

☐ The Wake Forest University's Political Speeches gateway (www.wfu. edu/~louden/Political%20Communication/Class%20Information/ SPEECHES.html) offers links to collections of political speeches.

☐ The United States Senate (www.senate.gov) includes speeches by U.S. senators.

☐ *Vital Speeches of the Day* (www.vsotd.com) features current speeches delivered in the United States and is published monthly.

Consider Personal Knowledge and Experience

Used effectively, your own knowledge and experience about your topic can serve important functions in a speech, drawing in listeners and creating a sense of connection with them. Sharing experiences and observations about work you've done, people you've known, or places you've visited can add a dimension of authenticity and credibility that a secondhand source might not.

Conduct Interviews

Oftentimes you can glean considerably more insight into a topic, and get more compelling material to bring to your audience, by speaking personally to someone who has expertise on the subject. However, getting the information you need from a subject does require research and advance planning, from deciding how you will record the interview to the questions you will ask.

- Begin by *learning about the person you will be interviewing* so that you can prepare appropriate and informed questions for him or her.

- *Prepare questions for the interview* in advance of the interview date.

- *Word questions carefully:*
  - Avoid *vague questions,* those that don't give the person being interviewed enough to go on. Vague questions waste the interviewee's time and reflect the interviewer's lack of preparation.
  - Avoid *leading questions,* those that encourage, if not force, a certain response and reflect the interviewer's bias (e.g., "Like most of us, are you going to support candidate X?"). Likewise, avoid *loaded questions,* those that are phrased to reinforce the interviewer's agenda or that have a hostile intent (e.g., "Isn't it true that you've never supported school programs?").
  - Focus on asking *neutral questions,* those that don't lead the interviewee to a desired response. Usually, this will consist of a mix of open, closed, primary, and secondary questions. See p. 668 for more details on open- and closed-ended questions.
- *Establish a spirit of collaboration at the start:*
  - Acknowledge the interviewee and express respect for his or her expertise.
  - Briefly summarize your topic and informational needs.
  - State a (reasonable) goal—what you would like to accomplish in the interview—and reach agreement on it.
  - Establish a time limit for the interview and stick to it.
- *Use active listening strategies (see Chapter 35):*
  - Don't break in when the subject is speaking or interject with leading comments.
  - Paraphrase the interviewee's answers when you are unclear about meaning and repeat back to him or her.
  - Ask for clarification and elaboration when necessary.
- *End the interview by rechecking and confirming:*
  - Confirm that you have covered all the topics (e.g., "Does this cover everything?").
  - Briefly offer a positive summary of important things you learned in the interview.
  - Offer to send the interviewee the results of the interview.

CHECKLIST

Preparing for the Interview

- ☐ Have I researched my interviewee's background and accomplishments?

- ☐ Do I have a written set of questions?

- ☐ Can the questions be answered within a reasonable time frame?

- ☐ Are my questions relevant to the purpose of my speech?

- ☐ Are my questions posed in a well-thought-out sequence?

- ☐ Are my questions free of bias or hostile intent?

- ☐ Are controversial questions reserved until the end of the interview?

- ☐ Have I obtained advance permission to record the interview?

- ☐ Do I have a working writing implement and ample notepaper, or functioning laptop or tablet?

- ☐ Have I made certain that any recording equipment I plan to use is in working order?

Distribute Surveys

A survey can be useful as both a tool to investigate audience attitudes and a source of primary material for your speech. Surveys are an especially effective source for speech topics focused on the attitudes and behavior of people in your immediate environment, such as fellow students' opinions on issues on or off campus or community members' attitudes toward local initiatives (for guidelines on creating surveys, see Chapter 36.)

Explore Secondary Sources

Along with possible primary sources, your speeches will most likely require the support of secondary sources as found in books, newspapers, periodicals, government publications, print or online reference works (such as encyclopedias, almanacs, biographical reference works, books of quotations, poetry collections, and atlases), and reputable blogs and social news sites.

FROM SOURCE TO SPEECH

Evaluating Web Sources

Check the Most Authoritative Websites First

Seek out the most authoritative websites on your topic. If your speech explores the NBA draft, start with the NBA's official website. For information on legislation, government statistics, health, the environment, and other relevant topics, check government-sponsored sites at the official U.S. government portal, www.usa.gov. Government-sponsored sites are free of commercial influence and contain highly credible primary materials.

Evaluate Authorship and Sponsorship

1. *Examine the domain in the Web address* — the suffix at the end of the address that tells you the nature of the site: educational (.edu), government (.gov), military (.mil), nonprofit organization (.org), business/commercial (.com), and network (.net). A tilde (~) in the address usually indicates that it is a personal page rather than part of an institutional website. Make sure to assess the credibility of each site, whether it is operated by an individual, a company, a government agency, or a nonprofit group.

2. *Look for an "About" link that describes the organization or a link to a page that gives more information.* These sections can tell a great deal about the nature of the site's content. Be wary of sites that do not include such a link.

3. *Identify the creator of the information.* If an individual operates the site — and such sites are now prolific in the form of blogs and professional profile pages — does the document provide relevant biographical information, such as links to a résumé or a listing of the author's credentials? Look for contact information. A source that doesn't want to be found, at least by e-mail, is not a good source to cite.

Check for Currency

4. *Check for a date that indicates when the page was placed on the Web and when it was last updated.* Is the date current? Websites that do not have this information may contain outdated or inaccurate material.

Check That the Site Credits Trustworthy Sources

5. *Check that the website documents its sources.* Reputable websites document the sources they use. Follow any links to these sources, and apply the same criteria to them that you did to the original source document. Verify the information you find with at least two other independent, reputable sources.

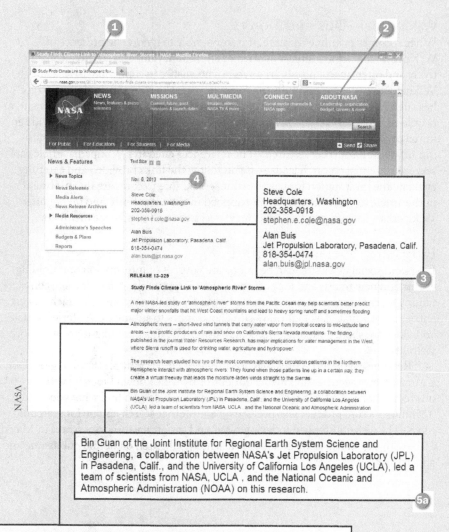

1

2

4 Nov. 8, 2013

3
Steve Cole
Headquarters, Washington
202-358-0918
stephen.e.cole@nasa.gov

Alan Buis
Jet Propulsion Laboratory, Pasadena, Calif.
818-354-0474
alan.buis@jpl.nasa.gov

5a
Bin Guan of the Joint Institute for Regional Earth System Science and Engineering, a collaboration between NASA's Jet Propulsion Laboratory (JPL) in Pasadena, Calif., and the University of California Los Angeles (UCLA), led a team of scientists from NASA, UCLA , and the National Oceanic and Atmospheric Administration (NOAA) on this research.

5b
"Atmospheric rivers are the bridge between climate and West Coast snow," said Guan. "If scientists can predict these atmospheric patterns with reasonable lead times, we'll have a better understanding of water availability and flooding in the region." The benefit of improving flood prediction alone would be significant. A single California atmospheric-river storm in 1999 caused 15 deaths and $570 million in damage.

NASA

Wikipedia—Dos and Don'ts

When it comes to online research, it is impossible to ignore the presence of Wikipedia, the world's largest experimental free encyclopedia, written collaboratively and often anonymously by anyone who wishes to contribute to it. Though Wikipedia's instant accessibility and vast range make it tantalizingly easy to consult, bear in mind that information may or may not be accurate at any given moment, as people edit material at will. As with any encyclopedia, Wikipedia may provide an initial overview of a topic, but to ensure accuracy, it should serve only as a starting-off point for further research.[3] The references cited in a Wikipedia article can serve as potential research leads — *if* you follow the links provided and carefully evaluate the information for trustworthiness. Be sure to compare the information in the article to credible sources *not* supplied in the entry itself, and do not offer Wikipedia — or any encyclopedia entry — as a source to audience members.

Blogs and Social News Sites

Blogs and social news sites can be important sources of information of unfolding events and new trends and ideas, if the source is reputable. A *blog* is a site containing journal-type entries maintained by individuals or groups in which newest entries appear first. A **social news site** allows users to submit news stories, articles, and videos to share with other users of the site. The most popular items win more visibility.

Reference only those sites that are affiliated with reputable (local, regional, or national) news agencies and media outlets, or by well-known bloggers with serious reputations. A blog-specific search engine can help you find what you need. Technorati's core product was previously an Internet search engine for searching blogs. The website stopped indexing blogs and assigning authority scores in May of 2014 with the launch of its new website, which is focused on online publishing and advertising.

CHAPTER

40

Citing Sources in Your Speech

A lerting the audience to the sources you use and offering ones that they will find authoritative is a critical aspect of delivering a presentation. When you credit speech sources, you:

- Increase the odds that audience members will believe in your message.
- Demonstrate the quality and range of your research to listeners.
- Demonstrate that reliable sources support your position.
- Avoid plagiarism and gain credibility as an ethical speaker who acknowledges the work of others.
- Enhance your own authority.
- Enable listeners to locate your sources and pursue their own research on the topic.

Ethically you are bound to attribute any information drawn from other people's ideas, opinions, and theories—as well as any facts and statistics gathered by others—to their original sources. Remember, you need not credit sources for ideas that are *common knowledge*—established information likely to be known by many people and described in multiple places (see p. 647).

Alert Listeners to Key Source Information

An **oral citation** credits the source of speech material that is derived from other people's ideas. For each source, plan on briefly alerting the audience to the following:

1. The *author* or *origin of the source* ("documentary film-maker *Ken Burns*..." or "on the *National Science Foundation website*...")

2. The *type of source* (journal article, book, personal interview, website, blog, online video, etc.)

Chapter 40, "Citing Sources in Your Speech," is taken from Dan O'Hair, Hannah Rubenstein, and Rob Stewart: *A Pocket Guide to Public Speaking*, Fifth Edition, pp. 70–77 (Chapter 10, "Citing Sources in Your Speech").

3. The *title* or a *description of the source* ("In the book *Endangered Minds...*"; or "In an article on sharks...")

4. The *date of the source* ("The article, published in the *October 10th, 2015*, issue..." or "According to a report on revising the SAT, posted online September 28, 2015, on the *Daily Beast...*")

Spoken citations need not include a complete bibliographic reference (exact title, full names of all authors, volume, and page numbers); doing so will interrupt the flow of your presentation and distract listeners' attention. However, do keep a running list of source details for a bibliography to appear at the end of your speech draft or outline.

Establish the Source's Trustworthiness

Too often, inexperienced speakers credit their sources in bare-bones fashion, offering a rote recitation of citation elements. For example, they might cite a source's name, but leave out key details about the source's background that could convince the audience to trust the source as credible (believable) and his or her conclusions as true (accurate).

Source credibility refers to our level of trust in a source's credentials and track record for providing accurate information. If you support a scientific claim by crediting it to an obscure personal blog, for example, listeners won't find it nearly as reliable as if you credited it to a scientist affiliated with a reputable institution.

Be aware that while a source that is credible is usually accurate, this is not always so.[1] Sometimes we have information that contradicts what we are told by a credible source. For instance, a soldier might read an article in the *Washington Post* about a conflict in which he or she participated. The soldier knows the story contains inaccuracies because the soldier was there. In general, however, the soldier finds the *Washington Post* a credible source. Therefore, *since even the most credible source can sometimes be wrong, it is always better to offer a variety of sources, rather than a single source, to support a major point.* This is especially the case when your claims are controversial.

Qualify the Source

A simple and straightforward way to demonstrate a source's credibility is to include a brief description of the source's qualifications to address the topic (a **"source qualifier"**), along with your oral citation (e.g., "researcher at Duke Cancer Institute," "columnist for the *Wall Street Journal*"). This will allow the audience to put the source in perspective. To see how you can orally cite sources in ways that listeners will accept and believe in them, see "From Source to Speech: Demonstrating Your Source's Credibility and Accuracy."

Avoid a Mechanical Delivery

Acknowledging sources need not interrupt the flow of your speech. On the contrary, audience members will welcome information that adds backing to your assertions. The key is to avoid a formulaic, or mechanical, delivery. Varying the wording and order in which you introduce a citation can help.

Vary the Wording

Avoid a rote delivery of sources by varying your wording. If you introduce one source with the phrase "According to...," switch to another construction ("As reported by...") for the next one. Alternating introductory phrases contributes to a natural delivery and provides the necessary variety listeners need.

Vary the Order

Vary the order in which you introduce a citation. Occasionally discuss the findings first, before citing the source. For example, you might state that "Caffeine can cause actual intoxication" and provide evidence to back it up before revealing the source(s) of it — "A chief source for this argument is a report in the July 5, 2015, issue of the *New England Journal of Medicine....*"

Types of Sources and Sample Oral Citations

Following are common types of sources cited in a speech, the specific citation elements to mention, and examples of how you might refer to these elements in a presentation. Note that each example includes an underlined source qualifier describing the source's qualifications to address the topic — for instance, "director of undergraduate studies for four years" or "research scientist at Smith-Kline." Including a source qualifier can make the difference between winning or losing acceptance for your supporting material.

FROM SOURCE TO SPEECH

Demonstrating Your Sources' Credibility and Accuracy

How Can I Lead the Audience to Accept My Sources as Credible and Accurate?

- If the source is affiliated with a respected institution, identify that affiliation.
- If citing a study linked to a reputable institution, identify the institution.
- If a source has relevant credentials, note the credentials.
- If the source has relevant real-life experience, mention that experience.

In the following excerpt from a speech about becoming a socially conscious consumer, the speaker omits information about his key sources that would help convince the audience that his evidence and sources are trustworthy:

> The force behind this new kind of partnership is called "cause marketing." According to the *Financial Times*, cause marketing is when a company and a consumer group—or a charity—tackle a social or environmental problem and create business value for the company at the same time. A survey on consumer responses to cause marketing was conducted by Nielsen. The poll found that two-thirds of consumers around the world would say they prefer to buy products and services from companies that have programs that give back to society. And over 46 percent of consumers were willing to pay more for goods and services from companies that are giving back.

Below we see a much more convincing use of the same sources.

> The force behind this new kind of partnership is called "cause marketing." According to the *Financial Times* Lexicon, an online dictionary found at the publication's website, in *cause marketing* a company and a consumer group—or a charity—tackle a social or environmental problem and create business value for the company at the same time. In March of 2012, the global marketing firm Nielson, which studies consumer behavior in more than one hundred countries, conducted a world-wide study on cause marketing. It found that two-thirds of consumers around the world say they prefer to buy products and services from companies that have programs that give back to society. And over 46 percent said that they were, and I'm quoting here from the survey question, "willing to pay more for goods and services from companies that are giving back."

1 The speaker states the date of the study in cause marketing and shows that it is relatively recent research.

2 Rather than merely mentioning the source's name (Nielsen), the speaker identifies the source as a reputable global marketing firm. Listeners are more likely to trust the source if it is connected to a trusted entity.

Two thirds (66%) of consumers around the world say they prefer to buy products and services from companies that have implemented programs to give back to society. That preference extends to other matters, too: they prefer to work for these companies (62%), and invest in these companies (59%). A smaller share, but still nearly half (46%) say they are willing to pay extra for products and services from these companies. These are the "socially conscious consumers," as defined by and focused upon in this report.

3 The speaker directly quotes from the source instead of paraphrasing, which provides stronger evidence and further credits the argument.

4 The speaker includes stronger language, like "a world-wide study," to emphasize the breadth of the agency's research.

Book

If a book has *two* or *fewer* authors, state first and last names, source qualifier, title, and date of publication. If *three* or *more authors*, state first and last name of first author and "coauthors."

> *Example:* In the book *1948: The First Arab-Israeli War*, published in *2008*, noted Israeli historian Benny Morris claims that…

> *Example:* In *The Civic Potential of Video Games*, published in 2009, Joseph Kahne, noted professor of education and director of the Civic Education Research Group at MillsCollege, and his two coauthors, both educators, wrote that…

Reference Work

For a reference work (e.g., atlas, directory, encyclopedia, almanac), note title, date of publication, author or sponsoring organization, and source qualifier.

> *Example:* According to *Literary Market Place 2015*, the foremost guide to the U.S. book publishing industry, Karen Hallard and her coeditors report that…

Print Article

When citing from a print article, use the same guidelines as you do for a book.

> *Example:* In an article entitled "How Junk Food Can End Obesity," published in the July 2013 issue of the *Atlantic* magazine, David H. Freedman, a journalist and author of the book Wrong: Why the Experts Keep Failing Us, argues that fast food chains such as McDonald's can offer lower-cost healthy foods than higher-priced health food stores…

Online-Only Publications

For online-only publications, use the book guidelines, and identify the publication as "online magazine," "online newspaper," or "online journal."

> *Example:* In an article on massive online open courses (MOOCs) posted on July 23, 2013, on the online magazine *Slate*, Gabriel Kahn, a professor at the University of Southern California and director of the Future of Journalism at Annenberg Innovation Lab…

Organization Website

Name the website, source qualifier, section of website cited (if applicable), and last update.

Example: On its website, last updated September 18, 2015, the Society of Interventional Radiology, a national organization of physicians and scientists, explains that radio waves are harmless to healthy cells...

If website content is undated or not regularly updated, review the site for credibility before use, using the criteria listed on pp. 694–695, "From Source to Speech: Evaluating Web Sources."

Blog

Name the blogger, source qualifier, affiliated website (if applicable), and date of posting.

Example: In a July 8, 2015, posting on *Talking Points Memo*, a news blog that specializes in original reporting on government and politics, editor Josh Marshall notes that...

Television or Radio Program

Name the program, segment, reporter, source qualifier, and date aired.

Example: Judy Woodruff, PBS Newshour co-anchor, described in a segment on the auto industry aired on June 2, 2015...

Online Video

Name the online video source, program, segment, source qualifier, and date aired (if applicable).

Example: In a session on "Mindfulness in the World" delivered at the Wisdom 2.0 Conference on February 26th, 2015, and broadcast on YouTube, Jon Kabat-Zinn, scientist, renowned author, and founding director of the Stress Reduction Clinic...

Credit Sources in Presentation Aids

Just as you acknowledge the ideas of others in the verbal portion of your speech, be sure to credit such material used in any accompanying presentation aids. When reproducing copyrighted material, such as a table or photograph, label it with a copyright symbol (©) and the source information. Even if it is not copyrighted, supporting material listed on a visual aid may require citation. You may cite this material orally, print the citation unobtrusively on the aid, or both.

Testimony (Lay or Expert)

Name the person, source qualifier, and date and context in which information was offered.

Example: On July 17, 2014, in Congressional testimony before the U.S. Senate Foreign Relations Committee, Thomas A. Shannon Jr., an attorney with the U.S. Department of State, described the exodus of unaccompanied minors from Central America...

Interview and Other Personal Communication

Name the person, source qualifier, and date of the interview/communication.

Example: In an interview I conducted last week, Tim Zeutenhorst, Chairman of the Orange City Area Health System Board, at Orange City Hospital in Iowa, said...

Example: In a June 23rd e-mail/letter/memorandum from Ron Jones, a researcher at the Cleveland Clinic...

CHECKLIST

Offering Key Source Information

- ☐ Have I identified the author or origin of the source?
- ☐ Have I indicated the type of source?
- ☐ Have I offered the title or description of the source?
- ☐ Have I noted the date of the source?
- ☐ Have I qualified the source to establish its reliability and credibility?

part 8

Public Speaking: Organization

Organizing the Body of the Speech

A speech structure is simple, composed of just three basic parts: an introduction, a body, and a conclusion. The **introduction** establishes the purpose of the speech and shows its relevance to the audience. The **body** of the speech presents main points that are intended to fulfill the speech purpose. The **conclusion** brings closure to the speech by restating the purpose, summarizing main points, and reiterating the speech thesis and its relevance to the audience. In essence, the introduction of a speech tells listeners where they are going, the body takes them there, and the conclusion lets them know the journey has ended.

Chapter 44 describes how to create effective introductions and conclusions. Here we focus on the elements of the speech body: *main points, supporting points,* and *transitions.*

Use Main Points to Make Your Claims

Main points express the key ideas of the speech. Their function is to represent each of the major ideas or claims being made in support of the speech thesis. To create main points, identify the most important ideas you want to convey. What major findings emerge from your research? Each of these ideas should be expressed as a main point.

Restrict the Number of Main Points
Research indicates that audiences are most comfortable taking in between two and seven main points.[1] For most speeches, and especially those delivered in the classroom, between two and five main points should be sufficient. As a rule, the fewer main points in a speech, the greater the odds that you will maintain your listeners' attention. If you have too many main points, further narrow your topic (see Chapter 37) or check the points for proper subordination (see pp. 710–711).

Chapter 41, "Organizing the Body of the Speech," is taken from Dan O'Hair, Hannah Rubenstein, and Rob Stewart: *A Pocket Guide to Public Speaking,* Fifth Edition, pp. 80–88 (Chapter 11, "Organizing the Body of the Speech").

Restrict Each Main Point to a Single Idea

A main point should not introduce more than one idea. If it does, split it into two (or more) main points:

Incorrect:	I.	West Texas has its own Grand Canyon, and south Texas has its own desert.
Correct:	I.	West Texas boasts its own Grand Canyon.
	II.	South Texas boasts its own desert.

Main points should be mutually exclusive of one another. If they are not, consider whether a main point more properly serves as a subpoint.

Express each main point as a *declarative sentence*—one that asserts or claims something. For example, if one of your main points is that children need more vitamin D, clearly state, "According to the American Academy of Pediatrics, children from infants to teens should consume more vitamin D." In addition, state your main points (and supporting points; see below) in *parallel form*—that is, in similar grammatical form and style (see p. 753). Phrasing points in parallel form helps listeners follow your ideas more easily while lending a rhythmic elegance to your words.

Use the Purpose and Thesis Statements as Guides

Main points should flow directly from your specific purpose and thesis statements (see pp. 710–677), as in the following example:

Specific Purpose: What you want the audience to learn or do as a result of your speech	"To show my audience, through a series of easy steps, how to meditate."		
Thesis: The central idea of the speech	"When performed correctly using just three steps, meditation is an effective and easy way to reduce stress."		
Main Points:	I.	The first step of meditation is the "positioning."	
	II.	The second step of meditation is "breathing."	
	III.	The third step of meditation is "relaxation."	

QUICK TIP

Save the Best for Last—or First

Listeners have the best recall of speech points made at the end of a speech (a phenomenon termed the "recency effect") and at the beginning of a speech
(the "primacy effect") than of those made in between (unless the ideas made in
between are much more striking than the others).[2] If it is especially important that
listeners remember certain ideas, introduce those ideas near the beginning of the
speech and reiterate them at the conclusion.

Use Supporting Points to Demonstrate Your Claims

Supporting points organize the evidence you have gathered to explain (in an informative speech) or justify (in a persuasive speech) the main points. Generate these
points with the supporting material you've collected in your research—examples,
narratives, testimony, facts, and statistics (see Chapter 38).

In an outline, supporting points appear in a subordinate position to main
points. This is indicated by *indentation*. Arrange supporting points in order of their
importance or relevance to the main point.

CHECKLIST

Reviewing Main and Supporting Points

☐   Do the main points flow directly from the speech goal and thesis?

☐   Do the main points express the key points of the speech?

☐   Is each main point truly a main point or a subpoint of another main point?

☐   Is each main point substantiated by at least two supporting points—or
      none?

☐   Do you spend roughly the same amount of time on each main point?

☐   Are the supporting points truly subordinate to the main points?

☐   Does each main point and supporting point focus on a single idea?

☐   Are the main and supporting points stated in parallel form?

Principles of Coordination and Subordination

- Assign equal weight to ideas that are coordinate.
- Assign relatively less weight to ideas that are subordinate.
- Indicate coordinate points by their parallel alignment.
- Indicate subordinate points by their indentation below the more important points.
- Every point must be supported by at least two points or none at all (consider how to address one "dangling" point by including it in the point above it).

Pay Close Attention to Coordination and Subordination

Outlines reflect the principles of **coordination and subordination**—the logical placement of ideas relative to their importance to one another. Ideas that are *coordinate* are given equal weight; **coordinate points** are indicated by their parallel alignment. An idea that is *subordinate* to another is given relatively less weight; **subordinate points** are indicated by their indentation below the more important points.

The most common format for outlining points is the **roman numeral outline**. Main points are enumerated with uppercase roman numerals (I, II, III…), while supporting points are enumerated with capital letters (A, B, C…), Arabic numerals (1, 2, 3…), and lowercase letters (a, b, c…), as seen in the following example (in phrase outline form; see p. 724) from a speech about using effective subject lines in business-related e-mails:

    I.   Subject line most important, yet neglected part of e-mail

        A.   Determines if recipient reads message

            1.   Needs to specify point of message

            2.   Needs to distinguish from spam

        B.   Determines if recipient ignores message

            1.   May ignore e-mail with missing subject line

            2.   May ignore e-mail with unclear subject line

   II.   Use proven techniques for effective subject lines

        A.   Make them informative

            1.   Give specific details

            2.   Match central idea of e-mail

            3.   Be current

        B.   Check for sense

            1.   Convey correct meaning

            2.   Reflect content of message

C. Avoid continuing subject line in text
   1. May annoy the reader
   2. May be unclear
       a. Could be confused with spam
       b. Could be misinterpreted

QUICK TIP

Spend Time Organizing Speech Points

Don't skimp on organizing speech points. Listeners' understanding of information is directly linked to how well it is organized,[3] and they will quickly lose interest when the speech is disorganized.[4] Listeners also find speakers whose speeches are well organized more believable than those who present poorly organized ones.[5]

Strive for a Unified, Coherent, and Balanced Organization

A well-organized speech is characterized by unity, coherence, and balance. Try to adhere to these principles as you arrange your speech points.

A speech exhibits *unity* when it contains only those points implied by the specific purpose and thesis statements (see pp. 676–677). The thesis is supported by main points, main points are strengthened by supporting points, and supporting points consist of carefully chosen evidence and examples.

A speech exhibits *coherence* when it is organized clearly and logically, using the principles of coordination and subordination to align speech points in order of importance (see "Principles of Coordination and Subordination," p. 710). In addition, the speech body should expand upon the introduction, and the conclusion should summarize the body. Within the body of the speech itself, main points should support the thesis statement, and supporting points should enlarge upon the main points. Transitions serve as mental bridges that help establish coherence.

Inexperienced speakers may give overly lengthy coverage to one point and insufficient attention to others; or they might provide scanty evidence in the speech body after presenting an impressive introduction. The principle of *balance* suggests that appropriate emphasis or weight be given to each part of the speech relative to the other parts and to the theme. The body of a speech should always be the longest part, and the introduction and conclusion should be of roughly the same length. Stating the main points in parallel form is one aspect of balance. Assigning each main point at least two supporting points is another. If you have only one subpoint, consider how you might incorporate it into the superior point. Think of a main point as a body and supporting points as legs; without at least two legs, the body cannot stand.

FROM POINT TO POINT

Using Transitions to Guide Your Listeners

Transitions direct your listeners from one point to another in your speech, leading them forward along a logical path while reinforcing key ideas along the way. Plan on using transitions to move between:

- The introduction and the body of the speech
- The main points
- The subpoints, whenever appropriate
- The body of the speech and the conclusion

Introduction

I.   Today I'll explore the steps you can take to create a greener campus...

(Transition: *So how do you go green?*)

Body

A.   Get informed — understand what is physically happening to your planet

(Transition: *Understanding the issues is only part of going green, however. Perhaps most important,...*)

B.   Recognize that change starts here, on campus, with you...

While transitions help guide your listeners from point to point, they can also do a lot more, including:

- Introduce main points
- Illustrate cause and effect
- Signal explanations and examples
- Emphasize, repeat, compare, or contrast ideas
- Summarize and preview information
- Suggest conclusions from evidence

Following is an excerpt from a working outline on a speech about campuses going green. Note how the student edits himself to ensure that he (1) uses transitions to help listeners follow along and retain his speech points and (2) uses transitions strategically to achieve his goal of persuading the audience.

(**Transition**: *Why are environmentalists targeting college campuses?*)

I.   College campuses generate the waste equivalent of many large towns...

(**Transition**: *As a result...*)

    A.   Colleges face disposal issues, especially of electronics...
    B.   Administrators face decisions about mounting energy costs...

(**Transition:** *Following are some ideas to create a greener campus. First...*)

II.   Promote a campus-wide recycling program

(**Transition:** *For example...*)

    A.   Decrease the availability of bottled water and disposable...
    B.   Insist on recycling bins at all residence halls...
    C.   Encourage computer centers to recycle...

(**Transition**: *Recycling is a critical part of going green. Decreasing the consumption of plastic and paper, installing recycling bins, and responsibly disposing of print cartridges will make a huge difference. Another aspect of going green is using sustainable energy...*)

III.   Lobby administrators to investigate solar, wind, and geothermal...
    A.   Make an argument for "eco-dorms..."
    B.   Explore alternative heating...

(**Transition**: *So far, we've talked about practical actions we can take to encourage a greener lifestyle on campus, but what about beyond the campus?*)

IV.   Get involved at the town government level
    A.   Town-grown communities...
    B.   Speak up and voice your concerns...

(**Transition**: *As you can see, we have work to do...*)

Conclusion

V.   If we want our children and our children's children to see a healthy earth, we must take action now...

Use Transitions to Give Direction to the Speech

Transitions are words, phrases, or sentences that tie the speech ideas together and enable the listener to follow the speaker as he or she moves from one point to the next. Transitions (also called *connectives*) are a truly critical component of speeches because listeners cannot go back and re-read what they might have missed. As you develop your speech, focus on creating transitions to shift listeners from one point to the next and signal to the audience that a new point will be made. Transitions can take the form of full sentences, phrases, or single words.

Use Transitions between Speech Points

Use transitions to move between speech points: from one main point to the next, and from one subpoint to another.

When moving from one *main point* to another, **full-sentence transitions** are especially effective. For example, to move from main point I in a speech about sales contests (*"Top management should sponsor sales contests to halt the decline in sales over the past two years"*) to main point II (*"Sales contests will lead to better sales presentations"*), the speaker might use the following transition:

> Next, let's look at exactly what sales contests can do for us.

Transitions between *supporting points* can be handled using single words, phrases, or full sentences as in the following:

> Next,...

> First,... (second, third, and so forth)

> Similarly,...

> We now turn...

> If you think that's shocking, consider this...

Transitions can also serve the dual function of signaling shifts between speech points and indicating relationships between ideas, as seen in the table on p. 715.

USE TRANSITIONAL WORDS AND PHRASES

- **To show comparisons:** Similarly; In the same way; Likewise; Just as
- **To contrast ideas:** On the other hand; And yet; At the same time; In spite of; However; In contrast
- **To illustrate cause and effect:** As a result; Hence; Because; Thus; Consequently
- **To illustrate sequence of time or events:** First, second, third…; Following this; Later; Earlier; At present; In the past
- **To indicate explanation:** For example; To illustrate; In other words; To simplify; To clarify
- **To indicate additional examples:** Not only; In addition to; Let's look at
- **To emphasize significance:** Most important; Above all; Remember; Keep in mind
- **To summarize:** In conclusion; In summary; Finally; Let me conclude by saying

Use Internal Previews and Summaries as Transitions

Previews briefly introduce audience members to the ideas that the speaker will address. In a speech introduction, the **preview statement** briefly mentions the main points and thesis of the speech (see p. 726 and p. 742). Within the body itself, speakers use an **internal preview** to signal a shift from one main point or idea to another:

> Victoria Woodhull was a pioneer in many respects. Not only was she the first woman to run her own brokerage firm, she was also the first to run for the presidency of the United States, though few people know this. Let's see how she accomplished these feats.

Similar to the internal preview, the **internal summary** draws together important ideas before the speaker proceeds to another speech point. Often, a speaker will transition from one major idea or main point to the next by using an internal summary and internal preview together:

> We've seen that mountain bikes differ from road bikes in the design of the tires, the seat, the gears, the suspension systems, and the handlebars. (*internal summary*) Now let's take a look at the different types of mountain bikes themselves. As you will see, mountain bikes vary according to the type of riding they're designed to handle—downhill, trails, and cross-country. Let's begin with cross-country. (*internal preview*)

See Chapter 43, "Outlining the Speech," for guidance on including transitions in the outline of your speech.

Selecting an Organizational Pattern

Of all of the aspects of speechmaking, the idea of organizational arrangements may seem the most confusing. But selecting and organizing speech points into a pattern is easier and more natural than it might seem. An organizational pattern helps the audience follow the speaker's ideas and link points together to maximum effect. Studies confirm that the way you organize your ideas affects your audience's understanding of them, so you'll want to make use of a pattern.[1] A good time to select one is after you've researched the speech and prepared preliminary main points.

Speeches make use of at least a dozen different organizational arrangements of main and supporting points. Here we look at six commonly used patterns: chronological, spatial, causal (cause-effect), problem-solution, topical, and narrative. There are three additional patterns of organization designed specifically for persuasive speeches: *Monroe's motivated sequence*, *comparative advantage*, and *refutation*.

Arranging Speech Points Chronologically

Some topics lend themselves well to the arrangement of main points according to their occurrence in time relative to one another. A **chronological pattern**, also called a *temporal pattern*, follows the natural sequential order of the topic under consideration. Topics that describe a series of events in time (such as events leading to development of a new vaccine) or follow a set of instructions (such as steps in installing solar panels) call out for this pattern. A speech describing the development of the World Wide Web, for example, calls for a chronological, or time-ordered, sequence of main points:

Chapter 42, "Selecting an Organizational Pattern," is taken from Dan O'Hair, Hannah Rubenstein, and Rob Stewart: *A Pocket Guide to Public Speaking*, Fifth Edition, pp. 89–95 (Chapter 12, "Selecting an Organizational Pattern").

Thesis Statement:	The Internet evolved from a small network designed for military and academic scientists into a vast array of networks used by billions of people around the globe.
Main Points:	I. The Internet was first conceived in 1962 as the ARPANET to promote the sharing of research among scientists in the United States.
	II. In the 1980s, a team created TCP/IP, a language that could link networks, and the Internet as we know it was born.
	III. At the end of the Cold War, the ARPANET was decommissioned, and the World Wide Web constituted the bulk of Internet traffic.[2]

Arranging Speech Points Using a Spatial Pattern

When describing the physical arrangement of a place, a scene, or an object, logic suggests that the main points can be arranged in order of their physical proximity or direction relative to one another. This calls for a **spatial pattern**. For example, you can select a spatial arrangement when your speech provides the audience with a "tour" of a particular place:

Thesis Statement:	El Morro National Monument in New Mexico is captivating for its variety of natural and historical landmarks.
Main Points:	I. Visitors first encounter an abundant variety of plant life native to the high-country desert.
	II. Soon visitors come upon an age-old watering hole that has receded beneath the 200-foot cliffs.
	III. Beyond are the famous cliff carvings made by hundreds of travelers over several centuries of exploration in the Southwest.

In a speech describing a geothermal heating and cooling company's market growth across regions of the country, a speaker might use the spatial arrangement as follows:

Thesis Statement:	Sales of geothermal systems have grown in every region of the country.
Main Points:	I. Sales are strongest in the Eastern Zone.
	II. Sales are growing at a rate of 10 percent quarterly in the Central Zone.
	III. Sales are up slightly in the Mountain Zone.

Arranging Speech Points Using a Causal (Cause-Effect) Pattern

Some speech topics represent cause-effect relationships. Examples include (1) events leading to higher interest rates, (2) reasons students drop out of college, and (3) effects of skipping vaccinations. The main points in a **causal (cause-effect) pattern of arrangement** usually take the following form:

I. Cause

II. Effect

Sometimes a topic can be discussed in terms of multiple causes for a single effect, or a single cause for multiple effects:

MULTIPLE CAUSES FOR A SINGLE EFFECT (Reasons Students Drop Out of College)		SINGLE CAUSE FOR MULTIPLE EFFECTS (Reasons Students Drop Out of College)	
I.	Cause 1 (lack of funds)	I.	Cause (lack of funds)
II.	Cause 2 (unsatisfactory social life)	II.	Effect 1 (lowered earnings over lifetime)
III.	Cause 3 (unsatisfactory academic performance)	III.	Effect 2 (decreased job satisfaction over lifetime)
IV.	Effect (drop out of college)	IV.	Effect 3 (increased stress level over lifetime)

Some topics are best understood by presenting listeners with the effect(s) before the cause(s). In a speech on health care costs, a student speaker arranges his main points as follows:

Thesis Statement:	In response to rising health care costs, large employers are shifting part of the expense to workers.	
Main Points:	I.	(Effect) Workers are now seeing higher co-pays and deductibles.
Main Points:	II.	(Effect) Raising the amount employees must contribute has restricted employer costs to just 5 percent this year.
	III.	(Cause) The Affordable Care Act mandates that large employers offer more of their workers health care plans.
	IV.	(Cause) Rising health care costs have lead to more expensive plans at all levels of coverage.

QUICK TIP

Blend Organizational Patterns

The pattern of organization for your subpoints can differ from the pattern you select for your main points. *Do keep your main points in one pattern—this will be the predominant pattern for the speech*—but feel free to use other patterns for subpoints when it makes sense to do so. For instance, for a speech about the history of tattooing in the United States, you may choose a chronological pattern to organize the main points but use a cause-effect arrangement for some of your subpoints regarding why tattooing is on the rise today.

Arranging Speech Points Using a Problem-Solution Pattern

The **problem-solution pattern** organizes main points to demonstrate the nature and significance of a problem followed by a proposed solution. Most often used in persuasive speeches, the problem-solution pattern can be arranged as simply as two main points:

I.   Problem (define what it is)

II. Solution (offer a way to overcome the problem)

But many problem-solution speeches require more than two points to adequately explain the problem and to substantiate the recommended solution:

I.   The nature of the problem (identify its causes, incidence, etc.)

II.   Effects of the problem (explain why it's a problem, for whom, etc.)

III. Unsatisfactory solutions (discuss those that have not worked)

IV.   Proposed solution (explain why it's expected to work)

Following is a partial outline of a persuasive speech about cyber-bullying arranged in a problem-solution format.

Thesis Statement:	To combat cyber-bullying, we need to educate the public about it, report it when it happens, and punish the offenders.

Main Point:	I. Nature of cyber-bullying
	    A. Types of activities involved
	        1. Name-calling, insults
	        2. Circulation of embarrassing pictures
	        3. Sharing private information
	        4. Threats
	    B. Incidence of bullying
	    C. Profile of offenders

Main Point:	II. Effects of cyber-bullying on victims
	    A. Acting out in school
	    B. Feeling unsafe in school
	    C. Skipping school
	    D. Experiencing depression

Main Point:	III. Unsuccessful attempts at solving cyber-bullying
	    A. Let offenders and victims work it out on their own
	    B. Ignore problem, assuming it will go away

Main Point:	IV. Ways to solve cyber-bullying
	    A. Educate in schools
	    B. Report incidents to authorities
	    C. Suspend or expel offenders

Arranging Speech Points Topically

When each of the main points is a subtopic or category of the speech topic, try the **topical pattern** (also called **categorical pattern**). Consider an informative speech about choosing Chicago as a place to establish a career. You plan to emphasize three reasons for choosing Chicago: the strong economic climate of the city, its cultural variety, and its accessible public transportation. Since these three points are of relatively equal importance, they can be arranged in any order without affecting one another or the speech purpose negatively. For example:

Thesis Statement:	Chicago is an excellent place to establish a career.
Main Points:	I. Accessible transportation II. Cultural variety III. Multiple industries

This is not to say that, when using a topical arrangement, you should arrange the main points without careful consideration. Any number of considerations can factor in your ordering of points, not least of which should be the audience's most immediate needs and interests. Perhaps you have determined that listeners' main concern is the city's multiple industries, followed by an interest in its cultural variety and accessible transportation.

QUICK TIP

Find Freedom with the Topical Pattern

Topical arrangements give you the greatest freedom to structure main points according to the way you wish to present your topic. You can approach a topic by dividing it into two or more categories, for example. You can lead with your strongest evidence or leave your most compelling points until you near the conclusion. If your topic does not call out for one of the other patterns described in this chapter, be sure to experiment with the topical pattern.

Arranging Speech Points Using the Narrative Pattern

Storytelling is often a natural and effective way to get your message across. In the **narrative pattern**, the speech consists of a story or series of short stories complete with character, setting, brief plot, and vivid imagery.

In practice, a speech built largely upon a story (or series of stories) is likely to incorporate elements of other designs. You might organize the main points of the story in an effect-cause design, in which you first reveal the outcome of what happened (such as a drunken driving accident) and then describe the events that led up to the accident (the causes).

Whatever the structure, simply telling a story is no guarantee of giving a good speech. Any speech should include a clear thesis, well-organized main points, and effective transitions, so be certain to include these elements as you organize the speech.

CHECKLIST

Determining an Organizational Pattern

Does your speech...

☐ Describe a series of developments in time or a set of actions that occur sequentially? Use the *chronological pattern*.

☐ Describe or explain the physical arrangement of a place, a scene, or an object? Use the *spatial pattern*.

☐ Explain or demonstrate a topic in terms of its underlying causes or effects? Use the *causal pattern*.

☐ Demonstrate the nature and significance of a problem and justify a proposed solution? Use the *problem-solution pattern*.

☐ Stress natural divisions or categories of a topic, in which points can be moved to emphasize audience needs and interests? Use a *topical pattern*.

☐ Convey ideas through a story, using character, plot, and settings? Use a *narrative pattern*, perhaps in combination with another pattern.

Outlining the Speech

Outlines are enormously helpful in putting together a speech, providing a framework for your speech materials and a blueprint for your presentation. In an **outline** you separate main and supporting points — the major speech claims and the evidence to support them — into larger and smaller divisions and subdivisions. Plotting ideas into hierarchical fashion based on their relative importance to one another and using indentation to visually represent this hierarchy will allow you to examine the underlying logic and relationship of ideas to one another. (For a review of the principles and of the mechanics of outlining, see Chapter 41.)

Plan on Creating Two Outlines

As you develop a speech, plan on creating two outlines: a working outline (also called a *preparation or rough outline*) and a speaking, or delivery, outline. Use the **working outline** to organize and firm up main points and, with the research you've gathered, develop supporting points to substantiate them. Completed, the working outline should contain your entire speech, organized and supported to your satisfaction.

Use a **speaking outline** to practice and actually present the speech. Speaking outlines contain the working outline in condensed form and are much briefer. Figure 43.1 provides an overview of the steps involved in outlining a speech.

Use Sentences, Phrases, or Key Words

Speeches can be outlined in sentences, phrases, or key words. Working outlines typically contain sentences, reflecting much of the text of the speech; speaking outlines use key words or short phrases.

In the **sentence outline format**, each main and supporting point is stated in sentence form as a declarative statement (e.g., one that makes an assertion about something). Following is an excerpt in sentence format from a speech by Mark B. McClellan on keeping prescription drugs safe:[1]

Chapter 43, "Outlining the Speech," is taken from Dan O'Hair, Hannah Rubenstein, and Rob Stewart: *A Pocket Guide to Public Speaking*, Fifth Edition, pp. 95–108 (Chapter 13, "Outlining the Speech").

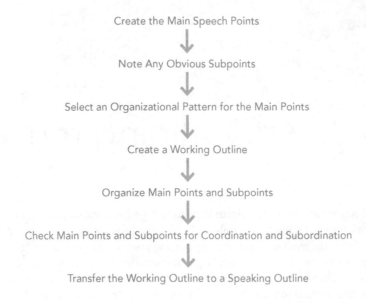

Create the Main Speech Points

↓

Note Any Obvious Subpoints

↓

Select an Organizational Pattern for the Main Points

↓

Create a Working Outline

↓

Organize Main Points and Subpoints

↓

Check Main Points and Subpoints for Coordination and Subordination

↓

Transfer the Working Outline to a Speaking Outline

FIGURE 43.1 Steps in Organizing and Outlining the Speech

I. The prescription drug supply is under attack from a variety of increasingly sophisticated threats.
    A. Technologies for counterfeiting—ranging from pill molding to dyes—have improved across the board.
    B. Inadequately regulated Internet sites have become major portals for unsafe and illegal drugs.

A **phrase outline** uses partial construction of the sentence form of each point. McClellan's sentence outline would appear as follows in phrase outline form:

I. Drug supply under attack
    A. Counterfeiting technologies more sophisticated
    B. Unregulated Internet sites

The **key-word outline** uses the smallest possible units of understanding to outline the main and supporting points. Keyword outlines encourage you to become familiar enough with your speech points that a glance at a few words is enough to remind you of exactly what to say:

I. Threats
    A. Counterfeiting
    B. Internet

Use a Key-Word Outline for Optimal Eye Contact

The type of outline you select will affect how you deliver a speech. The less you rely on reading any outline, the more eye contact you can have with audience members—an essential aspect of a successful speech. For this reason, experts recommend outlines containing key words or phrases over sentences, with the succinct key-word outline often being the preferred format. Key-word outlines permit not only the greatest degree of eye contact but also greater freedom of movement and better control of your thoughts and actions than either sentence or phrase outlines. With sufficient practice, the key words will jog your memory so that the delivery of your ideas becomes more natural.

Create a Working Outline First

Begin with a working outline before transferring your ideas to a speaking outline containing key words or shortened phrases, editing and rearranging as necessary as you work through the mass of information you've collected.

Prepare the body of the speech *before* the introduction, keeping the introduction (and the conclusion) *separate from* the main points (see sample outlines in this chapter). Since introductions serve to preview main points, you will first need to finalize them in the body. Introductions must also gain the audience's attention, introduce the topic and thesis, and establish the speaker's credibility (see Chapter 44). To ensure that you address these elements, use such labels as *Attention Getter*, *Topic and Thesis*, *Credibility Statement*, and *Preview Statement*.

SAMPLE WORKING OUTLINE

The following working outline is from a speech delivered by public speaking student Zachary Dominque. It includes all elements of the speech, including transitions, and reminders to show presentation aids (SHOW SLIDE) in magenta.

The History and Sport of Mountain Biking

Zachary Dominque
St. Edwards University

Topic:	Mountain Biking
General Speech Purpose:	To inform my listeners about the sport of mountain biking
Specific Purpose:	To help my audience gain an overview of and appreciation for mountain biking
Thesis Statement:	Mountain biking is a relatively new, exciting, and diverse sport.

Introduction
(Attention Getter)

I. Imagine that you're on a bike, plunging down a steep, rock-strewn mountain, yet fully in control.

II. Adrenaline courses through your body as you hurtle through the air, touch down on glistening pebbled streams and tangled grasses, and rocket upward again.

III. You should be scared, but you're not; in fact, you're having the time of your life.

IV. Like we say, Nirvana.

V. How many of you like to bike—ride to campus, bike for fitness, or cycle just for fun?

VI. You might own a bike with a lightweight frame and thin wheels, and use it to log some serious mileage—or possibly a comfort bike, with a nice soft seat and solid tires.

VII. Good morning, folks. My name is Zachary Dominque, and I'm a mountain biker.

VIII. I've been racing since I was eight years old and won state champion three years ago, so this topic is close to my heart.

(Preview Statement)

IX. Today, I'm going to take you on a tour of the exciting sport of mountain biking: I'll be your engine—your driver—in mountain bike–speak.

X. Our ride begins with a brief overview of mountain biking; then we'll do a hopturn—a turn in reverse— to learn about the sport's colorful history.

XI. Pedalling ahead in this beautiful autumn air, we'll chat about the various differences in design and function between mountain bikes and road bikes.

XII. We'll conclude our tour at a local bike shop, where you can compare downhill, trail, and cross-country mountain bikes.

XIII. These are the three main types of mountain bikes, designed for the three major types of mountain biking.

XIV. I hope by then that you'll catch a little bit of mountain biking fever and see why I find it such an exciting, intense, and physically challenging sport.

Transition:	Mountain biking is a sport that can be extreme, recreational, or somewhere in between. But no matter what kind of rider you are, it's always a great way to get out in the natural world and get the adrenaline going. To start, let me briefly define mountain biking.

Body

I. The website ABC of Mountain Biking offers a good basic definition: "Mountain biking is a form of cycling on off-road or unpaved surfaces such as mountain trails and dirt roads; the biker uses a bicycle with a sturdy frame and fat tires."

   A. The idea behind mountain biking is to go where other bikes won't take you.

      1. Mountain bikers ride on backcountry roads and on single-track trails winding through fields or forests.

      2. They climb up steep, rock-strewn hills and race down over them.

      3. The focus is on self-reliance, because these bikers often venture miles from help.

   B. According to the National Bicycle Dealers Association website, in 2013 mountain bikes accounted for 25 percent of all bikes sold in the United States.

      1. If you factor in sales of the comfort bike, which is actually a mountain bike modified for purely recreational riders, sales jump to nearly 38 percent of all bikes sold.

      2. Some 50 million Americans love riding their mountain bikes, according to data collected by the New England Mountain Bike Association.

Transition:	So you see that mountain biking is popular with a lot of people. But the sport itself is fairly new.

II. The history of mountain biking is less than 50 years old, and its founders are still around.

   A. The man in this picture is Gary Fisher, one of the founders of mountain biking. (SHOW PHOTO)

   B. According to *The Original Mountain Bike Book*, written in 1998 by pioneering mountain bikers Rob van der Plas and Charles Kelly, they, along with Fisher, Joe Breeze, and other members of the founding posse from the Marin County, California, area, were instrumental in founding the modern sport of mountain biking in the early 1970s.

   C. Mountain bikes—called MTBs or ATBs (for all-terrain bikes)—didn't exist then as we now know them, so as you can see in this picture of Gary Fisher, he's riding a modified one-speed Schwinn cruiser. (SHOW GARY)

      1. Cruisers, or "ballooners," aren't made to go off road at all.

      2. Nothing equips them to navigate trails, and their brakes aren't remotely equipped to handle stops on steep descents.

      3. But this is the type of bike Fisher and others started out with.

D. By the mid-1970s, growing numbers of bikers in California got into using modified cruisers to race downhill on rocky trails.

   1. They'd meet at the bottom of Mount Tamalpais, in Corte Madera, California.

   2. They'd walk their bikes a mile or two up its steep slopes, and hurl on down.

E. As even more people got involved, Charles Kelly and others organized the famed Repack Downhill Race on Mt. Tam.

   1. Held from 1976 to 1979, the Repack race became a magnet for enthusiasts and put the sport on the map, according to *The Original Mountain Bike Book.*

Transition:	The reason why the race was called "Repack" is a story in itself.

   2. The trail in the Repack race plummeted 1,300 feet in less than 2 miles, according to the Marin Museum of Biking website.

      a. Such a steep drop meant constant braking, which in turn required riders to replace, or "repack," their bikes' grease after nearly each run.

      b. As Breeze recounts in his own words: "The bikes' antiquated hub coaster brake would get so hot that the grease would vaporize, and after a run or two, the hub had to be repacked with new grease."

Transition:	As you might imagine, these early enthusiasts eventually tired of the routine.

F. The bikers had tinkered with their bikes from the start, adding gearing, drum brakes, and suspension systems.

G. In 1979, Joe Breeze designed a new frame—called the "Breezer"—which became the first actual mountain bike.

H. By 1982, as van der Plas and Kelly write in *The Original Mountain Bike Book*, standardized production of mountain bikes finally took off.

Transition:	Now that you've learned a bit of the history of mountain biking, let's look at what today's mountain bike can do. To make things clearer, I'll compare them to road bikes. Road bikes are the class of bikes that cyclists who compete in the Tour de France use.

III. Mountain bikes and road bikes are built for different purposes.

  A. Mountain bikes are built to tackle rough ground, while road bikes are designed to ride fast on paved, smooth surfaces.

    1. To accomplish their task, mountain bikes feature wide tires with tough tread.

    2. In contrast, road bike tires are ultrathin and their frames extremely lightweight.

      a. If you take a road bike off-road, chances are you'll destroy it.

      b. Without the knobby tread and thickness found on mountain bike tires, road bike tires can't grip onto the rocks and other obstacles that cover off-road courses.

  B. The handlebars on the bikes also differ, as you can see here. (SHOW HANDLEBARS)

    1. Mountain bikes feature flat handlebars; these keep us in an upright stance, so that we don't flip over when we hit something.

    2. The drop handlebars on road bikes require the cyclist to lean far forward; this position suits road cycling, which prizes speed.

  C. The gears and suspension systems also differentiate mountain bikes from road bikes.

    1. Mountain bikes use lower gears than road bikes and are more widely spaced, giving them more control to ride difficult terrain.

    2. As for suspension, road bikes generally don't have any kind of suspension system that can absorb power.

      a. That is, they don't have shock absorbers because they're not supposed to hit anything.

      b. Imagine riding over rocks and roots without shocks; it wouldn't be pretty.

    3. Many mountain bikes have at least a great front shock absorbing suspension system.

      a. Some have rear-suspension systems.

      b. Some bikes have dual systems.

Transition:	I hope by now you have a sense of the mountain bike design. But there are finer distinctions to draw.

IV. There are actually three different types of mountain bikes, designed to accommodate the three major kinds of mountain biking—downhill, trails, and cross-country.

Transition:	Let's start with downhill. (SHOW BIKE)

  A. Downhill bikes have the fewest gears of the three types of mountain bikes and weigh the most.

    1. That's because downhill biking is a daredevil sport—these bikers are crazy!

    2. They slide down hills at insane speeds, and they go off jumps.

B.   As described on the website Trails.com, downhill racers catch a shuttle going up the mountain, then speed downhill while chewing up obstacles.

C.   Think of downhill racing as skiing with a bike.

Transition:	Now let's swing by trails biking.

D.   Trails bikes look quite different than either downhill or cross-country bikes. (SHOW TRAIL BIKE)

  1.   They have very small wheels, measuring either 20, 24, or 26 inches, and smaller frames.

  2.   These differences in design help trail bikers do what they do best: jump over obstacles—cars, rocks, and large logs.

E.   The trail biker's goal is to not put a foot down on the ground.

F.   Trail bike racing is one of the few types of biking that's done by time, not all at a mass start.

Transition:	The third major type of mountain biking, cross-country, or XC cycling, is my sport. (SHOW XC)

G.   Cross-country biking is also the most common type of mountain biking—and the one sponsored by the Olympics.

  1.   That's right. According to Olympic.org, in 1996, mountain biking became an Olympic sport.

  2.   This was just two decades after its inception.

H.   With cross-country, you get the best of all worlds, at least in my humble opinion.

  1.   The courses are creative, incorporating hills and valleys and rough to not-so-rough terrain.

  2.   If done competitively, cross-country biking is like competing in a marathon.

  3.   Done recreationally, it offers you the chance to see the great outdoors while getting, or staying, in great shape.

I.   Cross-country bikes come in two forms.

  1.   XC bikes are very lightweight, with either full or partial suspension.

  2.   The Trails/Marathon XC hybrid bikes are a bit heavier, with full suspension; XC bikes are designed for seriously long rides.

Transition:	Well, it has been quite a tour, folks. **(Signals close of speech)**

Conclusion

I.   Our course began with an overview of mountain biking and a hopturn into a brief history of the sport.

II. We also learned about the differences between mountain bikes and road bikes, and the three major categories of mountain bikes. *(Summarizes main points)*

III. To me, mountain biking, and especially cross-country, is the perfect sport—fulfilling physical, spiritual, and social needs.

IV. It's a great sport to take up recreationally. *(Leaves audience with something to think about)*

V.   And if you decide to mountain bike competitively, just remember: ride fast, drive hard, and leave your blood on every trail. *(Memorable close)*

Works Cited

"Cycling, Mountain Biking," Olympics.org website, accessed February 15, 2015, www.olympic. org/Assets/OSC%20Section /pdf/QR_sports_summer/Sports_Olympiques_VTT_eng.pdf.

"The Economics and Benefits of Mountain Biking," New England Mountain Bike Association, accessed February 15, 2015, www.nemba.org.

"History of Mountain Biking," Marin Museum of Biking website, accessed February 15, 2015 http://mmbhof.org/mtn-bike-hall-of-fame/history.

"Industry Overview, 2013," National Bicycle Dealers Association, accessed February 15, 2015, http://nbda.com/articles/industry-overview-2012-pg34.htm.

"Types of Mountain Bikes," Trails.com, accessed February 15, 2015, www.trails.com/types-of-mountain-bikes.html.

Van der Plas, Rob, and Charles Kelly. *The Original Mountain Bike Book*. Minneapolis: Motorbooks, 1998.

"What Is Mountain Biking," ABC of Mountain Biking website, accessed February 15, 2015, www. abc-of-mountainbiking.com/mountain-biking-basics/whatis-mountain-biking.asp.

Prepare a Speaking Outline for Delivery

Using the same numbering system as the working outline, condense long phrases or sentences into key words or short phrases, including just enough words to jog your memory. Include any *delivery cues* that will be part of the speech (see below). Place the speaking outline on large (at least 4 × 6-inch) notecards, 8.5 × 11-inch sheets of paper, or in a speaker's notes software program or app (see Chapter 51). Print large enough, or use large-enough fonts, so that you can see the words at a glance.

Indicate Delivery Cues

Include any **delivery cues** that will be part of the speech. To ensure visibility, capitalize the cues, place them in parentheses, and/or highlight them.

Delivery Cue	Example
Transitions	(TRANSITION)
Timing	(PAUSE)
	(SLOW DOWN)
Speaking Rate/Volume	(SLOWLY)
	(LOUDER)
Presentation Aids	(SHOW MODEL)
	(SLIDE 3)
Source	(ATLANTA CONSTITUTION, August 2, 2015)
Statistic	(2015, boys to girls = 94,232; U.S. Health Human Services)
Quotation	Eubie Blake, 100: "If I'd known I was gonna live this long, I'd have taken better care of myself."

Practice the Speech

The key to the successful delivery of a speech using a key-word outline is practice. For more information on practicing the speech, see Chapter 48.

SAMPLE SPEAKING OUTLINE

The History and Sport of Mountain Biking

Zachary Dominque
St. Edwards University

Introduction
(Attention Getter)

I.   Imagine on bike, plunging rock-strewn, yet control.

II. Adrenaline, hurtle, touch downstream, rocket.

III. Be scared, but not—time of life.

IV. Nirvana.

V.   How many bike, fitness, fun?

VI. Might own lightweight, thin wheels, serious mileage—or comfort, soft seat, solid tires.

VII. Morning, Zachary, MTBer.

VIII. Eight; champion, heart.

(Preview Statement)

IX.   Today, tour, exciting sport of…engine, driver, MTB-speak.

X.   Ride begins brief overview; do hopturn—colorful history.

XI.   Pedaling ahead autumn, chat differences between mountain, road.

XII. Conclude shop, compare MTBs.

XIII. Three types bikes, designed for three…

XIV. Hope catch fever, exciting, intense, and physically.

> **Transition:**   MTB sport extreme…in-between. But no matter, always great way natural world, adrenaline. Start, define.

Body

I.   ABC/MB def: "MTB is a form of cycling on off-road or unpaved surfaces such as mountain trails and dirt roads; the biker uses a bicycle with a sturdy frame and fat tires."

   A.   The idea—go where others.

      1.   MTBs ride backcountry, single-track winding fields, forests.

      2.   Climb steep, rock-strewn, race down.

      3.   Self-reliance, miles from help.

   B.   National Bicycle Dealers Assoc., 2013 MTBs 25 percent sold.

      1.   Factor comfort, actually MTB modified recreational, sales 38 percent.

      2.   50 million love riding, data gathered NE MTB Assn.

> **Transition:**   So MTB popular people. But fairly new.

II. History MTB less 50, founders.

   A.   Gary Fisher, founders MTB. (SHOW PICTURE)

   B.   *Original Mountain Bike Book*, written 1998 by van der Plas, Kelly; they, along with Fisher, Breeze, other members posse Marin, instrumental founding modern sport early 1970s.

   C.   MTBs or ATBs (terrain)—didn't exist, so picture Fisher, modified Schwinn cruiser. (SHOW PICTURE)

      1.   Cruisers, "ballooners," off-road.

      2.   Nothing equips navigate, brakes equipped stops descents.

      3.   But bike Fisher, others started.

   D.   Mid-1970s, growing numbers using modified race downhill.

      1.   Meet bottom Tamalpais, CA.

      2.   Walk bikes mile up steep, hurl.

   E.   Even involved, Kelly, others organized Repack.

      1.   1976–1979, magnet enthusiasts, on map, *Original MTB*.

| Transition: | Reason called "Repack" story itself. |

2. Trail plummeted 1,300 feet 2 miles, according Breeze article posted MTB Fame website.

   a. Such drop constant braking, required riders replace, "repack," grease each run.

   b. Breeze recounts: "The bikes' antiquated hub coaster brake would get so hot that the grease would vaporize, and after a run or two, the hub had to be repacked with new grease."

| Transition: | Might imagine, early enthusiasts tired. |

F. Bikers tinkered, gearing, drum, suspension.

G. 1979, Breeze new frame—"Breezer"—first actual MTB.

H. 1982, as van der Plas, Kelly write in *Original MTB*, standardized took off.

| Transition: | Now learned history, let's look today's can do. Clearer, compare road. Class cyclists Tour de France use. |

III. MTB, road built different purposes.

   A. MTB tackle rough, road designed fast, paved, smooth.

      1. Accomplish task, wide tire, tough tread.

      2. In contrast, road ultrathin, frames lightweight.

         a. Take off-road, destroy.

         b. Without knobby tread, thickness MTB tires, road can't grip rocks, obstacles.

   B. Handlebars differ.

      1. MTB flat; upright stance, don't flip.

      2. Drop handlebars require lean forward; suits road cycling, prizes speed.

   C. Gears, suspension also differentiate.

      1. MTB lower gears, widely spaced—more control difficult terrain.

      2. As for suspension, road don't, absorb power.

         a. That is, don't have shock, not supposed to.

         b. Imagine without shocks; wouldn't be pretty.

      3. Many MTBs at least a great front.

         a. Some rear.

         b. Some dual.

| Transition: | Hope sense MTB design. But finer distinctions to draw. |

IV. Actually three types MTB, accommodate three kinds.

> **Transition:** Let's start with downhill.

A. Downhill fewest gears, weigh most.
   1. Because downhill daredevil—crazy!
   2. Slide insane, off jumps.
B. Trails.com, downhill racers catch shuttle going up, speed downhill chewing up.
C. Think racing skiing bike.

> **Transition:** Now let's swing by trails biking.

D. Trails bikes look different than either.
   1. Small wheels, 20, 24, or 26, smaller frames.
   2. Differences design help trail do best—jump obstacles—cars, rocks, large logs.
E. Trail goal not foot on ground.
F. Trail racing few types done by time, not mass.

> **Transition:** Third major type MTB, cross-country, or XC.

G. Cross-country most common—Olympics.
   1. That's right. In 1996…
   2. Just two decades inception.
H. With XC, best all worlds, humble.
   1. Courses creative, incorporating hills, valleys, rough, not-so.
   2. Competitively, XC like marathon.
   3. Recreationally, chance see outdoors, shape.
I. XC two forms.
   1. Lightweight, full or partial.
   2. Trails/Marathon XC hybrids heavier, full suspension; designed seriously long.

> **Transition:** Quite tour. **(Signals close of speech)**

Conclusion
I. Course began overview, hopturn history sport.
II. Also learned differences: mountain, road, three major categories of MTB, three types MTB accommodate fans. **(Summarizes main points)**
III. To me, MTB, especially XC, perfect—fulfilling physical, spiritual, social needs.
IV. Great take up recreationally. **(Leaves audience with something to think about)**
V. Decide bike competitively, remember: ride fast, drive hard, leave blood. **(Memorable close)**

CHECKLIST

Steps in Creating a Speaking Outline

- ☐ Create the outline on sheets of paper, large notecards, or software app.
- ☐ Write large and legibly using at least a 14-point font or easy-to-read ink and large letters.
- ☐ For each main and subpoint, choose a key word or phrase that will jog your memory accurately.
- ☐ Include delivery cues.
- ☐ Write out full quotations or other critical information.
- ☐ Using the speaking outline, practice the speech at least five times, or as needed.

part 9

Public Speaking: Starting, Finishing, and Styling

CHAPTER
44
Developing the Introduction and Conclusion

A compelling introduction and conclusion, although not a substitute for a well-developed speech body, are nevertheless essential to its success. A good opening previews what's to come in a way that engages listeners in the topic and speaker. An effective conclusion ensures that the audience remembers the message and reacts in a way that the speaker intends.

Any kind of supporting material—examples, stories, testimony, facts, or statistics; see Chapter 38—can be used to open and conclude a speech as long as it accomplishes these objectives.

Preparing the Introduction

The choices you make about the introduction can affect the outcome of the entire speech. In the first several minutes (one speaker pegs it at twenty seconds),[1] audience members will decide whether they are interested in the topic of your speech and whether they will believe what you say.

A speech introduction serves to:

- Arouse the audience's attention and willingness to listen.
- Introduce the topic and purpose.
- Establish your credibility to speak on the topic.
- Preview the main points.
- Motivate the audience to accept your speech goals.

Chapter 44, "Developing the Introduction and Conclusion," is taken from Dan O'Hair, Hannah Rubenstein, and Rob Stewart: *A Pocket Guide to Public Speaking*, Fifth Edition, pp. 110–116 (Chapter 14, "Developing the Introduction and Conclusion").

CHECKLIST

Guidelines for Preparing the Introduction

☐ Prepare the introduction after you've completed the speech body so you will know exactly what you need to preview.

☐ Keep the introduction brief—as a rule, no more than 10 to 15 percent of the entire speech.

☐ Practice delivering your introduction until you feel confident you've got it right.

Gain Audience Attention

An introduction must first of all win the audience's attention. They must believe the speech will interest them and offer them something of benefit. Some time-honored techniques of doing this include sharing a compelling story, establishing common ground, providing unusual information, posing a question, using humor, and offering a quotation.

Tell A Story

Noted speechwriter and language expert William Safire once remarked that stories are "surefire attention getters."[2] Stories, or *narratives*, that are directly relevant to your message encourage audience identification and involvement. Speeches that begin with brief stories of interesting, humorous, or real-life incidents also boost speaker credibility and promote greater understanding and retention of the speaker's message.[3] You can relate an entire story (if brief) in the introduction, or, alternatively, offer part of one, indicating you will return to it further on in the speech.

QUICK TIP

Show Them the Transformation

Stories often feature transformation—how people overcome obstacles or otherwise experience change.[4] One powerful means of gaining audience involvement is to tell a story in which others were changed by adopting beliefs and behaviors similar to those you are proposing in your speech. If you can think of a story that does this, your message is likely to be doubly persuasive.

Establish Common Ground

Refer to the occasion that has brought you together, and use your knowledge of the audience to touch briefly on areas of shared experience. Audiences are won over when speakers express interest in them and show that they share in the audience's concerns and goals. This creates goodwill and a feeling of common ground (or *identification;* see also Chapter 36).

Offer Unusual Information

"Sean Connery wore a wig in every single one of his Bond performances." Surprising audience members with unusual facts is one of the surest ways to get their attention. Some the most effective statements are based in statistics, a powerful means of illustrating consequences and relationships that can quickly bring points into focus, as in this opener by Chef James Oliver: "Sadly, in the next eighteen minutes when I do our chat, four Americans that are alive will be dead from the food they eat."[5]

Pose A Provocative Question

"How long do you think our water supply will last?" Posing a question of vital interest to the audience can be an effective way to draw the audience's attention to what you are about to say. These sorts of questions are usually rhetorical, in that they do not invite actual responses, but instead make the audience think. Sometimes a speaker will use a series of **rhetorical questions** to introduce different aspects of his or her topic.

Use Humor

Handled well, humor can build rapport and set a positive tone for the speech. But humor can also easily backfire. Telling a series of unrelated jokes without making a relevant point will detract from your purpose, and few things turn an audience off more quickly than tasteless humor. Strictly avoid humor or sarcasm that belittles others—whether on the basis of race, sex, ability, or otherwise. A good rule of thumb is that speech humor should always match the rhetorical situation.

Use A Quotation

A Czech proverb says, "Do not protect yourself by a fence but rather by your friends." A quotation that elegantly and succinctly expresses a theme of the speech will draw the audience's attention. Quotations can be culled from literature, poetry, and film, or directly from people you know.

State the Topic and Purpose

Once you've gained the audience's attention, use the introduction to alert listeners to the speech topic and purpose. Declare what your speech is about and what you hope to accomplish.

Topic and purpose are clearly revealed in this introduction by Marvin Runyon, former postmaster general of the United States:

> This afternoon, I want to examine the truth of that statement—"Nothing moves people like the mail, and no one moves the mail like the U.S. Postal Service." I want to look at where we are today as a communications industry, and where we intend to be in the days and years ahead.[6]

Establish Credibility as a Speaker

During the introduction, audience members make a decision about whether they are interested not just in your topic but also in you. They want to feel that they can trust what you have to say—that they can believe in your *ethos*, or good character. To build credibility, offer a simple statement of your qualifications for speaking on the topic. Briefly emphasize some experience, knowledge, or perspective you have that is different from or more extensive than that of your audience.

Preview the Main Points

Once you've revealed the topic and purpose and established your credibility, briefly preview the main points of the speech. This helps audience members mentally organize the speech as they follow along. An introductory **preview statement** is straightforward. You simply tell the audience what the main points will be and in what order you will address them. Save your in-depth discussion of each one for the body of your speech.

Robert L. Darbelnet effectively introduces his topic, purpose, and main points with this preview statement:

> My remarks today are intended to give you a sense of AAA's ongoing efforts to improve America's roads. Our hope is that you will join your voices to ours as we call on the federal government to do three things:
>
> Number one: Perhaps the most important, provide adequate funding for highway maintenance and improvements.
>
> Number two: Play a strong, responsible, yet flexible role in transportation programs.
>
> And number three: Invest in highway safety.
>
> Let's see what our strengths are, what the issues are, and what we can do about them.[7]

Motivate the Audience to Accept Your Goals

A final and critical function of the introduction is to motivate the audience to care about your topic and make it relevant to them. You may choose to convey what the audience stands to gain by the information you will share or convince audience members that your speech purpose is consistent with their motives and values. A student speech about the value of interview training shows how this can be accomplished:

> Why do you need interview training? It boils down to competition. As in sports, when you're not training, someone else is out there training to beat you. All things being equal, the person who has the best interviewing skills has got the edge.

CHECKLIST

Craft an Effective Introduction

- ☐ Use stories, unusual facts, quotes, or humor to capture the audience's attention and stimulate their interest.
- ☐ Establish a positive common bond with listeners, perhaps by referring to the purpose of the occasion.
- ☐ Alert listeners to the speech purpose and topic.
- ☐ Establish your credibility to address the topic.
- ☐ Preview the main points of the speech.
- ☐ Motivate listeners to accept your speech goals by conveying the benefits of your topic.

Preparing the Conclusion

Just as a well-crafted introduction gets your speech effectively out of the starting gate, a well-constructed conclusion gives you the opportunity to drive home your purpose and leave the audience inspired to think about and even to act upon your ideas. The conclusion consists of several elements that end the speech effectively. Conclusions serve to:

- Signal that the speech is coming to an end and provide closure.
- Summarize the key points.
- Reiterate the thesis or central idea of the speech.
- Remind the audience of how your ideas will benefit them.
- Challenge the audience to remember and possibly act upon your ideas.
- End the speech memorably.

Signal the End of the Speech and Provide Closure

People who listen to speeches are taking a journey of sorts, and they want and need the speaker to acknowledge the journey's end. They look for logical and emotional closure.

One signal that a speech is about to end is a transitional word or phrase: *finally, looking back, in conclusion, let me close by saying* (see Chapter 41). You can also signal closure by adjusting your manner of delivery; for example, you can vary your tone, pitch, rhythm, and rate of speech to indicate that the speech is winding down (see Chapters 47 and 48).

Summarize the Key Points

One bit of age-old advice for giving a speech is "Tell them what you are going to tell them (in the introduction), tell them (in the body), and tell them what you told them (in the conclusion)." The idea is that emphasizing the main points three times will help the audience to remember them. A restatement of points in the conclusion brings the speech full circle and gives the audience a sense of completion. Consider how Holger Kluge, in a speech titled "Reflections on Diversity," summarizes his main points:

> I have covered a lot of ground here today. But as I draw to a close, I'd like to stress three things.
>
> First, diversity is more than equity....
>
> Second, weaving diversity into the very fabric of your organization takes time....
>
> Third, diversity will deliver bottom line results to your businesses and those results will be substantial....[8]

Reiterate the Topic and Speech Purpose

The conclusion should reiterate the topic and speech purpose—to imprint it on the audience's memory. In the conclusion to a speech about the U.S. immigration debate, Elpidio Villarreal reminds his listeners of his central idea:

> Two paths are open to us. One path would keep us true to our fundamental values as a nation and a people. The other would lead us down a dark trail; one marked by 700-mile-long fences, emergency detention centers and vigilante border patrols. Because I really am an American, heart and soul, and because that means never being without hope, I still believe we will ultimately choose the right path. We have to.[9]

CHECKLIST

Guidelines for Preparing the Conclusion

- ☐ As with the introduction, prepare the conclusion after you've completed the speech body.

- ☐ Do not leave the conclusion to chance. Include it with your speaking outline.

- ☐ Keep the conclusion brief—as a rule, no more than 10 to 15 percent, or about one-sixth, of the overall speech. Conclude soon after you say you are about to end.

- ☐ Carefully consider your use of language. More than in other parts of the speech, the conclusion can contain words that inspire and motivate (see Chapter 45).

- ☐ Practice delivering your conclusion until you feel confident you've got it right.

- ☐ Once you've signaled the end of your speech, conclude in short order (though not abruptly).

Challenge the Audience to Respond

A strong conclusion challenges audience members to put to use what the speaker has shared with them. In an *informative speech*, the speaker challenges audience members to use what they've learned in a way that benefits them. In a *persuasive speech*, the challenge usually comes in the form of a **call to action**. Here the speaker challenges listeners to act in response to the speech, see the problem in a new way, or change both their actions and their beliefs about the problem.

Hillary Rodham Clinton makes a strong call to action in her conclusion to an address presented to the United Nations World Conference on Women:

> We have seen peace prevail in most places for a half century. We have avoided another world war. But we have not solved older, deeply rooted problems that continue to diminish the potential of half the world's population. *Now it is time to act on behalf of women everywhere.* If we take bold steps to better the lives of women, we will be taking bold steps to better the lives of children and families too.... Let this conference be our—and the world's—call to action.[10]

Bring Your Speech Full Circle

Picking up on a story or an idea you mentioned in the introduction can be a memorable way to close a speech and bring the entire presentation full circle. You can provide the resolution of the story ("what happened next?") or reiterate the link between the moral (lesson) of the story and the speech theme.

Make the Conclusion Memorable

A speech that makes a lasting impression is one that listeners are most likely to remember and act on. To accomplish this, make use of the same devices for capturing attention described for use in introductions — quotations, stories, questions, startling statements, humor, and references to the audience and the occasion.

CHECKLIST

Craft an Effective Conclusion

- [ ] Signal the start of the conclusion with a transition.
- [ ] End your speech soon after you signal you're about to close.
- [ ] Plan for a conclusion that is no more than about one-sixth of the time spent on the body of the speech.
- [ ] Reiterate your main points.
- [ ] Remind listeners of the speech topic and purpose.
- [ ] Reiterate the benefits of your topic.
- [ ] Include a challenge or call to action to motivate the audience to respond to your ideas or appeals, particularly if your goal is to persuade.
- [ ] Consider referring back upon story, unusual fact, or quotations you used in your introduction to provide a sense of closure and make a lasting impression.

Using Language

Words are the public speaker's tools of the trade, and the ones you choose to style your speech will play a crucial role in creating a dynamic connection with your audience. The right words help listeners understand, believe in, and retain your message.

Use an Oral Style

Speeches require an **oral style**—the use of language that is simpler, more repetitious, more rhythmic, and more interactive than written language.[1] Speeches therefore must be prepared for the ear—to be *heard* rather than read. This is particularly important because unlike readers, listeners have only one chance to get the message.

Strive for Simplicity

To ensure understanding, express yourself simply, without pretentious language or unnecessary **jargon** (the specialized, "insider" language of a given profession). Speak in commonly understood terms and choose the simpler of two synonyms: "guess" rather than "extrapolate;" "use" rather than "utilize." Use fewer rather than more words, and shorter sentences rather than longer ones. As speechwriter Peggy Noonan notes in her book *Simply Speaking:*

> Good hard simple words with good hard clear meanings are good things to use when you speak. They are like pickets in a fence, slim and unimpressive on their own but sturdy and effective when strung together.[2]

Chapter 45, "Using Language," is taken from Dan O'Hair, Hannah Rubenstein, and Rob Stewart: *A Pocket Guide to Public Speaking*, Fifth Edition, pp. 117–123 (Chapter 15, "Using Language").

> ## QUICK TIP
>
> ### Experiment with Phrases and Sentence Fragments
>
> In line with an oral style, experiment with using phrases and sentence fragments in place of full sentences. This speaker, a physician, demonstrates how short phrases can add punch to a speech: "I'm just a simple bone-and-joint guy. I can set your broken bones. Take away your bunions. Even give you a new hip. But I don't mess around with the stuff between the ears....That's another specialty."[3]

Make Frequent Use of Repetition

Repetition is key to oral style, serving to compensate for natural lapses in listening and to reinforce information. Even very brief speeches repeat key words and phrases. Repetition adds emphasis to important ideas, helps listeners follow your logic, and imbues language with rhythm and drama.

Use Personal Pronouns

Audience members want to know what the speaker thinks and feels, and to be assured that he or she recognizes them and relates them to the message. The direct form of address, using the personal pronouns such as *we*, *us*, *I*, and *you*, helps to create this feeling of recognition and inclusion. Note how Sheryl Sandberg, Chief Operating Officer of Facebook, uses personal pronouns to begin a speech on why there are too few women leaders:

> So for any of *us* in this room today, let's start out by admitting *we're* lucky. *We* don't live in the world *our* mothers lived in, *our* grandmothers lived in, where career choices for women were so limited....But all that aside, *we* still have a problem....Women are not making it to the top of any profession anywhere in the world.[4]

Choose Concrete Language and Vivid Imagery

Concrete words and vivid imagery engage audience members' senses, enlivening a speech. **Concrete language** is specific, tangible, and definite. Words such as "mountain," "spoon," "dark," and "heavy" describe things we can physically sense (see, hear, taste, smell, and touch). In contrast, **abstract language** is general or nonspecific, leaving meaning open to interpretation. Abstract words, such as "peace," "freedom," and "love," are purely conceptual; they have no physical reference. Politicians use abstract language to appeal to mass audiences, or to be noncommittal: "We strive for peace." In most speaking situations, however, listeners will appreciate concrete nouns and verbs.

Note how concrete words add precision and color:

Abstract:	The old road was bad.
Concrete:	The road was pitted with muddy craters and nearly swallowed up by huge outcroppings of dark gray granite.

Offer Vivid Imagery

Imagery is concrete language that brings into play the senses of smell, taste, sight, hearing, and touch to paint mental pictures. Vivid imagery is more easily recalled than colorless language,[5] and speeches containing ample imagery elicit more positive responses than those that do not.[6]

Adding imagery into your speech need not be difficult if you focus on using concrete and colorful adjectives and strong verbs. Substitute passive forms of the verb "to be" (e.g., *is, are, was, were, will be…*) with more active verb forms. Rather than "the houses were empty," use "the houses stood empty." You can use descriptive adjectives to modify nouns as well as verbs, as in *"dilapidated* house." President Franklin D. Roosevelt famously did this when he portrayed the Japanese bombing of Pearl Harbor as "the dark hour,"[7] conveying with one simple adjective the gravity of the attack.

Choose Strong Verbs

Mundane	Verb Colorful Alternative
look	behold, gaze, glimpse, peek, stare
walk	stride, amble, stroll, skulk
throw	hurl, fling, pitch
sit	sink, plop, settle
eat	devour, inhale, gorge

Use Figures of Speech

Figures of speech, including similes, metaphors, and analogies, make striking comparisons that help listeners visualize, identify with, and understand the speaker's ideas. A **simile** explicitly compares one thing to another, using *like* or *as:* "He works like a dog," and "The old woman's hands were as soft as a baby's." A **metaphor** also compares two things, but does so by describing one thing as actually *being* the other: "Time is a thief."

An **analogy** is simply an extended metaphor or simile that compares an unfamiliar concept or process to a more familiar one. For example, African American minister Phil Wilson used metaphoric language when he preached about the dangers of AIDS:

> Our house is on fire! The fire truck arrives, but we won't come out, because we're afraid the folks from next door will see that we're in that burning house. AIDS is a fire raging in our community and it's out of control![8]

As useful as analogies are, they can mislead audience members if used carelessly. A **faulty analogy** is an inaccurate or misleading comparison suggesting that because two things are similar in some ways, they are necessarily similar in others.

QUICK TIP

Avoid Clichés and Mixed Metaphors

Try to avoid predictable and stale metaphors and similes, known as **clichés**, such as "sold like hotcakes" (a clichéd simile) and "pearly white teeth" (a clichéd metaphor). Beware, too, of **mixed metaphors**, or those that compare unlike images or expressions: for example, "Burning the midnight oil at both ends" incorrectly joins the expressions "burning the midnight oil" and "burning the candle at both ends." Other figures of speech that contribute to vivid imagery include personification, understatement, irony, allusion, hyperbole, and onomatopoeia.

Choose Words That Build Credibility

Audiences expect speakers to be competent and credible. To project these qualities, use language that is appropriate, accurate, assertive, and respectful.

Use Words Appropriately

The language you use in a speech should be appropriate to the audience, the occasion, and the subject matter. Listeners view speakers who use General American (GA) English as more competent—though not necessarily more trustworthy or likable—than those who speak in a distinctive dialect (regional variation of speech).[9] At times, however, it may be appropriate to mix casual language, dialects, or even slang into your speech. Done carefully, the selective use of dialect, sometimes called **code-switching**, can imbue your speech with friendliness, humor, earthiness, honesty, and nostalgia.[10] The key is to ensure that your meaning is clear and your use is appropriate for your audience. Consider the following excerpt:

On the gulf where I was raised, *el valle del Rio Grande* in South Texas—that triangular piece of land wedged between the river *y el golfo* which serves as the Texas–U.S./Mexican border—is a Mexican *pueblito* called Hargill.[11]

Use Words Accurately

Audiences lose confidence in speakers who misuse words. Check that your words mean what you intend, and beware of **malapropisms**—the inadvertent, incorrect uses of a word or phrase in place of one that sounds like it[12] ("It's a strange receptacle" for "It's a strange spectacle").

Use the Active Voice

Voice is the feature of verbs that indicates the subject's relationship to the action. Speaking in the active rather than passive voice will make your statements—and the audience's perception of you as the speaker—clear and assertive instead of indirect and weak. A verb is in the *active voice* when the subject performs the action, and in the *passive voice* when the subject is acted upon or is the receiver of the action:

Passive:	A test was announced by Ms. Carlos for Tuesday.
	A president is elected every four years.
Active:	Ms. Carlos announced a test for Tuesday.
	The voters elect a president every four years.

Use Culturally Sensitive and Gender-Neutral Language

Be alert to using language that reflects respect for audience members' cultural beliefs, norms, and traditions. Review and eliminate any language that reflects unfounded assumptions, negative descriptions, or stereotypes of a given group's age, class, gender, ability, and geographic, ethnic, racial, or religious characteristics. Consider, too, whether certain seemingly well-known names and terms may be foreign to some listeners, and include brief explanations for them. Sayings specific to a certain region or group of people—termed **colloquial expressions** or *idioms*—such as "back the wrong horse" and "ballpark figure" can add color and richness to a speech, but only if listeners understand them.

Word your speech with gender-neutral language: Avoid the third-person generic masculine pronouns *(his, he)* in favor of inclusive pronouns such as *his* or *her, he* or *she, we, our, you, your,* or other gender-neutral terms.

QUICK TIP

Denotative versus Connotative Meaning

When drafting your speech, choose words that are both denotatively and connotatively appropriate to the audience. The **denotative meaning** of a word is its literal, or dictionary, definition. The **connotative meaning** of a word is the special (often emotional) association that different people bring to bear on it. For example, you may agree that you are "angry," but not "irate," and "thrifty" but not "cheap." Consider how the connotative meanings of your word choices might affect the audience's response to your message, including those of non-native speakers of English.

Choose Words That Create a Lasting Impression

Language artfully arranged and infused with rhythm draws listeners in and leaves a lasting impression on audience members. You can create a cadenced arrangement of language through **rhetorical devices** such as repetition, alliteration, and parallelism.

Use Repetition to Create Rhythm

Repeating key words, phrases, or even sentences at various intervals throughout a speech creates a distinctive rhythm and thereby implants important ideas in listeners' minds. Repetition works particularly well when delivered with the appropriate voice inflections and pauses.

In a form of repetition called *anaphora*, the speaker repeats a word or phrase at the beginning of successive phrases, clauses, or sentences. In his speech delivered in 1963 in Washington, DC, Dr. Martin Luther King Jr. repeated the phrase "I have a dream" eleven times in eight successive sentences, each with an upward inflection followed by a pause. Speakers have made use of anaphora since earliest times. For example, Jesus preached:

Blessed are the poor in spirit....

Blessed are the meek....

Blessed are the peacemakers....[13]

Repetition can help to create a thematic focus for a speech. Speakers often do this by using both anaphora and *epiphora* in the same speech. In **epiphora** (also called *epistrophe*) the repetition of a word or phrase appears at the end of successive statements. In a speech to his New Hampshire supporters, President Barack Obama used both anaphora and epiphora to establish a theme of empowerment (italics added):

> *It was* a creed written into the founding documents that declared the destiny of a nation: *Yes we can.*

> *It was* whispered by slaves and abolitionists as they blazed a trail toward freedom through the darkest of nights: *Yes we can.*

> *It was* sung by immigrants as they struck out from distant shores and pioneers who pushed westward against an unforgiving wilderness: *Yes we can.*[14]

Use Alliteration for a Poetic Quality

Alliteration is the repetition of the same sounds, usually initial consonants, in two or more neighboring words or syllables. Alliteration lends speech a poetic, musical rhythm. Classic examples of alliteration in speeches include phrases such as Jesse Jackson's "Down with dope, up with hope" and former U.S. Vice-President Spiro Agnew's disdainful reference to the U.S. press as "nattering nabobs of negativism."

Experiment with Parallelism

The arrangement of words, phrases, or sentences in a similar form is known as **parallelism**. Parallel structure can help the speaker emphasize important ideas, and can be as simple as orally numbering points ("first, second, and third"). Like repetition, it also creates a sense of steady or building rhythm. Speakers often make use of three parallel elements, called a *triad*:

> …of the people, by the people, and for the people…

> —Abraham Lincoln

Parallelism in speeches often makes use of **antithesis**—setting off two ideas in balanced (parallel) opposition to each other to create a powerful effect:

> One small step for a man, one giant leap for mankind.

> —Neil Armstrong on the moon, 1969

> For many are called, but few are chosen.

> —Matthew 22:14

CHECKLIST

Using Effective Oral Style

- ☐ Use familiar words, easy-to-follow sentences, and straightforward syntax.
- ☐ Root out culturally insensitive and gender-biased language.
- ☐ Avoid unnecessary jargon.
- ☐ Use fewer rather than more words to express your thoughts.
- ☐ Make striking comparisons with *similes*, *metaphors*, and *analogies*.
- ☐ Use the active voice.
- ☐ Repeat key words, phrases, or sentences at the beginning of successive sentences (*anaphora*) and at their close (*epiphora*).
- ☐ Experiment with *alliteration*—words that repeat the same sounds, usually initial consonants, in two or more neighboring words or syllables.
- ☐ Experiment with *parallelism*—arranging words, phrases, or sentences in similar form.

part 10

Public Speaking: Delivery

CHAPTER

46

Methods of Delivery

For most of us, anticipating the actual delivery of a speech feels unnerving. In fact, effective delivery rests on the same natural foundation as everyday conversation, except that it is more rehearsed and purposeful. By focusing on four key qualities of effective delivery, you can reduce your fears and make your presentations more authentic.

Keys To Effective Delivery

Effective delivery is the controlled use of voice and body to express the qualities of naturalness, enthusiasm, confidence, and directness.[1] Audiences respond most favorably to speakers who project these characteristics during delivery. As you practice delivering your speech, focus on these key qualities:

- *Strive for naturalness.* Rather than behaving theatrically, act naturally. Think of your speech as a particularly important conversation.

- *Show enthusiasm.* Inspire your listeners by showing enthusiasm for your topic and for the occasion. An enthusiastic delivery helps you feel good about your speech, and it focuses your audience's attention on the message.

- *Project a sense of confidence.* Focus on the ideas you want to convey rather than on yourself. Inspire the audience's confidence in you by appearing confident to them.

- *Be direct.* Engage directly with audience members. Demonstrate your interest and concern for listeners by establishing eye contact, using a friendly tone of voice, and animating your facial expressions, especially positive ones such as smiling and nodding whenever appropriate. (See Chapters 47 and 48 on techniques for using voice and body in a speech.)

Chapter 46, "Methods of Delivery," is taken from Dan O'Hair, Hannah Rubenstein, and Rob Stewart: *A Pocket Guide to Public Speaking*, Fifth Edition, pp. 126–129 (Chapter 16, "Methods of Delivery").

Select a Method of Delivery

For virtually any type of speech or presentation, you can choose from four basic methods of delivery: speaking from manuscript, speaking from memory, speaking impromptu, and speaking extemporaneously.

Speaking from Manuscript

When **speaking from manuscript**, you read a speech *verbatim*—that is, from prepared written text that contains the entire speech, word for word. As a rule, speaking from manuscript restricts eye contact and body movement, and may also limit expressiveness in vocal variety and quality. Watching a speaker read a speech can be monotonous and boring for the audience.

If you must read from prepared text—for example, when you need to convey a precise message, when you will be quoted and must avoid misinterpretation, or when addressing an emergency and conveying exact descriptions and direction—do what you can to deliver the speech naturally:

- Vary the rhythm of your words (see Chapter 47).
- Become familiar enough with the speech so that you can establish some eye contact.
- Use a large font and double- or triple-space the manuscript so that you can read without straining.
- Consider using some compelling presentation aids (see Chapter 50).

Speaking from Memory

The formal name for **speaking from memory** is **oratory**. In oratorical style, you put the entire speech, word for word, into writing and then commit it to memory. Memorization is not a natural way to present a message. True eye contact with the audience is unlikely, and the potential for disaster exists because there is always the possibility of forgetting. Some kinds of brief speeches, however, such as toasts and introductions, can be well served by memorization. Sometimes it's helpful to memorize a part of the speech, especially when you use direct quotations as a form of support. If you do use memorization, practice that portion of your speech so completely that you can convey enthusiasm and directness.

Speaking Impromptu

Impromptu speaking, a type of delivery that is unpracticed, spontaneous, or improvised, involves speaking on relatively short notice with little time to prepare. Many occasions require that you make remarks on the spur of the moment. An instructor may ask you to summarize key points from an assignment, for example, or a boss may invite you to take the place of an absent co-worker who was scheduled to speak on a new project.

Try to anticipate situations that may require you to speak impromptu, and prepare some remarks beforehand. Otherwise, maximize the time you do have to prepare on the spot:

- *Think first about your listeners.* Consider their interests and needs, and try to shape your remarks accordingly. For example, who are the people present, and what are their views on the topic?

- *Listen to what others around you are saying.* Take notes in a key-word or phrase format (see p. 724) and arrange them into main points from which you can speak.

- *Acknowledge the previous speaker.* If your speech follows someone else's, acknowledge that person's statements. Then make your points.

- *Stay on the topic.* Don't wander off track.

- *Use Transitions.* Use signal words such as "first," "second," and "third" to organize points and help listeners follow them.

As much as possible, try to organize your points into a discernible pattern. If addressing a problem, for example, such as a project failure or glitch, consider the *problem-solution pattern*—state problem(s), then offer solution(s); or the *cause-effect pattern* of organizational arrangement—state cause(s) first, then address effect(s); see Chapter 42 for various ways of using these patterns.

Speaking Extemporaneously

When speaking extemporaneously, you prepare and practice in advance, giving full attention to all facets of the speech—content, arrangement, and delivery alike. However, in an **extemporaneous speech**, instead of memorizing or writing the speech word for word, you speak from an outline of key words and phrases that isolates the main ideas that you want to communicate (see Chapter 43).

Because extemporaneous delivery is most conducive to achieving a natural, conversational quality, most speakers prefer it among the four types of delivery. Knowing your ideas well enough to present them without memorization or manuscript gives you greater flexibility in adapting to the specific speaking situation. You can modify wording, rearrange your points, change examples, or omit information in keeping with the audience and the setting. You can have more eye contact, more direct body orientation, greater freedom of movement, and generally better control of your thoughts and actions than any of the other delivery methods allow.

Speaking extemporaneously does present a possible drawback. Occasionally, even a glance at your speaking notes may fail to jog your memory on a point you wanted to cover, and you find yourself searching for what to say next. The remedy for this potential pitfall is frequent practice—rehearsing the speech about six times—using a key-word or phrase outline (see p. 724).

Choosing a Method of Delivery

When...	Method of Delivery
You want to avoid being misquoted or misconstrued, or you need to communicate exact descriptions and directions...	Consider *speaking from manuscript* (read the part of your speech requiring precise wording from fully prepared text).
You must deliver a short special occasion speech, such as a toast or an introduction, or you plan on using direct quotations...	Consider *speaking from memory* (memorize part or all of your speech).
You are called upon to speak without prior planning or preparation...	Consider *speaking impromptu* (organize your thoughts with little or no lead time).
You have time to prepare and practice developing a speech or presentation that achieves a natural conversational style...	Consider *speaking extemporaneously* (develop your speech in working outline and then practice and deliver it with a phrase or key-word outline).

CHECKLIST

Successful Delivery

☐ Strive for naturalness.

☐ Show enthusiasm.

☐ Project a sense of confidence and composure.

☐ Engage your audience by being direct.

☐ If you must read from a prepared text, do so naturally.

☐ In general, don't try to memorize entire speeches.

☐ When speaking impromptu, maximize any preparation time.

CHAPTER

47

Your Voice in Delivery

When delivering a speech, voice matters. Used properly, your voice is a powerful instrument of expression that can signal confidence and control, and enable you to communicate meaning exactly as you intend. As you practice, you can learn to modulate each of the elements of vocal delivery: volume, pitch, speaking rate, pauses, vocal variety, and pronunciation and articulation.

Adjust Your Speaking Volume

Volume, the relative loudness of a speaker's voice while delivering a speech, is usually the most obvious vocal element we notice about a speaker, and with good reason. We need to hear the speaker at a comfortable level. *The proper volume for delivering a speech is somewhat louder than that of normal conversation.* Just how much louder depends on three factors: (1) the size of the room and of the audience, (2) whether or not you use a microphone, and (3) the level of background noise. Speaking at the appropriate volume is critical to how credible your listeners will perceive you to be, so check that audience members can hear you. Be alert to signals that your volume is slipping or is too loud and make the necessary adjustments.

Vary Your Intonation

Pitch is the range of sounds from high to low (or vice versa). Anatomy determines a person's natural pitch—a bigger or smaller voice box produces a lower- or higher-pitched voice. But within these natural constraints, you can and should control pitch through **intonation**—the rising and falling of sound across phrases and sentences. Intonation is important in speechmaking because it powerfully affects the meaning associated with spoken words. For example, say "stop." Now, say "Stop!" Varying intonation conveys two very distinct meanings.

Chapter 47, "Your Voice in Delivery," is taken from Dan O'Hair, Hannah Rubenstein, and Rob Stewart: *A Pocket Guide to Public Speaking*, Fifth Edition, pp. 129–134 (Chapter 17, "Your Voice in Delivery").

Breathe from Your Diaphragm

To project your voice so that it is loud enough to be heard by everyone in the audience, breathe deeply from your diaphragm rather than more shallowly from your vocal cords. The reason? The strength of our voices depends on the amount of air the diaphragm—a large, dome-shaped muscle encasing the inner rib cage—pushes from the lungs to the vocal cords.

As you speak, intonation conveys your mood, level of enthusiasm, concern for the audience, and overall commitment to the occasion. Without intonation, speaking becomes monotonous. A monotone voice is a death knell to any speech.

The best way to avoid speaking in monotone is to practice and listen to your speeches with a recording device. If you have a recording device on your smart phone, you can use it to test your voice. You will readily identify instances that require better intonation.

Adjust Your Speaking Rate

Speaking rate is the pace at which you convey speech. The normal rate of speech for native English-speaking adults is roughly between 120 and 150 words per minute, but there is no standard, ideal, or most effective rate. If the rate is too slow, it may lull the audience to sleep. If your speech is too fast, listeners may see you as unsure about your control of the speech.[1]

Being alert to the audience's reactions is the best way to know whether your rate of speech is too fast or too slow. Some serious topics benefit from a slower speech rate; a lively pace generally corresponds with a lighter tone. An audience will get fidgety, bored, listless, perhaps even sleepy if you speak too slowly. If you speak too rapidly, listeners will appear irritated and confused, as though they can't catch what you're saying.

Control Your Rate of Speaking

To control your speaking rate, choose 150 words from your speech and time yourself for one minute as you read them aloud. If you fall very short of finishing, increase your pace. If you finish well before the minute is up, slow down. Practice until you achieve a comfortable speaking rate.

Use Strategic Pauses

Many novice speakers are uncomfortable with pauses. Like intonation, however, pauses can be important strategic elements of a speech. **Pauses** enhance meaning by providing a type of punctuation, emphasizing a point, drawing attention to a thought, or just allowing listeners a moment to contemplate what is being said.

As you practice delivering your speech, focus on avoiding unnecessary and undesirable **vocal fillers** such as "uh," "hmm," "you know," "I mean," and "it's like." These so-called disfluencies will make you appear unprepared and cause audience members to be distracted from the message. Rather than vocal fillers, use silent pauses for strategic effect.

Strive for Vocal Variety

Rather than operating separately, all the vocal elements described so far — volume, pitch, speaking rate, and pauses — work together to create vocal variety. Indeed, the real key to effective vocal delivery is to vary all these elements with a tone of enthusiasm. For example, as the great civil rights leader Martin Luther King Jr. spoke the now famous words "I have a dream," the pauses were immediately preceded by a combination of reduced speech rate and increased volume and pitch. Vocal variety comes quite naturally when you are excited about what you are saying to an audience, when you feel it is important and want to share it with them.

CHECKLIST

Practice Check for Vocal Effectiveness

- ☐ As you practice, is your vocal delivery effective?
- ☐ Is your voice too loud? Too soft?
- ☐ Do you avoid speaking in a monotone? Do you vary the stress or emphasis you place on words to clearly express your meaning?
- ☐ Is your rate of speech comfortable for listeners?
- ☐ Do you avoid unnecessary vocal fillers, such as "uh," "hmm," "you know," and "I mean"?
- ☐ Do you use silent pauses for strategic effect?
- ☐ Does your voice reflect a variety of emotional expressions? Do you convey enthusiasm?

Carefully Pronounce and Articulate Words

Few things distract an audience more than improper pronunciation or unclear articulation of words. **Pronunciation** is the correct formation of word sounds—examples of *mispronunciation* include, "aks" for "asked" (*askt*), and "jen yu wine" for "genuine" (jen yu in). **Articulation** is the clarity or forcefulness with which the sounds are made, regardless of whether they are pronounced correctly. Incorrect pronunciation and poor articulation are largely a matter of habit.

A common pattern of poor articulation is **mumbling**—slurring words together at a low level of volume and pitch so that they are barely audible. Sometimes the problem is **lazy speech**. Common examples are saying "fer" instead of "for" and "wanna" instead of "want to."

Like any habit, poor articulation can be overcome by unlearning the problem behavior:

- If you mumble, practice speaking more loudly and with emphatic pronunciation.
- If you tend toward lazy speech, put more effort into your articulation.
- Consciously try to say each word clearly and correctly.
- Practice clear and precise enunciation of proper word sounds. Say "articulation" several times until it rolls off your tongue naturally.
- Do the same for these words: "want to," "going to," "Atlanta," "chocolate," "sophomore," "California."

Use Dialect (Language Variation) with Care

Every culture has subcultural variations, or **dialects**, on the preferred pronunciation and articulation of its languages. In the United States, there is so-called "standard" or "General American English" (GAE), Ebonics (African American English), and Tex-Mex (a combination of Spanish and English spoken with a distinct Texas drawl). Although dialects are neither superior nor inferior to standard language patterns, the audience must be able to understand and relate to the speaker's language. As you practice your delivery, ensure that your pronunciation and word usage can be understood by all audience members.

CHECKLIST

Tips on Using a Microphone

☐   Perform a sound check with the microphone several hours before delivering your speech.

☐   When you first speak into the microphone, ask listeners if they can hear you clearly.

☐   Speak directly into the microphone; if you turn your head or body, you won't be heard.

☐   To avoid broadcasting private statements, beware of "open" mikes.

☐   When wearing a **lavaliere microphone** attached to clothing, speak as if you were addressing a small group. The amplifier will do the rest.

☐   When using a *handheld* or *fixed microphone*, beware of *popping*. Popping occurs when you use sharp consonants such as "*p*," "*t*," and "*d*" and the air hits the mike. To prevent popping, move the microphone slightly below your mouth and about six inches away.[2]

Your Body in Delivery

s we listen to a speaker, we simultaneously use our eyes and ears to evaluate messages sent by his or her **nonverbal communication**—body movements, physical appearance, and qualities of voice. As much if not more than listening to a speaker's words, we respond to his or her visual and aural cues. Thus it is vital to plan not only the words you will say but the physical manner in which you will deliver them.

Pay Attention to Body Language

Research confirms the importance of **body language**—facial expressions, eye behavior, gestures, and general body movements during the delivery of a speech. For example, audiences are more readily persuaded by speakers who emphasize eye contact, nodding at listeners, and standing with an open body position than by those who minimize these nonverbal cues.[1] Additionally, when speakers talk about their feelings and attitudes, one study suggests that the audience derives a mere *7 percent* of the speakers' meaning from the words they utter. The balance comes from the speakers' use of voice (38 percent) and body language and appearance (55 percent).[2]

Animate Your Facial Expressions

From our facial expressions, audiences can gauge whether we are excited about, disenchanted by, or indifferent to our speech—and the audience to whom we are presenting it.

Few behaviors are more effective for building rapport with an audience than *smiling*.[3] A smile is a sign of mutual welcome at the start of a speech, of mutual comfort and interest during the speech, and of mutual goodwill at the close of a speech. In addition, smiling when you feel nervous or otherwise uncomfortable can help you relax and gain heightened composure. Of course, facial expressions need to correspond to the tenor of the speech. Doing what is natural and normal for the occasion should be the rule.

Chapter 48, "Your Body in Delivery," is taken from Dan O'Hair, Hannah Rubenstein, and Rob Stewart: *A Pocket Guide to Public Speaking*, Fifth Edition, pp. 134–137 (Chapter 18, "Your Body in Delivery").

CHECKLIST

Tips for Using Effective Facial Expressions

☐   Use animated expressions that feel natural and express your meaning.

☐   Avoid a deadpan expression.

☐   Never use expressions that are out of character for you or inappropriate to the speech occasion.

☐   In practice sessions, loosen your facial features with exercises such as widening the eyes and moving the mouth.

☐   Establish rapport with the audience by smiling naturally when appropriate.

Maintain Eye Contact

If smiling is an effective way to build rapport, maintaining eye contact is mandatory in establishing a positive relationship with your listeners. Having eye contact with the audience is one of the most, if not *the* most, important physical actions in public speaking, at least in Western cultures. Eye contact does the following:

- Maintains the quality of directness in speech delivery.
- Lets people know they are recognized.
- Indicates acknowledgment and respect.
- Signals to audience members that you see them as unique human beings.

While it may be impossible to look at every listener, you can make the audience feel recognized by using a technique called **scanning**—moving your gaze from one listener to another and from one section to another, pausing to gaze at one person long enough to complete one thought. Be certain to give each section of the room equal attention.

Use Gestures That Feel Natural

Words alone seldom suffice to convey what we want to express. Physical gestures fill in the gaps, as in illustrating the size or shape of an object (e.g., by showing the size of it by extending two hands, palms facing each other), or expressing the depth of an emotion (e.g., by pounding a fist on a podium). Gestures should arise from genuine emotions and should conform to your personality.[4]

CHECKLIST

Using Gestures Effectively

- ☐ Use natural, spontaneous gestures.
- ☐ Avoid exaggerated gestures, but use gestures that are broad enough to be seen by each audience member.
- ☐ Eliminate distracting gestures, such as fidgeting with pens, jingling coins in pockets, drumming your fingers on a podium or table, or brushing back hair from your eyes.
- ☐ Analyze your gestures for effectiveness in practice sessions.
- ☐ Practice movements that feel natural to you.

Create a Feeling of Immediacy

In most Western cultures, listeners learn more from and respond most positively to speakers who create a perception of physical and psychological closeness, called **nonverbal immediacy**, between themselves and audience members.[5] The following behaviors encourage immediacy:

- Use an enthusiastic vocal delivery.
- Make frequent eye contact.
- Animate your facial expressions.
- Use natural body movements.

QUICK TIP

Use Movement to Connect

Audience members soon tire of listening to a **talking head** that remains steadily positioned in one place behind a microphone or a podium, so even in formal situations, use natural body movements. Use your physical position vis-à-vis audience members to adjust your relationship with them, establishing a level of familiarity and closeness that is appropriate to the rhetorical situation. Movement towards listeners stimulates a sense of informality and closeness; remaining behind the podium fosters a more formal relationship of speaker to audience.

Stand Straight

A speaker's posture sends a definite message to the audience. Listeners perceive speakers who slouch as being sloppy, unfocused, or even weak. Strive to stand erect, but not ramrod straight. The goal should be to appear authoritative but not rigid.

Practice the Delivery

Practice is essential to effective delivery. The more you practice, the greater your comfort level will be when you actually deliver the speech. More than anything, it is uncertainty that breeds anxiety. By practicing your speech using a fully developed speaking outline (see Chapter 43), you will know what to expect when you actually stand in front of an audience.

Focus on the Message

The primary purpose of any speech is to get a message across, not to display extraordinary delivery skills. Keep this goal foremost in your mind. Psychologically, too, focusing on your message is likely to make your delivery more natural and confident.

Plan Ahead and Practice Often

If possible, begin practicing your speech at least several days before you are scheduled to deliver it.

- Practice with your speaking notes, revising those parts of the speech that aren't satisfactory, and altering the notes as you go.
- Record the speech (see Quick Tip on p. 770).
- Time each part of your speech—introduction, body, and conclusion (see Chapter 44 for guidelines).
- Include any presentation aids you plan to use.
- Practice the speech about five times in its final form.
- Visualize the setting in which you will speak, and practice the speech under realistic conditions, paying particular attention to projecting your voice to fill the room.
- Practice in front of at least one volunteer, and seek constructive criticism.
- Schedule your practice sessions early in the process so that you have time to prepare.
- Dress appropriately for the rhetorical situation.

QUICK TIP

Record Two Practice Sessions

Videorecording two practice sessions can provide valuable feedback. As you watch your initial recording, make notes of the things you'd like to change. Before rerecording, practice several more times until you are comfortable with the changes you've incorporated. No one is ever entirely thrilled with his or her image on video, so try to avoid unnecessary self-criticism. Videorecord your speech a second time, paying close attention to the areas of speech delivery that you want to improve.

part 11

Public Speaking: Presentation Aids

CHAPTER

49

Speaking with Presentation Aids

Used judiciously, the visual reinforcement provided by presentation aids can help listeners to understand and retain information that is otherwise difficult or time-consuming to convey in words. Indeed, research confirms that most people process information best when it is presented both verbally and visually—a principle dubbed the "multimedia effect."[1] However, no matter how powerful a photograph, chart, or other aid may be, if it is unrelated to a speech point, is poorly designed, or simply duplicates what the speaker says, the audience will become distracted and actually retain less information than without it.[2]

Select an Appropriate Aid

A **presentation aid** can be an object, model, picture, graph, chart, table, audio, video, or multimedia. Choose the aid, or combination of aids, that will help your audience grasp information most effectively.

Props and Models

A **prop** can be any object, inanimate or even live, that helps demonstrate the speaker's points. A **model** is a three-dimensional, scale-size representation of an object. Presentations in engineering, architecture, and many other disciplines often make use these aids. When using a prop or model:

- In most cases, keep the prop or model hidden until you are ready to use it.

- Make sure it is big enough for everyone to see (and read, if applicable).

- Practice your speech using the prop or model.

Chapter 49, "Speaking with Presentation Aids," is taken from Dan O'Hair, Hannah Rubenstein, and Rob Stewart: *A Pocket Guide to Public Speaking*, Fifth Edition, pp. 140–144 (Chapter 19, "Speaking with Presentation Aids").

Pictures

Pictures (two-dimensional representations) include photographs, line drawings, diagrams, maps, and posters. A *diagram* or *schematic drawing* explains how something works or is constructed or operated. *Maps* help listeners visualize geographic areas and understand relationships among them; they also illustrate the proportion of one thing to something else in different areas.

Graphs, Charts, and Tables

A **graph** represents relationships among two or more things. A *line graph* uses points connected by lines to demonstrate how something changes or fluctuates in value. A *bar and column graph* uses bars of varying lengths to compare quantities or magnitudes. *Pie graphs* depict the division of a whole into slices. Each slice constitutes a percentage of the whole.

Pictograms use picture symbols (icons) to illustrate relationships and trends; for example, a generic-looking human figure repeated in a row can demonstrate increasing enrollment in college over time.

A **chart** visually organizes complex information into compact form. A **flowchart** diagrams the progression of a process or relationship helping viewers visualize a sequence or directional flow. A **table** (tabular chart) systematically groups data in column form, allowing viewers to examine and make comparisons about information quickly.

CHECKLIST

Create Effective Line, Bar, and Pie Graphs

- ☐ Label the axes of line graphs, bar graphs, and pictograms.
- ☐ Start the numerical axis of the line or bar graph at zero.
- ☐ Compare only like variables.
- ☐ Assign a clear title to the graph.
- ☐ Clearly label all relevant points of information in the graph.
- ☐ When creating multidimensional bar graphs, do not compare more than three kinds of information.
- ☐ In pie graphs, restrict the number of pie slices to a maximum of seven.
- ☐ Identify and accurately represent the values or percentages of each pie slice.
- ☐ In pictograms, clearly indicate what each icon symbolizes.
- ☐ Make all pictograms the same size.

Best Uses of Different Types of Graphs and Charts

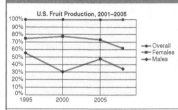

Line graph

To represent trends or information that changes over time

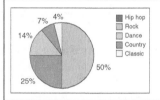

Bar graph

To represent trends or information that changes over time

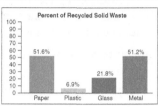

Pie graph

To show proportions, such as sales by region, shares

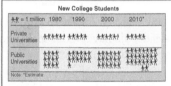

Pictogram

To show comparisons in picture form

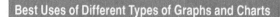

Flowchart

To show processes

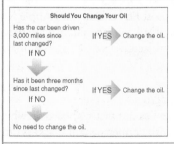

Table

To show large amounts of information in an easily viewable form

Audio, Video, and Multimedia

Audio and video clips—including short recordings of sound, music, or speech; and clips from movies, television, and other recordings—can motivate attention and help to move among and clarify points.[3] *Multimedia*, which combines stills, sound, video, text, and data into a single production, requires familiarity with presentation software programs such as Windows Movie Maker and Apple iMovie. (See Chapter 51 for guidelines on linking audio and video clips to slides.) This rich variety of information cues can potentially boost audience attention, comprehension, and retention.[4] One application of multimedia is **digital storytelling**—using multimedia to tell a story about yourself or others with resonance for the audience.

When incorporating audio and video into your presentation:

- Cue the audio or video clip to the appropriate segment before the presentation.
- Alert audience members to what they will be hearing or viewing before you play it back.
- Reiterate the relevance of the audio or video clip to your key points once it is over.
- Use the audio or video clip in a manner consistent with copyright.

Options for Displaying Presentation Aids

Many presenters create computer-generated aids shown with digital projectors or LCD displays. On the more traditional side, display options include chalkboards and whiteboards, flip charts, posters, and handouts.

Computer-Generated Aids and Displays

With software programs such as Microsoft PowerPoint and Apple Keynote, speakers can create slides to project using LCD (liquid crystal display) panels and projectors or DLP (digital light processing) projectors. See Chapter 51 for a discussion of how to use presentation software.

Chalkboards and Whiteboards

On the lowest-tech end of the spectrum lies the writing board on which you can write with chalk (on a chalkboard) or with nonpermanent markers (on a *whiteboard*). Reserve the writing board for impromptu explanations, such as presenting simple processes that are done in steps, or for engaging the audience in short brainstorming sessions. If you have the time to prepare a speech properly, however, don't rely on a writing board. They force the speaker to turn his or her back to the audience, make listeners wait while you write, and require legible handwriting that will be clear to all viewers.

Hold the Handouts

A **handout** conveys information that either is impractical to give to the audience in another manner or is intended to be kept by audience members after the presentation. To avoid distracting listeners, unless you specifically want them to read the information as you speak, wait until you are finished before you distribute the handout. If you do want the audience to view a handout during the speech, pass it out only when you are ready to talk about it.

Flip Charts

A **flip chart** is simply a large (27–34 inch) pad of paper on which a speaker can write or draw. This aid is often prepared in advance; then, as you progress through the speech, you flip through the pad to the next exhibit. You can also write and draw on the pad as you speak. Sometimes a simple drawing or word written for emphasis can be as or more powerful than a highly polished slide.

Posters

Speakers use *posters*—large paperboards incorporating text, figures, and images, alone or in combination—to illustrate some aspect of their topic; often the poster rests on an easel.

Incorporating Presentation Aids into Your Speech

- ☐ Practice with the aids until you are confident that you can handle them without causing undue distractions.
- ☐ Talk to your audience rather than to the screen or object—avoid turning your back to the audience.
- ☐ Maintain eye contact with the audience.
- ☐ Place the aid to one side rather than behind you, so that the entire audience can see it.
- ☐ Display the aid only when you are ready to discuss it.
- ☐ If you use a pointer, once you've indicated your point, put it down.
- ☐ In case problems arise, be prepared to give your presentation without the aids.

CHAPTER 50

Designing Presentation Aids

The visual appeal of a speaker's presentation aids is a critical factor in the audience's perception of his or her credibility, or ethos. Well-designed aids signal that the speaker is prepared and professional; poorly designed aids create a negative impression that is difficult to overcome.

As you generate aids, focus on keeping elements easy to read and consistently designed. Audience members can follow only one information source at a time, and visuals that are crowded or difficult to decipher will divert attention from your message.[1]

Keep the Design Simple

On average, audience members have only 30 seconds or less[2] to view an aid, so restrict text to a minimum and present only one major idea per aid:

- *Follow the six-by-six rule.* Use no more than six words in a line and six lines on one slide. This way the audience will spend less time reading the aid and more time listening to you (see "Buying a Used Car" on p. 779).

- *Word text in active verb form.* Use the active voice and parallel grammatical structure, e.g., "Gather Necessary Documents; Apply Early" (see Chapter 45 on language).

- *Avoid clutter.* Allow plenty of white space, or "visual breathing room" for viewers.[3]

- *Create concise titles.* Use titles that summarize content and reinforce your message.

Chapter 50, "Designing Presentation Aids," is taken from Dan O'Hair, Hannah Rubenstein, and Rob Stewart: *A Pocket Guide to Public Speaking*, Fifth Edition, pp. 144–148 (Chapter 20, "Designing Presentation Aids").

Cluttered Aid	Easy-to-Read Aid
Buying a Used Car	**Buying a Used Car**
1. Prepare in advance—know the market value of several cars you are interested in before going to shop.	1. Know the car's market value.
2. Do not get into a hurry about buying the first car you see—be patient, there will be others.	2. Don't hurry to buy.
3. It is recommended that you shop around for credit before buying the car.	3. Shop for credit before buying.
4. Inspect the car carefully, looking for funny sounds, stains, worn equipment, dents, etc.	4. Inspect the car carefully.
5. Ask for proof about the history of the car, including previous owners.	5. Get proof of the car's history.

QUICK TIP

Beware of "Chartjunk"

Certain kinds of information—especially statistical data and sequences of action—are best understood when visually presented. However, avoid what design expert Edward Tufte coined as "chartjunk"[4]—slides jammed with too many graphs, charts, and meaningless design elements that obscure rather than illuminate information. Use fewer rather than more slides and only those design elements that truly enhance meaning.

Use Design Elements Consistently

Apply the same design decisions you make for one presentation aid to all of the aids you display in a speech; this will ensure that viewers aren't distracted by a jumble of unrelated visual elements. Carry your choice of design elements—color, fonts, upper- and lowercase letters, styling (boldface, underlining, italics), general page layout, and repeating elements such as titles and logos—through each aid.

Select Appropriate Typeface Styles and Fonts

A *typeface* is a specific style of lettering, such as Arial or Times Roman. Typefaces come in a variety of *fonts*, or sets of sizes (called the *point size*), and upper- and lower cases. Designers divide the thousands of available typefaces into two major categories: serif and sans serif. *Serif typefaces* include small flourishes, or strokes, at the tops and bottoms of each letter. *Sans serif typefaces* are more blocklike and linear; they are designed without these tiny strokes.

Consider these guidelines when selecting and designing type:

- Check the lettering for legibility, taking into consideration the audience's distance from the presentation. On slides, experiment with 36-point type for major headings, 24-point type for subheadings, and *at least* 18-point type for text.
- Lettering should stand apart from the background. Use either dark text on light background or light text on dark background.
- Use a typeface that is simple and easy to read, not distracting.
- Use standard upper- and lowercase type rather than all capitals.
- As a rule, use no more than two different typefaces in a single visual aid.
- Use **boldface**, underlining, or *italics* sparingly.

QUICK TIP

Using Serif and Sans Serif Type

For reading a block of text, serif typefaces are easier on the eye. Small amounts of text, however, such as headings, are best viewed in sans serif type. Thus, consider a sans serif typeface for the heading and a serif typeface for the body of the text. If you include only a few lines of text, use sans serif type throughout.

Use Color Carefully

Skillful use of color can draw attention to key points, influence the mood of a presentation, and make things easier to see. Conversely, poor color combinations will set the wrong mood, render an image unattractive, or make it unreadable. Note the effect of these color combinations:

Effects of Color Combinations

Color	Effect in Combination
Yellow	Warm on white, harsh on black, fiery on red, soothing on light blue
Blue	Warm on white, hard to see on black
Red	Bright on white, warm or difficult to see on black

Color affects both the legibility of text and the mood conveyed. Following are some tips for using color effectively in your presentation aids:

- Keep the *background color* constant across all slides or other aids.
- Use *bold, bright colors* to emphasize important points.
- For typeface and graphics, use colors that contrast rather than clash with or blend into the background color; check for visibility when projecting. Audiences will remember information just as easily if white text appears on dark background or dark text on light background, so long as the design is appealing.[5]
- Limit colors to no more than three, with maximum of four in complex and detailed aids.

Consider Subjective Interpretations of Color

Colors can evoke distinct associations for people, so take care not to summon an unintended meaning or mood. For example, control engineers see red and think danger, whereas a financial manager will think unprofitability.

Consider, too, that the meanings associated with certain colors may differ across cultures. Western societies don black for funerals, while the Chinese use white. If you are presenting in a cross-cultural context, check the meanings of colors for the relevant nationalities.

CHECKLIST

Apply the Principles of Simplicity and Continuity

- ☐ Concentrate on presenting one major idea per visual aid.
- ☐ Apply design decisions consistently to each aid.
- ☐ Use type that is large enough for audience members to read comfortably.
- ☐ Use color to highlight key ideas and enhance readability.
- ☐ Check that colors contrast rather than clash.

Using Presentation Software

Public speakers can use a variety of powerful software tools to create and display high-quality visual aids. These programs include the familiar Microsoft PowerPoint and its Apple counterpart, Keynote, as well as the Web-based program Prezi.

Develop a Plan

Often the best place to begin planning your slides is your speaking outline (see p. 731). In general, a speaking outline will contain between two and seven main points, each of which is linked to at least two subpoints. Think through which points in your speech might be better explained to your audience with some kind of visual: decide what the content of your slides should be, how many slides you'll need, and how to arrange your slides. Review and edit slides as necessary using *Slide Sorter view* (in PowerPoint), *Lightable* or *Outline view* (in Keynote), or *path tool* (in Prezi).

Avoid Technical Glitches

Technical errors are always a hazard with presentation software and any hardware required to run it. Common risks include incompatibility of a PowerPoint or Keynote file with an operating system, an Internet connection failing while using Prezi, a display screen malfunction, or a computer drive freezing when attempting to play a media file. To avoid forcing the audience to wait as you try to fix technical problems, follow these steps:

Chapter 51, "Using Presentation Software," is taken from Dan O'Hair, Hannah Rubenstein, and Rob Stewart: *A Pocket Guide to Public Speaking*, Fifth Edition, pp. 148–154 (Chapter 21, "Using Presentation Software").

1. Save all the files associated with your presentation (i.e., images, sound, videos) into the same folder you will use in your presentation.

2. Check that the operating system of the computer you will use during your speech (e.g., Windows XP, Mac OS X) is compatible with the operating system used to create the aids.

3. Confirm that the version of the presentation software used to create the aids corresponds to the software on the computer you will use in the presentation; this will prevent distortions in your graphics, sound, and video.

4. Verify that you've saved the files to a source—a flash drive, CD, DVD, website, or e-mail—that will be recognized by the presentation computer.

5. Familiarize yourself with the layout and functioning of the presentation computer before the speech to facilitate smooth operation during the presentation.

6. Prepare a digital backup of your presentation in case of technical challenges.

Give a Speech, Not a Slide Show

Frequently we hear someone say, "I'm giving a PowerPoint (or a Prezi or Keynote) today," instead of "I'm giving a speech today." Some speakers hide behind presentation media, focusing attention on their aids rather than on the audience. They might erroneously believe that the display itself is the presentation, or that it will somehow save an otherwise poorly planned speech.[1] Other speakers become so involved in generating glitzy aids that they forget their primary mission: to communicate through the spoken word[2] and their physical presence.

Presentation aids certainly can and do help listeners process information and so enhance a speech, but only as long as you truly work to engage the audience and achieve your speech goal. Speaker and message, rather than any presentation media, must take center stage.

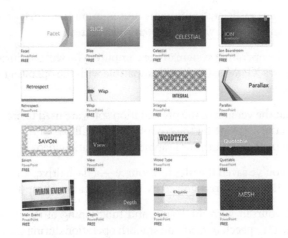

FIGURE 51.1 Design Templates in PowerPoint

FIGURE 51.2 Design Templates in Keynote

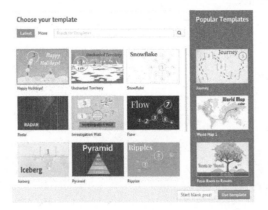

FIGURE 51.3 Design Templates in Prezi

Finding Media for Presentations

You can import still images, clip art, video, or sound directly into your aids by downloading your own files or those from the Internet. For downloadable *digital images*, try the following websites:

- Corbis Images (www.corbisimages.com): Contains more than two million photographs, prints, and paintings, 35,000 of which you can download for your personal use (for a fee).

- Google (www.google.com), Yahoo! (www.yahoo.com), and Bing (www. bing.com) offer extensive image searches.

The following sites contain free photographs and other still images:

- Flickr (www.flickr.com/creativecommons): Access to thousands of photographs shared by amateur and hobbyist photographers.

- Exalead (www.exalead.com/search/image): An innovative image search engine with over two billion images.

- American Memory (memory.loc.gov/ammem/index/html): Free access to still and moving images depicting the history of the American experience.

The following sites offer downloadable *music files* and *audio clips:*

- MP3.com (www.mp3.com)
- SoundClick (www.soundclick.com)
- Internet Archive (www.archive.org/details/audio)
- The Daily.WAV (www.dailywav.com)
- FreeAudioClips.com (www.freeaudioclips.com)
- SoundCloud (www.soundcloud.com)

The following sites contain useful *video clips:*

- CNN Video (www.cnn.com/video) and ABC News Video (abcnews. go.com/video): Especially useful for speech topics on current events or timely social issues.

- YouTube (www.youtube.com)
- New York Times (www.nytimes.com/video)
- Google Videos (video.google.com)
- Bing Videos (www.bing.com/videos/browse)
- Metacafe (www.metacafe.com)

FROM SLIDE SHOW TO PRESENTATION

Getting Ready to Deliver a PowerPoint, Keynote, or Prezi Presentation

To avoid technical glitches, practice delivering your speech with your presentation software and ensure compatibility with the venue's equipment.

Check the Venue

Before your speech, take stock of the equipment and room layout. See the annotated photo for tips on achieving a smooth delivery with digital aids.

1. **Locate power sources.** Ensure that cords can reach the presentation equipment, and consider taping them to the floor to keep them out of the way.

2. **Computer needs and compatibility.** Check that all files, from the slide show to audio and video clips, load successfully to the presentation computer. If possible, practice at least once on this computer.

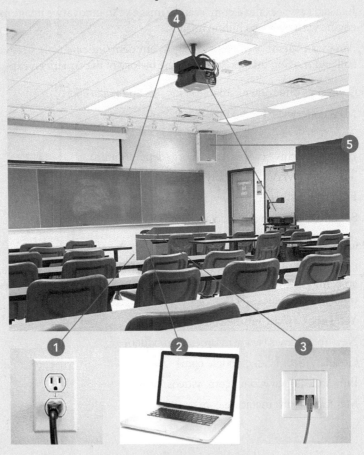

(clockwise from bottom) Jeff Presnail/Getty Images; Cinoby/Getty Images; Casper Benson/Getty Images; Purestock/Getty Images

3 **Internet access.** Have wireless log-in information available and/or a cable that reaches the Internet jack.

4 **Backup plan.** Create a contingency plan in case of computer failure; for example, print overhead transparencies from slide show, prepare to put information on board, or create handouts.

5 **Audio.** Determine how you will broadcast any audio aids, and check speaker volume before the speech.

Position Yourself Carefully

Choose a place to stand that gives the audience clear sightlines to you and your slide show. Stand such that you can face forward even when changing slides or gesturing toward your aids. This helps you connect with your audience, project your voice clearly, and prevents you from reading off your slides.

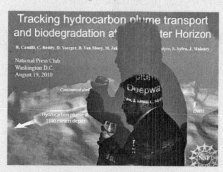

Mark Wilson/Getty; Getty Images

Needs improvement: This speaker's sideways stance discourages eye contact and indicates that he may be reading off his slides.

Good placement: This speaker can access the computer or gesture toward the slides without blocking the audience's sightlines.

Avoid Copyright Infringement

Be certain to abide by copyright restrictions when using visual and audio materials from the Internet or other sources. Recognize when material is available under fair-use provisions (see p. 649). Even if fair use applies, cite the source of the material in your presentation. Consult your school's information technology (IT) office for statements of policy pertaining to copyrighted and fair-use materials, especially from undocumented sources such as peer-to-peer (P2P) sharing:

- Cite the source of all copyrighted material in your presentation. For example, include a bibliographic footnote on the slide containing the material.
- Be wary of sites purporting to offer "royalty free" media objects; there might actually be other costs associated with the materials.
- When time, resources, and ability allow, create and use your own pictures, video, or audio for your presentation slides.

CHECKLIST

Tips for Successfully Using Presentation Software in Your Speech

- ☐ Don't let the technology get in the way of relating to your audience.
- ☐ Talk to your audience rather than to the screen.
- ☐ Maintain eye contact as much as possible.
- ☐ Have a backup plan in case of technical errors.
- ☐ If you use a pointer (laser or otherwise), turn it off and put it down as soon as you have made your point.
- ☐ Never shine a laser pointer into anyone's eyes. It will burn them!
- ☐ Incorporate the aids into your practice sessions until you are confident that they strengthen, rather than detract from, your core message.

Notes

A Pocket Guide to Public Speaking, Fifth Edition

Chapter 31

1. "Why Warren Buffett's Most Valuable Skill Wasn't from a Diploma," Fox on Stocks, December 19, 2012, accessed August 13, 2013 at **www.foxonstocks.com/ why-warrenbuffetts-most-valuable0skill-wasn't-from-a-diploma/**.

2. "It Takes More than a Major: Employer Priorities for College Learning and Student Success," Hart Research Associates (on behalf of The Association of American Colleges and Universities), April 10, 2013, **www.aacu.org/leap/documents/2013_ EmployerSurvey.pdf**.

3. "Youth Voting/Political Participation," Center for Information and Research on Civic Learning and Engagement (CIRCLE), accessed August 26, 2013, **www.civicyouth. org/ResearchTopics/research-topics/political-participation-and-voting/**; "Voter Turnout," FairVote/Center for Voting and Democracy, accessed August 26, 2013, **www. fairvote.org/voter-turnout#.Uhtfvhbt7Q0**.

4. For a discussion of Daniel Yankelovich's three-step process by which public judgments occur, see Yankelovich, *Coming to Public Judgment: Making Democracy Work in a Complex World* (Syracuse, NY: Syracuse University Press, 1991).

5. For a discussion of conversation stoppers and rules of engagement, see W. Barnett Pearce, "Toward a National Conversation about Public Issues," in *The Changing Conversation in America: Lectures from the Smithsonian*, eds. William F. Eadie and Paul E. Nelson (Thousand Oaks, CA: Sage, 2002), 16.

6. Robert Perrin, "The Speaking-Writing Connection: Enhancing the Symbiotic Relationship," *Contemporary Education* 65 (1994): 62–64.

7. Kristine Bruss, "Writing for the Ear: Strengthening Oral Style in Manuscript Speeches," *Communication Teacher* 26, no. 2 (April 2012): 76–81.

8. Lloyd F. Bitzer, "The Rhetorical Situation," *Philosophy and Rhetoric* (Winter 1968): 1–14.

Chapter 33

1. Graham D. Bodie, "A Racing Heart, Rattling Knees, and Ruminative Thoughts: Defining, Explaining, and Treating Public Speaking Anxiety," *Communication Education* 59 (2010): 70–105.

2. Ralph Behnke and Chris R. Sawyer, "Milestones of Anticipatory Public Speaking Anxiety," *Communication Education* 48 (April 1999): 165–72.

3. Christine Kane, "Overcoming Stage Fright — Here's What to Do," *Christinekane* (blog), April 24, 2007, **http://christinekane.com/blog/overcoming-stage-fright-heres- what-to-do/**.

4. Behnke and Sawyer, "Milestones of Anticipatory Public Speaking Anxiety."

5. David-Paul Pertaub, Mel Slater, and Chris Barker, "An Experiment on Public Speaking Anxiety in Response to Three Different Types of Virtual Audience," *Presence: Teleoperators and Virtual Environments* 11 (2002): 670–78.

6. Joe Ayres, "Coping with Speech Anxiety: The Power of Positive Thinking," *Communication Education* 37 (1988): 289–96; Joe Ayres, "An Examination of the Impact of Anticipated Communication and Communication Apprehension on Negative Thinking, Task-Relevant Thinking, and Recall," *Communication Research Reports* 9 (1992): 3–11.

7. Pamela J. Feldman, Sheldon Cohen, Natalie Hamrick, and Stephen J. Lepore, "Psychological Stress, Appraisal, Emotion, and Cardiovascular Response in a Public Speaking Task," *Psychology and Health* 19 (2004): 353–68; Senqi Hu and Juong-Min Romans-Kroll, "Effects of Positive Attitude toward Giving a Speech on Cardiovascular and Subjective Fear Responses during Speech on Anxious Subjects," *Perceptual and Motor Skills* 81 (1995): 609–10.

8. Elizabeth Quinn, "Visualization in Sport: Imagery Can Improve Performance," About. com: Sports Medicine, accessed August 29, 2007, **http://sportsmedicine.about.com/cs/sport_psych/a/aa091700a.htm**; Joe Ayres and Tim Hopf, "Visualization: Is It More Than Extra Attention?" *Communication Education* 38 (1989): 1–5; Joe Ayers and Tim Hopf, *Coping with Speech Anxiety* (Norwood, NJ: Ablex, 1993).

9. Joe Ayres, Chia-Fang "Sandy" Hsu, and Tim Hopf, "Does Exposure to Visualization Alter Speech Preparation Processes?" *Communication Research Reports* 17 (2000): 366–74.

10. Ayres and Hopf, "Visualization," 2–3.

11. Herbert Benson and Miriam Z. Klipper, *The Relaxation Response* (New York: HarperCollins, 2000).

12. Laurie Schloff and Marcia Yudkin, *Smart Speaking* (New York: Plume, 1991), 91–92.

13. Lars-Gunnar Lundh, Britta Berg, Helena Johansson, Linda Kjellén Nilsson, Jenny Sandberg, and Anna Segerstedt, "Social Anxiety Is Associated with a Negatively Distorted Perception of One's Own Voice," *Cognitive Behavior Therapy* 31 (2002): 25–30.

Chapter 34

1. *Oxford English Dictionary Online*, s.v. "responsibility," accessed June 17, 2013, **www.oed.com/view/Entry/163862?redirectedFrom=responsibility**.

2. Richard L. Johannesen, Kathleen S. Valde, and Karen E. Whedbee, *Ethics in Human Communication* (Long Grove, IL: Waveland Press, 2007).

3. Cited in Edward P. J. Corbett, *Classical Rhetoric for the Modern Student* (New York: Oxford University Press, 1990).

4. Shalom H. Schwartz, "An Overview of the Schwartz Theory of Basic Values," *Online Readings in Psychology and Culture* 2, no. 1 (2012), **http://dx.doi.org/10.9707/2307-0919.1116**.

5. Pew Center for People & the Press, "Trends in American Values: 1987–2012," June 4, 2012, **www.people-press.org/files/legacy-pdf/06-04-12%20Values%20Release.pdf**.

6. Douglas M. Fraleigh and Joseph S. Tuman, *Freedom of Speech in the Marketplace of Ideas* (New York: Bedford/St. Martin's, 1997).

7. W. Gudykunst, S. Ting-Toomey, S. Suweeks, and L. Stewart, *Building Bridges: Interpersonal Skills for a Changing World* (Boston: Houghton Mifflin, 1995), 92.

8. Michael Josephson, *Making Ethical Decisions: The Six Pillars of Character* (Josephson Institute of Ethics, 2002).

9. Ibid.

10. Ibid.

11. Rebecca Moore Howard, "A Plagiarism Pentimento," *Journal of Teaching Writing* 11 (1993): 233.

12. Francie Diep, "Fast Facts about the Japan Earthquake and Tsunami," *Scientific American*, March 14, 2011, **www.scientificamerican.com/article.cfm?id=fast-facts-japan**.

13. U.S. Copyright Office Web site, accessed June 19, 2014, **www.copyright.gov**.

14. U.S. Copyright Office, "Fair Use," accessed July 1, 2013, **www.copyright.gov/fls/fl102.html**.

Chapter 35

1. "An ILA Definition of Listening," *Listening Post* 53, no. 1 (1995): 4–5.

2. Laura A. Janusik and Andrew D. Wolvin, "24 Hours in a Day: Listening Update to the Time Studies," 23 (2009): 104–20; see also Richard Emanuel, Jim Adams, Kim Baker, E. K. Daufin, Coke Ellington, Elizabeth Fitts et al., "How College Students Spend Their Time Communicating," *International Journal of Listening* 22 (2008): 13–28.

3. Ibid.

4. Avraham N. Kluger and Keren Zaidel, "Are Listeners Perceived as Leaders?" *International Journal of Listening* 27, no. 2 (2013): 73–84; S. A. Welch and William T. Mickelson, "A Listening Competence Comparison of Working Professionals," *International Journal of Listening* 27, no. 2 (2013): 85–99.

5. Albert H. Hastorf and Hadley Cantril, "They Saw a Game: A Case Study," *Journal of Abnormal and Social Psychology* 49, no. 1 (1954): 129–34; Gordon W. Allport, and Lee J. Postman, "The Basic Psychology of Rumor," *Transactions of the New York Academy of Sciences* 8 (1945): 61–81.

6. Christian Kiewitz, James B. Weaver III, Hans-Bernd Brosius, and Gabriel Weimann, "Cultural Differences in Listening Style Preferences: A Comparison of Young Adults in Germany, Israel, and the United States," *International Journal of Public Opinion Research* 9, no. 3 (1997): 233–47, **search.proquest.com/docview/60068159?accountid=10965**; M. Imhof and L. A. Janusik, "Development and Validation of the Imhof-Janusik Listening Concepts Inventory to Measure Listening Conceptualization Differences between Cultures," *Journal of Intercultural Communication Research* 35, no. 2 (2006): 79–98.

7. Ibid.

8. Thomas E. Anastasi Jr., *Listen! Techniques for Improving Communication Skills* (Boston: CBI Publishing, 1982).

9. Ronald D. Gordon, "Communication, Dialogue, and Transformation," *Human Communication* 9, no. 1 (2006): 17–30.

10. James Floyd, "Provocation: Dialogic Listening as Reachable Goal," *International Journal of Listening* 24 (2010): 170–73.

Chapter 36

1. Pablo Briñol and Richard E. Petty, "The History of Attitudes and Persuasion Research," in *Handbook of the History of Social Psychology*, eds. Arie Kruglanski and Wolfgang Stroebe (New York: Psychology Press, 2011).

2. Richard E. Petty and John T. Cacioppo, *Attitudes and Persuasion: Classic and Contemporary Approaches* (Dubuque, IA: Wm. C. Brown, 1981); M. Fishbein and I. Ajzen, *Belief, Attitude, Intention, and Behavior: An Introduction to Theory and Research* (Reading, MA: Addison-Wesley, 1975); I. Ajzen and M. Fishbein, "The Influence of Attitudes on Behavior," in *The Handbook of Attitudes*, eds. Dolores Albarracín, Blair T. Johnson, and Mark P. Zanna (Mahwah, NJ: Erlbaum, 2005), 173–221.

3. Richard E. Petty, S. Christian Wheeler, and Zakary L. Tormala, "Persuasion and Attitude Change," in *Handbook of Psychology, Personality, and Social Psychology*, Vol. 5, eds. Theodore Millon, Melvin Lerner, and Irving B. Weiner (New York: John Wiley & Sons, 2003).

4. *The Stanford Encyclopedia of Philosophy*, s.v. "Belief," Winter 2011 edition, **http://plato. stanford.edu/archives/win2011/entries/belief/**.

5. "Human Values and Nature's Future: Americans' Attitudes on Biological Diversity," BlueStem Communications, accessed January 22, 2014, **http://bluestemcommunica tions.org/changing-behaviors-not-minds-a-communications-workshop/**.

6. Herbert Simon, *Persuasion in Society*, 2nd ed. (New York: Routledge, 2011).

7. Ibid.

8. Kenneth Burke, *A Rhetoric of Motives* (Berkeley, CA: University of California Press, 1969).

9. See, for example, "Millennials, Gen X and Baby Boomers: Who's Working at Your Company and What Do They Think about Ethics?" Ethics Resource Center, 2009 National Business Ethics Survey Supplemental Research Brief, http://ethics.org/files/u5/Gen-Diff.pdf; Dennis McCafferty, "Workforce Preview: What to Expect from Gen Z," *Baseline Magazine*, April 4, 2013, **www.baselinemag.com/it-management/slideshows/workforce-preview-what-to-expect-from-gen-z**; "Generations in the Workplace in the United States and Canada," Catalyst, May 1, 2012, **www.catalyst.org/knowledge/generations-workplace-united-states-canada**.

10. Jere R. Behrman and Nevzer Stacey, eds., *The Social Benefits of Education* (Ann Arbor: University of Michigan Press, 2000).

11. Pew Forum on Religion & Public Life, "U.S. Religious Landscape Survey: Religious Affiliation," February 1, 2008, **www.pewforum.org/2008/02/01/u-s-religious-landscape-survey-religious-affiliation/**.

12. Daniel Canary and Kathryn Dindia, eds., *Sex Differences and Similarities in Communication*, 2nd ed. (Mahwah, NJ: Erlbaum, 2006).

13. Matthew W. Brault, "Americans with Disabilities: 2010," Current Population Reports, U.S. Census Bureau; accessed January 22, 2014, **www.census.gov/content/dam/Census/library/publications/2012/demo/p70-131.pdf**.

14. U.S. Census Bureau, "U.S. Census Quick Facts," accessed December 12, 2014, **http://quickfacts.census.gov/qfd/states/00000.html**; U.S. Census Bureau, "New Census Bureau Interactive Map Shows Languages Spoken in America," August 6, 2013, **www.census.gov/newsroom/press-releases/2013/cb13-143.html**.

15. Inter-University Consortium for Political and Social Research, "World Values Survey, 1981–1984 and 1990–1993" (Irvine, CA: Social Science Data Archives, University Libraries, University of California, 1997). The 1990 World Values Survey covers four Asian countries (China, India, Japan, and South Korea) and eighteen Western countries.

16. Rushworth M. Kidder, *Shared Values for a Troubled World: Conversations with Men and Women of Conscience* (San Francisco: Jossey-Bass, 1994).

Chapter 38

1. Richard F. Corlin, "The Coming Golden Age of Medicine," *Vital Speeches of the Day* 68, no. 18 (2002).

2. Jonathan Drori, "Every Pollen Grain Has a Story," Filmed February 2010, TED video, 7:12, **www.ted.com/talks/jonathan_drori_every_pollen_grain_has_a_story.html**.

3. Quoted in Katharine Q. Seelye, "Congressman Offers Bill to Ban Cloning of Humans," *New York Times*, March 6, 1997, sec. A.

4. Mark Turner, *The Literary Mind* (New York: Oxford University Press, 1996).

5. Melinda French Gates, "Raising the Bar on College Completion," Keynote Address, American Association of Community Colleges, April 20, 2010, **www.gatesfoundation.org/media-center/speeches/2010/04/raising-the-bar-on-college-completion**.

6. Robert Lehrman, *The Political Speechwriter's Companion: A Guide for Writers and Speakers* (Washington, DC: CQ Press, 2010), quoted in Steven D. Cohen, "The Art of Public Narrative: Teaching Students How to Construct Memorable Anecdotes," *Communication Teacher* 25, no. 4, (2011): 197–204, doi: 10.1080/17404622.2011.601726.

7. Jim Carrey, Commencement Address, Maharishi University of Management, May 24, 2014, **www.mum.edu/whats-happening/graduation-2014/full-jim-carrey-address-video-and-transcript/**.

8. Derek P. Ellerman, "Testimony to Subcommittee on Human Rights and Wellness, Committee on Government Reform," U.S. House of Representatives, July 8, 2004, **www.polarisproject.org/what-we-do/policy-advocacy/national-policy/congressional-testimony/congressional-testimony-2004-derek-ellerman**.

9. Yaacov Schul and Ruth Mayo, "Two Sources Are Better Than One: The Effects of Ignoring One Message on Using a Different Message from the Same Source," *Journal of Experimental Social Psychology* 35 (1999): 327–45; Mike Allen, Rebecca Bruflat, Renée Fucilla, Michael Kramer, Steve McKellips, Daniel J. Ryan et al., "Testing the Persuasiveness of Evidence: Combining Narrative and Statistical Forms," *Communication Research Reports* 17 (2000): 331–36, cited in R. A. Reynolds and J. L. Reynolds, "Evidence," in *The Persuasion Handbook: Developments in Theory and Practice*, eds. James P. Dillard and Michael. Pfau (Thousand Oaks, CA: Sage, 2002), 427–44, doi: 10.4135/9781412976046.n22.

10. Rodney A. Reynolds and J. Lynn Reynolds, "Evidence," in *The Persuasion Handbook: Developments in Theory and Practice*, eds. James P. Dillard and Michael Pfau (Thousand Oaks, CA: Sage, 2002), 427–44, doi: 10.4135/9781412976046.n22.

11. "A380," Airbus, accessed July 7, 2013, **www.airbus.com/aircraftfamilies/passenger aircraft/a380family/**.

12. Cited in American Lung Association, *State of Tobacco Control 2014*, January 22, 2014, **www.stateoftobaccocontrol.org**.

13. "State and County QuickFacts," U.S. Census Bureau, accessed July 7, 2013, last revised January 6, 2014, **http://quickfacts.census.gov/qfd/states/08000.html**.

14. "State Unemployment Rates Decline in May 2013," National Conference of State Legislatures, January 28, 2014, **www.ncsl.org/issues-research/labor/state-unemploymentupdate.aspx**.

15. "Statistics and Facts about Facebook," Statista.com, February 11, 2015, **www.statista.com/topics/751/facebook/**.

16. Chuck Marr and Chye-Ching Huang, "Tax Foundation Figures Do Not Represent Typical Households' Tax Burdens," Center on Budget and Policy Priorities, April 2, 2013, **www.cbpp.org/cms/index.cfm?fa=view&id=3946**.

17. Roger Pielke Jr., "The Cherry Pick," Ogmius: Newsletter for the Center for Science and Technology Research 8 (2004), **http://sciencepolicy.colorado.edu/ogmius/archives/issue_8/intro.html**.

Chapter 39

1. Steve Coffman, "So What Now: The Future for Librarians," *Online Searcher*, January/February 2013, **www.infotoday.com/OnlineSearcher/Articles/Features/So-Now-What-The-Future-for-Librarians-86856.shtml**.

2. Elizabeth E. Kirk, "Information and Its Counterfeits," Sheridan Libraries of Johns Hopkins University, 2001, **www.library.jhu.edu/researchhelp/general/evaluating/counterfeit.html**.

3. Gregory Ferenstein, "Jimmy Wales, Wikipedia Go to College," *Fast Company*, July 6, 2011, **www.fastcompany.com/1765182/jimmy-wales-wikipedia-go-college**.

Chapter 40

1. Ralph Underwager and Hollida Wakefield, "The Taint Hearing," paper presented at the 13th Annual Symposium in Forensic Psychology, Vancouver, BC, April 17, 1997, **www.ipt-forensics.com/journal/volume10/j10_7.htm#en0**.

2. Institute for Writing and Rhetoric, "Sources and Citation at Dartmouth College," produced by the Committee on Sources, May 2008, **https://writing-speech.dartmouth.edu/learning/materials/sources-and-citations-dartmouth**.

Chapter 41

1. Gordon H. Bower, "Organizational Factors in Memory," *Cognitive Psychology* 1 (1970): 18–46.

2. Hermann Ebbinghaus, *On Memory: A Contribution to Experimental Psychology* (New York: Teachers College, 1813); Murray Glanzer and Anita R. Cunitz, "Two Storage Mechanisms in Free Recall," *Journal of Verbal Learning and Verbal Behavior* 5 (1966): 351–60.

3. Ernest Thompson, "An Experimental Investigation of the Relative Effectiveness of Organization Structure in Oral Communication," *Southern Speech Journal* 26 (1960): 59–69; C. Spicer and R. E. Bassett, "The Effects of Organization on Learning from an Informative Message," *Southern Speech Journal* 41 (1976): 290–99.

4. Raymond G. Smith, "Effects of Speech Organization upon Attitudes of College Students," *Speech Monographs* 18 (1951): 292–301.

5. Harry Sharp Jr. and Thomas McClung, "Effects of Organization on the Speaker's Ethos," *Speech Monographs* 33 (1966): 182ff; Eldon E. Baker, "The Immediate Effects of Perceived Speaker Disorganization on Speaker Credibility and Audience Attitude Change in Persuasive Speaking," *Western Speech* 29 (1965): 148–61.

Chapter 42

1. Raymond G. Smith, "Effects of Speech Organization upon Attitudes of College Students," *Speech Monographs* 18 (1951): 547–49; Ernest Thompson, "An Experimental Investigation of the Relative Effectiveness of Organizational Structure in Oral Communication," *Southern Speech Journal* 26 (1960): 59–69.

2. "Life on the Internet Timeline," Public Broadcasting System, accessed April 3, 2000, **www.pbs.org/internet/timeline/index.html**.

Chapter 43

1. Mark B. McClellan, Fifth annual David A. Winston lecture, National Press Club, Washington, DC, October 20, 2003, **www.fda.gov/newsevents/speeches/speecharchives/ucm053609.htm**.

Chapter 44

1. Jeremey Donovan, *How to Deliver a TED Talk* (CreateSpace Independent Publishing Platform, 2012).

2. William Safire, *Lend Me Your Ears: Great Speeches in History* (New York: Norton, 1992), 676.

3. Bas Andeweg and Jap de Jong, "May I Have Your Attention? Exordial Techniques in Informative Oral Presentations," *Technical Communication Quarterly* 7, no. 3 (Summer 1998): 271–84.

4. Nancy Duarte, *Harvard Business Review Guide to Persuasive Presentations* (Boston: Harvard Business Review Press, 2012).

5. James Oliver, "Teach Every Child about Food," Filmed February 2010, TED video, 21:53, **www.ted.com/talks/jamie_oliver**.

6. Marvin Runyon, "No One Moves the Mail Like the U.S. Postal Service," *Vital Speeches of the Day* 61, no. 2 (1994): 52–55.

7. Robert L. Darbelnet, "U.S. Roads and Bridges: Highway Funding at a Crossroads," *Vital Speeches of the Day* 63, no. 12 (1997): 379.

8. Holger Kluge, "Reflections on Diversity," *Vital Speeches of the Day* 63, no. 6 (1997): 171–72.

9. Elpidio Villarreal, "Choosing the Right Path," *Vital Speeches of the Day* 72, no. 26 (2007): 784–86.

10. Hillary Rodham Clinton, "Women's Rights Are Human Rights," speech delivered to the United Nations Fourth World Conference on Women, Beijing, China, September 5, 1995.

Chapter 45

1. Kristine Bruss, "Writing for the Ear: Strengthening Oral Style in Manuscript Speeches," *Communication Teacher*, 26, no. 2 (April 2012): 76–81.

2. Peggy Noonan, *Simply Speaking: How to Communicate Your Ideas with Style, Substance, and Clarity* (New York: Regan Books, 1998), 51.

3. Dan Hooley, "The Lessons of the Ring," *Vital Speeches of the Day* 70, no. 20 (2004): 660–63.

4. Sheryl Sandberg, "Why We Have Too Few Women Leaders," Filmed December 2010, TED video, 14:58, **www.ted.com/talks/sheryl_sandberg_why_we_have_too_few_women_leaders.html**.

5. Susan T. Fiske and Shelley E. Taylor, "Vivid Information Is More Easily Recalled Than Dull or Pallid Stimuli," *Social Cognition*, 2nd ed. (New York: McGraw Hill), quoted in Jennifer Jerit and Jason Barabas, "Bankrupt Rhetoric: How Misleading Information Affects Knowledge about Social Security," *Public Opinion Quarterly* 70, no. 3 (2006): 278–304.

6. Loren J. Naidoo and Robert G. Lord, "Speech Imagery and Perceptions of Charisma: The Mediating Role of Positive Affect," *Leadership Quarterly* 19, no. 3 (2008): 283–96.

7. Ibid; phrase taken from President Franklin Delano Roosevelt's 1933 inaugural address.

8. L. Clemetson and J. Gordon-Thomas, "Our House Is on Fire," *Newsweek*, June 11, 2001, 50.

9. Andrew C. Billings, "Beyond the Ebonics Debate: Attitudes about Black and Standard American English," *Journal of Black Studies* 36 (2005): 68–81.

10. Sylvie Dubois, "Sounding Cajun: The Rhetorical Use of Dialect in Speech and Writing," *American Speech* 77, no. 3 (2002): 264–87.

11. Gloria Anzaldúa, "Entering into the Serpent," in *The St. Martin's Handbook*, eds. Andrea Lunsford and Robert Connors, 3rd ed. (New York: St. Martin's Press, 1995), 25.

12. P. H. Matthews, *The Concise Oxford Dictionary of Linguistics* (New York: Oxford University Press, 1997).

13. Cited in William Safire, *Lend Me Your Ears: Great Speeches in History* (New York: Norton, 1992), 22.

14. "Barack Obama's New Hampshire Primary Speech," *New York Times*, January 8, 2008, **www.nytimes.com/2008/01/08/us/politics/08text-obama.html?r=0**.

Chapter 46

1. James A. Winans, *Public Speaking* (New York: Century, 1925). Professor Winans was among the first Americans to contribute significantly to the study of rhetoric. His explanation of delivery is considered by many to be the best coverage of the topic in the English language. His perspective infuses this chapter.

Chapter 47

1. MaryAnn Cunningham Florez, "Improving Adult ESL Learners' Pronunciation Skills," National Clearinghouse for ESL Literacy Education, 1998, accessed July 16, 2005, **www.cal.org/caela/esl_resources/digests/Pronun.html**.

2. Susan Berkley, "Microphone Tips," *Great Speaking* 4, no. 7 (2002), accessed July 16, 2005, **www.antion.com/ezine/v4n7.txt**.

Chapter 48

1. C. F. Bond and the Global Deception Research Team, "A World of Lies," *Journal of Cross-Cultural Psychology* 37 (2006): 60–74; Timothy R. Levine, Kelli Jean K. Asada, and Hee Sun Park, "The Lying Chicken and the Gaze Avoidant Egg: Eye Contact, Deception, and Causal Order," *Southern Communication Journal* 71 (2006): 401–11.
2. Robert Rivlin and Karen Gravelle, *Deciphering the Senses: The Expanding World of Human Perception* (New York: Simon & Schuster, 1998), 98; see also Anne Warfield, "Do You Speak Body Language?" *Training & Development* 55, no. 4 (2001): 60.
3. Eva Krumburger, "Effects of Dynamic Attributes of Smiles in Human and Synthetic Faces: A Simulated Job Interview Setting," *Journal of Nonverbal Behavior* 33 (2009): 1–15.
4. Alissa Melinger and Willem M. Levelt, "Gesture and the Communicative Intention of the Speaker," *Gesture* 4 (2004): 119–41.
5. Mike Allen, Paul L. Witt, and Lawrence R. Wheeless, "The Role of Teacher Immediacy as a Motivational Factor in Student Learning: Using Meta-Analysis to Test a Causal Model," *Communication Education* 55, no. 6 (2006): 21–31.

Chapter 49

1. Richard E. Mayer, *The Multimedia Principle* (New York: Cambridge University Press, 2001).
2. See discussion of the redundancy effect in Richard E. Mayer, ed., *The Cambridge Handbook of Multimedia Learning* (New York: Cambridge University Press, 2005).
3. Gary Jones, "Message First: Using Films to Power the Point," *Business Communication Quarterly* 67, no. 1 (2004): 88–91.
4. Kulwadee M. Axtell, "The Effect of Presentation Software on Classroom Verbal Interaction and on Student Retention of Higher Education Lecture Content," *Journal of Technology in Teaching and Learning* 4, no. 1 (2008): 21–23.

Chapter 50

1. Nancy Duarte, "Avoiding the Road to Powerpoint Hell," *Wall Street Journal*, January 22, 2011, **www.wsj.com**.
2. Ibid.
3. Ibid.
4. Edward Tufte, *The Visual Display of Quantitative Information* (Cheshire, CT: Graphics Press, 2001); Edward Tufte, "PowerPoint Is Evil," *Wired* 11 (2003), **www.wired.com/wired/archive/11.09/ppt2_pr.html**.
5. Ronald Larson, "Slide Composition for Electronic Presentations," *Journal of Educational Computing Research*, 31, no. 1 (2004): 61–76.

Chapter 51

1. D. Cyphert, "Presentation Technology in the Age of Electronic Eloquence: From Visual Aid to Visual Rhetoric," *Communication Education* 56, no. 2 (2007): 168–92; D. Cyphert, "The Problem of PowerPoint: Visual Aid or Visual Rhetoric?" *Business Communication Quarterly* 67, no. 1 (2004): 80–84.
2. J. Thomas, "PowerPoint Is Not the Problem with Presentations Today," March 21, 2010, *Presentation Advisors*, **http://blog.presentationadvisors.com/presentationadvisors/2010/03/powerpoint-is-not-the-problem-with-presentations.html**.

Works Cited

Habits of the Creative Mind

"About the Project." *7 Billion Others*. The GoodPlanet Foundation, n.d. Web. 27 Dec. 2013.

Abumrad, Jad, and Robert Krulwich. "An Equation for Good." *Radiolab*. WNYC. 15 Dec. 2010. Podcast. 21 Dec. 2013.

Alexander, Michelle. *The New Jim Crow: Mass Incarceration in the Age of Color Blindness*. New York: New Press, 2010. Print.

The Aristocrats. Dir. Paul Provenza. Think Film Company, 2005. Film.

Armstrong, Elizabeth M., and Ernest L. Abel. "Fetal Alcohol Syndrome: The Origins of a Moral Panic." *Alcohol and Alcoholism* 35.3 (May 2000): 276–82. Web. 29 Dec. 2013.

Arthus-Bertrand, Yann. *6 Billion Others: Portraits of Humanity from Around the World*. New York: Abrams, 2009. Print.

---. *Earth from Above*. 3rd ed. New York: Abrams, 2005. Print.

Bain, Ken. *What the Best College Students Do*. Cambridge, MA: Harvard UP, 2012. Print.

---. *What the Best College Teachers Do*. Cambridge, MA: Harvard UP, 2004. Print.

Bechdel, Alison. "Comics Reporter Interview #1—Alison Bechdel." Interview by Tom Spurgeon. Comicsreporter.com. *The Comics Reporter*, 18 Dec. 2012. Web. 8 Nov. 2014.

---. *Fun Home: A Family Tragicomic*. New York: Mariner, 2006. Print.

---. MacArthur Fellow Biography. MacArthur Foundation. Web. 8 Nov 2014.

---. quoted in Dwight Garner. "The Days of Their Lives: Lesbians Star in Funny Pages." Books of the Times. *New York Times,* 2 Dec. 2008. Web. 8 Nov. 2014.

Berger, John. "Why Look at Animals?" *About Looking*. New York: Random, 2011. Print.

Berthoff, Ann E. *Forming/Thinking/Writing: The Composing Imagination*. Montclair, NJ: Boynton/Cook, 1982. Print.

Blake, William. "Auguries of Innocence." *The Poetry Foundation*. Web. 16 Jan. 2014.

Bulwer-Lytton, Edward. *Paul Clifford*. *Gutenberg.org*. Project Gutenberg, 6 Nov. 2012. Web. 16 Jan. 2014.

---. *Richelieu, or, The Conspiracy: A Play in Five Acts*. *Openlibrary.org*. Web. 16 Jan. 2014.

The Bulwer-Lytton Fiction Contest. English Dept. San Jose State U, n.d. Web. 16 Jan. 2014.

Burke, Kenneth. *The Philosophy of Literary Form*. U of California. Berkeley: UP of California, 1941. Print.

Cain, Susan. *Quiet: The Power of Introverts in a World that Can't Stop Talking*. New York: Crown, 2012. Print.

Capote, Truman. *In Cold Blood*. New York: Random, 1965. Print.

---. "The Story Behind a Nonfiction Novel." Interview by George Plimpton. *New York Times*, 16 Jan. 1966. Web. 21 Dec. 2013.

Carroll, Lewis. *Alice's Adventures in Wonderland. Gutenberg.org.* Project Gutenberg, 8 Mar. 1994. Web. 18 Dec. 2013.

CK, Louis. "About Tig Notaro." *Louis CK*, 5 Oct. 2012. Web. 24 Jan. 2014.

Coates, Ta-Nehisi. "Considering the President's Comments on Racial Profiling." *Theatlantic. com.* Atlantic Monthly Group, 19 July 2013. Web. 27 Dec. 2013.

---. "Fear of a Black President." *Theatlantic.com.* Atlantic Monthly Group, 22 Aug. 2012. Web. 27 Dec. 2013.

Colette. quoted in Emily Temple. " 'My Pencils Outlast their Erasers': Great Writers on the Art of Revision." *Theatlantic.com.* Atlantic Monthly Group, 14 Jan. 2013. Web. 27 Dec. 2013.

Crutchfield, Susan. "Play[ing] her Part Correctly: Helen Keller as Vaudevillian Freak." *Disability Studies Quarterly* 25.3 (2005): n.pag. Web. 17 Jan. 2013.

Csikszentmihalyi, Mihaly. *Creativity: Flow and the Psychology of Discovery and Invention.* New York: Harper, 1996. Print.

Delbanco, Andrew. *College: What it Was, Is, and Should Be.* Princeton, NJ: Princeton UP, 2012. Print.

"Diane Arbus." *Wikipedia.* Wikimedia Foundation, 8 Dec. 2013. Web. 16 Jan. 2014.

Dissanayake, Ellen. "The Arts After Darwin: Does Art Have an Origin and Adaptive Function?" *Ellendissanayake.com.* U of Washington P, n.d. Web. 16 Jan. 2014.

Dreisinger, Baz. "Marching On: James McBride's *'Good Lord Bird.' " NYTimes.com.* New York Times, 15 Aug. 2013. Web. 4 Jan. 2014.

Duncker, Karl. "On Problem Solving." *Psychological Monographs* 58:5 (1945) Whole no. 270. Web. 3 June 2015.

Edwards, Betty. *Drawing on the Right Side of the Brain: A Course in Enhancing Creativity and Artistic Confidence.* New York: Tarcher, 1979. Print.

Ericsson, K. Anders, Ralf Th. Krampe, and Clemens Tesch-Römer. "The Role of Deliberate Practice in the Acquisition of Expert Performance." *Psychological Review* 100.3 (1993): 363–406. Web. 3 June 2015.

Fitzgerald, F. Scott. "Appendix A: Fitzgerald's Correspondence about The Great Gatsby (1922–25)." *The Great Gatsby.* Ed. Michael Nowlin. Peterborough, ON, Canada: Broadview, 2007. 185–87. Print.

Framework for Success in Postsecondary Writing. *Wpacouncil.org.* Council of Writing Program Administrators, n.d. Web. 27 Jan. 2014.

Freeza, Bill. "Is Drug War Driven Mass Incarceration the New Jim Crow?" *Forbes.com.* Forbes Media, 28 Feb. 2012. Web. 2 Jan. 2014.

Frost, Robert. "The Road Not Taken." The Poetry Foundation. Web. 4 June 2015.

Gaiman, Neil. "Advice to Authors." *Neilgaiman.com.* Harper Collins, n.d. Web. 6 Nov. 2014.

Galileo. *The Dialogue Concerning the Two Chief World Systems.* Trans. Stillmann Drake. New York: Modern Library, 2001. Print.

Gazzaniga, Michael S. "The Split Brain in Man." *Scientific American* 217.2 (1967): 24–29. Web. 3 June 2015.

"Genesis." *The English Standard Version Bible. ESVBible.org.* Crossway, 2015. Web. 16 Jan. 2014.

Gibson, William. *The Miracle Worker.* Playhouse 90, 1957. Teleplay.

---. *The Miracle Worker.* Dir. Arthur Penn. Playfilm Productions, 1962. Film.

---. *The Miracle Worker.* Samuel French, 1961. Play.

---. *Monday After the Miracle.* New York: Dramatists Play Service, 1983. Play.

Gladwell, Malcolm. *Outliers: The Story of Success.* New York: Little, 2008. Print.

---. *What the Dog Saw: And Other Adventures.* New York: Little, 2009. Print.

Gladwell, Malcolm, and Robert Krulwich. "Secrets of Success." *Radiolab.* WNYC. 26 July 2010. Podcast. 21 Dec. 2013.

Gonzales, Laurence. *Deep Survival: Who Lives, Who Dies, and Why.* New York: Norton, 2004. Print.

Gutkind, Lee. "Home." Lee Gutkind. Web. 5 Nov. 2014.

Hochschild, Adam. " 'Why's This So Good?' No. 61: John McPhee and the Archdruid." *Nieman Storyboard.* Nieman Foundation for Journalism at Harvard, 2 Oct. 2012. Web. 4 Jan. 2014.

Hohn, Donovan. *Moby-Duck: The True Story of 28,800 Bath Toys Lost at Sea and the Beachcombers, Oceanographers, Environmentalists, and Fools, Including the Author, Who Went in Search of Them.* New York: Viking, 2011. Print.

Johnson, Harriet McBryde. "Unspeakable Conversations." *NYTimes.com.* New York Times Magazine, 16 Feb. 2003. Web. 4 Jan. 2014.

Keller, Helen. *The Story of My Life. Gutenberg.org.* Project Gutenberg, 4 Feb. 2013. Web. 17 Jan. 2014.

---. *Teacher: Anne Sullivan Macy.* Garden City, New York: Doubleday, 1955. Print.

---. "Vaudeville Speech." quoted in Dorothy Hermann, *Helen Keller: A Life.* Chicago: U of Chicago P, 1998. Print.

---. *The World I Live In. Gutenberg.org.* Project Gutenberg, 1 Jan. 2009. Web. 17 Jan. 2014.

Kolbert, Elizabeth. *Field Notes from a Catastrophe: Man, Nature, and Climate Change.* New York: Bloomsbury, 2006. Print.

Lamotte, Anne. *Bird by Bird: Some Instructions on Writing and Life.* New York: Anchor, 1995. Print.

Lee, Colonel Robert E. "Colonel Robert E. Lee's Report Concerning the Attack at Harper's Ferry." 1859. *Famous Trials: The Trial of John Brown.* U of Missouri Coll. of Law, n.d. Web. 7 Jan. 2014.

Lepore, Jill. "Battleground America: One Nation, Under the Gun." *Newyorker.com.* New Yorker, 23 Apr. 2012. Web. 21 Jan. 2014.

---. *Book of Ages: The Life and Opinions of Jane Franklin.* New York: Knopf, 2013. Print.

---. Interview by Sasha Weiss and Judith Thurman. "Out Loud: Jane Franklin's Untold American Story." *Newyorker.com.* New Yorker, 30 June 2013. Podcast. 5 June 2015.

---. "Poor Jane's Almanac." *NYTimes.com.* New York Times, 23 Apr. 2011. Web. 23 Dec. 2013.

---. "The Prodigal Daughter: Writing, History, Mourning." *New Yorker,* 8 July 2013: 34–40. Print.

Lethem, Jonathan. "The Ecstasy of Influence: A Plagiarism." *Harpers.org.* Harper's Magazine, Feb. 2007. Web. 21 Jan. 2014.

Lightman, Alan. "The Accidental Universe." *Harpers.org.* Harper's Magazine, Dec. 2011. Web. 31 Dec. 2013.

Lincoln, Abraham. "Gettysburg Address." *Gutenberg.org.* Project Gutenberg, Web. 24 Jan. 2014.

The Matrix. Dir. Andy Wachowski and Lana Wachowski. Warner Bros., 1999. Film.

McBride, James. *The Good Lord Bird.* New York: Riverhead, 2013. Print.

---. Quoted in Julie Bosman. "Traveling with John Brown Along the Road to Literary Celebrity." *NYTimes.com.* New York Times, 24 Nov. 2013. Web. 7 Jan. 2014.

McPhee, John. "John McPhee, The Art of Nonfiction No. 3." Interview by Peter Hessler. *Paris Review* 192 (Spring 2010). Web. 1 Jan. 2014.

---. "Structure." *Newyorker.com.* New Yorker, 14 Jan. 2013. Web. 4 Jan. 2014.

Morrison, Toni. Interview by Elissa Schappell. "Toni Morrison, The Art of Fiction No. 134." *Theparisreview.org.* Paris Review 128 (Fall 1993). Web. 26 Dec. 2013.

Notaro, Tig. *LIVE.* Secretlycanadian.com. 3 Aug. 2012. MP3 file.

Obama, Barack. "Remarks by the President on the Nomination of Dr. Kim Jim for World Bank President." *Whitehouse.gov.* 23 Mar. 2012. Web. 27 Dec. 2013.

---. "Remarks by the President on Trayvon Martin." *Whitehouse.gov.* 19 July 2013. Web. 27 Dec. 2013.

Osifchin, Chris. "Abu Ghraib Ruminations." Message to Richard E. Miller. 29 Jan. 2014. E-mail.

Pink, Daniel. "The Puzzle of Motivation." TED. July 2009. Web. 11 Nov. 2014.

---. *A Whole New Mind: Why Right-Brainers Will Rule the Future.* New York: Riverhead, 2005. Print.

Plato. "The Apology." *Plato: Complete Works.* Eds. John M. Cooper and D. S. Hutchinson. Indianapolis: Hackett, 1997. 17–36. Print.

---. *The Republic.* Trans. G.M.E. Grube. 2nd ed. Indianapolis: Hackett, 1992. Print.

Pollan, Michael. "An Animal's Place." *NYTimes.com*. New York Times, 10 Nov. 2002. Web. 31 Dec. 2013.

---. *The Botany of Desire: A Plant's Eye View of the World*. New York: Random, 2001. Print.

Rose, Erik. Student Writing. n.d. TS. Rutgers UP. Contacted 12 Jan. 2014.

Sacks, Oliver. "The Mind's Eye." *Newyorker.com*. New Yorker, 28 July 2003. Web. 18 Jan. 2014.

Sagan, Carl. *Cosmos*. New York: Ballantine, 2013. Print.

Said, Edward. *Orientalism*. 2nd ed. New York: Vintage, 1994. Print.

Saint Anselm. *Basic Writings: Proslogium, Mologium, Gaunilo's In Behalf of the Fool, Cur Deus Homo*. Trans. S. N. Deane. 2nd ed. Peru, IL: Open Court, 1998. Print.

Schlosser, Eric. "Eric Schlosser." Interview by Robert Boynton. *The New New Journalism*. New York: Random, 2005. Print.

Shakespeare, William. *Romeo and Juliet*. *Gutenberg.org*. Project Gutenberg, 25 May 2012. Web. 24 Jan. 2014.

Simon, David. "HBO's 'Treme' Creator David Simon Explains It All for You." *Nola.com*. Times-Picayune, 11 Apr. 2010. Web. 15 Nov. 2014.

Singer, Peter. *Animal Liberation: A New Ethic for Our Treatment of Animals*. New York: Random, 1975. Print.

Skloot, Rebecca. "How Rebecca Skloot Built *The Immortal Life of Henrietta Lacks*." Interview by David Dobbs. *Theopennotebook.com*. The Open Notebook, 22 Nov. 2011. Web. 4 Jan. 2014.

---. *The Immortal Life of Henrietta Lacks*. New York: Crown, 2010. Print.

---. "What's the Most Important Lesson You Learned from a Teacher?" *Rebeccaskloot.com*. Rebecca Skloot, 8 May 2012. Web. 29 Dec. 2013.

Smith, Zadie. "Fail Better." *Theguardian.com*. Guardian, 13 Jan. 2007. Web. 20 Dec. 2013.

---. *NW*. London: Penguin, 2012. Print.

Sontag, Susan. "America Seen through Photographs, Darkly." *On Photography*. New York: Farrar, 1977. 27–50. Print.

---. "Looking at War." *New Yorker*, Dec. 2002: 82–98. Print.

---. "Regarding the Torture of Others." *NYTimes.com*. New York Times Magazine, 23 May 2004. Web. 20 Dec. 2013.

Sotomayor, Sonia. *My Beloved World*. New York: Knopf, 2013. Print.

Spiotta, Dana. *Stone Arabia*. New York: Scribner, 2012. Print.

Stern, Daniel. "Life Becomes a Dream." Rev. of *The Benefactor* by Susan Sontag. *NYTimes.com*. New York Times, 8 Sept. 1963. Web. 3 June 2015.

Stiver, Annie. "The Time is Ripe." Apr. 2012. TS. Rutgers UP. Contacted 29 Jan. 2014.

Talbot, Margaret. "Stealing Life." *Newyorker.com*. New Yorker, 22 Oct. 2007. Web.

Tharp, Twyla. *The Creative Habit: Learn It and Use It for Life.* New York: Simon, 2003. Print.

Thoreau, Henry David. "Walden." *Walden, and On the Duty of Civil Disobedience.* Project Gutenberg. Jan. 1995. Web. 26 Dec. 2013.

Toy Story. Dir. John Lasseter. Pixar Animation Studios, 1995. Film.

Trainer, Laureen. "The Missing Photographs: An Examination of Diane Arbus's Images of Transvestites and Homosexuals from 1957 to 1965." *Americansuburbx.com.* American Suburb X, 2 Oct. 2009. Web. 16 Jan. 2014.

Tremmel, Michelle. "What to Make of the Five-Paragraph Theme: History of the Genre and Implications." *TETYC* Sept. 2011. 29–41. Print.

Waking Life. Dir. Richard Linklater. Fox Searchlight, 2001. Film.

Walk, Kerry. "Teaching with Writing." Princeton Writing Program. Princeton U, n.d. Web. 27 Dec. 2013.

Wallace, David Foster. *This is Water: Some Thoughts, Delivered on a Significant Occasion, About Living a Compassionate Life.* Transcription of 2005 Kenyon Commencement Address—May 21, 2005. Purdue U, n.d. Web. 23 Dec. 2013.

Walzer, Michael. "Political Action: The Problem of Dirty Hands." *Philosophy and Public Affairs* 2.2 (1973): 160–80. Print.

Webster, Daniel W., and Jon S. Vernick. "Introduction." *Reducing Gun Violence in America: Informing Policy with Evidence and Analysis.* Eds. Daniel W. Webster and Jon S. Vernick. Baltimore, MD: Johns Hopkins UP, 2013. Print.

Woolf, Virginia. Letter to Vita Sackville-West. 26 Feb. 1939. MS. *Woolf in the World: A Pen and Press of Her Own.* Mortimer Rare Book Room. Smith College. Web. 31 Dec. 2013.

---. *A Room of One's Own. Gutenberg.org.* Project Gutenberg Australia. Web. 11 Nov. 2014.

---. "Street Haunting: A London Adventure." *Virginia Woolf: Selected Essays.* Oxford: Oxford UP, 2008. 177–87. Print.

---. *Three Guineas.* 1938. Blackwell Publishing. Web. 20 Dec. 2013.

"WPA Outcomes Statement for First-Year Composition." *Wpacouncil.org.* Council of Writing Program Administrators, n.d. Web. 27 Jan. 2014.

Zakaria, Fareed. "The Case for Gun Control: Why Limiting Access to Guns is Intelligent and American." *Time.com.* Time, 20 Aug. 2012. Web. 27 Jan. 2014.

---. "A Statement from Fareed." Fareed Zakaria GPS. *Globalpublicsquare.blogs.cnn.com.* CNN, 10 Aug. 2012. Web. 3 June 2015.

Acknowledgments

Habits of the Creative Mind

Coates, Ta-Nehisi. "Fear of a Black President." From the Atlantic. August 22, 2012. Reprinted by permission.

Council of Writing Program Administrators. Bulleted list of points taken verbatim from p. 1 of "Framework for Success in Postsecondary Writing." Council of Writing Program Administrators. Wpacouncil.org. Reprinted by permission.

Frost, Robert. Excerpt from "The Road Not Taken." The Poetry of Robert Frost. Copyright © 1969 Holt, Rhinehart & Winston, Inc.

Lepore, Jill. "The Last Amazon," originally published in *The New Yorker* (Sept. 22, 2014), adapted from *The Secret History of Wonder Woman* by Jill Lepore. Copyright © 2014 by Jill Lepore. Used by permission of Alfred A. Knopf, an imprint of the Knopf Doubleday Publishing Group, a division of Penguin Random House LLC. All rights reserved.

Said, Edward W. "Introduction" from *Orientalism*. Copyright © 1978 by Edward W. Said. Used by permission of Pantheon Books, an imprint of the Knopf Doubleday Publishing Group, a division of Penguin Random House LLC. All rights reserved.

Sontag, Susan. "Looking at War." Excerpt from *Regarding the Pain of Others*. Copyright © 2003 by Susan Sontag. Reprinted by permission of Farrar, Straus and Giroux, LLC.

Walzer, Michael. Excerpt 1 from "Political Action: The Problem of Dirty Hands." Philosophy and Public Affairs 2.2 (1973): 160–180. Philosophy & Public Affairs by Blackwell Publishing, Inc. Reproduced with permission of Blackwell Publishing, Inc. in the format Republish in a book via Copyright Clearance Center.

Webster, Daniel W., and Jon S. Vernick, eds. Foreword by Michael R. Bloomberg. *Reducing Gun Violence in America: Informing Policy with Evidence and Analysis*. pp. xxv–xxviii. Copyright © 2013 The Johns Hopkins University Press. Reprinted with permission of Johns Hopkins University Press.

Everything's An Argument, Seventh Edition

Doug Bandow. "A New Military Draft Would Revive a Very Bad Old Idea" from *Forbes*, July 16, 2012, copyright © 2012 by Forbes LLC. All rights reserved. Used by permission and protected by the Copyright Laws of the United States. The printing, copying, redistribution, or retransmission of this Content without express written permission is prohibited.

Sara Barbour. From "Kindle vs. Books: The Dead Trees Society," first published in the *Los Angeles Times*, June 17, 2011. Reprinted by permission of the author.

David Brooks. "It's Not about You" from the *New York Times*, May 31, 2011. Copyright © 2011 by The New York Times. All rights reserved. Used by permission and protected by the Copyright Laws of the United States. The printing, copying, redistribution, or retransmission of this Content without express written permission is prohibited.

Edye Deloch-Hughes. From "So God Made a Black Farmer Too," reprinted by permission of the author. http://eldhughes.com/2013/02/05/so-god-made-a-farmer-dodge-ram/

Jon Dolan. "Drake, 'Draft Day'" by Jon Dolan, from *Rolling Stone*, Issue 1207, April 24, 2014. Copyright © 2014 by Rolling Stone, LLC. All rights reserved. Used by permission.

Roger Ebert. From a review of *Toy Story* (1995). Used by permission of Ebert Digital, LLC.

Neil Irwin. "What the Numbers Show about N.F.L. Player Arrests" from the *New York Times*, September 13, 2014. Copyright © 2014 by The New York Times. All rights reserved. Used by permission and protected by the Copyright Laws of the United States. The printing, copying, redistribution, or retransmission of this Content without express written permission is prohibited.

Raven Jiang. "Dota 2: The Face of Professional Gaming" from the *Stanford Daily*, August 5, 2014, is reprinted by permission of the *Stanford Daily* and Raven Jiang.

Joyce Xinran Liu. "Friending: The Changing Definition of Friendship in the Social Media Era" by Joyce Xinran Liu, from *Vitamin IMC*, March 6, 2014. Reprinted by permission of the author.

Walter Russell Mead. From "It All Begins with Football," first published in the *American Interest*, December 4, 2011. Reprinted by permission of the author.

Virginia Postrel. "Let's Charge Politicians for Wasting Our Time" from *Bloomberg View*, June 3, 2014. Reprinted by permission of Bloomberg L.P. Copyright © 2014. All rights reserved.

Deborah Tannen. "Why Is 'Compromise' Now a Dirty Word?," first published in *Politico*, June 15, 2011. Copyright © Deborah Tannen. Used by permission of the author.

John Tierney. "Can a Playground Be Too Safe?" by John Tierney from the *New York Times*, July 18, 2011. Copyright © 2011 by The New York Times. All rights reserved. Used by permission and protected by the Copyright Laws of the United States. The printing, copying, redistribution, or retransmission of this Content without express written permission is prohibited.

Hayley Tsukayama. "My Awkward Week with Google Glass" from the *Washington Post*, April 29, 2014. Copyright © 2014 by The Washington Post Company. All rights reserved. Used by permission and protected by the Copyright Laws of the United States. The printing, copying, redistribution, or retransmission of this Content without express written permission is prohibited.

Sean Wilsey. From "The Things They Buried" from the *New York Times Book Review* section, June 18, 2006. Copyright © 2006 by The New York Times. All rights reserved. Used by permission and protected by the Copyright Laws of the United States. The printing, copying, redistribution, or retransmission of this Content without express written permission is prohibited.

Lan Xue. "China: The Prizes and Pitfalls of Progress" from *Nature* magazine, vol. 454, July 2008. Reprinted by permission from Macmillan Publishers Ltd. via the Copyright Clearance Center. Copyright © 2008 by Nature Publishing Group.